THE CONSTITUTION OF
INDEPENDENCE

The Constitution of Independence

The Development of Constitutional Theory in Australia, Canada, and New Zealand

PETER C. OLIVER

OXFORD
UNIVERSITY PRESS

OXFORD

UNIVERSITY PRESS

Great Clarendon Street, Oxford OX2 6DP

Oxford University Press is a department of the University of Oxford.
It furthers the University's objective of excellence in research, scholarship,
and education by publishing worldwide in

Oxford New York

Auckland Cape Town Dar es Salaam Hong Kong Karachi
Kuala Lumpur Madrid Melbourne Mexico City Nairobi
New Delhi Shanghai Taipei Toronto

With offices in

Argentina Austria Brazil Chile Czech Republic France Greece
Guatemala Hungary Italy Japan Poland Portugal
Singapore South Korea Switzerland Thailand Turkey Ukraine Vietnam

Published in the United States
by Oxford University Press Inc., New York

British Library Cataloguing in Publication Data

Data available

Library of Congress Cataloging-in-Publication Data

Oliver, Peter C. (Peter Crawford)
The constitution of independence : the development of constitutional theory in
Australia, Canada, and New Zealand / Peter C. Oliver.
p. cm.
Includes bibliographical references and index.
ISBN 0–19–826895–5 (hard cover : alk. paper) 1. Consitutional law—Australia. 2.
Constitutional law—Canada. 3. Constitutional law—New Zealand. I. Title.
K3165.O43 2005
342'.11241029—dc22   2004029483
ISBN 0–19–826895–5

1 3 5 7 9 10 8 6 4 2

Typeset by Newgen Imaging Systems (P) Ltd., Chennai, India
Printed in Great Britain
on acid-free paper by
Biddles Ltd., King's Lynn

To my family

Preface

Given the subject matter of this book, it may have been quite significant that, according to my slightly vague recollection, I was never asked to read anything by A.V. Dicey in first-year law at McGill University. The most significant legal event of that year—so important that classes were cancelled and a television installed in the Moot Court—was the Supreme Court of Canada's decision in *Reference re Resolution to Amend the Constitution*, otherwise known as the *Patriation Reference*. Following on the enactment of the Canada Act 1982 (UK) with its Schedule B, the Constitution Act, 1982, most constitutional lawyers naturally focused on the star of the constitutional piece, the Canadian Charter of Rights and Freedoms. Perhaps because of my historical training, or perhaps because of an aversion for the spotlight, I became fascinated instead by the new constitutional amending formula as found in Part V of the Constitution Act, 1982. It seemed to me that the amending formula was a mirror in which one could see so many of the tests and tensions that had characterised the preceding century or more of Canadian political and constitutional development.

Although I did study the Charter of Rights and Freedoms, with Professor Irwin Cotler, present Minister of Justice for Canada, and with Professors François Chevrette and André Morel, I also opted to do a long essay for Professor Stephen A. Scott, entitled 'Quebec and Constitutional Amendment'. This first effort on constitutional amendment led on to a doctoral dissertation at Oxford University (under the wise and good-humoured supervision of the late Geoffrey Marshall) entitled 'The Patriation and Amendment of the Constitution of Canada'.

At the time I completed my doctoral thesis, two books on Canadian constitutional amendment were well on their way towards publication. Furthermore, I found myself in the lively and congenial environment of the School of Law at King's College London rather than on location in Canada. For these and no doubt other reasons I did not seek to prepare my thesis for publication at that time. Instead, with encouragement from my colleague, Professor Keith Ewing, I decided to expand the thesis into an exercise in comparative law and theory. This decision has resulted in my reading and travelling more widely than I might otherwise have done. It has also allowed me to meet up again with Oxford friends in Australia, and to make new and rewarding academic contacts in Australia, Canada, New Zealand and the United Kingdom. I do not propose to attempt a list of all those whose friendship and good advice has assisted me so much. However, I do hope that I will be able to thank each of them in person before too long.

A number of immediate acknowledgements are necessary, however. This book would not have taken its present shape without the positive and informed influences of Stephen A. Scott, Geoffrey Marshall and Keith Ewing. My doctoral thesis was supported by the Faculty of Law, McGill University and by the SSHRC and FCAR. I have subsequently received funding from the Institute of Advanced Legal Studies, the University of London External Fund, the Canadian High Commission and both the School of Law and Centre of European Law, King's College London. Some of this funding enabled me to hire research assistants for short periods of time. I wish to record my thanks to Arash Amel, Andrew Copping, Katherine Harmer and Ron Levy for all their efforts and enthusiasm. My colleagues at King's College London have been wonderfully stimulating and encouraging throughout my career there. Robert Wintemute and Perry Keller have been particularly supportive regarding the preparation of this book. Carolina Cordero provided invaluable secretarial support and David Cordero was good enough to rescue my computer hard drive at a critical moment. In the final stages of preparing the manuscript I have benefited greatly from the advice of a number of constitutional experts in Australia, Canada, New Zealand and the United Kingdom. Many of them have read multiple instalments: Amanda Perreau-Saussine (Chapters 1, 3 and 4); Brian Slattery (Chapters 1 and 2), Ben Yong (Chapters 2, 8, 11 and 13), Tony Bradley (Chapters 3 and 4), Keith Ewing (Chapters 1, 3 and 4), Dick Risk (Chapters 5, 6 and 7), Phillip Joseph (Chapters 8, 11 and 13), Brian Opeskin (Chapters 11 and 13), George Winterton (Chapters 1, 2, 9, 10, 11 and 13) and Leslie Zines (Chapters 1, 9, 10, 11 and 13). I am also grateful to Adam Tomkins, Stephen Tierney, the late Michael Oliver, Alan Norrie, Timothy Macklem, Nicholas Kasirer, Fabien Gélinas, Conor Gearty, David Dyzenhaus and Robert Blackburn for their expert comments on earlier articles and other writing which relate to this book. I am also grateful to my students. Their questions and reactions over the years have played an important part in the development of the ideas discussed in this book. I, of course, am responsible in all cases for any remaining errors and omissions.

Oxford University Press has proved to be a patient and professional publisher. I am grateful to John Louth and Gwen Booth for helping me to get this project back on schedule, and to Louise Kavanagh, Alison Floyd, and Carolyn Fox for their assistance in making it presentable.

None of the chapters in this book has been published anywhere else in its present form; however, some chapters incorporate material from previous writings, adapted for inclusion here. Some of the discussion of Richard Latham's writing in Chapter 4 appeared originally in P. Oliver, 'Law, Politics, the Commonwealth and the Constitution: Remembering R.T.E. Latham, 1909–43' (2000) 11 KCLJ 153–89. Parts of Chapters 5, 6 and 7 are drawn from my doctoral thesis. Some of the New Zealand material in Chapters 8, 11 and 13 is drawn from P. Oliver, 'Cutting the Imperial Link—Canada and New Zealand' in P. Joseph (ed.) *Essays on the Constitution* (Wellington: Brookers, 1995) 368. The Canadian sections in Chapters 11 and 13 and some of the theoretical material in Chapter 12 appeared in similar form in P. Oliver, 'The 1982

Patriation of the Constitution of Canada: Reflections on Continuity and Change' (1994) 28 Rev Jur Thémis 875 and P. Oliver, 'Canada, Quebec and Constitutional Amendment' (2000) 49 UTLJ 519. A further part of Chapter 12 is drawn from P. Oliver, 'Sovereignty in the Twenty-First Century' (2003) 14 KCLJ 137.

This book is dedicated to my family, in both of the senses of the word that are mentioned in the Introduction to this book and in other senses as well. My sisters and their families, my parents and my grandparents have blessed me with all the love that anyone could hope for. By marriage, I am very lucky to have another supportive extended family close by. In Christy and Jeanna I have two children who are a constant wonder, delight and inspiration. If this book had to be dedicated to one person, it would be to my wife, Sophie, who has made everything possible.

Peter C. Oliver
Twickenham
1 August 2004

Contents

III. CONSTITUTIONAL INDEPENDENCE

List of Abbreviations

Amer Jo Comp L	American Journal of Comparative Law (US)
Austr LJ	Australian Law Journal (Aus)
Canta LR	Canterbury Law Review (NZ)
C du D	Cahiers du Droit (Can)
CLJ	Cambridge Law Journal (UK)
Cth	Commonwealth
Fed LR	Federal Law Review (Aus)
Imp.	Imperial
KCLJ	Kings College Law Journal (UK)
LQR	Law Quarterly Review (UK)
MLR	Modern Law Review (UK)
Monash U L Rev	Monash University Law Review (Aus)
NZLJ	New Zealand Law Journal (NZ)
NZPD	New Zealand Parliament, *Debates* (NZ)
NZULR	New Zealand Universities Law Review (NZ)
OJLS	Oxford Journal of Legal Studies (UK)
Otago LR	Otago Law Review (NZ)
Pub L Rev	Pubic Law Review (Aus)
Sup Ct L Rev	Supreme Court Law Review (Can)
UQLJ	University of Queensland Law Journal (Aus)
UTLJ	University of Toronto Law Journal (Can)
VUWLR	Victoria University of Wellington Law Review (NZ)
WA L Rev	Western Australia Law Review (Aus)

Table of Cases

Table of Statutes

1

Introduction

Constitutional continuity and constitutional independence

This is a book about how the well-behaved Dominions of the British Empire[1]—Australia, Canada and New Zealand—acquired their constitutional independence: how they anticipated it; how they went about it; and how they subsequently explained it. Whereas their tearaway siblings, Ireland and South Africa, took matters into their own hands and achieved what one Commonwealth writer has referred to as constitutional 'autochthony',[2] the remaining Dominion progeny were intent on showing respect for existing legal rules. In each case, constitutional independence was apparently achieved by means of an Act of the United Kingdom Parliament, although local enactments were important as well.

New Zealand was the first to take a bold initial step towards constitutional independence, in 1947, with the passage of the New Zealand Constitution Amendment (Request and Consent) Act 1947 (NZ) and the New Zealand Constitution (Amendment) Act 1947 (UK), but all three Dominions completed the action required to achieve constitutional independence in the mid-1980s. Canada began the constitutional process with the Canada Act 1982 (UK) (containing the Constitution Act, 1982 and its Charter of Rights and Freedoms), and Australia and New Zealand followed four years later with, respectively, the Australia Acts 1986 (UK and Cth) and the Constitution Act 1986 (NZ).

Before going further, I should perhaps explain what I mean in using the term 'constitutional independence'. As political scientists, historians, diplomats and civil servants will no doubt confirm, Australia, Canada and New Zealand acquired their political and international independence much earlier than the 1980s: 'political' independence, in the sense of their ability to make their own decisions regardless of formal legal rules, and 'international' independence, in the sense of how other countries viewed them. By 'constitutional' independence, I am referring to their ability in formal legal terms to determine with finality all

---

[1] Newfoundland was also a 'well-behaved' Dominion, though its constitutional development will not form part of the ensuing discussion. In terms of constitutional independence, the main focus of this book, Newfoundland's constitutional fortunes were joined with those of Canada as of 1949.

[2] K.C. Wheare, *The Constitutional Structure of the Commonwealth* (Oxford: Clarendon, 1960) ch. 4.

the rules, constitutional and other, in their respective legal systems. The fact, for example, that Australia, Canada and New Zealand remain (for the time being) monarchies, does not affect their constitutional independence given the fact that they can at any moment put a permanent end to that arrangement of their own volition. 'Constitutional' independence really establishes them as separate legal systems.

Sovereignty and legal system

The Constitution of Independence is also a book about sovereignty and legal systems. Both are central concepts in legal theory. 'Sovereignty' refers to the power of a person or institution to determine the law, and to have those determinations ultimately obeyed; to have the final word or to hold the trump card.[3] Traditionally, though not an essential part of the definition, it is the *untrammelled* or *unlimited* ability to do so, and usually it implicates courts and other institutions of administration and enforcement. 'Legal system' describes all the laws which are *related* to each other in a particular legal sense, i.e. they regulate their own creation, interpretation and amendment, and, at the most fundamental level, they must be heeded or recognised by lawyers, judges and officials.[4] To say this much is at the same time to say far too little. Theoretical claims of this type need to be unpacked and explored.

This is not a book of pure legal theoretical analysis. Rather, it is an attempt to chart the development of one of these theoretical concepts—sovereignty—in the three countries under study, with particular emphasis on how shifting understandings of sovereignty relate to independence. These three countries share the fact of being 'discovered', 'settled' or 'conquered' by Britain. As a matter of British law, they therefore fell under the sway of the British Crown and, as a matter of sovereign priority in the sense just mentioned, under the Crown-in-the Imperial British Parliament at Westminster.[5] This had implications for the evolution of Imperial and local legal systems. By means of its sovereign legal powers, the Imperial Parliament could legislate for the Empire, and therefore for the colonies that were or later made up Australia, Canada and New Zealand,

---

[3] For further discussion of the varied meanings of sovereignty, see P. Oliver, 'Sovereignty in the Twenty-First Century' (2003) 14 KCLJ 137.

[4] For further discussion of the theoretical aspects of legal system, see J. Raz, *The Concept of a Legal System* (2nd edn, Oxford: Clarendon Press, 1980); J. Raz, *Practical Reason and Norms* (Oxford: Oxford University Press, 1975) (reprinted with new postscript, 1990) 126 et seq. and ch. 5. The layperson's understanding of what it means to speak of a legal system is also relevant to this discussion, as will become apparent later in this Introduction.

[5] This Parliament will be referred to throughout this book using some of the different titles that are contained in the full description used here: the Imperial Parliament (in the period leading up to the Statute of Westminster, 1931); the United Kingdom or British Parliament; and (more neutrally) the Westminster Parliament. Each refers to the same institution, i.e. the House of Commons and House of Lords at Westminster acting in concert with the King or Queen of the day.

providing representative political institutions and an ultimate court of appeal (the Judicial Committee of the Privy Council). The Imperial Parliament could also act in a more concentrated way as a constituent assembly or constitution-making body for the Empire, as it did for New Zealand in 1852,[6] for Canada in 1867[7] and for Australia in 1900.[8]

The sovereign legislative and constitution-making powers of the Imperial Parliament provided the useful service of conferring supremacy and formal validity on these countries' constitutional arrangements. However, such sovereignty also presented these countries with a problem, one which related to both the concept of sovereignty and the concept of a legal system. According to orthodox understandings of parliamentary sovereignty, the Westminster Parliament could pass any law whatever and no institution, notably no subordinate institution and no court, could override that enactment.[9] This doctrine conveniently accounted for how the new constitutions of Australia, Canada and New Zealand acquired both validity and supremacy over local laws (as confirmed in the Colonial Laws Validity Act, 1865 (Imp.)). However, it made it difficult to explain how that same Westminster Parliament could eventually grant constitutional independence to these countries. A Westminster-enacted independence Act was certainly valid law, but it was always subject to repeal, express or perhaps even implied, by a later Act of that same Parliament, at least according to a corollary to the traditional view of parliamentary sovereignty which indicated that no one Parliament could bind any future Parliament.

This state of affairs seemed to indicate that independence from the 'Imperial' legal system could be *politically* real, in the sense that, certainly in the case of Australia, Canada and New Zealand, the Westminster government and Parliament never had nor was ever likely to have any real intention of reasserting its will in those countries' affairs. However, as a formal legal matter, independence was potentially illusory. The doctrine of parliamentary sovereignty seemed to indicate that the Westminster Parliament would forever retain its position as a ghostly legal presence, legally able to interfere in the affairs of its former colonies, unless those countries, their courts and other law-enforcing and -administering institutions rejected such interference in apparently extra-legal or revolutionary fashion.

---

[6] New Zealand Constitution Act, 1852 (Imp.) (which should be read together with the New Zealand Constitution Amendment Act, 1857 (Imp.)).

[7] British North America Act, 1867 (Imp.) (renamed the Constitution Act, 1867 in the Schedule to the Constitution Act, 1982).

[8] Commonwealth of Australia Constitution Act, 1900 (Imp.). We shall see in Ch. 2 below that the Imperial Parliament provided Constitutions for Canadian and Australian colonies before, respectively, 1867 and 1900.

[9] This orthodox understanding of sovereignty is usually associated with the writings of Professor A.V. Dicey, and especially his *An Introduction to the Study of the Law of the Constitution* E.C.S. Wade (ed) (10th edn, London: Macmillan, 1959). Dicey's writings and influence will be discussed in some detail in Ch. 3 below.

Rule of law and constitutional continuity: disguised revolutions and popular acceptance

The attraction of revolutionary or extra-legal explanations of constitutional independence should be evident from the foregoing account. If existing constitutional doctrine of a traditional variety—i.e. the orthodox view of parliamentary sovereignty—truly prevented a legally secure explanation of independence, then alternative non-legal doctrines would have to be identified. Whereas in the middle part of the twentieth century Australia, Canada and New Zealand might have been willing to leave the issue of their constitutional independence in some kind of legal limbo, by the end of the century, especially following the constitutional independence-securing legislation of the 1980s, a definitive and assertive explanation was generally required.

We will see how, in New Zealand after 1986, one of the dominant explanations of that country's constitutional independence was that there had been a 'disguised revolution' (of the type first noted by the English academic writer H.W.R. Wade in the 1950s).[10] Whereas before 1986 the New Zealand Constitution had been founded on the sovereignty of the Westminster Parliament, after the 'revolutionary' Constitution Act 1986 (NZ) it was said to be based on acceptance by the people of New Zealand. If ordinary New Zealanders could not really get their heads around the idea of a 'disguised revolution'—and why should they?—they could certainly relate to the idea of a constitution based in their own acceptance or rejection of it. Such reflections on what are generally called considerations of *legitimacy*[11] were especially important if *Aotearoa/ New Zealand*[12] was going to come to terms with the long-standing issues of *Māori-Pākehā* relationships and governance, issues previously obscured by the contrasting clarity of an apparently absolute Westminster-based sovereignty. We will revert to these issues in Part III. However, those New Zealanders with legal training, while perhaps in agreement with the prevailing emphasis on legitimacy, might nonetheless have been forgiven for asking what had happened to the concept of the rule of law in this process of disguised revolution. Certainly the government lawyers who provided advice on the purpose and eventual form of the New Zealand Constitution Act 1986 had felt that the process was anything

---

[10] H.W.R. Wade, 'The Basis of Legal Sovereignty' [1955] CLJ 172.

[11] For a wide-ranging and thorough discussion of the concept of legitimacy in the New Zealand context, see F.M. Brookfield, *Waitangi and Indigenous Rights: Revolution, Law and Legitimation* (Auckland: Auckland University Press, 1999).

[12] The name *Aotearoa/New Zealand* is used here to acknowledge that this country is still very much in the process of working out *Māori-Pākehā* constitutional relationships for the future. The English name, New Zealand, is used throughout this book so as to avoid confusion, given the historical focus and frequent use of nineteenth and early twentieth-century sources in which that title is invariably used. It should not be taken to express any political preference for traditional attitudes with regard to New Zealand's constitutional future.

but revolutionary. They had done their level best to follow what they perceived to be the then-existing rules regarding how to achieve constitutional change. What seemed to be lacking, however, was an explanation, necessarily a partly theoretical one, of how the absolute and apparently continuing sovereignty of the Westminster Parliament had been terminated (from a New Zealand perspective if not from a British perspective) and replaced by local constitutional machinery.

In Australia, explanations of constitutional independence post-1986 were less often couched in the language of revolution, disguised or otherwise, but they nonetheless showed a strong tendency towards extra-legal analysis. H.W.R. Wade, who popularised the notion of disguised revolution,[13] claimed that the ultimate principles in a legal system were extra-legal, in the sense that they were political or historical facts.[14] In the early years following the enactment of the Commonwealth of Australia Constitution Act in 1900, Australian lawyers and constitutional commentators had based the validity and supremacy of their Constitution in the sovereignty of the Imperial Parliament at Westminster and therefore, in Wade's terms, on the political and historical facts which originally established that Parliament's sovereignty. However, the emergence of an Australian Constitution in 1900 had not only been a product of Westminster enactment. Unlike the Canadian and New Zealand Constitutions which had preceded it, the Australian Constitution had been drafted by Australians in elected Constitutional Conventions and ratified by the Australian people voting in referendums in the future states. Could it not be said that *this* important political and historical process of legitimising the Constitution also represented the ultimate legal foundation of the Australian Constitution? This account has had strong support in Australia, not least from the High Court. However, the dominant view, at least prior to 1986, seems to have been that too much constitutional history would have to be rewritten to claim that popular ratification was the true legal foundation for the Australian constitutional system. The matter is very different following enactment of the Australia Acts 1986 (UK and Cth). A leading view in Australia at the moment is precisely that the Constitution *is* based in popular sovereignty. It is as if the twin horses of Westminster and popular sovereignty had been running side by side since 1900 with the constitutional rider in the Westminster saddle. When Westminster sovereignty was terminated in 1986, the constitutional rider simply hopped over to the popular sovereignty horse and carried on as before. Ordinary Australians are probably far happier conceiving of constitutional foundations in terms of their own acceptance of it, though this account raises difficult questions regarding who the Australian people are and have been, notably where aboriginal Australians are concerned. As in New Zealand, however, those with legal training,

---

[13] Wade (1955) (n. 10 above) 191: 'When sovereignty is relinquished in an atmosphere of harmony, the naked fact of revolution is not so easy to discern beneath its elaborate legal dress.'
[14] Wade (1955) (n. 10 above) 189.

notably the government lawyers who advised on the 1986 constitutional independence process, may still wonder whether and if so how the dramatic jump from Westminster to popular sovereignty respected the central constitutional principle of the rule of law, i.e. of legality and the achievement of change—even constitutional change—by legal means. While it would be foolish to ignore popular political factors and the question of legitimacy, it would also be odd if legal explanations were not available for this most important of legal changes.

Concern for the rule of law is most apparent in the Canadian story. The attainment of Canadian constitutional independence in 1982 is wrapped up with the fifty-year search for an appropriate and politically acceptable constitutional amending formula. By the late 1970s the search had been complicated by the fact that an avowedly separatist party had become the government in the predominantly French-speaking province of Quebec. In the face of such a long legacy of failure and frustration, and presented with what it judged to be an implacable government in Quebec, Prime Minister Trudeau's federal government resolved itself to 'patriate' the Canadian Constitution unilaterally. That is, it would by-pass the provinces and ask the Canadian House of Commons and Senate to request a final Act from the United Kingdom Parliament that would simultaneously terminate that body's law-making powers for Canada, replace them with a domestic general amending formula and set out a Charter of Rights and Freedoms, the last serving to fulfil one of Trudeau's political ambitions and to ensure the popularity of the otherwise controversial process. Some academic commentators at the time suggested that the Trudeau government should reject the out-dated Westminster constitutional amendment process in favour of an Irish-style constitutional novation—i.e. a new constitutional start founded on the vote of the people in a referendum.[15] After all, they argued, if the Constitution is ultimately based on the acceptance of the Canadian (Irish, Australian or New Zealand) people, then should not the constitution-making and -amending procedure reflect this fact? Despite the good political sense contained in this argument, it never took hold in Canada, whether in the Trudeau government or in the wider community of constitutional comment. Although the point was seldom articulated, the reason for the reluctance to exchange respect for the existing pre-1982 constitutional rule on constitutional amendment (Westminster enactment) for a constitutional novation based on the consent of the Canadian people (approval by referendum) was fairly obvious. Few federalists, and certainly not the fervently federalist Prime Minister Trudeau, wanted to hand separatists an inexpensive pass out of the federation. If the federal government had chosen popular ratification over respect for the existing constitutional rule of law, then it would have been much more difficult to object to a Quebec government

---

[15] See, e.g., E. McWhinney, *Canada and the Constitution, 1979–82* (Toronto: University of Toronto Press, 1982) 46 and G. Rémillard, *Le Devoir [de Montréal]*, 26 June 1980, 13. Rémillard was a law professor at the University of Laval at the time but was later to become the Minister of Intergovernmental Affairs in the Quebec government.

eventually doing the same if ever the people of that province voted in favour of independence.[16]

Having the constitutional cake and eating it too: sovereignty and legal system reconsidered

Removing the issues from their historical context in Australia, Canada and New Zealand for a moment, there would seem to be objectively strong reasons for recognising as constitutional foundations both respect for the rule of law (and the constitutional continuity that accompanies it) *and* popular acceptance. As a rule, polities have a strong preference for rule-following, even where significant change is sought. New constitutional beginnings, or constitutional novations as they have been termed here, tend to be favoured only out of necessity, following defeat in war (Germany) or success in revolution (France, the USSR, the United States). Even countries which had good reasons to draw a line between their constitutional past and future have tended where possible to encourage respect for the rule of law by maintaining constitutional continuity. One thinks most recently of Eastern European countries after 1989 and South Africa post-apartheid. Ironically, in the context of this book's preoccupations, it was in part the stubborn persistence of the formal sovereignty of the Westminster Parliament that contributed to De Valera and others' sense that Ireland required a new constitutional start.[17]

Was it not possible to have the constitutional cake and eat it too: to respect the rule of law and thereby maintain constitutional continuity while achieving constitutional independence, a new beginning and a foundation based on popular acceptance? The argument in this book is that it certainly is possible.

Beyond charting the development of constitutional ideas, especially relating to sovereignty, in Australia, Canada and New Zealand, one of the purposes of this book is to illustrate how theories of sovereignty interact with concepts of a legal system. The traditional or Diceyan understanding of absolute and continuing sovereignty has an analogue in Kelsen's theory of a legal system.[18] Both appear to mean that, so long as constitutional rules are followed, only one legal system prevails, in our case an 'Imperial' legal system presided over by the Westminster Parliament. Any break in this rule-following may achieve independence but only by what H.W.R. Wade called a 'disguised revolution' or by what Kelsen referred

---

[16] In this respect, now see *Reference re Secession* [1998] 2 SCR 217.

[17] Wheare (1960) (n. 2 above) 89 et seq.

[18] See H. Kelsen, *General Theory of Law and State*, A. Wedberg (trans.) (Cambridge: Harvard University Press, 1949) esp. 110 et seq. Kelsen's ideas on law, legal system, *Grundnorm* (basic norm), etc. were developed in numerous publications over his long and prolific lifetime. The references to the *General Theory of Law and State* are preferred here, as this was the version which H.L.A. Hart referred to in *The Concept of Law* (Oxford: Clarendon Press, 1961; 2nd edn, 1994). Hart's (and Kelsen's) legal thought will be discussed in greater detail in Ch. 12 below.

to as the assumption of a new *Grundnorm* and therefore a new legal system. On this account it is impossible to have the constitutional cake and eat it too.

However, Dicey's account of parliamentary sovereignty and Kelsen's theory of a legal system are by no means universally accepted, though their influence was undoubtedly strong. One alternative to Dicey's absolute, continuing sovereignty is what H.L.A. Hart termed 'self-embracing' sovereignty.[19] According to the latter version, the sovereignty of a body such as the Westminster Parliament extends even so far as to imposing limits on itself. The prevalence of absolutist political theories of sovereignty and the reluctance of Parliament to even attempt limits on itself contributed to the assumption that Parliament was legally prohibited from doing so. There was an easy slippage between Parliament never having attempted to and Parliament being legally prohibited from doing so. Challenges to the traditional conception of sovereignty had to be dressed up in procedural and exceptional form, and even these tended to be discounted.[20]

As the early chapters of this book reveal, the Dicey picture of sovereignty was so dominant in the United Kingdom and across the Empire and Commonwealth that constitutional commentators struggled to explain how the one legal system of the Empire could ever, by legal means, break up into many independent legal systems. The Balfour Declaration and the Statute of Westminster 1931 avoided the legal nettle of calls for constitutional independence, and wrapped it up instead in the flexible material of constitutional convention. While constitutional convention could achieve a perfectly satisfactory level of independence in practice, it was never likely to be an acceptable peg on which to hang full and permanent constitutional independence. The ghost-like formal legal presence of the Westminster Parliament was far too likely to rankle even if it was seldom if ever roused into interfering behaviour. Was there an alternative conception of sovereignty which could support an alternative account of the evolution of Imperial and local legal systems?

An alternative account

As we have just seen, dominant theories of sovereignty and legal system were and perhaps still are the main obstacles to explaining independence in a way which takes in both respect for the rule of law and the removal of the newly independent constitution from the sphere of influence of the old. One common response to this is to treat the dominant theories as given and to respond accordingly. For a former British colony which is determined to assert its independence, escape from the continuing sovereignty of the Westminster Parliament is achieved by the sort of disguised revolution identified by Dicey's

[19] Hart (1st edn, 1961; 2nd edn, 1994) (n. 18 above) ch. 7, section 4.
[20] For further discussion of the points made in this paragraph see Oliver (2003) (n. 3 above).

foremost apologist H.W.R. Wade, or if necessary by recourse to deliberate breach of constitutional rules.[21] Escape from Kelsen's legal system is explained by Kelsen himself: if the legal system is not altered according to the rules of that system (and traditional assumptions were that this was perhaps legally impossible in any event) then a new system and a new *Grundnorm* has to be presumed.[22] What were the alternatives to these revolutionary accounts of independence?

As already noted, the alternative to Dicey's continuing sovereignty was self-embracing sovereignty. Hart was surely right in observing that these versions of sovereignty are equally coherent. Continuing sovereignty has a long and deeply entrenched legacy in the United Kingdom[23] and therefore in the Empire as well. Reasons for the entrenched nature of these ideas lay in the constitutional struggles of earlier centuries.[24] Whatever the history of the Westminster Parliament's sovereignty, an array of possible approaches to it emerged in the twentieth century.

First, the dominant approach in the United Kingdom was to assume that Parliament's sovereignty was continuing and that it must forever be so. Even a procedural inroad proposed in the early and middle part of the twentieth century—the manner and form theory whereby a sovereign Parliament could specify the manner and/or the form of its legislation[25]—could ultimately be blocked by Parliament's continuing ability to prevail on all-important substantive matters.

The dominant approach was always based more on dogma than on authority.[26] Such authority as there was looked very weak when scrutinised more carefully. It was therefore possible that, though the absolute and continuing sovereignty of Parliament had been dominant for so long, Parliament had unused (and therefore hidden) powers of a self-embracing nature, powers which would allow it to limit itself to some extent provided that it *clearly* indicated an intention to do so. This was the second approach. The existing authority lined up against this approach (see the *Vauxhall Estates*,[27] *Ellen Street Estates*[28] and *British Coal Corporation*[29] cases) was weak precisely because Parliament had never made a clear attempt to do so. However, when later it did so (in section 2 of the European Communities Act 1972), such limitation proved to be effective (as

[21] See, e.g., J. Finnis, 'Revolutions and Continuity of Law' in A.W.B. Simpson, (ed.) *Oxford Essays in Jurisprudence* (2nd ser., Oxford: Clarendon Press, 1973) 44.

[22] Kelsen (1949) (n. 18 above) 110 et seq.

[23] See J. Goldsworthy, *The Sovereignty of Parliament* (Oxford: Oxford University Press, 1999), and for a critical assessment of the same see Oliver (2003) (n. 3 above).

[24] Goldsworthy (1999) (n. 23 above).

[25] See I. Jennings, *The Law and the Constitution* (5th edn, London: University of London Press, 1959) ch. 4 and G. Marshall, *Parliamentary Sovereignty and the Commonwealth* (Oxford: Clarendon Press, 1957).   [26] Dicey himself referred to it as dogma: Dicey (1959) (n. 9 above) 71.

[27] *Vauxhall Estates v Liverpool Corporation* (1932) 1 KB 733 (Div Ct).

[28] *Ellen Street Estates v Minister of Health* (1934) 1 KB 597 (CA).

[29] *British Coal Corporation v The King* (1935) AC 500 (PC).

confirmed by the *Factortame*[30] and, more recently, *Thoburn* cases[31]). According to this approach, the Westminster Parliament successfully limited itself when it terminated its ability to legislate for New Zealand, Canada and Australia. It may be that this approach is closer than ever to being accepted, even in the United Kingdom. However, at the time these countries achieved their constitutional independence it was certainly not accepted. As late as 1981, the Supreme Court of Canada in the *Patriation Reference*[32] had appeared to confirm the contrary, in stating that the Westminster Parliament's powers to legislate for Canada were still unlimited, untrammeled and undiminished. Even if one brings the *Factortame* and *Thoburn* cases into the frame, one reading of their combined impact is that, provided Parliament expresses itself clearly enough, it can still enact whatever it wishes, including (it would seem) new legislation for former colonies and former Dominions.

A third approach takes the coherence of the second approach for granted but makes no assumptions regarding the extent to which it has presently taken hold in the United Kingdom.[33] It asserts that a self-embracing interpretation of the Westminster Parliament's powers was latent—misunderstood because never employed.[34] In Hart's terms, the core of parliamentary sovereignty was reasonably clear—Parliament could enact any law whatever—but penumbral issues still needed to be explored.[35] Recently a number of writers[36] (judges among them)[37] have suggested that certain imaginary and as yet unenacted legislation by Parliament is beyond the pale, i.e. beyond what the courts should or would recognise. That is one sort of penumbral issue. However, it is clear that until such scenarios are presented concretely we cannot know with certainty what the courts' approach will be. Another sort of penumbral issue, more relevant to

---

[30] *Factortame v Secretary of State for Transport (No 2)* [1991] AC 603 (HL).

[31] *Thoburn v Sunderland City Council* [2003] QB 151 (Div Ct).

[32] *Reference re Resolution to Amend the Constitution* [1981] 1 SCR 753.

[33] As we shall see in Ch. 4 below, British proponents of the 'new view', such as Geoffrey Marshall, naturally wanted to prove that the 'new' or even the 'revised' view was valid not only for independence-seeking self-governing colonies and Dominions, but also for the United Kingdom. The logic behind this was, of course, entirely sound; however, there was no practical necessity that it be so. The 'new' and 'revised' views canvassed in Ch. 4 have always been more popular outside the United Kingdom than in.   [34] See Oliver (2003) (n. 3 above).

[35] On 'core' and 'penumbra' in the 'rule of recognition', see Hart (1961; 2nd edn, 1994) (n. 18 above) ch. 6, section 3 and ch. 7, section 4.

[36] T.R.S. Allan, 'The Limits of Parliamentary Sovereignty' [1985] Public Law 614; T.R.S. Allan, *Law, Liberty and Justice: The Legal Foundations of British Constitutionalism* (Oxford: Clarendon Press, 1993); M.J. Detmold, *The Unity of Law and Morality: A Refutation of Legal Positivism* (London: Routledge & Kegan Paul, 1984); M.J. Detmold, *The Australian Commonwealth: A Fundamental Analysis of Its Constitution* (Sydney: Law Book Company, 1985). A book-length refutation of the historical and philosophical basis for these views can be found in Goldsworthy (1999) (n 23 above).

[37] R. Cooke, 'Fundamentals' (1988) NZLJ 158 (formerly Cooke P of the New Zealand Court of Appeal and now Lord Cooke of Thorndon, a British Law Lord); J. Laws, 'Law and Democracy' [1995] Public Law 72; J. Laws, 'The Constitution, Morals and Rights' [1996] Public Law 622 (now Laws LJ of the English Court of Appeal); H. Woolf, 'Droit Public—English Style' [1995] Public Law 57 (formerly Master of the Rolls, now Lord Chief Justice of England).

our concerns, was that Parliament could limit its own powers if *it* ever attempted to do so. Common sense and perhaps authority dictated that it would have to do so clearly. Independence legislation enacted by Westminster was one such limitation. We have already identified this possibility (see the second approach). The distinctive feature of the approach being discussed here is that even if the United Kingdom adopts the first approach or a version of the second approach which leaves open the possibility of future clear legislation by the Imperial Parliament, all relevant actors in Australia, Canada and New Zealand would reject such legislation even in the unlikely event of its enactment. The Supreme Court of Canada indicated as much in the *Quebec Veto Reference* of 1982 when it stated that, following the Canada Act 1982 (UK), amendment of the Canadian constitution was uncontroversially and irreversibly a Canadian matter.[38] The third approach therefore relies on the possibility of separate legal systems—those of Australia, Canada, New Zealand *and* the United Kingdom—having a different perspective on the same neutral fact or event: a constitutional independence-conferring Act of the Westminster Parliament.

There is no point in telling Australians, Canadians and New Zealanders what they should think about their constitutions. However, it may be important, if it is at all possible to do so, to indicate that these countries' apparent respect for the rule of law over many years is compatible with their constitutional independence, new beginnings and popular acceptance. It would be surprising if this were not the case. If the argument is made out, it should not be viewed as only the latest victory for law's empire. Instead we may see how thin and inadequate respect for the rule of law can look if not accompanied by some measure of real authority and legitimation. What emerges from this account is that the rule of law is an important principle but by no means a sufficient and entirely satisfying one.[39]

Puzzles regarding legal systems

The comments regarding legal system need to be unpacked a bit further if the ideas which tie this book together are to be made at all clear from the outset.

We have already seen that according to Kelsen's influential theory of legal systems, a breach of legal continuity implies a new *Grundnorm* and a new legal system. The flip-side of this point is that respect for legal continuity implies an enduring *Grundnorm* and an enduring legal system. In the case of the Empire this presents the 'well-behaved' Dominions and other former colonies of the Empire with a dilemma. If Kelsen's legal theory were the only determinant,

---

[38] *Reference re Objection to a Resolution to Amend the Constitution* [1982] 2 SCR 793. See also *Secession Reference* (n. 16 above) 46. For Australia, see *Sue v Hill* (1999) 199 CLR 462, paras 60–65.

[39] For further discussion see the Conclusion of this book (Ch. 14) and Oliver (2003) (n. 3 above) 174 et seq.

they would have been presented with a pair of unattractive options: follow the constitutional rules and be condemned to perpetual membership of the Imperial legal system; or break away from that legal system but at the cost of ignoring constitutional rules of the highest order.[40] Some Commonwealth countries deliberately took the second option, viewing it as a necessary price to pay.[41]

Why is it that achieving independence with respect for the existing constitutional rules means that the previous legal system persists? This seems particularly strange where, as in the Canadian case and as in virtually all other moments of Commonwealth independence, independence legislation not only declares that no future Act of the Westminster Parliament should be recognised as law, but also substitutes new constitutional amendment procedures in place of the former constituent role of Westminster.

The problem is effectively one of amending the amending formula. For Australia, Canada and New Zealand (and for other former colonies) the Westminster Parliament which first enacted the Dominion (or other colonial) constitution remained an ultimate, if not supreme, procedure for amending that constitution.[42] Independence legislation usually involved exercising the Westminster amending formula one more time so as to end this constitutional amending role and substitute a new ultimate procedure. In a broader analysis of amending amending formulae, the Danish legal philosopher Alf Ross had concluded that such processes could not be strictly legal. Described somewhat simplistically at this stage, Ross observed that it was illogical for the new amending formula simultaneously to derive its validity from a superior norm in the legal hierarchy (the old (Westminster) amending formula) *and* replace that norm, thereby claiming equivalent hierarchical status. If amendment of an amending formula was legally recognised despite these logical problems, then according to Ross the event was better termed 'magical' as opposed to legal.[43] There are strong echoes of Wade's 'disguised revolution' here.

As we shall see in Chapter 12, Ross eventually changed his view, with help from a fairly cumbersome re-interpretation of the content of the *Grundnorm*.[44]

---

[40] For a critical discussion of this issue, see J. Raz, *The Authority of Law* (Oxford: Oxford University Press, 1979) 100.   [41] See Finnis (1973) (n. 21 above).

[42] 'Of these two ideas, supreme criterion and ultimate rule, the first is the easiest to define. We may say that a criterion of legal validity or source of law is supreme if rules identified by reference to it are still recognised as rules of the system, even if they conflict with rules identified by reference to other criteria, whereas rules identified by reference to the latter [i.e. ultimate rule] are not so recognised if they conflict with the rules identified by reference to the supreme criterion . . . The sense in which the rule of recognition is the *ultimate* rule of a system is best understood if we pursue a very famililar chain of legal reasoning . . . we [then reach] a rule which . . . provides criteria for the assessment of the validity of other rules; but it is also unlike them in that there is no rule providing criteria for the assessment of its own legal validity.' Hart (1961; 2nd edn, 1994) (n. 18 above) ch. 6, section 1: 'Rule of Recognition and Legal Validity'.

[43] A. Ross, *On Law and Justice* (London: Stevens, 1958) 81.

[44] A. Ross, 'On Self-Reference and a Puzzle in Constitutional Law' (1969) 78 Mind 1.

An intervening contribution to the debate from H.L.A. Hart was more significant and ultimately more convincing.[45] Hart pointed out that Ross had wrongly imposed the strict rules of logic on law without recognising law's added dimensions. Whereas a chain of logical proof is susceptible to a one-dimensional analysis involving numbered propositions set out on a page, legal analysis adds at least one further dimension—the dimension of time. While, strictly speaking, it may be illogical for a new amending formula simultaneously to derive its validity from a superior norm in the legal hierarchy *and* to replace that norm thereby claiming hierarchical equivalence, the problem is avoided if one adds this temporal dimension. The constitution is amended according to the old amending formula at T1 thereby successfully conferring legal validity on a new amending formula; and it is later amended according to the new amending formula because the constitution at T2 specifies a new procedure for constitutional amendment (as a direct result of the process accomplished at T1). On paper, T2's derivation from and claim of equivalence to T1 looks problematic, but laid out over the dimension of time the problem is resolved. There is nothing wrong with a constitution being amended according to rules which govern at one moment, and being later amended according to rules which govern at a later moment, even if the later amending rules are derived from an earlier version.

All of this will need to be explained in greater detail in Chapter 12. However, the upshot is that, first, self-embracing processes are coherent, and secondly, new independent legal systems can be created out of old legal systems even when the relevant constitutional rules are followed to the letter. An amending formula can both validate a new amending formula and terminate itself, and accordingly the Westminster Parliament can both validate a new Constitution, including new or enhanced amendment procedures, and terminate its role for that Constitution. This allows the former Imperial legal system to break up into many independent legal systems, not only by unilateral proclamation but also by legal devolution.

Some will say that the logical problem identified by Ross and others cannot be so quickly put aside. In a sense this is true, as we shall see. However, the persistence of the problem has nothing like the dramatic consequences that used to be alleged. Effectively, what we are seeing here is a confusion between two different senses of the word 'legal system'. A similar confusion exists if one speaks of 'family' in ordinary speech contexts. In asking what or who is a member of a legal system or family, there is uncertainty as to whether one is speaking in terms of the present moment (those who are still active and able to influence legal or family affairs) or in terms of the past as well (thereby including those who while not now 'alive' are nonetheless part of the explanation for the legal system or family's coming into existence). It is perfectly sensible both to acknowledge that the validity of law in, say, Canada, is derived in an important sense from a legal

---

[45] H.L.A. Hart, 'Self-Referring Laws' in H.L.A. Hart (ed.) *Essays in Jurisprudence and Philosophy* (Oxford: Oxford University Press, 1983) 170.

connection to the United Kingdom Parliament *and* to claim that since 1982 at
the latest the United Kingdom Parliament has had no ability whatsoever to
interfere in Canadian legal affairs. This is similar to the way in which we say that
any one of us owes his or her existence to those higher up in the family tree, while
at the same time denying that our ancestors hold any ongoing overwhelming or
ghost-like power over us in our day-to-day affairs.

It is true to say that legal connections are not essential in the way that blood
connections are. We have already seen how many legal systems opt to draw a line
and make a new start. For example, constitutionally speaking, the United States
basically ignores its undeniable historical connection to the United Kingdom.
The new start is not, however, a condition of constitutional independence. The
point being made here is that, just as in family relations, it is possible both to
acknowledge connections or links to the past and to claim independence of
action in the present. There may be good reasons for denying past connections,
especially where they conjure up something negative, but there is no requirement
to do so, certainly no logical requirement. I have emphasised that in law the
connection to the past often carries with it a signal of respect for legality and for
the rule of law. Where legality has been abused and the purposes of the rule of
law thereby turned on their heads, there may be good reason to start afresh,
precisely so as to signal a new resolve to respect not just the rule of law in the
narrow sense of legality, but also to show respect for more substantive senses of
the rule of law having to do with human rights and respect for human dignity.[46]

Just as with sovereignty, then, there would seem to be a number of different
approaches to the idea of legal system in the Empire/Commonwealth: first,
acceptance of ongoing membership in the Imperial/United Kingdom legal system with convention as protection for independence; secondly, rejection of such
membership and assertion of a new legal system based on a new constitutional
foundation, apparently at the cost of legal continuity; thirdly, acceptance of a
legal connection to the Imperial/United Kingdom legal system as part of the
explanation of validity of many (notably constitutional) laws, but rejection of
any ongoing ability of the Imperial/United Kingdom Parliament to interfere by
any legal means in the newly independent legal system.

While the first approach to legal system will appeal to traditionalists, and the
second to nationalists, the third should at least appeal to those who wish to
understand what was probably intended by those who devised the independence
processes in Australia, Canada and New Zealand.[47] While this approach is by no
means favoured for that reason alone, it would be surprising if lawyers could not
explain what lawyers have done for many, many years, at least in the Empire and
Commonwealth.

---

[46] For an example of this type of argument regarding post-1945 Germany, see L. Fuller,
'Positivism and Fidelity to Law—A Reply to Professor Hart' (1958) 71 Harvard L Rev 630.

[47] Furthermore, traditionalists should value its appeal to legal continuity, while nationalists
should value its affirmation of constitutional independence.

Why reconsider constitutional independence in the Commonwealth?

In order to explain and defend the thesis that respect for the rule of law and constitutional continuity are compatible with independence and new constitutional foundations, it will be necessary to examine some historical background as well as some theoretical assumptions. The structure of the book is set out at the end of this introductory chapter. Before doing so, it may be helpful, even essential for many readers, to explain what I take to be the interest in pursuing such an analysis.

We have already seen that this sort of study may add new dimensions to consideration of the connections between sovereignty and legal system. Sovereignty contains more possibility than that contained in absolute, continuing sovereignty—the traditional and orthodox understanding of sovereignty in British constitutional law. Self-embracing understandings of sovereignty began to emerge when polities opted to place constitutional limits on government, notably since the writing of the United States Constitution. Imperial constitutional law initially remained immune to such influences, as reflected in the late nineteenth-century writings of Dicey. However, nineteenth-century colonial constitutional draftsmanship and twentieth-century constitutional theory began to reveal greater possibility. It is one of the themes of this book that self-embracing, relativised, non-zero-sum understandings of sovereignty are closely related to the legal processes by which legal systems break up or come together.

'Break up' relates to the Empire and Commonwealth. 'Come together' refers to a topic of greater current interest: the European Union. In the Imperial and Commonwealth context, the radically self-embracing independence process usually included both the conferral of powers of constitutional amendment and relinquishment by the conferring body of any future ability to accomplish constitutional change in the newly independent legal system. In the EU context, self-embracing change of this type allows a Member State to accomplish the less radical but equally important process of conferring power on European institutions by means of that Member State's supreme constitutional powers and relinquishing (though often on uncertain terms)[48] some of its claims to hierarchical superiority, thereby leaving legal systems which clearly overlap. While Commonwealth and European constitutional development flow in different directions and therefore present many separate problems, the self-embracing process of constitutional change is similar if not identical.[49]

---

[48] We shall see that uncertainty, especially in the middle quarters of the twentieth century, was a feature of Canadian and, especially, New Zealand and Australian constitutional experience. The nature of this uncertainty is discussed in greater detail in Part III below.

[49] See N. MacCormick, *Questioning Sovereignty: Law, State, and Practical Reason* (Oxford: Oxford University Press, 1999) esp. chs 6 and 7. For a critical assessment which makes a start at drawing the Commonwealth-European comparisons, see Oliver (2003) (n. 3 above).

The Commonwealth experience is in one sense admittedly *passé*, at least as far as mainstream constitutional analysis is concerned. It was not always so. For most of the last century the top British (or United Kingdom-based) constitutional minds applied their talents to the task of analysing Empire and Commonwealth developments.[50] Sovereignty was a key factor but so too was the concept of a legal system. Broadly speaking, the *single* legal system with the Westminster Parliament at its apex was gradually breaking up into many separate legal systems. And whereas at the beginning of the process it was clear that the Imperial Parliament at Westminster prevailed and equally clear at the end of the process that the Constitutions of the now independent former colonies were unassailable, in the intervening years there had been considerable uncertainty. The process which presently fascinates many of the best British and non-British constitutional minds is a transition of the reverse sort. In Europe, many sovereign legal systems have begun a process of surrendering some of their sovereignty in order to create the European Union, an entity which is acknowledged to have the characteristics of a separate legal order. The existence of a separate legal order does not necessarily imply the domination of a new, single sovereign legal order, i.e. the perfection of a transition from many legal systems into one. It may come to that; but for the moment Europe finds itself in a middle period of centripetal uncertainty, not dissimilar to that which was experienced in a centrifugal direction in the Commonwealth.

There are important differences, of course, which will be crucial to our analysis. For instance, whereas it is of no practical difficulty that the Australian, Canadian or New Zealand courts take a different view to the British courts on questions of the Westminster Parliament's ongoing sovereignty (see, for example, *Manuel v Attorney-General*)[51] because their spheres of authority no longer overlap, it is potentially troublesome, to say the least, if the British (German or Italian) courts take a different view to the European Court of Justice—their spheres of authority certainly do overlap. And yet, as Neil MacCormick has observed, even in twenty-first century Europe there may be more potential for living constructively with that uncertainty than is generally acknowledged.[52]

Studying the process of constitutional independence also tells us something about *law* and legal system. Unusual situations such as revolutions, *coups d'état* and defying the mother country (as Ireland, South Africa and others did) are well known to reveal important lessons about our legal understandings. It is less obvious, but I would argue just as revealing, that apparently peaceful transitions also teach us important lessons. With revolutions and the like the assumptions on which change is based are close to the surface: a new rule of recognition or a new *Grundnorm*. With peaceful transitions the lessons are below the seemingly

[50] Amongst the many legal/constitutional commentators, one thinks, in particular, of A.V. Dicey, James Bryce, Arthur Berriedale Keith, Ivor Jennings, R.T.E. Latham, H.W.R. Wade, K.C. Wheare, S.A. de Smith, John Finnis and Geoffrey Marshall.
[51] [1983] Ch 77, 87 (H Ct), 99 (CA).   [52] MacCormick (1999) (n. 49 above).

unchanged surface, and assumptions need to be unpacked. For instance, does the fact that the rules (or principles) regarding legal transition to independence are uncertain prior to independence make the eventual process extra-legal in some sense? If the rule of recognition is a question of fact in any legal system, is it nonetheless possible for procedures of legal change within that system to contribute to the alteration of this ultimate rule? Is it possible for the same legal process to be viewed in one way in one legal system and in an opposite way in another legal system?

Finally, it may be interesting and important to look at this Commonwealth process of transition in order to come to a better understanding of how law and legal system interact with politics and society. A major preoccupation of this book is to provide a legal, necessarily partially theoretical, answer to how lawyers can explain a famous legal process: the orderly break-up or building-up of new legal systems. However, this legal task will have failed if it leaves readers with the sense that a purely legal analysis exists (in the sense of it being sufficient for most purposes).

In fact it is the tendency of lawyers to look at law and legal system as inherently valuable, neutral and sufficient that has contributed to otherwise avoidable misunderstandings and injustices, some of which are only belatedly being put right. Legal systems, it is said, are cognitively open but normatively closed, i.e. they are potentially open and aware of social, economic, scientific, cultural and political forces, but they are ultimately governed by their own self-created and self-amended rules. While law's potential for cognitive openness may be true in a sociological sense, the culture of legal practice and legal education too often encourages us to focus only on the normative, legal-logical side of things, and to leave the cognitive aspect underdeveloped. Given the complexity of the world, this filtering out of information is to some extent essential. However, there is a difference between necessary filtering and self-justifying denial.

We will see that both at the beginning and at the end of our story—at the moment of reception and on the acquisition of independence—the orderliness of the legal rules disguises not revolution but the unavoidable contingency of the legal process. In order for English law to take hold in what became Australia, Canada and New Zealand there was no need to exclude aboriginal law. Only the traditional, absolutist model of sovereignty could make it seem so, but there was nothing inevitable about that model, as has been argued above. Contemporary constitutionalism has revealed that difference can coexist in constitutional structures which deny any entity the legal power to dominate the others.[53] At the moment of independence there were at least two opposing ways of interpreting the relevant Westminster enactment, one which allowed the sovereignty of the Westminster Parliament to endure, even if controlled by rigid convention, and

[53] See J. Tully, *Strange Multiplicity: Constitutionalism in an Age of Diversity* (Cambridge: Cambridge University Press, 1995). See also MacCormick (1999) (n. 49 above).

another which required that that sovereignty terminate, at least as far as any future local purposes were concerned. Both models are workable. Furthermore, it seems an excessively Imperial conception of law which deems itself self-sufficiently equipped to decide between the two. Unless we fall back on the use of force, we must ask what, besides the use of force, sustains a legal system, what it is that explains why we do or do not think of what exists at the beginning and what exists at the end of the story as one legal system.[54] This takes us into questions of history, politics, authority and legitimacy, broadly understood. This book will not pursue these questions in any detail; however, they should always be borne in mind.

The structure of this book

The book is divided into three Parts. The first Part examines both the legal structure of the Empire and the dominant constitutional ideas which held it together. Chapter 2 Considers how English law came to be received in foreign lands and how self-government came to be established. The basic texts and rules of the Imperial Constitution will be discussed here, together with the early constitutional development of the three countries under study. This will provide some of the context for the discussion of Imperial constitutional ideas which takes up Chapters 3 and 4. It also allows the five chapters in Part II to begin with the heart of the matter—the prospect of constitutional independence in each of those countries—rather than with extended preliminaries.

The topics covered in Chapter 2 are diverse and, in some cases, very difficult. I am not presenting original, primary-source historical research here. My goal is simply to provide an introduction to Imperial political and constitutional history to readers who are unfamiliar, while at the same time highlighting issues which will re-emerge in later discussions. The topic has new freshness due to the fact that writers specialising in aboriginal rights have re-examined this area in recent years; and not surprisingly, some of their conclusions sit uncomfortably with more traditional and orthodox views. As far as constitutional theory is concerned, the main theme here is the tendency, even by Australians, Canadians and New Zealanders, to seek pan-Imperial or pan-Commonwealth explanations for the development of the larger legal system. There is no lack of diversity but even the most single-minded constitutional commentators tend to see themselves, through much of the period covered in these chapters, as engaged in a broader as opposed to purely national enterprise. In this they are distinguishable from their Irish and South African counterparts.

The balance of Part I, made up of Chapters 3 and 4, will examine Imperial or British constitutional theory. Chapter 3 will set out the orthodox view of

---

[54] See Finnis (1973) (n. 21 above) 69 et seq.

parliamentary sovereignty, i.e. the idea associated with A.V. Dicey, that Parliament—and therefore the Imperial Parliament—can make any law whatever, and that no institution can challenge Parliament's ability to do so. So long as local courts and local populations were willing to accept this principle, the Westminster Parliament could act as constituent assembly for the Empire, enacting constitutions for New Zealand in the 1850s, Canada in the 1860s and Australia at the turn of the century. It also had the ability to amend these constitutions even (so long as one accepted the orthodox view) in a country such as Australia which had adopted its own constitutional amendment procedures. Dicey himself could be unforgiving of those in remote parts of the Empire who did not appreciate these basic facts. The domination of traditional thinking about sovereignty also limited the range of possible options when it came to reducing the egalitarian sentiments of the Balfour Declaration to legal form. Much of the writing at the time of the Statute of Westminster 1931 illustrates these difficulties. While the jurisprudence of countries such as South Africa and Ireland took an independent turn, the view from the centre—the Judicial Committee of the Privy Council—was formal, legal and traditional. Writers such as Bryce and Berriedale Keith perpetuated this tradition for the most part.

Chapter 4 will discuss the writings of constitutional theorists who challenged the Diceyan orthodoxy. Spearheaded by Ivor Jennings, this view was never so well expressed as by his younger University of London colleague, Richard Latham, son of the Chief Justice of Australia and lecturer at King's College, London. This book will be unique in attributing much of the hard intellectual work on the 'new' and 'revised' view of parliamentary sovereignty to Latham (whose promising academic and professional career was tragically cut short in 1943). It will benefit from the detailed archival research into Latham's life and work that I have undertaken independently of this book project.[55] Jennings' and Latham's insight could be pinned down to the fact that asserting Parliament's sovereignty (*à la* Dicey) assumed knowledge of something called 'Parliament'. The courts can only know what Parliament is because of custom, now incorporated into the common law. Just as Parliament can alter by legislation the common law relating to contract, so can it alter the common law (and custom) relating both to Parliament's existence and to the exercise of its sovereignty. H.L.A. Hart would later provide this last view with the convenient label 'self-embracing' sovereignty, so as to contrast it with the traditional Dicey position of 'continuing sovereignty'. If Parliament could alter the nature of its own sovereignty then there appeared to be no reason why it could not add more onerous procedural requirements to its power of enactment or even limit the possible subject matter of its legislation. More specifically, for Commonwealth purposes, it could provide that Westminster must not pass legislation for a Dominion

---

[55] See P. Oliver, 'Law, Politics, the Commonwealth and the Constitution: Remembering R.T.E. Latham, 1909–43' (2000) 11 KCLJ 153.

unless it stated that such was done with the request and consent of the country concerned (see Ceylon Independence Act 1947, section 1(1)); or it could declare, as in the Nigeria Independence Act 1960, section 1(2) that '[n]o Act of the Parliament of the United Kingdom passed on or after [independence] shall extend, or be deemed to extend, to [the newly independent country]'. If these words could be taken at face value, then the problem of Commonwealth devolution and post-Westminster Parliament independence would seem to be solved. For the citizens of the newly independent countries these esoteric matters were beyond their concern.

Constitutional lawyers had more difficulty explaining what had occurred, as we shall see. Writers such as Geoffrey Marshall and K.C. Wheare in the 1950s and early 1960s revealed that there was a full range of approaches and attitudes to the achievement of constitutional independence. And such uncertainty continues to suffuse considerations regarding the United Kingdom's own sovereignty within the European Union. The analysis in Chapter 4 also brings this traditional view of sovereignty up to date, in part by focusing on the writings of Dicey's most powerful apologist, H.W.R. Wade. The latter's contributions to the theoretical debate continue to spur on United Kingdom discussions regarding sovereignty and Europe.

This survey of pan-Commonwealth and United Kingdom constitutional theory will reveal a number of relevant factors:

(1) the mesmerising simplicity of Dicey's theory of sovereignty and its continued hold on constitutional thinking, especially in courts and government;

(2) the powerful critique of that theory presented by adherents of the 'new' and 'revised' view, notably in their attempts to explain the process of Commonwealth devolution and independence;

(3) the acceptance of the 'new' and 'revised' views in academic circles but rejection or only partial acceptance beyond those circles—the tendency to grant, if at all, that the Westminster Parliament may be able to limit the territorial range of its competence or the manner and form of its legislation but that the power to undo such limitations remained with the United Kingdom Parliament ('continuing' sovereignty in other words);

(4) given the absence of wide acceptance of 'self-embracing' sovereignty, attempts to explain Commonwealth devolution from the point of view of the centre (i.e. Westminster and the United Kingdom) were frustrated— satisfactory explanations had to emerge instead from local constitutional theory, which is the subject of Part II.

Part II builds on the general historical and theoretical background material provided in Part I. The chapters in Part II look, first, at how those concerned with the Constitution in Australia, Canada and New Zealand—lawyers, judges,

politicians or constitutional commentators—contemplated the possibility of
cutting the legislative links with the Imperial Parliament. Research here indicates
that 'independent' (in relation to the Imperial and British orthodoxy) theoretical
takes on this possibility, and on the related issues of sovereignty and legal system,
were rare. In general, the 'Imperial theory'—Diceyan notions of parliamentary
sovereignty—presented an intellectual straitjacket for constitutional reformers.
This manifested itself in various arguments: (a) that independence legislation
was a futile gesture; (b) that independence could be successfully achieved by an
Act of Parliament but that Westminster would retain a ghostly presence (or, in
constitutional terms, the latter would have to remain in place all the while
respecting a strong convention against unwarranted interference); (c) that
building on the last point, the newly 'independent' constitution could only
retain its legal validity and supremacy if the Westminster Parliament remained
part of the local legal system.

Secondly, Part II will consider how, following the enactment (although not
the immediate adoption) of the Statute of Westminster 1931 and the subsequent
years of accelerating de-colonisation, a growing number of constitutional
writers in Australia, Canada and New Zealand began to accept that legislative
independence could be achieved, even by legal means. High-sounding phrases
such as 'the basic norm' and 'constituent power' were set out in academic
commentary to justify such views. Given the esoteric nature of such subject
matter, there was little or no opportunity for legislative or judicial confirmation
of the legal weight of the arguments on which they depended. Government
advisers tended instead to cling to the fact that other Commonwealth countries
appeared to have successfully achieved their independence by means of Westminster legislation and that the same should be possible for them.

Thirdly, despite the paucity of references to these matters, it will be useful
nonetheless to consider the role of the judiciary in making sense of such fundamental constitutional matters. Each country achieved strikingly different levels
of judicial independence at different points in this century. New Zealand has
only very recently ended appeals to the Judicial Committee of the Privy
Council,[56] but even before this occurred New Zealand courts were not shy to
develop innovative approaches to constitutional theory. Both the Canadian and
Australian courts have commented directly on the sources of legislative authority
under their respective constitutions, the highest Canadian court having done so
in detailed fashion in the 1981 *Patriation Reference*. Australian courts were
especially articulate on these issues in the decade preceding 1986, and have
remained so after 1986.

Fourthly, Part II will describe the process surrounding termination of
Westminster's power to legislate for Australia, Canada and New Zealand.

---

[56] Supreme Court Act 2003 (NZ), s. 42 of which ended appeals to the Privy Council in respect
of 'any civil or criminal decision of a New Zealand court made after 31 December 2003'. The
newly created Supreme Court of New Zealand (s. 6) began hearings on 1 July 2004 (s. 55).

In Canada this was caught up with a more elaborate, high profile constitutional reform project which included the Charter of Rights and Freedoms. In Australia and New Zealand, the process attracted less popular attention but was of no less concern in government circles. In all three countries the severing of the Imperial legislative ties provoked in-depth discussion of constitutional fundamentals in academic journals, textbooks, and occasionally even in judicial comment. Fifthly and finally, this Part will consider these discussions in some detail, focusing initially on official explanations for what had occurred.

Part III attempts to explain constitutional independence and to analyse its consequences. It begins (in Chapter 11) with a detailed discussion of the attempts by constitutional commentators in Australia, Canada and New Zealand to explain the fundamental changes which occurred in 1982 and 1986. While a great deal of descriptive writing was published at this time, this Part focuses on those writers who attempted to explore more carefully the legal, political and social forces that were at play.

This Part also attempts (in Chapter 12) an independent explanation of the independence of legal systems. The assumption made here is that constitutional independence can be explained, first, by observing that questions of sovereignty are closely related to issues which are central to the concept of a legal system; and secondly, by asserting the independence of local constitutional theory. A credible explanation for independence can be set out in a series of propositions. The virtue of this explanation is that it provides a legal account of that which lawyers, politicians and the public apparently assume: that Australia, Canada and New Zealand are now independent and that that independence was achieved by legal means. However, it is not surprising to state that explanations for independence—legal, political, popular or other—are as varied as they are unexpected. The following propositions require elaboration. However, it may be useful to set them out at this stage in the book so as to alert the reader to the argument which eventually emerges:[57]

(1) That despite initial doubts on the matter, it is now accepted that both continuing and self-embracing interpretations of the ultimate rule of a legal system are coherent (as discussed by H.L.A. Hart in *The Concept of Law* and elsewhere). This means that, from a local perspective, the United Kingdom Parliament can be seen either to remain perpetually at the apex of the legal systems or to provide for its own replacement as ultimate amending procedure.

(2) That, understood in self-embracing terms, the United Kingdom Parliament can simultaneously confer legal validity on the local constitution, and, without undermining that validity, disappear (immediately or eventually) from the legal map of those constitutional systems. John Finnis has described this 'principle of continuity' in the following terms: 'A law once validly brought into being, in

[57] Footnotes have been omitted here as they appear at the end of Ch. 12 below, where a slightly more elaborate version of these propositions is repeated.

accordance with criteria of validity *then in force*, remains valid until either it expires according to its own terms or terms implied at its creation, or it is repealed in accordance with conditions of repeal in force *at the time of repeal.*' If this principle is accepted, applying either to the self-reflexive provisions of the constitutional amendment procedure or to legislation generally, then it seems also to imply that there is no need to keep the United Kingdom as an active component of the local legal system.

(3) That, as Joseph Raz has pointed out, Hans Kelsen's use of constitutional continuity as the proper criterion of the identity of a legal system does not fit the facts: 'A country may be granted independence by a law or another country authorising its laws; nevertheless, its laws form a separate legal system.' The *Grundnorm* or basic norm is of interest in providing a genealogy of certain legal rules in the system, and for accounting for their validity and normativity, but as long as one accepts the possibility of self-embracing change, one should expect to uncover in local constitutional history institutions and laws which are no longer active parts of the present legal system, however vital their role may have been in the past. Constitutional continuity indicates respect for the constitutional rule of law, and, from a positivist perspective, a link to the historically-first constitution and the *Grundnorm*. It does not indicate that all the members of the family tree are alive and well, and ready and able to assert their ancestral priority.

(4) That H.L.A. Hart's notions of the ultimate rule of recognition and of differing perspectives explain how the Westminster Parliament can be seen as having continuing sovereign powers from a United Kingdom perspective and spent self-embracing sovereign powers from an Australian, Canadian or New Zealand perspective. From the external perspective the United Kingdom and the local interpretations of the same Westminster processes are clearly incompatible, but as separately functioning internal perspectives this incompatibility is of no consequence. However, Hart's account does not explain how or why the ultimate rule of recognition can be said to evolve, as clearly it must have done over the twentieth century, as the accounts in Parts I and II indicate.

(5) That more recent writing regarding the concept of a legal system reveals that the allegiance of the primary law-applying agencies (courts) is an important factor in predicting how the ultimate rule of recognition will be perceived and where the boundaries of the legal system will be drawn. Raz emphasises that 'whatever form one's ultimate account of continuity takes, it must, in view of the relation between law and state, be based on the interaction of legal and non-legal norms, and the extent and manner of their change'. Neil MacCormick's recent writing regarding Member State/EU constitutional relations endorses the point about the interaction of legal and non-legal norms, but re-emphasises the role of primary law-making agencies (legislatures) in determining how the rule of recognition changes.

(6) That if the ultimate rule of recognition is a customary rule whose core content is judicially established (i.e. the Queen-in-Parliament is sovereign), but whose penumbra is uncertain (i.e. is that sovereignty continuing or self-embracing?), one would expect it to evolve in advance of judicial determination in step with social and political developments in the local country in question.

(7) That in the case of Australia, Canada and New Zealand key factors and principles—such as international status, judicial independence, the connection between the local population and the local constitution, democratic account-ability, responsible government, etc.—point towards an interpretation of the ultimate rule of recognition which justifies constitutional independence. A self-embracing interpretation of Westminster's powers (at least from the local point of view) fulfils this function. Increasing attachment to this interpretation can be identified in the development of constitutional theory in each of the countries even if a consensus has yet to emerge. If ever a local court were asked or was tempted on its own initiative to describe the nature of Westminster's powers at the moment that Parliament apparently transferred its constituent powers to Australia, Canada or New Zealand, the self-embracing interpretation would seem to explain the intricate legal workings of that which politics and history will have already confirmed.

Chapter 13 will apply the analysis just developed to the facts of constitutional development in Australia, Canada and New Zealand. The point will not be to insist on this account as the only viable one, but rather to propose it as one way of accounting for both constitutional continuity *and* constitutional independence. Whereas there are similarities in the explanations proposed for Canadian and New Zealand constitutional independence, Australian developments require special treatment, particularly in relation to the idea that popular sovereignty is the new basis for the Australian Constitution.

The concluding chapter will consider how traditional ideas in constitutional theory—sovereignty, legal system and rule of law—relate to more contemporary theoretical concerns: authority, legitimacy, democracy and the like. However, we do well to keep these concerns in mind from the outset. We now turn to the beginning of the story: the establishment of the Imperial legal system in Australia, Canada and New Zealand.

PART I

THE IMPERIAL CONSTITUTION

2

The Imperial Dominions

Acquisition of sovereignty and 'reception' of English law

How is it that English or, as we shall occasionally call it, Imperial law came to apply in Australia, Canada and New Zealand? The problem is usually referred to as one of 'reception'. The term has a genteel sound to it. This gentility is removed in some post-modern and critical accounts of law and legal system by referring to 'the founding moment of violence'.[1] The point is that there is certainly no inevitability associated with the fact that the English common law and other non-aboriginal forms of law now dominate the Australian, Canadian and New Zealand legal systems. It is a contingent fact, explainable only by the occurrence of certain extraordinary events. Far from amounting to reception (in the sense of a welcoming), these events more closely approximate an 'imposition', which even in its more polite sense captures the important point that even if the British and their laws were sometimes greeted by aboriginal populations with curiosity and good will, accommodation of a new, and it

---

[1] J. Derrida, 'Force of Law: The "Mystical Foundation of Authority"' in D. Cornell, M. Rosenfeld and D. Carlson (eds) *Deconstruction and the Possibility of Justice* (New York: Routledge, 1992) 1, 35–6, 40–1. The use of this expression is not intended to imply that legal systems in Australia, Canada and New Zealand were created solely or mainly by overt physical violence. It is, however, intended to convey how the insertion of powerful legal constructs—those of sovereignty and legal system in this case—radically and permanently altered relations on the ground. As we shall see, expressions of equality and friendship with aboriginal populations transformed themselves into sovereign determinations by Imperial (or colonial) legislatures and courts which often went against aboriginal understandings. Looked at from the perspective of each setback for aboriginal peoples, the moment of 'violence' to their understandings and expectations lay not simply in the present of the legislatures' or courts' determinations; it lay most profoundly in the establishment of those institutions' sovereignty and in the pre-emptive founding of the legal system of which they are a part. See, e.g., Brennan J. in *Mabo v Queensland (No 2)* (1992) 175 CLR 1, 69: 'The Crown's acquisition of sovereignty over the several parts of Australia [and with it the jurisdiction of the High Court of Australia] cannot be challenged in an Australian municipal court.' A similar process of recognising aboriginal rights without questioning the original acquisition of British (later Canadian) sovereignty occurred in *Delgamuukw v British Columbia* [1997] 3 SCR 1010, on which see J. Borrows, *Recovering Canada: The Resurgence of Indigenous Law* (Toronto: University of Toronto Press, 2003) ch. 7 or J. Borrows, ' "Because it does not make sense": sovereignty's power in the case of *Delgamuuk v The Queen 1997*' in D. Kirkby and C. Coleborne (eds) *Law, History, Colonialism: The Reach of Empire* (Manchester: Manchester University Press, 2001) 190. For a discussion of similar issues in New Zealand, see P. McHugh, *The Māori Magna Carta: New Zealand Law and the Treaty of Waitangi* (Auckland: Oxford University Press, 1991) ch. 2.

must be said, assertive European culture was always going to be difficult, to say the least.

Consistent with the idea of 'imposition', the rules[2] regarding acquisition of new territories and 'reception'[3] of British law were determined, not by British settlers and the aboriginal populations that the former encountered, but by European-inspired international law or by British law. International law was relevant *vis-à-vis* other European powers that might have wished to challenge Britain's claim to a particular colonial acquisition—the question of 'external sovereignty', as it is sometimes referred to.[4] Aboriginal populations were not able to avail themselves of a system of 'international' law which often did not recognise their own tribes and nations. British law, within the frame of a pre-sumed 'internal'[5] Imperial sovereignty, was relevant where Imperial courts, British and local, were called upon to decide not just whether British law applied, but also how and to what extent. For instance, and as we shall see, British law determined whether the British Crown could legislate in the new colony by prerogative, or whether the Crown had to defer to local legislative will.

As it happened, the international and British rules regarding acquisition of new territories and reception of European laws were similar in the main. This analysis is an approximation of the British version. The main distinction that had to be made in these rules was that between 'settled' and 'conquered' colonies. In the case of settled colonies, i.e. where British settlers found a colony in an 'uninhabited' country (according to the British perspective), the settlers' law—or at least such British statute and English common law as was applicable to their new situation—came to the new land with them. In one writer's words, 'as soon as the original settlers had reached the colony, their invisible and inescapable cargo of English law fell from their shoulders and attached itself to the soil on which they stood'.[6]

---

[2] The use of the term 'rules' requires some qualification here and elsewhere in this chapter. First, these 'rules' were in a very unsettled state throughout the eighteenth and much of the nineteenth century (as demonstrated, e.g., by the need for the Colonial Laws Validity Act, 1865) and underwent quite significant evolution and change throughout this entire period. Secondly, the rules were generated by a very considerable and highly complex body of legal practice and opinion, in an ever-expanding and somewhat heterogeneous British Empire, including areas in the Caribbean, North America, Africa, India, and South-East Asia. I am grateful to Brian Slattery for pointing out the need for this qualification, even if the general and basic nature of this chapter does not always reflect the necessary level of nuance.

[3] Though somewhat inapt for the reasons mentioned, the usual term, 'reception', will be used from here on.

[4] See, e.g., N. MacCormick, *Questioning Sovereignty: Law, State, and Practical Reason* (Oxford: Oxford University Press, 1999) 126.   [5] MacCormick (1999) (n. 4 above) 126.

[6] R.T.E. Latham, 'The Law and The Commonwealth' in W.K. Hancock (ed.) *Survey of British Commonwealth Affairs*, Vol. 1 (London: Oxford University Press, 1937) 510, reprinted with a Foreward by W.K. Hancock but with otherwise unaltered pagination as R.T.E. Latham, *The Law and the Commonwealth* (Oxford: Oxford University Press, 1949) 517. Latham also pointed out that Scotsmen were deemed to be Englishmen overseas, in that it was the English common law and not Scots law that featured in that invisible cargo, a matter which seemed particularly unfair given the large number of Scottish explorers and settlers.

One might have thought that the law regarding 'discovery' and newly 'settled' colonies would be of little relevance to Australia, Canada and New Zealand where aboriginal populations had for a long time inhabited[7] the lands in question.[8] However, in the case of Australia and parts of Canada (and, on one view, the South Island of New Zealand), discovery and settlement were indeed the main reasons for the application of British law in those lands. Explanations for this aberration diverge; however, the conclusion was, in an important sense, all that mattered, at least at the time. For along with British law came the absolutist notions of sovereignty that were a characteristic of European nation states' world-view at the time of exploration and colonisation.[9] Current recognition that aboriginal peoples not only inhabited but also governed the lands in question is relevant to re-examination of constitutional theory, but it takes place within a legal context where the existence of a settler-created legal system is already taken for granted, at least as a matter of (settler) law.[10]

The other way in which British law could attach in a colony was by means of conquest and/or cession. This was the case, for example, in central Canada when, at the end of the Seven Years War in 1763, the defeated France ceded virtually all of its North American territorial possessions to Great Britain. According to one interpretation of New Zealand events, the Treaty of Waitangi amounted to cession by Māori chiefs (at least by those of the North Island) to Great Britain.

The main difference between acquisition by conquest (and cession) rather than by settlement was that, in the former case, the existing legal system remained intact[11] unless and until modified or abrogated by the British Crown or

---

[7] On agri*culture* as evidence of settlement from a European perspective see P. Goodrich, 'Terminal legality: Imperialism and the (de) composition of law' in D. Kirkby and C. Coleborne (eds) *Law, History, Colonialism: The Reach of Empire* (Manchester: Manchester University Press, 2001) 1. On aboriginal and Imperial relations more generally, see B. Slattery, 'Aboriginal Sovereignty and Imperial Claims' (1991) 29 Osgoode Hall LJ 1.

[8] 'There is a view that the sovereignty of the Crown over Te Waipounamu [New Zealand's South Island] stems from "right of discovery" and not from an act of cession by treaty. This view, which has periodic currency in public argument about treaty rights and race relations, causes a certain amount of hilarity amongst Ngāi Tahu who rhetorically ask, "Discovery by whom?" The proposition, however misinformed, has its serious side...' Tipene O'Regan, 'The Ngāi Tahu Claim' in I.H. Kawharu, *Waitangi: Māori and Pākehā Perspectives of the Treaty of Waitangi* (Auckland: Oxford University Press, 1989) 234, 239–40.

[9] See J. Tully, *Strange Multiplicity: Constitutionalism in an Age of Diversity* (Cambridge: Cambridge University Press, 1995).

[10] See *Mabo v Queensland (No 2)* (1992) 175 CLR 1, 69, where aboriginal title was re-considered but where Australian sovereignty was not placed in question. See also *Delgamuukw v British Columbia* [1997] 3 SCR 1010 and *New Zealand Maori Council v Attorney-General* [1987] 1 NZLR 641. The numerous recent unsuccessful attempts to set up *Māori* sovereignty against New Zealand sovereignty have been collected in a recent unreported decision of the New Zealand High Court: *David Lee Morunga v New Zealand Police*, 16 March 2004. I am grateful to Philip Joseph for providing a copy of this unreported case.

[11] Changes to local law were in the meantime subject to the terms of cession, however, 'the common law recognized the effect of a treaty of cession, usually signed after a conquest. To arrive at the "cession rule" one merely applied the conquest rule, with the added *caveat* that changes in local law were subject to the terms of the treaty'. M.D. Walters, 'British Imperial Constitutional Law and Aboriginal Rights: A Comment on *Delgamuukw v. British Columbia*' (1992) 17 Queen's LJ 350, 361.

Parliament. Also, in conquered and ceded territories, the British Crown could rule by proclamation, at least until representative institutions had been set up, at which time the rights of the settlers would revert to those cherished by all British subjects since the Glorious Revolution, i.e. a prohibition on Crown legislation without Parliament (except in those residual areas of the prerogative where such legislation was permitted even in Britain). However, for our purposes, these differences and others were of lesser importance. Both settlement and conquest (cession) succeeded in establishing British legal authority and legal institutions in the countries in question, thereby making them part of the larger Imperial legal system in which the Imperial Parliament was sovereign. And even in the case of conquered (or ceded) lands where legislation by Crown proclamation was an option, legislation by the Imperial Crown-*in-Parliament* was always possible and would in such an event prevail.

The fact that Australia, Canada and New Zealand became part of the larger Imperial legal system, in which Imperial parliamentary sovereignty operated, meant that resolution of controversies regarding local populations—French settlers and aboriginal peoples, for example—would, strictly speaking, take place in an uneven, contradictory or paradoxical context. For instance, British settlers might negotiate with aboriginal populations in a spirit of equality and mutual respect, but British courts were duty bound to prefer any version of events which the common law recognised as having precedence, most notably that version provided for in the sovereign Acts of the Imperial Parliament. Canons of interpretation could be developed eventually to protect the assumptions of equality,[12] but, as with all questions of construction, if the sovereign Imperial Parliament wished to express itself clearly enough, its will would prevail.

The contradictory and paradoxical nature of British colonial relations can be seen in two seminal documents: the Royal Proclamation of 1763 and the Treaty of Waitangi of 1840. The first of these was an exercise by the British Crown of its prerogative to legislate for a conquered (or ceded) territory, in this case the vast territory of Quebec. The Proclamation of 1763, amongst other things, recognised aboriginal tribes and nations as representatives of their peoples and possessors of their lands; however, at the same time, it contradicted the equality and mutual respect suggested by the Proclamation by referring to those same lands as 'such Parts of *our* Dominions and Territories':

And whereas it is just and reasonable, and essential to Our Interest and the Security of Our Colonies, that the several Nations or Tribes of Indians, with whom We are connected, and who live under Our Protection, should not be molested or disturbed in the Possession *of such Parts of Our Dominions and Territories* as, not having been ceded to, or purchased by Us, are reserved to them, or any of them, as their Hunting Grounds . . . [13]

[12] See, e.g., *Calder v British Columbia (Attorney-General)* [1973] SCR 313.
[13] Royal Proclamation, RSC 1985, App. II, No. 1 (emphasis added). For discussion, see Canada, *Report of the Royal Commission on Aboriginal Peoples*, Vol. 1, *Looking Forward Looking Back* (1996) ch. 5, section 2.

The Treaty of Waitangi, arguably the most important document in New Zealand history, contains similar contradictory or paradoxical provisions. Its first article referred in English to cession 'to Her Majesty the Queen of England absolutely and without reservation all the rights and powers of *Sovereignty* which the said Confederation or Individual Chiefs respectively exercise or possess, or may be supposed to exercise or possess over their respective Territories as the sole Sovereigns thereof'. However, in *Māori*, translated back to English, this same article read 'The Chiefs of the Confederation and all the Chiefs not in that Confederation cede without reservation to the Queen of England forever the *Governorship* of all their lands'.[14] Whatever the exact meaning of 'sovereignty' and 'governorship', a tension soon emerged. The second article then reserved to the *Māori* signatories 'full exclusive and undisturbed possession of their Lands and Estates Forests Fisheries and other properties'.[15]

It was therefore unclear whether the equality and mutual respect manifested in the words and actions of so much formal aboriginal-settler interaction, or the hierarchy and subordination of some of the legal language, represented the true state of affairs. However, these ambiguities were often lost on the British and colonial courts, at least in the early stages of aboriginal-settler cohabitation. One thinks, for example, of Prendergast CJ in *Wi Parata v Bishop of Wellington*[16] in which the Treaty of Waitangi was declared to be, legally speaking, 'a simple nullity'. In Canada, a doctrine of aboriginal rights developed whereby courts recognised aboriginal peoples' possession of their lands and their right to continue to occupy and use them until they ceded them to the Crown through a formal treaty-like process. However, as one writer has stated, 'it is doubtful that there was the same mutuality of understanding with regard to the part of the doctrine, so essential to the British, that asserted the Crown's fundamental sovereignty over the Indian territories'.[17] The Judicial Committee of the Privy Council provided early clarification of the matter by indicating that Indian title was merely 'a personal and usufructuary right, dependent on the good will of the Sovereign'.[18] The reason for the weak aboriginal right, at least in the eyes of the common law, was that, in Philip Joseph's words, 'acquisition of a territory in sovereignty import[ed] more . . . than *imperium*—the right of

---

[14] R.J. Walker, 'The Treaty of Waitangi as the Focus of Māori Protest' in I.H. Kawharu (ed.) *Waitangi: Māori and Pākehā Perspectives of the Treaty of Waitangi* (Auckland: Oxford University Press, 1989) 263 (emphasis added).

[15] See F.M. Brookfield, 'The New Zealand Constitution: The Search for Legitimacy' in I.H. Kawharu (ed.) *Waitangi: Māori and Pākehā Perspectives of the Treaty of Waitangi* (Auckland: Oxford University Press, 1989) 1, 4.

[16] (1877) 3 NZ Jur (NS) 72 at 78 (SC). More recently, see e.g. *Attorney-General v Ngati Apa* [2003] 3 NZLR 643 (CA).

[17] P. Russell, 'High Courts and the Rights of Aboriginal Peoples: The Limits of Judicial Independence' (1998) 61 Sask L Rev 247, 356.

[18] See *St Catherine's Milling and Lumber Co v The Queen* (1888) 14 App Cas 46, quoted in Russell (1998) (n. 17 above) 257–8.

government. It also import[ed] *dominium*—the Crown's paramount ownership of its territory'.[19]

The account which has been set out thus far is largely based on what Mark Walters has referred to as the rules of 'simple conquest' and 'simple settlement'.[20] The assumption of this 'simple' model was that ultimately one sovereignty and one legal system had to prevail. We shall see in the next chapter how closely this assumption was tied into the orthodox Imperial theory propounded by writers such as Professor A.V. Dicey. More recently, constitutional writers in Australia, Canada and New Zealand have identified strains of an alternative account— what Walters calls 'complex conquest' and 'complex settlement'[21]—according to which less absolutism and more legal pluralism were possible.[22] British law was of course introduced, or received, for British settlers 'as their birthright';[23] however 'continuity of some indigenous law for aboriginal peoples' was also possible.[24] This approach was arguably much more appropriate where, notably in Australia and many parts of Canada, contact between settlers and aboriginal peoples was so limited that speaking of discovery and settlement, much less conquest or cession, had a considerable level of unreality to it.

Such new and complex approaches have especially important consequences where land claims, and associated rights, are concerned. Cases such as *Mabo* and *Delgamuukw* provide evidence of these consequences. However, it is quite a leap from recognising continuity in aboriginal land claims, and associated rights, to claiming a legally protected sphere of sovereignty or constitutional independence for aboriginal peoples. This sort of arrangement is certainly conceivable in law— it exists in federalism and in the relative sovereignties of international law.[25] However, we shall see that the dominance of a more traditional and absolutist version of sovereignty, and a corresponding aversion to pluralism where legal systems are concerned, has heavily conditioned the terms of current debates. Recognition of enduring property rights is one thing; recognition of enduring constitutional rights equivalent to sovereignty is quite another. Contemporary constitutionalism shows a willingness to embrace the latter, but the hold

---

[19] P.A. Joseph, *Constitutional and Administrative Law in New Zealand* (2nd edn, Wellington: Brookers, 2001), 32, citing *Oyekan v Adele* [1957] 2 All ER 785 (PC).

[20] Walters (1992) (n. 11 above) 366.   [21] ibid., 373.

[22] See, e.g., B. Slattery, *Land Rights of Aboriginal Canadian People, as Affected by the Crown's Acquisition of Their Territories* (Doctoral Dissertation, Oxford University, 1979); 'The Independence of Canada' (1983) 5 Sup Ct L Rev 369, 'Ancestral Lands, Alien Laws: Judicial Perspectives on Aboriginal Title' (Saskatoon: University of Saskatchewan Native Law Centre, 1983) and 'Understanding Aboriginal Rights' (1987) 66 Can Bar Rev 727; K. McNeil, *Common Law Aboriginal Title* (Oxford: Clarendon Press, 1989); and P. McHugh, *The Aboriginal Rights of the New Zealand Maori at Common Law* (Doctoral Dissertation, Cambridge University, 1987) and *The Maori Magna Carta: New Zealand and the Treaty of Waitangi* (Auckland: Oxford University Press, 1991).

'Less absolutism' and 'more legal pluralism' were famously present in the decisions of Marshall CJ of the United States Supreme Court, notably *Worcester v The State of Georgia* (1832) 31 US (6 Peter's Reports) 515.   [23] Walters (1992) (n. 11 above) 376.

[24] ibid., 376.   [25] Tully (1995) (n. 9 above) 195.

of traditional constitutionalism is sometimes overwhelming, at least for the moment.

Self-government and Imperial law[26]

It was this unchallengeable sovereignty in the Crown (when acting by prerogative) and ultimately in the Crown-*in-Parliament* (when acting by legislative enactment) that eventually operated the constituent process for the three countries in question. New Zealand was, in 1852, the first of them to acquire a national constitution, although colonies in what were to become Canada and then Australia had by this time already acquired constitutions and institutions, and were well on their way to achieving responsible government. For the purposes of this survey chapter, we shall focus on the acquisition of national constitutions, though it will be important to remember, in the case of Canada and Australia, that smaller entities came together to achieve the status of nationhood with which we are now familiar.

New Zealand

As Philip Joseph has noted, it is 'the extension of British sovereignty [that] indelibly determined New Zealand's constitutional character', and therefore it is 'ironic that the method by which it became a Crown colony is destined to be disputed'.[27] It is at least clear that New Zealand was not acquired as a result of conquest. However, if the Treaty of Waitangi (and therefore 'cession') is deemed to be the critical event in the acquisition of British sovereignty over New Zealand, then, as we have seen, the rules of acquisition and reception by conquest would in any event apply.

Given the significance of the Treaty of Waitangi in the New Zealand social, political and legal consciousness, the fact that British officials and *Māori* chiefs representing at least some of New Zealand signed a solemn agreement in 1840 is bound to be of great importance, legal and other, come what may. However, unless we are intent on and capable of re-writing history, which clearly we are not, it is vital to remember that there was a strong alternative explanation for the establishment of British sovereignty and reception of British law in New Zealand;

---

[26] The country surveys which follow rely to a considerable degree on the leading general textbooks on constitutional law in each of New Zealand, Canada and Australia. For New Zealand, I have relied on Philip A. Joseph, *Constitutional and Administrative Law in New Zealand* (2nd edn, Wellington: Brookers, 2001), for Canada, Peter W. Hogg, *Constitutional Law of Canada* (4th edn (looseleaf), Toronto: Thomson Carswell, 1997), and for Australia, T. Blackshield and G. Williams, *Australian Constitutional Law and Theory* (Annandale: Federation Press, 2002) and Leslie Zines, *Constitutional Change in the Commonwealth* (Cambridge: Cambridge University Press, 1991). I record this debt with gratitude, though of course I remain responsible for misreadings and/or misrepresenations. [27] Joseph (2001) (n. 26 above) 30.

and the fact that this explanation was for such a long time preferred by that same law gave it an undoubted advantage and, for the time being, legal precedence.[28]

In the case of New Zealand, the dominant legal version is roughly as follows.[29] In early 1840, Governor Sir George Gipps of New South Wales issued three proclamations. The first of these extended the boundaries of New South Wales to include any territory which might be acquired in New Zealand.[30] The second and third proclamations stated that Captain Hobson had been appointed Lieutenant Governor and that, as of proclamation, title to land purchased privately from the *Māori* would not be recognised by the Crown.[31]

The process which culminated in the signing of the Treaty of Waitangi began in February 1840, initiated by the new Lieutenant Governor, William Hobson. On 5–6 February 1840 he convened an assembly of native chiefs and obtained signatures, at this stage from fifty-odd chiefs from the northern parts of New Zealand. Over the ensuing months, the signatures of other chiefs were sought and, by October 1840 when the Treaty was sent to Her Majesty Queen Victoria (chief of the British, so to speak) over 500 chiefs had signed. The signed proclamation was then published on 2 October 1840. Hobson had in the meantime issued two proclamations, dated 21 May 1840, asserting British sovereignty over New Zealand. The first claimed sovereignty over the North Island as a result of the cession by North Island chiefs in the Treaty of Waitangi; the second claimed sovereignty over the South Island and other smaller islands by virtue of discovery and settlement.[32]

To complete the picture, in June 1840 the Legislative Council of New South Wales passed an Act extending its laws to New Zealand, and on 7 August 1840, the Imperial Parliament enacted the New South Wales Continuance Act 1840 in which it provided for New Zealand eventually to be made a separate colony by Letters Patent. The Imperial Act also authorised the establishment of a Legislative Council in New Zealand consisting of nominated members. Finally, on

---

[28] The competition between the Treaty of Waitangi explanation and an alternative, favoured British and settler explanation, is in some ways similar to the competition between the Australian people and the Westminster Parliament as explanations for the legal foundation of the Australian Constitution. This point was flagged in Ch. 1 above and will be discussed in greater detail in Part III. The fact that the Westminster Parliament explanation tended to be preferred, and the fact that its preference is an important element of the story that will be told in this book, in no way eliminates the importance of the powerful alternative explanation. If New Zealand concludes that the Treaty of Waitangi is constitutionally foundational, and if Australia concludes that the people are sovereign, then that is very much their prerogative. It will be nonetheless important to recall that these countries were, for a time, running two horses alongside each other, with the legal rider initially very much in the more traditional mount.

[29] See Joseph (2001) (n. 26 above) ch. 2.

[30] This was done by virtue of Letters Patent issued in 1839 by which the boundaries of New South Wales were altered so as to include 'any territory which is or may be acquired in sovereignty by Her Majesty ... within that group of Islands ... know as New Zealand'. Joseph (2001) (n. 26 above) 37.   [31] ibid., 37.

[32] In the *Māori Council* case in the 1980s two judges of the New Zealand Court of Appeal viewed the Hobson proclamation as definitive in establishing British sovereignty. *New Zealand Māori Council v Attorney-General* [1987] 1 NZLR 641, 671 and 690 (*per* Richardson and Somers JJ).

24 November 1840, Hobson was, by Letters Patent, appointed *Governor* of New Zealand, and the new colony was officially proclaimed in existence as of 3 May 1841.

As we have seen, had the legally recognised form of acquisition been cession, then New Zealand courts would have been obliged to recognise and apply *Māori* law, and there is scant evidence of this having occurred. However, it seems somewhat unreal to apply standard colonial law and formal legal logic to this situation. Although British politicians in the 1830s and 1840s (the era of emancipation of slavery movements) were increasingly inclined to respect aboriginal populations, they were probably not as yet prepared to recognise communal or tribal customs as law, leaving the normal rules of cession free to compete against a legal void,[33] one which British law could conveniently fill.[34]

So either by a culturally skewed version of cession, or simply by occupation and settlement, the New Zealand courts quickly confirmed that in their view English law applied from the creation of the colony. Any doubts on this score, and as we have seen there could be many, were removed, at least in law, by enactment of the English Laws Act, 1858 (Imp.) which, as subsequently re-enacted in 1908, deemed the inheritance of English law to have dated from 14 January 1840, prior to the signing of the Treaty of Waitangi.[35]

Given the sort of constitutional beginnings that have been described, it is not surprising that New Zealanders (aboriginal or settler) were not directly involved in the making of their constitutional texts. The first Constitution for New Zealand was the Letters Patent granted 16 November 1840, sometimes referred to as the Charter of 1840.[36] It was these Letters Patent, as we have seen, that established an appointed Executive Council to advise Governor Hobson, and an appointed Legislative Assembly (of only six) rather than the representative assembly that would have been expected in a settled colony. (The Canadian

---

[33] See, e.g., Prendergast CJ in *Wi Parata v Bishop of Wellington* (1877) 3 NZ Jur (NS) 72, 77: 'On the foundation of this colony, the aborigines were found without any kind of civil government, or any settled system of law . . .

Had any body of law or custom, capable of being understood and administered by the Courts of a civilised country, been known to exist, the British Government would surely have provided for its recognition . . .'

[34] Joseph (2001) (n. 26 above) notes, at 39–40, that British subjects in settled colonies were entitled to representative government. Creation of an appointed assembly required a special Act of Parliament to override the settlers' right. Had cession been the operative assumption, then no legislation would have been necessary, the Crown being thereby entitled to set up non-representative institutions by prerogative. The fact that the Imperial Parliament chose to legislate may be evidence of nothing more than the colonial office acting out of an abundance of caution, because in either case legislation sufficed. At 40 Joseph quotes the Permanent Under Secretary to the Colonial Office, James Stephen, assuming that representative institutions were New Zealanders' right by common law while also noting that in New Zealand's existing circumstances it would be premature, hence the need for (1) a proclamation bringing New Zealand initially under the wing of New South Wales which already possessed a non-representative legislature, and (2) enacting Imperial legislation in the form of the New South Wales Continuance Act 1840 providing for a non-representative legislature once New Zealand became a separate colony.

[35] Joseph (2001) (n. 26 above) 39.   [36] ibid., 96.

colonies, for instance, had representative assemblies, and were at the time of New Zealand's national birth rebelling to obtain not just representative but also *responsible* government.) A representative council would require new legislation from the Imperial Parliament.

Express Imperial legislative authorisation came in the form of the Constitution Act, 1846 (Imp.). The Governor, Sir George Grey, was charged with bringing the new system into operation. Far from supporting the scheme, he petitioned the Secretary of State in London for legislation suspending the 1846 Constitution, and this request was acceded to, with appropriate legislation following, all without a representative legislature being constituted.

Representative government was eventually achieved with the enactment of the New Zealand Constitution Act 1852 (Imp.), until 1986 the key document in New Zealand's 'unwritten' or 'uncodified' Constitution. It created a General Assembly (later termed Parliament) whose constituent units were the Governor, an appointed Legislative Council and an elected House of Representatives. Initially, the 1852 Act was not open to amendment by ordinary legislative process. However, the New Zealand Constitution Amendment Act 1857 (Imp.) empowered the New Zealand General Assembly (or Parliament) to amend all but twenty-one of the sections of the 1852 Act. Joseph states that the 1857 amendments to the 1852 Act were in part responsible for the 'Constitution Act' losing its special legal status.[37] From approximately that time, the New Zealand Constitution was said to be 'unwritten', and similar in this respect to that of the United Kingdom.

Canada

Canada was next to achieve a national constitution, in 1867, though as noted earlier, its constituent parts—the colonies of Canada (formerly the separate colonies of Upper (later Ontario) and Lower (later Quebec) Canada), New Brunswick and Nova Scotia[38]—had had representative institutions and constitutive documents for some time by then.[39] The justification for acquisition of British sovereignty and therefore the mode of reception differed in each case,[40] although the imposition of the ultimate sovereignty of the Imperial Parliament was the bottom line and end result in all cases.

---

[37] Joseph (2001) 114.

[38] Manitoba (1870), British Columbia (1871), Prince Edward Island (1873) and Newfoundland (1949) remained outside Confederation for the moment. New provinces (Saskatchewan and Alberta) would be carved out of Rupert's Land and the Northwest Territories in 1905.

[39] See W.P.M. Kennedy, *The Constitution of Canada: An Introduction to Its Development and Law* (2nd edn, London: Humphrey Milford, Oxford University Press, 1931) chs V–XIX.

[40] 'Conquest' in the case of those territories defeated in 1759 and ceded to Britain by the Treaty of Paris 1963 (i.e. present day Ontario and Quebec) and settlement elsewhere. Some provinces, e.g. Nova Scotia, were conquered, and yet came to be considered as settled colonies. See Hogg (1997) (n. 26 above) ch. 2.

The British North America Act, 1867 (Imp.), renamed the Constitution Act, 1867 in 1982, was the product of three years of dedicated discussions involving political representatives in the British North American colonies. It created a federal country with four provinces—initially New Brunswick, Nova Scotia, Ontario and Quebec—as its constituent federal parts. As Peter Hogg has confirmed,[41] at Confederation the various reception dates and differing laws of the uniting colonies remained unchanged. Section 129 of the 1867 Act ensured that the laws existing at the time of union in the colonies of Canada, Nova Scotia and New Brunswick continued in force. That which had changed was that these laws could now be altered either by the federal Parliament (under powers granted in section 91 of the 1867 Act and elsewhere) or by a provincial legislature (under powers granted in section 92 or elsewhere).

The details of these constitutional arrangements are of less interest to us here. They can be found in any text on Canadian constitutional law, and clearly some of these elements will emerge as the rest of this story unfolds. A more pertinent question for our purposes was how the key constitutional document of this new nation came into existence, legally speaking. A few potential models can be immediately ruled out. It was not the case, as it had been in a New Zealand that had only very recently begun to be occupied and governed by British settlers, that the Constitution was essentially drafted and enacted in London and then made available to the colony for its intended local operation. Canadian political representatives had been heavily involved from the beginning of the Confederation project, as befitted what was by then a fairly mature polity. Nor was the United States (and, later, Australian) model followed, whereby a constitutional text agreed by political representatives was then referred back to the constituent states for approval by Convention, such that it could be said, even in a qualified sense, that 'the People' had ratified the Constitution. It is true that the Canadian 'Fathers of Confederation', as they were known, were elected political representatives, according to the (by modern standards) unrepresentative electoral rules of the mid-nineteenth century. But once they had agreed on the content of the new Constitution it was not returned to the people, or even to the colonies concerned, for ratification. Such ratification occurred, if ratification is the right word at all in the circumstances, only after the 1867 Act had been enacted and the new country proclaimed. Only at that time did each province, according to its political circumstances, hold elections in which the people could express, retroactively, their assent or dissent to the new project. In Nova Scotia, for example, the pro-federation representatives lost the election, with the result that Confederation was for a time threatened. Nova Scotia eventually decided to remain part of the project,[42] and the main changes to the new federation were instead in the form of additions to the new country: Manitoba in 1870, British

---

[41] ibid., para. 2-11.
[42] On Nova Scotia's response to Confederation, see Kennedy (1931) (n. 39 above) ch. XIX.

Columbia in 1871, Prince Edward Island in 1873, Alberta and Saskatchewan in 1905 and Newfoundland in 1949. Only Newfoundland allowed its people to vote on joining Confederation, making it difficult to sustain the argument that, legally speaking, Confederation is based on the sovereignty of the people, as in the United States and (possibly, as we shall see) in Australia.

The Canadian people did not, in any strong sense, assent to the 1867 Act. Aboriginal peoples in the (expanding) territory of Canada certainly did not consent either. What then is the legal explanation for the validity of the Canadian Constitution and the creation of a new Canadian legal system? The 1867 Act was enacted by the Imperial Parliament in Westminster. According to the rules of the Imperial legal system, of which the various parts of Canada had become a part according to the rules described earlier, the Imperial Parliament at Westminster could legislate not just for the United Kingdom, but also for the colonies. When it performed the latter function its enactments were known as Imperial statutes. As Peter Hogg has noted,[43] neither reception (in any particular sense) nor adoption by the colonial legislature explained the validity of these statutes in the early colonial period; this emerged rather *ex proprio vigore* (by virtue of their own force). Imperial statutes were then a continuing reminder of the 'founding violence' upon which the Imperial legal system was based, grounded as they were by the original claim to sovereignty over the colonial territories. The difference between Imperial statutes and received statutes may need further elaboration.

In Canada (Australia and New Zealand) there were effectively two classes of United Kingdom statutes in operation.[44] The first class was made up by statutes which had been enacted for United Kingdom purposes, but which became part of a colony's laws by way of reception, until such time as the colonial legislature chose to repeal or amend such laws. The second class comprised statutes which had been expressly passed to deal with colonial affairs: Imperial statutes.[45] These statutes could not be amended by the colonial legislature, and the British North America Act, 1867 was such a statute. As recently as 1865, the Colonial Laws Validity Act, itself an Imperial statute, had confirmed this arrangement, stating that colonial laws were void if they were repugnant to an Imperial statute (though not void if they were repugnant to a received statute or rule of the common law). We will have more to say in this section about the Colonial Laws Validity Act, 1865 in discussing Australian matters.

The concepts of Imperial statutes and repugnancy presented an odd picture in the context of emerging nationhood, whether in Canadian, Australian or New Zealand circumstances. However, in the absence of the realistic capacity (New Zealand) or the political will to create a constitution in the American way

---

[43] Hogg (1997) (n. 26 above) paras 2-16 and 2-17.   [44] ibid., para. 2-17.
[45] ibid., para. 2-17: 'They became law in the colony by their own terms, whether or not they were also in force in England (some were and some were not), and whether or not they were enacted before the date upon which the colony received English laws.'

(Canada) or the desire to sever the British connection (Australia), enactment of a constitution in the form of an Imperial statute was the only simple way of achieving a level of validity, supremacy and entrenchment that was and is normally associated with constitutional texts. Therefore the New Zealand Constitution Act, 1852, the Canadian Constitution Act, 1867 and later, the Commonwealth of Australia Constitution Act, 1900, as Imperial statutes, took precedence over incompatible domestic legislation.[46]

In Canada, where no general constitutional amendment formula had been provided for in the 1867 Act, constitutional amendments had to be accomplished by resort to the same procedure that enacted the Constitution initially, i.e. enactment of a statute by the Imperial Parliament. Whatever the true reasons for the absence of such a mechanism, it was clear that a range of legislative competence, most significantly the power to modify the 1867 Act, remained in the hands of the Imperial Parliament. The events of 1867 did not alter the hierarchy of Imperial and colonial law that had been so recently confirmed and clarified by the Colonial Laws Validity Act, 1865.

Australia

Australia was the last of the three countries in this study to acquire national status and a national constitution. The events of just over a century ago have been recalled, and in some cases re-enacted, over recent years in Australia, both as part of normal celebrations and as a part of the exceptional process that was the Australia republic debate.[47]

Presented with the examples of New Zealand and Canada, and with the rules on reception and Imperial law discussed earlier, a brief introduction to Australian circumstances is fairly easily done. The same voyages that had provided a pretext for British claims to New Zealand created 'what would now be described as an inchoate title'.[48] The Netherlands and France could have made similar claims to discovery, but it was occupation by British settlers that clinched the matter, at least from the perspective of European-dominated international law. Given that same international law's reluctance to recognise aboriginal nations and their laws, British occupation could be viewed as discovery and

[46] Judicial review of legislation, which was the product of Chief Justice John Marshall's genius in the United States (see *Marbury v Madison* (1803) 1 Cranch 137 (USSC)), came naturally, e.g. to federal Australia/Canada, where courts were called upon to decide whether a statute enacted by the Commonwealth/federal or state/provincial levels of government was consistent with the division of powers set out in the Constitution. In unitary New Zealand (despite some federal aspects early on), the New Zealand Parliament was the only qualified local legislator, and one which had been empowered to amend freely all but 21 sections of the 1852 Act (which from 1875 reduced to 15 'entrenched' sections), giving it a supremacy comparable to the United Kingdom Parliament so long as it legislated consistently with the bare framework set out in relevant Imperial statutes.

[47] See, e.g., the various publications produced by the Constitutional Centenary Foundation regarding this debate.

[48] A. Castles, *An Australian Legal History* (Sydney: Law Book Company, 1982) 20.

peaceful settlement rather than conquest.[49] The British law on the matter followed this approach as well, with the result that Governor Phillip, who received his first commission in 1787, travelled to New South Wales under the assumption that English law would apply, in accordance with the law on settlement (as opposed to that concerning conquest or cession).

In January 1788 a ceremony was held in what is now Sydney, to assert the British Crown's independent right to control New South Wales. In Brennan J's words in the *Mabo* case:

The hypothesis being that there was no local law already in existence in the territory, the law of England became the law of the territory (and not merely the personal law of the colonists). Colonies of this kind were called 'settled colonies'. Ex hypothesi, the indigenous inhabitants of a settled colony had no recognised sovereign, else the territory could have been acquired only by conquest or cession. The indigenous people of a settled colony were thus taken to be without laws, without a sovereign and primitive in their social organisation.[50]

Even though New South Wales was treated as a settled rather than a conquered or ceded colony, it was clearly a settled colony of a special type. After all, in its earliest days it was a penal colony. This fact has been used to explain why, unlike the situation which should have prevailed in a settled colony, where Englishmen were entitled to expect representative institutions unless an Act of the Imperial Parliament provided otherwise, much of the law-making in New South Wales was exercised by the Governor, as if by prerogative (and therefore contrary to the rules of settlement). As one Australian writer has noted, 'the basis, and the only legal basis of the absolute dictatorship of the Governor was that he was in law to be regarded as Superintendant-General or Head Gaoler'.[51]

For some time, therefore, it was not clear whether New South Wales could truly be treated as a 'settled colony' for the purposes of applying English law.[52] This situation was eventually clarified in 1828 by the passage of An Act to Provide for the Administration of Justice in New South Wales and Van Diemen's Land (Imp.). Section 24 of this Act made it clear that New South Wales and what we now know as Tasmania were to be placed on the same footing as settled colonies as of 28 July 1828. That which applied to New South Wales would also eventually apply to Victoria, which was carved out of the larger state

---

[49] In *Cooper v Stuart* (1889) 14 AC 286 (JCPC) Lord Watson stated, at 291, as follows:

The extent to which English law was introduced into a British Colony, and the manner of its introduction, must necessarily vary according to circumstances. There is a great difference between the case of a Colony acquired by conquest or cession, in which there is an established system of law, and that of a Colony which consisted of a tract of territory practically unoccupied, without settled inhabitants or settled law, at the time when it was peacefully annexed to the British dominions. The Colony of New South Wales belongs to the latter class.

[50] *Mabo v Queensland (No. 2)* (1992) 175 CLR 1, 36.

[51] H.V. Evatt, 'The Legal Foundations of New South Wales' (1938) 11 Austr LJ 409, 421.

[52] A. Castles, 'The Reception and Status of English Law in Australia' (1963) 2 Adelaide L Rev 1, 2.

in the 1850s. Queensland, another entity separated from New South Wales, dates its reception of English law from 1828. South Australia was also created out of the original boundaries of New South Wales, but 'subsequent enactments and decisions . . . have confirmed that the application of English law to that State is to be considered "as if this province never had any association with the mother colony" '.[53] English law therefore applies in South Australia as of 28 December 1836, the date which was specified by legislation. The relevant date for reception of English law in Western Australia is 1 June 1829. The fact that South Australia and Western Australia were in fact 'settled colonies' and New South Wales and Tasmania treated as such meant that each state inherited a vast amount of English law.

By way of summary, New South Wales, Tasmania, Victoria and Queensland date reception of English statute law from July 1828, Western Australia from June 1829 and South Australia from December 1836. The common law, however, was deemed to have been received at the moment of settlement, i.e. from the late eighteenth century, and this as a result of the Australian Courts Act, 1828 (Imp.). So as Sir Victor Windeyer observed in a 1962 article,[54] in most states, reception of English law begins in 1828 as a result of the Australian Courts Act; 'But', he said, 'we must not think of it as the source of that inheritance. The source is the common law itself. The law of England had come to Australia with the First Fleet, forty years before 1828. Section 24 was inserted in to the [Australian Courts] Act . . . to get over a particular difficulty. It fixes a date. It does not originate a doctrine.'[55]

As many times as one reads these by-now familiar accounts of the acquisition of British sovereignty and reception of English law, it is hard not to be struck each time by the sheer boldness, even arrogance—or at least the fantastical conjuring quality—of these rules. With the wave of a wand, or more literally with the planting of a cross, flag or a sword, the deed was done and the power and might of a legal system took its invisible but overwhelming place.

As the nineteenth century wore on, each of the Australian colonies acquired bicameral legislatures along New Zealand, Canadian, and indeed, British lines. Although these institutions were created, directly or indirectly, by the sovereign Imperial Parliament at Westminster, and were therefore hierarchically inferior to it, they came to be seen as omnicompetent legislatures in their own right, in the image of the body that created them.[56] 'Omnicompetent', that is, within the limits set out by Imperial law.

---

[53] Castles (1963) (n. 52 above) 3.

[54] V. Windeyer, ' "A Birthright and Inheritance"—The Establishment of the Rule of Law in Australia' (1962) Tasmanian Univ L Rev 635.   [55] Windeyer (1962) (n. 54 above) 636.

[56] For instance, as confirmed by the Privy Council in *R v Burah* (1878) 3 AC 889, though they were clearly creations of the Imperial Parliament, colonial legislatures were not to be viewed in any sense as 'delegates'. Had this not been the case, the frequent legislative practice of delegating to a Minister (or in the *Burah* case, the Lieutenant-Governor) the precise application of a particular legislative policy, would not have been possible, given that it would violate the principle *delegatus*

What were the limits set out by Imperial law? In the middle of the nineteenth century, a particularly single-minded judge in South Australia, Benjamin Boothby,[57] had insisted that the laws of a colonial legislature had to be consistent not only with Imperial statute law, but also with English common law.[58] Relief from Boothby's reign of legal uncertainty came in the form of the Colonial Laws Validity Act, 1865 (Imp.) which was noted in the briefest terms earlier. To repeat and elaborate, the 1865 Act made it clear that statutes passed by colonial legislatures could override received British statutes and common law. However, it also made it clear that such legislatures could *not* enact laws which were repugnant to (i.e. inconsistent with) Imperial statutes, defined in section 2 of the Act as those 'made applicable to such Colony by . . . express Words or necessary Intendment'. Examples of such Imperial statutes were the New Zealand Constitution Act, 1852, the Canadian Constitution Act, 1867, and the Commonwealth of Australia Constitution Act, 1900.

It must be said that the hierarchical picture painted above is the formal, legal version. The way that it worked in practice became steadily more respectful of local concerns. While it remained true that the Westminster Parliament could pass any sort of statute it wished, the emerging convention was that it would only legislate for the self-governing Dominions if they requested and consented to the legislation in question. It was the governments of Australian colonies, then, having produced a constitutional compromise for a new nation in Convention and having presented it to the people in these colonies for approval, that requested that the Commonwealth of Australia Constitution Act 1900 be enacted as a statute of the Imperial Parliament, thereby granting it supreme status in Australia.

The nature of the Dominions' ongoing subordination

What then was the status of Australia, Canada and New Zealand at the turn of the nineteenth century? We have already seen that by virtue of the subordinate

---

non potest delegare. The *Burah* doctrine was repeated by the Privy Council in the Canadian case, *Hodge v The Queen* (1883) 9 AC 117. Sir Barnes Peacock, for the Board, stated unequivocally that provincial legislatures 'are in no sense delegates of or acting under any mandate from the Imperial Parliament'. He went on to state that, within the limits set out by Westminster in the British North America Act, 1867, 'the local legislature is supreme, and has the same authority as the Imperial Parliament' (*Hodge*, 132.)

[57] Castles (1963) (n. 52 above) 23 quotes Boothby's biographer, by way of partial defence of his subject, as follows: 'His learning, if it was neither as deep as a well, nor as wide as a Church door, was at least as extensive as that of the average barrister who was a candidate for a colonial judgeship.'

[58] Joined by his colleague Gwynne J, though often opposed by Chief Justice Hanson, Boothby J obstructed the initiatives of the South Australia Legislature off and on for a period of ten years. As quoted by Castles (1963) (n. 52 above) 24–5, Governor Daly of South Australia wrote despairingly to the British government in 1865 to the effect that 'no one can tell under what laws he is living or what will, in any given instance, be the decision of the Supreme Court'.

status, in formal legal terms, of their central constitutional texts, and given the continued force of the doctrine of repugnancy under the Colonial Laws Validity Act, 1865, these Dominions were still clearly subordinate parts of an overarching and all-embracing Imperial legal system under which or in which the legislative will of the Imperial Parliament would always prevail.

It was less controversial that the rules of the Imperial legal system set out in the Colonial Laws Validity Act, 1865 should apply to New Zealand. After all, its key constitutional texts—the New Zealand Constitution Act 1852 and the New Zealand Constitution Amendment Act 1857—were enacted by the Imperial Parliament *prior* to the 1865 Act. However the Canadian Constitution Act, 1867 and the Commonwealth of Australia Constitution Act, 1900 were both subsequent Acts of that same Parliament, and one might therefore have expected the doctrine of implied repeal to apply to the 1865 Act, thereby eliminating the rule regarding repugnancy set out therein. In Canada's case the reason for a continuing repugnancy rule was relatively clear. Section 129 of the Constitution Act, 1867 provided that pre-Confederation laws that were in force in the uniting provinces remained in force, and it gave the legislature with the appropriate jurisdiction (under the new federal division of powers) the ability to repeal, abolish or alter such laws. However, the same section protected from such repeal, abolition or alteration such laws 'as are enacted by or exist under Acts of Parliament of Great Britain or of the Parliament of the United Kingdom of Great Britain and Ireland'.[59] The paramountcy of Imperial statutes, and thus the doctrine of repugnancy, was thereby preserved in Canada.[60]

The matter was potentially more complicated in the case of Australia. Again, the issue arose because the enactment of the main constitutional text, the Commonwealth of Australia Constitution Act, 1900 was enacted subsequent to the Colonial Laws Validity Act, 1865. Consequently, it was possible to argue that because the 1900 Act of the Imperial Parliament could be said to have impliedly repealed the 1865 Act, the Commonwealth was unconstrained even by inconsistent Imperial statutes. In *Union Steamship Co of New Zealand Ltd v Commonwealth*,[61] the High Court of Australia held that the repugnancy doctrine continued to apply to the Commonwealth.[62] The Australian delegates had

[59] Hogg (1997) (n. 26 above) para. 3-4.

[60] Taken literally, section 129 could have denied Canadian legislatures the power to amend, alter or repeal *any* British statute, whether or not it was an Imperial statute. However, this interpretation was never adopted and, in any event, the restriction on amending pre-Confederation statutes was removed by s. 2(2) of the Statute of Westminster, 1931, as we shall see. See Hogg (1997) (n. 26 above) paras 3-4n and 3-6n.   [61] (1925) 36 CLR 130.

[62] This did not stop the High Court from going to considerable lengths to avoid a finding of inconsistency with Imperial law where it saw fit. See, e.g., *Commonwealth v Limerick Steamship Co Ltd* (1924) 35 CLR 69, as explained by *Commonwealth v Kreglinger and Fernau Ltd* (1926) 37 CLR 393. See Blackshield and Williams (2002) (n. 26 above) 136–7.

made assurances to this effect to the British government prior to the creation of the Commonwealth.[63]

Besides the doctrine of repugnancy, which is clearly of central importance in this book, the Dominions were subject to further limitations in the early stages of their constitutional development. Leaving the doctrine of repugnancy first and foremost, the second doctrine which affected them was the doctrine of extra-territoriality, according to which legislation was invalid unless it had a sufficient connection to the geographical area of the legislating colony. As one Australian textbook has pointed out,[64] a more extreme version of this doctrine was that invalidity would arise if *any* part of the legislation in question operated outside that territory. The doctrine of extraterritoriality seemed to contradict the assumption that, as stated by the Privy Council in *Hodge v The Queen*,[65] 'within [its] limits of subjects and area the local legislature is supreme' with 'the same authority as the Imperial Parliament . . . would have had under like circum-stances', i.e. 'authority as plenary and as ample . . . as the Imperial Parliament in the plenitude of its power possessed and could bestow'.[66] In British law, the 'sovereignty' or 'supremacy' of the British Parliament implied that its law-making power had no territorial limit. So far as the Australian Commonwealth Parliament was concerned, the grant of legislative power under section 51(xxix) of the Constitution seemed on its terms to require extraterritorial operation.[67]

Not surprisingly, the doctrine of extraterritoriality had always been contro-versial. For those countries to which the Statute of Westminster applied imme-diately, the doctrine ceased to have effect as of 1931, as we shall see. However, for countries like Australia and New Zealand which initially chose not to adopt the Statute, the Privy Council decision in *Croft v Dunphy*[68] had considerable

---

[63] In *China Ocean Shipping Co v South Australia* (1979) 145 CLR 172, 209, Stephen J described the pre-Federation attitude as follows:

. . . in London in 1900 the form of covering cl 5 of the . . . Bill was a point of contention, the matter in issue being whether the clause made it sufficiently clear that laws enacted by the Commonwealth Parliament would be 'colonial laws' subject to the provisions of the Colonial Laws Validity Act, 1865 (Imp). The Imperial Government wished to leave 'no room for doubt as to the paramount authority of the Imperial legislation', while, as Quick and Garran observe at 350 of their Annotated Constitution, the Australian framers of the Commonwealth Bill had not 'thought necessary to declare that the Constitution should be read in conjunction with the Colonial Laws Validity Act. It was assumed, as a matter of course, that that would be done.' The Australian delegates, determined to avoid any change, even to the covering clauses, of a document so long debated in Australia and which had just been approved by referendum of the Australian people, contended that the Bill in fact left no room for doubt: 'The Commonwealth appear to the Delegates to be clearly a "Colony" and the Federal Parliament to be a "Legislature" within the meaning of the Colonial Laws Validity Act' they observed in their memorandum to the Colonial Office and of this they succeeded finally in convincing the Imperial Crown Officers.

[64] Blackshield and Williams (2002) (n. 26 above) 138.   [65] (1883) 9 AC 117 (PC).
[66] ibid., 132.

[67] Section 51(xxix) 'external affairs', whereas other grants of power under the Australian Constitution could happily be interpreted as having only territorial application (e.g. 'industrial disputes' in s. 51(xxxv) not applying to disputes on Australian ships outside Australian waters).
[68] [1933] AC 156.

importance. This Canadian case saw Lord Macmillan state on behalf of the Board: 'Once it is found that a particular topic of legislation is among those upon which the Dominion Parliament may competently legislate . . . their Lordships see no reason to restrict the permitted scope of such legislation by any other consideration than is applicable to the legislation of a fully Sovereign State.'[69] Despite the apparent clarity of this decision, Australian courts failed to apply it in its strongest sense, in part because the reasoning in the *Croft* case was thought to depend upon the Statute of Westminster which the Commonwealth did not adopt until 1942 (with effect from 1939), New Zealand until 1947, and which the Australian states never adopted. Aikman has noted that after New Zealand adopted the Statute of Westminster in 1947, the Court of Appeal of New Zealand took that as a cue to adopt the more generous interpretation of extraterritorial powers that had been approved by the Judicial Committee of the Privy Council in *Croft v Dunphy*.[70]

The third and fourth limitations on Dominions were, respectively, reservation and disallowance by the Crown under its prerogative. Provisions in all colonial constitutions provided for 'reservation' and 'disallowance' of legislation enacted by colonial legislatures. The Governor might be instructed (or might choose), when presented with a colonial Bill, to 'reserve' it for Her Majesty's pleasure. This meant that the Bill in question would be referred to the British government to consider whether it should be allowed to become law. Each of the Constitutions contained specific instances where powers of reservation of Bills for the Royal Assent were expressly set out. In these cases reservation was obligatory (for example, in New Zealand, sections 57, 65, 68, and 69 of the 1852 Act,[71] and in Canada, sections 55 and 57 of the 1867 Act)[72]. In all other matters, reservation of Bills was discretionary. Where no Imperial interest was affected, the Governor was entitled simply to take the advice of his Ministers; however, in cases where such interests were concerned, reservation did occur, and Bills were amended if the Imperial government voiced an objection.[73] In the case of Australia, a 1907 Imperial Act, the Australian States Constitution Act, 1907, set out classes of laws that were to be reserved.[74] Commonwealth conventions had in fact eliminated the practical effect of these powers of reservation before the Statute of Westminster, 1931.[75]

[69] ibid., 163.
[70] C.C. Aikman, in J.L. Robson (ed.) *New Zealand: The Development of its Laws and its Constitution* (2nd edn, London: Stevens, 1967) 58.   [71] Joseph (2001) (n. 26 above) 104–5.
[72] Hogg (1997) (n. 26 above) para. 3-2 notes that reservation occurred 21 times between 1867 and 1878, but never occurred subsequently (when royal instructions were changed). Of the 21 cases of reservation, six denials of Royal Assent followed. Section 90 of the 1867 Act provides for reservation and disallowance of provincial legislation, but the power is exercisable by the Canadian federal government, not by the United Kingdom government, so, as Hogg says, 'no issue of Canadian independence is thereby raised'.   [73] See Joseph (2001) (n. 26 above) 105.
[74] Australia, *First Report of the Constitutional Commission*, Vol. 1 (Canberra: Australian Government Publishing Service, 1988) para. 2.115.
[75] e.g. the power of disallowance had been rendered inoperative as a result of the convention that refusal of assent to reserved Bills was conditional upon consultation with and consent by the

In addition, the Queen, i.e. the British government, could 'disallow' legislation passed by colonial legislatures, usually within two years of its enactment.[76] Upon being disallowed an Act ceased to be a law. These powers of the British Crown (i.e. government) were exercised only in rare cases where Imperial or foreign interests were involved, such as laws which discriminated against the people of other countries.[77] Zines has noted that a strange product of Australia having the ability from the moment of federation to amend its own Constitution is that provisions regarding reservation and disallowance have remained part of the Australian Constitution for much longer than they otherwise would have done, similar provisions having been repealed by the Westminster Parliament at the request of other Dominions.[78] Section 58 of the Australian Constitution gives the Governor General the power to reserve a proposed Commonwealth law for the Queen's assent, and section 59 authorises the Queen to disallow any law within one year from the Governor General's assent. Restriction, or more likely, removal, of these provisions would require a constitutional amendment under section 128 of the Constitution. Australia's poor track record with constitutional amendments, as well as the expense of the process in relation to such an essentially harmless principle, makes the venture seem unattractive. It should be pointed out, however, that the Queen is advised in such matters not by the British government but by the Australian government. This makes the exercise of reservation and disallowance procedures extremely unlikely.[79]

In summary, then, the main indicators of the Dominions' subordinate status were the following: the doctrine of repugnancy as confirmed and clarified by the Colonial Laws Validity Act, 1865; the doctrine of extraterritoriality; and reservation and disallowance. New Zealand authors pre-1947 regularly added a further category, namely certain inabilities regarding amendment of the Constitution, as set out in the New Zealand Constitution Act, 1857.[80] However, as

Dominion concerned. See Wheare, *The Statute of Westminster and Dominion Status* (5th edn, Oxford: Oxford University Press, 1953), 123. Conventions in this spirit in relation to both disallowance and reservation were laid down at the Imperial Conference of 1926. See K.C. Wheare ibid., 127–30.

[76] Australia, *First Report of the Constitutional Commission*, (n. 74 above) para. 2.115.

[77] Hogg (1997) (n. 26 above) para. 3-2 notes that in Canada's case disallowance occurred only once, in 1873.

[78] Zines (1991) (n. 26 above) 23. Equivalent state provisions were repealed by the Australia Act 1986.

[79] Zines (1991) (n. 26 above) 24, puts forward a possible scenario in which a recently elected government, blocked by ordinary legislative means from repealing an earlier government's legislation (as, e.g., by Senate refusal), might seek to have the legislation disallowed by the Queen. Zines rightly observes that this colonial relic is therefore useful only as a means of subverting responsible government, and, not surprisingly, the Constitution Commission has recommended the repeal of ss. 58 and 59. Australia, *First Report of the Constitutional Commission* (n. 74 above) para. 2.172.

[80] See, e.g., A.E. Currie, *New Zealand and the Statute of Westminster 1931* (Wellington: Butterworths, 1944) para. 12-5.

R.O. McGechan has pointed out,[81] any inability regarding amendment of the Constitution was really a special case of the doctrine of repugnancy.

Balfour and the Statute of Westminster

By the 1920s, following a World War in which Dominion armies had fought in separate units and Dominion leaders had separately signed the peace treaty at Versailles, there were increasing calls for an end to the ongoing vestiges of subordination to the Mother Country. Canada was most insistent, while New Zealand and Australia were fairly reluctant parties to this campaign to end subordination.[82] Other Dominions, such as South Africa and Ireland, were at least as keen as Canada, and so the campaign moved ahead.

Whether as protagonists or as passengers, the self-governing Dominions together sought to acquire the full attributes of nationhood. In order to deal with this issue and others, the Imperial Conference met in 1926 and agreed on what was to become known as the Balfour Declaration. The Balfour Declaration acknowledged that Great Britain and the Dominions were 'autonomous Communities within the British Empire, equal in status, in no way subordinate one to another in any aspect of their domestic and external affairs, though united by a common allegiance to the Crown, and freely associated as members of the British Commonwealth of Nations'.[83] The understanding was that formerly 'colonial' legislatures were no longer *subordinate* to the United Kingdom Parliament but rather *coordinate*. They, together with the United Kingdom, were equal under the Crown.[84]

The problem with the forward-looking sentiments of the Balfour Declaration was that they were difficult to convert into legal form, and this for at least two reasons, one general, the other parochial. First, given the then-dominant understandings of parliamentary sovereignty, it was impossible to imagine any legal restraint on the sovereignty of the Westminster Parliament. We will have much more to say about this in the next chapter. Accordingly, the Statute of Westminster, 1931 in many ways side-stepped the issue. The preamble to the

---

[81] R.O. McGechan, 'Status and Legislative Inability' in J.C. Beaglehole (ed.) *New Zealand and the Statute of Westminster* (Wellington: Victoria University College, 1944) 65, 98.

[82] See W.J. Hudson and M.P. Sharp, *Australian Independence: Colony to Reluctant Kingdom* (Melbourne: Melbourne University Press, 1988). [83] Cmnd 2768 (1926).

[84] As Professor W.P.M. Kennedy has pointed out, this description of relationships within the Empire corresponded to the understanding put forward by Americans in their disputes with Great Britain leading up to the American War of Independence. W.P.M. Kennedy, *Some Aspects of the Theories and Workings of Constitutional Law* (New York: Macmillan, 1932) 59. The subtle distinction between allegiance to the British Parliament and allegiance to the British Crown was not accepted by the British authorities leading up to the war with the American colonies, and subordination to the Imperial Parliament became the nineteenth-century norm. The Balfour Declaration proposed a new relationship whereby each Dominion was deemed to be equal to Great Britain.

1931 Statute set out the new position of the Dominions *vis-à-vis* the United Kingdom as recognised by the Balfour Declaration in 1926. The text of the Statute did not, however, terminate the ability of the United Kingdom to legislate for the Dominions; instead, it set out the newly restricted terms on which the United Kingdom Parliament could do so.[85] Section 4 of the Statute provided as follows:

4.   No Act of Parliament of the United Kingdom passed after the commencement of this Act shall extend, or be deemed to extend, to a Dominion as part of the law of that Dominion, unless it is expressly declared in that Act that that Dominion has requested, and consented to, the enactment thereof.

Subsequently, in the case of *British Coal Corporation v The King*, Lord Sankey, by way of obiter dictum, interpreted this provision as if it kept alive the legal (if unlikely) possibility of unrequested and unconsented to Imperial legislation for a Dominion, insisting that 'the Imperial Parliament could, as a matter of abstract law, repeal or disregard section 4 of the *Statute*'.[86]

In terms of the two most important indicia of subordination noted above— repugnancy and extraterritoriality—the 1931 Statute dealt with them in the following way. First, section 2 eliminated the doctrine of repugnancy by, in subsection (1), providing that the Colonial Laws Validity Act, 1865 'shall no longer apply to any law made after the commencement of this Act by the Parliament of a Dominion', and in subsection (2) stating unequivocally that 'no law and no provision of any law made after the commencement of this Act by the Parliament of a Dominion shall be void or inoperative on the ground that it is repugnant to the law of England'. Together these provisions undid both the statutory and the common law bases for the doctrine of repugnancy. Secondly, section 3 'declared and enacted that the Parliament of a Dominion has full power to make laws having extraterritorial operation'.

What about the parochial reasons for the difficulty in converting the Balfour Declaration into law? It has already been noted that any inability to amend a Constitution was really just a special case of the doctrine of repugnancy. However, it was, notably for Canada, a special case of a particularly intractable nature. Federal and provincial representatives had met in Canada as early as 1927 in order to devise a mutually satisfactory domestic amendment procedure, but no agreement had been reached by 1930–1. Such an agreement was to prove highly elusive. As a result it was necessary to retain the possibility of recourse to the Parliament at Westminster in order to accomplish at any moment in the future amendments to the United Kingdom legislative texts which formed part of the Canadian Constitution. As far as Canada was concerned, the Statute of

---

[85] For analysis, see G. Marshall, *Constitutional Conventions* (Oxford: Oxford University Press, 1984) 188n.

[86] [1935] AC 500, 520–22 (PC). It will be argued in Ch. 3 below that this case is not as convincing with regard to authority for Parliament's continuing sovereignty as its proponents assume.

Westminster, 1931 appeared to maintain the *status quo ante*. After much discussion, a provision which eventually became section 7(1) of the 1931 Statute was approved.[87] This provision effectively left the United Kingdom Parliament at the apex of the Canadian legal system; and, as we know, it would take over fifty years before Canadians could settle on a new procedure to amend the constitution of Canada and repeal section 7(1).

Compared to Canada, South Africa and the Irish Free State, New Zealand and Australia were, respectively, reluctant and less interested with respect to the Statute of Westminster, as we shall see in Chapters 8 and 9. Both countries would probably have been content to see the new spirit of equality develop at the level of Commonwealth convention.[88] Accordingly, although they took part in the negotiations, they ensured that section 10(1) of the 1931 Statute provided that the key sections should not apply to them unless and until adopted.[89] Immediately upon enactment in 1931, however, section 8 of the Statute of Westminster applied to both Australia and New Zealand, providing that: 'Nothing in this Act shall be deemed to confer any power to repeal or alter the Constitution or the Constitution Act of the Commonwealth of Australial or the Constitution Act of the Dominion of New Zealand otherwise than in accordance with the law existing before the commencement of this Act.'

Australia's federal nature was deemed to require special arrangements, if and when it adopted the 1931 Statute. Whereas section 7(2) ensured that the liberating effect of the Act extended to the Canadian Provinces, section 9 preserved the legal position which had applied to the Australian states prior to 1931. Adoption of the 1931 Statute meant adoption of section 9 which preserved this arrangement, so the Australian states' legal position would not lose its subordinate character *vis-à-vis* Westminster until 1986.

New Zealand showed its complete preference for the *status quo* where the Statute of Westminster was concerned. Section 10 of the Statute ensured that the sections 2, 3, 4, 5 and 6—the core provisions—would not have any effect in New Zealand until the New Zealand Parliament decided to adopt the Statute.

With the pronouncement of the Balfour Declaration and the passage of the Statute of Westminster, we see, at least for the Dominions, the end of the Empire and the beginnings of the Commonwealth. It was no longer, from this point on, appropriate to speak of 'the Imperial tie', the 'Imperial prerogatives', or the 'Imperial Parliament'.[90] Even though, as we shall see, the Westminster

---

[87] '7.—(1) Nothing in this Act shall be deemed to apply to the repeal, amendment or alteration of the *British North America Acts, 1867 to 1930*, or any order, rule or regulation made thereunder.'

[88] e.g. we have already seen how convention brought reservation and disallowance powers under Dominion control. See Wheare (1953) (n. 75 above).

[89] Section 10(2) went so far as to provide that the Parliaments of Australia and New Zealand could revoke any such adoption.

[90] See L. Zines, 'The Growth of Australian Nationhood and its Effects on the Powers of the Commonwealth' in L. Zines (ed.) *Commentaries on the Australian Constitution* (Sydney: Butterworths, 1977) 1, 39.

Parliament (the neutral term for the United Kingdom Parliament that is often employed in this book) retained formal legal powers, both in its own eyes, and in the eyes of Australia, Canada and New Zealand, constitutional conventions changed significantly. To write off these informal constitutional changes as irrelevant legally speaking would be a great mistake, though we do not propose to enlarge on the topic here.[91]

Also occurring in this period, besides the important legal and conventional changes regarding the United Kingdom Parliament, were closely related developments regarding the Judicial Committee of the Privy Council. The acquisition of judicial independence will be the subject of the next section.

Gradual acquisition of judicial independence

At the top of the hierarchy of Imperial courts was the Judicial Committee of the Privy Council. Initially a creation entirely of prerogative, in the nineteenth century it was placed on a statutory footing. The Judicial Committee Act of 1833 set up, in statutory form, the appeal to His Majesty in Council and regulated the manner in which it should be heard.[92] The Judicial Committee Act of 1844 expressly extended the jurisdiction of the Privy Council, stating that Her Majesty could provide by Order in Council 'for admission of any appeal or appeals to Her Majesty in Council from any judgments, sentences, decrees, or orders of any Court of justice within any British Colony or Possession abroad'. This was a statement in the widest terms of Her Majesty's ability to hear appeals, and Her subjects' right to ask for leave to appeal. These statutes effectively put into legislative form the jurisdiction which had previously existed as a matter of prerogative.[93]

By 1926, in each of Australia, Canada (where appeals from the superior courts of the states and provinces were concerned) and New Zealand, the right of the subject to appeal without obtaining special leave had been restricted or abolished. Restriction usually amounted to some minimal requirement as to the amount in dispute. However, in the case of appeals from the High Court of Australia, the right to appeal without special leave had been completely abolished.[94]

In the case of Canadian appeals, with or without leave, in criminal cases, a Canadian Act of 1888 had purported to abolish them. The parties in the 1926

---

[91] For discussion of the emerging Commonwealth conventions at an early stage, see R.T.E. Latham, 'The Law and The Commonwealth' in W.K. Hancock (ed.) *Survey of British Commonwealth Affairs*, Vol. 1 (London: Oxford University Press, 1931) 517, reprinted with a foreword by W.K. Hancock but with otherwise unaltered pagination as R.T.E. Latham, *The Law and the Commonwealth* (Oxford: Oxford University Press, 1949). For analysis at a later period of development see Marshall (1984) (n. 85 above).

[92] See Wheare (1953) (n. 75 above) 89. On the history of appeals to the Privy Council, see D.B. Swinfen, *Imperial Appeal* (Manchester: Manchester University Press, 1987).

[93] ibid., 89–90.   [94] ibid., 91.

Canadian case of *Nadan v The King*[95] accepted that the appeal without special leave had thereby been effectively abolished. And although the case actually turned on whether the appeal by special leave had also been eliminated, the Privy Council was also prepared to assume that appeal without special leave no longer existed. So only the Australian states, the Canadian provinces and New Zealand continued at this stage to permit subjects in those jurisdictions the right to appeal without special leave.

The question which then arose for consideration was whether any of Australia, Canada and New Zealand had the power to restrict or abolish the appeal by special leave. As Wheare has put it, there were three problems with this, or three obstacles. First, the right of the Privy Council to grant special leave was a prerogative right, and it was established that for a colonial legislature to restrict or abolish a prerogative right it would have to not only legislate in clear enough terms, but it would also have to be given the necessary power to do so by an Imperial Act.[96] Secondly, even if the colonial legislature had such a power, the legislation purporting to restrict or abolish the prerogative to grant special leave would be repugnant to the 1833 and 1844 Imperial statutes and therefore void for that repugnancy. And thirdly, restricting or abolishing the prerogative to grant special leave would have to be extraterritorial in nature and would be void for that further reason. In *Nadan v The King*, the Privy Council decided that the Canadian Parliament had clearly tripped up on two of these obstacles, i.e. repugnancy and extraterritoriality.[97]

It was only in 1935 that the Privy Council came to deal with the first obstacle. It decided that in the case of Canada, the 1867 Act had conferred on the Canadian Parliament the power to regulate 'the Criminal Law'[98] and to provide for 'a General Court of Appeal for Canada'.[99] Together these provisions indicated that, at least by necessary intendment, if not expressly, the Canadian Parliament had the power to restrict or abolish even the prerogative power to grant special leave to appeal. The problem then lay with repugnancy and extraterritoriality. New Zealand, the Australian states and the Canadian provinces all had the same obstacles to overcome. Only the Australian Commonwealth, by section 74 of the Constitution, had been empowered to make laws limiting the matters in which special leave to appeal might be sought (although such laws had to be reserved).[100] And furthermore, in Australia's case, the appeal with special leave could have been abolished by the ordinary process of constitutional amendment, i.e. section 128.

The Statute of Westminster, 1931 did not expressly cover the issue of special leave to the Privy Council.[101] However, it did remove two of the obstacles

---

[95] [1926] AC 482 (PC).   [96] Wheare (1953) (n. 75 above) 94.

[97] According to Wheare (1953) (n. 75 above) 94–6, a reasonable interpretation of the *Nadan* case was to the effect that the Canadian Parliament had also tripped on the first obstacle, i.e. inability to deal with the prerogative, however the Privy Council subsequently ruled in *British Coal Corporation v The King* (1935) AC 500 (PC) that the matter had been left undecided.

[98] Constitution Act, 1867, s. 91(27).   [99] ibid., s. 101.

[100] Wheare (1953) (n. 75 above) 95–6.   [101] ibid., 198.

which have just been mentioned. As stated above, section 2 of the Statute removed the problem regarding repugnancy, and section 3 did the same regarding extraterritoriality.

As we have just seen, the Privy Council in the *British Coal Corporation* case held that the Canadian Parliament had always had power under the 1867 Act to restrict or eliminate the prerogative in this matter. While this resolved the issue regarding termination of the appeal with special leave in so far as criminal matters were concerned, appeals in civil cases persisted. However in 1939[102] the Canadian Parliament drafted a Bill abolishing appeals in civil cases. This Bill was referred initially to the Supreme Court of Canada and then to the Privy Council for a decision on whether it might be valid. If it were valid, it would abolish appeals in civil and criminal matters, whether from the Supreme Court of Canada or from the superior courts of the provinces. The alleged grant of power to do this was based, as before, on section 101 of the 1867 Act. which empowered Parliament 'to provide for the constitution, maintenance, and organisation of a General Court of Appeal for Canada . . . *notwithstanding anything in this Act*'. The same power had been used to establish the Supreme Court of Canada. The last phrase in section 101 was important in that it allowed the Privy Council to say that the Canadian Parliament had the power to abolish appeals with special leave 'notwithstanding' the fact that the provinces had been given jurisdiction, in section 92 of the 1867 Act, over the administration of justice in the province. Thus as of 1949, the year of the Privy Council's decision and final enactment of the referred legislation, the Privy Council ceased to be the highest court for Canadian appeals.

As we have seen, for Australia, matters were different. Before the enactment of the Statute of Westminster, the legal inequality represented by a continuing appeal to the Privy Council by special leave could have been ended, according to Wheare,[103] in one of three ways: first, legislation by the Commonwealth Parliament aimed at limiting such appeals;[104] secondly, by means of section 128, i.e. the procedure for constitutional amendment under the Australian constitution; and thirdly, section 74 of the Constitution could itself have been eliminated by means of constitutional amendment, and Commonwealth legislation could then have been passed subject to no potential Imperial obstacle. After adoption of the Statute of Westminster the same three options remained available; however, sections 2 and 3 of the Statute, regarding repugnancy and extraterritoriality, respectively, permitted Australia to repeal the Judicial Committee Acts of 1833 and 1834 should they have been deemed to preserve the appeal by special leave even after the adjustments to the Australian Constitution mentioned above. Of course, the Statute of Westminster, even once adopted, did not extend the powers conferred

---

[102] Wheare (1953) (n. 75 above) 199.　　　[103] ibid., 222.

[104] Such legislation would have had to be reserved by the Governor General under the terms of the Australian Constitution, but according to the emerging convention Royal Assent would certainly not have been withheld. Wheare (1951) (n. 75 above) 222n.

in sections 2 and 3, in particular, to the states of Australia. Hence, the states would be subject to appeals to the Privy Council by special leave until 1986.

It was not until 1968 (and 1975) that the Australian Commonwealth began to clarify matters regarding the Judicial Committee, however. The combined effect of the Privy Council (Limitation of Appeals) Act 1968 and the Privy Council (Appeals from the High Court) Act 1975 was to end appeals to the Privy Council from the High Court, federal and territorial courts and all state courts exercising federal jurisdiction.[105] In another example of the sort of 'constitutional and legal conundrum' that such a situation could produce, the High Court signalled that it no longer viewed itself as bound by Privy Council decisions.[106] This gave rise to a potential conflict of authority, given that cases still arose under state law in which a party could opt to appeal either to the High Court or to the Privy Council.[107]

New Zealand's situation regarding appeals to the Judicial Committee of the Privy Council can be dealt with more briefly. Before the enactment of the Statute of Westminster the restriction or elimination of appeals by special leave was impossible owing to the doctrines of repugnancy and extraterritoriality. As we have seen, these obstacles were removed by sections 2 and 3 of the 1931 Statute, and when New Zealand adopted the Statute in 1947, this became the case for that country as well. For a variety of reasons, however, New Zealand opted not to end appeals to the Privy Council until very recently.[108] As we shall see, this may have had implications regarding whether it was possible to confirm that New Zealand had in fact achieved full constitutional independence even after 1986, because on one view of the matter, it was the highest court in the legal system which locked such independence into place. As Philip Joseph said, writing in 1993: 'Only the final right of appeal to the Judicial Committee of the Privy Council weighs New Zealand with its colonial past, and that may not be forever.'[109] In 1987, the independent-minded then-President of the New Zealand Court of Appeal, Sir Robin (now Lord) Cooke, stated that failure to abolish the appeal and 'accept responsibility for our own national legal destiny . . . would be to renounce part of our nationhood'.[110]

As of 2004, however, New Zealand's judicial independence has been placed beyond doubt. Constitutional questions in Australia, Canada and New Zealand, including questions regarding constitutional independence, are now decided by those countries' highest courts, and by them alone.

---

[105] Zines (1991) (n. 26 above) 11.   [106] ibid., 10.

[107] See *Viro v R* (1978) 141 CLR 88 (H Ct).

[108] Now see the Supreme Court Act 2003 (NZ) which terminates appeals to the Privy Council (s. 42) and establishes a Supreme Court of New Zealand (s. 6). The new Supreme Court commenced its functions on 1 July 2004 (s. 55). Section 49 of the 2003 Act provided that, *inter alia*, the Judicial Committee Acts of 1833 and 1844 ceased to have effect as part of the law of New Zealand.

[109] P. Joseph, *Constitutional and Administrative Law in New Zealand* (Sydney: Law Book Company, 1993) 415.

[110] Sir Robin Cooke, 'The New Zealand National Identity', *New Zealand Law Conference Papers* (1987) 268, 271, quoted in Joseph (1993) (n. 109 above) 415.

3

Parliamentary Sovereignty
in the Empire and Commonwealth:
Dicey's Dominions and Dogmas

This chapter and the one which follows examine the sort of British and Imperial constitutional theory that has had such an impact on the development of constitutional law and theory in Australia, Canada and New Zealand. We have already had a glimpse of the importance of theoretical assumptions in Chapter 2, where the law governing reception, or imposition, of English law was touched upon. We saw there that there was nothing inevitable[1] about rules of international law and Imperial constitutional law which dictated that new lands— conquered, ceded or settled—be ultimately subject to the prerogative of the British Crown (and therefore the British government) and the supremacy of the British or Imperial Parliament at Westminster.

The growing Imperial legal system was, in practice, dependent on the willingness of local garrisons and local judges to make good their allegiance to the United Kingdom and its law. A soldier manifests his allegiance in the familiar ways that fill up the text of school history books. The judge manifests his allegiance in less obvious ways, some of which are perhaps not fully understood even by him or her. Especially when deciding what we might now call 'hard cases', judges fall back on the most fundamental assumptions of their legal education and training. As we shall see, the achievement of constitutional independence was, and perhaps still is, one such 'hard case'.

While it would be fascinating to investigate systematically the decisions of judges in the United Kingdom and in Australia, Canada and New Zealand in order to tease out their most fundamental assumptions regarding constitutional theory, I do not propose to proceed in this way. Instead, in the chapters which

[1] By way of striking contrast, see, e.g., the decisions of John Marshall CJ regarding the position of American Indian tribes *vis-à-vis* the United States legal system. John Marshall, *The Writings of Chief Justice Marshall on the Federal Constitution* (Boston: James Monroe, 1839) esp. 419–48. For an approving summary of Marshall's approach, see J. Tully, *Strange Multiplicities: Constitutionalism in an Age of Diversity* (Cambridge: Cambridge University Press, 1995) 117–24.

follow, I focus on the main texts and other documents of constitutional law which would have been available to all judges, lawyers and officials, and treat these sources as indicative of such fundamental assumptions. This approach seems justified for at least three reasons. First, the main texts and other important documents of constitutional law would form the core of materials used to educate lawyers, whether that education was formal or informal. Secondly, texts which purport to be authoritative do so in part by claiming to provide an accurate reflection of *existing* attitudes of judges and other officials. These texts are therefore a readily available means of accessing such attitudes. To the extent that such texts may instead represent their authors' individual and contestable interpretations, a third point may be relevant. There is a natural tendency amongst all but the most talented and independent-spirited judges, lawyers and officials, to turn to the fundamentals of their legal education or to authoritative texts when dealing with hard cases, instead of exploring issues from first principles. To the extent that the method employed in this book is not justified as a general statement of legal attitudes, it should at least reveal points of interest regarding intellectual trends in the leading texts.

Chapters 5 to 10 will examine constitutional theory in Australia, Canada and New Zealand: how the possibility of independence was theoretically constrained; how these countries contemplated independence despite such constraints; and how they eventually achieved constitutional independence. Chapter 11 will consider how they then explained what they had done. Underlying the discussion in these seven chapters is a well-established British strain of writing on constitutional issues. Where constitutional independence is concerned, the central preoccupation is to do with sovereignty, principally the sovereignty of the Imperial Parliament at Westminster. Implications for our other central preoccupation—legal systems—tended to be subsumed under considerations of sovereignty and will be noted in just that way. One of the deficiencies of Imperial, Commonwealth and British constitutional theory was just this lack of thinking about the concept of a legal system. The analysis in Chapter 12 will attempt to remedy that situation sufficiently in order to lay out the basics of a number of viable understandings of the acquisition of constitutional independence in Chapter 13.

Parliamentary sovereignty personified: Albert Venn Dicey

'In 1900', wrote Geoffrey Marshall in 2003, 'Dicey's account of the principle of parliamentary sovereignty would have gained general assent'.[2] A.V. Dicey was, of course, Vinerian Professor of English Law at Oxford University and

---

[2] G. Marshall, 'The Constitution: Its Theory and Interpretation' in V. Bogdanor (ed.) *The British Constitution in the Twentieth Century* (Oxford, Oxford University Press, 2003) 29, 42.

author of multiple editions of *An Introduction to the Study of the Law of the Constitution*.[3]

Dicey famously expressed this principle of parliamentary sovereignty[4]—which he admitted was also a 'dogma'—in a definition which set out both its positive and its negative aspects:

The principle of parliamentary sovereignty means neither more nor less than this, namely, that Parliament . . . had, under the English constitution, the right to make or unmake any law whatever; and, further, that no person or body is recognised by the law of England as having a right to override or set aside the legislation of Parliament.[5]

Applied to the Empire, it is easy to see how this principle provided cement both for the Imperial legal system and for its ultimate legislator, the Imperial Parliament, at the apex of that system.

One of the most convincing signs of Dicey's influence—a sort of intellectual Empire of its own—was the extent to which Marshall's statement, just quoted, was true not just in the United Kingdom but also across the British Empire. Not only was Dicey's *Law of the Constitution* widely read in its many editions, but Dicey himself clearly took an interest in the constitutional rules of the Empire, as is apparent from the frequent references to colonial examples in his works. His greatest preoccupation was Ireland,[6] but he also surveyed the Empire, notably the self-governing Dominions, for new constitutional developments and egregious constitutional views. When, for instance, Chief Justice Draper of Ontario suggested that the 'exclusive' grant of legislative power in sections 91 and 92 of the British North America Act, 1867 might exclude the Imperial Parliament altogether,[7] Dicey's eventual reply was dogmatic and unforgiving. He wrote that

---

[3] A.V. Dicey, *An Introduction to the Study of the Law of the Constitution*, 10th edition by E.C.S. Wade (London: Macmillan, 1959) will be used in this book (hereinafter *Law of the Constitution*). E.C.S. Wade also edited the 9th edition (1939). The other editions (1st edn, 1885; 2nd edn, 1893; 3rd edn, 1890; 4th edn, 1893; 5th edn, 1897; 6th edn, 1902; 7th edn, 1908; and 8th edn, 1915) were all published in Dicey's lifetime. Dicey died in 1922.

[4] Dicey's dogmatic insistence on an absolute version of sovereignty was no doubt connected to his views on the Irish question. He was convinced that divided or limited sovereignty, including federalism, for the United Kingdom would be a mistake. Dicey therefore associated sovereignty with political stability, as many had done before him. See M. Loughlin, *Public Law and Political Theory* (Oxford: Clarendon Press, 1992) 148. Dicey was well aware of the importance of politics and 'public opinion' to constitutional law; however, he was 'unable to invest [the force of this point] with juristic significance' due to 'his adherence to legal positivism'. M. Loughlin, *The Idea of Public Law* (Oxford: Oxford University Press, 2003) 67n.   [5] Dicey (1959) (n. 3 above) 41.

[6] See, e.g., A.V. Dicey, *A Leap in the Dark: A Criticism of the Principles of Home Rule as Illustrated by the Bill of Rights 1893* (1st edn, 1893) (2nd edn, London: John Murray, 1911) which was dedicated 'to Irish Unionists'. At p. 4, Dicey set out the basics of parliamentary sovereignty: 'As a matter of legal theory Parliament has the right to legislate for any part of the Crown's dominions. Parliament may lawfully impose income tax upon the inhabitants of New South Wales; it may lawfully abolish the Constitution of the Canadian Dominion.' Admittedly, here Dicey was making the point that Parliament's power was theoretical not real in the Dominions, whereas in Ireland its power was at that point still real and effective.

[7] *R v Taylor* (1875) 36 UCR 183, 220 (QB). This case and the issue of 'exclusive' grants of legislative authority will be discussed further in Chs 5 and 6 below. Essentially, Chief Justice

this 'curious idea' would not have presented itself to Chief Justice Draper 'if even learned lawyers had not occasionally failed to realise that the parliament at Westminster is a Sovereign legislature'.[8]

Being a sovereign legislature meant, for example, that 'if Parliament were tomorrow to impose a tax, say on New Zealand or on the Canadian Dominion, the statute imposing it would be a legally valid enactment'.[9] In fact, according to Dicey, 'no lawyer questions that Parliament could legally abolish any colonial constitution... and the colonial, no less than the English, courts completely admit the principle that a statute of the Imperial Parliament binds any part of the British dominions to which the statute is meant to apply'.[10] Dicey's assertive, clear and apparently authoritative writing seemed to demand the sort of widespread acceptance that it is generally thought to have achieved.[11]

While the Imperial Parliament was a sovereign legislature, legislatures in the colonies, including self-governing Dominions such as Australia, Canada and New Zealand, were 'subordinate' or 'non-sovereign' law-making bodies. The attributes of non-sovereign law-making bodies—'the marks or notes of legislative subordination'—were the opposite of sovereign attributes: the existence of laws affecting the constitution which a subordinate law-making body must obey and cannot change; the existence of a clear distinction between ordinary and fundamental (or constitutional) laws; and the existence of some persons (courts) having authority to pronounce on the validity or constitutionality of laws passed by the subordinate law-making body.[12]

Dicey knew as well as anyone, that the evolving conventions of the Empire meant that the sovereign Parliament would only legislate for self-governing Dominions where requested to do so, but he left no doubt as to the hierarchical nature of the formal Imperial legal system. If need be, and even in defiance of convention, the Westminster Parliament could make law across the globe-spanning, sun-never-setting expanse of the British Empire. And if Dicey's statements about *judicial* acceptance of a constitutional role premised on the sovereignty of the Imperial Parliament were correct, then the effectiveness of this system of legal subordination was not in doubt.

Draper's argument was that the 'exclusive' grant of federal powers in s. 91 excluded not the provincial legislatures but the Westminster Parliament.

[8] A.V. Dicey, 'Book Review' (1898) 14 LQR 199. Dicey was not above passing out compliments to constitutional commentators in the colonies. He offered the following praise of Professor Hearn of Melbourne, spoiled only partially by the sting in its tail: '...he would be universally recognised among us as one of the most distinguished and ingenious exponents of the mysteries of the English constitution, had it not been for the fact that he made his fame as a professor, not in any of the seats of learning in the United Kingdom, but in the University of Melbourne.' Dicey (1959) (n. 3 above) 20.   [9] ibid., 67.

[10] ibid., 113.

[11] According to Loughlin, Dicey's 'outstanding achievement' in 'the British context' was 'to formulate constitutional law as a discrete set of rules (that is, positive law)'. Loughlin, *The Idea of Public Law* (2003) (n. 4 above) 43.   [12] Dicey (1959) (n. 3 above) 92.

One of the most controversial parts of Dicey's constitutional picture was that the non-sovereign Dominion legislatures found themselves in surprising company for the scientific and dispassionate purposes of constitutional classification. Dicey placed the Parliaments of Australia, Canada and New Zealand comfortably alongside the Parliaments of Belgium and France (which owing to the limitations placed on them by their constitutions were not sovereign), but somewhat incongruously alongside 'railway companies, school-boards, town councils, and the like'.[13] The reason for the classification was that, despite their differences, they were all non-sovereign law-making bodies. In the face of criticism of his classification, Dicey was unrepentant. He could, of course, see the profound differences between, say, a school-board and a national Parliament, but if they shared the constitutional characteristic of being non-sovereign bodies, then the classification was appropriate: 'A man differs from a rat. But this does not make it the less true or the less worth noting that they are both vertebrate animals.'[14]

The hierarchical positioning of the sovereign Westminster Parliament and the subordinate Dominion (and other) legislatures is central to Dicey's constitutional model. Despite the haughty language used in parts of his analysis, his picture provided answers to difficult constitutional questions, and was seized upon by constitutional analysts in part for that reason. For example, United Kingdom legislation such as the British North America Act, 1867 was amendable by the sovereign body which enacted it—the Westminster Parliament—but was binding on and generally speaking unamendable by the subordinate legislatures in Ottawa and the Canadian provinces. The distinction between constitutional and ordinary laws was therefore clear; and furthermore, courts were called upon to pronounce on the validity or constitutionality of ordinary laws according to their conformity with constitutional law so identified. The Commonwealth of Australia Constitution Act, 1900 (Imp.) provided for amendment by Australian processes, but its validity and supremacy was generally seen to depend upon its status as an Act of the Westminster Parliament. In New Zealand the Wellington Parliament had a sort of omnicompetence that made it resemble its Westminster parent; however, it was an act of the sovereign Imperial Parliament, the New Zealand Constitution Act, 1852 (Imp.), which had made that state of affairs clear. In the early part of the twentieth century, the constitutional law of the self-governing Dominions seemed to turn on Dicey's assumptions.

One part of Dicey's constitutional model that we have not yet discussed lies at the centre of the difficulties Australia, Canada and New Zealand have had in anticipating, achieving and accounting for their constitutional independence. This is the idea that no Parliament can bind a future Parliament,[15] which in Dicey's terms was a corollary of the main principle of parliamentary sovereignty. Of course, if no Parliament could bind a future Parliament, then as a matter of

[13] Dicey (1959) (n. 3 above) 93.   [14] ibid., 92n.   [15] ibid., 67–8.

strict law, as opposed to political reality, the Parliament which granted constitutional independence could always change its mind and reassert its authority. And any court which admitted the principle of parliamentary sovereignty would therefore have to heed Westminster once again. On this account, constitutional independence seemed unavoidably precarious.

The reasons for this single limitation on Parliament's legal sovereignty were, according to Dicey, both logical and historical, and I propose to focus on the former. The logical reason why 'Parliament cannot so bind its successors by the terms of any statute, as to limit the discretion of a future Parliament'[16] was that 'a sovereign power, cannot, *while retaining its sovereign character*, restrict its own powers by any particular enactment'.[17] If sovereign power is understood to mean absolute and unrestricted power, as it was by Dicey, then it is hard to dispute his logic: if a sovereign Parliament successfully places a limit on itself then it is no longer sovereign in this absolute sense. If we focus on the italicised phrase in the previous quotation, Dicey might seem to be leaving open the possibility that, provided a sovereign Parliament was clear about its intention to surrender some of its powers and thereby lose its sovereign character (in the absolute sense of sovereignty), it could go ahead and do so. However, Dicey's logic also excluded partial surrender of powers by a sovereign legislature. ' "Limited Sovereignty", in short, is in the case of a Parliament as of every other sovereign, a contradiction in terms.'[18] Just in case it might have been thought that the contradiction was of the logical type first mentioned, Dicey sets the matter straight: 'Let the reader note . . . the impossibility of placing a limit on the exercise of sovereignty' and further on, 'sovereignty is not limitable'.[19] And yet, as numerous commentators pointed out subsequently, it is not at all illogical for a sovereign body to exercise that sovereignty by placing limits on itself. Whether having successfully done so it deserves the name 'sovereign' is a separate question, but clearly any 'impossibility' of placing such limits is dogmatic rather than logical. In many readers' minds, however, the obvious force of Dicey's first logical statement, regarding the impossibility of a sovereign power limiting itself while remaining sovereign in the same absolute sense, may have lent undue weight to the misleading second statement, regarding the impossibility of a sovereign power ever placing such limits.

For other readers, concerns about, say, the apparent impossibility of a sovereign Westminster Parliament ever limiting its own powers in order to grant constitutional independence to the self-governing Dominions and other colonies were seemingly satisfactorily addressed by Dicey's assertion that a sovereign Parliament could abdicate its sovereignty. However, this apparently helpful concession by Dicey came in an inconveniently rigid form: 'A sovereign power can divest itself of authority in two ways, and (it is submitted) *in two ways only.*

---

[16] ibid., 67, quoting Todd, *Parliamentary Government in the British Colonies* (1st edn, 1880) 192 with full approval.   [17] Dicey (1959) (n. 3 above) 68n (emphasis added).
[18] ibid., 68n.   [19] ibid., 68n.

It may simply put an end to its own existence . . . A sovereign power again may transfer sovereign authority to another person or body of persons.'[20] Given his prescriptions regarding 'the impossibility of placing a limit on the exercise of sovereignty', it seems clear that such a transfer, like the divesting of authority, would have had to have been absolute.[21] Dicey did not elaborate, but it would seem that in order to achieve what some (though not Dicey himself) might call 'limited sovereignty', a sovereign Parliament would have to terminate its powers entirely in favour of a newly promulgated constitution involving such limited powers.[22] Therefore, attentive readers of Dicey will have seen that the abdication or transfer of sovereignty is not at all a simple or convenient matter. More cursory readers, encouraged perhaps by Dicey's reassurance that the United Kingdom Parliament could divest itself of its own sovereignty, would none-theless have been somewhat bemused as to how this could be so given Dicey's other assertions regarding the nature of sovereignty and the inability of a sov-ereign parliament to bind itself.[23]

Dicey claimed to be no theoretician. For that he relied on others: 'All that can be urged as to the speculative difficulties of placing any limits whatsoever on sovereignty has been admirably stated by Austin . . . '[24] Dicey saw his own work as empirical: 'Our whole business is now to carry a step further the proof that, under the English constitution, Parliament *does constitute* such a supreme legislative authority of sovereign power as, according to Austin . . . must exist in every civilised state.'[25] However, despite his disclaimers regarding theoretical intentions, Dicey's writing had profound theoretical influence. As we have seen it went beyond empirical observation in bringing Austinian notions of absolute sovereignty into the legal sphere and in presenting them as the only logical understanding of parliamentary sovereignty in particular. As a result, Dicey succeeded in embedding those traditional, orthodox and absolutist theoretical understandings regarding parliamentary sovereignty in the minds of generations of readers, both in Britain and in the Empire at large.

[20] Dicey (1959) (n. 3 above) 69n. See also Dicey (1911) (n. 6 above) 28n.

[21] See G. Marshall, *Parliamentary Sovereignty and the Commonwealth* (Oxford: Clarendon Press, 1957) 38 concurring that this is the only possible reading of Dicey on this point. See also H.W.R. Wade, 'The Basis of Legal Sovereignty' [1955] CLJ 172, 196n, where Dicey's most convincing apologist admits that Dicey does not adequately explain how his ideas on divesting or abdicating power square with his insistence that Parliament cannot bind itself.

[22] See James Bryce's elaboration of this point in his *Studies in History and Jurisprudence*, vol. I (Oxford: Oxford University Press, 1901), 206–7n.

[23] It is perhaps easier to understand the idea of abdicating or transfering sovereignty in terms of international law. Two factors, one theoretical and one practical, made the recourse to international law problematic: first, if parliamentary sovereignty necessarily involved the allegiance of law-applying institutions (principally courts), then so long as those institutions professed a loyalty to the Westminster Parliament, the problem of constitutional independence would persist; secondly, in Australia, Canada and New Zealand, courts took the legal powers of the Westminster Parliament, and the implications of those powers, very seriously. See, e.g. *Reference re Resolution to amend the Constitution* [1981] 1 SCR 753 and *Sue v Hill* (1999) 199 CLR 462.

[24] Dicey (1959) (n. 3 above) 61.   [25] ibid., 61 (emphasis added).

Furthermore, Dicey had help in this task. Influential early twentieth-century writers such as James Bryce and Arthur Berriedale Keith either agreed with Dicey or perhaps deferred to him, in most cases taking a very similar line on the question of Parliament's ultimate legal sovereignty that interests us. Bryce had a particularly strong influence in Australia, where his *The American Common-wealth* had been required reading for participants in the Conventions of the 1890s which drafted the Australian Constitution. Berriedale Keith's influence was of a more general nature, owing to the fact that he was a prolific writer, who also benefited from the profile of his publishers—Oxford University Press and Macmillan & Co.—in gaining a similar international readership to Dicey and Bryce.

Constitutional orthodoxy in university and government: James Bryce

James Bryce was Regius Professor of Civil Law at Oxford University for twenty-three years, from 1870 to 1893. He therefore overlapped with Dicey, who was Vinerian Professor of English Law from 1882 to 1909. In his Valedictory Lecture, Bryce referred to Dicey as a 'distinguished man whose powers...are now recognised over the English-speaking world'.[26]

Bryce was also politcally active and influential. As Under-Secretary for Foreign Affairs in Gladstone's third ministry, he was called upon to defend the proposed scheme for the government of Ireland which not only called for a separate Irish Parliament but, by clause 39, provided that the Act establishing this arrangement should be alterable only with the consent of the Irish Parliament. In debate, some members of the Westminster Parliament criticised the Bill as an unprecedented attempt to limit the authority of Parliament. Bryce spoke for the government, making clear that the Bill did not derogate in any way from the sovereignty of Parliament:

We shall retain as a matter of pure right the power to legislate for Ireland, for all purposes whatsoever, for the simple reason that we cannot divest ourselves of it. There is no principle more universally admitted by constitutional jurists than the absolute omnipotence of Parliament. This omnipotence exists because there is nothing beyond Parliament, or behind Parliament...There is one limitation and one only upon our omnicompetence and that is that we cannot bind our successors. If we pass a statute purporting to extinguish our right to legislate on any given subject, or over any given district, it may be repudiated and repealed by any following Parliament—aye even by this present Parliament on any later day.[27]

---

[26] J. Bryce, *Studies in History and Jurisprudence*, Vol. II (Oxford: Oxford University Press, 1901) 506.

[27] Parliamentary Debates (10 May 1886), quoted in Marshall (1957) (n. 21 above) 65–6.

Clause 39 was therefore merely 'a parliamentary compact . . . an engagement made by a statute, which although it cannot legally bind a succeeding Parliament, or even the existing Parliament, has the effect of imposing a moral obligation not to act contrary to the statute'.[28] The logic of these statements was entirely in conformity with the views set out by Dicey just one year earlier in the first edition of his *Law of the Constitution*, a work with which Bryce and the government's advisers would certainly have been familiar.

If these were Bryce's views when speaking for the Gladstone government, what were his own views as expressed in his books and lectures? A well-known passage from his *Studies in History and Jurisprudence* in which he discusses the possibility of 'entrenching' the British Constitution provides an indication:

Those who have suggested that the United Kingdom ought to embody certain parts of what we call the British Constitution in a Fundamental Statute (or Statutes) and to declare such a statute unchangeable by Parliament, or by Parliament acting under its ordinary forms, seem to forget that the Act declaring the Fundamental Statute to be fundamental and unchangeable by Parliament would itself be an Act like any other Act, and could be repealed by another ordinary statute in the ordinary way. All that this contrivance would obtain would be to impose an additional stage in the process of abolition or amendment, and to call attention both of the people and the legislature in an emphatic way to the fact that a very solemn decision was being reversed. Some may think that such security if imperfect, would be worth having. The restraint would, however, be a moral not a legal one.[29]

In a footnote to this passage, Bryce noted that 'soon after the above lines were written, the point they deal with came up in Parliament in a practical form', in the debate on the Irish Home Rule Bill of 1886. Regarding the imagined possibility of debarring Parliament from recalling its grant of power to Ireland or from legislating as it pleased 'over the heads of the Irish legislature', Bryce repeated the government line without reservation: 'It was generally agreed by lawyers that Parliament could not so limit its own powers, and that no statute it might pass could be made unchangeable, or indeed could in any way restrict that power of future Parliaments.'[30]

While a grant of constitutional protection for Ireland (or it would seem for any self-governing Dominion or colony) and any entrenchment of part of the British Constitution were ruled out by Bryce, he was more creative when it came to then-popular proposals to create a sort of federal Imperial scheme or Confederation of Empire:

If this idea were ever to take practical shape, it would probably be carried out by a statute establishing a new Constitution for the desired Confederation, and creating the Federal Assembly. Such a statute would be passed by the Parliament of the United Kingdom, and (being expressed to be operative over the whole Empire) would have full legal effect for the Colonies as well as for the mother country. Now if such a statute assigned to the

---

[28] Parliamentary Debates (10 May 1886), quoted in Marshall (1957) (n. 21 above) 65–6.
[29] Bryce (Vol. I, 1901) (n. 22 above) 206–7.   [30] ibid., 206–7n.

Federal Assembly certain specified matters . . . taking them away from the present and future Parliament as well as from the parliaments of the several Colonies (or perhaps of the Federal Assembly itself), it is clear that the now unlimited powers of the British Parliament would have to be reduced . . . Parliament would not be fully sovereign; and if either the British or Colonial Parliament passed laws inconsistent with statutes passed by the Federal Assembly in matters assigned to the latter, the Courts would have to hold the transgressing laws invalid.[31]

This scheme appeared to allow for the sort of limited sovereignty and judicial review of Westminster legislation that Dicey had excluded. In fact, Bryce too was quick to reassert the Dicey orthodoxy in a footnote: 'It may of course be observed . . . that the British Parliament, while it continues to be elected as now, may be unable to divest itself of its general power of legislating for the whole Empire, and might therefore repeal the Act by which it had resigned certain legislative matters to the Federal Assembly and resume them for itself.'[32] This was the Irish issue reappearing in another context, and the response was the same. Any protection for Ireland or for the Empire under a federal scheme would have to be political—'no Parliament can be supposed capable of the breach of faith which such a repeal would involve'—rather than legal. If legal protection were required, a much more elaborate constitutional transition would have to take place, again seemingly inspired by Dicey's ideas on the abdication or transfer of sovereignty. Bryce, however, applied his ingenuity not to reconsidering the nature of Parliament's sovereignty but to the sort of more elaborate scheme which his more orthodox views deemed essential:

Upon the general question whether Parliament could so enact any new Constitution for the United Kingdom as to debar itself from subsequently repealing the Constitution, it may be suggested, for the consideration of those who relish technicalities, that Parliament could, if so disposed, divest itself of its present authority by a sort of suicide, i.e., by repealing all the statutes under which it is now summoned, and abolishing the common-law right of the Crown to summon it, and thereupon causing itself forthwith dissolved, having of course first provided means for summoning such an assembly, or assemblies, as the new Constitution created. There would then be no legal means of summoning another Parliament of the old kind, and the new Constitution, whatever it was, would therefore not be liable to be altered save in such a manner as its own terms provided.[33]

---

[31] ibid., 246.   [32] ibid., 246n.

[33] ibid., 207n. Bryce develops the same idea further on when discussing a possible Federation of the United Kingdom, ibid., 248:

If such a scheme provided, as it probably would provide, for an exclusive assignment to the local legislatures of local affairs, so as to debar the Imperial Parliament from interfering therewith, it would destroy the present Flexible British Constitution and substitute a Rigid one for it. Care would have to be taken to use proper legal means of extinguishing the general sovereign authority of the present Parliament, as for instance by directing the election for the new Federal Legislature to be held in such a way as to effect a breach of continuity between it and the old Imperial Parliament, so that the latter should absolutely cease and determine when the new Constitution came into force. Upon this scheme also it would be for the Courts of Law to determine whether in any given case either the Federal or one of the Local Legislatures had exceeded its powers.

Sovereignty here appeared to be such a powerful and resilient beast that nothing could be left to chance in making sure that it was well and truly dead before creating something new in its place.

While Bryce was in the main true to Dicey's orthodox standards where the Westminster Parliament was concerned, Bryce showed some flexibility in his more general writing on sovereignty. Like Dicey he agreed that 'the Imperial Parliament has an unquestioned right to legislate for every part of the British Dominions so as to override all local legislation'.[34] And we have just seen how difficult it would be, in Bryce's view, for the Imperial Parliament ever to end this sovereignty. However, unlike Dicey and other orthodox writers on sovereignty, Bryce placed less emphasis on the absolute or untrammelled nature of that sovereignty, preferring the ability to have the last word (though not necessarily on all matters) as the true indicator of sovereignty.[35] Accordingly, unlike Dicey, Bryce found it possible, without contradiction, to speak of 'limited sovereignty' or, as he termed it 'partial sovereignty':

In every country the legal Sovereign is to be found in the authority, be it a Person or a Body, whose expressed will binds others, and whose will is not liable to be overruled by the expressed will of any one placed above him or it. The law may, in giving this supremacy, limit it to certain departments, and may divide the whole field of legislative or executive command between two or more authorities. The sovereignty of each of these authorities will then be, to the lawyer's mind, a *partial sovereignty. But it will none the less be a true Sovereignty, sufficient for the purposes of the lawyers.* He may sometimes find it troublesome to determine in any particular instance the range of action allotted to each of the several Sovereign authorities. But so also is it sometimes troublesome to decide how far a confessedly inferior authority has kept within the limits of authority conferred upon it by the supreme authority.[36]

Dicey would have regarded this as a nonsense, whereas Bryce's prior in-depth study of the American Constitution would have made it seem uncontroversial. Bryce went further. He could even conceive of some part of the totality of sovereignty being excluded altogether from legislative hands:

We have already seen that Legal Sovereignty may be limited or divided. But it is further to be noted that the totality of possible legal sovereignty may, in a given State, not be vested either in one sovereign or in all the sovereign bodies and persons taken together. In other words, there may be some things which by the constitution of the State no authority is competent to do, because those things have been placed altogether out of the

---

[34] Bryce (Vol. I, 1901) (n. 22 above) 525–6.

[35] This was the type of definition of sovereignty that was proposed in Ch.1 above, the Introduction to this book. It should be noted that once it is acknowledged that absoluteness is not an essential attribute of sovereignty, then Dicey's logical objections to limiting that sovereignty fall by the wayside.   [36] Bryce, Bryce (Vol. II, 1901) (n. 26 above) 54 (emphasis added).

reach of legislation ... And we may imagine a case in which a Constitution has been enacted with no provision for any legal method of amending it.[37]

With Bryce, therefore, limited sovereignty was conceivable in theory. However, for him, the fully sovereign Westminster Parliament could only achieve a state of limited sovereignty with great disruption to the existing constitution, and with considerable practical trouble.

Whereas Dicey and Bryce wrote before the Balfour Declaration and the Statute of Westminster, the writings of the third person in the orthodox tradition at the turn of the twentieth century, Arthur Berriedale Keith, straddled these critical political and legal events.

British writing on sovereignty before and after Balfour and the Statute of Westminster: Arthur Berriedale Keith

Berriedale Keith's three-volume, *Responsible Government in the Dominions* was published in the lead-up to World War I, in 1912,[38] before Irish Home Rule and before the most significant developments regarding Dominion status. Despite being positively encyclopaedic on Imperial matters, it was not a particularly controversial text on matters of theory. In fact such matters were seldom addressed. At this time, it was not unusual, for example, to state: 'The Imperial Parliament has not, of course, given up its right to legislate for the whole Empire.'[39] Far from viewing Imperial legislation as a threat, Berriedale Keith was still impressed with its possibility. He emphasised how useful it was to have the Westminster Parliament available as need be to serve as a pan-Empire legislator. He refused to join others in seeing responsible government as a one-way development in favour of the Dominions and other colonies, because, after all, 'the people and the Crown are ultimately one people and one Crown'.[40] As this quotation suggests, Berriedale Keith was interested in the possibility of Imperial federation. He even considered the idea of an Imperial Court of Appeal.[41] All these pan-Imperial schemes were eventually to come to nought, however, and Berriedale Keith's writing slowly adjusted to this reality.

As we have already seen in Chapter 2, the Balfour Declaration and Statute of Westminster, 1931 set out, respectively, the political and legal equality of the United Kingdom and the Dominions, so far as it was possible to do so. By way of reminder, the Balfour Declaration and the Preamble to the Statute of Westminster had attempted to set out in political or conventional form the idea that the Dominions and the United Kingdom were equal under the Crown. Establishing the same point in law was fiendishly difficult if the orthodoxy

---

[37] ibid., 58.
[38] A. Berriedale Keith, *Responsible Government in the Dominions*, Vols 1–3 (Oxford: Clarendon Press, 1912).   [39] Berriedale Keith (Vol. 3, 1912) (n. 38 above) 1316.
[40] ibid., 1453.   [41] ibid., 1528.

regarding the sovereignty of the Westminster Parliament was to be taken seriously, and of course Dicey, Bryce, Berriedale Keith and others had seen to that
quite nicely. Various sections of the 1931 Statute removed obstacles that had
previously stood in the way of Dominion equality: repugnancy, reservation,
disallowance and extraterritoriality. Section 4 appeared to go further by declaring
that 'no Act of the United Kingdom Parliament . . . shall extend, or be deemed to
extend, to a Dominion as part of the law of that Dominion, unless it is expressly
declared . . . that the Dominion has requested, and consented to, the enactment
thereof'. Without pre-judging the various interpretations that were eventually
given to this section, it was clear that the section stopped short of an unambiguous attempt to limit the Westminster Parliament. In fact it had all the
appearance of a more sophisticated version of just the sort of moral commitment
by the Westminster Parliament that Bryce had referred to regarding Ireland in
1886. The increased sophistication lay in the fact that section 4 appeared to
reverse the interpretative presumption of the Colonial Laws Validity Act, 1865
('Acts of Parliament . . . shall . . . be said to extend to any Colony when it is made
applicable . . . by the express Words or necessary Intendment of any Act of
Parliament') by replacing it with a deeming provision based on declaration
of Dominion request and consent. However, this left open the real possibility of,
or at least the real possibility of a credible interpretation of, section 4 favouring
an ongoing power in the Westminster Parliament to legislate for the Dominions
and other colonies.

With South Africa and Ireland pushing hard for legal equality in substance,
and other Dominions such as Canada not far behind, why was section 4
so weak? The answer would appear to lie in the seemingly immovable theoretical
obstacle placed in the way of real legal equality by the orthodox theory
regarding Westminster parliamentary sovereignty. As Geoffrey Marshall has
related,

In and after 1931 . . . many constitutional lawyers, however desirable they might find the
'root principle of equality governing the free association of the members of the British
Commonwealth of Nations', were yet compelled to insist upon the legal impossibility of
an irrevocable auto-limitation of United Kingdom sovereignty. The resulting conflict
between academic logic and the facts of political life is an effective reminder that the
traditional linguistic garb in which the theory of sovereignty has been clothed is an
embarrassing apparel for a Parliament which passed the Statute of Westminster to make
Dominion independence a legal reality.

The language in which propositions about legal sovereignty have been formulated is
inevitably a language which leans upon traditional (and questionable) pieces of
vocabulary in jurisprudence and political science.[42]

Elsewhere, Marshall has noted that there was more uncertainty and debate
in the United Kingdom tradition of sovereignty thinking than is sometimes

---

[42] Marshall (1957) (n. 21 above) 38.

acknowledged.[43] Jeffrey Goldsworthy, writing more recently, in contrast, gives the impression that the traditional, absolutist view of sovereignty has had a clear run of things since the late seventeenth century if not before.[44] I have tried to argue elsewhere that despite its apparent simplicity, sovereignty is a mask for an array of difficult, even fundamental, legal (and other) questions.[45] We have already seen that Bryce was willing to display some flexibility in his sovereignty 'language', to use Marshall's term. Berriedale Keith showed the same willingness, as we shall see. However, both were as firm as Dicey on the impossibility of a sovereign Westminster Parliament binding a future Parliament, and that difficulty presented a significant obstacle for those contemplating Dominion equality and eventual constitutional independence.

When Berriedale Keith wrote his *Sovereignty of the British Dominions* in 1929, the Balfour Declaration was already three years old and plans were well under way to prepare the Statute of Westminster. Berriedale Keith showed some of Bryce's new-found flexibility in employing the term 'sovereignty' in his initial discussion of the problem of sovereignty. First, 'it is both useful and legitimate to recognise two aspects of [state] sovereignty, internal and external'.[46] Secondly, 'it is necessary to admit that sovereignty can be divided, and that in any country both internal and external sovereignty may be shared by various authorities'.[47] In case it be thought that such shared sovereignty applied to others but not to the United Kingdom, he made clear that 'so long as the Imperial Parliament has supreme authority to legislate for the whole of the Empire ... it is clear that there is some division of sovereignty between the United Kingdom and the Dominions'.[48] This passage may have referred to 'external sovereignty', but in the legal system that was the Empire the distinction between internal and external sovereignty was blurred in any event.

As noted earlier, our main concern is not so much with sovereignty and semantics, but with the orthodox idea that no Parliament can bind a future Parliament. Goldsworthy's historical research makes clear how often this idea was repeated through the generations, with the rationale frequently stated in terms of allowing each successive generation to determine its own future uninhibited by the limitations of a previous generation.[49] This was all very well for the United Kingdom,[50] but applied to the Dominions and other colonies with independent-minded aspirations, this same idea made their desire to determine their own futures precarious.

---

[43] G. Marshall, *Constitutional Theory* (Oxford: Clarendon Press, 1971) ch. 3, and Marshall (2003) (n. 2 above).

[44] J. Goldsworthy, *The Sovereignty of Parliament* (Oxford: Oxford University Press, 1999).

[45] P. Oliver, 'Sovereignty in the Twenty-First Century' (2003) 14 KCLJ 137.

[46] A. Berriedale Keith, *The Sovereignty of the British Dominions* (London: Macmillan, 1929) 1.

[47] ibid., 1.   [48] ibid., 2.   [49] Goldsworthy (1999) (n. 44 above) 105.

[50] Although, as John Finnis has pointed out, those who assert that each generation should be entirely free to make its own laws too often fail to explain why those same generations should for all time be *denied* the ability to protect fundamental values by entrenching them to some extent. It is

Writing in 1929, Berriedale Keith was adamant that the rule as stated remained intact, and that these non-sovereign or subordinate entities could not cause their own independence to come about. He approached the issue from two perspectives. First, he was clear that the Dominions have no right to secede from the Empire. 'It is . . . manifest that, under the existing constitutional law of the Empire, no Dominion has the power to secede of its own volition, and that no Dominion Act . . . would have the slightest power to sever the British connexion . . . they have no power to terminate that membership without the legal intervention of the Imperial Parliament.'[51] The second perspective picked up on the final part of the perspective just set out. The only institution in the Empire which enjoyed true constituent power was the Imperial Parliament: 'The second fundamental limitation on the power of the Dominion Parliaments lies in their inability to exercise unfettered constituent power which belongs to the Imperial Parliament of the United Kingdom. That Parliament has no superior, and it cannot bind itself.'[52] One might have thought that a truly constituent power could do whatever it wanted, including limit itself,[53] but Dicey's logic was in firm command of Berriedale Keith's reasoning here, despite Berriedale Keith's apparent escape from rigid understandings of sovereignty elsewhere in his writing.

Berriedale Keith echoed Dicey's language in reporting that a Dominion such as Canada was effectively 'helpless', having only a 'scintilla of constituent power' itself, and certainly not enough ever to achieve its independence on its own.[54] Australia was no better off: 'the State and the Commonwealth Parliaments taken together do not possess even for Australia the constituent power of the Imperial Parliament'.[55] Even the assent of the Australian people was not enough. Only New Zealand could hope to alter its Constitution as it saw fit, but even its powers were 'not beyond doubt'.[56] It remained to be seen whether the Statute of Westminster could change all this.

Berriedale Keith first discussed the effects of the Statute of Westminster in his 1933 work, *The Constitutional Law of the British Dominions*[57] and in his 1935 work, *The Government of the British Empire*;[58] however, full treatment of the topic awaited his 1938 rewriting of *The Sovereignty of the British Dominions*, now entitled, somewhat optimistically, *The Dominions as Sovereign*

---

not enough simply to assert that each generation must have a clean slate. See J. Finnis, 'Scepticism, Self-Refutation and the Good of Truth' in P.M.S. Hacker and J. Raz (eds) *Law, Morality and Society: Essays in Honour of H.L.A. Hart* (Oxford: Clarendon Press, 1977) 247, 255.

[51] Berriedale Keith (1929) (n. 46 above) 185, 196.   [52] ibid., 197.

[53] As most constituent bodies do when they propose a new constitutional structure which often excludes future recourse to the constituent process, substituting for it a new constitutional amendment process.   [54] Berriedale Keith (1929) (n. 46 above) 199.

[55] ibid., 204.

[56] ibid., 206. See Ch. 2 above regarding the reasons for the New Zealand Parliament's relatively free hand.

[57] A. Berriedale Keith, *The Constitutional Law of the British Dominions* (London: Macmillan, 1933).

[58] A. Berriedale Keith, *The Governments of the British Empire* (London: Macmillan, 1935).

States.[59] There, in a chapter entitled 'The Dominions and the United Kingdom: Imperial Sovereignty and the Statute of Westminster', Berriedale Keith once again revealed his willingness to discuss sovereignty in relative terms. He acknowledged that, following the 1931 Statute, 'establishment of complete sovereignty in the sense of independence of Imperial intervention is not wholly complete', but that 'the essential elements of such sovereignty had been attained'.[60] And he went on to detail these essential elements under fourteen headings.

However, despite his more flexible use of the vocabulary of sovereignty, Berriedale Keith could not shake the stubborn logic of Dicey's theory of parliamentary sovereignty. 'The Statute', he acknowledged, 'removes for the future the essential restrictions of the validity of Dominion legislation'. However, 'the mere fact that the Imperial Parliament can remove restrictions implies that it can at will reimpose them'. Berriedale Keith referred to this fact as 'a fundamental difficulty which afforded no logical mode of solution'.[61] The 'only method', therefore, was not a legal method but a political one: to control the Imperial Parliament by constitutional convention. Section 4 of the Statute was only understandable to Berriedale Keith as reflecting this convention:

No doubt the clause [section 4] may be regarded as invalid, since it purports to hamper the action of future Parliaments . . . Unquestionably in strict law, if a subsequent Act of Parliament applied *nominatim* to any Dominion, the omission of the requisite statement of concurrence would be unavailing to prevent it applying to the Dominion.[62]

Berriedale Keith's reasoning echoed that of the orthodox interpretation of the Judicial Committee of the Privy Council decision in *British Coal Corporation v The King*,[63] as we shall see in a moment. It seemed to exclude the acquisition of Dominions' constitutional independence by means of an Act of the Westminster Parliament.

A close reading of Berriedale Keith exposed a possible way forward. In his discussion of the careful drafting of section 2 of the Statute of Westminster (which provided that the Colonial Laws Validity Act, 1865, and with it the doctrine of repugnancy to Imperial statutes, would not apply after 1931) he noted that it was still deemed necessary for the Westminster Parliament to legislate 'in respect of matters taking place in the Dominions and affecting British subjects when present therein'. Section 2(2) had ensured that this was possible. 'The essential difference between the old system and the new', opined Berriedale Keith, 'lies in the fact that such British legislation as is contemplated

---

[59] A. Berriedale Keith, *The Dominions as Sovereign States: Their Constitutions and Governments* (London: Macmillan, 1938). Berriedale Keith indicated in the Preface that he felt that the time was right to rewrite what he had said in *The Sovereignty of the British Dominions* and *The Constitutional Law of the British Dominions*. By this he meant that both South Africa and the Irish Free State had taken decisive action on the back of or in defiance of the Statute of Westminster.

[60] Berriedale Keith (1938) (n. 59 above) 62.   [61] ibid., 86.   [62] ibid., 87–8.

[63] *British Coal Corporation v The King* [1935] AC 500.

as still possible would be enforceable only in British Courts, and not as under the old system in the courts of the Dominions'.[64] However, if local courts were going to take a different view to that of their British counterparts, something in the theory of the constitution would have to move beyond the Dicey orthodoxy, and for the moment that orthodoxy seemed to been in a process of consolidation rather than disintegration, in part as a result of a spate of 1930s case law on the issue.

Leading cases on parliamentary sovereignty in the 1930s

It has often been said that Dicey had no judicial authority for the dogma regarding absolute and continuing parliamentary sovereignty. In the 1930s, three cases were decided which together have done most of the work of justifying this dogma for the balance of the twentieth century (and beyond). They addressed the aspect of parliamentary sovereignty which was at the heart of constitutional independence for the Dominions and other colonies, i.e. the rule that the sovereign Westminster Parliament could never effectively bind its successors.

Two of these cases, *Vauxhall Estates v Liverpool Corporation* and *Ellen Street Estates v Minister of Health*,[65] concerned the same provision in the Acquisition of Land (Assessment of Compensation) Act 1919. That Act set out a compensation scheme which applied where public authorities compulsorily purchased land. Section 7(1) of the Act stated: 'The provisions of the Act or order by which the land is authorised to be acquired, or of any Act incorporated therewith, shall, in relation to the matters dealt with in this Act, have effect subject to this Act, and so far as inconsistent with this Act those provisions shall cease to have or shall not have effect.' It should be noted immediately that this was by no means a clear attempt to bind a future Parliament if it was an attempt at all. Instead the 1919 Act seemed to contemplate that authorisation for compulsory purchases could come, first, from pre-1919 legislation with provisions already in effect, or, secondly, from pre-1919 legislation with provisions not yet in effect. According to this credible interpretation of Parliament's intention in enacting the 1919 Act, there was no attempt to bind a future Parliament. The marginal notes to section 7(1) confirmed as much.

Nonetheless, when the Housing Act 1925 attempted to legislate on the compensation issue dealt with in the 1919 Act by reducing the compensation payable, counsel for the claimants in the *Vauxhall* and *Ellen Street* cases, Mr H.A. Hill, argued as forcefully as he could that section 7(1) tied the hands of the 1925 and other future Parliaments so far as compensation schemes of this

---

[64] Berriedale Keith (1938) (n. 59 above) 75.

[65] *Vauxhall Estates v Liverpool Corporation* [1932] 1 KB 733 (Div Ct) and *Ellen Street Estates v Minister of Health* [1934] 1 KB 590 (CA).

type were concerned. Both the Divisional Court in *Vauxhall* and the Court of Appeal in *Ellen Street* ruled that section 7(1) did not have this effect. Two of the six judges who heard the two cases (Avory LJ in the *Vauxhall* case and Talbot J in the *Ellen Street* case) took the view that the 1919 Act was not intended to require that its compensation scheme be preferred to another compensation scheme proposed in the future. Their more general comments about a Parliament's ability to bind a future Parliament were clear obiter dicta therefore. The remaining four judges (Humphreys J and Macnaughten J in the *Vauxhall* case and Scrutton LJ and Maugham LJ in the *Ellen Street* case) left open whether the Act was future-directed and concluded that any such future-directed application was sufficiently contradicted by the later Act. Their more general comments about a Parliament's ability to bind a future Parliament could only apply to the 1919 Parliament's (probably unintended or accidental) attempt to do so. Despite this, these cases came to be seen as clear and uncontroversial authority for the rule that no Parliament can bind a future Parliament. The words of Maughan LJ have been cited on countless occasions, despite the fact that, somewhat like Dicey's words before, their force and categorical nature went far beyond what the facts appeared to justify: 'The Legislature cannot, according to our constitution, bind itself as to the form of subsequent legislation.'[66]

The third case that makes up the trilogy from the 1930s is the *British Coal Corporation* decision of the Privy Council which has been referred to earlier in this chapter and in Chapter 2. In that case, the Privy Council was asked to decide whether Canadian legislation barring appeals to the Privy Council by way of special leave was valid after the Statute of Westminster, 1931 despite having been declared invalid prior to 1931 in the case of *Nadan v The King*.[67] In the *British Coal Corporation* case, the Privy Council decided that the earlier case had been based solely on two grounds: (1) the fact that the Canadian legislation was repugnant to an Imperial statute (here, the Privy Council Acts 1833 and 1844); and (2) the fact that the Canadian legislation could only be effective if construed as having extraterritorial operation. Both of these grounds were eliminated as a result of the Statute of Westminster, 1931. This was enough to decide the case contrary to *Nadan*; however, Lord Sankey went further. Noting that any remaining limitation on Dominion legislatures would have to come from the 1931 Statute itself, he briefly discussed section 7 of the Statute, a provision that was inserted at the request of Canada, as we have seen. It excluded from the competence of the Canadian federal and provincial legislatures any power of 'repeal, amendment or alteration' of the Canadian constitution. Lord Sankey then made an often-quoted assertion, by way of obiter dictum:

It is doubtless true that the power of the Imperial Parliament to pass on its own initiative any legislation that it thought fit extending to Canada remains in theory unimpaired; indeed, the Imperial Parliament could, as a matter of abstract law, repeal or disregard s. 4

---

[66] *Ellen Street Estates* (n. 65 above) 597.   [67] *Nadan v The King* [1926] AC 482.

of the Statute. But that is theory and has no relation to realities. In truth, Canada is in enjoyment of the full scope of self-government. Its legislature was invested with all necessary powers for that purpose by the Act, and what the Statute did was to remove the two fetters which have already been discussed.

This appears to be, and probably was, a statement of orthodox theory regarding the Westminster Parliament's enduring legal powers. However, it should also be noted that Lord Sankey made these remarks specifically with reference to Canada, a Dominion which, by means of section 7 of the Statute, had opted to retain the Westminster Parliament at the apex of its constitutional arrangements in order to amend its Constitution, at least until it could agree on a domestic general amending formula for itself. Most commentators, in agreement with Lord Sankey, took the view that section 7 had the effect of ensuring that section 4 of the Statute did not apply to Canada. Therefore it was quite true that, as a result of Canada's decision to preserve the *status quo ante*, the Westminster Parliament could pass any law whatever for Canada, at least as a matter of law. As the enduring general procedure for amendment of the Constitution of Canada, the Westminster Parliament possessed the master key to all manner of change, constitutional and (directly or indirectly) other. Political realities, and well-established conventions, dictated that nothing could be done without Canadian request and consent, but, in Canada's case, the legal situation really was other-wise, as the Supreme Court of Canada would confirm in the 1981 *Patriation Reference*.[68] As long as section 7 remained in force, it would be hard (though clearly not impossible) to deny that the full sovereignty of the Westminster Parliament was exercisable in Canada, even beyond matters of constitutional amendment. However, it was quite another thing to say that section 4 of the Statute could be disregarded in relation to, say, South Africa and Ireland, or, eventually, in relation to Australia and New Zealand. Even if Lord Sankey thought that the Westminster Parliament could ignore section 4 in relation to those countries, he probably would not have been so reckless as to say it even by way of obiter dictum. The fact that he did so is indicative of the orthodox cast of mind that was so prevalent at the time. However, in terms of binding authority for the general proposition that it is said to stand for—that the Westminster Parliament cannot bind itself—it is far weaker than is all too often assumed.

Before concluding this discussion, we should consider one further case: *Attorney-General for New South Wales v Trethowan*.[69] It is an appropriate case to end on because, paradoxically, it opened up potential for what became known as the 'new view' of parliamentary sovereignty—the subject of the next chapter—while, at the same time, confirming the primacy of the orthodox view. The case emerged as a result of New South Wales legislation in 1929 which provided that

---

[68] *Reference re Resolution to Amend the Constitution* [1981] 1 SCR 753. This case will be discussed in detail in Ch. 7 below.

[69] *Attorney-General for New South Wales v Trethowan* [1932] AC 526 (PC).

no Bill to abolish the New South Wales Legislative Council could be presented to the Governor-General for assent unless it had been approved in a referendum. Crucially, the Act also provided that the same rule should apply to a Bill amending the Act. The following year, a newly-elected Labor government sought to repeal the 1929 legislation and abolish the Legislative Council. The required legislation—in the form of two Bills[70]—passed both Houses of the New South Wales Legislature. Injunctions were immediately sought in order to prevent these two Bills from being presented to the Governor-General without their having been approved in referendum. The New South Wales Supreme Court granted the interim injunctions and declared that neither Bill could be presented to the Governor-General without a referendum.[71] The New South Wales government promptly appealed to the High Court of Australia, which accepted the New South Wales Court's reasoning but carefully avoided the question of the interim injunction.

Rich J of the High Court was clear that the effectiveness of the New South Wales 1929 legislation turned entirely on section 5 of the Colonial Laws Validity Act, 1865.[72] He was also clear that, because 'the Legislature of New South Wales is not sovereign . . . no analogy can be drawn from the position of the British Parliament'.[73] Some of his comments seemed to belie that assertion, as when he stated: 'There is no reason why a Parliament representing the people should be powerless to determine whether the constitutional salvation of the State is to be reached by cautious and well-considered steps rather than by rash and ill considered measures [and that there was] no difference in this respect between a unitary and a federal system.'[74] Rich J's distinction between the United Kingdom Parliament and other Parliaments depended on Dicey's distinction between sovereign and subordinate legislatures.

Only Dixon J was prepared to consider the entrenchment point with regard to the United Kingdom Parliament. Dixon J accepted the distinction between sovereign and subordinate legislatures, or, respectively, legislatures with supremacy over the law and legislatures which were under the law, as he preferred to put it. However, he did not think that this distinction ended the matter:

Because of the supremacy of the Imperial Parliament over the law, the Courts merely apply its legislative enactments and do not examine their validity, but because the law

---

[70] The first Bill repealed the attempted 1929 entrenchment, and the second Bill abolished the Legislative Council.   [71] *Trethowan v Peden* (1930) 31 SR (NSW) 183.

[72] Section 5 of the 1865 Act empowered a colonial (and therefore state) legislature to alter [its] Constitution and generally to 'make Laws respecting the Constitution, Powers, and Procedure of such Legislature; provided that such Laws have been passed in such Manner and Form as may from Time to Time be required by any Act of Parliament . . . or Colonial Law for the Time being in force in the said Colony'.

[73] *Attorney-General for New South Wales v Trethowan* (1931) 444 CLR 395, 418.

[74] *Trethowan* (H Ct) 420. Rich J's democratic reasoning demonstrates the force of the point made earlier regarding each generation's right to fashion its own constitutional set-up, *including* some level of entrenchment.

over which the Imperial Parliament is supreme determines the powers of a legislature in a Dominion, the Courts must decide upon the validity as well as the application of the statutes of that legislature. *It must not be supposed, however, that difficulties would vanish if the full doctrine of parliamentary supremacy could be invoked.* An Act of the British Parliament which contained a provision that no Bill repealing any part of the Act including the part so restraining its own repeal should be presented for the royal assent unless the Bill were first approved by the electors, would have the force of law until the Sovereign actually did assent to a Bill for its repeal. In strictness it would be an unlawful proceeding to present such a Bill for the royal assent before it had been approved by the electors. If, before the Bill received the assent of the Crown, it was found possible, as appears to have been done in this appeal, to raise for judicial decision the question whether it was lawful to present the Bill for that assent the Courts would be bound to pronounce it unlawful to do so. *Moreover, if it happened that, notwithstanding the statutory inhibition, the Bill did receive royal assent, although it was not submitted to the electors, the Courts might be called upon to consider whether the supreme legislative power in respect of the matter had in truth been exercised in the manner required for its authentic expression and by the elements in which it had come to reside.*[75]

Whatever the true state of affairs for the United Kingdom, Dixon J agreed with the majority of the High Court that section 5 of the Colonial Laws Validity Act, 1865 settled the matter as far as the New South Wales legislature was concerned. However, as a result of his thoughtful analysis of section 5, Dixon J and the High Court 'might have stumbled onto a more fundamental constitutional principle not dependent on s. 5 . . . but inherent in the very idea of lawmaking'.[76] This principle was that 'the process of making law is itself a process necessarily regulated by law; and accordingly that *any* purported exercise of lawmaking power will be valid only if it is carried out in accordance with the procedures which the law for the time being requires'.[77] We will see in the next chapter how these ideas were developed into 'new' and 'revised' views of parliamentary sovereignty.

On appeal to the Privy Council, it was held that the requirement of a referendum was binding on the legislature of New South Wales until it had been abolished by a law passed in the requisite 'manner and form' (as authorised by section 5 of the Colonial Laws Validity Act, 1865). If one clung to the Diceyan distinction between sovereign and subordinate legislatures, then the *Trethowan* case was simply confirmation of the importance of that distinction. However, if one followed Dixon J's lead and accepted that the issue in question was one that related to all legislatures, sovereign or non-sovereign, then the *Trethowan* case

[75] *Trethowan* (H Ct) 426 (emphasis added).

[76] T. Blackshield and G. Williams, *Australian Constitutional Law and Theory* (3rd edn, Annandale: Federation Press, 2002) 495.

[77] Blackshield and Williams (2002) (n. 76 above) 495 (emphasis added). See also *Harris v Minister of the Interior* [1952] 2 SALR 428 (App Div) in which the binding operation of the 'manner and form' requirements could not rely on s. 5 of the Colonial Laws Validity Act, 1865 as a result of s. 2 of the Statute of Westminster. The *Harris* case is discussed in detail by G. Marshall, *Parliamentary Sovereignty and the Commonwealth* (Oxford: Clarendon Press, 1957) ch. 11. See also *Bribery Commissioner v Ranasinghe* [1965] AC 172 (PC).

was full of potential, notably, for our purposes, in considering how the Westminster Parliament might grant independence to its Dominions and other colonies.[78]

It is now time to consider the unorthodox part of Imperial theory in greater detail. Under a number of different titles—the 'new view', 'the manner and form school', 'the revised view', etc.—they presented a powerful alternative to Dicey's and Dicey's followers' traditional perspective. And although they won many adherents, notably in academic circles, their impact on the legal mainstream, in both the United Kingdom and in Australia, Canada and New Zealand, was surprisingly limited, especially given the general cogency of their arguments. There may be a need to revert to some of these arguments in order to explain constitutional independence in a satisfactory manner, as we discuss in greater detail in Part III.

---

[78] See Wade (1955) (n. 21 above) 180. 'It should be noted . . . that Jennings [*The Law and the Constitution*] and Friedmann [(1950) 24 Austr LJ 103] are in agreement in rejecting as irrelevant any distinction between sovereign and subordinate legislatures—which was one of the principal points of Dicey's analysis—and in taking *Trethowan's* case as an example which will serve for the Parliament of the United Kingdom just as well as for the Parliament of New South Wales'. Wade (1955) (n. 21 above) 180n, points out that three of the five judges in the *Trethowan* case 'state[d] clearly the ordinary rule that Parliament cannot bind its successors, without any qualification'.

4

Theories of Parliamentary Sovereignty
After 1931: New and Revised

New thinking about parliamentary sovereignty in the twentieth century

It is tempting to assert in the first years of the twenty-first century, as Geoffrey Marshall did regarding the first years of the twentieth, that Dicey's account of the doctrine of parliamentary sovereignty still has general assent.[1] If this assertion is at all true it testifies to the enduring persuasiveness of Dicey's account. Government documents still regularly assert, in relation to devolution to Scotland and the incorporation of the European Convention on Human Rights, for example, that 'no UK Parliament can bind its successors'.[2] A recent publication by Jeffrey Goldsworthy, *The Sovereignty of Parliament*, reaffirms the traditional, absolutist, orthodox or Diceyan account as both historically and philosophically preferable.[3]

To the extent that Dicey still dominates, this is remarkable, especially given the tests that the twentieth century presented for the theory, notably Commonwealth independence and participation in a new European legal order. Regarding the Commonwealth, the most recent statement by a British court was agnostic on the question of whether Parliament could have bound itself in the Statute of Westminster.[4] And even if the court of a former Dominion or colony could answer this question in the affirmative, a British court would probably have to toe the traditional Dicey line and assume that reply in the negative. Regarding the new European legal order, the *Factortame* decision[5] prompted even the most devoted Dicey apologist to acknowledge that the traditional theoretical order had ended.[6] Others are still unconvinced, taking the

[1] G. Marshall, 'The Constitution: Its Theory and Interpretation' in V. Bogdanor (ed.) *The British Constitution in the Twentieth Century* (Oxford: Oxford University Press, 2003) 29, 42.
[2] United Kingdom, Scottish Office, *Scotland's Parliament* (White Paper) (1997) (Cm 3658) 12. See also, United Kingdom, Home Secretary, *Rights Brought Home: The Human Rights Bill* (White Paper) (October 1997)(Cm 3782) ch. 2.
[3] J. Goldsworthy, *The Sovereignty of Parliament* (Oxford: Oxford University Press, 1999).
[4] *Manuel v Attorney-General* [1983] Ch 77 (Megarry V-C) and 87 (Slade, Cumming-Bruce and Eveleigh LJJ).   [5] *Factortame v Secretary of State for Transport (No 2)* [1991] AC 603 (HL).
[6] H.W.R. Wade (1991) 107 LQR 1 and (1996) 112 LQR 568.

United Kingdom's 'ultimate sovereignty'—as embodied in a clear statute repealing or repudiating the key components of the European Communities Act 1972—as an indicator that Dicey's doctrine is alive and well.[7]

The fact that so many claim that the orthodox view of parliamentary sovereignty is still hail and hearty may represent the sort of bravado that so often precedes total collapse. Only time will tell. It is more important for our purposes to set a tone which should be kept in mind for the balance of this chapter if not for the balance of the book. The passage of the Statute of Westminster, 1931 saw the development of new theories regarding parliamentary sovereignty. The nature of these theories will be the subject of the better part of this chapter. However, it should be remembered that, as powerful as these theories may have been, they never took firm hold in the United Kingdom. The same was true, as we shall see, in Australia, Canada and New Zealand, until recently, that is.

It may be useful to attempt a fairly simple classification of the theories which challenged the orthodox view of parliamentary sovereignty after 1931. The most famous of these was the 'new view'. 'Its essence', as stated by the late Geoffrey Marshall in a recently published essay, 'lies in the supposition that legal supremacy relates essentially to the possession of an unlimited area of power, but that rules that simply define the procedures through which legal changes are effected are not fetters or limits on power and do not constitute restrictions on sovereignty.'[8] The 'new view' allowed the British lawyer or theorist to believe simultaneously in the absolute substantive sovereignty of the United Kingdom Parliament and in the possibility of restraint concerning the manner and form by which that sovereign power is used.[9] In his talks on the subject, Geoffrey Marshall used to say that the English (because legal sovereignty is truly an English obsession) 'prefer to live in half-way houses'—hence, the appeal of the new view, exemplified below by the writings of Ivor Jennings.

However, outside the world of familiar English pragmatism, it is quite easy to see how, if and when push came to shove, a choice between houses was required.[10] If a 'sovereign'[11] Parliament imposed requirements on how it was to

---

[7] 'A narrower explanation is that the 1972 Act created a rule of construction requiring courts to apply UK legislation consistently with Community law, except where an Act expressly overrides Community law.' A.W. Bradley and K.D. Ewing, *Constitutional and Administrative Law* (13th edn, Harlow: Pearson, 2003). See also A. Tomkins, *Public Law* (Oxford: Clarendon Press, 2002). 　　　　　　　　　　　　　　　　　　　　[8] Marshall (2003) (n. 1 above) 46.

[9] G. Marshall, *Constitutional Theory* (Oxford: Clarendon Press, 1971) 42.

[10] See G. Winterton, 'The British Grundnorm: Parliamentary Supremacy Re-examined' (1976) 92 LQR 591.

[11] Definitions of sovereignty—and therefore Parliament's sovereignty—are many and varied (see P. Oliver, 'Sovereignty in the Twenty-First Century' (2003) 14 KCLJ 137). The orthodox view, discussed in Ch. 3 above, sees the absoluteness, or the full scope and ambit, of Parliament's powers as essential. The definition of sovereignty used in Ch. 1 above emphasised instead the idea of 'having the last word', even if the 'last word' does not apply to every imaginable matter. Limitations of the first type of sovereignty are thought to present problems, given that the sovereign ceases to be such if the limitation takes effect. Limitations of the second type of sovereignty do not present such problems, given that the sovereign's power is relative rather than absolute in any event.

enact laws in future for certain purposes, then it was not too difficult to imagine a court eventually having to choose between recognising the will of a future Parliament normally constituted or refusing to recognise the will of that body because improperly constituted. Seemingly inoffensive procedural requirements for the proper expression of Parliament's will reappear as significant substantive limits on Parliament as normally constituted: either the traditional Parliament's will merits recognition by the courts or it does not.

A more direct take on this issue is represented in what Marshall has recently termed the 'revised' or 'self-embracing' theory of sovereignty.[12] The latter term refers to what H.L.A. Hart viewed as the equally logical alternative to 'continuing' (or orthodox, traditional and absolutist) sovereignty.[13] The well-known paradox of sovereignty means that if a person or body is sovereign either it must not limit itself so as to avoid losing that sovereignty, in which case it is a 'continuing' sovereign; or it is truly unlimited in what it can do, in which case its sovereignty is 'self-embracing', in that its sovereignty *includes* the ability to impose restraints on itself. The self-embracing sovereign would then cease to be sovereign in the sense of having absolute and unlimited power, but it would remain sovereign, or some prefer to say supreme, in the sense of having the last word on a significant range of questions or competences. This last type of sovereignty is familiar to constitutional systems around the world, in that constitution-making bodies regularly transfer their 'sovereign' constituent powers to constitutional set-ups characterised by federalism, bills of rights, specified constitutional amendment procedures and other forms of limitation.[14] And even when the constitutional amendment procedures in these constitutions are themselves amended, the understanding is always that the new procedure replaces the old in self-embracing fashion, not that the first procedure continues to apply, as would be the case with 'continuing' sovereignty.[15]

British constitutional thinking is a long way from conceiving of parliamentary sovereignty in these terms. This means that the revised or self-embracing version has tended to exist only in explicitly theoretical writing, such as that of H.L.A. Hart,[16] John Finnis[17] or Joseph Raz;[18] or it has tended to underlie some

---

[12] Marshall (2003) (n. 1 above) 47.

[13] 'Self-embracing' sovereignty and 'continuing' sovereignty were briefly discussed in Ch. 1 above. See H.L.A. Hart, *The Concept of Law* (Oxford: Clarendon Press, 1961) (2nd edn, 1994) ch. 7, section 4.

[14] See J. Tully, *Strange Multiplicities: Constitutionalism in an Age of Diversity* (Cambridge: Cambridge University Press, 1995) 193–5.

[15] For further discussion regarding continuing and self-embracing sovereignty see Oliver (2003) (n. 11 above).

[16] H.L.A. Hart, 'Self-Referring Laws' in H.L.A. Hart (ed.) *Essays in Jurisprudence and Philosophy* (Oxford: Oxford University Press, 1983) 170.

[17] J. Finnis, 'Revolutions and Continuity of Law' in A.W.B. Simpson (ed.) *Oxford Essays in Jurisprudence* (2nd Series, Oxford: Clarendon Press, 1973) 44.

[18] J. Raz, *The Concept of a Legal System* (2nd edn, Oxford: Clarendon, 1980); J. Raz, *The Authority of Law* (Oxford: Oxford University Press, 1979).

of the writing of theorists in the new view. The new view was essentially a lawyer's argument, designed to drive a strategic wedge in the overwhelmingly dominant orthodox theory. However, some constitutional writers, notably Richard Latham,[19] Jennings' colleague at the University of London, saw that the wedge would eventually split open the supposedly unbreakable orthodox sovereignty whole.

In response to writers such as Jennings and Latham, attempts were made to reassert and reinforce the orthodox view of parliamentary sovereignty. The most notable attempt to do so was by H.W.R. Wade in an article entitled 'The Basis of Legal Sovereignty'.[20] This article had the advantage of explaining developments such as the acquisition of independence by means of Acts of the Imperial Parliament while reaffirming the traditional Dicey view of parliamentary sovereignty. This 'solution' could only be achieved, however, at the expense of acknowledging that the acquisition of independence amounted to a legal revolution disguised beneath the fancy legal dress of independence legislation.[21] Following Wade, even writers more sympathetic to the 'new view' tended to concede that, as the fact of independence was undeniable, there was no real need to provide a clear legal explanation for it. The courts and legal opinion of the United Kingdom would take one view—the traditional—and the courts and legal opinion of the independent Commonwealth would take another view. No clear explanation for the latter view was offered, except to say that 'freedom once conferred could not be revoked'.[22] Writers in the 1950s and early 1960s such as Wheare,[23] de Smith[24] and even to some extent Marshall,[25] tended towards this sort of fatalistic approach to the issue of parliamentary sovereignty in the context of Commonwealth independence.

We will now look at the new and revised view of parliamentary sovereignty in greater detail. This is where our analysis of Imperial and British constitutional theory will end, because we should then be prepared to examine Australian,

---

[19] See R.T.E. Latham, 'The Law and The Commonwealth' in W.K. Hancock (ed.) *Survey of British Commonwealth Affairs*, Vol. 1 (London: Oxford University Press, 1937) 517, reprinted with a foreword by W.K. Hancock but with otherwise unaltered pagination as R.T.E. Latham, *The Law and the Commonwealth* (Oxford: Oxford University Press, 1949).

[20] H.W.R. Wade, 'The Basis of Legal Sovereignty' [1955] CLJ 172.   [21] ibid., 191.

[22] The quotation is from a South African case, *Ndlwana v Hofmeyr* (1937) AD 229, 237, but it has been widely adopted by British and Commonwealth courts and commentators. It should be noted that while its rhetorical force is powerful, its value in terms of a legal explanation for independence is virtually non-existent. As a legal argument, it adds little to the more traditionally expressed obiter dictum in the *British Coal Corporation* case (1935) AC 500 (PC) which was discussed in Ch. 3 above.

[23] K.C. Wheare, *The Statute of Westminster and Dominion Status* (5th edn, Oxford: Oxford University Press, 1953) and K.C. Wheare, *The Constitutional Structure of the Commonwealth* (Oxford: Clarendon Press, 1960).

[24] S.A. de Smith, *The New Commonwealth and its Constitutions* (London: Stevens & Sons, 1964).

[25] G. Marshall, *Parliamentary Sovereignty and the Commonwealth* (Oxford: Clarendon Press, 1957).

Canadian and New Zealand constitutional theory leading up to constitutional independence in a more complete intellectual context. Between the early 1960s and the 1980s when constitutional independence was achieved, writers such as Hart, Finnis, Raz and, again, Marshall, continued to push the debate on, but their debates took place in books and journals having to do with jurisprudence and legal philosophy, and to that extent their influence on the opinions of more practically-minded constitutional commentators in Australia, Canada and New Zealand was felt to a far lesser extent. We shall see in Part III that some of this more theoretical writing provided some of the inspiration for post-independence attempts to explain constitutional fundamentals.

Even more recently, in what Marshall refers to (with characteristic irony) as a 'still newer view',[26] a collection of British and Commonwealth academics and judges has begun to develop the idea that some principles are so fundamental that the common law and its judges must make sure that even Parliament cannot encroach on them.[27] This, of course, is a full-frontal attack on the traditional theory of parliamentary sovereignty, and it has provoked attacks from many quarters as being historically,[28] philosophically[29] and politically[30] misguided. At this point, it is important to notice that whereas the revised or self-embracing view of sovereignty contemplates limits on Parliament imposed *by Parliament*, the 'still newer view' recommends limits imposed by the common law, i.e. *by judges* acting alone.

Parliamentary sovereignty is to a great extent about the relationship between Parliament and the courts. And it is true to say that unless the common law recognises the self-embracing powers of Parliament, the revised theory cannot make any further progress. However, there is a great difference between courts agreeing to recognise that which a Parliament has enacted, even in the form of self-limitation, and those same courts deciding to impose limitations at their own initiative. These and other issues underlie the evolving debate on parliamentary sovereignty in the twentieth century. We begin with Dicey's most determined critic, Ivor Jennings.

The 'new view' of parliamentary sovereignty: Ivor Jennings

In the preface to the final edition of *The Law and the Constitution*,[31] Ivor Jennings looked back on the legal-intellectual heritage which had influenced his

---

[26] Marshall (2003) (n. 1 above) 49.

[27] e.g. Cooke P of the New Zealand Court of Appeal (as he then was), the Australian High Court in the late 1980s and early 1990s, Sir John Laws, Trevor Allan and Michael Detmold.

[28] See Goldsworthy (1999) (n. 3 above).   [29] ibid.

[30] See T. Campbell, K.D. Ewing and A. Tomkins (eds) *Sceptical Essays on Human Rights* (Oxford: Oxford University Press, 2001).

[31] I. Jennings, *The Law and the Constitution* (5th edn, London: University of London Press, 1959). The fifth edition has been preferred in this discussion of Jennings, simply because it

early studies and early teaching experiences.[32] He noted that the 'orthodox' theory regarding 'fundamental principles of English constitutional law'[33] was dominated by Dicey and his 'inarticulate major premises'.[34] With the help of Cambridge commentators such as Maitland, the new version of the 'orthodox' theory became one which 'assumed that Dicey's views were fundamentally correct, but that they needed qualification at the margin'.[35] Jennings confessed that his own teaching of public law, beginning in 1925 at the University of Leeds, was founded on this new, essentially Diceyan, orthodoxy. It was in part his initial studies of Imperial and Commonwealth constitutional law which had caused him to reconsider. He 'soon discovered that matters such as ... the relations between the United Kingdom and the rest of the Commonwealth could not satisfactorily be fitted into the "orthodox" version of English constitutional law'.[36] Following on his move to the London School of Economics in 1929, 'further reading ... convinced me that if there were any "heretics" they were to be found amongst those who regarded themselves as "orthodox"'.[37] He therefore set about considering 'the ideas of a past generation ... to show how ill-adapted they seem to the present generation'.[38] We shall look first at the problems which Jennings identified in 'orthodox' constitutional theory regarding parliamentary sovereignty, before focusing on the particular problems thrown up by Imperial and Commonwealth constitutional affairs.

Jennings' main theoretical problem with Dicey was that Dicey had separated political and legal sovereignty without leaving the political idea of sovereignty behind. 'Sovereignty', in the political sense as developed by Bodin, Hobbes, Bentham and Austin, was 'supreme power' unrestrained by law, or absolute power, as we have been referring to it until now. Although the concept may at one time have seemed to fit the facts of English political life, for Jennings Parliament was not even a sovereign in this political sense, 'for there are many things, as Dicey and Laski both point out, which Parliament cannot do'.[39] What of legal sovereignty? Jennings was prepared to distinguish the political and the

represents the most advanced rendition of Jennings' thinking on sovereignty. However, it is important to bear in mind that the first edition of *The Law and the Constitution* appeared in 1933, just one year after the Judicial Committee of the Privy Council decision in *Attorney-General for New South Wales v Trethowan* [1932] AC 526. For a historically-informed analysis of the shifting pattern of Jennings' thought through the various editions of *The Law and the Commonwealth*, see K.D. Ewing, *'The Law and the Constitution*: Manifesto of the Progressive Party' (2004) 67 MLR 734.

[32] For a recent account of Jennings' life and legacy, see A.W. Bradley, 'Sir William Ivor Jennings: A Centennial Paper' (2004) 67 MLR 716.   [33] Jennings (1959) (n. 31 above) v.
[34] ibid., v.   [35] ibid., v.   [36] ibid., v.   [37] ibid., v–vi.   [38] ibid., vi.

[39] ibid., 147. Jennings was clearly influenced by his L.S.E. colleague, H.J. Laski. Laski wrote a great deal about sovereignty in the early part of the twentieth century. See, e.g., H.J. Laski, *The Foundations of Sovereignty and Other Essays* (London: Allen & Unwin, 1921). Laski's writings have not been discussed in any detail in this book because, for whatever reason, they were never as influential in Commonwealth constitutional commentary as those of Dicey, Bryce, Berriedale Keith, Jennings and the others discussed in this chapter. For discussion of Laski and his influence on Jennings and others, see M. Loughlin, *Public Law and Political Theory* (Oxford: Clarendon Press,

legal, but he strongly disagreed with Dicey's acceptance that 'legal sovereignty' could qualify as sovereignty. Instead, in his view, 'legal sovereignty' in England was not sovereignty at all, if sovereignty was to retain its traditional sense. It was not supreme or absolute power, as Bodin and others had conceived of it; rather, it was 'a legal concept, a form of expression which lawyers use to express relations between Parliament and the courts'.[40] Far from being a supreme or absolute power unconstrained by law, for Jennings Parliament owed its legal existence to law, i.e. to the common law.[41] And according to the common law, the English courts 'will always recognise as law the rules which Parliament makes by legislation; that is, rules made in the customary manner and expressed in the customary form'.[42] ' "Legal sovereignty" is merely a name indicating that the legislature has for the time being power to make laws of any kind in the manner required by law.'[43] Jennings illustrated this point with help from *Attorney-General for New South Wales v Trethowan*,[44] a case which was discussed at some length in Chapter 3.

So whereas Dicey saw the Westminster Parliament as supreme or absolute, and therefore unique, fundamental and unchangeable, Jennings saw it as a legislature much like other legislatures, i.e. deriving its powers from law and capable of limitation, including self-limitation. We see here an immediate contrast of approaches on issues which are of central importance in this book: the distinction between sovereign and non-sovereign legislatures and the question whether Parliament can bind a future Parliament.

Regarding sovereign and non-sovereign legislatures, Jennings reminded us that, from Dicey's perspective, if sovereignty is supreme or absolute power, then 'any powers which are not vested in the sovereign must be derived from it' and be subordinate to it.[45] However, if Parliament is not a supreme or absolute power

---

1992) 169 et seq. Loughlin notes, at 170, that Laski 'was highly critical of the abstract legal idea of absolute legal sovereignty, arguing that it could not form a realistic basis for political relationships. Authority in the state is inherently federal since the state is simply one association amongst many'.

[40] Jennings (1959) (n. 31 above) 149.

[41] Strictly speaking, Parliament owes its existence to custom; however, custom is in turn controlled by the common law.   [42] Jennings (1959) (n. 31 above) 149.

[43] ibid, 152–3. Jennings made this point even more forcefully in the third edition of *The Law and the Commonwealth*:

The powers of Parliament are not expressed in an Act of Parliament. Nevertheless it is admitted, as Dicey admits, that the powers do come from the law. The law is that Parliament may make any law in the manner and form provided by the law. The manner and form is provided, at present, either by the common law or by the Parliament Act of 1911. But Parliament may, if it pleases, provide another manner and form. Suppose, for instance, that the present Parliament enacted that the House of Lords should not be abolished except after a majority of electors had expressly agreed to it, and that no Act repealing that Act should be passed except after a similar referendum. There is no law to appeal to except that Act. The Act provides a new manner and form which must be followed unless it can be said that at the time of its passing that Act was void or of no effect.

See I. Jennings, *The Law and the Commonwealth* (3rd edn, London: University of London Press, 1943). For comment, see Ewing (2004) (n. 31 above) 145.

[44] [1932] AC 526 (PC).   [45] Jennings (1959) (n. 31 above) 150.

and is instead derived from law, as Jennings believed, then Parliament is in the same category as other legislatures. 'The question then becomes one of the variety of legislative powers which these bodies possess',[46] and determination of this question of *relative* power was the job of courts. It turned out, of course, that the Westminster Parliament had more powers than, say, the United States Congress or the Australian and Canadian Parliaments, but this was now a question of degree rather than one of classification. Each of these Parliaments, including the Westminster Parliament, was, to use Dicey's jarring analogy, a different type of invertebrate—but they all were invertebrates.

Jennings' elimination of confusions caused by the inappropriate use of political conceptions of sovereignty in law allowed him to explain and understand contemporary legal uses of the term 'sovereignty' in places where Dicey's reaction would have been one of disdain:

> ... in modern constitutional law, it is frequently said that a legislature is 'sovereign within its powers'. This is, of course, pure nonsense [as it was for Dicey] if sovereignty is supreme [or absolute] power, for there are no 'powers' of a sovereign body; there is only the unlimited power which sovereignty implies. But if sovereignty is merely a legal phrase for legal authority to pass any sort of laws, it is not entirely ridiculous to say that a legislature is sovereign in respect of certain subjects, for it may then pass any sort of laws on those subjects, but not on any other subjects.[47]

Even if one accepted Jennings' argument that the law determined Parliament's powers, it remained possible that *the law* simply allowed Parliament to pass any law whatever, as Dicey had suggested. Here, too, Jennings was doubtful, however. He asserted that Dicey 'had failed to prove that the law made ... Parliament a sovereign law-making body' and that no one else had succeeded in doing so either.[48] To a large extent, this was because the courts had been sensible enough not to challenge Parliament, and Parliament sensible enough not to enact extreme statutes. However, given that 'a lawyer ought to be able to say what the answer of the courts would be',[49] Jennings had to admit that 'the modern trend [was] towards admitting the supremacy of Parliament over the common law', even if he did not follow that trend.[50]

Assuming that others were right and that Parliament was supreme over the common law, could *Parliament* ever change that situation by choosing to limit its own powers? This was the second question referred to earlier, i.e. whether Parliament could bind a future Parliament. Dicey's dominant view was stated in the previous chapter. His view that Parliament cannot bind itself was, as Jennings admitted, 'a perfectly correct deduction from the nature of a supreme

---

[46] ibid., 150.

[47] ibid., 150. Jennings' understanding made sense of the term 'sovereignty' as it is often employed in a federal system, such as Canada, where provinces are said to be fully sovereign within their own sphere.   [48] ibid., 156.

[49] ibid., 159.   [50] ibid., 160.

[or absolute] power',[51] in Bodin's political sense of the term. However, if Jennings was right about legal sovereignty being simply 'a name indicating that the legislature has for the time being power to make laws of any kind in the manner [and form] required by the law', then 'the "legal sovereign" may impose legal limitations upon itself, because its power to change the law includes the power to change the law affecting itself'.[52] The *British Coal Corporation*,[53] *Vauxhall Estates*[54] and *Ellen Street Estates*[55] cases were not authority for Parliament's inability to limit its own powers; rather they were evidence of the fact that 'the courts would not be anxious to read limitation into the power of Parliament'.[56]

For the orthodox follower of Dicey, section 4 of the Statute of Westminster, 1931 could only be an interpretative provision. For Jennings, it was a 'manner and form' limitation, meaning that the declaration of Dominion request and consent in that section was a legally enforceable condition. On the first analysis, the courts would interpret Westminster legislation as not applying to a Dominion in the absence of the declaration. On the second Jennings' analysis, the courts would refuse to recognise it as an Act of Parliament. The result was the same in practice; however, if Jennings' analysis was correct, then all sorts of other Parliamentary self-limitation were possible, including the type of self-limitation that would appear in independence legislation as of the late 1940s. This independence legislation required actual request and consent or local enabling legislation if the Westminster Parliament were ever to legislate again for the newly independent states.[57] Accordingly, it was no surprise to see that this was how Jennings interpreted the independence legislation for India and Pakistan:

Case law, logic, and the progress of the laws of the Commonwealth suggest that the [orthodox] theory [of parliamentary sovereignty] is an academic formulation which does not fit the law of England. The genius of the common law has been its capacity to produce common-sense solutions for political problems; and the common-sense answer to the Indian problem is that in 1947 the Parliament of the United Kingdom prevented itself from legislating for British India without the consent of the new Dominions, which have now become republics incapable of giving that consent. In other words, the 'sovereign' Parliament limited its 'sovereignty'.[58]

There is no doubt that Jennings would have viewed Westminster legislation of the Canada Act 1982 or Australia Act 1986 (UK) variety as further clear evidence of Parliament's ability to bind itself.

[51] Jennings (1959) (n. 31 above) 152.   [52] ibid., 252.

[53] *British Coal Corporation v The King* (1935) AC 500 (PC).

[54] *Vauxhall Estates v Liverpool Corporation* (1932) 1 KB 733 (Div Ct).

[55] *Ellen Street Estates v Minister of Health* (1934) 1 KB 597 (CA).

[56] Jennings (1959) (n. 31 above) 163.

[57] See, e.g., Indian Independence Act, 1947, s. 6(4): 'No Act of Parliament of the United Kingdom . . . shall extend, or be deemed to extend, to either of the new Dominions as part of the law of that Dominion, unless it is extended thereto by a law of the Legislature of the Dominion.'

[58] Jennings (1959) (n. 31 above) 167–8.

Jennings' attack on Dicey's orthodoxy was radical on many fronts, as we have seen. However, Jennings' ideas on Parliament limiting itself were focused on the idea of 'manner and form' limitation. Jennings did not explore to the same extent the possibility of Parliament imposing self-embracing substantive limitations on itself. The beginnings of that task were left to Richard Latham.

First signs of a 'revised view' of parliamentary sovereignty: R.T.E. Latham

One of Jennings' junior colleagues at the University of London was R.T.E. Latham, Rhodes Scholar, Fellow of All Souls and son of the then Chief Justice of Australia, Sir John Latham. In the years 1936–9 Latham was based at King's College, London. It is fairly certain that he taught alongside Jennings at the Masters level for a seminar course entitled 'Constitutional Law of the British Empire'.[59] It was during this time that Latham wrote his two most important contributions to the literature on parliamentary sovereignty: 'What is an Act of Parliament?'[60] and 'The Law and The Commonwealth'.[61] These contributions followed Jennings' lead in questioning the orthodox theory,[62] but they took the 'new view' further and exposed its more radical possibilities. They therefore represent the first contributions to that which was referred to earlier as the 'revised' or 'self-embracing' theory of parliamentary sovereignty. Sadly, Latham died in active service during World War II, but his influence has lived on mostly due to the posthumous republication of *The Law and The Commonwealth* in monograph

---

[59] King's College, London, *Calendars for 1937–38, 1938–39, 1939–40* (Bungay, Suffolk: Richard Clay, 1938–40) 143, 183, 181.   [60] [1939] *King's Counsel* 152.

[61] R.T.E. Latham, 'The Law and the Commonwealth' in W.K. Hancock (ed.) *Survey of British Commonwealth Affairs*, Vol. I, *Problems of Nationality 1918–36* (Oxford: Oxford University Press, 1937) 510–630, reprinted with unaltered pagination and layout as R.T.E. Latham, *The Law and the Constitution* (Oxford: Oxford University Press, 1949).

[62] Latham was no sycophant, however. He frequently criticised Jennings in print, notably regarding what Latham saw as Jennings' attempts to break down the distinction between law and convention. See P. Oliver, 'Law, Politics, the Commonwealth and the Constitution: Remembering R.T.E. Latham, 1909–43' (2000) 11 KCLJ 153, 174–5. Latham was quite clear in his own mind that he wished to reject traditional thinking on sovereignty. In a letter to his father in 1936 while writing his chapter for the Hancock book, Latham reported a disagreement that he had had with a Canadian colleague, and in so doing distanced himself in no uncertain terms from writers such as Arthur Berriedale Keith:

I am having a hard time preventing the young Canadian who is writing the short Chatham House book from confounding an unmitigated Austinianism, and introducing the facts which limit the sovereignty of the Imperial Parliament as a disorderly appendix. That, of course, is the Keith method, which is why, with all his meticulous accuracy in detail he can't get anything like the right perspective. Perhaps a Professor of Sanskrit can't help seeing only the beginnings of things and not their present shape.

National Library of Australia, *Sir John Latham Collection*, Series 10/22 June 1936.

form.[63] It is worth discussing this work in some detail below. It may be more helpful, however, to deal with his later, shorter and less developed work first.

The later publication, 'What is an Act of Parliament?', was mostly about the impossibility of legal sovereignty, a point that had been emphasised by Jennings. Latham examined the issue more deeply, however. Like Jennings, Latham's main point was that in order for law to be obeyed it must be intelligible. Accordingly, it was not sufficient to say, as Dicey did, that (the King- or Queen-in) Parliament is sovereign, because this tells us far too little about Parliament and its Acts. Latham set out three proofs of the impossibility of legal sovereignty which were missing from simplistic orthodox analysis, some of which resonate with H.L.A. Hart's later description of the (ultimate) rule of recognition.[64] The first proof was that 'there must be principles in the constitution prescribing what form of the sovereign's acts will be recognised as valid'.[65] This was the question of 'authenticity', and it brought with it, somewhat incongruously in an English context, 'the inevitability of judicial review of legislation'.[66] The second proof was that there must be rules governing the succession of the sovereign, in order at least to designate which King or Queen is to be the requisite Sovereign-in-Parliament.[67] The third proof was that there must be rules governing 'procedure in the sovereign assembly'.[68] He illustrated the point as follows:

It is not impossible to ascertain the will of an individual without the aid of rules: he may be presumed to mean what he says, and he cannot say more than one thing at one time. But the extraction of a precise expression of will from a multiplicity of human beings is, despite all the realists say, and artificial process and one which cannot be accomplished without arbitrary rules. It is therefore an incomplete statement to say that in a state such and such an assembly of human beings is sovereign. It can only be sovereign when acting in a certain way prescribed by law. At least some rudimentary 'manner and form' is demanded of it: the simultaneous cry of the rabble, small or large, cannot be law, for it is unintelligible. The minimum would be rules prescribing some sort of majority—simple plurality, absolute majority, unanimity or some arbitrary portion—coupled with rules for the election of a chairman.[69]

In addition to the rules implied by Latham's three proofs, 'there must be a rule *laying down how these rules may be changed* . . . And all these rules, whether readily alterable, alterable with difficulty, or unchangeable . . . are logically prior to the sovereign, for only to the extent that they are observed do they exist'.[70]

Latham's insight was crucial. Once we realise that the statement 'Parliament is sovereign' begs the questions 'what is Parliament?', 'when does it change?', and 'how does it speak?', then the two key interpretations of sovereignty later identified by Hart ('continuing' and 'self-embracing') come rapidly into focus.

---

[63] See Oliver (2000) (n. 62 above).

[64] Hart discusses the 'ultimate rule of recognition' in *The Concept of Law* (2nd edn, Oxford: Clarendon Press, 1994) 107.   [65] Latham (1939) (n. 61 above) 153.

[66] ibid., 152.   [67] ibid., 153.   [68] ibid., 153.   [69] ibid., 153.

[70] ibid., 153–4 (emphasis added).

Either Parliament as presently constituted (House of Commons, House of Lords, Speakers, majority voting, etc.) is frozen for all time as a legally untouchable and logically prior rule as in Dicey's version of continuing sovereignty; or Parliament itself has the self-embracing power to determine its own composition, transition and legislation, including the 'manner and form' of such legislation. Anticipating Hart's ideas of core and penumbra in the (ultimate) rule of recognition, Latham was quick to observe, contrary to all the prevailing assumptions of his time, that 'there is quite astonishing lack of certainty on this central point of our law'.[71] Latham, along with Jennings, was primarily concerned to develop the 'manner and form' aspect of the new view, but Latham simultaneously exposed the fact that the 'manner and form' question was itself sitting on a deep fault line in constitutional theory.[72]

Latham's awareness of this 'fault line' was evident in his discussion of *Attorney-General for New South Wales v Trethowan*:

If, therefore, the decision in *Trethowan's Case* that the legislature could bind itself follows logically from the fact that its law must be made in the manner and form required by law, *that consequence must follow also for the British Parliament. The exact length to which this argument goes must be carefully observed.* It does not deny directly the hallowed rule that Parliament cannot prohibit itself from legislating on any subject, or from repealing any law. It only pushes to its logical conclusion the recognised competence of Parliament to regulate validly and in a manner binding for the future its own composition . . . That is to say, *it maintains simply that Parliament can bind itself for the future by a law relating to the manner and form of its own legislation process, though not by any other kind of law—though it clearly follows that it can in effect prohibit itself from legislating on any specified topic, by prescribing for legislation on that topic a special legislative process which, though theoretically practicable, is practically impossible.*[73]

Latham here identified both the importance of the distinction between procedural and substantive limitations, and the difficulty in maintaining that distinction, both in theory and in practice.[74]

Most of these ideas had been developed a few years earlier in Latham's more detailed study, 'The Law and the Commonwealth'. This is not the place to set out the brilliance of this essay in detail. A brief sampling may suffice. Part of its current relevance lies in Latham's attempt to describe a legal order which existed and evolved somewhere between international law and national legal systems, much as the European legal order does today.

Latham introduced the discussion of modern Commonwealth law with a warning that philosophy and politics were to play a part in his account, noting that in 'the frontier regions', further from 'the centre of established doctrine',

---

[71] ibid., 154.   [72] ibid., 161.

[73] (1931) 44 CLR 395 (H Ct), [1932] AC 526 (PC). Latham (1939) (n. 61 above) 161 (emphasis added).

[74] On the theoretical difficulty, see G. Winterton, 'The British Grundnorm: Parliamentary Supremacy Re-examined' (1976) 92 LQR 591.

'to require self-sufficiency of legal scholarship is to ensure not its chastity but its sterility'.[75] He then reminded his readers to avoid what Hart later referred to as 'formalistic' error, i.e. assuming that there is a set legal answer to any legal question that can be imagined in advance of judicial determination.[76] In stating that this is 'the implicit traditional theory of English law, though possibly not of British speculation' Latham may have been referring in part to the tendency of constitutional lawyers such as Dicey to make up for the paucity of case law by providing apparently authoritative answers to as-yet-undecided issues.[77]

In order to discuss the legal aspect of the Commonwealth after the Statute of Westminster, 1931, Latham needed a tool which was not readily available in the Imperial or Commonwealth legal theory of his time.[78] It was the need for such theoretical grounding that must have drawn Latham to the work of Hans Kelsen. Latham acknowledged that he was indebted to Kelsen for this part of his analysis,[79] but Latham was quick to add that he did not subscribe to Kelsen's over-emphasis on the purely rational or formal elements in law at the expense of sociological, political and other non-legal perspectives. Kelsen's *Grundnorm*, or basic norm, might be ultimate in law, but, in Latham's view, its validity depended on non-legal considerations, including 'ethics, religion, political principle, tradition, and mere blind reflex loyalty'.[80]

Latham then moved on to discuss the United Kingdom and Commonwealth *Grundnorm*, firmly rejecting here the Austinian version of sovereignty which was then prevalent. The following passage was referred to, even as early as the 1950s, as an 'almost classical' statement of a more modern (both 'new' and 'revised') view of sovereignty:

Where the purported sovereign is any one but a single actual person, the designation of him must include the statement of the rules for the ascertainment of his will, and these rules, since their observance is a condition of the validity of his legislation, are rules of law logically prior to him. Further, *the mere assertion of the omnipotence of a sovereign leaves completely uncertain the fundamental question whether or not he can bind himself*; but the addition of a ruling in either sense on this point makes the basic rule of the system something more than a mere designation of the sovereign.[81]

---

[75] Latham (1937/1949) (n. 61 above) 521.   [76] Hart (1994) (n. 64 above) ch. 7, section 4.

[77] Latham (1937/1949) (n. 61 above) 522. Elsewhere, Latham noted, 524: 'In the English system of case law, fundamental principles are not stated . . . Clearly, in such a system there is no certainty that the most fundamental principle . . . will be reached and declared by the courts. It may be that no case will arise which necessitates resort to the ultimate rule.'

[78] Hart (1994) (n. 64 above) 296, observed that 'Latham was the first to interpret the constitutional development of the Commonwealth in terms of the growth of a new basic norm with a "local root"'.

[79] For a discussion of Latham's thoughts and contact with Kelsen, see Oliver (2000) (n. 62 above) 181.   [80] Latham (1937/1949) (n. 61 above) 522n.

[81] ibid., 523 (emphasis added). For references to this quotation in similar terms, see, e.g., Wade (1955) (n. 21 above) 187, E.C.S. Wade, 'Introduction' to A.V. Dicey, *An Introduction to the Study of the Law and the Constitution* (10th edn, London: Macmillan, 1959) xl–xli and H. Gray, 'The Sovereignty of Parliament Today' (1953) 10 UTLJ 54, 63: 'A passage which has become almost classical.'

This passage anticipated 'What is an Act of Parliament?', and it indicated how clearly Latham saw the continuing and self-embracing interpretations of sovereignty later identified by Hart.[82] It also recognised the importance of the fact, alluded to earlier, that the exact content of Parliament's sovereignty may be uncertain pending judicial determination:

Clearly in such a system there is no certainty that the most fundamental principle, the *Grundnorm*, will be reached and declared by the courts. It may be that no case may arise which necessitates resort to the ultimate rule. Yet at any time such a case may arise, for by definition the *Grundnorm* is a rule of law, and, also by definition, since it is a rule of law, it must be capable of declaration and application by the courts.[83]

In 'a field as little tilled by judicial decision as the ultimate constitutional theory of the Common Law'[84] all sorts of dogma could be propounded without the obstacle of decided cases. 'That this field is unexplored in England may be seen from the striking fact that Dicey was unable to cite a single decided case as authority for his classic exposition of the sovereignty of Parliament.'[85]

Latham developed this insight regarding what Hart later referred to as the 'ultimate rule of recognition' in a legal system; however, Latham then moved beyond by considering a question glossed over by Hart: how and why does the ultimate rule of recognition shift?[86] Latham attributed the shifts to 'the influence of . . . judges' general philosophies' which tend to emerge more in 'high constitutional decisions' than in any others.[87] Latham then went on to use language which would be more familiar to readers of Hart later on:

If this tendency [of judges' philosophies emerging in constitutional decisions] is so marked . . . it is to be expected that decisions on the ultimate question, decisions defining the *Grundnorm*, will reflect still more strongly the basic beliefs of the judges themselves. It may then be said, and not in any cynical way, that the *Grundnorm* of a case-law system is *simply the sum of those principles which command the ultimate allegiance of the courts.* This loose definition opens up possibilities of indeterminacy of *Grundnorm* and of shifting of *Grundnorm* which will be illustrated in the next few pages.[88]

In those 'next few pages' Latham examined the law and jurisprudence of Commonwealth countries, principally the Dominions, to determine whether formal legal unity existed. He was less interested in well-behaved Australia, Canada and New Zealand, all of which avoided challenging the Imperial and

---

[82] Hart (1994) (n. 64 above) 149.   [83] Latham (1937/1949) (n. 61 above) 524–5.
[84] ibid., 525.   [85] ibid., 525.
[86] For discussion of how Hart excludes this important question from his concept of law, see J. Finnis, 'Revolutions and Continuity of Law' in A.W.B. Simpson (ed.) *Oxford Essays in Jurisprudence*, 2nd Series, (Oxford: Clarendon Press, 1973) 44.
[87] Latham (1937/1949) (n. 61 above) 525.
[88] ibid., 525 (emphasis added). Compare Hart (1994) (n. 64 above) 115: 'What is crucial is that there should be a unified or shared official acceptance of the rule of recognition containing the system's criteria of validity.'

Commonwealth *Grundnorm* at that time. Their tearaway siblings, Ireland and South Africa, were his real fascination. Much like Berriedale Keith, he noted that separatist tendencies were 'in strict law impossible' given the 'established constitutional doctrine' that the Westminster Parliament cannot effectively bind itself to respecting such independence.[89] However, unlike Berriedale Keith, he recognised that escape from this dilemma was possible so long as, first, the local (here, South African) legal system had the 'courage and tact' to adopt a different view, namely the sort of 'new' and self-embracing view of sovereignty that had been noted by Jennings and developed by Latham.[90] In so doing, the South Africans would be setting up 'a fiction that the Statute of Westminster was a complete and irrevocable abdication of the power of the Imperial Parliament'.[91] And even though in some eyes this sort of conduct did 'violence to law or to history, probably both', there was 'much to be said for stealth and subtlety as methods of revolution, if revolution there must be'.[92]

In Ireland, Latham saw an even more direct interest in fundamental constitutional questions. Irish men and women were speaking openly about an independent Irish source for their legal system: 'The *Grundnorm* has descended into the market place', in Latham's memorable phrase.[93] However, he saw more consistency in the Irish approach than the South African, given that the claim of an independent Irish source had been consistently made since at least the creation of the Irish Free State.[94] The South Africans had come to their separatist tendencies much later. Latham concluded that it was the 'extreme fundamental vagueness' of Imperial and Commonwealth law that rendered possible the shifting of the basic norm in South Africa and Ireland.[95] This vagueness could be explained, first, by the empirical character of the common law method, and secondly, by the fact that constitutional development in the Commonwealth had tended to operate in 'the alternative field of constitutional convention' rather than in the far less arable terrain of general constitutional law.[96]

South Africa and Ireland had exploited the uncertainty regarding the sovereignty of the Westminster Parliament in the context of a Statute of Westminster which was clearly not intended to terminate that Parliament's powers. Their independent constitutional theory was therefore based on revolution, fiction or a controversial reading of history. However, it was possible through Latham's analysis to imagine that Australia, Canada and New Zealand might eventually

---

[89] Latham (1937/1949) (n. 61 above) 530.   [90] ibid., 530.   [91] ibid., 534.

[92] ibid., 534. It is important to note that the revolution label applied first, because what we now know as continuing sovereignty was the 'established constitutional doctrine', and secondly, because the Statute of Westminster was clearly never intended to be such an abdication of power. However, it seems clear that Latham could contemplate both a self-embracing interpretation of the paradoxical concept of sovereignty and an enactment by the Westminster Parliament that could have a true independence-directed intention, and that in such a case the revolution label would not apply.   [93] Latham (1937/1949) (n. 61 above) 534–5.

[94] ibid., 540.   [95] ibid., 540.   [96] ibid., 540.

base their constitutional independence around an independent constitutional theory that reflected the real *uncertainty* in the ultimate rule of recognition and the real *coherence* of a self-embracing conception of the Westminster Parliament's powers. Even if the United Kingdom clung to a continuing conception of its Parliament's powers, as Latham was inclined to accept, other conceptions were coherent and viable within what Hart would later call the penumbra of the ultimate rule of recognition, and available therefore to Dominion legal understandings provided that they and their courts were prepared to take an independent view.

Latham conceded that according to 'established constitutional doctrine . . . it was in strict law impossible for the Imperial Parliament to put it beyond its power to repeal any of its Acts'.[97] He described as follows the effects of this doctrine on prospects for Commonwealth independence:

Any measure of emancipation at the hands of the Imperial Parliament would therefore suffer from the vital flaw that it was revocable at the Imperial Parliament's pleasure. According to established theory, nothing that Westminster could do would remove this taint from its gifts. In other words, the revocability in strict law of Dominion emancipation seemed to be irradicable . . .[98]

Latham's scepticism regarding strict law and established doctrine is evident here and throughout *The Law and the Commonwealth*. In the footnotes to the passages quoted immediately above, he listed himself with Jennings as one of the critics of Dicey.[99] Latham accepted that the orthodox view was established and that certain conclusions flowed from it if that was so, but he did not concede its validity. His discussions of South Africa and Ireland showed that it was possible for a Dominion to assert a local root and thereby 'remove from the law of that Dominion the theoretical possibility that any or all of the laws of that Dominion might at any time be overborne by imperial legislation'.[100] But South Africa and Ireland had taken a revolutionary path to this solution even if it had been well disguised. Was it possible for such a solution to be achieved without revolution? Latham clearly thought so. He was prepared to accept that even Canada, with its deliberately chosen[101] ongoing role for the Westminster Parliament in fundamental constitutional amendment, could have a different *Grundnorm* to that of the United Kingdom even as early as 1937:

For already, in constitutional convention, the Imperial Parliament exercises these powers not on its own behalf, but as the mere agent of the Dominion. *It is not at all impossible that the law of a Dominion should come to regard the Imperial Parliament's legislative power within the borders of the Dominion as now derivative—delegated by tolerance, if not expressly—if only it can explain how its former supremacy was terminated.*[102]

---

[97] ibid., 530.   [98] ibid., 530.   [99] ibid., 530n.   [100] ibid., 586.
[101] See s. 7 of the Statute of Westminster, 1931 and discussion in Ch. 2 above.
[102] Latham (1937/1949) (n. 61 above) 525 (emphasis added).

The Statute of Westminster did not provide such an explanation but another statute, interpreted in the way that Latham and Jennings acknowledged was possible, could certainly do so.

As it turned out, Latham's bold statement went further than even the Supreme Court of Canada was willing to go in 1981, perhaps because, as Latham said elsewhere, courts tend to look for explicit directions before they will assign a different root or *Grundnorm*.[103] Even in the absence of explicit directions, it was possible for a new root to emerge gradually 'just as the existence of a system of law as a system involves the postulating of a *Grundnorm*, so the working of the system involves the rendering of the *Grundnorm* explicit'.[104] However, given the 'archaic inflexibility of the general constitutional law of the Empire',[105] very explicit directions were likely to be required, and those explicit directions only emerged in the 1980s for the countries under study.

There is much more in Latham that is worth reading and considering, but at least half a dozen new or newly polished ideas can be identified by way of general summary: first, there is the fact that legal rules, perhaps especially constitutional rules of a fundamental type, often remain uncertain in important parts despite constitutional lawyers' speculative attempts to fill in the gaps; secondly, that until a court pronounces authoritatively on such uncertainties, the issue remains unresolved; thirdly, that the (unresolved) issue of self-embracing versus continuing sovereignty logically precedes the power of the so-called sovereign parliament; fourthly, that it is possible for the local legal order to adopt the unorthodox, but no less coherent and viable, view of the Westminster Parliament's powers; fifthly, that the recognition of different basic norms or ultimate rules implies the emergence of separate legal systems; and sixthly, that the (shifting) content of the basic norm is determined by allegiance of the relevant courts. Some of these insights were used by Hart in his *The Concept of Law*, and virtually all of them will be put to use in this book, as we shall see in Chapter 12.

The orthodox theory of parliamentary sovereignty restored: H.W.R. Wade

One would have been forgiven for thinking that, in the face of such attacks, the orthodox theory was on the wane. Constitutional writers such as Jennings and Latham were against it, and developments in the Commonwealth seemed to be against it. Dicey was in need of an apologist; and not just one who could restate his doctrine of parliamentary sovereignty, but one who could pitch that restatement at the level of theory as well. Just as Latham took Jennings' ideas to a deeper theoretical level, so H.W.R. Wade uncovered the theoretical foundations

---

[103] Latham (1937/1949) (n. 61 above) 543.   [104] ibid., 540.   [105] ibid., 540.

of Dicey's doctrine. Wade published an article entitled 'The Basis of Legal Sovereignty' in 1955.[106] This article is perhaps one of the most frequently cited in British constitutional law and theory. It apparently responded to a perceived need in many constitutional readers and commentators to restore their faith in Dicey in the face of, and despite, events such as the Statute of Westminster and the phenomenon of independence in the Commonwealth. How did Wade manage this?

Wade's defence of Dicey proceeded at two levels, one based on authority and the other based on theory. Regarding the first, Wade cited a trio of cases that had been unavailable to Dicey and which have been discussed at the end of Chapter 3: *Vauxhall Estates*,[107] *Ellen Street Estates*[108] and *British Coal Corporation*.[109] Whereas Jennings had viewed these cases as unconvincing dicta, Wade saw the famous passages so often quoted from each as essential to the decision in each case and therefore binding.[110] However, the theoretical argument presented by Wade is of greater interest to us.

For the purposes of joining issue more effectively, Wade reduced Jennings' argument to a three-point proposition: '(1) The authority of Acts of Parliament depends on the common law; (2) Parliament can change the common law in any way whatever; (3) Therefore Parliament can change the legal rules on which the authority of Acts of Parliament rests.'[111] Wade acknowledged that this argument was 'alluring' and 'skilfully set out',[112] but he saw no difficulty in refuting it. He conceded more than Dicey by admitting that the rule that 'Parliament can bind its successors as to manner and form' was 'a perfectly possible state of affairs',[113] but based on Wade's reading of the authorities noted above and 'a long line of professional opinions'[114] dating back at least as far as the seventeenth century, he was convinced that Dicey's rendition of the rule was right. Furthermore, and most crucially in terms of Wade's theoretical plan, the idea of Parliament's 'continuing sovereignty'[115]—captured by Dicey's assertion that no Parliament can bind a future Parliament—was 'legally ultimate; its source [being] historical only, not legal'.[116] Elsewhere he referred to it as 'simply a political fact'.[117] Whether one wanted to call it a common law rule or not, it was 'unique in being unchangeable by Parliament'.[118] It was beyond the reach of statute because it was

---

[106] H.W.R. Wade, 'The Basis of Legal Sovereignty' [1955] CLJ 172.
[107] *Vauxhall Estates v Liverpool Corporation* (1932) 1 KB 733 (Div Ct).
[108] *Ellen Street Estates v Minister of Health* (1934) 1 KB 597 (CA).
[109] *British Coal Corporation v The King* (1935) AC 500 (PC).
[110] i.e. Wade noted that counsel in the *Vauxhall* and *Ellen Street* cases had argued that, in enacting the Acquisition of Land (Assessment of Compensation) Act, 1919, the 1919 Parliament had tried to insulate itself against implied repeal, and Wade argued that, where the *British Coal Corporation* case was concerned, the 1931 Parliament had also attempted to control the form of later legislation. [111] Wade (1955) (n. 106 above) 187.
[112] ibid., 184.   [113] ibid., 185.   [114] ibid., 184.   [115] ibid., 187.
[116] Salmond, *Jurisprudence*, 10th edn, by Glanville Williams, 155, quoted with approval by Wade (1955) (n. 106 above) 187.   [117] Wade (1955) (n. 106 above) 189.
[118] ibid., 189.

'itself the source of authority of statute'.[119] If it were to be changed at all, that would have to be 'by revolution, not by legislation'.[120]

Conceiving of the 'ultimate legal principle' of 'continuing' parliamentary sovereignty in this way in turn assisted Wade in explaining Dicey's distinction between sovereign and subordinate legislatures and legislation:

The distinction between sovereign and subordinate legislation is therefore this: sovereign legislation depends for its authority on an 'ultimate legal principle,' i.e., a political fact for which no purely legal explanation can be given; subordinate legislation depends for its authority on some ulterior legal power for which a legal explanation can be given. Analytically this is a clear distinction, and many of its results are explained by Dicey in the course of his comparison between sovereign and non-sovereign law-making bodies.[121]

Perhaps the distinction was clear, but the true question was whether it corresponded to the reality of British and Commonwealth constitutional law.

Unlike Latham, Wade seemed convinced that the 'ultimate legal principle' was not only unchangeable by legal means but clear as well. This assertion of clarity was essential given Wade's claim elsewhere that Parliament's continuing sovereignty was 'in one sense a rule of the common law, but in another sense— which applies to no other rule of the common law—it [was] the ultimate political fact upon which the whole system hangs'.[122] For if Latham was right about this ultimate rule being unclear, then the sense in which it was a rule of the common law became far more important; for it would be up to judges—in Britain but also in the Commonwealth—to clarify its content. We are reminded of Jennings' assertion that parliamentary sovereignty was essentially about a relationship between Parliament and the courts. If that relationship was frozen in time, as Wade asserted, then nothing but a revolution could change it; but if it was in flux, like the rest of the common law, then its evolution was as much a legal matter as the evolution of any other common law constitutional rule.

Sticking with Wade's analysis for the moment, it remains to describe how he explained the undeniable fact that the Parliament which was said to be incapable of binding itself had passed a growing list of independence Acts. Did Wade's neo-Diceyan analysis render all independence granted in such a manner pre-carious? Wade thought not. In the unlikely event of the United Kingdom Parliament passing post-independence legislation for the former colony 'English judges would be bound to uphold...Parliament's power'; however, such legislation would be ineffective in the newly independent former colony, the courts there having 'thrown off their allegiance to the United Kingdom Parliament'.[123] This would mean that 'a revolution had...taken place' on the

---

[119] Wade (1955) 187n, citing Latham 'Where the purported sovereign...' on this point, ignoring the fact that while Latham saw the rules regarding Parliament's sovereignty as prior, he was not nearly as convinced as Wade that 'continuing' parliamentary sovereignty was the rule.
[120] Wade (1955) (n. 106 above) 189.   [121] ibid., 189.   [122] ibid., 188.
[123] ibid., 191.

back of a new set of 'political events'.[124] The constitution and statutes of the independent nation were no longer justified in terms of their 'legal pedigree',[125] for that rested upon the (now rejected) authority of the United Kingdom Parliament. The local courts would have to seek their own ultimate legal principles: 'they must invent them, for they have to fill a vacuum'.[126] And 'in this, they have a perfectly free choice, for legally the question is ultimate'.[127]

One was entitled to ask why so many of the Commonwealth countries had gone to the trouble of obtaining their constitutional independence by means of Acts of the United Kingdom Parliament if these were in reality ineffective. Was their respect for the rule of law at the highest constitutional level a charade? Wade's famous response seemed to confirm that it was: 'When sovereignty is relinquished in an atmosphere of harmony, the naked fact of revolution is not so easy to discern beneath its elaborate legal dress'.[128]

We shall see later that Wade's theory could be criticised, even contradicted, effectively; however, for a period of time in the middle decades of the last century, Wade's approach influenced not only the re-affirmation of Diceyan principles but also the character of the new and revised view response to Commonwealth developments. The new and revised view was personified in Geoffrey Marshall, while the traditional approach was apparent in the writings of K.C. Wheare.

Parliamentary sovereignty and Commonwealth independence: Geoffrey Marshall and K.C. Wheare

In the 1950s and early 1960s a number of important books appeared which focused entirely on Commonwealth constitutional development and which took the notion of Commonwealth independence seriously.[129] Earlier writers such as Latham had taken the early independent-spirited moves of South Africa and Ireland seriously but had hung on to the possibility of some sort of pan-Commonwealth legal system for the remaining colonies. By the late 1950s it was clear that the devolution of power in the Commonwealth was a one-way track, and the literature began to reflect this fact. Furthermore, the influence of Dicey's most convincing apologist, H.W.R. Wade, was strong. Even writers who did not necessarily agree with Wade (or Dicey) were attracted by Wade's response to the dilemma of Commonwealth independence: British courts would take one view

---

[124] ibid., 191.   [125] ibid., 191.   [126] ibid., 192.   [127] ibid., 192.
[128] ibid., 191.
[129] G. Marshall, *Parliamentary Sovereignty and the Commonwealth* (Oxford: Clarendon Press, 1957) and K.C. Wheare, *The Constitutional Structure of the Commonwealth* (Oxford: Clarendon Press, 1960). See also K. Robinson, 'Authochthony and the Transfer of Power' in K.E. Robinson and A.F. Madden (eds) *Essays in Imperial Government* (Oxford: Blackwells, 1963) and S.A. de Smith, *The New Commonwealth and its Constitutions* (London: Stevens & Sons, 1964).

of Parliament's continuing sovereignty, and local courts in the newly independent countries of the Commonwealth would take another view.

The Wade-inspired argument appeared in different guises. In other words, Wade's court-based/different-points-of-view solution could be used by pessimistic exponents of the new view as well as by pragmatic exponents of the orthodox view. Geoffrey Marshall, writing in 1957, was one of the most articulate proponents of the 'new' and 'revised' view. However, he despaired at British and (with notable exceptions) Commonwealth failure to see the sense in the new and revised theory and to break away from orthodox assumptions. He tended to conclude, therefore, that the local courts would have to recognise their constitutional independence by whatever means they could. Perhaps this reaction was quite natural for someone whose preoccupation, after all, was bound up less with explaining Commonwealth constitutional independence and more with changing what he viewed as misguided orthodox British understandings of parliamentary sovereignty.

In contrast, the Australian-born K.C. Wheare, like Latham, showed considerable interest in local constitutional perspectives of Commonwealth former colonies; but, unlike Latham, Wheare basically took the ascendancy of the orthodox point of view for granted. Against the grain of Commonwealth writing, Wheare noted a tendency to *underestimate* the importance of strict law and to over-emphasise the importance of convention—and by strict law he meant the strict Dicey view.[130] Wheare fully understood the need for Commonwealth countries to get out from under the independence-limiting power of the Westminster Parliament, but in his view only the courts could see to it that this happened, by rejecting that Parliament's sovereignty in response to new 'political facts'.[131]

In other words, constitutional commentators of both the new and the orthodox persuasions increasingly resorted to an essentially pragmatic response to the question of constitutional independence (the courts of the newly independent country would somehow find a way to ignore post-independence Westminster legislation), without explaining how these local courts would account for what had occurred in law. Marshall knew what the explanation should be—i.e. some version of the new or revised view—but he seemed adamant that the new or revised explanation should be good not only for newly independent Commonwealth countries but for the United Kingdom as well. If an explanation based on the self-embracing nature of Parliament's sovereignty was excluded for lack of consensus, then what sort of explanation was available for these local courts? Marshall had some ideas, as we shall see, but even he was not convinced that these explanations were entirely satisfactory given the ascendancy of orthodox Diceyan ideas. If a newly independent colony used the

---

[130] K.C. Wheare, *The Statute of Westminster and Dominion Status*, (5th edn, Oxford: Oxford University Press, 1953) 4.   [131] ibid., 155–6.

Westminster Parliament to obtain its independence, then a satisfactory under-standing of that independence would have to include an explanation of how that Parliament's powers had been terminated *vis-à-vis* the local legal system. If such an explanation were unavailable due to lack of movement in theoretical assumptions regarding parliamentary sovereignty, then alternative explanations would have to take continuing Westminster sovereignty as given and therefore ground themselves elsewhere. Such explanations could be 'good enough' for most constitutional observers and commentators in newly independent coun-tries, but they would fail the test of accounting for the validity of the newly independent legal system *in accordance with constitutional continuity and respect for the rule of law*. And yet continuity and respect for the rule of law were by all accounts central to what these countries had set out to achieve in pursuing their constitutional independence by legal means.

Wheare too knew what the final answer should be where constitutional independence was concerned, whether it was consistent with United Kingdom understandings or not, but he did not provide an alternative to the revolutionary sort of explanation made popular by Wade. Without such an explanation, Wade's Dicey-inspired thesis regarding independence as disguised legal revolu-tion was likely to become the new default explanation.

Having isolated the main points of concern, it may be helpful to look more closely at Marshall and Wheare in order to get a better feel for the sort of constitutional analysis that dominated legal thinking on the subject from the 1950s onwards.

Geoffrey Marshall's 1957 work, *Parliamentary Sovereignty in the Common-wealth*, was a typically rigorous look at the subject. Marshall was clearly unim-pressed by the so-called pedigree of orthodox British understandings of parliamentary sovereignty, and much of his writing showed clear sympathy for both the new view and the revised (or self-embracing) theory. Contrary to Dicey and Wade (and, more recently, contrary to Jeffrey Goldsworthy), Marshall argued that there was much more uncertainty and debate in the English and British tradition of parliamentary sovereignty than orthodox thinkers were prepared to acknowledge. He noted that 'remarks about "absolute and uncon-trollable" authority seem sometimes to have been repeated as a kind of juristic platitude, even by writers inclined to theories of "limited government"'.[132] Marshall also pointed out some ironies in terms of the authority used by orthodox writers. Dicey, for example, noted that the nineteenth-century writer, Sidgwick, was 'full of interest' despite 'differing a certain extent from the view put forward in [*The Law of the Constitution*]'.[133] In fact, as Marshall observed, Sidgwick's analysis differed more than 'a certain extent'; it was a foundation for

---

[132] Marshall (1957) (n. 129 above) 48–9 quoting Halifax and Swift. Coke, Blackstone and Bentham were also shown to be ambivalent on the absolute or continuing nature of sovereignty.

[133] A.V. Dicey, *An Introduction to the Study of the Law of the Constitution* by E.C.S. Wade (10th edn, London: Macmillan, 1959) 70n.

the new view. Sidgwick argued that 'it would be at least misleading to say that there is no legal limit to [Parliament's] power; since the very structure of this supreme legislature, being legally determined, may practically limit its power of acting'.[134] Although in fact the sovereign Parliament's substantive powers might not be restricted by legal rules, 'in another sense it has legal limits of great importance, since it is prevented from acting, except under certain conditions by the legal rules determining its structure and procedure'.[135] The new view could not be more clearly stated. Salmond, on whom Wade relied to such a great extent,[136] was shown by Marshall to be in fact the most unorthodox of thinkers, leading the new view on towards its later revised or self-embracing phase. In an appendix to his famous *Jurisprudence*, Salmond asked: 'If the law can regulate the manner of the exercise of legislative power why not also its matter? . . . What would be the effect of a statute providing that no statute should be repealed save by an absolute majority of all members in each House? Would it not create good law?' And elsewhere: 'That the sovereign power may be legally controlled within its own province is a self-contradictory proposition; that its province may have legally appointed bounds is a distinct and valid principle.'[137] As Marshall exclaimed: 'This is more than doubt; it is heresy!'[138]

Marshall himself clearly stated that 'a rule which envisages and provides for its own revision or transformation is certainly conceivable'.[139] However, he went further, arguing that 'by close discussion of the true conclusion to be drawn from existing authority and thereafter by pointing to analogies and to the inconvenient conclusions and terminology of the opposite doctrine that [a rule which envisages and provides for its own revision or transformation] *exists* in the United Kingdom'.[140] Whatever academic sources said, and these were more divided than usually admitted, 'judicial materials for a history of the [orthodox] doctrine of parliamentary sovereignty [were] extremely meagre'.[141]

On the point that is of greatest interest to us, whether Parliament can bind itself, such judicial materials were of more recent vintage; however, Marshall remained unconvinced. Cases such as *Vauxhall Estates* and *Ellen Street Estates* had been interpreted as supporting propositions far broader than their facts could justify, in his view: 'The terms of the 1919 Act did not by any means state an unambiguous intention of the legislature to safeguard its provisions against future repeal, and it could be said with some justification that this was not the intention of the Act.'[142] It remained the case, however, that these decisions together with the *British Coal Corporation* case left the vast majority of English constitutional commentators convinced that the Dicey/Wade orthodoxy was still in place.

---

[134] Marshall (1957) (n. 129 above) 63, quoting H. Sidgwick, *Elements of Politics*, 2nd edn.
[135] ibid., 63.   [136] Wade (1955) (n. 106 above) 187.
[137] Marshall (1957) (n. 129 above), 60–1 (quoting J. Salmond, *Jurisprudence*, 10th edn, 495–6, 478).
[138] ibid., 61.   [139] ibid., 45.   [140] ibid., 46 (emphasis added).   [141] ibid., 68.
[142] ibid., 36.

Much of *Parliamentary Sovereignty and the Commonwealth* was devoted to detailing how, outside the United Kingdom, especially in South Africa,[143] the orthodox theory was under serious attack. However, Marshall could also not help but observe that the orthodox theory was in many countries deeply entrenched. For example, though *Trethowan* was an Australian case so often cited in support of the new view, this did not mean that Australia had adopted the new or revised approach. Far from it, as we shall see in Part II. The same was true of New Zealand and Canada.

This did not stop Marshall from taking the view that Commonwealth developments provided support for the new and revised view. On his reading, Commonwealth constitutions rejected the Dicey/Wade idea of subordinate status supposedly assigned to them: 'In no part of the Commonwealth does the present role of the British Parliament rise higher than that of the wielder of a delegated legislative authority.'[144] Marshall's theoretical sympathies could hardly have been clearer in the following passage discussing attitudes towards orthodox British constitutional theory in the Commonwealth (however, his attribution of these same attitudes to Commonwealth lawyers was based for the most part on his hope that constitutional developments, first among them the gradual abolition of the Privy Council appeal, would eventually see them onto the right path):

It may be an important convention that a particular set of organs or processes is selected as apt to bear the title 'sovereign', but it is a convention and not a requirement of logic or nature which inclines to this way of talking. That there are historical reasons in plenty for the convention is undeniable, but they are ideologically parochial reasons and hardly respectable in a Commonwealth which does not accept the vocabulary of Dicey or of English jurisprudence as mandatory. At the present time the application of the Diceyite vocabulary to differing sets of legal arrangements is extremely uncertain. Described as a search for the 'source of law', the 'seat of sovereignty', or the 'nature of the *Grundnorm*', the question has the air of a philosophical exercise—what one Canadian author has called 'a tickling of the ears with legal dogma'.[145] But as a problem about the legal arrangements by which constitutional change is provided for and regulated in any society the inquiry is one with an obvious practical significance. The history of the Commonwealth constitutional development is a history of English juristic conventions exerting pressure upon differing sets of provision for change. Here the centripetal effect of decisions by the Privy Council is clear. With the abolition of the Appeal on almost all major constitutional issues arising within the Commonwealth, the evolution of

---

[143] In particular, see *Harris v Minister of the Interior* [1952] (2) SA 428. This case provided clear support for the 'new' view, if not for the 'revised' view as well, and Marshall paid close attention to it. See Marshall (1957) (n. 129 above) ch. XI. Although this case rightly attracted attention throughout the Commonwealth, it did not dislodge the orthodox theory from its dominant position, as we shall see in Part II below.   [144] Marshall (1957) (n. 129 above) 87.

[145] See W.P.M. Kennedy, 'The Imperial Conferences, 1926–1930' (1932) 190 LQR 191, 205: 'No one disputes the sovereignty of Parliament, and anyone is welcome to tickle the ears of believers with legal dogma.' For discussion of Kennedy's views, see Ch. 6 below.

a different vocabulary appears possible. It is certainly feasible and perhaps increasingly useful to attempt a description of Commonwealth constitutions without any reference to the location of sovereignty and without conducting a search for a sovereign entity in every case.

What we see in this passage is Marshall's wish that Commonwealth countries and their newly 'supreme' courts would reject the strictures of Dicey's vocabulary and corresponding theoretical assumptions. Perhaps this hope was encouraged by Irish and, especially, South African independent-spiritedness in developing their own constitutional understandings,[146] and by the gradual termination of Privy Council appeals. However, if courts in Australia, Canada and New Zealand carried on maintaining orthodox attitudes regarding Westminster parliamentary sovereignty, then it was hard to see how Marshall's hope could be realised. And such attitudes proved to be surprisingly hardy, as we shall see.[147]

Even if Commonwealth judges, lawyers and officials could not always, or even often, see their way to adopting the new or revised view, the solution to achieving constitutional independence was clear in Marshall's view, even if, as with Wade's solution, the legal explanation for that transition was lacking:[148]

... all that is necessary for the phrases 'totally distinct *Grundnorm*' or 'local and national root for municipal law' correctly to describe the legal situation is that the way in which a Commonwealth court applies the law should be consistent with the regarding of rules laid down in a local instrument as being basic rules of that legal system. If memories of the 'source' of a constitution in an historical sense offend nationalist sentiment, it may, none the less be a matter of some moment to secure specific proclamations of independence and adopt a more congenial enacting formula than that of the Queen in Parliament. Here there is a choice of vocabulary. In terms of [the] myth of the turtle and the elephant a number of choices is available. There might be 'a divine turtle, deriving its authority from God; or a provincial autonomy turtle, calling itself the compact theory; or an Anglo-French turtle calling itself a treaty between races; or ... a popular turtle labelled "We the People" '.[149]

The realism and pragmatism of Marshall's comments were quite justified. Constitutional independence *could* be achieved by these means. However, so long as Australia, Canada and New Zealand were dominated by orthodox assumptions it was hard to see how their courts' recognition of the primacy of their constitutions ahead of the Westminster Parliament could be anything more than the assertion of a new political fact much as Wade had suggested. The *legal* explanation for constitutional independence, consistent with the rigorous respect for the rule of law alluded to earlier, was not available so long as British and

---

[146] See *Harris* (1952) (n. 143 above).

[147] In particular, see *Reference re Resolution to Amend the Constitution* [1981] 1 SCR 753 which is discussed in detail in Ch. 7 below.   [148] Marshall (1957) (n. 129 above) 101–2.

[149] ibid., 102 (quoting F.R. Scott, 'The Redistribution of Imperial Sovereignty' in *Transactions of the Royal Society of Canada*, June 1950, 33, reprinted in F.R. Scott, *Essays on the Constitution* (Toronto: University of Toronto Press, 1977) 244).

Commonwealth understandings of Westminster parliamentary sovereignty were not ready *together* to change in the direction of new and revised theory. Without a coherent legal explanation for their constitutional independence, it was not clear how even Commonwealth courts liberated from the centripetal domination of the Privy Council could go about explaining how the Westminster Parliament had lost its sovereign control. Marshall would go on proposing legal explanations throughout his career, but his assumption and emphasis was always that British and Commonwealth understandings should change in unison. Change in both was proving difficult.

While Marshall was only beginning his academic career in 1957, K.C. Wheare was coming to the end of his years of prolific writing on Commonwealth and general constitutional matters. For our purposes, the books which are of particular interest, are his *The Statute of Westminster and Dominion Status*, by now in its fifth edition, and his *The Constitutional Structure of the Commonwealth*.[150]

The Statute of Westminster and Dominion Status revealed Wheare's orthodox leanings regarding parliamentary sovereignty. We have already noted that Wheare believed that convention tended to be over-emphasised and strict law underestimated in most writing and thinking about Commonwealth constitutional developments.[151] This could be interpreted as a rebuke to those who focused excessively on Lord Sankey's mention of 'political reality' in the *British Coal Corporation* case, at the expense of the law. Strict or not, the law was the law.

Wheare's traditional views were clearest in his discussion of the effect of section 4 of the Statute of Westminster. This section was not in his view an attempt to diminish or abolish the power of the Westminster Parliament to legislate for the Dominions. Instead it was a rule of construction directed at the courts. This left what Wheare referred to regularly as 'the overriding legislative control of the Imperial Parliament'[152] perfectly intact:

[Section 4] does not render it legally impossible for the United Kingdom Parliament to legislate for a Dominion without the request and consent of the Dominion. On the basis of the theory of sovereignty which was accepted by the Courts of the United Kingdom and all of the Dominions except [Ireland] in 1931, there seems no doubt that section 4 of the Statute is ineffective in law to restrict the United Kingdom Parliament to the sphere of legislating for a Dominion only with the request and consent of that Dominion . . . If at any time since the passing of the Statute, the United Kingdom Parliament were to pass an Act which contained no express declaration that it had been passed with the request and consent of a Dominion but which contained sufficient expression of intention, in terms, to indicate that it should apply to a Dominion, notwithstanding any law of the Dominion to the contrary, then that Act must be accepted by the Courts as prevailing over the Acts of the Dominion Parliament, even if subsequently enacted, and

---

[150] Wheare (1953) (n. 130 above) and Wheare (1960) (n. 129 above).
[151] Wheare (1953) (n. 130 above) 4.   [152] ibid., 74, 84.

as amounting to a repeal pro tanto of section 4 of the Statute of Westminster. The rule of construction is impliedly amended or repealed.[153]

This was as orthodox a statement as could be imagined, but if section 4 of the Statute of Westminster was only intended to be rule of construction—and there were very good reasons for believing that this was so—then Wheare's views were not so much evidence of orthodox thinking as sound legal advice. However, Wheare was equally clear that the Westminster Parliament could not have used the Statute of Westminster to limit its powers *vis-à-vis* the Dominions even if it had wanted to do so:

On [the] accepted view of the sovereignty of the United Kingdom Parliament, 'no law it makes can deprive it of its supremacy over that law. The last expression of its legislative will repeals all prior inconsistent laws'. It is not necessary for the United Kingdom Parliament to repeal section 4 of the Statute explicitly. It has merely to legislate for a Dominion, and that legislation frees it from the restriction voluntarily accepted and expressed in section 4. The position was recognised and stated by Lord Sankey in the *British Coal Corporation Case* . . . Lord Sankey's words indicate that the reconciliation of the accepted theory of legal sovereignty with the accepted fact of constitutional equality is not easy. For law is law in the Courts, whether it be abstract or concrete, theoretical or real. And so long as the theory is accepted by the Courts, for so long it will be impossible to dismiss the difficulties which arise in strict law by a reference to 'abstract law' or to a theory which 'has no relation to the realities'.[154]

This attitude to parliamentary sovereignty appeared to leave no possibility of legal escape from the Imperial legal system. What of the possible 'get-out' represented by the phrase 'so long as the theory is accepted by the Courts'? Wheare clearly recommended such a route, though the escape was probably not legal at all. Wheare was writing here before H.W.R. Wade but the language and the conclusion were strikingly similar:

. . . it is well to examine what is meant by the 'indestructible sovereignty of the King in Parliament over the law throughout the King's Dominions'. This sovereignty is indestructible by Parliament. And the Courts have accepted this. Sovereignty may belong to the United Kingdom Parliament by nature but it is effective only in so far as and for so long as the Courts recognise Parliament to be sovereign. Parliamentary sovereignty is a result of the law declared by the Courts; it is an expression of the legal relation between Parliament and the Courts. *If it is asked why the Courts did and do recognise Parliament as sovereign, the answer is that they did and do as a result of a particular political situation.* And if the particular political situation should warrant it in the future, there is no doubt that the Courts could qualify or reject the legal sovereignty of the United Kingdom Parliament. In other words the sovereignty is indestructible by Parliament but not by the Courts. Applying this analysis to section 4 of the Statute, it may be conceived that should the United Kingdom Parliament attempt to repeal section 4, the Dominion courts might

---

[153] ibid., 153–4. Contrast Jennings (1959) (n. 31 above) 163.

[154] Wheare (1953) (n. 130 above) 154, quoting O. Dixon, *Australian Law Journal*, Vol. X, Supplement, 98, and Lord Sankey in *British Coal Corporation*.

reject the accepted theory of sovereignty and might interpret section 4 not merely as a rule of construction but as a restriction upon power . . . It is clear, however, that a Dominion Court, without adopting *such a revolutionary view* of the legal effect of section 4, and merely by treating the section as no more than a rule of construction, can go to great lengths in refusing to regard such an Act as impliedly repealing that section.[155]

Wheare seemed to offer two choices for independence-minded Dominions or colonies: a revolutionary (or extra-legal) explanation; or the preservation of independence by strapping down the Imperial Parliament like some sort of Gulliver, using the ropes provided by rules of convention and statutory interpretation. And yet Wheare readily acknowledged that in the latter case, the all-powerful Imperial Parliament could easily break the fragile bonds by which it was controlled. Was there no legal means by which constitutional independence could be achieved and guaranteed?

The fifth edition of *The Statute of Westminster and Dominion Status* was the last. Its successor volume, thoroughly reconceived, was *The Constitutional Structure of the Commonwealth*. The emphasis in this book was much less on the emerging status of Dominions and other former colonies and more on the frank acknowledgement that autonomy and equality had been achieved (by whatever route). However, Wheare had by no means escaped from the orthodox understandings of parliamentary sovereignty which had caused him to offer legal revolution or strong conventions and statutory interpretation as the only viable ways of explaining constitutional independence. Wheare noted in his Preface that Geoffrey Marshall had read and commented on the manuscript.[156] However, there was only limited evidence that Wheare had taken on board Marshall's new and revised arguments regarding sovereignty. Wheare now viewed orthodox/new-view differences as a genuine matter for argument, but he had by no means switched sides in the debate.

The main points of interest in Wheare's *The Constitutional Structure of the Commonwealth* are contained in three important chapters entitled 'Equality', 'Autonomy' and 'Autochthony'. In the chapter on 'Equality' Wheare noted how, between 1926 and 1947, members of the Commonwealth had been extraordinarily reluctant to use the word 'independence'.[157] The first official usage of the term was in the Indian Independence Act, 1947 (Imp.) and, later that same year, in the Ceylon Independence Act, 1947 (Imp.). Such legislation presumed equality of status, but how was this achieved? Wheare had considered such questions for some time, and was therefore able to see the sorts of difficult issues which hid beyond the lay person's view:

When independence is to be granted to a Commonwealth country one of the most important questions to be dealt with at the outset is the inequality which arises from the

---

[155] Wheare, quoting O. Dixon, *Australian Law Journal*, Vol. X, Supplement, 155–6 (emphasis added). Wheare was in fact cited with approval in Wade (1955) (n. 21 above) 189n.

[156] Wheare (1960) (n. 129 above) vi.   [157] ibid., 20.

existence of a power in the parliament of the United Kingdom to make laws for that country. The simple and straightforward course, in the eyes of a layman, would be for parliament to enact that this power is hereby abolished in respect of the Commonwealth country, and that it will never be exercised or revived again. Lawyers, however, have doubted the efficacy of this step. They hold that the power is inalienable and they demonstrate this by asserting that, since one parliament cannot bind its successors, a later parliament would always be at liberty to revive and exercise the power, whatever a predecessor might have declared or promised. Whether this view is sound is a matter of argument. None the less, the inequality has not so far been tackled by a head-on approach. Instead the legislation has attempted not to abolish the power but to ensure that, if it is exercised, it will be ineffective, unless the legislature of the Member of the Commonwealth concerned consents to it. What has been attempted, in short, is not to abolish the power but, in the words of the Imperial Conference of 1930, to find an 'appropriate method of reconciling the existence of this power with the established constitutional position' of equality.[158]

In Wheare's view, 's. 4 of the Statute of Westminster [and other similarly worded independence Acts passed by the Westminster parliament] [had] been misunderstood at times because it has been thought that their intention was to abolish or nullify the power of the Parliament at Westminster to make laws extending to another Member of the Commonwealth'. This, said Wheare, was 'not their intention'. 'They were enacted on the assumption that the Parliament at Westminster [still] had that power and that it could be exercised.'[159] What would happen then in the unlikely event that Westminster enacted legislation for a Member of the Commonwealth in seeming contradiction to the supposed equality and independence? Wheare could not say for certain:

It is impossible to say what interpretation a court in a Commonwealth Member would adopt if these issues were raised before it. The possibility is so remote that it may seem fruitless to consider it. A court in the United Kingdom would be faced with a decision whether it should prefer a later act of parliament to an earlier act of parliament when two conflicted and it is difficult to see how it could avoid preferring the later act. A court in the overseas Member concerned, however, might decide that since the British act . . . did not contain a declaration of request and consent . . . it was not part of the law of that Member, and therefore no question arose of preferring a later British act to an earlier British act.[160]

Again, the emphasis was on statutory interpretation. And even though the court of the Member in question took an independent view in this hypothetical case, that court would still presumably be bound by a crystal clear intention in the British Act.

Wheare's ultimate solution was for the Member in question to use powers given to it under section 2 of the Statute of Westminster, 1931 to repeal the 1931 Statute itself so as to protect what the 1931 Statute had given it. However,

---

[158] Wheare (1960) (n. 129 above) 25.   [159] Wheare (1960) (n. 129 above) 27.
[160] ibid., 32.

if the powers of the Westminster Parliament were as unrestricted as Wheare had indicated, and more importantly, if local courts had not abandoned their allegiance to the orthodox theory, then it was still hard to see how even this solution could succeed in securing equality and independence. Wheare acknowledged as much in stating that 'there were always possible nightmares for the nationalistic legalist, so long as there existed, even in paralysed form, some organ at Westminster that could make laws extending to other Members of the Commonwealth'.[161]

Wheare then went on to discuss 'autonomy', by which he meant 'the capacity to adopt and adapt your own constitution'.[162] He observed that autonomy raised 'the whole question of the authority and supremacy of the constitutions of Members of the Commonwealth, once those constitutions lose any superior status they may have enjoyed as acts of the parliament of the United Kingdom'.[163] In the past it had been possible to rely on 'the overriding supremacy of legislation by or under the authority of the parliament at Westminster'.[164] When this went, what took its place? Wheare's answer was that 'the supremacy of the constitution is based upon logic, not upon its origin'.[165] In other words, the Constitution of, say, Australia, remained supreme over the Australian Commonwealth Parliament 'not because it was an act of Parliament of the United Kingdom', but 'because it is the constitution, and as such must be construed as logically prior to any measure passed by the parliament which owes its existence and power to the constitution'.[166] On this basis, the Constitution of Australia, and along with it the Constitution of Canada as well, would have remained supreme even if the safeguarding sections 7, 8 and 9 of the Statute of Westminster had not been enacted.

Wheare's final independence-related chapter bore the then-unfamiliar title 'Autochthony'. Wheare's term has since become very popular in Commonwealth constitutional writing.[167] 'Autochthony' referred to the fact that the constitution 'sprung from the land itself' or was 'constitutionally rooted in . . . native soil'.[168] Most importantly it was 'not imported from the United Kingdom'.[169] Those who assert that their constitution is autochthonous claim more than equality and autonomy. They claim 'something stronger': 'self-sufficiency', 'constitutional autarky' and the fact that their constitution has 'force of law and, if necessary, of supreme law within their territory through its own native authority and not because it was enacted or authorized by the parliament of the United Kingdom'.[170]

---

[161] ibid., 35.   [162] ibid., 58.   [163] ibid., 58.   [164] ibid., 58.   [165] ibid., 68.
[166] ibid., 68.
[167] See, e.g., A. Dillon, 'A Turtle by Any Other Name: The Legal Basis of the Australian Constitution' (2001) 29 Fed LR 241, 243; P.W. Hogg, *Constitutional Law of Canada* (4th edn (looseleaf), Toronto: Thomson Carswell, 1997) 3–10; and P.A. Joseph, *Constitutional and Administrative Law in New Zealand* (2nd edn, Wellington: Brookers, 2001) 453 et seq.
[168] Wheare (1960) (n. 129 above) 89.   [169] ibid., 89.   [170] ibid., 89.

From the perspective of the reception or imposition of English law in Australia, Canada and New Zealand, this claim to autochthony seemed to represent a naïve or arrogant constitutional argument. If these countries' laws were not linked to the original claim of the British sovereign, then the law which sprang from the land itself was aboriginal law and custom not settler law. However, the theory of autochthony came equipped with an organic metaphor which explained this seemingly contradictory claim to a home grown, yet non-aboriginal law. The constitution and other important laws may have originally grown in the United Kingdom but they had been transplanted onto native branches and had subsequently taken root in native soil. The tendency to ignore aboriginal law was still arrogant, perhaps, but it was in no way naïve.

The most obvious candidates for autochthony were countries such as Ireland, which in the late 1930s had effected what was essentially a constitutional novation. Australia, Canada and New Zealand had not ever employed such methods. Wheare was quick to note that this did not for a moment mean that the latter countries 'accept without question the view that their own constitutions are not rooted in their own soil'.[171] For example, the Australians could argue that 'if their constitution obtained its life in the seed bed at Westminster, and was transplanted to Australia, it [had] struck root in the Australian soil, and it [owed] its life now to Australia not to Britain'.[172] The same could be said by Canadians and New Zealanders.

The autochthonous story opened up new possibilities for local courts to explain constitutional independence. They could say that 'it is the law because it is the law', or that 'it is law because [citizens] accept it as law'.[173] However, the inclusion of a part of the story taking in first life and subsequent transplantation meant that the local courts 'could also answer . . . that it is the law because it was enacted by the parliament of the United Kingdom'.[174] The first two explanations were autochthonous and legally revolutionary, while the last was non-autochthonous, legally orthodox and for that reason problematic, both in terms of simple independence and, *a fortiori*, autochthony. The 'only satisfactory reply' for those who remained unhappy with the possibility of a United Kingdom Parliament-based explanation was to claim, with a quick change of analogy, 'that the painter was cut, so to speak, at the Westminster end'.[175] However, as we have seen 'the Westminster end' did not apparently accept its ability to cut the painter. But perhaps it was sufficient if the local courts accepted that it could do so, if only they could lay claim to an adequate legal explanation.

The most surprising part of Wheare's discussion of autochthony was not that newly-independent countries wished to explain their constitutions by new means, including most notably, acceptance by the local population. The surprise

[171] Wheare (1960) (n. 129 above) 108.   [172] ibid., 108.   [173] ibid., 109.
[174] ibid., 109.
[175] ibid., 110. We shall see in Chs 11 and 13 below that this claim has been made regarding the Australia Act 1986 (UK).

was that they were apparently prevented from supplementing the local basis for present acceptance of the constitution with an account of the historical and formal legal basis for the constitution's existence and initial validity for fear that this would place constitutional independence in jeopardy. Denial or de-emphasising of history is one thing, but denial of attempts to abide by rules is a somewhat contradictory form of behaviour for lawyers, judges and officials. And yet this is what the orthodox theory seemed to impose on those who naturally wanted to secure their constitutional independence.

We leave off this discussion of Imperial or British constitutional theory with a strong sense of the enduring power of the orthodox theory. This very power provoked theorists to explain even the most scrupulously legal independence processes as legal revolutions, and prompted local constitutional commentators to search for autochthonous alternatives to Westminster enactment. The new or revised view seemed to offer an explanation for independence, if theoretical understandings and legal precedent allowed the Westminster Parliament to limit its own powers. However, the new or revised view had by no means taken hold in the United Kingdom,[176] and until it had done so local constitutional commentators seemed to view it with great mistrust, as we shall see. Perhaps they assumed or wished, like Marshall, that a change from orthodox to new or revised understandings would have to occur by generally accepted consensus in the United Kingdom and elsewhere in the Commonwealth. After all, the theory related to the powers of *one Parliament*. Or perhaps they feared that the legal explanation of their constitutional independence would always be threatened with collapse or failure, so long as it was possible for British courts to revert to orthodox reasoning. In Part III we shall see that there was a way for newly independent colonies to have their cake and eat it too, i.e. to claim both constitutional continuity *and* constitutional independence. In Part II, however, we see that Australia, Canada and New Zealand struggled under the influence of orthodox Imperial constitutional theory for the better part of the twentieth century.

---

[176] An influential United Kingdom exponent of the new view was R.F.V. Heuston, *Essays on Constitutional Law* (2nd edn, London: Stevens, 1964).

PART II

CONSTITUTION TO INDEPENDENCE

5

Canada I: Confederation and the Imperial Theory

Confederation and the absence of a general procedure for constitutional amendment

The Canadian part of this story begins in the 1850s and 1860s, one of the most active periods of constitution-making that the Empire has seen. New Zealand had acquired its Constitution and the newly federated Canada would have one too, though for different reasons. However, an obvious component of the New Zealand model was missing in Canada. Why was it that what was then referred to as the British North America Act, 1867 (Imp.) made no express provision for a general amendment procedure?[1] Clearly, the missing provision was not an oversight. The drafters would have been familiar with both Article V of the Constitution of the United States and New Zealand's Constitution Act, 1857; and elsewhere in the 1867 Act they had seen fit to include Class 1 of section 92, which governed amendments to the constitutions of the provinces. As surprising as it may seem, especially from the perspective of constitutional independence, it is generally agreed that the Fathers of Confederation were content to allow the British Parliament to amend the British North America Act, 1867 which it had created, just as that Parliament had altered the constitutional statutes relating to the British North American colonies in the past. As we shall see, this decision to leave the main constituent powers with the Imperial

---

[1] For further discussion of Canadian constitutional amendment, including the absence of a general amending formula in the British North America Act, 1867 (Imp.), see B. Pelletier, *La Modification Constitutionnelle au Canada* (Scarborough: Carswell, 1996) esp. 23n; J.R. Hurley, *Amending Canada's Constitution: History, Processes, Problems and Prospects* (Ottawa: Canada Communication Group, 1996) esp. ch. 2; P. Oliver, 'Canada, Quebec and Constitutional Amendment' (2000) 49 UTLJ 519; E. Forsey, *Freedom and Order* (Toronto: McClelland & Stewart, 1974) esp. 228–30; J.-Y. Morin and J. Woehrling, *Les Constitutions du Canada et du Quebec du Régime Français à nos Jours* (Montreal: Thémis, 1994) Tome I, esp. 371–2; P. Gérin-Lajoie, 'Du pouvoir d'amendement constitutionnel au Canada' (1951) 29 Can Bar Rev 1136; W. Lederman, 'Canadian Constitutional Amending Procedures: 1867–1982' (1984) 32 Amer Jo Comp L 339; G. Rémillard, 'L'historique du rapatriement' (1984) 23 C du D 1; W.S. Livingston, *Federalism and Constitutional Change* (Oxford: Oxford University Press, 1956); and P. Gérin-Lajoie, *Constitutional Amendment in Canada* (Toronto: University of Toronto Press, 1950) 49.

Parliament contributed to the assumption that constitutional understandings regarding the Canadian constitution were also necessarily Imperial, an assumption which could only be encouraged by the existence of a continuing role for the Judicial Committee of the Privy Council.

Despite the absence of a general procedure for constitutional amendment, the 1867 Act was highly significant in terms of constitutional independence, in that it had been put together at the initiative of political representatives in the British North American colonies and had involved their collaboration throughout. Only the formal drafting and the final sanction, the latter effected by enactment at the Parliament in Westminster, were not accomplished by Canadian hands. Still, one would have thought that Canadians in 1867 would have wished to guard the product of their hard work from later interference by the Imperial Parliament, even if that interference was highly unlikely as a matter of constitutional convention.

In fact, reliance on the Imperial Parliament appears to have satisfied opposing, even contradictory, requirements: flexibility and stability, strong central government and distrust of the centre. There are fairly reliable indications that the framers of the Canadian Constitution were influenced by events in the United States. As early as 1858, three Canadian politicians presented the Secretary of State for the Colonies with a memorandum on the idea of Confederation and referred to the possibility of amendment by the Imperial Parliament as preferable to the American model:

It will be observed that the basis of Confederation now proposed differs from that of the United States in several important particulars. It does not profess to be derived from the people but would be the Constitution provided by the Imperial Parliament, thus affording the means of remedying any defect, which is now practically impossible under the American Constitution.[2]

It should be noted that the American Constitution was not amended from 1804 until 1865 and was widely thought to be excessively rigid at the time this memorandum was written. By the time the Confederation debates were fully under way, the Americans had engaged in a bloody civil war and amended their Constitution in a way which might well have alarmed their more conservative northern neighbours. Canada had experienced its own periods of unrest as recently as 1837–8. As Paul Gérin-Lajoie has observed: 'No doubt, this psychological situation... evoked a desire for stronger authority among the British North American provinces and for more permanency in their political institutions.'[3] It seemed that the Imperial Parliament could be at once a means of remedying any defect in the new Constitution and a force of stability and reason.

---

[2] See Canada, Senate, *Report*, by W.F. O'Connor (Ottawa, 1939; reprinted 1961) (hereinafter cited as O'Connor (1939)); P.B. Waite, *The Life and Times of Confederation*, (Toronto: University of Toronto Press, 1962).   [3] Gérin-Lajoie (1950) (n. 1 above) 37.

The decision to leave the power to amend the Constitution with the Imperial Parliament also appears to have been influenced by local political factors. John A. Macdonald, future Prime Minister and most active proponent of the union of the British North American colonies, spoke out initially in favour of a unitary form of government and continued to encourage strong central power, even after a federal model had been chosen. Gérin-Lajoie and others[4] have suggested that Macdonald deliberately avoided the question of an amending process in the knowledge that the power to *initiate* amendments might then be left to the federal Parliament, as indeed turned out to be the case.

In the course of the Confederation debates which took place at Quebec in 1864, Macdonald referred to the tensions in the United States' constitutional past and spoke in favour of a clear constitutional division of powers between the 'General Legislature' and the 'Local Legislatures'.[5] That presumably would assure stability. But once the maximum central power that was then politically feasible had been set out clearly, Macdonald was apparently in favour of the sort of flexible constitution ensured by the traditional method of amendment. And to achieve that he proposed that the British (and presumably the Imperial) model be maintained: 'We should keep before us the principles of the British Constitution. It (our constitution) should be a mere skeleton and framework that would not bind us down. We have now all the elasticity which has kept England together.'[6]

Not surprisingly, there is also evidence that other more provincial elements in the emerging federation distrusted Macdonald's brand of centralist politics. But they too were satisfied to leave amendment beyond the control of a new Canadian Parliament, and therefore beyond the control of any centripetal Canadian interest.[7]

Leaving the process of constitutional amendment aside (and therefore with Westminster) allowed the framers of the Constitution to balance the conflicting political claims which were an inevitable part of their discussions. The Confederation debates contain few references to the possibility of future constitutional change, but the most famous reference captures the sense in which the Imperial Parliament represented not only a procedure for any constitutional change which might be required in the future but also a means of mediating various opposing Canadian interests should that ever be required. Thomas D'Arcy McGee, in the course of the debates, made the following statement which is frequently cited in support of the view that the framers of the Constitution *intended* to leave amendment with the Imperial Parliament: 'We go to the Imperial Government, the common arbiter of us all, in our true Federal

---

[4] ibid., 38 and, e.g., N. McL. Rogers, 'The Constitutional Impasse' (1934) 41 Queen's Q 482.

[5] J. Pope, *Confederation: Being a Series of Hitherto Unpublished Documents Bearing on the British North America Act* (Toronto: Carswell, 1895) 58.   [6] ibid., 59.

[7] See Hon. P.J.T. O'Hearn, 'Nova Scotia and Constitutional Amendment' (1966–7) 12 McGill LJ 433, 434.

metropolis—we go there to ask for our fundamental Charter. We hope, by having that Charter that can only be amended by the authority that made it, that we will lay the basis of permanency for our future government.'[8] But even McGee's bold statement revealed some ambiguity when examined more closely, perhaps an ambiguity which was intended by such an able orator. First, it was not clear in what sense the Imperial Parliament was likely to remain the type of arbiter which it had been in the past in its earlier, paternalistic role as colonial power.[9] Even in the period immediately preceding 1867, opposing Canadian parties called on Westminster to mediate their interests. For example, the product of the framers discussions—the Quebec Resolutions—ostensibly represented an unalterable set of principles (just as it would be for the framers of the Australian Constitution)[10] which would serve as a basis for the British North America Act, 1867.[11] But clearly the drafting process which was to take place in London was likely to produce points of contention. One view of Imperial arbitration was expressed in a letter sent by the Lieutenant Governor of Nova Scotia to his counterpart in the United Canadas:

It appears to myself and the members of my Government that, to avoid the probable multified divergence of opinion in each Legislature, inseparable from discussing a variety of details in several independent Parliaments, despite of a general agreement in the main objects and principles of the general scheme, it is better for these Provinces to avail themselves of the friendly arbitrament of the Queen's Government and send Delegates to consult with the latter during the preparation of the proposed Imperial Bill.[12]

Members of the Nova Scotia legislature hoped to take advantage of the 'arbitrament of the Imperial Government'[13] in order to 'improve' the Confederation package.[14] Some francophone politicians from the pre-1867 colony of Canada feared that such improvements might benefit only their Maritime partners.[15] The anglophone Canadian delegate at the London meetings, Alexander Galt, ensured that certain improvements were made on behalf of his interests before declaring himself bound by the Quebec Resolutions, except perhaps regarding certain outstanding Maritime claims.[16] Clearly, this first

---

[8] Livingston (1956) (n. 1 above) 21. Quoted in Gérin-Lajoie (1950) (n. 1 above) 4.

[9] 'Maternalistic' is probably a more apt description, and one which anticipates later discussions. If 1867 represented, as was often said, 'the birth of a nation', then there remained the problem of determining when the new nation came of age, acquired full legal rights, etc. Gérin-Lajoie (1950) (n. 1 above) writing in the middle of the twentieth century, still regularly used the phrase 'the Mother Parliament' when referring to Westminster.

[10] For an account of the Australian process, see Ch. 8 below.

[11] D'Arcy McGee, speaking to the Canadian legislature indicated this assumption at an early stage: 'It is for the Imperial Parliament to act upon [the Address adopted by the Canadian Parliament] . . . That body that can cause the several propositions to be moulded into a measure which will have the form of law, and these resolutions may probably be the *ipsissima verba* of the measure they will give us and the other Provinces.' Thomas D'Arcy McGee, *Speeches and Addresses: Chiefly on the Subject of British American Union* (London: Chapman and Hall, 1865) 287.

[12] O'Connor (1939) (n. 2 above) Annex II, 29.   [13] See Waite (1962) (n. 2 above) 276.
[14] ibid., 276.   [15] ibid., 276.   [16] O'Connor (1939) (n. 2 above) Annex 4, 44.

example of conflicting local interests revealed that if 'arbitrament' by the Mother Parliament were to continue as part of the political, if not the legal, process of constitutional amendment, then it would be a significant and highly difficult role for the United Kingdom authorities to play.[17]

A second, related point could be made regarding McGee's famous pronouncement on how the new Canadian constitutional text would be amended. There was considerable ambiguity in the phrase 'that Charter that can only be amended by the authority that made it [the constitution]'. Clearly, in the legal sense, the Imperial Parliament was to 'make' the Canadian constitution, and this was probably what McGee meant. But in a very real sense, the delegates from the British North American colonies had themselves made their Constitution, and they would have a role in the process of amending it, although one which neither McGee nor Canadians in the century to come could define with any precision.

The 'Imperial' and 'Independence' theories

This chapter and the next will concentrate on the differing attitudes regarding the prospect of Canada acquiring its constitutional independence. According to one view, referred to as the 'Imperial theory' and discussed in this chapter, the process for amending the Constitution of Canada was left in the hands of the United Kingdom Parliament in 1867 and remained there until 1982. That process—regarding what some would call the master-key of the Canadian Constitution—would therefore be governed by United Kingdom understandings of the power of the Westminster Parliament. A second view, referred to as the 'Independence theory' and examined in Chapter 6, suggested that the Constitution and the amendment process became subject to increasing Canadian control, and that it should have been governed by long-standing principles such as federalism and the rule of law, and by emerging principles such as independence and protection of minorities. These theories underpinned the arguments presented by the different parties which came before the Supreme Court of Canada in *Reference re Resolution to Amend the Constitution*,[18] and ultimately it can be said that the Imperial theory prevailed.

The *Patriation Reference* will be considered in some detail in Chapter 7. The remainder of this chapter will examine the prevalence of the Imperial theory in Canadian nineteenth- and twentieth-century constitutional thinking.

The most basic characteristic of the Imperial theory is captured in the widespread usage of the word 'patriation', by which is meant the process which allowed control over the Constitution to be brought home to Canada. Choosing

---

[17] As indeed proved to be the case. See, e.g., United Kingdom, House of Commons, *First, Second and Third Reports of the Foreign Affairs Committee* (21 January, 15 April, 22 December, 1981) (London: HMSO, 1981).   [18] [1981] 1 SCR 753 (hereinafter *Patriation Reference*).

to speak of 'patriation' gave the impression that the Constitution of Canada remained in the United Kingdom until all the means of controlling it, principally the process for its amendment, had been returned to Canadian soil. Until that time, the implicit understanding was that it should also be governed by British, or at best Commonwealth, constitutional theory, notably that part of the theory concerning sovereignty that was examined in Part I.

In a 1965 White Paper, the Minister of Justice, the Honourable Guy Favreau objected to the term *'repatriation'*[19] which was in common usage at the time, as it misleadingly 'implie[d] the return to Canada of something that was here originally'. He noted that in fact 'the full responsibility for our Constitution has never been vested in Canada'.[20] He made reference to earlier attempts to 'work out a way by which "a Canadian Constitution" might be "domiciled" in Canada'.[21] In a speech entitled 'Constitutional Amendment in a Canadian Canada' delivered one year earlier, Favreau's comments had been more emotive in reference to this notion of domicile. The tenses used in the speech reflected the Minister's misplaced optimism regarding the chances of success of the domestic amending formula which he was proposing at that time:

But the [proposed] formula . . . marks the birth in Canada of a new climate of political discussion. That climate, *for the first time*, is unmistakably Canadian. As long as our country's fundamental law remained domiciled abroad, a cloud of doubt, humiliating doubt, obscured our homeland's sovereignty. However deep the affection we all feel for the great island beyond the seas that sent us one of our founding peoples, we could no longer, as a proud and independent nation, allow our Constitution to stand subject, even formally, to an absentee Parliament. The pilgrimage to London was an intolerable anachronism . . . [22]

Favreau's notion of domicile is useful because it takes in a number of the other important attributes of the Imperial theory. According to some stronger versions, Canadian political independence did not arrive until 1982 when the Constitution finally fulfilled the requirements of a Canadian domicile.[23] Furthermore, the Imperial theory made it difficult to speak of a *Canadian* amending formula. Despite the fact that in 1931 a Canada which was acknowledged to have autonomous status internationally *chose* to leave the mechanism for amendment of its Constitution with Westminster, in legal terms

---

[19] The French word, *rapatriement*, is still commonly used, while in English 'patriation' became the standard. See, e.g., Rémillard (1984) (n. 1 above). See also Oliver (2000) (n. 1 above).

[20] Hon. Guy Favreau, *The Amendment of the Constitution of Canada* (Ottawa: Queen's Printer, 1965) 50.   [21] ibid., 51.

[22] Hon. Guy Favreau, 'Constitutional Amendment in a Canadian Canada' (1966–7) 12 McGill LJ 384, 392–3 (emphasis added). The proposal, known as the Fulton-Favreau formula in recognition of the two Ministers of Justice who had had a hand in its conception, was abandoned in 1965 when the Premier of Quebec, Jean Lesage, announced his Province's decision to reject this 'patriation' scheme. See the Lesage-Pearson letters in (1966–7) 12 McGill LJ 592.

[23] Although, the logic of this strong version made it difficult to see how, even after 1982, there was not at least a theoretical possibility of the 'Mother Parliament' reasserting her authority.

the nature of the relationship could still be seen as one of Empire and colony, and the key documents of the fundamental law of Canada could be seen merely as a collection of Imperial legislation, recorded in the statute books at Westminster. According to this view, the rules governing the modification of such legislation were naturally those rules applicable to all Westminster legislation. If the undeniable Canadian attributes of federalism, protection of minorities, self-government and international recognition could not be found in this legislation, then they could exist only at the level of convention or politics. In law, the courts (the Judicial Committee and later even the Supreme Court of Canada) were apparently obliged to respect the principles of the British (and Imperial) Constitution, and those included the central notions of parliamentary sovereignty and the rule of law. Finally, if the Constitution was domiciled in the United Kingdom, then it was appropriate to interpret it not only according to its own terms but also consistently with British or at least Commonwealth constitutional theory and, by implication, with that body of law and theory which applied to all Commonwealth nations.[24] In effect, in so far as the theory was operative, it called upon the Supreme Court of Canada to act with regard to Imperial legislation not as a Canadian court responding to developments in Canadian legal and political culture, but as a stand-in for the Judicial Committee of the Privy Council, the highest court of the Empire which (as we shall see in Chapter 7) the Supreme Court of Canada in fact replaced, at least for Canadian appeals.

The true characteristic of the Imperial theory, then, was not alegal; in fact, it was positively legal. It did not consider the potential implications of such factors as federalism, independence, protection of minorities and legitimacy precisely because, strictly speaking, it was not required to do so. The Constitution which was in the making was domiciled in the United Kingdom, not in Canada, and until agreement could be had to bring it home, Canadians, even Canadian courts, were powerless, so the theory went, to modify the situation which Favreau and others described as 'anachronistic' and 'humiliating'. It was fundamentally a very conservative theory. However, its critics needed more arguments than those traditionally put forward to say that this is a bad thing. After all, perhaps even the Supreme Court of Canada should be very wary of boldly reforming the constitutional rules at the highest level.[25] The Imperial theory may, however, be vulnerable to criticism if it cannot explain the change of constitutional domicile— or 'patriation'—which was desired from a very early point in Canadian constitutional history but which did not occur completely until 1982.

Clearly, there was much in the way of justification for the Imperial theory. As we saw in the discussion regarding the absence of an amending formula,

---

[24] Important legislation included the Colonial Laws Validity Act, 1865 (Imp.) and the Statute of Westminster, 1931 (Imp.), but perhaps even more important was a very impressive body of Imperial constitutional theory. See Chs 3 and 4 above.

[25] This point will be dealt with more fully in Ch. 7 below.

the Fathers of Confederation appear intentionally to have left control over the 1867 Act with the Imperial Parliament. They also accepted implicitly the jurisdiction of the Judicial Committee of the Privy Council which acted as a final court of appeal on issues concerning the vires of federal or provincial legislation, even after the creation of the Supreme Court of Canada in 1875.

If we take a brief look at the development of Canadian constitutional theory since 1867, it should not surprise us to see strong indications of the Imperial theory in early writings. It should also not surprise us to see that the early thinking on this subject was heavily influenced by ideas coming from the centre of the Empire, i.e. the United Kingdom. Writing in 1867, John Gooch captured the sense in which both the law and theory of the Canadian Constitution were tightly connected to the United Kingdom: 'This Constitution of Canada by reason of its enactment as an Act of Parliament of the United Kingdom, is integrated as a Branch of the ancient constitution of the Empire, i.e., the mother trunk projects in the direction of these colonies an arm of its strength—and may it prove our strong arm, please God.'[26]

However, especially early on, before Dicey's intellectual empire had been firmly established, some Canadian writers displayed evidence of both Imperial *and* Independence theory thinking. The first detailed legal analysis of the Canadian Constitution, D.A. O'Sullivan's *A Manual of Government in Canada* was published in 1879.[27] A second edition appeared in 1887.[28] O'Sullivan, a Toronto practitioner and prominent law official in the Roman Catholic Church,[29] was in some ways quite independent spirited, though it is hard to gauge the extent to which he was aware of being so. He showed sympathy for the view that 'exclusive authority' in section 91 of the 1867 Act pre-empted even the Imperial Parliament from (ever)[30] legislating under the powers listed there, apparently in opposition to the idea that the Westminster Parliament was incapable of binding itself. In the first and second editions, O'Sullivan regularly referred to the way in which sovereignty in Canada was divided between Imperial, Canadian and provincial authorities. These were 'separate and distinct sovereignties acting separately and independently of each other within their

---

[26] J. Gooch, *Manual or Explanatory Development of the Act for the Union of Canada, Nova Scotia and New Brunswick in one Dominion under the Name of Canada, Synthetical and Analytical: With the Text of the Act Etc, and Index to the Act and the Treatises* (Ottawa: G.E. Desbarats, 1867) 1.

[27] D.A. O'Sullivan, *A Manual of Government in Canada; or, The Principles and Institutions of our Federal and Provincial Constitutions* (Toronto: J.C. Stuart, 1879).

[28] D.A. O'Sullivan, *Government in Canada: The Principles and Institutions of our Federal and Provincial Constitutions: The BNA Act 1867 Compared with the United States Constitution, With a Sketch of the Constitutional History of Canada* (2nd edn, Toronto: Carswell, 1887).

[29] R.C.B. Risk, 'Constitutional Scholarship in the Late Nineteenth Century: Making Federalism Work' (1996) 46 UTLJ 427.

[30] O'Sullivan (1887) (n. 28 above) 98, added the word 'ever' to the relevant passage from the first edition: 'in regard to these [powers listed in section 91] the English legislature has no concern, and have deprived themselves of the right of *ever* interfering' (emphasis added).

respective spheres'.[31] This way of speaking about sovereignty contradicted the traditional absolutist Austinian view. During the interval between O'Sullivan's first and second editions, Dicey's *Law of the Constitution* appeared, reaffirming the Austinian version in a new, more legal guise. O'Sullivan had clearly read Dicey's famous book, but the Canadian was not willing to abandon his heretical views on sovereignty in the second edition. He persisted in referring to 'a three-fold division of sovereignty', 'separate and distinct'.[32] However, a certain amount of uncertainty or schizophrenia had crept into the analysis.

The problem was that the Preamble to the 1867 Act made clear that Canada's was 'a Constitution similar in principle to that of the United Kingdom', and yet its federal structure made it seem more similar to that of the United States. O'Sullivan, like other Canadian constitutional writers after him,[33] rebuked Dicey for implying that the 1867 Act was more American than British in inspiration, and for describing the Preamble statement as 'official mendacity'. And yet O'Sullivan's federalist and relative usage of the term 'sovereignty' could be said to vindicate Dicey's observation.[34] O'Sullivan made up for his equivocation on 'sovereignty' by reasserting in true Dicey fashion the absolute sovereignty of the Westminster Parliament: 'The British legislature has no division of powers, it legislates on all classes of subjects and there is no limit to its powers...it is omnipotent.'[35] Furthermore, the Canadian legislatures, federal and provincial, 'deriv[ed] their power from the same sovereign authority'.[36] O'Sullivan was clearly torn between his American and British influences, as further on in the text, he expanded on this idea of derivation to include an element of popular sovereignty: 'Both [the federal and the provincial] powers were derived from the will of the people of Canada, acting under British authority, and these powers cannot be altered but by that same will and authority.'[37]

The unapologetic way in which passages originally written for the first edition referred to federal and provincial 'sovereignty' was followed by more tentative new writing in the second edition in which new worries appear. For example, in elaboration on the distribution of powers, O'Sullivan stated that 'the parliament of Canada stands midway between the sovereignty of the British parliament and what is sometimes called the sovereignty of the local legislatures', commenting at the same time that 'the accepted meaning of the term sovereignty as used by constitutional lawyers in England is not readily adjusted to the jurisprudence of any country governed under a purely federal system'.[38] O'Sullivan's intellectual anguish was evident elsewhere. 'All the American constitutional writers speak of

---

[31] O'Sullivan (1879) (n. 27 above) 59.   [32] O'Sullivan (1887) (n. 28 above) 20.

[33] See, e.g., W.H.P. Clement, *The law of the Canadian Constitution* (Toronto: Carswell, 1892; 2nd edn, 1904; 3rd edn, 1916) 3; A.H.F. Lefroy, *The Law of Legislative Power in Canada* (Toronto: Toronto Law Book and Publishing, 1897–8) xliii–iv.   [34] O'Sullivan (1887) (n. 28 above) 3n.

[35] ibid., 12.   [36] ibid., 7.   [37] ibid., 22.

[38] ibid., 96. See also 97: 'central and state governments are each sovereign within their own limits,—a description, however, which falls short of the English theory of sovereign power, inasmuch as it is limited'.

divided sovereignty', he noted in a footnote, 'while the English writers from Austin down regard this as a contradiction in terms'.[39] In the end O'Sullivan was inclined to downplay the power of Westminster as 'nominal'[40] and to emphasise the powers of Canadian authorities, the latter having 'complete, absolute and supreme' powers 'within their respective limits'.[41]

Canadian constitutional writers following O'Sullivan persisted in using the term 'sovereignty' more flexibly than Austinian or Diceyan usage would recommend. However, O'Sullivan had begun to take matters further, suggesting perhaps that Westminster had 'deprived itself of the right of *ever* interfering'[42] with matters of federal and provincial competence and exploring a sense of constitutional derivation linked to 'the will of the people of Canada'.[43] These early green shoots of Independence theory did not take hold. Instead we begin to see the Imperial theory establishing itself much more firmly.

The Imperial theory takes hold

Strong evidence of the Imperial theory having taken hold can be found in the two textbook writers who followed on O'Sullivan's early efforts. W.H.P. Clement, another Toronto legal practitioner (and later British Columbia judge), published three editions of *The Law of the Canadian Constitution* between 1892 and 1916.[44] A.H.F. Lefroy, also a Toronto practitioner, was Oxford educated and, as of 1900, a professor of law at the University of Toronto. Between 1897 and 1920, roughly the period in which Clement was writing, Lefroy published four textbooks on Canadian constitutional law.[45]

Unlike O'Sullivan, who was inclined to emphasise the independent aspects of Canada's constitutional arrangements, Clement was intent on reasserting Imperial orthodoxy, especially in the first two editions of *The Law of the Canadian Constitution*. Whereas O'Sullivan showed sympathy for the view that the Imperial Parliament had forever renounced legislative competence in areas granted to the federal Canadian legislature in the 1867 Act, Clement removed the doubt:

We have spoken of the want of legal limit to the power of the 'national' government under the British Imperial system. The expression is perhaps hardly accurate—the want which really exists is the want of legal limit to the legislative power of the British

---

[39] O'Sullivan (1887) (n. 28 above), 9n.   [40] ibid., 99.   [41] ibid., 107.
[42] ibid., 98.   [43] ibid., 22.
[44] Clement (1892) (n. 33 above). See Risk (1996) (n. 29 above) 429.
[45] Lefroy (1897–8) (n. 33 above); also by Lefroy, *Canada's Federal System* (Toronto: Carswell, 1913); *Leading Cases in Canadian Constitutional Law* (Toronto: Carswell, 1914; 2nd edn, 1920); and *A Short Treatise on Canadian Constitutional Law* (Toronto: Carswell, 1918). See R.C.B. Risk, 'A.H.F. Lefroy: Common Law Thought in Late Nineteenth-Century Canada: On Burying One's Grandfather' (1991) 41 UTLJ 307 and R.C.B. Risk, 'The Scholars and the Constitution: P.O.G.G. and the Privy Council' (1996) 2 Manitoba L.R. 496.

Parliament . . . No judge within the Empire can legally limit the British Parliament as a legislative body, or treat its enactments as ultra vires . . . [46]

Clement continued: 'The "sphere of authority" of the British Parliament, as a law-making body for the Empire, is legally unlimited, and within that unlimited sphere it may exercise its law-making powers in whatever fashion may appear proper to it.'[47] Dicey could not object to any of this. Clement was also clear on the supposed corollary to Parliament's absolute sovereignty: 'No power even its own, can tie the hands of the Imperial Parliament; and the boundaries set to colonial freedom of action in one session of that parliament may be enlarged in the next, and again restricted in a third.'[48]

Clement kept to essentially the same line on these points in the second edition. His third edition began similarly:

In the study of the Canadian Constitution the first fact which challenges attention is that the Dominion of Canada is a British colony . . . It was no part of the scheme of Confederation to alter in any essential respect the colonial relationship . . . and there is nothing in the Act to indicate a surrender in any degree by the British Parliament of that cardinal principle of the Constitution, the supreme legislative authority of the British Parliament over and throughout the Empire.[49]

This was as orthodox a statement of constitutional theory as one might find. However, in the third edition, Clement pursued two paths of inquiry which promised something in the way of an Independence theory.

First, Clement referred to the United Kingdom Parliament as a 'constituent assembly',[50] and as 'the constitution-maker for the colonies'.[51] Perhaps there were things that the United Kingdom Parliament could do as a constituent assembly that were different from what it could do (or not do) as a mere Parliament. Pointing himself down a path which might lead to constitutional independence, he asked: 'To what extent have constituent powers been bestowed upon the Canadian legis-latures?'[52] Sadly, from a Canadian perspective, he had little to provide by way of reply.

Secondly, Clement in his third edition discussed the force of Imperial legisla-tion from two perspectives, a 'British View' and a 'Colonial View', rough equivalents of the Imperial and Independence theories introduced in this chapter.[53] The 'British View' simply involved 'legislative supremacy over the

---

[46] Clement (1892) (n. 33 above) 11, and similarly 55–6:

For the whole British Empire, legislative sovereignty resides in the Imperial Parliament, and when that body undertakes to legislate for the colonies generally, or for any one of them in particular, its enactments are a law unto such a colony, binding its inhabitants, and peremptorily requiring recognition by the judges in its courts; and no colonial legislature has power, directly or by side wind, to alter, in one jot or tittle, any such Imperial enactment.

See also Clement (1904) (n. 33 above) 25 for a more compact statement of the same.

[47] Clement (1892) (n. 33 above) 12.
[48] ibid., 56, citing Dicey's *Law of the Constitution*. See also Clement (1904) (n. 33 above) 25.
[49] Clement (1916) (n. 33 above) 1.   [50] ibid., 3, 29.   [51] ibid., 32.   [52] ibid., 3.
[53] ibid., ch. VI.

colonies', a principle 'now thoroughly established in the constitutional law of the Empire'.[54] However, the 'Colonial View' was more varied. 'Remarkable' as it was, he observed 'that at each step in Canada's constitutional progress it has been contended that the Imperial Parliament in legalising such a step had surrendered, so far as related to Canada, some portion of its paramount authority'.[55] We will look at some of these contentions in Chapter 6. Clement left no doubt, however, that there was 'ample' recognition of the British view in the colonies, and this was clearly his view as well, at least in so far as the Canadian colony was concerned.

Clement's contemporary, A.H.F. Lefroy, wrote widely in matters of Canadian constitutional law, but he was less forthcoming as to the theoretical assumptions underpinning his work. The most authoritative commentator on Lefroy's legacy notes that he 'never speculated in any rigorous and abstract way about questions of sovereignty, although the general structure of his thought and his jurisprudence courses suggest that he accepted without question that there always must be a sovereign power'.[56] Lefroy's *The Law of Legislative Power in Canada* was made up of a series of Propositions, the twelfth of these being that the 'powers of legislation conferred upon the Dominion Parliament and the Provincial Legislatures, respectively, by the British North America Act, are conferred subject to the sovereign authority of the Imperial Parliament'.[57] Lefroy adopted freely Dicey's vocabulary of sovereignty and subordination where the Imperial Parliament and the Canadian legislatures were concerned.[58] His only criticism of Dicey was to join others in affirming that Canada could be both federal and 'similar in principle' to the United Kingdom. Lefroy's criticism of Dicey was apt and thorough in this regard, but Lefroy nonetheless felt obliged to begin the paragraph following the criticism in somewhat contrite fashion, referring deferentially to 'the last two editions of [Dicey's] brilliant lectures on the *Law of the Constitution*'.[59]

The orthodox writers, such as Clement and Lefroy, had echoes in Canadian political developments in the early part of the twentieth century. Senior Canadian officials began at this time to consider the possibility of finding a domestic procedure for amending the Constitution.[60] By the mid-1920s it had become a matter of great importance. The strong hold of the Imperial theory is evident in most of these discussions. For example, it was assumed by many that even after Canada obtained a domestic procedure for amending the Constitution, it would remain possible for the Westminster Parliament to assert its continuing

---

[54] Clement (1916) (n. 33 above) 52.   [55] ibid., 60.

[56] Risk (1991) (n. 45 above) 323.

[57] Lefroy (1897–8) (n. 33 above) 208. This appears as Proposition 13 in Lefroy (1913) (n. 45 above) 51.   [58] Lefroy (1897–8) (n. 33 above) 248.

[59] ibid., xliv.

[60] See P. Gérin-Lajoie, *Constitutional Amendment in Canada* (Toronto: University of Toronto Press, 1950) 221–2 and M. Ollivier, *L'avenir constitutionnel du Canada* (Montreal: Albert Lévesque, 1935) 130.

sovereignty. The problem in all its logical complexity had been explained as early as 1925 by the then Leader of the Opposition, the Right Honourable Arthur Meighen, a highly regarded thinker if somewhat ineffectual political leader. His terms seem to distinguish politics or convention ('constitutional right') from law:

... if all were unanimous that we abandon recourse to the British Parliament altogether, and through some system at home, vest in the various legislatures and the Parliament the right to amend the Constitution, would we really be farther ahead than we are now? The Prime Minister says, and I support him to the full, that we have to-day an absolute constitutional right to fix the terms of our Constitution. Speaking for the people of Canada, satisfying the British Parliament that we so speak—and there is no difficulty doing this if the voice of objection is not heard—we have the right as a Parliament to decide what goes into that Act and what stays out. Such is our position to-day. Hon. gentlemen say 'Yes, but that only rests on the foundation of constitutional right; by law we still have to go around the route to the British Parliament; and we do not want to rest on the insecure basis of mere constitutional right. We want our legal rights plainly defined before the world.' Let us inquire into that contention. In my judgment our legal position would not be one whit stronger in that case than it is now. True, it is by virtue of constitutional right that we can now dictate virtually any amendments to the Act, provided we speak for all Canada and the voice of minorities raises no objection. But the sanction of constitutional right within this British Empire is just as firm, just as lasting, and just as dependable as the voice of law itself. But I go farther. *When we have gone through all this and got our substituted system, when we have obtained the legal right to amend in our several Parliaments this British North America Act, the legal foundation is not one iota better than it was before. Why do I say that? Though the British North America Act may be amended, in such a way as to give the Parliament of Canada, after a long series of provincial approvals, the right to amend the Act, after that is all done the legal power would still remain in the British Parliament to change the Act at will. And nothing could restrain them* save a regard for constitutional authority. In other words, we would still be protected by constitutional right and constitutional right alone; *the legal power in the British Parliament would remain to amend the Act or to repeal it.* So that, after all, the sanction we would have would be the very sanction we now enjoy.[61]

The proposed enactment which was the subject of debate was only a partial amending formula for Canada, so, in spite of Meighen's hypothetical consideration of the matter, no end to the Westminster Parliament's powers to amend the Constitution of Canada was yet contemplated.[62] However, if one accepted the main tenets of orthodox sovereignty theory, it was difficult to avoid the thrust of Meighen's argument: no matter what Canada proposed, the Westminster Parliament would retain an ultimate power to legislate.

---

[61] Canada, House of Commons, *Debates* (19 February 1925) 336–7 (emphasis added). See R. MacGregor Dawson (ed.) *Constitutional Issues in Canada* (London: Oxford University Press, 1933) 21.   [62] See Gérin-Lajoie (1950) (n. 60 above) 226n.

The Imperial theory after the Statute of Westminster

The most important opportunity to provide such a legal text limiting the apparently unlimited powers of the Parliament at Westminster came with the process which led up to the passage of the Statute of Westminster, 1931. Canadian politicians, meeting at successive federal-provincial conferences were unable to agree on a domestic procedure for amending the Constitution of Canada and chose therefore to preserve the *status quo ante* by means of section 7 of the Statute.[63] If there had been any doubt before, regarding the continuing ability of the United Kingdom Parliament to legislate for Canada, at least where it was amending that country's fundamental law, those doubts had been removed by the words of section 7(1), as we have seen in Chapter 2.

The preamble to the 1931 Statute taken together with the Balfour Declaration of 1926 clearly recognised the autonomous political status which Canada had acquired. Section 7(3) of the Statute and the notes of the preparatory conferences confirmed the political importance of provincial approval for any constitutional change which might affect the federal nature of the country. But the words of section 7(1) stated that 'Nothing in this Act' could be deemed to apply to the amendment of the Imperial statutes which together made up Canada's Constitution. According to the Imperial theory, which was still very much dominant, changes of a political nature could not have any impact on the unaltered sovereignty of the United Kingdom Parliament in this domain.

That which was even more disturbing, at least at the theoretical level, was that the same orthodox Imperial understanding of parliamentary sovereignty even rendered the *legal* limitations contained in the text of the 1931 Statute formally precarious. As the Privy Council stated in the *British Coal Corporation* case,[64] as a matter of abstract theory the Westminster Parliament could always reclaim its power to legislate in all respects for the former colonies. On the strongest version of the Imperial theory, the Westminster Parliament could legislate on any matter for Canada. This was judged to be the case, in law at least, by the Parliamentary Counsel of the Senate, writing in 1939, eight years after the passage of the Statute of Westminster, 1931:

It is not open to doubt that the Imperial Parliament may, so far as constitutional *law* is concerned, legislate for Canada, notwithstanding the British North America Act, and without Canada's consent or request, indeed against Canada's will, to as full an extent as it may see fit. Nor can there be any doubt that, notwithstanding the Statute of Westminster, the Imperial Parliament may so far as such *law* is concerned, as fully, freely

---

[63] Gérin-Lajoie (1950) (n. 60 above) ch. 1, shows that s. 7 may not have even succeeded in doing what it set out to do because of the specific references to the British North America Acts, 1867–1930.

[64] *British Coal Corporation v The King* [1935] AC 500. For a reassessment of the importance of this case, see discussion in Ch. 3 above.

and extensively so legislate. The British North America Act and the Statute of Westminster, alike, are in eye of the law, merely statutes of Parliament and—at law—no Parliament can bind either itself or a future Parliament.[65]

There was also, of course, a strong convention which made it very unlikely that the Westminster Parliament would legislate to such a full extent in Canadian matters. However, in the Canadian case, the question whether the Statute of Westminster had limited the Imperial Parliament's powers was moot in another sense. Presumably, any direct interference in Canadian affairs which the United Kingdom Parliament might have wished to accomplish could have been done indirectly through its power to amend Canadian constitutional texts, a power explicitly maintained in section 7(1).

Despite the fact that Canadians had been unable to agree upon a domestic procedure for constitutional amendment for inclusion in the Statute of Westminster, 1931, the attempts to find such a procedure did not abate. Numerous proposals emerged in the years immediately following passage of the 1931 Statute. While the greatest parts of these proposals were concerned with substance, it is possible to see nonetheless the various influences of the constitutional understandings which are characteristic of the Imperial theory. The most revealing aspect of these proposals, in terms of constitutional theory, was the manner by which the transfer of ultimate legislative authority might take place.

In 1935, for example, the Ontario government presented to the Federal-Provincial Conference a proposal for a Canadian amending procedure in which a suggestion appeared regarding the United Kingdom Parliament. The suggestion was later reported in summary form and with commentary by Paul Gérin-Lajoie:

(f) Recourse to the Parliament of the United Kingdom for the enactment of constitutional amendments should accordingly be abolished except as regards amendments to the amending process; the Ontario proposal also set forth that no alteration should be made in this process except by consent of the federal Parliament and of the legislatures of all the Provinces. The Ontario proposal attached much importance to the retaining of the United Kingdom Parliament 'as the arbitor [sic] in this matter of vital concern'. *This peculiar feature was considered necessary in order to ensure the continuance of the method of amendment proposed.*[66]

It appears that the Ontario government wished in so far as possible to remove the United Kingdom Parliament as the ultimate constitutional authority in the Canadian Constitution, but this account also indicates that the continued role of Westminster was deemed necessary in order to accomplish any future alteration *of the amending process itself*, and perhaps even to ensure the ongoing status of such a process as part of Canadian fundamental law. One must be wary of

---

[65] O'Connor (1939) (n. 2 above) Annex 5, 17 (O'Connor's emphasis).
[66] Gérin-Lajoie (1950) (n. 60 above) 246 (emphasis added).

reading too much into these proposals, but it seems that the Ontario government saw the British, Diceyan notion of what came later to be known as continuing sovereignty [67] as the only model available to Canada. And furthermore, it may have felt that if the United Kingdom disappeared from the Canadian constitutional structure, the Canadian constitution would lose its fundamental or supreme legislative status at the same time. The safer and perhaps the more desirable option on this view was to maintain the Imperial link.

The prevalence of the British notion of parliamentary sovereignty in two generations of Canadian constitutional scholars can be seen in Gérin-Lajoie's account in 1950 of Maurice Ollivier's 1935 proposals regarding the Canadian Constitution. Ollivier had suggested that Canadians should draft a new constitution based on the 1867 Act. According to Gérin-Lajoie's account of it, the main object of this proposal was 'to bring about the repeal of the British North America Acts and to have the Canadian Constitution embodied exclusively in a Canadian Act in order that it might not be any more subject, in law, to amendment by the Parliament of the United Kingdom'.[68] Gérin-Lajoie noted the problem with this proposal 'in strict law'. His comments indicated that that law was based on British principles which were, apparently, equally applicable to Canada:

Dr. Ollivier seems to have forgotten that, as a matter of abstract law, Westminster could amend or repeal any Canadian acts as well as any British acts relating to Canada. (See in this respect the illuminating pages of Jennings, *The Law and the Constitution*, pp. 148–51.) By constitutional convention, however, the supremacy of Westminster—which is a legal fiction—is limited to the extent of precluding Parliament from amending or repealing without the request or Canada, the British North America Acts as well as any Canadian statute (either embodying the Constitution or not). The enactment in Canada of a Canadian Constitution (for instance, by concurrent statutes of the federal Parliament and the Provinces) and the repeal of the present British acts on the subject would therefore operate only a change of form. This change is, no doubt, highly desirable in many respects. *But it would not affect at all, from a strictly legal and abstract point of view, the supremacy of the Parliament of the United Kingdom over the Canadian Constitution.*[69]

Once again, the predominance of British constitutional theory, even regarding Canadian constitutional matters,[70] can be seen, even to the point of making it apparently impossible to cut the Imperial link.[71] The Honourable Arthur

---

[67] See discussion in Chs 1 and 3 above.   [68] Gérin-Lajoie (1950) (n. 60 above) 240–1.

[69] Gérin-Lajoie (1950) (n. 60 above) 241n (emphasis added). Only the parenthetical reference to Jennings hints at any doubt in Gérin-Lajoie's mind on this matter.

[70] As we shall see in discussing the Independence theory, it was open to Canadians, after Balfour and the Statute of Westminster if not before, to regard the Westminster Parliament as part of the *Canadian* machinery for amendment of its Constitution, and to consider it therefore as a matter of *independent* Canadian constitutional theory.

[71] This, of course, may account for the form of s. 4 of the Statute of Westminster, 1931 which made no reference to the *termination* of Imperial power, leaving that to be taken care of by the 'request and consent' provisions. See G. Marshall, *Parliamentary Sovereignty and the Commonwealth*

Meighen in the 1920s, the Parliamentary Counsel for the Senate in the 1930s and Gérin-Lajoie's writing in the 1940s are all excellent examples of an Imperial theory view.

Gérin-Lajoie had a proposal of his own which was inspired in part by the report of a sub-committee to the Federal-Provincial conferences of 1935–6. The sub-committee had proposed that the Statute of Westminster, 1931 be amended to remove section 7(1) and to empower the Parliament of Canada to enact a consolidated Constitution (a proposed amending clause having already been enacted as a new section 148 of the 1867 Act) which would not operate as new law but would be construed as declaratory of the law as existing at the time of such enactment.[72] Gérin-Lajoie specified that the consolidated Constitution should only be a rearrangement of the 1867 Act not a restatement or reform, and that it be brought into force by an Act of the federal Parliament concurred in by the legislatures of all the provinces of Canada. He did not mention the removal of section 7(1) of the 1931 Statute. Instead, he concluded, with a reference to the comments set out immediately above, that this scheme 'would not remove, in strict law, the supremacy of the Parliament of the United Kingdom over the Constitution of Canada'.[73]

Also writing in 1950, F.R. Scott agreed that schemes of this type could not easily escape the supremacy of the Westminster Parliament:

In my view, this kind of procedure still suffers from its relationship to the Statute of Westminster, which is an exclusively United Kingdom statute. The Canadian constitution thus created would seem to depend upon the sovereign Parliament as of old. While the Statute of Westminster was intended to free the former colonies from certain legal fetters, it nevertheless preserved the law-making power of the United Kingdom Parliament over the very nation it was attempting to free.[74]

Scott also described (perhaps for the first time in Canada, at least in such explicit terms) the hold which British constitutional theory had on Canadian constitutional understandings:

What was this basic principle, this fundamental rule, which showed such remarkable tenacity? Dicey first made it a widely understood idea. The opening sentence of chapter I of his *Law of the Constitution* declares simply that 'The sovereignty of Parliament is (from the legal point of view) the dominant characteristic of our political institutions.' This principle means, he continues, that Parliament (i.e. the United Kingdom Parliament) had the right to make or unmake any law whatever, and further that no person or body is

(Oxford: Oxford University Press, 1957), 146n and K.C. Wheare, *The Statute of Westminster and Dominion Status*, (5th edn, Oxford: Oxford University Press, 1953).

[72] Gérin-Lajoie (1950) (n. 60 above) 247–8.　　　[73] ibid., 277–8.

[74] F.R. Scott, 'The Redistribution of Imperial Sovereignty' in *Transactions of the Royal Society of Canada*, 44, Series III, June 1950, 27–34, reprinted in F.R. Scott, *Essays on the Constitution* (Toronto: University of Toronto Press, 1977) 244, 250. Dr Gérin-Lajoie changed his views in reaction to Professor Scott's article: see P. Gérin-Lajoie, 'Du pouvoir d'amendement constitutionnel au Canada' (1951) 29 Can Bar Rev 1178.

recognized by the law of England as having a right to override or set aside the legislation of Parliament. Hence it follows that the constitutions of the various Dominions and colonies, created by laws enacted in this Parliament, are binding upon the courts and people of the territory covered by them, and can only be 'made or unmade' by this same authority which first gave them the force of law.[75]

He observed that the legal rules were tempered to a great extent by convention, and that the system had worked well enough to that point. However, he insisted that:

'This system . . . obviously leaves in existence the ancient doctrine of Imperial sovereignty. The inequality of the relationship has become more and more apparent as the international status of the Dominion has risen. While the active interference of British governments in Canadian affairs has withered away, the hard core of legal dependence has been unconscionably slow in dying, and is not yet dead.[76]

Scott was unique among constitutional lawyers of the period in recognising that Canadian legal independence would require the development of a distinct Canadian legal understanding, including its own *Grundnorm*, to use Kelsen's formulation which was at that time gaining currency. That distinct understanding was also crucial to what will later emerge as the Independence theory, and, accordingly, it will be necessary to return to Scott's argument in Chapter 6. It is sufficient for the moment to point out that, according to Scott's view of the matter, Canada would only be entitled to its own *Grundnorm* after the enactment of a Canadian independence Act, a final United Kingdom statute at Canada's request which would declare that all jurisdiction over Canada vested in the United Kingdom Parliament would cease, and thereby establish 'once and for all the solid fact of Canada's legal sovereignty vis-à-vis Great Britain'.[77] He was less clear as to how this change in *Grundnorm* would take place or, perhaps more importantly, how a Canadian court would account for the change in legal terms. Likening the *Grundnorm* to the turtle upon which, according to eastern myth, the elephant (constitution) sits, he stated that Canadians must simply 'pull out the old turtle and slip a new one in its place, so that not even a tremor need be felt in the superstructure'.[78]

It was not clear how this sleight of hand was actually to take place nor was it evident who were the 'Canadians' who would do it. One might have looked to the Supreme Court of Canada, by then the highest Canadian court with no appeal beyond it to the Privy Council. But as we shall see, a majority of the Court was not prepared, even in 1981, to manhandle the old turtle, at least not overtly. Also, even though Scott's views presented the possibility of an eventual break from the Imperial connection (a possibility ignored or denied in versions of the Independence theory which we have examined thus far), his writing did

---

[75] Scott (1950) (n. 74 above) 245.   [76] Scott (1950) (n. 74 above) 246.   [77] ibid., 250.
[78] ibid., 249. The turtle analogy was referred to by Marshall (1957) (n. 71 above) 103 (see Ch. 4 above for discussion).

not overtly acknowledge the logical extension of his theory, i.e. the possibility that a new Canadian *Grundnorm* had already been in existence, unrecognised, since 1931, if not since 1867. Such a radical perspective anticipates the Independence theory. It was buried in Scott's thinking and not at all current in the 1950s, as we shall see. The Imperial theory still dominated Canadian constitutional thinking.

The Imperial theory and the ongoing search for a Canadian amending formula

The Constitutional Conferences of 1950 authorised a Continuing Committee of Attorneys-General 'to study the methods and techniques whereby a Canadian Constitution can be domiciled in Canada as a purely Canadian instrument'.[79] The Continuing Committee did not succeed. For the next thirty years, numerous Canadian committees would grapple with the problem. The results and the rhetoric usually confirmed the traditional view that it would not be possible to think of 'a truly Canadian Constitution, domiciled in Canada as a purely Canadian instrument' until the anachronistic and humiliating role of the United Kingdom Parliament could be terminated. Far less attention was paid to the problem of the position of the United Kingdom Parliament *vis-à-vis* Canada *after patriation*—Scott and others had allayed if not eliminated those concerns— but the dominance of Westminster and British constitutional understandings were scarcely challenged in the meantime.

The Conference of Attorneys-General meeting in 1960[80] continued to wrestle with the problem of patriating the Constitution and divesting the United Kingdom Parliament of its legislative powers regarding Canada. Draft 'transfer', 'savings' and 'renunciation' clauses were prepared in order to *transfer* power from the United Kingdom Parliament, *preserve* the power of the Parliament of Canada and of the legislatures, and *end* the right of the United Kingdom Parliament to make laws for Canada or have them extend to Canada. In the end, what became know as the Fulton formula of 1961 only contained savings and renunciation clauses, transfer possibly too problematic.[81]

After a change of government at the federal level, the Fulton formula was transformed into what became known as the Fulton-Favreau formula. The

---

[79] Quoted in Favreau (1965) (n. 20 above) 51.

[80] See Letter from E.D. Fulton to Attorneys-General of all the Provinces, 25 October 1960, reprinted with drafts of the transfer clause, saving clause, renunciation clause, limitation clause, and delegation clause in A.F. Bayefsky (ed.) *Canada's Constitution Act, 1982 and Amendments: A Documentary History*, Vol. I (Toronto: McGraw-Hill Ryerson, 1989), 1–3.

[81] Letter from E.D. Fulton to Attorneys-General of all the provinces, 30 November 1961, reprinted with attachment: An Act to Provide for the Amendment of the Constitution of Canada, in Bayefsky (1989) (n. 80 above) 13–5.

communiqué of the Federal-Provincial Conference of 1964 announced[82] unanimous agreement on:

a formula to repatriate the Constitution of Canada. This formula, when it has become law, will mean that any future amendment of the Constitution will be made in Canada instead of by the Parliament of the United Kingdom. As a result, our Constitution will have become, for the first time in the history of Canada, truly and wholly Canadian.

The savings and renunciation clauses were virtually unaltered. A new preamble declared that Canada requested and consented to the proposed enactment. The explanatory notes stated that: 'Section 7 of the Statute of Westminster exempts the British North America Acts from this requirement [i.e. request and consent], but since the amending formula contains a renunciation clause applicable to the United Kingdom Parliament, it is considered appropriate to include the recital.'[83] This indicated that in the view of the Minister of Justice of Canada, and in accordance with the Imperial theory, Canadian request and consent had *not* been a legal requirement, in Canadian legal terms, for constitutional amendments to that point.

The Fulton-Favreau formula was not adopted. In 1967, a Canadian constitutional commentator could still write: 'One would think it clear . . . that the U.K. Parliament, which now retains by virtue of section 7(1) of the *Statute of Westminster, 1931*, unrestricted power to *dispose* of legislative power in Canada, *ipso facto* retains an unrestricted right to *exercise* that power.'[84] At about the same time, an adviser to the Quebec government and future judge of the Supreme Court of Canada, Louis-Philippe Pigeon, expressed the view that the renunciation clause in the Fulton-Favreau formula would not even have been entirely effective. After citing the usual authority for the proposition that a Parliament cannot bind itself, he stated that only the enactment of a Constitution by *Canadian* legislation would definitively end the legislative power of the United Kingdom Parliament in the Canadian legal system. He presumed that Canadian courts would then be legally obliged to ignore legislation passed by Westminster, although he did not explain how that would be so. One might have presumed that the theory of continuing parliamentary sovereignty to which the author subscribed (citing British authority) would have required the Canadian courts to take notice.[85]

In 1971, a new attempt to 'patriate' the Constitution failed to achieve adequate support. The federal government responded immediately to this set-back by establishing a Special Joint Committee of the Senate and the House of

---

[82] Communiqué of the Federal-Provincial conference, 14 October 1964, reprinted with attachment: An Act to Provide for the Amendment in Canada of the Constitution of Canada, in Bayefsky (1989) (n. 80 above) 16.   [83] Favreau (1965) (n. 20 above) 34.

[84] S.A. Scott, 'Constituent Authority and the Canadian Provinces' (1966–7) 12 McGill LJ 528, 572.

[85] L.-P. Pigeon, 'Le sens de la formule Fulton-Favreau' (1966–6) 12 McGill LJ 403, 411–12.

Commons on the Constitution of Canada. The Committee's final report, tabled in March of 1972, revealed strong indications of the ongoing influence of the Imperial theory.[86] The Committee reported that even though the British North America Act, 1867 had served the country well, it was 'the constitution of a colony'.[87] In order to remove the anachronistic role of the United Kingdom Parliament, the Committee recommended a novel procedure which had apparently been agreed to at the meetings prior to the failed 1971 initiative.[88] It is perhaps worth quoting at length from the Committee's description and explanation of that procedure in order to reveal the extent to which the Imperial theory dominated the Committee's thinking:

following agreement among the governments of Canada as to an amending formula and as to any substantive changes, the Parliament of Canada and all the Provincial Legislatures would pass resolutions authorizing the Governor-General to issue a proclamation containing a formula and any substantive changes agreed to; before the issuance of the proclamation the British Parliament would be asked to take all necessary steps to ensure the legal validity of the procedures including nullification of any British statutes, present or future, which purport to affect the Canadian Constitution; finally, the Governor-General's proclamation would be timed to coincide with the effective date of the British renunciation of jurisdiction.

The complexity of these procedures results from the desire, on the one hand, to avoid having a new Canadian Constitution brought into being solely by an act of the British Parliament, and the fear, on the other hand, that, if it was not so grounded, there might be a legal gap which might conceivably lead to a court's invalidating the whole new Constitution. The effect of the agreed procedures is to have the negative action which removes Canada from the jurisdiction of the British Parliament and the positive action by which we proclaim our new Constitution occur simultaneously so that both legal continuity and national autonomy are safeguarded.

There are no precedents in such an area, and one can only speculate about possible judicial reaction to the procedures. Nevertheless, since there is no apparent deficiency in them, it is hard to believe that any Canadian judge would strain language or law to invalidate them, since they would represent the solemnly expressed will of all the legislative bodies in Canada. We are therefore prepared to accept the suggested procedures for patriation of the Constitution without any fears that they would not be held legally viable.[89]

The Special Joint Committee's observations and these complex procedures resembled somewhat the proposals of the 1936 Federal-Provincial Conference and the suggestions of Gérin-Lajoie in 1950, and they also revealed the full extent to which the Imperial theory and its accompanying rhetoric were still deeply

---

[86] Canada, Special Joint Committee of the Senate and the House of Commons on the Constitution of Canada, *Final Report* (March 1972), reprinted in Bayefsky (1989) (n. 80 above) 224–308.   [87] ibid., 230.

[88] See Canada, Constitutional Conference, Statement of Conclusions, Working Session No. 3, 8–9 (February 1971), reprinted in Bayefsky ibid., 210–13.

[89] Canada, Special Joint Committee of the Senate and the House of Commons on the Constitution of Canada, *Final Report* (March 1972), reprinted in Bayefsky ibid., 231–2.

ingrained in Canadian attitudes toward 'patriation'.[90] If the Canadian Constitution was truly colonial, then the Committee was justified in taking care to safeguard national autonomy. But unless the colonial theory could be discarded along with it, then it was hard to see how even these ingenious procedures could accomplish the task. In the end, the Committee placed its faith in the Canadian courts. While the procedures might indeed have been valid, it was not clear from the Committee's account by what theory the courts could be expected to avoid the theoretical possibility of unwanted reassertion of the Imperial power.

As the federal government became more frustrated with the ongoing failure of the Provinces to agree upon a domestic amending formula, the Imperial theory rhetoric became deliberately more colonial, and hence borrowed heavily from the language which we have already associated with the Imperial theory. It was as if the federal authorities wished to shame the country into action. Prime Minister Trudeau referred to the existing amendment process via Westminster as 'demeaning for an independent country, but a legal necessity since we have never remedied the omission in the legislation of 1867'.[91]

Perhaps the strongest expression of the Imperial theory can be found in the testimony of the federal Minister of Justice, the Honourable Jean Chrétien, in his testimony before the 1980 Special Joint Committee of the Senate and House of Commons on the Constitution of Canada. The Minister was defending the government's unilateral effort to 'patriate' the Constitution and to add a new amending formula and Charter of Rights and Freedoms. It was of course in the federal government's interest to emphasise the unlimited power of the British Parliament and the absence of any legal requirement of Canadian participation. In response to questions regarding the role of the British Parliament, the Minister made the following statement:

Mr. Chrétien: . . . I have said that from a legal point of view, the British Parliament could theoretically decide to completely revert the Canadian Constitution from A to Z. It could decide tomorrow to accept the theory of your leader to the effect that Canada is a community of communities and can do away with the Federal Government.[92]

Further along in his testimony, the Minister acknowledged that the situation was unprecedented and that there was no binding legal authority on the matter:

Mr Chrétien: You are talking about precedents. I do not know where you found your precedents because we have never repatriated the Constitution, so there are no precedents.
. . .
   There is no jurisprudence; we are in the process of making it.

[90] For a more independent-spirited interpretation of the Special Joint Committee's recommendations, see B. Strayer, *Patriation and Constitutional Legitimacy* (Saskatoon: College of Law, University of Saskatchewan, 1982).

[91] See, e.g., Rt Hon. Pierre Elliott Trudeau, *A Time for Action: Toward the Renewal of the Canadian Federation*, reprinted in Bayefsky (1989) (n. 80 above) 457.

[92] Canada, Parliament, *Minutes and Proceedings of the Special Joint Committee of the Senate and House of Commons on the Constitution of Canada* (Chairs: Senator Harry Hays and Serge Joyal, MP) (1980–81) 4:27 (hereinafter Special Joint Committee (1980–1)).

From the strictly legal point of view, the Canadian Constitution is a British law and we maintain that the power to decide the future of the Canadian Constitution rests with the British Parliament . . . [93]

Other advisers to the federal government had expressed the view that even the Supreme Court of Canada might feel itself powerless to question the validity of United Kingdom legislation for Canada, even where such legislation was requested in accordance with what could be seen as the existing *Canadian* procedure for amending the Constitution. In what became known as the Kirby Memorandum, Michael Kirby, adviser to Prime Minister Trudeau and Secretary to the Cabinet for Federal-Provincial relations, expressed the following views in a document dated 30 August 1980, only a few months before the federal government's unilateral 'patriation' initiative:

As to the question of validity, it is the view of the Department of Justice that a law passed by the U.K. Parliament to patriate the Constitution, with an amendment formula and other changes, could not be successfully attacked in the courts. It seems abundantly clear that the legal power remains for the U.K. Parliament to enact such a law for Canada . . . [94]

The author of the memorandum nonetheless saw strategic advantage in having the federal resolution passed and United Kingdom legislation enacted 'before a Canadian court had occasion to pronounce on the validity of the measure'.[95]

As we shall see in Chapter 7, the Supreme Court of Canada would rule on the legal validity of the federal initiative before the United Kingdom Parliament had had the opportunity to act, but the majority reasons gave every indication that a Canadian court, even the Supreme Court of Canada, would have to recognise the validity of *any* legislative action by the United Kingdom Parliament amending the Canadian constitution.

In order to appreciate fully the problems with such an understanding of the Canadian Constitution it will be useful to turn now to the Independence theory. Before doing so, it is worth pointing out that throughout the long discussions regarding the Westminster Parliament's continuing sovereignty and the absence of a Canadian-based amendment procedure, there was very little mention of an alternative source of sovereignty in the Canadian people. According to British constitutional theory, sovereignty lay with the Westminster Parliament, and those who subscribed to the Imperial theory had to make do with that. But it was by no means far-fetched to suggest that sovereignty rested with the people, and that Canada could come by a new, domestic amendment procedure by means of a constituent assembly and/or referendum. Canada's neighbour, the United States, and her present and former Commonwealth siblings, Australia and

---

[93] Special Joint Committee (1980–1) 4:93–4.

[94] Reprinted in L. Cohen, P. Smith, P. Warwick (eds) *The Vision and the Game: Making the Canadian Constitution* (Calgary, 1987) 113, 121.

[95] Quoted by Mr Beatty in a question to the Minister of Justice, 1980–81 Special Joint Committee (1981–2) 4:49.

Ireland, had both drawn on this model, to a greater or lesser extent. The possibility of popular approval of a new Constitution was certainly discussed in Canada, as we shall see in Chapter 6, but the perceived weakness of this approach and general lack of interest in it may well have had something to do with the pervasiveness of the Imperial theory and its accompanying British constitutional notions.

6

Canada II: An Independent Constitutional Theory

The 'Independence' theory

The 'independence' in this theory refers both to the political independence of Canada, which is deemed by some proponents of the theory to have produced certain legal consequences, and to the more general idea that an independent Canadian understanding of the constitutional texts was available and potentially applicable through the courts in cases such as *Reference re Resolution to Amend the Constitution*.[1] Of course, if political *and* constitutional independence had been acquired in the 1920s or any time thereafter, there would not have been an issue regarding the independence of Canadian constitutional theory; it would have been taken for granted. However, as matters turned out, and as we have seen in the discussion of the Imperial theory, Canadians showed a marked reluctance to develop an independent theory until 1982 when the last vestiges of an omnipotent Parliament at Westminster had been (apparently) removed.

In one sense, it can be said, in spite of the comment just made, that Canada has always had its own constitutional theory. The constitutional writing and thinking regarding the British North America Act, 1867 could fall into this category. Both the Supreme Court of Canada and the Judicial Committee of the Privy Council have interpreted Canadian constitutional texts on the basis of certain background Canada-specific assumptions, regarding, for example, the requirements of federalism and the protection of minorities.[2] But the development of a distinct and independent Canadian constitutional theory, in the sense in which it is understood here, required more. The argument here advanced is that Canadian constitutional theory only went so far; in fact, the mainstream of Canadian legal thinking stopped short of theorising its constitutional foundations, including the constitutional amendment process. As long as the latter process was routed through Westminster, then apparently only British constitutional

---

[1] [1981] 1 SCR 753 (hereinafter *Patriation Reference*).

[2] The 1998 Secession Reference makes it clear that Canada-specific principles such as these have been at work in Canadian constitutional law for some time. More generally applicable principles such as constitutionalism, the rule of law and democracy have also been at work according to the Court. *Reference re Secession of Quebec* [1998] 2 SCR 217.

theory could govern. This proposition was seldom overtly stated, as we have seen, but its effect in stunting the development of Canadian constitutional thought, especially regarding constitutional amendment, was a constant, culminating in the *Patriation Reference*, which we will examine in Chapter 7. More 'independent' thinking might have taken into account considerations such as the legitimacy of the fundamental body of law in the eyes of all Canadians (English, French, aboriginal and multicultural communities, etc.), interpretation of that law with a mind to the facts of an evolving Canadian society, and generally acceptance of the possibility of separate British and Canadian understandings of Canadian constitutional instruments, whether such instruments originated in the United Kingdom or not.

As we have seen in the discussion of the Imperial theory, as viewed through the prism of Canadian constitutional amendment, Canadian understandings of the law were heavily constrained by a view of the Constitution as a British statute, governed by the law and theory generally applying to British statutes. It is quite conceivable that even a fully liberated and independent Canadian theory could nonetheless have viewed the constitutional amendment process as lacking any sufficiently clear legal signposts to justify any other conclusion than that the sovereign Westminster Parliament had been retained as the ultimate constituent power for Canada after 1931 and until 1982. But as we have seen, in many cases, the dominance of the Imperial theory made the very idea of a separate Canadian legal understanding of the role of Westminster seem impossible, or at least incredible.

The central theme in the Independence theory version of Canadian constitutional history was that the Constitution was a Canadian document, despite the fact that it had been formally brought into law by the Imperial Parliament and would for a time be interpreted in important ways by the highest Imperial court, the Judicial Committee of the Privy Council. The undeniable and ongoing link to the United Kingdom did not stop a relatively small number of Canadian constitutional commentators from considering the Constitution in its Canadian context. Some early observers worried about its legitimacy. Some proponents of a domestic amending formula felt that any modification should be ratified by the people. Others felt that no matter what formula was chosen it would have to be agreed upon and reflect the federal fact in Canada. These sentiments did not automatically engage the law, but they did reveal an understanding of a Constitution with strong roots in Canadian soil.

With time, even legal theories were to emerge, based to a large extent on the important events of 1926–31. Some Canadian constitutional commentators tentatively suggested that even the Privy Council could interpret Canada's fundamental law in a manner which took into account a changing Canadian reality. A distinctive Canadian interpretation foreshadowed the boldest step toward the possibility of uniquely Canadian rules regarding validity. Constitutional thinkers such as W.P.M. Kennedy and F.R. Scott provided a framework for this approach; and W.R. Lederman and former Supreme Court of Canada judge, Ivan Rand developed it into an independent Canadian understanding of constitutional theory which went well beyond the text of the 1867 Act (and even the Statute of Westminster, 1931). While Lederman's views in particular, representing a strong version of the Independence theory, were not accepted in the mainstream of Canadian constitutional thinking, and were ultimately rejected in the *Patriation Reference*, they did have some impact, perhaps in forcing the more probing constitutional thinkers to take a stand on the issue of an independent Canadian constitutional theory on amendment. Weaker versions of the Independence theory appeared in the writings of Peter Hogg from the 1970s onwards.

Perhaps as a result, in part, of these refreshing and liberating developments in Canadian constitutional thinking in the latter part of the twentieth century, federal and provincial politicians discussing the possibility of a domestic amending formula seem gradually to have worried far less about the feasibility of an eventual final break with the United Kingdom Parliament; and the proposed texts reflected this new confidence. The 'liberating developments' came to be questioned, however, partially as a result of a slightly cynical tack taken by the Trudeau government in the 1970s and early 1980s in response to its natural frustration with failed negotiations regarding 'patriation', the new amending formula and the various substantive amendments which were being proposed (principally a Charter of Rights and Freedoms). With the election of an avowedly separatist government in Quebec in 1976, the prospects for success seemed even more dim. The federal government began to resuscitate the idea that the United Kingdom Parliament was ultimately the constituent assembly for Canada, and that, accordingly, that Parliament could bring any proposal, even a unilateral federal proposal, into law. We have already seen the strong Imperial theory language used by the Minister of Justice in the parliamentary hearings on the unilateral proposal which the federal government eventually put forward.

Of course, the federal government was not wholly successful. We will see in Chapter 7 how the Supreme Court of Canada articulated much of the content of the Independence theory as part of its majority opinion on constitutional *convention*. Constitutional conventions were supposedly unenforceable by courts, but the Supreme Court of Canada's authority was such that the federal government had no alternative but to return to the negotiating table and come to an agreement which satisfied the requirements of Canadian federalism. While the *Patriation Reference*, and particularly the majority judgment regarding constitutional convention perhaps rescued the legitimacy of the 'patriation' project, it also left the Independence theory in its *legal* incarnation in shreds. Many questions were asked after the 1982 patriation process about how, in law, 'patriation' and 'independence' had come about. Some of those questions will be considered in Part III.

The Independence theory from Confederation to the Statute of Westminster

As mentioned earlier, the Independence theory was only rarely articulated early on in Canadian constitutional history. Perhaps its most obvious precursor was the sentiment, even at the time of Confederation, that called for *Canadian* acceptance of the British North America Act, 1867 as opposed to simple, formal legal process through the Imperial Parliament. This sentiment at least revealed an understanding of legitimacy and the existence of a Canadian attachment to the Constitution which was separate from an understanding of it as a British legal text, and, more importantly, separate from the standard Westminster-centred thinking on Canada's residual Westminster-based constitutional amendment procedure. Even during the discussions prior to Confederation, there were some who felt that the Confederation scheme should not be enacted by the Imperial Parliament before the electorate of the colonies concerned had been consulted. Joseph Howe of Nova Scotia expressed this view in a letter to Lord Russell:

In England no important change in the machinery of government is made without an appeal to the country. In the United States no amendment can be made to the constitution which is not sanctioned by two-thirds of the members of both Houses, and ratified by a majority of the electors.

Your Lordship will readily understand how our people would feel if their institutions, enjoyed for a century, were swept away by a surprise, without the constituencies, who have worked them peacefully and successfully, being consulted.[3]

Howe's argument, while not expressed in legal terms, served as a counterpoint to his central Canadian counterparts', Galt and McGee, emphasis on the Imperial Parliament as effectively the creator and protector of the 1867 Act.[4]

In the late nineteenth century two constitutional arguments arose which did not directly involve the question of amendment and constituent power, but which clearly had implications in that direction. First, in the 1870s, Chief Justice Draper of Ontario argued that that 'exclusive' grant of federal powers in section 91 of the 1867 Act excluded not the provincial authorities but rather the Imperial Parliament.[5] We have seen in the previous chapter that O'Sullivan took the view that this might mean that the Imperial Parliament

---

[3] Quoted in Hon. P.J.T. O'Hearn, 'Nova Scotia and Constitutional Amendment' (1966–67)12 McGill LJ 433, 435. Howe's examples from comparative constitutional law were not wholly accurate; however, the idea of a constitution being connected to a particular polity and therefore to a group of electors was a potentially powerful one, as American and Australian experience has revealed.

[4] See statements by Galt and McGee in Ch. 5 above and set out in P. Gérin-Lajoie, *Constitutional Amendment in Canada* (Toronto: University of Toronto Press, 1950) 4.

[5] *R v Taylor* (1875) 36 UCR 183, 220 (QB).

was forever prohibited from legislating in areas handed over to the Canadian authorities in sections 91 and 92 of the 1867 Act, but for reasons largely to do with the dominance of the Imperial theory, this view never attracted support.

Secondly, in the early 1890s, the Minister of Justice, Sir John Thompson, argued before the Colonial Secretary that Canadian legislative authorities had the power by virtue of sections 91 and 92 of the 1867 Act to repeal Imperial statutes passed prior to 1867 and to legislate as they saw fit in the legislative power granted to them. This argument was rejected by the Colonial Secretary, and it never attracted support amongst Canadian constitutional commentators; however, as late as 1905, the Supreme Court of Canada stated that it was 'still open for discussion whether the Parliament of Canada, having been given exclusive jurisdiction to legislate...may not by virtue of that jurisdiction be able to override Imperial legislation antecedent to the British North America Act, 1867'.[6] The independence-directed force of these arguments was somewhat undermined by concessions such as Thompson's to the effect that 'nobody can doubt that the parliament of Great Britain can at any time... repeal or amend the British North America Act, or exercise, in relation to Canada, its legislative powers over the subjects therein mentioned'.[7]

As we have seen, the absence of a domestic procedure in the 1867 Act was not seen as an important national issue until well into the twentieth century. But, as Gérin-Lajoie indicated, lack of interest did not mean that the issue had disappeared entirely from the political and constitutional agenda.[8] In 1883, an article in *The Bystander*, a Toronto periodical, stated that the power of constitutional amendment ought to be vested in Canada and be entrusted to the sovereign people.[9] At the turn of the century, J.S. Ewart called for Canada to acquire the fullest possible autonomy in the Commonwealth,[10] including a domestic procedure for amendment of the Constitution.[11] According to

---

[6] *Imperial Book Co v Black* (1905) 35 SCR 488, quoted in W.H.P. Clement, *The Law of the Canadian Constitution* (3rd edn, Toronto, Carswell, 1916) 63.

[7] Report to Governor General by Sir John Thompson, 3 August 1889, quoted in A.H.F. Lefroy, *The Law of Legislative Power in Canada* (Toronto: Toronto Law Book and Publishing, 1897–8) 222.

[8] See Gérin-Lajoie (1950)(n. 4 above) 221 et seq.

[9] Quoted ibid., 221: The Bystander, N.S., No. 4 (1883) 261–2.

[10] J.S. Ewart, *The Kingdom of Canada, Imperial Federation, The Colonial Conferences, the Alaska Boundary and other Essays* (Toronto: Morang & Co, 1908) 25:

I mean that we are to be as independent as the United Kingdom itself; that our Parliament shall be as omnipotent...as the Parliament at Westminster; that Downing Street shall have no more control over our legislation than Parliament Hill at Ottawa has over British statutes; that, even as Sir Elzear Taschereau and his [Supreme Court of Canada] colleagues exercise no supervision over British litigation, so also the Privy Council shall cease to interfere with us; in short, we shall be a nation 'self-existent, autonomous, sovereign', and 'capable of maintaining relations with all other governments'.'

[11] Gérin-Lajoie (1950) (n. 4 above) 221. See Ewart (1908) (n. 10 above). See also M. Ollivier, *L'avenir constitutionnel du Canada* (Montreal, 1935) 130.

Gérin-Lajoie: 'These were isolated cases and were considered as the claims of extremists if not real anti-imperialists'.[12]

It was only with World War I and its aftermath that the search for a domestic amending formula became a pressing national concern. Sir Clifford Sifton (a former Minister in the government of Wilfrid Laurier) suggested two possible methods of overcoming what he referred to as 'an anachronism and an absurdity'.[13] As a first possibility, he proposed a Conference of elected representatives from all parts of the country which would draft a new Constitution for approval by the people. A second possibility involved a Committee of federal and provincial delegates which would hear submissions from a wide range of constitutional lawyers before drafting a new constitution and submitting it to the people.[14] The idea of popular ratification of constitutional amendments or new constitutions resurfaced from time to time prior to 1982 but was doomed to be ignored in the face of the apparently overwhelming and exclusive legal requirement of passage through Westminster.

It was only in 1922 that the Independence theory found its first intellectual standard bearer. W.P.M. Kennedy may have acquired much of his affinity for Canadian constitutional law while collaborating with A.H.F. Lefroy,[15] but his theoretical framework could not have been more different. Not only did Kennedy reject the orthodox absolutist conception of sovereignty,[16] he viewed it as a stumbling block to constitutional progress in Canada and

---

[12] Gérin-Lajoie (1950) (n. 4 above) 221. Despite his strikingly independent vision for Canada, Ewart (1908) (n. 10 above) 58, accepted the strict legal position (emphasis added):

In form, our constitution is an imperial statute; in reality, it is the declaration of our own wish. In form, the Imperial Parliament can abrogate or alter our constitution as it pleases; in reality, the Imperial Parliament would as probably legislate for France as for Canada, except at Canada's request; in reality, we can to-morrow if we like, give ourselves any constitution that we care to assume.

As a matter of form, we are part of the British Empire. As a matter of living fact, we are an independent nation . . . we are masters of our own destiny [and] free politically and practically as any nation in the world to do exactly what we like.

[13] Quoted in Gérin-Lajoie (1950) (n. 4 above) 222.

[14] See Sir Clifford Sifton, 'Some Canadian Constitutional Problems' (1922) 3 Can Hist Rev 3. See also Ollivier (1935) (n. 11 above) 130 and Gérin-Lajoie (1950) (n. 4 above) 222.

[15] W.P.M. Kennedy, *The Constitution of Canada: An Introduction to its Development and Law* (London: Oxford University Press, 1922) x. Kennedy and Lefroy had collaborated on A.H.F. Lefroy, *Short Treatise on Canadian Constitutional Law* (Toronto: Carswell, 1918), Kennedy providing 'An Historical Introduction'. Kennedy was at that time Professor of Modern History at the University of Toronto. In 1922, he moved to the Faculty of Arts and Science where he taught history and political science, including a course on 'Federal Constitutions'. In 1927 he became Professor of Law and Federal Institutions, remaining in the Law School for the rest of his career, and serving as Dean throughout most of the next two decades. See R.C.B. Risk, 'The Many Minds of W.P.M. Kennedy' (1998) 48 UTLJ 353.

[16] See Kennedy (1922) (n. 15 above): 'Absolute sovereignty in the last resort proves to be an illusory but most perilous claim in the face of the facts of interdependence.' (p. vii); 'The older doctrine of sovereignty admitted no third course, but the active criticism of recent political thought working on such material as modern federations, leagues and unions so abundantly provide, rejects that absolutism.' (p. 454); 'In the last resort absolute power is a mystic doctrine which has relevance

the Empire.[17] He saw Canada's explorations regarding the limited and relative sovereignty of federalism and Imperial interdependence as a model for the world.[18] His theoretical approach had more in common with the realist or sociological intellectual traditions.[19] Over and over again, he stated that theory would have to conform to fact rather than vice versa.[20] And although he had no doubt that Britain would accept the fact of Canadian independence if Canadians opted for that, he clearly favoured a middle path or 'third course'[21] between 'complete independence or permanent inferiority of status'[22]—in fact the very solution that was about to be arrived at in the Balfour Declaration and Statute of Westminster, 1931.

Regarding two notoriously difficult constitutional conundrums, Kennedy was strikingly unfazed. First, on the seldom-asked question regarding how Canada might achieve its constitutional independence, Kennedy acknowledged that it could not be done by 'a federal Act of Parliament', but he stated quite matter-of-factly that 'an Act of the imperial Parliament' could 'constitutionally abrogate' Canada's 'constitutional dependence'.[23] He had no patience for 'theoretical difficulty which for many minds prevents a just appreciation' of Canada's present and potential place in the Empire.[24] Presumably, fact would triumph over

---

neither to men nor to states. Instead of the fiction of absolute sovereignty . . . we must be content with the reality of relative autonomy.' (p. 456).

[17] ibid.: 'The theoretical difficulty which for many minds prevents a just appreciation of the present position of Canada and the empire [is] the old view that political sovereignty by its very nature is one and indivisible.' (p. 454); 'Supposing Austinian doctrine of sovereignty had been rigidly accepted in the past, what a barrier it would have placed in the way of modern federalism within and without the British empire!' (p. 454); '[I]t is the insistence of the older doctrine of sovereignty, one exclusive and indivisible, which is the greatest stumbling-block in the way of the evolution of the greater unities which political exigencies, as distinct from political dogma, require to-day.' (pp. 455–6); 'We must not be swept off our feet by problems, by dilemmas, by political antinomies and all the stock-in-trade of theorists and of doctrinaires.' (p. 457).

[18] ibid.: 'Canada as a political unity has a distinctive, to some it may seem anomalous character. It is well worth studying . . . as a most significant illustration of that real and yet not absolute sovereignty which defies the older theories of government and thereby leads us to a truer conception of the state . . . the evolution of Canadian government has constituted a decisive challenge to the absolute Austinian doctrine of sovereignty.' (p. vii)

[19] For a fuller discussion of Kennedy's intellectual assumptions, see Risk (1998) (n. 15 above) 368–70.

[20] See Kennedy (1922) (n. 15 above): 'If the formula declares that there must be one single ultimate residence of all sovereign powers within a state, and the facts reveal a dual or multiple residence, so much the worse for the formula.' (p. 454); 'Necessity modifies our over-simple and over-rigid theories . . . We must therefore make our theory of sovereignty conformable to these facts.' (p. 455); 'And if the resulting development contradicts fond theories of sovereignty, these may be offered up, in thankfulness for the unity maintained and achieved, as a cheerful and willing sacrifice.' (p. 457). [21] ibid., 454.

[22] ibid., 454.   [23] ibid., 448.

[24] ibid., 454. See also W.P.M. Kennedy, 'The Imperial Conferences, 1926–1930' (1932) 190 LQR 191, 205: 'It is somewhat pathetic . . . to read addresses and such-like discoursing on the sovereignty of Parliament in this connection. It would lead me far afield to take up this barren challenge. No one disputes the sovereignty of Parliament, and anyone is welcome to tickle the ears of believers with legal dogma.'

theoretical dogma once again. Secondly, on the more familiar question whether the Westminster Parliament still had absolute power to legislate for Canada as Dicey and others had claimed, Kennedy's eventual reply was categorical and typical of his realist perspective: 'The position can be made clear, unequivocal and without reserve: any attempt by the Parliament of the United Kingdom to legislate for Canada apart from a request from and with the consent of Canada would simply mean a declaration of independence. I leave it at that.'[25]

Kennedy's independence-directed assertions ring especially true to modern ears, but they seemed to ignore an additional fact. Even if unwanted Westminster legislation would ultimately be rejected, and even if independence could be achieved, Kennedy did not indicate how judges and lawyers would explain what had occurred, especially given their preference for respecting the rule of law. Kennedy had broken the silence, but it would be up to later writers to attempt explanations. A further reason for Kennedy's reticence on these issues was that, like Ewart, no matter how independent his theoretical perspective, his strong practical preference was not for outright independence but for the sort of inter-dependence within the Commonwealth that both the Balfour Declaration and the Statute of Westminster, 1931 were designed to produce. After the achievement of that objective, Kennedy's constitutional writing became noticeably orthodox,[26] though he never subscribed to the Austin-Dicey aspect of that orthodoxy.[27]

---

[25] Kennedy (1932) (n. 24 above) 206. See also W.P.M. Kennedy, *The Constitution of Canada 1534–1937: An Introduction to its Development Law and Custom* (2nd edn, London: Oxford University Press, 1938) 521–2, where the passage quoted appeared again; however, 'I leave it at that' was replaced the equally emphatic 'Legal principles, if such exist, must yield to social facts'.

[26] See, e.g., W.P.M. Kennedy, 'Interpreting the Statute of Westminster' in W.P.M. Kennedy (ed.) *Essays in Constitutional Law* (London: Oxford University Press, 1934) 165:

It is hardly necessary to say that in strict law the parliament that enacted [the Statute of Westminster] can repeal. That fact the parliament of the United Kingdom cannot get rid of without a complete reconstruction of the commonwealth, which is not in question . . . however . . . the legal powers of the parliament at Westminster are effectually limited in this connexion by the desire and wishes of the dominions . . . This point has been admirably put by Professor Keith in words which may well become a permanent source of political illumination, in an essay which is perhaps the most brilliant and statesmanlike exposition of the situation. 'Legally,' he says, 'as Bacon long ago perceived, the imperial parliament cannot limit the powers of any successor, but it is equally clear that it can declare a constitutional principle which will be far more binding than any mere law'.

In opposition to the view preferred by himself and Berriedale Keith, Kennedy cited W. Ivor Jennings, *The Law and the Constitution* (1933) ch. iv.

[27] W.P.M. Kennedy 'Theories of Law and the Constitutional Law of the British Empire' in W.P.M. Kennedy, *Essays in Constitutional Law* (London: Oxford University Press, 1934) 18: 'No one seriously follows John Austin and sovereignty is as dead as Queen Anne.' See also W.P.M. Kennedy, 'Law as Social Science' (1934) South African LJ 100, concerning the teaching of constitutional law, 'I eliminate all the archeology of Anson and Dicey', and concerning the teaching of jurisprudence, 'We spend no time over the historical or analytical jurisprudence. Austin, Salmond and such-like make way for sociological jurisprudence as expounded by modern French, German and American jurists.' (p. 101), quoted in Risk (1998) (n. 15 above) 372.

The latter part of this discussion of Kennedy has already taken us beyond the Balfour Declaration and Statute of Westminster. We now consider the balance of Independence theory writing after 1931.

The Independence theory after the Statute of Westminster

As we have already seen in Chapter 5, both the Balfour Declaration and the Statute of Westminster, 1931 made surprisingly little impact on the prevailing Canadian constitutional theory. The dominant view was that Canada had indeed achieved a high degree of autonomy through these events, but that as a result of section 7 of the Statute, the *status quo ante* applied. The Westminster Parliament alone remained capable of amending most parts of the Canadian Constitution.

The debates of the time had, however, provoked some national self-examination in the discussions by Canadian constitutional thinkers on the question of what the *status quo ante* in fact was. It was accepted that, as a matter of constitutional convention, the Westminster Parliament would have to ratify any amendment proposed by Canada, but there was some doubt as to whether there was any law with respect to the requisite source and sanction of Canadian amendment initiatives. In the early 1930s, a theory which was known as the 'compact theory' of Confederation reached its zenith, having peaked once before in the 1880s. The compact theory had its earliest expression in the provincial rights movement which had considerable political impact in the years after Confederation.[28] The theory taught that the 1867 Act had been a compact or contract between the uniting colonies, now provinces, and that any modification of that contract would require the consent of all the provinces. There was, of course, a problem in the fact that all nine provinces (making up Confederation in the 1930s) had not been present at the negotiating table in 1866–7, but this was not seen by its proponents to take away from the essential thrust of the theory, i.e. that the legitimacy of the Canadian Constitution lay in the country's constituent parts—the provinces.

The compact theory had been presented in its most prominent and articulate form by Premier Howard Ferguson of Ontario. In a letter and memorandum to Prime Minister R.B. Bennett, he asserted that the Canadian Constitution was really 'the crystallization into law by an Imperial statute of an agreement made by the provinces' and that 'this agreement should not be altered without the consent of the parties to it'.[29] The memorandum went on to refer to the 'unwritten

---

[28] See R.C. Vipond, *Liberty and Community: Canadian Federalism and the Failure of the Constitution* (Albany: State University of New York Press, 1991). For a discussion of the 'compact theory' and its meaning in Canadian political writing, see E.R. Black, *Divided Loyalties* (Montreal: McGill-Queen's Press, 1975).

[29] 'Letter and memorandum of Hon. Howard Ferguson, Premier of Ontario, to the Prime Minister of Canada' set out in Canada, Senate, Report Relating to the British North America Act,

Constitution' and cited both history and judicial precedent in support of the vital role of the provinces with respect to amendment of the written constitutional text wherein provincial powers were delineated. The memorandum did not indicate whether the rule of unanimous provincial consent which flowed from the compact theory was legal or conventional, but clearly the makings of a legal argument were present.

This theory had the potential to add a new, and essentially Canadian, layer to the interpretation of the United Kingdom legislation making up the Canadian Constitution. And clearly if it had done so, it would have amounted to an important first step along the way to a Canadian understanding of constitutional amendment which went beyond the narrower confines of the British constitutional theories based on Westminster sovereignty.

However, the compact theory was immediately discredited by a number of Canadian critics. The most devastating and much-quoted attack was an article by Queen's University Norman Rogers.[30] Rogers was concerned, as were many others, that the theory would act as a roll of 'barbed-wire' in the way of Canadian constitutional development.[31] However, in criticising the compact theory he also gave his support to the Imperial theory by stating that, legally, only the Imperial Parliament was behind the 1867 Act and that nothing in history, practice or judicial precedent had changed that. The Rogers view of the matter was later endorsed by such commentators as the Parliamentary Counsel to the Senate, W.F. O'Connor[32] and the Law Clerk of the House of Commons, Maurice Ollivier. Ollivier bemoaned the rigidity inherent in the compact theory and added a chapter to one of his books in which he set out the various arguments against it.[33] This would not be the last time that a Canadian theory intended to provide Canadian parameters for the Westminster amendment process would be discredited in order to reduce the obstacles in the way of patriation.[34]

As we have seen in earlier discussions of this period regarding the Imperial theory, Canadian writing on constitutional fundamentals continued to be

---

1867, by W.F. O'Connor (Ottawa 1939; reprinted 1961) Annex 4, 134–9 (hereinafter O'Connor (1939)).

[30] Norman McL. Rogers, 'The Compact Theory of Confederation' (1931) 9 Can Bar Rev 400.

[31] ibid., 417.

[32] O'Connor (1939) (n. 29 above) Annex 4, 151:

... when the [1867] Bill was introduced and promoted, whereupon that sole outstanding compact stood fully and faithfully performed, so that when the Bill was enacted there was no outstanding compact or treaty, explicit or implicit of any kind whatever, but only an Imperial statute, into which all previous communings had merged and become as if they had never been.

. . .

Now, as in the beginning deliberately intended, the Imperial Parliament is, in my opinion, the arbiter and executor as between this Dominion and its provinces as to when and how and to what extent, if at all, the British North America Act shall be amended.

[33] Ollivier (1935) (n. 11 above) 18. See ch. V: 'Notre Constitution n'est pas un contrat.'

[34] This phenomenon was seen earlier, in Ch. 5 above, in the comments of the federal authorities prior to the 1980 attempt to patriate the Constitution unilaterally.

influenced to a very large extent by the idea of the ultimate, untrammelled and continuing sovereignty of the United Kingdom Parliament. The first author of a book-length discussion of Canadian constitutional amendment, Paul Gérin-Lajoie confirmed the essential elements of an Imperial theory, as we saw in Chapter 5. The Canadian Constitution was a British statute and, legally, it would continue to be dealt with according to the British constitutional rules, including the related rule of parliamentary sovereignty which was enforced by British and (so it was presumed) by loyal Canadian courts as well.[35]

Perhaps the most important opening for a possible independent Canadian theory of the Constitution was the idea presented by F.R. Scott in his 1950 article, 'The Redistribution of Imperial Sovereignty' which was referred to in Chapter 5.[36] Scott's idea of a new Canadian *Grundnorm* reduced the anxiety which had earlier prevailed regarding Canada *ever* being able to shake off the Imperial link (and that was perhaps its main importance), but it also presented possibilities for the development of a uniquely Canadian theory of the Constitution even prior to the formal independence-granting event.

Scott pointed out that Dicey's idea of sovereignty of Parliament had shown 'remarkable tenacity'.[37] He noted that even where a Dominion or colonial Constitution contained a permission to the local legislature to amend its Constitution (as with the then-recent amendments of 1949 which gave the federal Parliament in Canada the power to amend parts of the Canadian Constitution),[38] there was always the possibility that the permission might be withdrawn. This was the logic of 'the binding force of the doctrine of Imperial sovereignty'.[39] As we have seen, Scott did not deny 'the unlimited law-making power of the United Kingdom'.[40] In his view, it could only be tempered by the conventions by which the legislators of the Westminster Parliament might feel constrained. Even the Statute of Westminster, 1931, or the events which preceded it, did not make law out of convention, and in Scott's view, the new system 'obviously [left]

---

[35] Gérin-Lajoie (1950) (n. 4 above) 135 stressed in his study that Canadian request and consent and even provincial consent in certain circumstances were constitutionally required for amendment but he was careful to point out that such requirements were of a conventional sort. The only requirement of law was enactment by the Parliament at Westminster: 'The necessity of... enactment at Westminster is the one feature of the amending process which is determined entirely by law proper and does not result in any way from convention. Any attempt to alter the Constitution or to override it by other means would be repudiated and declared null and void by the courts.' Gérin-Lajoie was prepared to develop Canadian constitutional thinking regarding amendment to take into account such considerations as independence, federalism and legitimacy, but only at the level of convention. The ultimate legal process and the legal thinking governing it were matters for the Westminster Parliament and the ample United Kingdom-dominated literature regarding the latter's proper role. It is not surprising that Dr Gérin-Lajoie's highly influential study on amendment fits so well with the traditional approach of the majority on the legal questions in the Patriation Reference, as we shall see in Ch. 7 below.

[36] F.R. Scott, 'The Redistribution of Imperial Sovereignty' in Transactions of the Royal Society of Canada, June 1950, reprinted in F.R. Scott, *Essays on the Constitution* (Toronto: University of Toronto Press, 1977) 244.   [37] Scott (1950)(n. 36 above) 245.

[38] British North America Act (No. 2), 1949 (UK) (now repealed).

[39] Scott (1950) (n. 36 above) 245.   [40] ibid., 245.

in existence the ancient doctrine of Imperial sovereignty'.[41] It will be obvious from earlier discussions that this was strong Imperial theory.

That which was potentially liberating in Scott was his elaboration of the idea of a new Canadian *Grundnorm*, or basic norm. The idea of the *Grundnorm* is well known now, but until that moment, it had not made an entry into the mainstream of Canadian constitutional thinking. Scott expressed his indebtedness to R.T.E. Latham whose 'brilliant essay', 'The Law and the Commonwealth',[42] had applied Kelsen's approach in order to find a *Grundnorm* for the Commonwealth. Scott acknowledged the existing Commonwealth *Grundnorm* but also saw the possibility of a new version for Canada in due time:

> The process can be described . . . by saying that whereas till now we have had but one *Grundnorm*, one fundamental law for the Commonwealth, namely the ultimate proposition that all laws emanating from the United Kingdom Parliament must be obeyed in all the courts of the Commonwealth, in future we shall have many totally distinct systems of law each with its own *Grundnorm*, which may well vary from country to country. To borrow another analogy from the well-known eastern myth, we may say that until now all legal rules in Canada . . . have derived their validity from the elephant of the B.N.A. Act, which stood firmly upon the turtle of the sovereignty of the United Kingdom Parliament. Beneath the turtle nothing further has existed to support a stable universe. Now the various Dominions are getting their own turtles, and we are looking for a Canadian turtle.[43]

Scott did not explain how a Canadian court would explain or sanction this swapping of turtles, and, more importantly for our immediate purposes, he did not explain why it was that a Canadian *Grundnorm* had not already developed if not by 1867 then at least since 1926–31.[44]

Although Scott had not approved of the immediate development of a Canadian *Grundnorm*, he apparently calmed those who had been concerned that it would never be possible to sever the so-called Commonwealth or Imperial *Grundnorm*. In an article published soon after that of Scott, Gérin-Lajoie adopted Scott's approach. Gérin-Lajoie stated that once Canada had acquired the means to amend its own Constitution, Canadians would be masters, even in legal terms, of their development, and not even the Westminster Parliament

---

[41] Scott (1950) (n. 36 above) 245.

[42] R.T.E. Latham, 'The Law and The Commonwealth' in W.K. Hancock, (ed.) *Survey of British Commonwealth Affairs*, Vol. 1 (London: Oxford University Press, 1931) 517, reprinted with a Foreword by W.K. Hancock but with otherwise unaltered pagination as R.T.E. Latham, *The Law and the Commonwealth* (Oxford: Oxford University Press, 1949). For a detailed assessment of Latham's contribution, see Ch. 4 above and P. Oliver, 'Canada, Quebec and Constitutional Amendment' (2000) 49 UTLJ 519.   [43] Scott (1950) (n. 36 above), 246.

[44] Scott did not go into any detail in describing Kelsen's theory, but one can presume that Scott understood the *Grundnorm* as a logical premise, and not therefore one which could easily or regularly adapt or evolve in response to various non-revolutionary extrinsic developments. Latham appeared to subscribe to an evolutionary view of the *Grundnorm*. It may be that Scott did not see any clear legal markers even to justify an evolution in the *Grundnorm*.

would be able to affect that independence.[45] This too needed further explaining, as we shall see in Part III.

The Independence theory developed

Perhaps for the reasons set out by constitutional commentators such as Scott and Gérin-Lajoie, the government advisers appeared to be less concerned with the question of terminating the effects of even the remarkably tenacious doctrine of Imperial sovereignty.[46] While government literature continued to bemoan the humiliating anachronism of an unpatriated Constitution, the proposed independence legislation of the early 1960s dealt with the matter in a more straightforward manner than, say, many of the schemes which had been devised in the 1930s.[47] As we have seen, however, the common understanding in all these proposals was that the Constitution and even its *Grundnorm*, were domiciled in the United Kingdom until the new domestic amending formula had been found. But even the hope-turned-belief that a complete and irreversible transfer of sovereignty could take place should perhaps be identified as the next step in an Independence theory that was only just beginning to be developed in detail. The fuller articulation of an Independence theory, at least as an *immediate* or pre-patriation possibility, waited on two important Canadian constitutional thinkers for its most forceful exposition: former justice of the Supreme Court of Canada and Dean of the Faculty of Law of the University of Western Ontario, the Honourable Ivan Rand, and Queen's University law professor, W.R. Lederman.

In the Oliver Wendell Holmes Lecture delivered in 1960 at the Harvard Law School and later published in the *Canadian Bar Review*, Ivan Rand set out a

---

[45] See P. Gérin-Lajoie, 'Du pouvoir d'amendement constitutionnel au Canada' (1951) 29 Can Bar Rev 1136, 1178n.

[46] G. Marshall, *Constitutional Conventions* (Oxford: Oxford University Press, 1984) 205 explains that by 1960, British constitutional draftsmen had come to assume that British parliamentary sovereignty with respect to a former colony could be terminated by means of a final Independence Act (e.g. the Nigeria Independence Act of 1960). Their Canadian counterparts may have shared this assumption.

[47] See, e.g., the Ollivier proposal described in Gérin-Lajoie (1950) (n. 4 above) 240–1. For uncomplicated newer proposals see the 1961 Fulton Formula, s. 7 and the 1964 Fulton-Favreau Formula, s. 10 in A.F. Bayefsky (ed.) *Canada's Constitution Act, 1982: A Documentary History*, Vol. I, (Toronto: McGraw-Hill Ryerson, 1989) 14, 17. The 1965 White Paper explained the transitional process in uncomplicated fashion:

The purpose of the proposed amending formula . . . is to transfer to legislative authorities in Canada—acting whether singly or in combination—complete and exclusive power of amendment over the whole of the Constitution of Canada. The formula would thus terminate all authority now vested in the Parliament of the United Kingdom to enact statutes forming part of Canadian law.

Hon. G. Favreau, *The Amendment of the Constitution of Canada* (Ottawa: Queen's Printer, 1965) 10. See, however, the complex federal solution to this problem recommended by the Special Joint Committee in 1972 in Bayefsky (1989) 231–2.

theory of the Constitution which was based on the legal significance of the events of 1926–31. Rand saw the Statute of Westminster, 1931 not so much as a law-creating text, but rather as 'the formal confirmation of the substance of the existing state of things',[48] specifically the fact that Canada 'had come formally of age'.[49] The question which would have come more naturally to the minds of a Canadian audience was whether such confirmation could have any legal force given the continuing sovereignty of the Westminster Parliament and the pre-servation of that Parliament's power to amend the Canadian Constitution after 1931. Rand's answer was that Canada's coming of age had legal effects, and that unwanted interference by the United Kingdom Parliament, even regarding amendment of the Constitution, would be ignored by a Canadian court, even if this meant a Wade-style disguised legal revolution:

> The question may be raised of the political *and legal* force of resolutions passed by Imperial Conferences [of 1926 and 1930] and confirmed by legislation. It cannot, in my view, be less than this: that they are to be treated as creating constitutional commitments of a permanent nature, which once approved and entered upon become irrevocable as self-executing conventions, placed, by that fact, beyond repudiation. They have not become the subject of juridical examination but that might happen. *Should, for example, the British Parliament, of its own initiative, purport to repeal the Act of 1931 what would be the position of Canadian legislation and of Canadian courts? The answer must be that the purported repeal would not be recognized....* The acceptance of the convention concludes resort to conflicting statutory power; if that were not so, the bonds of colonial relation embodied in statutes could never constitutionally be dissolved, there could be no ter-mination by statutory enactment, a link of that nature would be perpetual; even express renunciation could be revoked. Actual or constructive revolution would then be the only means of establishing a status of independence. But treaties can effect finalities in the transfer of titles or the recognition of sovereignty; and there is nothing in the nature of such a convention that prevents a similar result in the creation of a constitutional title to independence by which a status is created the modification of which is withdrawn from future parliamentary competence. The relation between kingdom and colony is founded on the idea of ultimate evolution to independence; and the statutory removal of legis-lative subordination becomes a formal renunciation of suzerainty; the disappearance of paramountcy becomes the recognition and investment of sovereign power.[50]

Was this not the espousal of a Canadian *Grundnorm* that was already operative in 1960, at the time of Rand's lecture (and apparently since 1931)? The con-ventions that Rand refers to do not appear to be constitutional conventions; rather they are conventions in the nature of treaties. And even if understood as constitutional conventions in the Diceyan sense, they were clearly conventions with a difference, in that they could be seen, in Rand's eyes, to determine the very rules of validity used by Canadian courts. They had 'crystallised', to use a

---

[48] Hon. Ivan C. Rand, 'Some Aspects of Canadian Constitutionalism' (1960) 38 Can Bar Rev 135, 139.   [49] ibid., 138.
[50] ibid., 148–9 (emphasis added).

term which would become popular at a later moment. That which might be a convention in British terms (no legislation for Canada to be enacted by the Westminster Parliament without Canadian request and consent) could at the same time be a basic rule of constitutional law in Canadian terms. That was a powerful and potentially liberating idea.[51]

In order to explain the peculiarity of an independent Canada having left the power to amend the Constitution of Canada with the United Kingdom Parliament, Rand provided a powerful analogy. He no longer saw Westminster as an omnipotent legislator, but rather as 'a bare legislative trustee'.[52] The United Kingdom Parliament could be seen to have been given a power to deal with the Constitution of Canada but only in a manner which was consistent with the wishes of an otherwise sovereign and independent Canada, which in turn was absolutely entitled to call for personal control over the constitutional trust property whenever it might wish.[53]

If the United Kingdom Parliament acted as a bare legislative trustee, then there was still some question as to who might be the beneficiary. Was it Canada as a whole, speaking through the voice of its federal Parliament, or was it Canada as a whole, as represented by both the federal and provincial levels of government?[54] The demise of the compact theory of Confederation had made it difficult to argue that unanimous provincial consent was required, by law or convention, but clearly an argument was available to the effect that at least some provincial consent was required. Had not section 7(3) of the Statute of Westminster been designed to protect the federal division of powers? These and other arguments were eventually developed by Professor Lederman in the 1970s and resurfaced as part of the dissenting provinces' arguments in the *Patriation Reference*.

In the 1960s, however, Lederman had not yet come to the more independent perspective he would subsequently espouse. In a 1967 article, he set out some of

---

[51] It is significant that this view should come from a former Supreme Court of Canada justice who had served through the transformation from Privy Council to Supreme Court of Canada as the highest court of Canadian appeal. The Privy Council had a natural desire to interpret different constitutions according to one Imperial constitutional theory, even if it sometimes stated the contrary. The Supreme Court of Canada taking over as highest constitutional court would have less interest in maintaining theoretical and doctrinal coherence, constitutionally speaking, Commonwealth-wide. It could be more interested in Canadian concerns and could develop a uniquely (or independent) Canadian constitutional theory. That which the more activist Rand might have been willing to do in the late 1950s was ultimately not to appeal to a more conservative Supreme Court in the early 1980s.

[52] Rand (1960) (n. 48 above) 145.

[53] A bare legislative trustee deals with the trust property not according to the original wishes of the settlor (unless the settlor is also the absolutely entitled beneficiary as in a nomineeship), but according to the (by now) absolutely entitled beneficiary. This beneficiary can call for the property to be transferred to him or her at any time, according to his or her convenience. Although the legal title still remains with the trustee, that beneficiary's absolute beneficial title causes him or her to be viewed as the owner for all intents and purposes.

[54] Aboriginal Canadians did not have a constitutional voice at this stage of Canada's constitutional development. That was to come, admittedly to a limited extent, only after 1982.

the principles which would later enable him to develop an understanding of the law regarding constitutional fundamentals that related more specifically to the Canadian reality.[55] In other respects, however, he appeared at this stage to accept some of the precepts of the Imperial theory.

It is significant that Lederman began his argument with a reminder that the legal system is based on what Kelsen referred to as the *Grundnorm* or basic norm.[56] This placed his thinking on the line developed by F.R. Scott. Lederman subscribed to the view that the Constitution must be found not only in the (British) statute book, but also in general principles and the common law.[57] In commenting on the Favreau White Paper, which as we have seen[58] was laden with Imperial theory language, Lederman admitted that there was 'a respect in which the Canadian Constitution is not now and never has been at home', specifically in the sense that in certain cases amendment of the Constitution required that steps be taken in the United Kingdom. But his analysis made plain that the legal rules regarding amendment were governed by an independent Canadian understanding:

... we see that our basic law of amendment has been made by longstanding official precedent, custom and practice modifying the constitutional law of the old British Empire ... Anyone who doubts the validity and force of such custom, convention and practice should read again the preamble to the Statute of Westminster, 1931, which makes it clear that even that statute purports to be declaratory of a basic 'constitutional position' already 'established' by other means than statute ... [59]

The Fulton-Favreau process had not provoked questions regarding the idea of a legal requirement of Canadian request and consent in addition to the provincial agreement which might be said to make up that request and consent. Accordingly, in 1967, Lederman did not have to develop his ideas on those issues. One decade later, however, there was increasing talk of the supposed legality of a unilateral federal initiative to 'patriate' the Constitution, and this provoked Lederman's most forceful interventions. Some background information may be necessary.

It should be pointed out first that while the discrediting of the compact theory had quieted the claim that unanimous provincial consent was required in law, there were still those who believed that there was a strong convention, or at least a frequent practice, to that effect. A most important, if qualified, statement of this convention or practice could be found in the Favreau White Paper of 1965:

The fourth general principle is that the Canadian Parliament will not request an amendment directly affecting federal-provincial relationships without prior consultation

---

[55] W.R.Lederman, 'The Process of Constitutional Amendment for Canada' (1966–7) 12 McGill LJ 371, reprinted in W.R. Lederman, *Continuing Constitutional Dilemmas* (Toronto: Butterworths, 1981) 81 (hereinafter Lederman (1966–7) cited to 1981 pagination).

[56] ibid., 82.   [57] ibid., 82.

[58] Favreau (1965) (n. 47 above). See Ch. 5 above for discussion.

[59] Lederman (1966–7) (n. 55 above) 84.

and agreement with the provinces . . . The nature and degree of provincial participation in the amending process, however, have not lent themselves to easy definition.[60]

Unanimous consent from the Provinces had been one of the hallmarks of the Fulton-Favreau formula and ultimately the refusal of only two provinces had sunk the project. There were many who felt that even such a conventional rule would prevent Canada from ever agreeing on 'patriation' and a domestic amending formula. The next major proposal, the Victoria formula of 1971,[61] contained a more flexible amending formula proposal, but it too was thwarted by a lack of unanimous provincial consent. As we have seen, throughout the 1970s many federal officials were intent on reminding Canadians of the humiliating and anachronistic fact of the continued link to the United Kingdom Parliament for amendment of key parts of the Constitution. It also became common for federal documents to point out that whatever past practice had been, the federal Parliament was still constitutionally entitled to proceed unilaterally to Westminster. The Special Joint Committee of the Senate and the House of Commons on the Constitution tabled a report in March of 1972 in which it made the following statement:

The present amending procedure is humiliating to an independent state, but it is nevertheless effective. Amendment formally takes place by act of the British Parliament, which follows the constitutional convention that the United Kingdom Parliament will make any amendment to the British North America Act which is requested by the Government of Canada. Such a request is traditionally preceded by a joint address of both Houses of the Parliament of Canada. Some argue that there is a secondary convention that the Canadian Parliament will request amendments only with unanimous consent of all the provinces, or of the provinces affected where not all provinces are involved. However, the British Parliament has shown, by its refusal to entertain objections from Provincial Governments in disputed cases, that it will follow the request of the Canadian Parliament without reference to the views of the Provinces. It seems therefore safe to assert that, as a matter of mixed law and convention, the Parliament of Canada possesses the unilateral power to change the Constitution. Nevertheless Parliament has chosen not to exercise that power . . . [62]

In a letter to the provincial Premiers, dated 31 March 1976, Prime Minister Trudeau repeated this view,[63] and by 1978 it had been incorporated in the 'observations' of the Federal-Provincial Relations Office, a branch of the federal

---

[60] Favreau (1965) (n. 47 above) 15.

[61] Canada, Constitutional Conference, *Statement of Conclusions* (8–9 February 1971), reprinted in Bayefsky (1989) (n. 47 above) 210.

[62] Canada, Parliament, Special Joint Committee of the Senate and the House of Commons on the Constitution of Canada, *Final Report*, 16 March 1972 (Chairmen: Senator G.L. Molgat, Mr Mark MacGuigan, M.P.), reprinted in Bayefsky (1989) (n. 47 above) 231.

[63] Letter from P.E. Trudeau to provincial Premiers (31 March 1976), reprinted in Bayefsky (1989) (n. 47 above) 314: 'we are satisfied that . . . action by the Parliament of Canada does not require the consent of the provinces . . .'; 'at present it is the federal Parliament alone which goes to Westminster, and the degree of consultation of or consent by the provinces is only a matter of convention about which there can be differences of view'.

government. The 'observations' were borrowed to a large extent from the earlier 'principles' of the Favreau White Paper, but significant additions appeared in the later formulation:

The fourth observation is that, *although not constitutionally obliged to do so*, the Government of Canada, before asking Parliament to adopt a Joint Address, sought and obtained the consent of all provinces on the three amendments . . . that involved the distribution of powers.[64]

The statement regarding absence of constitutional obligation indicated that if ever the federal government decided to abandon its practice of obtaining provincial consent it would meet no legal impediment, and even changes altering the distribution of powers could be validly enacted if passed by the United Kingdom Parliament. If there was any scope for development of an Independence theory, the federal government appeared to be wilfully blind to it.

The Independence theory prior to Patriation

In an article published in 1978, Lederman provided a contrary opinion, and in so doing expanded on the ideas which had been put forward in the 1960s by Rand and himself.[65] He began his 1978 piece by stating that constitutional law (and therefore constitutional theory) is intimately related to the people whose affairs it governs: 'For me, constitutional law arises out of our whole history and tradition as a people, and one must constantly relate these rules and principles of law and government to the organic life of our national community, from which they derive their validity.'[66] Regarding the law of constitutional amendment, he insisted that far from lacking an amending formula, Canada actually had 'in Canadian constitutional law a full-fledged amending process'.[67] According to Lederman's account, this process had evolved over the nation's history. In 1867: 'The original power of the British Parliament to change the B.N.A. Act, one of its own statutes, was plenary and unlimited.'[68] Over time, however, the rules on amendment had evolved to the point where 'this plenary power [was] now exercised by the British Parliament only in response to and in accordance with a proper request from Canada, and not on its own initiative'.[69] The rules regarding the 'proper request' had also evolved to the point where it could be said that the Constitution at least required substantial provincial compliance in cases involving changes to the federal-provincial relationship. In support of this

---

[64] Canada, Federal-Provincial Relations Office, *The Canadian Constitution and Constitutional Amendment* (1978), reprinted in Bayefsky (1989) (n. 47 above) 459, 468 (emphasis added).

[65] W.R. Lederman, 'Constitutional Amendment and Canadian Unity' in *Special Lectures of the Law Society of Upper Canada 1978: The Constitution and the Future of Canada* (Toronto, 1978), reprinted in Lederman, *Continuing Canadian Constitutional Dilemmas* (n. 55 above) 91.

[66] Lederman (1978) (n. 65 above) 92.   [67] ibid., 97.   [68] ibid., 97.

[69] ibid., 97.

evolution, Lederman emphasised that the Statute of Westminster, 1931 purported to declare constitutional principles already established, and he noted that there were weighty judicial precedents[70] in which the process of 'crystallization of constitutional usage into a rule of constitutional law'[71] had been recognised and described. Lederman stressed that such rules of constitutional law would have the greatest impact in governing political practice, but he denied that such was their only purpose:

There may be some doubts about the status of these rules. Are they full-fledged constitutional laws or are they something less? Are they merely political conventions of the constitution that do not have the force of law and which can, to some extent at least, be varied or disregarded? *In my view these rules are basic constitutional laws in every sense* and should be recognized as such by the governments and parliaments concerned, including the British.[72]

In the end, however, Lederman acknowledged, of course, that only the Supreme Court of Canada would be able to determine the matter.[73] However basic these rules were, they were clearly not recorded in an unambiguously clear text. In some cases, it was clearly possible to say that they had already achieved the level of convention. But in the case of the most important, most vital rules of the constitution it was crucial, in Lederman's view, that they be referred to as law and respected as law, even in advance of their formal recognition by the courts or eventual formulation in a legal text.

Perhaps Lederman did not expand on these ideas as much as many would have liked. But his argument was fundamental, especially to the development of what has been described as an Independence theory. It allowed that Canadian conventions regarding Canadian request and consent or substantial provincial agreement could evolve into basic rules of the Constitution. It also permitted a *separate* analysis of British and Canadian constitutional law, which was something that the Imperial theory inhibited. The practice of amending the 1867 Act only with Canadian request and consent could develop into and remain a convention in British constitutional law and for British courts; however, it could at the same time evolve from convention into law in so far as the Canadian Constitution and Canadian courts were concerned. As long as one accepted the possibility of independent British and Canadian constitutional theory, the difference was possible. There might be objections as to the soundness of constitutional analysis in the different cases, but the possibility could not be denied. And ultimately it would be up to the courts of Canada to decide.

As we shall see, part of the problem which many constitutional lawyers might have had with this analysis is that once a practice has been identified as a

---

[70] *Reference re Weekly Rest in Industrial Undertakings Act* [1936] 3 DLR 673, 678–9 (*per* Sir Lyman P. Duff, CJC), and *Attorney-General for Ontario v Attorney-General for Canada* [1947] AC 127, 153–4 (*per* Lord Jowitt).
[71] *Reference re Weekly Rest in Industrial Undertakings Act* (1936) (n. 70 above) 678–9.
[72] Lederman (1978) (n. 65 above) 95 (emphasis added).   [73] ibid., 103.

convention it may not then simply become law by further practice; it must be formally enacted[74] or linked to another legal rule[75] in order for the courts to recognise it as law proper. This is a reasonable analysis, especially where one is examining a single legal system. However, in the case of new legal systems which have emerged from older legal systems, it may be that that which is a convention in the older system (Britain) may at the same time be a fundamental rule of the new legal system (Canada), i.e. a prerequisite of its independence, as seen from the younger system's point of view. Such fundamental rules may never be recorded in statute or determined by courts but, according to one view of the matter, it is nonetheless appropriate for commentators to describe them as law if they are very confident that a court would, for example, immediately recognise the rule if ever asked to do so.[76] The rule regarding request and consent from Canada for constitutional amendment by the Westminster Parliament is a good example.

Some of the points made above were recognised by Peter Hogg who, as Lederman noted in the footnotes to his 1978 article,[77] disagreed with Lederman's assertion regarding the full-fledged constitutional status of some basic practices but at least acknowledged that apparent conventions could be transformed into law by judicial recognition. In the first edition of his highly influential Canadian constitutional law text published in 1977, Hogg stated his own opinion regarding the convention requiring Canadian request and consent: 'If the Parliament at Westminster enacted a statute purporting to alter the law of Canada without the request and consent of Canada, the courts would not deny validity to that statute.'[78] That statement, reflecting the Imperial theory assumptions, amounted to a prediction of the behaviour of Canadian courts. With characteristic sensitivity to the range of alternative arguments, Professor Hogg considered another potential scenario: 'If a court did give a remedy for a breach of convention, for example, by declaring invalid a statute enacted for Canada by the United Kingdom Parliament without Canada's request or consent . . . then we would have to change our language and describe the rule which used to be thought of as a convention as a rule of the common law.'[79] Hogg could have added that a British court might refuse to recognise the same convention.

[74] See, e.g., the Parliament Act 1911 (UK) which, *inter alia*, converted the conventional rule that the House of Lords should not block money bills into a legal rule.

[75] See *Attorney-General v Jonathan Cape Ltd* [1976] QB 752 in which the convention of collective ministerial responsibility received legal protection as a result of its being connected to the already-existing law of confidence, appropriately enlarged and adapted for public law purposes.

[76] Some commentators acknowledge the problem of deciding whether or not to recognise rules which, however important they are, have not been recognised by courts or legislatures. See Latham (1937) 521. For further discussion regarding different legal system perspectives and uncertainty in the ultimate rule of recognition, see Ch. 12 below.   [77] Lederman (1978) (n. 65 above) 95.

[78] P.W. Hogg, *Constitutional Law of Canada* (Toronto: Carswell, 1977) 7.

[79] ibid., 8. See p. 17n: 'There is little doubt the imperial Parliament could disregard the convention, although it is possible that Canadian courts might refuse to recognize as Canadian law a statute enacted in breach of the convention.'

In general, however, Hogg's opinions were those which have been aligned under the Imperial theory. He stated, for instance, in no uncertain terms: 'The provinces have no legal role in the amending process, and their interests can be affected by the unilateral action of the federal Parliament.'[80] He acknowledged that 'This is intolerable to the provinces, and . . . is inconsistent with orthodox conceptions of federalism',[81] but he considered only the possibility that 'the practice of securing provincial consent to amendments altering the distribution of powers [had] hardened into a binding convention'.[82] In no sense could it be seen to engage the law.

It would be inappropriate to assign the entirety of Hogg's writing to either the Imperial or the Independence theory, and of course there is no need to do so. His legal instincts as expressed in the first edition of his text were conservative, in the sense that he did not predict that the Canadian courts would invalidate unwanted United Kingdom legislation. This conclusion along with others appeared to set him with the Imperial theorists. Hogg clearly recognised the possibility of an independent Canadian constitutional understanding of constitutional problems based on the principles flowing from factors such as federalism, independence and legitimacy. However, he did not feel that there was sufficient justification for recognition of such factors in the law relating to Canadian constitutional amendment, whatever their value might be in considering constitutional conventions. Hogg examined in some detail the legal and theoretical problems associated with 'patriation', and we will have occasion to consider his analysis in Chapter 11.

Popular sovereignty considered

Before moving on to consider the traces of an Independence theory in the *Patriation Reference*, it may be appropriate to consider one final pre-patriation manifestation of the Independence theory: the idea of direct recourse to the Canadian people. We have seen the referendum proposal earlier in the ideas of Sir Clifford Sifton. In 1949, Gérin-Lajoie also mentioned the idea of a referendum as part of a proposed constitutional amendment ratification process, though in the end he did not endorse it.[83] The possibility of recourse to referendums[84] in search of legitimacy for a constitution reflected a sensitivity to the Canadian basis for the Constitution, regardless of the traditional legal requirement of enactment of amendments by Westminster. In that sense, the idea was closely connected to the Independence theory. But if proponents of referendums still insisted that, in law, amendment had to go through the Westminster

---

[80] ibid., 19.   [81] ibid., 19.   [82] ibid., 20.

[83] Gérin-Lajoie (1950) (n. 4 above) 267–77.

[84] In the United Kingdom, the pedantic debate about 'referenda' versus 'referendums' has been resolved in favour of the latter, at least as far as United Kingdom law is concerned.

Parliament, then clearly the British idea of Parliamentary sovereignty held sway over the Canadian legitimising process. Thus even the federal government in 1980–1, wedded as it was (if only for convenience) to an Imperial theory view, proposed various referendum-based methods of choosing a new amending formula and amending the Constitution, but it did so only as a part of a process which drew its legal validity, in the federal legal advisers' eyes, from Westminster.[85]

A strong Independence theory was, however, evident in the writings of those who suggested that British parliamentary sovereignty was not the operative ultimate rule of the Canadian legal system. They suggested that a new Constitution could, if necessary, derive its legal validity solely from the sovereign people in a referendum. Clearly this way of thinking had little to do with classical British constitutional theory and much more to do with American thinking. An example of this view could be found in the writing of Edward McWhinney. In his post-patriation publication, *Canada and the Constitution, 1979–82*,[86] McWhinney expressed views which he had made known before 1982, stating confidently that recourse to the people of Canada in order to 'patriate' the Constitution would have been not only more legitimate but legal as well, even without the final sanction of Westminster:

In an era of constitutional democracy, constituent power comes from the people, and there is little reason to believe that had Prime Minister Trudeau proceeded boldly by going directly to the people with a new constitutional project, the courts or any other authority would have stood in the way of any resounding endorsement. A legally unimpeachable, popular source of sovereignty would thus have been established (in place of or as a supplement to the older imperial basis, now presumably fallen into disuse), just as it had been in the United States and in France.'[87]

Had Canada followed this route it would have joined what McWhinney referred to as 'a clear trend, observable throughout the world and without exception to "bring the people in" to any process for drafting and adoption of a new constitutional charter, or even for substantial renewal of an old one'.[88] It should be noted that McWhinney's ideas had their echo in French Canada in the writings of Gil Rémillard, Professor of constitutional law and later Minister of Justice for the Province of Quebec.[89]

The importance of the referendum alternative is not that it would certainly have been accepted as legal by the Canadian courts, but rather that it represented

[85] See October 1980 proposed resolution, s. 38(3) and s. 42; February 1981 proposed resolution, s. 42(3) and s. 46; and April 1981 proposed resolution, s. 43(3) and s. 47, reprinted in (1984–5) 30 McGill LJ 753 et seq.

[86] E. McWhinney, *Canada and the Constitution, 1979–82* (Toronto: University of Toronto Press, 1982). See also E. McWhinney, 'The How, When and Why of Constitution-Making: The Machinery for Developing a New Constitution' in G.-A. Beaudoin *et al.* (eds) *Mécanismes pour une nouvelle constitution* (Ottawa: Éditions de l'Université d'Ottawa, 1981) 65.

[87] McWhinney (1982) (n. 86 above) 46.

[88] ibid., 121.   [89] See *Le Devoir [de Montréal]*, 26 juin 1980, 13.

an attempt to think about the Canadian constitution in terms other than those of Westminster-based sovereignty. As we know, the federal government eventually stuck by its strict interpretation of constitutional validity and proceeded via Westminster. That approach was eventually recognised by the Supreme Court of Canada, but, as we have seen, other possibilities for an independent Canadian constitutional theory were encountered along the way.

In the preceding chapters, two theories have been described and documented. The purpose in doing this was to understand better the constitutional transition of 1982. It is to that event that we now turn in an attempt to explain 'patriation' and Canadian constitutional independence. It may be useful to provide a summary of the Imperial and Independence theories as we have encountered them so far while anticipating the appearance of those theories in the *Patriation Reference*.

The Imperial theory viewed the Canadian law of the Constitution in its textual or enacted form. Prior to 1982, as a result of the failure in 1867 and 1931 to enact a written, Canadian-based amending formula, amendment of the Constitution of Canada could in vital respects only take place by using 'the old machinery' of the Westminster Parliament. As long as this anachronistic and, to some, humiliating situation persisted, it would be correct to say, according to the Imperial theory understanding, that the Canadian Constitution remained domiciled in the United Kingdom. We have seen that, consistent with this idea of British domicile, constitutional considerations, especially those regarding amendment, were highly influenced by the main tenets of British constitutional theory, notably the doctrine of absolute, untrammelled and continuing Parliamentary sovereignty. In the *Patriation Reference*, as we shall see, a majority of the Supreme Court of Canada appeared to affirm this notion of Westminster Parliamentary sovereignty and, in doing so, adopted the attitude of a *British or Imperial* court toward that Parliament. The Supreme Court of Canada seemed to make clear that it would not review or declare invalid any legislation emanating from Westminster so long as that Parliament retained its untrammelled powers *vis-à-vis* Canada. Considerations of Canadian independence, federalism and legitimacy, for example, could not engage the law, although they might be relevant in the development and recognition of constitutional conventions. Any rule regarding the requirement and nature of Canadian request and consent for constitutional amendments was apparently only a convention. The Imperial theory did not take on board the idea that a rule could be, at one and the same time, a convention of the British Constitution but an enforceable law of the Canadian Constitution. It would have been up to the Supreme Court of Canada to declare it so, but that Court was not willing to do so. As we shall see in Chapter 7, there may have been good reasons for its reticence, given the highly political nature of such a decision and the Court's non-elected status. More surprising than its cautious decision was the narrowness of its theoretical framework. As long as the Canadian Constitution remained domiciled in Britain,

Canadian constitutional theory was subsumed, at the highest level, by British (or Commonwealth) theory.

Furthermore, neither the Imperial theory nor the judges in the *Patriation Reference* who appeared to subscribe to it, provided an explanation for how the untrammelled powers of the Westminster Parliament could be terminated. Earlier this century it was assumed by some not to be possible or desirable. Later some legislators and their advisers devised intricate schemes in order to cut the knot. Since 1982 and the *Quebec Veto Reference*[90] the Supreme Court of Canada and most Canadians assumed that the Canada Act 1982 (UK) had successfully terminated the United Kingdom Parliament's power to legislate for Canada. This conclusion was hard to align with the idea of the untrammelled powers of that Parliament that had been acknowledged by the Supreme Court of Canada in the earlier *Patriation Reference*. Consistent with its earlier posture, the Supreme Court presumably planned to rely on British (or at least Commonwealth) explanations for the 1982 process. We shall see in Part III that there were problems with such explanations, but that alternative explanations, based more in the Independence theory, were available.

The Independence theory began with the assumption that, regardless of the fact that the Canadian Constitution was amended via Westminster, it was a Canadian set of rules. These rules were primarily contained in constitutional texts which were agreed upon by Canadians, but in important respects the Canadian Constitution was unwritten or yet to be determined. In so far as it was unwritten and yet to be determined it was evolving in accordance with Canadian developments such as independence, federalism and the changing attitudes of the Canadian public. Accordingly, the Constitution was domiciled in Canada and was governed by a distinct Canadian constitutional understanding. The same was true of the rules regarding constitutional amendment, regardless of the fact that a vital part of the legal amendment mechanism was Westminster-centred. Canadians had retained that mechanism perhaps by default in 1867, but they had clearly chosen it in 1931, and accordingly it should have been governed by Canadian interpretations of it, just as was the case with all other parts of the constitutional structure. Questions such as whether as a matter of law Canada had to request and consent legislation from Westminster, whether that consent had to come from the provinces as well or whether Westminster could have been avoided altogether by recourse to the Canadian people, should not have been rigidly cast as law or convention, usually consistently with British understandings, but they should have been (at least since 1949) matters for the Supreme Court of Canada to decide. As we shall see in Chapter 7, the so-called convention of substantial provincial consent could have been a rule of law had the Supreme Court of Canada chosen to recognise it as such. The Independence theory admitted this possibility whatever its plausibility in fact, whereas the

---

[90] *Reference re Objection to a Resolution to Amend the Constitution* [1982] 2 SCR 793.

Imperial theory did not. According to the Imperial theory, of course, the powers of the Westminster Parliament were untrammelled, and legislation for Canada emanating from it could not be declared invalid. The Independence theory would have justified the Supreme Court in declaring invalid that which a British court would have been obliged to recognise. The Independence theory experienced a stunted growth prior to 1982 because of the dominance of the idea of a British-domiciled Canadian Constitution governed to a great extent by British constitutional notions, but since 1982 it has come into its own. The Independence theory may still be useful to us in order to explain what happened in 1982. If the Westminster-based mechanism prior to 1982 was simply a type of amending formula chosen by Canadians, at least since 1931, then like most amending procedures in modern constitutions, perhaps it could provide for its own replacement. We will consider that issue in Part III.

7

Canada III: The *Patriation Reference*

The Judicial Committee of the Privy Council and the Supreme Court of Canada

The acquisition of judicial independence was considered briefly in Chapter 2. We saw there that the Privy Council's role was severely limited even as early as 1901 where the Commonwealth of Australia was concerned. We saw also that the Privy Council only ceased to have a role as the highest appeal court for New Zealand in December 2003. Only Canada went through a radical change in its highest court in the twentieth century. Given the importance of courts in ensuring that parliamentary sovereignty takes effect, such a change deserves closer attention.

As we have seen, the Privy Council was the final court of appeal from all the colonial courts in the nineteenth century, having been constituted by legislation of the Imperial Parliament in 1833 and 1844 to perform this role. Its authority in Canada was preserved by section 129 of the British North America Act, 1867 and perpetuated even after the creation of the Supreme Court of Canada in 1875.[1] In 1888, the Canadian government passed a statute which purported to abolish appeals to the Privy Council in criminal cases. In 1926, in *Nadan v The King*,[2] the Privy Council held that the 1888 statute was invalid, basing its decision primarily on the necessary effect of section 2 of the Colonial Laws Validity Act, 1865 (Imp.). Viscount Cave LC stated the following: 'In their Lordships' opinion [the impugned section] of the Canadian Criminal Code . . . is repugnant to the Acts of 1833 and 1844 which have been cited, and is therefore void and inoperative by virtue of the Act of 1865.'[3]

With the passage of the Statute of Westminster, 1931, and in particular section 2(1) of that Statute, it became possible for the Parliament of Canada to repeal, amend or alter all Imperial statutes (other than those listed in section 7(1)) in so far as these were part of Canadian law. Accordingly, Parliament re-enacted

---

[1] The creation of the Supreme Court of Canada was authorised by s. 101 of the 1867 Act which empowered the Parliament of Canada to 'provide for the Constitution, Maintenance, and Organization of a General Court of Appeal for Canada'. See Supreme Court and Exchequer Courts Act, 1875, SC 1875, and Supreme Court Act, RSC 1970, c. S–19.

[2] *Nadan v The King* [1926] AC 482.   [3] ibid., 492–3.

the statute of 1888 which had been invalidated in the *Nadan* case, and once again the legislation was challenged.

In *British Coal Corporation v The King*,[4] Viscount Sankey LC stated that the difficulties with the Canadian legislation, as described in the *Nadan* case 'could only be overcome by an Imperial statute', and it was the Judicial Committee's task to determine whether the Statute of Westminster, 1931 accomplished this adequately.[5] It may be useful to set out a large portion of Viscount Sankey's response, including the famous passage already discussed in Chapter 3:

It is true that before the Statute [of Westminster], the Dominion Legislature was subject to the limitations imposed by the Colonial Laws Validity Act and by s. 129 of the [1867] Act, and also by the doctrine forbidding extra-territorial legislation, though that is a doctrine of somewhat obscure extent. But these limitations have now been abrogated by the Statute. There now remain only such limitations as flow from the Act itself, the operation of which as affecting the competence of Dominion legislation was saved by s. 7 of the Statute, a section which excluded from the competence of the Dominion and Provincial Parliaments any power of 'repeal, amendment or alteration' of the Act. But it is well known that s. 7 was inserted at the request of Canada and for reasons which are familiar. It is doubtless true that the power of the Imperial Parliament to pass on its own initiative any legislation that it thought fit extending to Canada remains in theory unimpaired: indeed, the Imperial Parliament could, as a matter of abstract law, repeal or disregard s. 4 of the Statute. But that is a theory and has no relation to realities. In truth Canada is in enjoyment of the full scope of self-government: its Legislature was invested with all the necessary powers for that purpose by the Act, and what the Statute did was to remove the two fetters which have already been discussed.

. . .

Their Lordships can see no valid reason since the Statute why the power to regulate or prohibit this type of appeal should not be held to be vested in the Dominion Parliament . . . [6]

Even if the judgment of the Privy Council in the *British Coal Corporation* case confirmed that the constitutional independence of Canada was still doubt in theory so long as section 7 remained in place, it made clear that appeals from Canada to the Privy Council could be further limited or abolished altogether.

In 1939, the Parliament of Canada took steps to abolish all Privy Council Appeals. A Bill was introduced in which it was provided that: 'The Supreme Court shall have, hold and exercise exclusive ultimate appellate civil and criminal jurisdiction within and for Canada; and the judgment of the Court shall, in all cases, be final and conclusive.'[7] The federal Parliament even proposed to

---

[4] *British Coal Corporation v The King* [1935] AC 500 (PC).   [5] ibid., 516.

[6] ibid., 520–2. It should be even clearer by now that this obiter dictum was intended not as an unconditional legal affirmation of the Imperial Parliament's continuing, absolute and untrammelled sovereignty but as confirmation that Canada had chosen in 1931 to allow the Westminster Parliament to maintain its constituent powers *vis-à-vis* the Canadian Constitution, possibly even (given the words of s. 7) in defiance of s. 4.

[7] Bill 9, *An Act to Amend the Supreme Court Act*, 4th Session, 18th Parliament, 1939.

eliminate *per saltum* appeals, i.e. appeals to the Privy Council coming directly from *provincial* courts, pursuant to *provincial* legislation. Finally, provision was made for the repeal of the Judicial Committee Acts of 1833 and 1844 in so far as they affected Canada.

The Bill was referred to the Supreme Court of Canada for an opinion as to its validity. That Court ruled that the Parliament of Canada was competent to enact the Bill,[8] and the Privy Council eventually confirmed that view,[9] with the result that appropriate legislation was enacted and came into force in 1949. Cases commencing after 1949 could no longer proceed to the Privy Council. It is important to note that, to the extent that the Constitution of Canada was and continues to be modified by decisions of the highest court, the termination of Privy Council appeals brought a further measure of constitutional control into Canadian hands.[10]

Challenge to the patriation process in the courts

The search for a formal domestic procedure for amending the Canadian Constitution was ongoing throughout the better part of the twentieth century. Following the first failed attempt at the Dominion-Provincial Conference of 1927, various renewed efforts took place in 1931, 1935, 1950, 1960, 1964 and 1971, the last two of these coming tantalisingly close to agreement.[11] A final phase began in the late 1970s and had produced no consensus by 1980, prompting Prime Minister Trudeau to attempt to proceed unilaterally, i.e. by the sole initiative of the federal Parliament. This initiative was intended to achieve a three-fold objective: 'patriation' of the Constitution; a comprehensive set of procedures for constitutional amendment; and a new Charter of Rights and Freedoms. Two provinces and one federal opposition party supported this bold move, but the Official Opposition and the eight remaining provinces objected. The provinces of Manitoba, Newfoundland and Quebec asked their respective Courts of Appeal to consider the constitutionality of the federal initiative. Only the Newfoundland Court of Appeal ruled in favour of the

---

[8] *Reference as to the Legislative Competence of the Parliament of Canada to Enact Bill No. 9 of the Eighteenth Parliament of Canada Entitled 'An Act to Amend the Supreme Court Act'* [1939] SCR 49.
[9] *Attorney-General of Ontario v Attorney-General of Canada* [1947] AC 127 (PC).
[10] We will see in Chs 12 and 13 below how important it was for the Supreme Court of Canada to take over the ultimate responsibility for Canadian judicial law-making. Whereas the Judicial Committee of the Privy Council was naturally inclined to decide matters in a manner which was likely to be equally applicable elsewhere in the Commonwealth, the Supreme Court of Canada was in no way bound to do so. In the *Patriation Reference*, the majority on the legal question acted much as the Privy Council might have done, as we shall see, but we can now predict with some confidence that the current Supreme Court of Canada would be at pains to establish its post-patriation independence in judicial thinking.
[11] For a summary of these efforts, see J.R. Hurley, *Amending Canada's Constitution: History, Processes, Problems and Prospects* (Ottawa: Canada Communication Group, 1996).

dissenting provinces' position,[12] but the decisions of all three Courts of Appeal were appealed to the Supreme Court of Canada. The decision of that Court proved to be one of the most important in Canadian history.

The *Patriation Reference* brought together many of the seemingly disparate elements of Canadian constitutional history which have been highlighted in Chapters 5 and 6. The Supreme Court of Canada, the highest Canadian court and, since the termination of appeals to the Privy Council, also the ultimate judicial authority regarding Canada's 'Imperial' legal business, was called upon to determine the legal and conventional rules applicable to repeal, amendment or alteration of the Canadian Constitution, the very matters which had been omitted from the 1867 Act and excluded from the operation of the Statute of Westminster, 1931. In a very real sense, then, the Court was presented with a constitutional issue which had been sheltered from formal legal treatment since 1867, but which in practice had evolved and matured along with the Canadian nation.

The questions before the Court can be summarised as follows. First, would the federal proposal, if enacted, affect federal-provincial relationships or the powers, rights or privileges of the provinces? Secondly, was there a constitutional convention requiring the consent of the provinces before the Senate and House of Commons lay before the Parliament of the United Kingdom a measure to amend the Constitution of Canada affecting federal-provincial relationships? And thirdly, was there a legal requirement regarding such provincial consent?[13] It may be helpful to summarise the various conclusions arrived at by the shifting majorities and minorities in the case, before examining their reasons in more detail, and connecting those reasons to the Imperial and Independence theories canvassed in Chapters 5 and 6.

The Court dealt with legal and conventional questions separately. Questions one and three, the legal questions, were therefore treated together. The Attorney-General of Canada had conceded that the federal-provincial relationship would be affected by the federal proposal, and consequently the legal analysis really focused on the third question. A majority[14] which included then Chief Justice Laskin concluded that there was no *legal* limit on the authority of the federal Parliament to request the amendment of the Constitution of Canada by the Parliament at Westminster. It rejected the argument that certain practices can crystallise into law, and it refused to enshrine by means of judicial legislation a legal principle of provincial consent. Many arguments were considered regarding

---

[12] *Reference re Amendment of the Constitution of Canada (No 2)* (1981) 118 DLR (3d) 1 (Nfld CA). See also *Reference re Amendment of the Constitution of Canada* (1981) 117 DLR (3d) 1 (Man CA) and *Reference re Amendment of the Constitution of Canada (No 3)* (1981) 120 DLR (3rd) 385 (Que CA).

[13] A fourth question relating only to the Province of Newfoundland is not relevant to our discussion and will be ignored.

[14] The majority on the legal question will be referred to as the majority (law). It included Laskin CJC and Dickson, Beetz, Estey, McIntyre, Chouinard and Lamer JJ.

the legal effects of the Statute of Westminster, 1931. The majority (law) favoured the view that, regarding constitutional amendment, the 1931 Statute was designed to leave things as they had been before. There was nothing in that Statute which could be said to cast any doubt in law on the 'undiminished authority of the Parliament of the United Kingdom over the *British North America Act*'.[15] This unqualified statement came straight from the Imperial theory tradition.

The minority on the legal question[16] turned the problem on its head. Rather than considering the unlimited powers of the Westminster Parliament and the absence of legal limits on the ability of the federal Parliament to pass resolutions, the minority (law) asked a familiar rule of law question having to do with legality:[17] was there any affirmative legal rule that could be identified which permitted the Senate and House of Commons to cause the Canadian Constitution to be amended in such a radical way without the consent of the Provinces? Having no statutory basis for doing so, and having no power to implement measures contrary to the 1867 Act, it was equally beyond the power, or ultra vires, of the two federal houses to accomplish such a modification of the Constitution of Canada through the agency of the Imperial Parliament.

As noted above, question two regarding conventions was treated separately. A new majority of the Court[18] determined that there was a convention that would have required 'a substantial measure of provincial consent'[19] prior to passage of the resolution containing the federal proposal. The majority (convention) declined to express a view as to the precise number of provinces which would suffice.

The *minority* on the question of convention[20] denied even the existence of such a convention. These judges, who included the forceful personality of Laskin CJC, first made clear their aversion to considering a question which was traditionally beyond the scope of legal determination. However, they decided to deal with the matter of conventions given the exceptional nature of the constitutional reference and given the extensive reasons of the majority (convention). The minority limited its views to a convention requiring the consent of all provinces, judging that the majority's finding of a convention of 'substantial . . . provincial consent' went beyond the terms of the reference. In the end, the minority (convention) concluded that there was no convention of the first type.

---

[15] *Patriation Reference*, 801.   [16] Martland and Ritchie JJ (hereinafter the minority (law)).

[17] This form of rule of law questioning goes back at least as far as Camden CJ in *Entick v Carrington* (1765) 19 State Trials 1030. In Canada, it is supported by *Roncarelli v Duplessis* (1959) 15 DLR (2d) 689.

[18] Martland, Ritchie, Dickson, Beetz, Chouinard and Lamer JJ (hereafter the majority (convention)). It is important to note that Dickson, Beetz, Chouinard and Lamer JJ were also part of the majority (law).   [19] *Patriation Reference*, 905.

[20] Laskin CJC and Estey and McIntyre JJ (hereinafter minority (convention)).

The Imperial theory in the *Patriation Reference*

If some of the observations in Chapter 5 were thought to be too strongly put, or expressed in caricature, it is worthwhile to look at the *Patriation Reference* for a particularly strong example of the influence of the Imperial theory.

The members of the majority (law) made clear that the issue before them was 'an unprecedented situation'.[21] The federal government had never before attempted unilaterally to patriate the Constitution by means of the United Kingdom Parliament, and the Supreme Court of Canada had never before been asked to rule on the law governing such an initiative. The Court had said in the *Senate Reference*[22] that any changes to the Constitution affecting the federation as a whole had to be enacted by the United Kingdom Parliament. However, the *Senate Reference* concerned an attempt by the federal government to accomplish such changes not via Westminster but by ordinary legislation of the federal Parliament using powers granted to it in the British North America (No 2) Act, 1949.

The *Patriation Reference* therefore provided the Court with an 'unprecedented' opportunity to describe the rules which governed amendment of the Canadian Constitution via Westminster. As we shall see, a majority of the Court viewed only the Canadian-based part of the process as a matter for its concern. Political practices which could have been recognised even at that stage as part of the Canadian *law* of constitutional amendment were deemed instead to be conventions, and hence not enforceable by a court of law. The legal rules governing the passage of a Canadian amendment through the Westminster Parliament were seen less as part of the Canadian law of constitutional amendment (and hence subject to interpretation by Canadian courts in accordance with Canadian principles and theory), and more as matters of British constitutional law and practice, which effectively excluded them from review by any court which accepted the doctrine of parliamentary sovereignty. It is entirely possible that even if the Court had viewed the Westminster Parliament as a part of an essentially Canadian process it might have denied that that process was governed by legal rules regarding a requisite level of provincial consent; however, for our purposes, it is significant to note that the issue was deemed to be a matter for the Westminster Parliament, there being no notion of ultra vires and judicial review in British and Imperial theory, at least where the Westminster Parliament was concerned.[23]

On the legal, as opposed to the conventional, branch of the *Patriation Reference*, the Court was asked two basic questions. These have been identified in

---

[21] *Patriation Reference*, 807.

[22] *Reference re Authority of Parliament in Relation to the Upper House* [1980] 1 SCR 54 (hereinafter *Senate Reference*).

[23] That situation has changed where directly effective European law is concerned.

the brief summary which was set out above. As noted there, it was conceded that the first legal question (whether or not the proposed federal initiative would, if enacted, affect federal-provincial relationships) should be answered in the affirmative.[24] The second legal question was framed differently by Newfoundland and Manitoba on the one hand and by Quebec on the other hand. Newfoundland and Manitoba asked generally whether 'the agreement of the provinces [is] constitutionally required for *amendment of the Constitution of Canada*'.[25] Quebec focused to a greater extent on the Canadian-based part of the process which initiated the amendment process: 'Does the Canadian Constitution empower . . . the Senate and the House of Commons of Canada to cause the Canadian Constitution to be amended without the consent of the provinces . . . ?'[26] It was perhaps in response to this second, more convenient, way of formulating the question that the majority chose to divide it into two separate issues:

(1) the authority of the two federal Houses to proceed by Resolution where provincial powers and federal-provincial relationships are thereby affected and (2) the role or authority of the Parliament of the United Kingdom to act on the Resolution. The first point concerns the need of legal power to initiate the process in Canada; the second concerns legal power or want of it in the Parliament of the United Kingdom to act on the Resolution when it does not carry the consent of the Provinces.[27]

There was nothing inherently misleading in this manner of separating the issues. It simply divided initiation and ratification. As we shall see, however, it permitted the Court to consider initiation as a matter for Canadian judicial consideration but to deny any such competence regarding the process of (Westminster-based) ratification. Once it could be established that the Westminster Parliament had been designated to enact and to modify the Canadian Constitution, the manner in which it did so could not be a matter for Canadian courts. The majority made two pertinent observations:

First, we have an anomaly that although Canada has international recognition as an independent, autonomous and self-governing state, as, for example, a founding member of the United Nations, and through membership in other international associations of sovereign states, yet it suffers from an internal deficiency in the absence of legal power to alter or amend the essential distributive arrangements under which legal authority is exercised in the country, whether at the federal or provincial level. When a country has been in existence as an operating federal state for more than a century, the task of introducing a legal mechanism that will thereafter remove the anomaly undoubtedly raises a profound problem. Secondly, *the authority of the British Parliament or its practices and conventions are not matters upon which this Court would presume to pronounce.*[28]

---

[24] See *Patriation Reference*, 767.   [25] Patriation Reference, 762 (emphasis added).
[26] *Patriation Reference*, 763.   [27] *Patriation Reference*, 773.
[28] *Patriation Reference*, 774 (emphasis added).

Although it is obvious why a Canadian court would not want to pronounce on the authority, practices and conventions of a foreign Parliament, it is not clear why it should not do so where that foreign Parliament is, for amendment purposes, an integral part of the local constitutional system. That which is valid law for the United Kingdom need not be similarly so in Canada unless the 'anomaly' and 'internal deficiency' of the absence of a domestic amending formula means that not only the process but also the law, interpretation and theory governing that process lie beyond the jurisdiction of Canadian courts until 'patriation'.[29] It is hard to see how such an approach was consistent with Canadian political independence, an independence which, at least since 1949, included an independent Canadian judiciary. A more satisfactory approach from a Canadian point of view might have been to claim the ability to pronounce on the validity of the enactments of the United Kingdom Parliament in terms of Canadian law, but to conclude perhaps that no rules regarding provincial consent had been provided and that it was not up to the Court to provide them. The result would have been the same, but the analysis would have differed in important ways. For example, the Court might have wanted to say in a later case that Canadian *law* required that enactments of the Westminster Parliament amending the Canadian Constitution be preceded by Canadian request and consent.[30] This conclusion was excluded if the Court could not pronounce on the authority of the British Parliament.

From all the evidence, it appears that the majority (law) was not inclined to find a legal rule requiring provincial consent under any view of the matter. Provincial consent was at best a matter of convention and, as such, not enforceable by the courts. Of course, such an analysis begged the question. Once the matter had been deemed to be conventional it was by definition beyond the Court's purview.[31] However, the majority adopted a strict and formal approach to such questions in stating: 'What is desirable as a political limitation does not translate into a legal limitation, without expression in imperative constitutional text or statute.'[32]

---

[29] *Patriation Reference*, 766.

[30] Even this possibility is ruled out by the minority (convention). These reasons therefore represent a very strong version of the Imperial theory. *Patriation Reference*, 855–6. It is important to remember that there was by no means any certainty at the time of the *Patriation Reference* that patriation would occur. It was therefore possible that a Westminster-based amendment process could have remained part of the Canadian constitutional system for many years to come. With that in mind, the Supreme Court of Canada's reasons did not make very reassuring reading for Canadian nationalists.

[31] This same point is made by W. Conklin, *Images of a Constitution* (Toronto: University of Toronto Press, 1989) 71.

[32] *Patriation Reference*, 784. This is a very narrow definition of the Constitution. It appears to ignore the fact that at least one part of the Constitution, that which H.L.A. Hart would call the rule of recognition, is derived in part from practice, although it may be identified and clarified by a court and thus made legal; H.L.A. Hart, *The Concept of Law* (Oxford: Clarendon Press, 1961; 2nd edn., 1994) ch. 6. The *Patriation Reference* was an opportunity for the Supreme Court of Canada to articulate the Canadian rule of recognition, but the majority (law) appeared unwilling to do so; or

In considering whether such 'express or imperative constitutional text or statute' could be found, the majority turned to the bipartite division of the legal issue set out earlier. It considered, first, the authority or power of the two federal powers to initiate the amendment resolution affecting the federal-provincial relationship and, secondly, the role or authority of the United Kingdom Parliament. As we shall see, on the first part of the issue, the majority appeared to be highly influenced by a British interpretation of the 1867 Act of the British Parliament, and on the second, the majority seemed to view the authority of that same British Parliament as being beyond the competence of a Canadian court.

Turning to the first part of the issue, one notes that the majority stressed that the 1867 Act was silent as to the power of initiation of constitutional amendments, and that such silence could justify neither a positive nor a negative conclusion regarding the federal Parliament's ability. Examination of this question should not necessarily have involved any British considerations, but, oddly enough, the views of a former British Solicitor-General of 1940 were cited at some length. Presumably, British interpretations of the 1867 Act were still deemed to be relevant for Canadian purposes. In response to a question regarding provincial consent to the 1940 'unemployment insurance amendment', which directly affected provincial legislative power, Sir William Jowitt was quoted as saying[33] that he did not know whether the Provinces had consented but that, even in 1940, the provinces appeared to have expressed a desire that the old system of a request by the Parliament of Canada and enactment at Westminster continue:

... at the request of Canada this old machinery still survives until something better is thought of, but we square the legal with the constitutional position by passing these Acts only in the form that the Canadian Parliament require and at the request of the Canadian Parliament.

...

In reply to the hon. Member ... I do not know what the view of the Provincial Parliaments is. I know, however, that when the matter was before the Privy Council some of the Provincial Parliaments supported the Dominion Parliament. It is sufficient justification for the bill that we are morally bound to act on the ground that we have here the request of the Dominion Parliament and that we must operate the old machinery which has been left over at their request in accordance with their wishes.

Given the silence of the 1867 Act and the lack of justification for interpreting that silence one way or another, the majority (law) then dealt with the question of whether the Supreme Court of Canada could, by its own initiative, 'enshrine

perhaps, even more distressingly, it viewed the British rule of recognition as binding. This point will be developed further in Part III. See also W. Lederman, 'The Supreme Court of Canada and Basic Constitutional Amendment' in K. Banting and R. Simeon (eds), *And No One Cheered: Federalism, Democracy and the Constitution Act* (Toronto: University of Toronto Press, 1985) 176, 180, where he criticises the Supreme Court majority (law) as being positivist and historically static.

[33] *Patriation Reference*, 787.

as a legal imperative a principle [of unanimous provincial consent] for constitutional amendment':

The stark legal question is whether this Court can enact by what would be judicial legislation a formula of unanimity to initiate the amending process which would be binding not only in Canada but also on the Parliament of the United Kingdom with which amending authority would still remain. It would be anomalous indeed, overshadowing the anomaly of a Constitution which contains no provision for its amendment, for the Court to say retroactively that in law we have had an amending formula all along, even if we have not hitherto known it; or, to say, that we have had in law one amending formula, say from 1867 to 1931, and a second amending formula that has emerged after 1931.[34]

This formulation of the 'stark legal question' is as close as the majority came to recognising the possibility of a distinctive Canadian legal interpretation of its fundamental constitutional statute. As the Court acknowledged elsewhere in the judgment, the question was 'unprecedented'. Presumably, the Court should have been entitled to declare the true state of the law, whether or not that corresponded with the practice which had obtained until that moment.[35] And presumably, if there were sufficiently compelling reasons in law to do so, the Court could have also concluded that there had a been one amending formula before 1931 and another after that moment. There were numerous elements, both formal and informal, in Canada's rapid and complex constitutional development which could have been highlighted in order to justify such conclusions. These conclusions, whatever their merit in law, could only be seen as *anomalous* if the unaltered position of the formal amending authority—the United Kingdom Parliament—was deemed to be determinative. That Parliament had, of course, gone through a certain evolution of its own since 1867. But there was apparently nothing in its evolution which could be said to have limited its ability to modify its own legislative acts, unless a specific legislative text could be said to have done so, and from that perspective it would indeed have been anomalous to imply new legal limits, especially given the wording of section 7 of the 1931 Statute. It would only cease to be so if it the Court felt that it were possible to look at the role and authority of the United Kingdom Parliament for Canadian purposes as being different from its role and authority for United Kingdom purposes, and, more importantly, as being an appropriate subject of Canadian judicial consideration. Instead, the majority (law)'s attitude was just that recommended by Dicey one century earlier: obedience to the Westminster Parliament.

It appeared, then, that the majority (law) was unwilling to deal with the first issue in a manner which would require it to describe the content of the rule

---

[34] *Patriation Reference*, 787.
[35] The Court was to take such bold action four years later in *Reference re Manitoba Language Rights* [1985] 1 SCR 721.

regarding initiation of amendments, despite the fact that the matter had never been dealt with before. In the absence of a positive legal text covering the matter, any court-initiated determination would amount to judicial legislation. Of course, the *minority* (law) allowed itself to see in the absence of a legal text a corresponding *absence* of authority to do that which appeared to violate one of the principles of Canadian constitutional law, i.e. federalism.

Having refused to describe the content of the 'initiation' aspect of the amendment process, it was not likely that the Court would be any less reluctant regarding the second issue: the role and authority of the United Kingdom Parliament. The highest Canadian court showed itself unwilling to define, even for Canadian purposes, the limits, if any, of Westminster Parliament power.

As we shall see below, the dissenting provinces presented strong arguments in favour of a distinctive Canadian legal interpretation of the role and authority of the United Kingdom Parliament. Elements of these arguments were considered in the discussion of the Independence theory. In its strongest version, the Independence theory dictated that federal considerations, and hence provincial consent, should be a legally relevant part of the amendment process. Briefly put, since the 1867 Act made no formal provision for amendment, neither the federal Parliament nor the provincial legislatures could be said to have been given the power to amend the most fundamental parts of the Constitution, principally those parts where the rights of both levels of government were guaranteed. Accordingly, the consent of both levels would be required before a Canadian court (or a court acting for Canada pre-1949, in the case of the Privy Council) could recognise such a Westminster-enacted amendment as Canadian law. To do otherwise would have been to violate that part of Canadian constitutional design which had certainly been confirmed by 1867, that is, its federal nature. Only later, sometime during the first half of the next century, would the addition of a requirement of proper Canadian consent be more easily argued, in recognition of Canadian equality and autonomy *vis-à-vis* the United Kingdom.

Not surprisingly, these and other similar arguments did not convince the majority (law). Some possible reasons for this have been discussed. The majority required a clear formal, legal indication, recognisable as such in relation to the Westminster Parliament, to justify such conclusions and these were not forthcoming. The Balfour Declaration reference to 'autonomous communities' was judged to be a purely political statement from which the argument in favour of provincial consent could seek no nourishment.[36] If the Declaration had any impact it would have to be 'regarded as retroactively having that effect by reason of the ultimate enactment of the Statute of Westminster'.[37]

Upon this Statute, then, lay the burden of revealing that 'an equality of status as between the Dominion and the Provinces *vis-à-vis* the United Kingdom Parliament' had come into existence and that 'the theretofore untrammeled

---

[36] *Patriation Reference*, 790.   [37] *Patriation Reference*, 790.

legislative authority of that Parliament in relation to Canada where provincial interests [were] concerned' had been attenuated.[38] We can at least be sure that the majority felt that the argument regarding the 1867 Act and the federal principle had no toe-hold even by 1931. The untrammelled authority of the Westminster Parliament was the rule.

With respect to the Statute of Westminster, 1931, the majority saw no justification for the view that a requirement of provincial consent had been imposed on the activity of the United Kingdom Parliament regarding the amendment of the 1867 Act. The preamble to the Statute pertained primarily to Canada as a whole, not the provinces. Section 2 repealed the Colonial Laws Validity Act, 1865 and empowered Canada, and pursuant to section 7(2), the provinces, to repeal or amend any British legislation that was or would be made applicable to them. As section 7(3) made clear, this only applied to the enactment of laws in relation to matters within the competence of each. Amendment of the greatest part of the Canadian Constitution had never been within the competence of either. In the view of the majority (law),[39] section 7(1)

... appeared ... to maintain the *status quo ante*; that is, to leave any changes in the *British North America Act* ... to the prevailing situation, namely, with the legislative authority of the United Kingdom Parliament being left untouched ... 'the old machinery' remained in place ...

In the end, the majority (law) was of the view that 'as of 1930, there was certainly no rule of law with respect to constitutional amendment' and 'No change was effected in the legal position by the Statute of Westminster'.[40]

The idea that there was never 'a rule of law with respect to constitutional amendment' is a constant in the reasons of the majority, and it is an important characteristic of the Imperial theory. The contrary point of view, as we shall see, required that the Supreme Court of Canada see the Canadian Constitution as *complete*, including rules on amendment which, in terms of its general procedure, happened to involve the United Kingdom Parliament. Accordingly to this view, the Supreme Court of Canada would have been entitled to determine the conditions according to which an amendment to that Canadian Constitution was to be deemed valid. As emphasised earlier, even a Court less influenced by the Imperial theory might legitimately have felt that such a decision went beyond the proper judicial function, but, equally, it might have inferred, for example, a requirement of provincial consent after 1867 and an absolute requirement of Canadian request and consent following 1931. But any of these determinations of the rules for the validity of Canadian constitutional amendment required that the whole of the Constitution, including its amendment procedures, be an appropriate subject of judicial enquiry. As we have seen, the majority in the *Patriation Reference* viewed that Constitution differently. In the majority's view,

---

[38] *Patriation Reference*, 790.   [39] *Patriation Reference*, 794–5.
[40] *Patriation Reference*, 797.

the Westminster Parliament was a process unto itself, and a foreign process at that, governed by its own rules. Expressed in that way, it was an unobjectionable point of view. What the majority failed, or was unwilling to consider, was that Westminster could be seen and judged differently for *Canadian purposes*, i.e. as part of a complete Canadian Constitution (though one not entirely Canada-based in its machinery).

Instead, as already stated, the majority viewed the Canadian Constitution as incomplete:

At least with regard to the amending formula the process here concerns not the amendment of a complete constitution but rather the completion of an incomplete constitution.

We are involved here with a finishing operation, with fitting a piece into the constitutional edifice; it is idle to expect to find anything in the *British North America Act* that regulates the process that has been initiated in this case.[41]

Canadian independence, or the autonomy and equality which came to be recognised in the former colony's relationship with the United Kingdom, manifested itself not in the ability of Canadian courts to determine what amounted to the ultimate rule of the Canadian Constitution; instead, in the majority's view,[42] it justified only

... a procedure which takes into account the intergovernmental and international link between Canada and Great Britain. There is no comparable link that engages the Provinces with Great Britain ... The legal competence of [the British] Parliament, for the reasons already given, remains unimpaired, and it is for it alone to determine if and how it will act.

There was apparently nothing in the Statute of Westminster, 1931 which could be seen to remove that full, 'unimpaired' and 'undiminished' competence in the Westminster Parliament: 'Whatever the [1931] statute may import as to intra-Canadian conventional procedures, there is nothing in it or in the proceedings leading up to it that casts any doubt in law as to the undiminished authority of the Parliament of the United Kingdom over the British North America Act.'[43] The majority (law) insisted that by 1931 Canada had the rights of an independent nation in international law. This had been recognised in 1923, confirmed in Imperial Conferences and sanctified in the Statute of Westminster, 1931. In the majority (law)'s view, 'The remaining badge of subservience, the need to resort to the British Parliament to amend the British North America Act, although preserved by the Statute of Westminster, did not carry any diminution of Canada's legal right in international law.'[44] That which remained unclear was why the need to resort to the United Kingdom Parliament also required that the

---

[41] *Patriation Reference*, 799. As Conklin (1989) (n. 31 above) 73, observes, the idea that the Canadian Constitution is incomplete is related to the majority (law)'s apparent understanding of the constitutional 'law as enactment'.   [42] *Patriation Reference*, 799.

[43] *Patriation Reference*, 801.   [44] *Patriation Reference*, 802.

courts of an apparently independent country deny their ability to determine the rules regarding the validity *for Canadian purposes* of the enactments of that foreign legislature, especially when those enactments were part of a Canadian constitutional amendment process. And yet that appeared to be the majority (law)'s approach:

History cannot alter the fact that in law there is *a British statute* to construe and apply in relation to a matter, fundamental as it as, that is not provided for by the statute.

. . .

There is here . . . an unprecedented situation in which *the one constant since the enactment of the British North America Act in 1867 has been the legal authority of the United Kingdom Parliament to amend it.* The law knows nothing of any requirement of provincial consent, either to a resolution of the federal Houses or as a condition of the exercise of United Kingdom legislative power.[45]

Presumably, if a situation is unprecedented, then it is up to the courts to declare or interpret the law even, or perhaps especially, where the fundamental law of the country is silent. It is one of the ironies of the *Patriation Reference* that that which was described as a conventional rule by a different majority of the Supreme Court of Canada—i.e. the requirement of a substantial provincial consent— could have been declared as a condition of validity for Canadian purposes of an otherwise valid enactment of the Westminster Parliament.[46]

In effect, that which the Court eventually described as a constitutional convention could have been used as the content of the ultimate rule of the Canadian Constitution. In this exceptional context, it may well have been correct to speak of a convention for United Kingdom purposes (and courts) and a rule of law for Canadian purposes (and courts). The Imperial theory left no room for such an argument.

It has been acknowledged throughout that there may have been very good reasons for the Supreme Court of Canada to refuse to identify a legal rule regarding provincial consent, even in circumstances where it recognised its authority to declare the law in this fashion in the appropriate case. First, the rule of substantial provincial consent was vague and imprecise. Secondly, the courts may have seen themselves as lacking the legitimacy to define the law in the absence of formal indication. And thirdly, there may simply have been insufficient justification under any view of the matter to have inferred some type of provincial consent requirement.

It was not so much the result which is important for our analysis. Rather it was the approach that is so revealing. The majority (law) did not even seem to have acknowledged that it was in the process of defining the ultimate rule of the

---

[45] *Patriation Reference*, 803, 807 (emphasis added).

[46] This argument has been developed by F. Gélinas, 'Les conventions, le droit et la Constitution dans le renvoi sur la "sécession" du Québec: le fantôme du rapatriement' (1997) 57 Rev du Barreau 291. See also F. Gélinas, *Constitutional Adjudication and the Independence of Canada: Issues of Principle, Convention, and Law*, Doctoral Dissertation, Oxford, 1995.

Canadian Constitution. Ultimate legal control over that Constitution had been left in the hands of the United Kingdom Parliament. The rules regarding its amendment were the rules of that Parliament. Whatever the rule of recognition applicable to that Parliament in order to determine the validity of its legislative enactments, it was not deemed to be a matter for the Canadian courts. By following the Imperial theory's tenets, the Supreme Court of Canada showed an unwillingness to acknowledge that it was possible for an enactment of the United Kingdom Parliament regarding the amendment of the Canadian constitution to be valid according to British law but invalid according to Canadian law.

The importance of the Imperial theory approach can perhaps be best explained by examining the difficulties which it could be seen to have in providing satisfactory answers in three situations, two of which were mentioned in the *Patriation Reference*. The last was its most beguiling consequence.

The majority (law) stated that during the course of argument the Attorney-General of Canada was asked whether the federal government could, in theory, 'procure an amendment to the British North America Act that would turn Canada into a unitary state'.[47] The Attorney-General answered in the affirmative. The logic of his argument required it. The majority (law) stated simply that this was not what the present Resolution envisaged. Presumably, if there had been a means of discounting such a possibility in law, the majority would have stated it. But the logic of the Imperial theory dictated that there could be no objection in law to an Act of the United Kingdom Parliament which accomplished even such a radical alteration of the country's constitutional structure. The conventions of the Canadian Constitution and international comity made the prospect unlikely. One might also have wanted to say that in such an event the courts would find a way to declare it unconstitutional. But then that was the problem. There appeared to be no ready answer within the Imperial theory.

A second situation emerged in the strong Imperial theory line kept to by the minority (convention). In that judgment, the logic of the Imperial theory was taken to its extreme. The minority (convention) considered the theoretical possibility of a statute enacted for Canada by the United Kingdom Parliament without Canada's request or consent, in contravention of a well-established convention against such action, being invalidated by a Canadian court. Peter Hogg's open-minded consideration of this possibility (set out in Chapter 6) was quoted with disapproval.[48] The minority rejected this view forcefully. Presumably, such a statute would have been valid, in the minority (convention)'s view, in both British and Canadian law. There was no room within the Imperial theory for the view that that which might be a convention in the United Kingdom (the United Kingdom Parliament will not pass a law amending the constitutional statutes for Canada without Canadian request and consent) could

---

[47] *Patriation Reference*, 855–6.   [48] *Ibid.*

be a legal requirement in Canada (the Canadian courts will not recognise the validity of a United Kingdom Parliament law amending the Canadian constitutional statutes without evidence of Canadian request and consent). Without a Canadian court having pronounced on the issue, it is uncertain whether such a rule would have been considered a convention or part of the ultimate rule of the Canadian constitution. And, however unlikely the prospect of such legislation was, if one could have confidently predicted that Canadian courts would have declared such legislation invalid, it seems misleading to have insisted on referring to it in Canadian terms as a convention, despite the fact that that might have been the most accurate description in British terms. The Imperial theory made this distinction illegitimate, however.

The minority (convention) joined the majority (law) in viewing the Canadian constitution as an incomplete body of law:

In view of the fact that the . . . argument has been raised . . . it should be noted, in our view, that the federal constitutional proposals, which preserve a federal state without disturbing the distribution or balance of power, would create an amending formula which would enshrine provincial rights on the question of amendments on a secure, legal and constitutional footing, and would extinguish, as well, any presently existing power on the part of the federal Parliament to act unilaterally in constitutional matters . . . *Its effect is to complete the formation of an incomplete constitution by supplying its present deficiency, i.e. an amending formula, which will enable the Constitution to be amended in Canada as befits a sovereign state.*[49]

This statement, along with statements of its type which were highlighted in the majority (law), presented a third problem for the Imperial theory. If the Parliament of the United Kingdom was governed by British constitutional understandings, then in what sense could it effectively transfer the power to amend the Canadian Constitution to Canada? Over a year later, the *Quebec Veto Reference* appeared to indicate that the process which was successfully played out in 1981–2 was now 'irreversible'. We can be quite certain that the Supreme Court of Canada would reject as invalid any attempt to undo the Canada Act 1982 or to amend the Canadian Constitution by means of a statute of the United Kingdom Parliament. However, the Imperial theory makes this very hard to explain because of its failure to separate and distinguish Canadian and British constitutional theory. Not long after 1982, British courts accepted the theoretical possibility of a re-assertion of the power of the United Kingdom Parliament to legislate for independent countries,[50] and noted that they would have to heed such legislation, though courts of the independent countries would not. However, if Canadian courts continued to heed the Imperial theory, then they too would have to respect such a reassertion of legislative authority. This was the logic of the *Patriation Reference* and the Imperial theory, both of which appeared

---

[49] *Patriation Reference*, 873 (emphasis added).
[50] See Megarry VC in *Manuel v Attorney-General* [1983] Ch 77, 87.

to place the United Kingdom Parliament beyond the reach of judicial review, even for Canadian purposes.

The standard modern analysis of this problem by British and Canadian constitutional commentators is that 'Imperial' legislation of this (unlikely) sort, would simply be ignored by the Canadian courts.[51] This seems unchallengeable. However, the enduring effects of the Imperial theory would make it hard for these same courts to explain this convincingly, except by a resort to British constitutional theory where such an explanation is difficult. As we shall see in discussing the Independence theory in the *Patriation Reference*, the Supreme Court of Canada may have missed a chance to pull together the threads of a distinctive Canadian theory of the Constitution. It may also be the case that Canadians have to revert to at least part of that independent Canadian theory to explain in a convincing way the 'irreversibility' of the 1982 patriation process.

The Independence theory in the *Patriation Reference*

The minority (law) dealt solely with the question of the Ottawa Parliament's legal empowerment to proceed unilaterally by means of a resolution requesting legislative action by the United Kingdom Parliament. Arguments regarding the allegedly full legal authority of the United Kingdom Parliament to amend the Canadian Constitution were noted but not discussed in any detail. If we are to presume any conclusion by the minority (law), it would probably be one in favour of such a full legal authority. But the minority (law) was not obliged to deal with such questions because it chose to resolve the question on a purely internal, Canadian basis. The 1867 Act provided no answer to the question whether the federal Parliament was empowered to cause the Constitution of Canada to be amended without the consent of the provinces. The issue was 'unique'.[52] However, a combination of the Preamble to the 1867 Act, the division of powers set out in the Act and the jurisprudential treatment of the Constitution indicated that 'the dominant principle of Canadian constitutional law is federalism'.[53] Furthermore, it was up to the courts to preserve the integrity of the Constitution, including its federal structure.

The minority then turned its attention to the federal authorities' power to pass resolutions and noted that the power had never before been exercised for the purpose of curtailing provincial legislative authority without provincial consent.

---

[51] See, e.g., G. Marshall, *Constitutional Theory* (Oxford: Oxford University Press, 1971) 63 and P.W. Hogg, *Constitutional Law of Canada* (4th edn (looseleaf) Toronto: Thomson Carswell, 1997) 3–14.   [52] *Patriation Reference*, 815.
[53] *Patriation Reference*, 821.

The legal issue could be rephrased as being:

... whether the established incompetence of the federal government to encroach on provincial powers can be avoided through the use of the resolution procedure to effect a constitutional amendment passed at the behest of the federal government by the Parliament of the United Kingdom.[54]

It was noted that at no time in the past had amendments directly affecting the federal-provincial relationship been enacted without federal consultation with, and the consent of, all the provinces.[55] It was possible to conclude therefore that 'normal constitutional principles recognizing the inviolability of separate and exclusive legislative powers were carried into and considered an integral part of the operation of the resolution procedure'.[56] The Balfour Declaration and the Statute of Westminster, 1931 were discussed only to point out that Canada's independent sovereign status did not alter the fact that the nation remained federal in nature. The Balfour Declaration and 1931 Statute certainly did not mean that the federal Parliament acquired sole control over the exercise of that sovereignty.[57] And regarding amendment of the Constitution of Canada: 'The effect of s. 7(1) was to preserve the Imperial Parliament as the legal instrument for enacting amendments to the B.N.A. Acts, 1867–1930. This clearly had no effect on the existing procedure which had been used to obtain the amendment of the B.N.A. Act.'[58]

The minority (law) then considered the federal power to pass resolutions in its modern context. It was first noted that the British authorities which stated that internal parliamentary procedures were not the proper subject of judicial enquiry were of no help in determining the proper Canadian judicial attitude. Resolutions of the type under consideration were not matters of internal procedure but rather the means by which one level of government in a federal system could attempt to abridge the powers of the other level. The minority (law) pointed out that the constitutional power which allowed the federal Parliament to determine the rule of procedure applicable to the House of Commons and Senate was limited by the federal division of power: 'because ... Parliament's power to legislate was limited in extent, it could not grant to the Senate and the House of Commons powers which it did not itself possess'.[59] Parliament could only confer powers in so far as they were 'consistent with and not repugnant to' the 1867 Act.[60] The conclusion demanded by this analysis was that the Senate and House of Commons were purporting to exercise a power which they did not in fact possess. The two Houses of Parliament could not be permitted to 'accomplish indirectly, through the intervention of the United Kingdom Parliament, that which the Parliament of Canada itself [was]

---

[54] *Patriation Reference*, 824.
[55] *Patriation Reference*, 830.
[56] *Patriation Reference*, 831.
[57] *Patriation Reference*, 835.
[58] *Patriation Reference*, 835.
[59] *Patriation Reference*, 838.
[60] *Patriation Reference*, 839.

unable to do',[61] and it was 'the duty of [the] Court to consider this assertion of rights with a view to the preservation of the Constitution'.[62]

After a review of other cases in which the Supreme Court of Canada had put forward 'judicially developed principles and doctrines',[63] the minority ruled that it was the proper function of the Court in its role of protecting and preserving the Canadian Constitution to declare that the two Houses of the Canadian Parliament could not claim the power unilaterally to effect an amendment to the 1867 Act. The resolution at issue in the *Patriation Reference* could only be an effective expression of Canadian sovereignty if it had the support of both levels of the federal structure.

The majority (convention) framed its reasons in a tightly-written judgment. It employed Dicey's distinction between law and conventions and noted that the latter are not enforced by the courts.[64] The requirements for establishing a convention were taken from Ivor Jennings: precedents, actors treating the rule as binding, and a reason for the rule.[65] As for precedents, the majority (convention) recognised a strong indication of a requirement of unanimity.[66] The actors, however, could only be said to have accepted a binding rule of substantial provincial consent.[67] The reason for the rule was, of course, the federal principle.[68]

In a statement which, according to another direction of analysis, might have formed a new *legal* rule, the majority (convention) stated that: 'The federal principle cannot be reconciled with a state of affairs where the modification of provincial legislative powers could be obtained by the unilateral action of the federal authorities.'[69] However, the so-called convention requiring substantial provincial consent could not be considered as law as long as the judges accepted the determination made by the majority (law) regarding that which could be recognised by the courts. As we have seen, the majority (law) required 'an imperative constitutional text or statute' before it would have been able to recognise as law the limitation contained in a convention of substantial provincial consent.[70] The majority (law) rejected the notion that the 'leap from convention to law' could be explained 'almost as if there was a common law of constitutional law, but originating in political practice'.[71]

It is interesting to note in this respect that the majority (convention) adopted an understanding of a convention according to which Peter Hogg was quoted as saying that 'a convention is a rule which is regarded as obligatory by the officials to whom it applies'.[72] The common law is also a set of rules which is regarded as obligatory by judicial officials, and therefore these rules may require

[61] *Patriation Reference*, 840.   [62] *Patriation Reference*, 840.
[63] *Patriation Reference*, 844.   [64] *Patriation Reference*, 880.
[65] *Patriation Reference*, 888. See Ivor Jennings, *The Law and the Constitution* (5th edn, London: University of London Press, 1959) 134–6.   [66] *Patriation Reference*, 894.
[67] *Patriation Reference*, 905.   [68] *Patriation Reference*, 905.
[69] *Patriation Reference*, 906.   [70] *Patriation Reference*, 784.
[71] *Patriation Reference*, 784.   [72] *Patriation Reference*, 883.

special consideration. In the United Kingdom, of course, the rule that the courts will heed enactments of the Queen-in-Parliament is itself a part of the common law. It is regularly regarded as obligatory by English judges. As we know, Canadian judges have in the past ruled that they feel bound to uphold the principles of federalism, and some of these decisions were set out in the minority (law) reasons. This happens most often precisely where there is no 'imperative constitutional text or statute' but where the law calls out for an answer. Something which was initially part of the realm of political practice (say in the early years after 1867 before the first decisions of the Supreme Court of Canada and the Judicial Committee of the Privy Council) became a part of the law of the Constitution through the common law, i.e. because the judges of those courts saw it as a binding rule or principle. It is perhaps misleading, then, to speak of a hard and fast division between law and convention at the highest level, especially in Canada where judicial review is more extensive than in the United Kingdom, precisely because of the federal nature of the former.

It is important to make a qualification here. We generally think of the common law as that which can be modified by statute. Where the common law concerns the Constitution, however, it can only be altered by the authority which is competent to amend the Constitution. In the United Kingdom, the authority is still with the Westminster Parliament, but in Canada it is controlled by the special rules on amendment. At this level, it is perhaps inappropriate to speak of the common law. Constitutional theorists and some constitutional lawyers prefer to speak of the *Grundnorm* or the ultimate rule of recognition. Had the majority (law) acknowledged that it was considering the most fundamental rules of the Canadian Constitution, the conclusion regarding substantial provincial consent which was reached by the majority (convention) might well have served to shed light on the ultimate rule of Canadian constitutional amendment. To this rule, the majorities (law and convention) might have wanted to add the rule that no amendment to the Canadian Constitution accomplished by means of the United Kingdom Parliament could be valid unless requested and consented to by the proper Canadian authorities. The strength of the prevailing Imperial theory may have prevented them from doing so. There are strong reasons, mostly relating to a sense of constitutional propriety, which make the judiciary reluctant to make rules at the most fundamental levels of the Constitution; but likewise there are circumstances when it may be obliged to do so in order to preserve the principles upon which the Constitution is based, most importantly, the rule of law.

The Aftermath of the *Patriation Reference*

The decision of the Supreme Court of Canada in the *Patriation Reference* presented the Trudeau government with a dilemma. It could embrace the judgment of the majority (law) and go ahead with the constitutional project relying on bare legality. Or it could return to the federal-provincial bargaining table and make renewed attempts at coming to the type of deal which would also satisfy the conventional requirement of substantial provincial consent.

It may be useful at this point to mention that, throughout the period of constitutional uncertainty which had existed since the declaration of a unilateral federal initiative in October 1980, discussions were also heating up in the Parliament at Westminster. On 5 November 1980 the Foreign Affairs Committee of the House of Commons, under the Chairmanship of Sir Anthony Kershaw, decided to 'inquire into the role of the United Kingdom Parliament in relation to the British North America Acts, and to report'.[73] The Committee heard evidence from British experts and received written memoranda from interested individuals and bodies, including the governments of five Canadian provinces. The dissenting Canadian provinces were at the same time active in lobbying British MPs on the matter of the impropriety of the unilateral action of the Canadian federal Parliament. The United Kingdom Parliament was being asked, in effect, to act as 'arbiter' in much the same way as it had been perhaps expected to do by some of the framers in 1867. Canadian independence had intervened, however, and the British authorities were acutely aware of the delicacy of the situation.

The First Kershaw Report provided twelve conclusions. Among those conclusions was the assertion that the only way for the United Kingdom Parliament to reconcile its own exclusive powers to amend fundamental parts of the Canadian constitution with Canada's sovereign independence was to exercise those powers in accordance with constitutional requirements, taking into account, therefore, the federal character of Canada's constitutional system.[74] Then came the startling conclusion that the United Kingdom Parliament would be 'bound to exercise its best judgment in deciding whether the [Canadian Parliament's] request, in all circumstances, conveys the clearly expressed wishes of Canada as a federally structured whole'.[75]

The United Kingdom government appeared to take a different view of the matter. In a reply to the First Kershaw Report, the United Kingdom government stated that it would act in accordance with a request from the federal Parliament of Canada and would urge the United Kingdom Parliament to do likewise.[76]

---

[73] United Kingdom, House of Commons, *First Report from the Foreign Affairs Committee: British North America Acts: The Role of Parliament* (London, 21 January 1981) vi (hereinafter the First Kershaw Report).   [74] First Kershaw Report (1981) xii, Conclusions 3 and 4.

[75] First Kershaw Report (1981) Conclusion 9.

[76] United Kingdom, House of Commons, 'Observations by the Secretary of State for Foreign and Commonwealth Affairs on the First Report from the Foreign Affairs Committee', Cmnd 8450 in *Sessional Papers* (1981) para. 13.

Also in response to the First Kershaw Report, the Canadian government issued a background paper in March 1981[77] in which it made clear its opinion that the United Kingdom Parliament was bound to accede to any request relating to amendment made by the Parliament of Canada. The Kershaw Committee issued a lengthy reply in April 1981 in which it repeated and further documented its own position.[78]

By September 1981, then, the Trudeau government was staring at two large obstacles to its unilateral federal initiative. The Supreme Court of Canada had declared the initiative legal but contrary to convention, and there was no guarantee that the United Kingdom Parliament's acquiescence would be automatic. The Canadian Prime Minister decided to convene a federal-provincial meeting for early November 1981 in order to make another attempt at finding a proposal which could attract sufficient provincial support. The first ministers and their officials met on 2 November 1981, and by 5 November they had made the compromises necessary to ensure the support of nine out of ten provinces. Unfortunately, the dissenting province was the predominantly French-speaking province of Quebec, and the government of that province decided to refer the matter of the new agreement to its Court of Appeal for a decision as to the constitutionality of a fundamental amendment to the Constitution in the absence of Quebec's consent.

Meanwhile the patriation project went ahead. In early December 1981, the resolution was approved by the Canadian Parliament and transmitted to the United Kingdom. In a third and final Report, dated 22 December 1981, the Kershaw Committee recommended that 'it would be proper for the United Kingdom Parliament to enact the proposals, notwithstanding that they will directly affect the Canadian Provinces and are dissented from by one of those Provinces, Quebec'.[79] The Prime Minister of Quebec, René Lévesque, wrote to the British Prime Minister, Margaret Thatcher, requesting that the Parliament of the United Kingdom delay enactment of the proposed legislation until the Canadian courts had had the opportunity to rule on the constitutionality of proceeding without Quebec's approval.[80] The British Prime Minister's reply, transmitted in early January 1982, stated that the United Kingdom Parliament would not delay the progress of the Canada Bill.[81]

The Parliament at Westminster finally completed its 'Canadian business' on 25 March 1982, and four days later Queen Elizabeth II assented to the Canada Act 1982 (UK). Schedule B to that Act set out the Constitution Act, 1982 and

---

[77] Canada, Parliament, *The Role of the United Kingdom Parliament in the Amendment of the Canadian Constitution* (Ottawa, 1981).
[78] United Kingdom, House of Commons, *Second Report of the Foreign Affairs Committee, Supplementary Report on the British North America Acts: The Role of Parliament* (15 April 1981).
[79] United Kingdom, House of Commons, *Third Report on the British North America Acts: The Role of Parliament* (22 December 1981) v.
[80] A copy of the letter is reprinted in (1984–5) 30 McGill LJ 708.   [81] ibid., 724.

provided Canada with the most significant addition to its Constitution since the British North America Act, 1867.[82] Section 2 of the Canada Act 1982 stated boldly that 'No Act of the Parliament of the United Kingdom passed after the Constitution Act, 1982 comes into force shall extend to Canada as part of its law', and the marginal notes underlined this point succinctly: 'Termination of power to legislate for Canada'.[83] If the Act was truly all that it purported to be, it would have been difficult to imagine a more crucial constitutional text, at least in Canadian terms.

On 17 April 1982, at a windy ceremony on Parliament Hill in Ottawa, Canada, Queen Elizabeth II proclaimed the Constitution Act, 1982 in force.[84] The opening words of the proclamation gave further indication of the importance of the event:

> WHEREAS in the past certain amendments to the Constitution of Canada have been made by the Parliament of the United Kingdom at the request and with the consent of Canada;
>
> AND WHEREAS it is in accord with the status of Canada as an independent state that Canadians be able to amend their Constitution in Canada in all respects;
>
> AND WHEREAS it is desirable to provide in the Constitution of Canada for the recognition of certain fundamental rights and freedoms and to make other amendments to the Constitution;
>
> AND WHEREAS the Parliament of the United Kingdom has therefore, at the request and with the consent of Canada, enacted the Canada Act, which provides for the patriation and amendment of the Constitution of Canada;
>
> . . .

Such official-sounding phrases begged to be given clearer meaning. In what sense had the Parliament of the United Kingdom acted 'at the request and *with the consent of Canada*'?[85] What was the relationship between Canada's 'independence' and her ability to amend her Constitution at home? To what extent were the newly recognised 'fundamental rights and freedoms' themselves subject to

---

[82] Renamed Constitution Act, 1867 (see Schedule to Constitution Act, 1982).

[83] The Department of Justice annotations alongside s. 2 of the Canada Act 1982 state: 'This clause terminates the power of the United Kingdom Parliament to legislate for Canada, thereby patriating the Canadian Constitution. The formula used is the standard formula now used in modern independence instruments.' Canada, Department of Justice, Annotated Canada Bill 1982 (1982). For a description of the design behind the Canada Act 1982 from an insider's perspective, see B. Strayer, *The Patriation and Legitimacy of the Canadian Constitution* (Saskatoon: College of Law, University of Saskatchewan, 1982). Section 2 of the Canada Act 1982 needs to be read in conjunction with (a) Part V of the Constitution Act, 1982 which sets out a new 'code' on Canadian constitutional amendment to replace the former mix of United Kingdom and Canadian law, convention and parliamentary procedure, and (b) s. 52(1) of the Constitution Act, 1982 which states: 'The Constitution of Canada is the supreme law of Canada, and any law that is inconsistent with the provisions of the Constitution is, to the extent of the inconsistency, of no force or effect.'

[84] The Constitution Act, 1982, with the exception of s. 23(1)(a) in respect of Quebec, came into force on this date. See SI/82–97, reprinted in (1984–5) McGill LJ 725.   [85] Emphasis added.

the new rules on amendment? What was the 'patriation' of the Constitution of Canada? Had not the Constitution always been in Canada? And had not amendment always been possible? In what way did the new provisions on amendment change the rules?

As noted above, the first formal attempt to question the 'patriation' process had already been initiated by the government of the province of Quebec. On 25 November 1981, as the government of Canada prepared to submit a Resolution to the Parliament of Canada requesting the introduction in the Parliament of the United Kingdom of a Bill entitled the Canada Act, the government of Quebec had presented a reference case to the Quebec Court of Appeal in which it challenged the legitimacy of proceeding to patriation and amendment of the Constitution of Canada over the objection of the province of Quebec. On 7 April 1982, just days before the scheduled proclamation of the Constitution Act, 1982, the Quebec Court of Appeal rendered a unanimous opinion in which it rejected the arguments of the Quebec government.[86] The case moved on to the Supreme Court of Canada and thereby provided the country's highest Court with a first opportunity to comment on the constitutional transformation which had by then taken place.[87] A unanimous full Court agreed with the Court of Appeal and made the following declarations in the course of its reasons:

> The Constitution Act, 1982 is now in force. *Its legality is neither challenged nor assailable.* It contains a new procedure for amending the Constitution of Canada which *entirely replaces* the old one in its legal as well as in its conventional aspects. Even assuming therefore that there was a conventional requirement for the consent of Quebec under the old system, it would no longer have any object or force.[88]

Once again, a series of questions emerged, ones which could not even be hidden behind the straightforward, reassuring language of the Court. Even if the legality of the 1982 Constitution was not challenged, could its legality be truly unassailable? Would even the highest Court of Canada decline to declare the 'patriation' and amendment invalid if the legal process had been flawed?[89] Or did the stamp of the United Kingdom Parliament put the process beyond the Canadian courts' jurisdiction? And in what sense did the new procedure for amending the Constitution for Canada 'entirely', and irrevocably one presumes, 'replace' the old one? Presumably the United Kingdom Parliament which accomplished the deed could undo it at a later time, especially when one considered the *Patriation Reference*'s many statements regarding the unlimited and undiminished power of the Westminster Parliament.

---

[86] *Re: Objection to a Resolution to Amend the Constitution* [1982] CA 33.

[87] *Re: Objection to A Resolution to Amend the Constitution* [1982] 2 SCR 793 (hereinafter the *Quebec Veto Reference*).   [88] *Quebec Veto Reference*, 806 (emphasis added).

[89] As it was prepared to do regarding Manitoba statutes passed according to a flawed process. See *Reference re Manitoba Language Rights* [1985] 1 SCR 721.

Many of these questions will be addressed in Part III, both by the various Canadian constitutional commentators surveyed in Chapter 11 and by the analysis proposed for Canada in Chapter 13. However, before considering Canadian explanations of constitutional independence, we turn to the pre-1986 constitutional experience of the other two countries under study. For reasons which will emerge later,[90] New Zealand will be considered first, followed by Australia.

[90] See Ch. 13 below.

8

New Zealand: Waitangi, Westminster and Wellington

Early constitutional arrangements in New Zealand

In Chapter 2 we saw the confusion that surrounded New Zealand's founding, including the contested importance of the Treaty of Waitangi. Like all legal systems, the New Zealand legal system remained cognitively aware of those who claimed that Waitangi was legally and constitutionally significant, but normatively the legal system was all but closed to such arguments. That situation has changed in the past thirty years. However, during the early part of New Zealand's constitutional development, the Treaty of Waitangi was hardly visible even between the lines of mainstream legal and constitutional commentary. Taking our cue from that commentary, we therefore begin this account of early constitutional arrangements in New Zealand by focusing on the various Imperial enactments that were enacted as of the 1850s.

Unlike Canada, New Zealand acquired the ability to amend its constitutional texts at an early stage in its constitutional development. The Westminster-enacted New Zealand Constitution Act, 1852 (Imp.)[1] gave the New Zealand General Assembly[2] the power 'to make laws for the peace, order, and good government of New Zealand, provided that no such laws be repugnant to the law of England'[3] and apparently,[4] by section 68, made it lawful for the General Assembly 'to alter from time to time any provisions of this Act' subject to reservation for the signification of royal pleasure. By 1857 newly expanded powers of constitutional amendment were granted. In section 2 of the New Zealand Constitution Amendment Act, 1857,[5] the Imperial Parliament provided that 'it shall be lawful for the said General Assembly of New Zealand by any Act or Acts

---

[1] Hereinafter the Constitution Act, 1852.

[2] I have used the terms General Assembly and New Zealand Parliament interchangeably in this chapter, usually preferring the former description earlier on in New Zealand history and the latter description into the twentieth century.   [3] Section 53.

[4] P. Joseph, *Constitutional and Administrative Law of New Zealand* (2nd edn, Wellington: Brookers, 2001) 107, indicates that other commentators misinterpret the 1852 Act by stating that the General Assembly had no power to amend the Act.

[5] Hereinafter the Constitution Act, 1857.

from time to time to alter, suspend, or repeal all or any of the provisions of [the 1852 Act], except as are herein specified', and accordingly repealed the above-mentioned section 68. Only twenty-one sections were excluded from the amending powers of the General Assembly, and it was generally accepted that only the Imperial Parliament could amend these so long as the 1857 Act remained unaltered.[6]

In any event, the powers of the General Assembly were limited in ways which went beyond an inability to legislate in areas covered by the entrenched provisions. It could not legislate with extraterritorial effect and its Bills were subject to reservation and disallowance. However, for our purposes, the main additional limitation was that it could not legislate repugnantly to the law of England. This fundamental rule of the Imperial legal system was set out in the proviso to section 53 of the 1852 Act: 'provided that no such laws be repugnant to the law of England'. As Aikman would later state, the doctrine of repugnancy:

> ... was itself an expression of a broader principle, the legislative supremacy of the United Kingdom Parliament. The prohibition against repugnancy was the only respect in which the legislative supremacy of the United Kingdom Parliament actually limited the legislative competence of the New Zealand Parliament. Nevertheless, the United Kingdom Parliament had the power, limited only by convention, to enact statutes extending to New Zealand without consulting the New Zealand Government and even in opposition to the wishes of the New Zealand Government or Parliament.[7]

Indeed it was the prohibition against repugnant legislation which protected the entrenched sections of the Constitution Act, 1852 by preventing the New Zealand General Assembly from claiming for itself a full power of amendment.[8]

---

[6] In fact, in 1862 the Imperial Parliament gave power to repeal one of those entrenched sections, and that power was exercised in 1873. Another 5 sections were rendered inoperative by the passage of the Abolition of Provinces Act, 1875 (NZ) and were repealed by the Statute Law Revision Act, 1892 (UK). The remaining 15 sections ceased to be entrenched upon the enactment of the New Zealand Constitution (Amendment) Act, 1947 (UK). The increasingly limited degree of entrenchment explains why the New Zealand Parliament is often considered to be 'sovereign' or 'supreme' in much the same way as the United Kingdom Parliament. See Joseph (2001) (n. 4 above) 107–8 and C.C. Aikman, 'Parliament' in J.L. Robson (ed.) *New Zealand: The Development of its Laws and its Constitution* (2nd edn, London: Stevens, 1967) 40, 55 (hereinafter Aikman (1967)).   [7] ibid., 59–60.

[8] ibid., 59. The Colonial Laws Validity Act, 1865 (Imp.), by s. 2, clarified but also reasserted the overriding supremacy of the Imperial Parliament. See K.C. Wheare, *The Statute of Westminster and Dominion Status* (5th edn, Oxford: Oxford University Press, 1953) 79. An argument had been made, based on s. 5 of the 1865 Act, to the effect that New Zealand was thereby granted full power, or self-sufficiency, regarding its Constitution. See R.O. McGechan, 'Status and Legislative Inability' in J.C. Beaglehole (ed.) *New Zealand and the Statute of Westminster* (Wellington: Victoria University College, 1944) 65, 100–2. and J. Hight and H.D. Bamford, *Constitutional History and Law of New Zealand* (Christchurch: Whitcombe and Tombs, 1914) 346. J.F. Northey, 'The New Zealand Constitution' in J. F. Northey (ed.) *The A.G. Davis Essays in the Law* (London: Butterworths, 1965) 149, 154–6 provides a useful summary of the arguments for and against. Those who argued 'for' claimed that the expansion of the General Assembly's powers operated in such a way as to remove the restriction over amendment of the entrenched provisions in the

Change in the Empire-Colony relationships would have to await the Statute of Westminster, 1931.[9]

What were the theoretical assumptions of New Zealand lawyers, judges and officials in this early period? One way of gauging such attitudes was to look at the sorts of textbooks that would have been consulted at this time. By far the most influential book in the early period of New Zealand constitutional history—that is, before the Statute of Westminster, 1931—was Hight and Bamford's *Constitutional History and Law of New Zealand*.[10] Hight, the historian, and Bamford, the barrister and law lecturer, revealed the sort of orthodox theoretical assumptions that one would have expected to find in the early part of the twentieth century, and which were characteristic of the Imperial theory.[11]

Given limitations on the New Zealand General Assembly's powers, such as repugnancy and extraterritoriality,[12] it was not surprising that Hight and Bamford affirmed both the sovereignty of the Imperial Parliament and the subordinate status of the General Assembly: 'It is evident that [the powers conferred on the General Assembly by the Constitution Act, 1852] are not unlimited like those of the Imperial Parliament.'[13] However, they acknowledged that so long as the General Assembly respected the limits imposed on it as a result of its subordinate status, its powers were extensive: 'within the limits of its powers the Parliament of a self-governing Dominion is supreme—its powers are plenary ... and in making laws for "the peace, order and good government" of the Dominion it may use any means it pleases'.[14]

But Hight and Bamford were quick to add that 'the limitations imposed on the powers of the Dominion Parliament are real and important'. In the first place, 'it has not the attribute of full sovereignty'; and secondly, 'the Dominion can legislate only for the Dominion itself, whilst the British Parliament can legislate for any part of the British possessions or British subjects wherever situated'.[15] Thirdly, 'no laws made by the Parliament of the Dominion shall be repugnant to the laws of England'.[16] And finally, 'a Colonial Parliament is subject to certain restrictions on its power to alter the Constitution'.[17] Dicey,

---

Constitution Act. Whatever the merit of these arguments, the fundamentals of the Westminster-Wellington relationship had not been altered. Hight and Bamford (1914) (above) 346, who noted the possibility of an argument based on s. 5 of the 1865 Act in their 1914 textbook, recognised nonetheless 'the legislative sovereignty of the Imperial Crown-in-Parliament'.

[9] New Zealand constitutional commentators and reformers proceeded on the assumption that the arguments based on s. 5 were not sufficiently solid to be relied upon exclusively. See, e.g., Hight and Bamford (1914) (n. 8 above) 346; McGechan (1944) (n. 8 above) 102. The same assumption is made in this chapter.   [10] Hight and Bamford (1914) (n. 8 above).

[11] For discussion of the Imperial theory in the Canadian context see Ch. 5 above.

[12] For further discussion, see Ch. 2 above.

[13] Hight and Bamford (1914) (n. 8 above) 344.   [14] ibid., 344.   [15] ibid., 344.

[16] ibid., 345.

[17] ibid., 345. As noted above, the Constitution Act, 1857 gave the General Assembly the power to vary the Constitution, with several important exceptions. Hight and Bamford discussed whether s. 5 of the Colonial Laws Validity Act, 1865 could have been said to provide the amendment powers

The Law of the Constitution was cited by way of authority.[18] Hight and Bamford did not discuss the prospect of constitutional independence. We shall see that this was far from New Zealanders' minds at this time.[19]

Balfour, Westminster and beyond

When the Balfour Declaration and Statute of Westminster, 1931 came to be considered, New Zealand showed its preference for the *status quo*. Whereas other Dominions, such as Canada, the Irish Free State and South Africa, were anxious to take full advantage of the freedom and equality there offered, section 10 of the 1931 Statute ensured that the core provisions (sections 2–6) would not have any effect in New Zealand until the New Zealand Parliament decided to adopt the Statute. To borrow Sir Geoffrey Palmer's words, 'reluctance to take power when it is offered is not often met with in constitutional history'.[20] Some comment-ators have expressed the view that New Zealand would have been quite satisfied if the whole project of assuring Dominion equality had failed. Writing in 1944, J.C. Beaglehole noted the New Zealand government's lack of interest in the 1931 Statute in the following terms: 'I have no confidential information at my disposal, and I can give no authority for the statement—but I have a very strong impression that the government of New Zealand in 1931 would have been far from disappointed had the discussions over the Statute, and the Statute itself, then come to an unpremeditated and sudden end.'[21]

The parliamentary debates on the 1931 Statute provide an insight into New Zealand constitutional thinking of the time. Prime Minister Forbes felt that he had 'correctly interpreted public opinion' in assuming that there was no need to alter a constitutional position 'which has proved thoroughly satisfactory in its

---

held back by the 1857 Act, but they concluded that the matter was unclear, and that it would have to be resolved by the courts, and eventually by the Privy Council (p. 346).

[18] Hight and Bamford (1914) (n. 8 above) 344n.

[19] A nineteenth-century example of New Zealand's lack of independent-minded constitutional spirit was Sir John Bell, speaking at the Australasian Federation convention in 1890. He said that the colonies were bound to the United Kingdom by 'the fondest ties of affection', but beyond that 'we are also attached by something more permanent and durable, that is by the conviction that our connection with the old country will best serve our material interests and be the best safeguard of our liberties'. Official Record of the Proceedings and Debates of the Australasian Federation Conference, 1890, Melbourne and Sydney, 1890, 182, quoted in W.J. Hudson and M.P. Sharp, *Australian Independence: Colony to Reluctant Kingdom* (Melbourne: Melbourne University Press, 1988) 35. It should be noted that such sentiments were not unique to New Zealand. Equally devoted statements could be found in Australia and Canada in this period.

[20] Rt Hon. Sir G. Palmer, *New Zealand's Constitution in Crisis: Reforming Our Political System* (Dunedin: John McIndoe, 1992) 45. For Australian hesitations and the reasons behind them, see Ch. 9 below.

[21] J.C. Beaglehole, 'The Statute and Constitutional Change' in Beaglehole (ed.) (1944) (n. 8 above) 63.

operation in the past'.[22] New Zealanders valued the British connection on the whole, with its trading and defence advantages, and not surprisingly most of their representatives' interventions related to those concerns. Legal issues relating to sovereignty were dealt with at a more figurative, even emotional, level. The speeches in the debate referred to 'the Old Country', 'the Motherland' and even 'Mother dear', and in one case bemoaned 'the disintegration of the British Empire'.[23] Some speakers were forward-looking in their recognition that New Zealand would eventually have to shed its 'swaddling clothes'.[24] One also finds fairly classical statements of Diceyan sovereignty and Imperial theory, as was normal for that age. With reference to section 4 of the 1931 Statute which on its face limited the right of the United Kingdom Parliament to legislate for the Dominions, Mr Downie Stuart noted: 'Legally this clause can have no effect, as the Imperial Parliament cannot divest itself of its sovereignty in that way . . . there is here an attempt to accomplish the impossible.'[25]

In the Governor General's speech of 1944, the government finally announced its intention 'to place before Parliament the question of the adoption of the Statute of Westminster, the enactment of which would bring New Zealand into line with the other self-governing Dominions'.[26] Adoption would, it was announced, have the dual advantage of 'remov[ing] doubts in the eyes of the foreign powers regarding the Sovereign status of New Zealand' and of 'removing existing legal drafting and administrative difficulties both in New Zealand and in the United Kingdom'.[27] Ever since 1931, inabilities regarding constitutional amendment had been of little practical concern compared to the inconvenience of having to request help from Westminster regarding legislation with extra-territorial application, the latter being particularly necessary and often urgent in the context of World War II. In the end the government did not proceed with adoption at that time, in part because of the perceived propaganda advantage which might have been offered to the enemy if one of the allies had been seen to be distance itself from Britain.[28]

[22] Quoted in speech by Mr H.F. Holland (New Zealand, Parliament, *Debates*, (NZPD) 5th Session, 23rd Parliament, 1931, 601) in which the future party leader teased the Prime Minister for bringing home 'an unwanted foundling, and vehemently he protests his own innocence in the matter of paternal responsibility', but also disagreed with the latter's gauging of New Zealand public opinion, noting instead 'wide public sentiment' in favour of greater legislative autonomy.

[23] NZPD, 5th Session, 23rd Parliament, 1931, 585 (Rushworth).

[24] ibid., 580 (Carr): 'I welcome a move towards political autonomy among the component parts of the British Commonwealth. That may seem a rash thing to say, but I think it is time we, as New-Zealanders, began to free ourselves from swaddling clothes. We are so proud to be more English than the English that there is just a danger that we may fail for all time to develop a pride in an individuality of our own—in a measure of independence of our own.' See also NZPD, 5th Session, 23rd Parliament, 1931, 601 (Holland). Reluctance to sever the Imperial link was also persistent in Australia and Canada at this time, though to differing degrees.

[25] NZPD, 5th Session, 23rd Parliament, 1931, 552.

[26] NZPD, 1st Session, 27th Parliament, 1944, 7.   [27] ibid., 7.

[28] B.S. Gustafson, *Constitutional Changes Since 1870* (Auckland: Heinemann, 1969) 9: 'Although the New Zealand Labour Government announced in 1944 its intention of adopting

Despite the lack of legislative progress at that time there was renewed interest in adoption of the Statute as a matter of academic study. Given the state of constitutional theory in this period, it was not clear whether adoption would end New Zealand's subordination to the United Kingdom Parliament as a matter of law. This question was considered in detail by Professor R.O. McGechan in a lecture published in 1944.[29] In terms of the approaches identified in discussing Canada's constitutional development, McGechan's lecture drew primarily from the Imperial theory perspective; however, glimpses of perspectives closer to the Independence theory emerged from time to time.

McGechan began by asserting that 'neither the enactment nor the adoption of the Statute [of Westminster]' involved 'any alteration whatsoever in our status'.[30] The only point of the whole operation was to 'put our legislative house in order'.[31] He noted that one sometimes heard 'wild assertions' to the effect that adoption of that Statute in New Zealand meant 'cutting the painter'.[32] In an imperious style reminiscent of Dicey, he dismissed such talk as 'either meaningless' or indicative of 'abysmal ignorance of the present international and constitutional status of the dominions'.[33] Whatever the Balfour Declaration said, 'the Imperial Parliament is a sovereign body, and the New Zealand Parliament a non-sovereign one'.[34] 'The New Zealand Parliament had not the capacity to make or unmake any law.'[35]

After discussing the various existing limitations on the New Zealand Parliament, and the uncertainty regarding that Parliament's ability to amend all of the New Zealand Constitution, McGechan moved on to what he saw as the fundamental post-adoption question—which he did not promise to answer: 'If we adopt the Statute of Westminster, will the Parliament of the United Kingdom retain its legislative supremacy?'[36] McGechan proposed to leave 'abstract and theoretical' issues aside and to approach the matter more practically, but of course abstract theory influenced that which was deemed practically and legally possible.[37] In any event, the answer to the fundamental question, in his view, depended on how one interpreted sections 4 and 2(2) of the Statute of Westminster. Section 4 clearly preserved a competence in the Westminster Parliament 'to legislate for New Zealand whenever asked to do so by New Zealand'.[38] But the more important problem—'legal not political', as McGechan observed—was 'whether the Imperial Parliament will continue competent to legislate for New Zealand *against the wishes of*

the Statute, it delayed doing so until 1947. This delay was caused partly by fears that enemy propaganda might misinterpret the move and partly by uncertainty as to the intentions of the National Party Opposition, which had left the War Cabinet.'

[29] R.O. McGechan, 'Status and Legislative Inability' in J.C. Beaglehole (ed.) *New Zealand and the Statute of Westminster* (Wellington: Victoria University College, 1944) 65.   [30] ibid., 77.
[31] ibid., 77.   [32] ibid., 78.   [33] ibid., 78.
[34] ibid., 78. McGechan added, 'I am using the phrase legislative sovereignty in the Dicey sense of capacity to make or unmake any law'.   [35] ibid., 78.
[36] ibid., 103.   [37] ibid., 103.   [38] ibid., 103.

New Zealanders'.[39] McGechan's practical answer to that question was that section 2(2) would permit New Zealand immediately to nullify the unwanted imperial legislation.[40] The true question, then, as McGechan put it, was 'whether the Imperial Parliament can repeal or annul the Statute of Westminster'.[41] The answer to that question had been given, at least as a matter of abstract theory, by the Privy Council in the *British Coal Corporation* case,[42] although McGechan pointed out that the Privy Council's view 'has not been left unchallenged among constitutionalists in their dominions'.[43] Despite his practical inclinations, McGechan had to admit that 'the theoretical problem [noted in *British Coal Corporation*] remains and goes to the fundamentals of our constitutions'.[44] The problem turned on 'whether the nature of legislative sovereignty logically involves capacity or incapacity for partial abdication'.[45] McGechan concluded prophetically that these questions 'may well provide a legal controversy for several decades'.[46]

New Zealand understandings of the adoption of the Statute of Westminster

The New Zealand Parliament finally adopted the Statute of Westminster in 1947. Three legislative provisions accomplished the task. First, the Statute of Westminster Adoption Act 1947 (NZ)[47] reversed the effect of section 10 of the Statute of Westminster and thereby gave effect, most importantly, to the provisions dealing with repugnancy (section 2), extraterritoriality (section 3) and Dominion request and consent (section 4). Section 3(1) of the Adoption Act 1947 (NZ) declared that the request and consent referred to in section 4 of the 1931 Statute 'shall be made and given by the Parliament of New Zealand, and not otherwise'. A second New Zealand enactment, the New Zealand Constitution Amendment (Request and Consent) Act 1947 (NZ)[48] provided the requisite request and consent for a final piece of Westminster legislation for

---

[39] ibid., 103–4 (emphasis added).   [40] ibid., 103.   [41] ibid., 104.

[42] *British Coal Corporation v The King* [1935] AC 500 (PC).

[43] He cited the famous statement of the South African Court of Appeal in *Ndlwana v Hofmeyr* (1937) AD 229, that 'freedom once given cannot be taken away'. He also noted an article by W.N. Harrison, published in *Australian Law Journal*, January/February 1944, as support for the view that, in McGechan's summary 'the true meaning of s. 4 of the Statute is that the Imperial Parliament had purported to divest itself of the power to legislate for the Dominions, and that the Imperial Parliament is competent to do this. If both of these propositions are sound, repeal of the Statute, as law of the Dominion, is beyond the Imperial Parliament's powers.' McGechan (1944) (n. 29 above) 105. McGechan's own solution once again revealed his practical bent: 'No doubt the Boston Tea Party is the best sanction against the repeal of the Statute of Westminster' (p. 104).

[44] McGechan (1944) (n. 29 above) 104.   [45] ibid., 105.   [46] ibid., 105.

[47] Hereinafter the Adoption Act 1947 (NZ).

[48] Hereinafter the (Request and Consent) Act 1947 (NZ).

New Zealand, the New Zealand Constitution (Amendment) Act 1947 (UK).[49]
The latter conferred constituent powers[50] on the New Zealand Parliament that
would otherwise have been denied it due to the effect of section 8 of the 1931
Statute. Section 1 of the (Amendment) Act 1947 (UK) repealed the Constitution Act, 1857 and made it 'lawful for the Parliament of New Zealand ... to
alter, suspend or repeal, at any time, all or any of the provisions of the
New Zealand Constitution Act 1852'. How did these provisions affect the
state of constitutional subordination which had existed until that point? And
furthermore, could it now be said that New Zealand was constitutionally
self-sufficient?

The White Paper which accompanied the adoption legislation was somewhat ambiguous with respect to the theoretical points that interest us.[51] The
authors were at pains to emphasise, as was the government,[52] that the 1947
constitutional proposals were not in any way revolutionary. They enabled
New Zealand to obtain 'full legislative capacity' through adoption of the
Statute of Westminster and true 'legislative autonomy' with the enactment by
the United Kingdom Parliament of the (Amendment) Act 1947.[53] Self-
sufficiency seemed assured on this version, but the authors also appeared to
cling to the orthodoxy of continuing subordination. They reasserted, without
specifically mentioning the case, the *British Coal Corporation* doctrine by
stating that 'without ... request and consent the United Kingdom Parliament
is constitutionally, *though not legally*, incapable of concerning itself with
matters appertaining to New Zealand self-government'.[54] And elsewhere they
stated that, while conventions put the Imperial connection on 'a more substantial basis', the legal picture was still apparently one of 'legal subordination
of the Parliament of the people of New Zealand to the Parliament of the
people of the United Kingdom'.[55] In this version, then, it appeared that
subordination persisted, and that legislative capacity and autonomy (based on
an assumption of Westminster restraint) were the most that New Zealand
could expect. Dicey was still casting a long shadow over New Zealand constitutional thinking.

What did the legislators make of this proposal? On behalf of the government,
Prime Minister Fraser was at pains to emphasise, quoting A. Berriedale Keith,
that adoption was 'not revolutionary': 'it simply "establishe[d] as law that which

---

[49] Hereinafter the (Amendment) Act 1947 (UK).

[50] The nature of these constituent powers will be discussed in greater detail in Part III.

[51] New Zealand, House of Representatives, *The Statute of Westminster: Notes on the Purpose and
Effect of the Adoption by New Zealand Parliament of Sections 2, 3, 4, 5 and 6 of the Statute of
Westminster and the New Zealand Constitution Amendment (Consent and Request) Bill* in New
Zealand, House of Representatives, *Journals*, 1st Session, 28th Parliament, 1948, App., Vol. 1
(hereinafter White Paper (1947)).

[52] NZPD, 1st Session, 28th Parliament, 1947, 562 (Prime Minister Fraser).

[53] White Paper (1947) (n. 51 above) 5–6.   [54] ibid., 4 (emphasis added).

[55] ibid., 5.

had before rested on convention" '.[56] The Prime Minister recognised that until 1947 'the New Zealand Parliament still exist[ed] as subordinate in some way to the British Parliament', and then went on to state that it was his desire to see to it that 'even implied subordination should be eliminated altogether'.[57] This seemed to go much further than the White Paper.

It was clear from the (Request and Consent) Act 1947 (NZ) that New Zealand contemplated an ongoing link with the United Kingdom Parliament, or at least the possibility of that link, but that need not have imported subordination. Mr Mason, the Attorney-General, explained that that Act was designed to avoid a situation where 'indirectly, legislation might be imposed without reference to this Parliament'.[58] The Prime Minister's remarks confirmed that this arrangement was not to imply subordination: 'for the future, no Bill passed by the British Parliament will apply to New Zealand unless New Zealand is a consenting party to it and takes the necessary action'.[59]

It is difficult to determine whether the request and consent requirements were placed in the Bill because recourse to the United Kingdom Parliament was thought likely, or simply because the possibility was expressly mentioned in section 4 of the 1931 Statute and therefore needed to be controlled.[60] Furthermore, one cannot be sure whether the Prime Minister and Attorney-General were speaking in terms of the law or conventions of the Constitution. Given the

---

[56] NZPD, 1st Session, 28th Parliament, 1947, 562. The Attorney-General, Mr Mason, agreed: '[The Statute of Westminster] puts into statutory form what was previously a convention. One cannot become emotional over that circumstance; it does not provoke anything in the nature of a revolution.' (p. 540)

[57] NZPD, 1st Session, 28th Parliament, 1947, 532. Dr Finlay took a similarly robust line, stating that adoption of the measures would 'give us the sole right to legislate for New Zealand. No longer will it be possible for the Imperial Parliament to pass legislation extending to New Zealand' (p. 548). Mr Algie, himself a former Professor of Law (see Northey (1965) (n. 8 above) 164), expressed the commonly-held fear that 'by adopting this Statute in its entirety we would sever the link between the Old Country and ourselves' (p. 551). However, later in his speech he tried to allay that fear:

It has been suggested that by adopting this Statute we might be cutting the painter. That argument cannot be thrown over lightly, but I should like to give my two answers to it. First of all, let us bear in mind that fact that it is curious to talk of cutting the painter with the Old Land when it was the Old Land herself who handed us the weapons with which to do the cutting. The Old Land had said to us, 'Here is the Statute of Westminster. We are adopting it. You take it and adopt it, too, if you like.' Now, we cannot be said to be cutting the painter when we do no more than England herself has invited us to do. (p. 552).

[58] NZPD, 1st Session, 28th Parliament, 1947, 542.   [59] ibid., 563.

[60] The Attorney-General's remarks indicate the former explanation, while Mr Webb explaining the Bill following the Prime Minister suggested the latter. NZPD, 1st Session, 28th Parliament, 1947, 564. The Leader of the Council, the Hon. Mr Wilson, also suggested the latter: 'With the passing of the [Statute of Westminster Adoption] Bill, it will not be possible for the United Kingdom Government to pass legislation affecting New Zealand' (p. 870). However, later in his speech he quoted from the Explanatory Memorandum which repeated the s. 4 procedure (p. 871). In his explanation of the New Zealand Constitution (Request and Consent) Bill he left the impression that the legislation was intended to make New Zealand fully sovereign: 'It is a mark of a sovereign Legislature that it has full power to deal with its own constitution. If New Zealand is a fully sovereign State, it is necessary that we should have full power to deal with our

understandings of sovereignty which prevailed at the time, it is not surprising that section 4 request and consent procedures were accepted as a matter of course. The more important development was the assumption of full legislative competence and autonomy. Whether that amounted to an end to even the theoretical possibility of subordination was a question which could not be answered with full consideration of the relevant option, until New Zealand Constitutional theory had evolved a little further.[61]

The evolution in New Zealand understandings of the legal effects of 1947 can be charted through a reading of the first and second editions of a highly influential commentary on the New Zealand Constitution, first published in 1954 as part of *The British Commonwealth* series.[62] In the introductory chapter, by K.J. Scott and J.L. Robson and later by C.C. Aikman and J.L. Robson, the authors asserted that 'the New Zealand Parliament acquired plenary powers in 1947', and that as a result 'the New Zealand Constitution became in all essential respects the same in content as the British'.[63] It was not clear from this statement whether 'plenary powers', which clearly connoted self-sufficiency, also included a sense of ultimate supremacy, even *vis-à-vis* the Westminster Parliament.

The second chapter on 'Parliament', written first by Scott and later by Aikman, provided some insight into this question. The first edition included an account in the Imperial theory tradition which seemed to acknowledge the continuing sovereignty of the United Kingdom Parliament, a sovereignty limited only by Westminster self-restraint or conventions.[64] The second edition, published in 1967, took a bolder course which was more characteristic of the Independence theory. It acknowledged that in the pre-1947 past, New Zealand's

---

Constitution . . . It is an essential quality of a sovereign State that it shall have [the ability to deal fully with the Constitution of New Zealand]. The only means by which these doubts can be resolved is by an enactment by the Parliament of the United Kingdom.' (pp. 876–7).

[61] Mr Doidge's view was as follows. He referred to the project as 'a legal bill of divorcement if required' (NZPD, 1st Session, 28th Parliament, 1947, 535), and later: 'All that the Statute does is to provide a facility for a breakaway from the Empire, if there is such a desire—and there is certainly no such desire in this country. We are proud of the granite strength of our loyalty, proud of our British heritage enshrined as it is in the British Throne. With us, loyalty to the Motherland is an instinct as deep as religion.' (p. 538).

[62] J.L. Robson (ed.) *New Zealand: The Development of its Law and Constitution* (London: Stevens, 1954; 2nd edn, 1967).   [63] ibid. (1st edn, 1954); (2nd edn, 1967) 1.

[64] . . . but prior to the Statute of Westminster the United Kingdom Parliament also had the power, limited only by convention, to enact statutes extending to New Zealand without consulting the New Zealand Government and even in opposition to the wishes of the New Zealand Government or Parliament. This power can be said to have been abolished (*if we assume that the United Kingdom Parliament will continue to be unwilling to enact amending legislation*) by section 4 of the Statute of Westminster.

K.J. Scott, 'Parliament' in Robson (1st edn, 1954) (n. 62 above) 30, 46 (emphasis added). The afterthought was both cryptic and somewhat disturbing if it meant that New Zealand's constitutional autonomy depended entirely upon Westminster's restraint. A footnote moderated the effect somewhat by suggesting an out: 'Possibly s. 4 is binding on the United Kingdom Parliament. Zelman Cowen, "Parliamentary Sovereignty and the Limits of Legal Change" *Australian Law Journal*, September 22, 1952, 237, 240.' Scott in Robson (1st edn, 1954) (n. 62 above) 46.

autonomy had been dependent upon Westminster's respect for convention, but it also suggested that since 1947 that autonomy was secure, even as a matter of law. By section 4 of the Statute of Westminster, the United Kingdom Parliament 'surrendered' its 'power . . . to enact legislation extending to New Zealand without consulting the New Zealand Government or Parliament'.[65] And although the Privy Council in the *British Coal Corporation* case had expressed the view that the United Kingdom Parliament could ignore or repeal section 4, it was 'most unlikely that a Commonwealth court would regard any such legislation as extending ". . . to a Dominion as part of the law of that Dominion" '.[66] Aikman added that, in New Zealand, section 3(1) of the (Adoption) Act 1947 (NZ) had in effect amended section 4 of the Statute. Read in this light, section 3(1) seemed categorical: '*the request and consent* of New Zealand to the enactment of any Act of the Parliament of the United Kingdom *shall be made and given by the Parliament of New Zealand and not otherwise*'.[67] If this could be taken to mean that, at least as a matter of New Zealand law, nothing less than true request and consent would do, then perhaps the United Kingdom Parliament was now legally subordinate to the New Zealand Parliament. It will be necessary to return to this difficult argument in Part III.

In his own textbook, published posthumously in 1962,[68] Scott held to a rigid Diceyan-Imperial theory line.[69] He asserted that, on its face, section 4 of the Statute of Westminster required only a declaration of New Zealand request and consent, not request and consent in substance.[70] Accordingly, though section 3(1) of the (Adoption) Act 1947 (NZ) might have had the effect of preventing any other *New Zealand* authority from purporting to speak for that country for the purposes of section 4, the former provision could not limit the power of the United Kingdom any more than section 4 itself could. Scott's admission that a New Zealand court might find 'some way' around these obstacles clearly lacked conviction.[71]

---

[65] Aikman in Robson (2nd edn, 1967) (n. 62 above) 60.   [66] ibid., 60.   [67] ibid., 60.
[68] K.J. Scott, *The New Zealand Constitution* (Oxford: Oxford University Press, 1962).
[69] See O. Hood Phillips, Book Review (1964) 80 LQR 290, 291: 'On the general question whether a Parliament that has power to legislate on any given subject by the ordinary legislative process has power to deny itself that power, Professor Scott propounds the orthodox view skillfully and to us convincingly.'
[70] Scott (1962) (n. 68 above) 18–19 (emphasis added):

The United Kingdom Parliament still has power to enact legislation extending to New Zealand as part of the law of New Zealand. No provision on the statute-book of either the United Kingdom or New Zealand could be deemed to have abrogated this power; and the only provision that could be deemed to have diminished it is section 4 of the Statute of Westminster. A United Kingdom Act containing a declaration, in terms of section 4, that New Zealand had requested and consented to its enactment would extend to New Zealand as part of the law of New Zealand. *For the sake of completeness it has to be said that this would be the case even if the declaration were contrary to fact, for in terms of section 4 an Act is excepted not if New Zealand has requested and consented to it but if it contains a declaration that New Zealand had requested and consented to it.*

[71] ibid., 18.

Scott's insistence on taking the Westminster-centered and Dicey-influenced approach to these questions would have been that much more disturbing from a New Zealand point of view, were it not for the fact that he was quick to see the importance of a practical argument, identified earlier by McGechan, i.e. the ability of the New Zealand Parliament, using section 2(2) of the Statute, to put right immediately any such unwanted legislative interference by Westminster.[72] The ultimate question, then, was whether the United Kingdom Parliament could repeal section 2 and restore the earlier colonial law rule of subordination. Scott and Aikman were clearly divided on this point. During the 1960s and early 1970s, the wind seemed to shift temporarily away from Scott.

In his 1965 essay 'The New Zealand Constitution',[73] J.F. Northey provided an illuminating account of the then-existing state of constitutional affairs in New Zealand. His main preoccupation in this essay was the possibility of a written constitution for New Zealand, but this topic gave him ample opportunity to comment on the sorts of theoretical issues which interest us.

Northey began by noting a certain constitutional naivety amongst New Zealand constitutional lawyers of the period. Whereas Australian, Canadian and South African lawyers were 'well trained . . . in the subtleties of constitutional law', very few 'New Zealand lawyers of twenty years' standing would admit the possibility of limitations, procedural or otherwise, on the legislative authority of Parliament'.[74] Northey, however, displayed detailed knowledge of the debate between orthodox constitutional theorists such as Wade, and the various adherents to the 'new view' (including H.R. Gray).[75] While Northey expressed 'no wish to enter the lists in support of either view',[76] he clearly saw the force of the 'new view' arguments. However he 'conceded that, because New Zealand Courts are unfamiliar . . . it might be difficult to persuade them that the point of view expressed by Professor Gray is tenable'.[77]

This unfamiliarity and uncertainty regarding fundamental constitutional matters inevitably affected prospects for Northey's project of a written constitution, but it also affected the interpretation of the events of 1947 described earlier. The effect of the two New Zealand Acts and single UK Act of 1947 was 'to make clear that all former limitations on legislative power had been or could in future be removed by the [New Zealand Parliament].[78] Northey went so far as to say that most New Zealand lawyers 'would be prepared to acknowledge without much, if any, hesitation that the 1947 legislation removed all remaining limitations on the legislative competence of the [New Zealand Parliament]'.[79] But the matter was 'not altogether free from doubt'.[80] The apparent reason for doubt was that section 53 of the 1852 Act only empowered the New Zealand

---

[72] Scott (1962) (n. 68 above) 19–20.

[73] J.F. Northey, 'The New Zealand Constitution' in J.F. Northey (ed.) *The A.G. Davis Essays in Law* (London: Butterworths, 1965) 150.   [74] ibid., 150.

[75] ibid., 164, citing H.R. Gray and J.D.B. Mitchell.   [76] ibid., 165.   [77] ibid., 170.

[78] ibid., 158.   [79] ibid., 159.   [80] ibid., 159.

Parliament to legislate for the 'peace, order and good government of New Zealand'. Section 3 of the Statute of Westminster removed the pre-existing limitation regarding extraterritorial legislation, but section 3 did not in and of itself expand the vires of section 53 to include legislation with extraterritorial intent. Nor could section 53 expand its own powers. The issue therefore turned on whether the New Zealand Constitution (Amendment) Act 1947 (UK) handed over to the New Zealand Parliament plenary constituent power regarding New Zealand, or whether the New Zealand Parliament's power to amend or repeal any portion of the 1852 Constitution was limited to its prior competence under section 53. Northey was inclined to believe that the powers granted to the New Zealand Parliament in 1947 included the ability to amend section 53 itself.[81] It was not surprising therefore that he was willing to give the 'new view' the benefit of the doubt. Northey's suspicion, however, was that most New Zealanders 'showed no awareness' of what had been achieved in 1947.[82]

Soon after Northey's discussion of these matters, the issue took on new urgency and importance, with the result that many New Zealand lawyers became familiar with some of the issues just discussed. Others would wait until 1986 before exploring the foundations of the New Zealand Constitution.

The New Zealand Constitution Amendment Act 1973 (NZ) and the Constitution Act 1986 (NZ)

During the late 1960s a new controversy emerged. The sovereignty of the New Zealand Parliament was placed in doubt by the case of *R v Fineberg* in just the sort of way that Northey had anticipated.[83] In the *Fineberg* case, Moller J had suggested that, as the New Zealand Parliament's powers were limited to 'peace, order and good government' under section 53 of the Constitution Act, 1852, Parliament could not be said to have the same powers as the United Kingdom Parliament, and, accordingly, laws passed by the New Zealand Parliament—specifically laws having extraterritorial effect—could be challenged as being outside its powers.[84] There were numerous bases on which this decision could be dismissed or criticised,[85] but at the time it was felt necessary to clarify matters. The result was the New Zealand Constitution Amendment Act 1973.

Section 2 of the New Zealand Constitution Amendment Act 1973 repealed the former section 53 of the Constitution Act, 1852 and replaced it with a provision stating that Parliament had 'full power to make laws'. If the earlier section 53 represented the totality of Parliament's powers then it was hard to see

---

[81] ibid., 160.   [82] ibid., 179.   [83] *R v Fineberg* [1968] NZLR 119 *per* Moller J.
[84] ibid., 122.   [85] See Joseph (2001) (n. 4 above) 447 et seq.

how that could grow into 'full powers' without the aid of the United Kingdom Parliament. But if the events of 1947 had truly ended New Zealand's subordinate legal status and made her Parliament entirely self-sufficient, then clearly the local Parliament could act to remove any apparent legislative disability. The government of the day seemed to have acted on the latter assumption.[86] Even if Parliament had been restricted in its legislative capacity under section 53, its constituent powers were arguably unrestricted on the terms of the (Amendment) Act 1947 (UK). Those powers had already been used in 1950 to abolish the Legislative Council.[87] Furthermore, the reference in the new section 53 to 'full powers' seemed to capture and codify both aspects of Parliament's plenary powers: the full power to legislate on any matter whatever and the ultimate power to make and amend constitutional provisions.

In the early 1980s, Parliament had cause once again to exercise its putative constituent powers, at a time when Canada and Australia were also putting their constitutional houses in order. New Zealand had its own reasons to act, prompted largely by the turbulent transfer of power in the final days of the Muldoon government (1975–84). As part of a larger package of constitutional reform, the new Labour government included an enactment that sought to terminate any residual power of the United Kingdom Parliament to legislate for New Zealand.

If the orthodox understanding of that Parliament's sovereignty typical of the Imperial theory still held sway, then it was possibly a futile gesture, at least in legal terms. However, if the (Amendment) Act 1947 (UK) had transferred constituent or amending powers to the New Zealand Parliament (the very powers that had been used in 1973), leaving the United Kingdom Parliament as an alternative but subordinate constituent or amending body alongside the New Zealand Parliament after 1947, then the Constitution Act 1986 (NZ) terminated even this residual role for the United Kingdom Parliament. How did it go about doing so?

The work of preparing the necessary legislation was given to the Officials Committee on Constitutional Reform. Its recommendations, particularly the Second Report, provided a rich source of information regarding the powers of the New Zealand Parliament. The Committee readily acknowledged that before 1947 the New Zealand Parliament had been 'clearly subordinate' to the

---

[86] See New Zealand, Parliament, *Explanatory Note to the New Zealand Constitution Amendment Bill, No 57–1*, 1973. See also Joseph (2001) (n. 4 above) 452:

The Government advisors believed the General Assembly was competent to alter or repeal [s. 53] by virtue of s. 1 of the 1947 Amendment Act (UK) . . . In their view, this was more than a liberalizing provision for removing the United Kingdom entrenchment limitation on the s. 53 powers; rather it was an independent grant of legislative (constituent) power for amendment or repeal of the 1852 Act, of which s. 53 was part. They regarded s. 1 as unfettered by any substantive limitation which may have hedged the s. 53 powers. On this analysis, the 1947 Amendment Act altered the rule of succession of rules in New Zealand and provided for the supercession or amendment of its rule of recognition.

[87] Legislative Council Abolition Act 1950 (NZ).

Parliament of the United Kingdom,[88] but it insisted that after 1947 the relationship had changed due to the combined effect of section 4 of the 1931 Statute and section 3 of the (Adoption) Act 1947.[89] The Officials Committee appeared to subscribe to the view proposed by Professor Aikman to the effect that, after 1947, New Zealand could not be made subject to unrequested United Kingdom legislation. Even K.J. Scott had acknowledged that New Zealand had a veto over any such legislation by virtue of section 2 of the 1931 Statute. From 1947 on, then, even the United Kingdom Parliament's residual constituent powers had been subordinate to the will of the New Zealand Parliament. By 1986, in the Committee's view, 'the continued power of the United Kingdom Parliament to legislate for New Zealand, even residually and as agent for the New Zealand Parliament, [was] incompatible with New Zealand's present status'.[90]

It flowed naturally from the above analysis that it was up to the New Zealand Parliament, as the supreme constituent authority in the New Zealand legal system, to declare that the United Kingdom Parliament's powers were terminated. This was accomplished by section 15(2) of the Constitution Act, 1986: 'No act of the Parliament of the United Kingdom passed after the commencement of this Act shall extend to New Zealand as part of its law.' The revocation of the Statute of Westminster, 1931, in so far as it applied to New Zealand, removed the only other possible source of United Kingdom Parliament power *vis-à-vis* New Zealand. Section 26(1) also repealed the (Amendment) Act 1947 (UK) and with it the first gift of full constituent powers to the New Zealand Parliament; however, as noted earlier, it was possible to view the 1973 Act as having incorporated those powers in the new section 53. Section 15(1) made sure that these 'full powers' were perpetuated: 'The Parliament of New Zealand continues to have full power to make laws.'[91]

When the proposed Bill came before Parliament it solicited surprisingly little comment.[92] Members may have been satisfied with the Minister of Justice's assurances that the Bill was mostly a restatement and updating of the law.

---

[88] New Zealand, Department of Justice, *Reports of an Officials Committee on Constitutional Reform: Second Report* (1986) 28 (hereinafter Officials Committee (1986)).

[89] 'Under United Kingdom law an Act could extend to inter alia New Zealand if it "expressly declared" the request and consent of New Zealand. It was technically a matter of form and construction. In section 3 of the Statute of Westminster Adoption Act, the New Zealand Parliament *clearly implied a substantive concept of request and consent*, and one which took the form of an Act of Parliament. *In theory our Parliament had arguably already transcended section 4 of the 1931 Act.*' Officials Committee (1986) 29 (emphasis added).

[90] Officials Committee (1986) 29.

[91] According to the Officials Committee (1986): 'It is...the unrestricted statement of the legislative power...that makes unnecessary the retention of the 1947 Acts concerned with the amendment of the Constitution Act. That power is contained within the broad terms of [s. 15(1)].' (p. 30). For further discussion of the need to retain the 1947 Act, see Part III.

[92] NZPD, 2nd Session, 41st Parliament, 1986. Mr McClay noted, at 5852, that only 8 individuals or organisations made submissions and few Members of Parliament elected to speak on the Bill.

One member, a future Attorney-General, had difficulty fitting the Bill within the Diceyan framework of his legal education:

Mr GRAHAM: I wish to raise one or two matters with the Minister about the Bill, but I do so with trepidation because I am dragging up memories from my law studies 25 years ago and I appreciate that the Minister is learned in the law. It appears to me that the English Statute of Westminster . . . meant that the English Parliament could enact laws for New Zealand . . . and as I understand the position the English Parliament could now, however unlikely it is, pass a law, provided it contained a declaration that New Zealand had requested and consented to the enactment—even if it had not. I know that is unlikely, but the point of the argument is that if a power does exist in England at present to enact laws for New Zealand our Parliament ought to invite the United Kingdom Parliament to revoke that power. I very much doubt that it will be sufficient for New Zealand merely to declare that henceforth it will make its own laws and that no English statute that is enacted from now on will apply to New Zealand. It is a rather esoteric point, but it appears to me—and I ask the Minister to reply—that the English Parliament ought to be asked to revoke the Statute of Westminster so far as it relates to New Zealand.[93]

This 'esoteric point' seemed entirely relevant if one had been educated according to Diceyan understandings of the absolute and continuing sovereignty of Parliament. And even if the views of Dicey's critics were accepted, it was natural to want to know when the United Kingdom Parliament had relinquished its powers. Nor was Graham satisfied with the Minister of Justice's reassurances to the effect that United Kingdom legislation was not required:

Mr GRAHAM: I realize that the adoption part of the Statute of Westminster is repealed by the Bill, but there is still an inherent right in the English Parliament to enact laws that affect New Zealand, and that should not be so. We may be able to declare our own constitutional rights in the matter, but if there is a residual power in the English Parliament only the English Parliament can revoke that right. It may willingly do so, and it is proper that it should do so.[94]

But Graham's concerns did not appear to have preoccupied others.

This account of New Zealand's more recent constitutional development appeared to indicate that New Zealand had found a way out of orthodox understandings of the sovereignty of the Westminster Parliament. However, a further challenge remained for New Zealand constitutional law and theory. With the Westminster Parliament now entirely removed from the operative New Zealand legal system as a result of the 1986 Act, questions emerged regarding how in future to explain the validity of New Zealand's law, notably its key constitutional statutes. We will postpone this discussion until Chapter 11. We shall see there that a majority of New Zealand constitutional theorists favour

---

[93] NZPD, 2nd Session, 41st Parliament, 1986, 1357–8.
[94] NZPD, 2nd Session, 41st Parliament, 1986, 1358.

a 'revolutionary' explanation of their country's constitutional foundations, in much the same way as H.W.R. Wade had proposed in the 1950s. Before turning to explanations for constitutional independence after 1982 and 1986, we need to complete the study of the anticipation and achievement of constitutional independence by looking at Australia's unique experience.

9

Australia I: Colonies, Conventions and the Constitution

Early constitutional arrangements

Australia was the last of the three countries under study to acquire a national Constitution. Like pre-1867 Canada, Australian constitutional development had not been held back by the absence of a continent-wide polity. The movement from representative institutions to responsible government in the late nineteenth century had simply proceeded at the level of individual Australian colonies rather than at the national level.

Since the mid-nineteenth century, there had been proposals, mostly British,[1] to develop national institutions, but these had come to nothing due to a lack of local support. An early prominent example was Earl Grey's proposal to establish a general executive and legislative authority for Australia. Grey, the Colonial Secretary in Lord John Russell's administration, 'took constitution-making for his hobby'.[2] In communications beginning in 1847, Grey had proposed a number of innovations, including a General Assembly to deal with customs duties, roads, railways and other matters of general Australian interest. Grey's ideas were met 'with a storm of indignation' in the colony of New South Wales.[3] The Australian colonists were 'especially alarmed at the suggestion of indirect election which would take away the instalment of representative institutions which they had lately won'.[4] Grey professed no desire to impose unwelcome constitutional changes on the colonies, but he persisted nonetheless. He was particularly concerned with the illogical generation of different tariffs as a result of neighbouring colonies having separate powers in this regard. In 1849, the Committee for Trade and Plantations agreed that a uniform tariff was

---

[1] See however, J.D. Lang, *Freedom and Independence for the Golden Lands of Australia* (London: Longman, Brown, Green & Longmans, 1852) which called for federation and independence, i.e. a republican United States of Australia. See Sir R. Garran, *The Making and Working of the Constitution* (Sydney: New Century Press, 1932) 6.   [2] Garran (1932) (n. 1 above) 4.
[3] R. Quick and R. Garran, *The Annotated Constitution of the Australian Commonwealth* (reprint of 1901 edition) (Sydney: Legal Books, 1976) 82.   [4] ibid., 82.

desirable. The Committee also proposed a General Assembly to be composed of representatives from all the colonies.[5]

The Committee's views and Grey's determination, despite protestations to the contrary, resulted in the Constitution Bill of 1850. Moore reports that 'neither in Parliament nor in the colonies was the measure cordially received'.[6] The legislative aspects of the proposal required parliamentary approval. The General Assembly clauses were accepted by the House of Commons but were eventually withdrawn from the House of Lords. Despite the unpopularity of the Bill, Grey went ahead with the executive aspect, which did not need legislation. He appointed Sir Charles Fitzroy[7] 'Governor-General of all her Majesty's Australian possessions including the colony of Western Australia'. Fitzroy was also appointed governor of each colony so that he could visit any of them. Lieutenant-governors in each colony were instructed to communicate with the Governor-General in matters of common interest. However, Grey left the Colonial Office in 1852 and this 'nursing policy' was abandoned. In 1855 lieutenant-governors became governors again.[8] Fitzroy's authority was only nominal and never exercised.[9] Any future reform would wait on colonial initiative.

It did not take long for such an initiative to emerge. In 1857, leading members of the New South Wales and Victoria governments sent a Memorial to the Secretary of State under the title 'General Association for the Australian Colonies'. In it, they set out a scheme for 'a permissive bill for the establishment of the General Assembly'.[10] Labouchere, Lord Palmerston's Colonial Secretary, had learned Grey's lesson regarding meddling in Australian affairs. Despite lobbying in London on behalf of the scheme,[11] Labouchere left it to committees in the New South Wales and Victoria legislatures to consider the matter further. The Victorian committee came out particularly strongly in favour, and it was agreed that all the Australian colonies should meet in a conference in 1860. However, Queensland, South Australia and, by then, New South Wales, were all less keen on the idea, and the proposed conference never took place.[12]

In 1870 the idea re-emerged. Charles Gavan Duffy obtained a Royal Commission in Victoria to inquire into the best means for accomplishing a federal union of Australian colonies. It was not lost on Australian colonists that Canadian colonies had come together in 1867.

By the 1880s federation was 'in the air'.[13] As if to symbolise the idea, a New South Wales-Victoria railway was being built. Also, Queensland had pre-empted potential German claims by taking possession of New Guinea.

[5] W. Harrison Moore, *Constitution of the Commonwealth of Australia* (London: John Murray, 1902) 20.   [6] ibid., 21.

[7] In the mid-1840s, as Governor of New South Wales, Fitzroy had called for the coordination of Australian colonies by a British-appointed functionary in the name of trade. (Moore (1902) (n. 5 above) 19.)   [8] ibid., 21.

[9] Garran (1932) (n. 1 above) 5.   [10] Moore (1902) (n. 5 above) 23.

[11] Garran (1932) (n. 1 above) 6.   [12] Moore (1902) (n. 5 above) 23–5.   [13] ibid., 30.

The Secretary of State, Lord Derby, repudiated Queensland's move, pointing out that such action required 'federation of the colonies into one united whole which would be powerful enough to undertake and carry through tasks for which no one colony is presently sufficient'.[14] Accordingly, in December 1883, Ministers from all the Australian colonies, New Zealand and Fiji met to discuss 'The Annexation of Neighbouring Islands, and the Federation of Australasia'. James Service, premier of Victoria, spoke strongly in favour of full federation, but others were not yet convinced. Samuel Griffith, premier of Queensland, suggested a Federal Council instead, and a draft Bill to that effect was adopted by all but New South Wales and Fiji. An address to the Queen was prepared, and as a result the Federal Council of Australasia Act, 1885 (Imp.) was enacted. James Bryce criticised it as 'a very scanty, fragmentary and imperfect sketch of a federal constitution',[15] but it was an important step nonetheless, if only as a staging post. In actual fact, the Federal Council did little. Neither New South Wales nor New Zealand attended any of its meetings. It had no executive and no revenue, and it did little to promote the federal cause.

Promotion of the federal cause was left to influential politicians such as New South Wales' Henry Parkes who for some time had supported the idea of federation. Parkes had spoken out in favour of federation at an intercolonial conference in Melbourne in 1867, the year of Canadian Confederation.[16] Parkes visited Canada and the United States in 1882 and was impressed with what he saw. On his return to Australia he began to prepare public opinion, using scare stories about the inadequacy of Australian defences and the like.[17] In 1889 he judged that the moment was right, making a speech at Tenterfield that 'sent a thrill through Australia'.[18] Parkes turned on the Federal Council, referring to it as 'a rickety body'.[19] Instead he proposed a National Convention to frame a Constitution creating a federal government and Parliament.

Parkes' proposal attracted enough support for an Intercolonial Conference to be convened in Melbourne in February 1890. At that Conference, supporters of federation convinced sceptics that the Federal Council was no longer sufficient. Parkes developed themes that he had touched on at Tenterfield, coining the famous phrase: 'The crimson thread of kinship runs through us all.' Parkes was possibly affected by 'the spice of vanity from which the greatest are not immune',[20] but more importantly he had caught or created a mood. It was also

---

[14] Quoted in Moore (1902) (n. 5 above), 30.

[15] J. Bryce, *Studies in History and Jurisprudence*, Vol. 1 (Oxford: Clarendon Press, 1901) 473, quoted in Garran (1932) (n. 1 above) 8.   [16] Garran (1932) (n. 1 above) 6.

[17] ibid., 8.

[18] ibid., 9. Parkes' speech was made on the occasion of the opening of the Sydney-Brisbane railway. Never one to hold back on rhetorical flourishes, Parkes spoke of 'the crimson fluid of kinship pulsing through all iron veins'. Quoted in R. French, 'The Constitution and the People' in G.J. Lindell, C. Saunders and R.S. French (eds) *Reflections on the Australian Constitution* (Sydney: Federation Press, 2003) 65.   [19] Quoted in French (2003) (n. 18 above) 65.

[20] Garran (1932) (n. 1 above) 8.

significant that the Melbourne Conference was open to the public. This ensured that press coverage of the proceedings was extensive. Public participation and public opinion were vital to the ten-year process which led to the Australian federal Constitution.

The Melbourne Conference ended with a motion which recognised the value of the Federal Council over the previous seven years, but which called for 'union of the colonies, under one legislative and executive government on principles just to the several colonies'.[21] Finally, the members of the Conference resolved to go back to their respective legislatures and convince their colleagues to send delegates to a National Australasian Convention empowered to pursue the federal constitutional scheme.

The Conventions and the Commonwealth of Australia Constitution Act, 1900 (Imp.)

The Melbourne Intercolonial Conference led directly to the first Constitutional Convention which met in Sydney in March and April of 1891. Delegates to the Convention were elected by the colonial legislatures. The Convention set to work on agreeing resolutions. These resolutions and the discussions on them were based on 'a comparative study of the federal Constitutions of the United States, Canada and Switzerland, together with the political experience of the members of the Convention in the working of the Constitutions of the six colonies'.[22] Throughout the Convention, various delegates spoke of the importance of appealing to the people of the colonies. Alfred Deakin was particularly clear on this point: 'We know from the outset the bar of public opinion before which we are to be judged, and we know from the commencement of our labours that the conclusion of them rests in other hands than ours—in the hands of no less a body than the assembled peoples of all the Australasian colonies.'[23] Eventually a drafting committee produced 'A Draft Bill to Constitute the Commonwealth of Australia', and this was approved by the Convention. This document was substantially what became the 1900 Constitution.[24]

Despite the impressive start in Sydney, the Constitution Bill adopted by the Convention soon ran into political troubles. Change of government, notably in New South Wales, caused the project to lose momentum. Beyond the politics of shifting political support, Quick and Garran noted that political issues of a more fundamental nature were at stake:

It soon became clear that neither the parliaments nor the people would accept the work of the Convention as final. [There was] a vague feeling of distrust of the Constitution, as the work of a body somewhat conservative in composition, only indirectly representative of

---

[21] Quoted in French (2003) (n. 18 above) 65.   [22] Garran (1932) (n. 1 above) 10.
[23] *Convention Debates*, Sydney, 1891, 29.   [24] Moore (1902) (n. 5 above) 42.

the people, and entrusted with no very definite or detailed mandate even by the parliaments which created it.[25]

In the end, the Convention process was to need a kick-start from outside the formal process. At a conference at Corowa organised by the Australasian Federation League and the Australian Natives' Association,[26] John Quick proposed a motion designed to address the issues of political legitimacy referred to above. The motion was accepted in the following terms:

That in the opinion of this conference the Legislature of each Australasian colony should pass an Act providing for *the election of representatives* to attend a statutory Convention or Congress to consider and adopt a bill to establish a Federal Constitution for Australia, *and upon the adoption of such Bill or measure it be submitted by some process of referendum to the verdict of each colony.*[27]

The importance of the motion was that it proposed involvement of the people in both the election of Convention representatives and the approval of a product of such Convention by means of referendum.

The 'Corowa plan' was discussed and accepted by the premiers at their Conference in 1895. It was decided that each colony should enact enabling legislation to choose ten delegates to represent it at a Convention dedicated to drafting a federal Constitution. If the Convention produced a draft Constitution it would be submitted to each colonial legislature, following which the Convention would reconvene to consider proposed amendments. The final draft of the Constitution would then be put to the people in a referendum in which acceptance by the voters of at least three colonies would be required. If accepted, the Constitution would then be submitted to the Crown.

Enabling legislation was first submitted to the New South Wales legislature to make sure that the largest colony was committed to the process, and then others followed suit. The Convention reconvened at Adelaide in 1897 in slightly ragged style. Queensland was not represented, because it could not agree a mechanism for selection. Western Australia appointed its representatives rather than electing them. And New Zealand, which had shown interest in federation since 1891, decided not to attend at all.[28]

At Adelaide in March 1897 the draft Constitution Bill from 1891 was adopted as a foundation for discussion. As contemplated by the enabling legislation, proceedings were adjourned so that the colonial legislatures could consider the Bill and propose amendments. The Convention then reconvened in Sydney in September 1897 to consider nearly 300 amendments, though such

[25] Quick and Garran (1901) (n. 3 above) 144.

[26] It is important to note that 'natives' at this time meant 'white' Australians. See H. Irving, *To Constitute a Nation: A Cultural History of Australia's Constitution* (Cambridge: Cambridge University Press, 1999) 135.

[27] Quick and Garran (1901) (n. 3 above) 153 (emphasis added).

[28] The New Zealand delegates indicated that they were not interested in federation, equating the number of reasons against it to the number of miles (1,200) separating New Zealand from Australia.

was the difficulty of this task that reconsideration and revision of the Bill was only completed in an extended session of the final Convention at Melbourne in January–March 1898. Again as contemplated, the Bill was presented for adoption by the electors of each colony.

The Bill was approved by the electors of the requisite three colonies—Victoria, South Australia and Tasmania—in 1898, but the majority in favour in New South Wales was not sufficient to meet statutory requirements as to minimum numbers of voters. The size and importance of New South Wales was acknowledged by an unwillingness to go ahead without it. New elections in New South Wales meant new political dynamics regarding the Constitution Bill. New amendments were agreed by all six colonies at a premiers conference at Melbourne in January 1899, and the new Bill was put to the electors once again. Voters in Victoria, South Australia, Tasmania and New South Wales voted for the Bill, as did voters in Queensland later in the year, and each colony adopted an address to the Crown accordingly. Western Australia held out for further concessions and did not therefore hold a referendum in 1899. The referendum in Western Australia went ahead with positive results in July 1900, and an address to the Crown was passed soon after requesting that the colony be included as a State in the new Commonwealth.

In terms of constitutional theory, we will see in Chapter 10 that many Australians take seriously the possibility that their Constitution is grounded, politically *and* legally, in the sovereignty of the Australian people. The above account indicates that there is ample support for this interpretation in terms of the way in which the Constitution was prepared and adopted.[29] It is also reflected in the Preamble to the Commonwealth of Australia Constitution Act, which stated that 'the people of New South Wales, Victoria, South Australia, Queensland, and Tasmania, humbly relying on the blessing of Almighty God, have agreed to unite in one indissoluble Federal Commonwealth'.

What of the alternative explanation, whereby ultimate legal validity was provided by the Imperial Parliament at Westminster? The Framers of the Australian Constitution were well aware of the American model of revolutionary constitutional beginnings based in popular sovereignty, but they had no appetite for it. As Helen Irving relates, 1900 was more of a marriage[30] between the various colonies rather than an attempt to become independent. The vast majority

---

[29] J. Brown, 'The Australian Commonwealth Bill' (1900) 61 LQR 24, 31–2 set out a striking selection of quotations from leading politicians regarding the importance of popular participation:

'I welcome the constitution as the most magnificent institution into which the chosen representatives of a free and enlightened people have ever breathed the spirit of popular sentiment and of national hope.'—Mr Kingston.

'Nothing can be done under the constitution which is contrary to the will of the people.'—Sir Edward Braddon.

'It is a constitution framed for a free people.'—Mr Barton.

'If ever there was a people's constitution it is this one.'—Mr Holder.

[30] Irving (1999) (n. 26 above) 211.

of Australians still felt a genuine attachment to Britain and the monarchy.[31] Their preference was for legality and constitutional continuity. They had obtained their powers of government from the Imperial Parliament at Westminster, and they naturally assumed that they would have to go there again in order to obtain authorisation for the new federal Constitution. However, they had every intention of ensuring that the Bill which Westminster enacted was the Bill which the people of Australia had approved in referendum.

The premiers chose delegates who could assist and explain the Bill when it went before the Westminster Parliament. These delegates saw their role as defending the Constitution from British interference. They were very nearly successful in this task. The Colonial Office initially recommended that the Bill be accepted 'as is', but Joseph Chamberlain, the Colonial Secretary, wanted changes that would protect both his cherished Empire and investment therein.[32] The Bill contained a section severely limiting appeals to the Judicial Committee of the Privy Council, and this proved to be troublesome. Chamberlain gave a sympathetic reception to the various petitions and letters sent to his office demanding that this section be altered. The Australian delegates were adamant that no change should be made. As Irving relates, in their view 'the Constitution had been approved by the Australian people at referendums . . . it had passed through the colonial Parliaments', and 'if it were amended, they might have to begin all over again'.[33] In the end a compromise was agreed.[34] The future section

[31] Irving (1999) (n. 26 above) 205.

[32] Imperial law officers also expressed doubt as to the applicability of the Colonial Laws Validity Act, 1865 to the Commonwealth. A proposed amendment to cover the point was eventually dropped, it being assumed that the Constitution Act would not operate a repeal of the previous Act, despite the former being an Imperial Act later in date than the former. W. Anstey Wynes, *Legislative and Executive Powers in Australia* (Sydney: Law Book Company, 1936) 59.

[33] Irving (1999) (n. 26 above) 14.

[34] The italicised parts of cl. 74 of the Draft Constitution (agreed at the Melbourne Convention (1898)) were amended and replaced by the present s. 74. The square brackets indicate the present wording of s. 74 only where that wording differs from cl. 74:

74. *No appeal shall be permitted to the Queen in Council in any matter involving the interpretation of this Constitution or of the Constitution of a State, unless the public interests of some part of Her Majesty's Dominions, other than the Commonwealth of a State, are involved.*
[74. No appeal shall be permitted to the Queen in Council from a decision of the High Court upon any question, howsoever arising, as to the limits inter se of the Constitutional powers of the Commonwealth and those of any State or States, or as to the limits inter se of the constitutional powers of any two or more States, unless the High Court shall certify that the question is one which ought to be determined by Her Majesty in Council.

The High Court may so certify if satisfied that for any special reason the certificate should be granted, and thereupon an appeal shall lie to Her Majesty in Council on the question without further leave.]

Except as provided in this section, this Constitution shall not impair any right which the Queen may be pleased to exercise by virtue of her Royal Prerogative to grant special leave of appeal from the High Court to Her Majesty in Council. *But the Parliament may make laws limiting the matters in which such leave may be asked.* [The Parliament may make laws limiting the matters in which such leave may be asked, but proposed laws containing any such limitation shall be reserved by the Governor-General for Her Majesty's pleasure.]

74 was altered accordingly (as were two of the covering clauses) and the Bill was passed by the Westminster Parliament, coming into effect on 1 January 1901. In strict legal terms, the final version of the Commonwealth of Australia Constitution Act, 1900 could only be the product of the Imperial Parliament. However, to understand it exclusively in strict legal terms would be to ignore ten years of popular political commitment to the Constitution by the people and political institutions of Australia.

Even if the Constitution of the Commonwealth of Australia Act 1900 owed its legality to the Imperial Parliament, the people and political institutions could claim ownership of the Constitution by virtue of section 128, according to which that same Constitution was 'not to be altered except' as therein provided. Section 128 required approval of the alteration by each House of Parliament (or, in special circumstances, one House) and by the Australian people voting in state referendums (approval of the alteration by a majority of electors voting in a majority of states and by a majority of electors overall). 'Not to be altered except' seemed to exclude even the Imperial Parliament. However, that conclusion seemed to contradict the supposed sovereignty of the latter Parliament. According to the orthodox Diceyan understanding, whatever the Australian Constitution might say, the Act of 1900 could not bind a future Westminster Parliament, and the Australian legislatures, including the section 128 procedure, could only be considered 'subordinate legislatures'.

The Commonwealth of Australia Constitution Act, 1900 had created a Constitution for the new federation. However, in terms of constitutional arrangements for the original Australian colonies, the new Constitution basically left the states as they were, in contrast to the Canadian Constitution Act, 1867 which incorporated the four founding colonies into the new constitutional arrangements. The Australian colonies, now states, had their Constitutions recognised in section 106 of the 1900 Act: 'The Constitution of each State of the Commonwealth shall, subject to this Constitution, continue as at the establishment of the Commonwealth . . . until altered in accordance with the Constitution of the State.' Amendment of state Constitutions was governed by those Constitutions rather than by section 128 of the Commonwealth Constitution.[35] The details of these constitutional arrangements would be especially important at the time of the enactment and adoption of the Statute of Westminster and just prior to the enactment of the Australia Acts 1986 (Cth and UK).

It may now be appropriate to consider how contemporary Australian constitutional commentators viewed the new Australian Constitution, both in terms of the reasons for its validity and the reasons or prospects for constitutional independence.

---

[35] Because a State Constitution could be amended in accordance with s. 106 of the Australian Constitution, strictly speaking, s. 106 and therefore state Constitutions, could be amended in accordance with s. 128. On the history of state constitutions, see A. Twomey, *The Constitution of New South Wales* (Annandale: Federation Press, 2004).

Australian constitutional understandings prior to the Statute of Westminster, 1931

Alongside Quick and Garran, perhaps the most influential commentator on the Australian Constitution in the early years after 1900 was Harrison Moore, Dean of the Faculty of Law at the University of Melbourne and author of *The Constitution of the Commonwealth of Australia*.[36] The first edition of this work was published in 1902, only a year after the Australian Constitution had come into force, and too early for Australian courts to have added anything but a trickle of interpretation. Much of the work was therefore historical. He discussed the sources of Australian law, including the rules regarding settled colonies, discussed in Chapter 2. Moore's description of the 'The History of Australian Federation' has been used to support the previous two sections of this chapter. Moore concluded this account with a firm statement of the importance of popular input into the new federal Constitution of Australia: 'The Federation of Australia was a popular act, an expression of the free will of the people of every part of it, and therein, as in some other respects, it differs in a striking manner from the federation of the United States, of Canada, and of Germany.'[37]

One might then have anticipated references to the foundation of the Australian Constitution in popular sovereignty, but this would have been not only to ignore the constraints of Moore's legal education and the constitutional understandings of the time, but also to treat the events of 1900 as more about independence than federation. *'Federation'* not 'independence' was 'a popular act', according to the statement by Moore just quoted. In terms of the relationship between Australia and the Imperial Parliament, however, Moore was seemingly orthodox, an adherent of what in the consideration of the development of Canadian constitutional theory was termed the Imperial theory.

In a chapter entitled 'The relation of the legislative authorities (the Imperial Parliament, the Commonwealth Parliament, the State Parliaments) and the Validity of Laws'[38] Moore was clear that they formed a 'hierarchy' with the Imperial Parliament at the apex:[39] 'The Imperial Parliament remains paramount, and is capable now, as at all times previously, of legislating for this as for all parts of the dominions of the Crown.' He then addressed the very Canadian unorthodoxy that Dicey had criticised (as related in Chapters 3 and 6), and Moore showed no sympathy for egregious errors of this type: 'The view that obtained some currency in Canada, that the "exclusive" powers conferred by the British North America Act, 1867, meant exclusive of the Imperial Parliament, is

---

[36] W. Harrison Moore, *Constitution of the Commonwealth of Australia* (London: John Murray, 1902); W. Harrison Moore, *Constitution of the Commonwealth of Australia* (2nd edn, Melbourne: Charles F. Maxwell, 1910) (reprinted by Legal Books, 1997, with an introduction by George Winterton).   [37] Moore (1902) (n. 36 above) 61.
[38] ibid., ch. X.   [39] ibid., 167.

now so far discredited that it is unnecessary to discuss the grounds upon which it is based . . .'[40]

In the Chapter on 'The Alteration of the Constitution' Moore was equally orthodox in his assertions. He noted that 'all constitutional alteration . . . must be "for the Commonwealth", and no alteration of the Constitution may be repugnant to any Imperial Act in operation in the Commonwealth, unless, expressly, or by implication, power over such an Act has been given by the Imperial Parliament'.[41] One such Imperial Act, over which the Commonwealth had no power according to Moore, was the Constitution of the Commonwealth of Australia Act, as opposed to the Australian Constitution itself. The latter owed its existence and validity to Covering Clause IX which stated: 'The Constitution of the Commonwealth shall be as follows.' In Moore's words, 'the Commonwealth is established in virtue of this part of the Act, and it would appear to be dissoluble only by Imperial Act'.[42]

Regarding the Constitution itself, however, 'no part [was] withdrawn from the power of the Commonwealth'.[43] There was 'no doubt, that the whole Constitution could be repealed under section 128, and that without any provision being made to substitute anything for it'.[44] Moore justified his confidence here by citing Dicey: 'It seems an irresistible conclusion, that, as Professor Dicey (Law of the Constitution, 5th edition, p. 65) says, "The impossibility of placing a limit on the exercise of sovereignty does not in any way prohibit, either logically, or in matter of fact, the abdication of sovereignty"'.[45] Moore's comments here relate only to Australian powers under section 128, but one wonders whether he was already asking questions regarding how the Imperial Parliament might eventually grant full constitutional independence to Australia. Moore's other writing at the time indicated that eventual constitutional independence was within his contemplation, but that he was inclined to close doors leading in that direction rather than open them, assuming, that is, that we can take what he says at face value.

Moore had anticipated his more in-depth study by producing a short article on the Constitution Bill in the January 1900 issue of *The Law Quarterly Review*.[46] In the main, it was a familiar tour through the Bill pointing out its main features. It contained some interesting bits of trivia. Moore reported that the Canadian title 'Dominion' had been rejected because the Australian union

---

[40] ibid., 167.   [41] ibid., 320–1.   [42] ibid., 321.   [43] ibid., 321.
[44] ibid., 321.   [45] ibid., 321–2.
[46] W. Harrison Moore, 'The Commonwealth of Australia Bill' (1900) 16 LQR 35. This article was in fact a reply to a series of articles on the Constitution Bill by the Canadian constitutional writer A.H.F. Lefroy: 'The Commonwealth of Australia Bill' (1st Article) (1899) 58 LQR 155; (Second Article) (1899) 59 LQR 281. In the same series, Brown (1900) (n. 29 above) 24:

The Australian Commonwealth Bill embodies the political ideals of a Constitutional Assembly, convened in the closing years of the nineteenth century, and favoured by conditions which afforded a unique opportunity for the achievement of grand constitutional results. All history for precedent! All the world-wide literature of political science as a guide!

was to be of a different kind. 'Rightly or wrongly' the title 'Dominion' was thought to suggest 'that prevalence of the central power which is the mark of the Canadian union'.[47] The title 'Commonwealth' was said to have been proposed by Henry Parkes in 1891 as a tribute to Cromwell and the men of the Commonwealth period. In other minds, the title was 'associated with Mr Bryce's work on the American Commonwealth'.[48] Moore reassured the readers of *The Law Quarterly Review* that the 'discussion in the Convention as to the title of the Union was sufficient to divest it of any republican significance'.[49]

There is little in this article which helps us determine Moore's theoretical assumptions. However, there are occasional glimpses. One such passage was also noteworthy because of its prophetic nature. Moore here identified the power which was eventually employed to enact the Commonwealth version of the Australia Act 1986:

> There is one power conferred upon the Commonwealth Parliament . . . which seems to me more far-reaching and perhaps more dangerous than those which are merely concerned with external affairs. The 38th Article [the present section 51 (xxxviii)] of legislation includes the power to 'exercise within the Commonwealth at the request or with the concurrence of the Parliaments of all the States concerned, any power which can at the establishment of this Constitution be exercised only by the Parliament of the United Kingdom . . .' This article may lead to serious trouble. Claims to legislative independence have been founded on lighter grounds than this; and . . . the theoretical power of the Imperial Parliament to recall constitutional powers is not one of great practical value. Under this article it would seem that the Commonwealth Parliament might, at the request of a State Parliament, repeal any Act of the Imperial Parliament applicable in the colony; in other words, the Commonwealth and State parliaments, acting together, might nullify Imperial legislation. Here, if anywhere, the Imperial Parliament may in future be said to have intended to divest itself of authority. It is not enough that we may be able to show by abstract reasoning that this is not or could not be the case.[50]

This is a surprising and ambiguous passage. If Moore really believed in the theoretical, but formal legal power of the Imperial Parliament to 'recall' Australian constitutional powers and if 'abstract reasoning', presumably of the Diceyan variety, could demonstrate that a subordinate legislature cannot (without express or implied power) nullify Imperial legislation, then presumably he should have been confident that the courts would view the matter similarly— unless, that is, Moore was more interested in 'claims to legislative independence' and the 'serious trouble' that they represented than he was willing here to admit. If that had been the case, one might have expected such independent-minded statements to unfold in the second edition of *The Constitution of the Commonwealth of Australia*, but that was not to be the case. That work was stoutly Diceyan, perhaps even to a greater extent than the first edition. Moore was by

---

[47] Moore (1900) (n. 46 above) 35.   [48] ibid., 35.   [49] ibid., 35.
[50] ibid., 39–40 (emphasis added).

then able, for example, to dismiss any 'doubt or speculation as to the theoretical origin or legal foundation of the Commonwealth and the Constitution'.[51]

Part IV of the second edition, 'The Powers of the Commonwealth Government', was full of references to subordinate legislatures and contrasts between the United States sovereignty of the people model and the British/Australian alternative.[52] However, Moore's writing often seemed to pose hidden questions for readers willing to make links. For instance, his discussion of the Imperial Parliament's constituent powers followed by an account of constituent powers under section 128 raised questions, unvoiced by Moore, about whether and when the former might give way to the latter. A closer look at these passages may assist here.

Moore began by noting that 'the real nature of the power' exercised by the Imperial Parliament was obscured by the fact that its sovereign power 'to make paramount laws on all subjects whatever' involved 'uniformity in the mode of exercising' that power.[53] Despite the uniformity of procedure, the Imperial Parliament was exercising very different powers: 'legislative' for the most part, but in establishing a colonial Constitution by Act of Parliament, 'constituent'.[54] The important legal principle which followed from this distinction was that the colonial legislature created by such constituent powers possessed sovereign powers of self-government (subject to control by the Imperial government in the form of disallowance) not merely powers delegated to it by the Imperial Parliament in its legislative mode.[55] Colonial legislatures such as those in Australia had 'plenary powers' with limitations only in 'certain definite restrictions'.[56] Plenary powers would not *per se* carry a power to alter the Constitution itself, but such a power had been conferred in the case of the Australian Commonwealth: 'The power to amend the Constitution of the Colony...exists as a distinct power from the ordinary power of legislation...it seems that the "constituent power" is so far distinct from the "legislative", that ordinary acts of legislation are controlled by the Constitution until is has been amended.'[57] Putting the two constituent legislatures together, one cannot help but wonder whether the Imperial Parliament in its constituent role could hand over any residual powers regarding Australia to the relevant Australian institutions, or whether the constituent powers in section 128 could remove any such residual limitations by its own action. Moore did not develop the point other than to note, as he did in the first edition, that, according to Dicey, abdication of sovereignty was possible.[58]

Another highly influential text in the early period of the Australian constitution was Quick and Garran's *Annotated Constitution of the Australian*

---

[51] Moore (1910) (n. 36 above) 66–7, quoted in A. Dillon, 'A Turtle By Any Other Name: The Legal Basis of the Australian Constitution' (2001) 29 FL Rev 241, 244.
[52] Moore (1910) (n. 36 above) 243–7.   [53] ibid., 249.   [54] ibid., 249.
[55] ibid., 249–50.   [56] ibid., 255.   [57] ibid., 256.   [58] ibid., Part X.

Commonwealth.[59] As the title suggests, this weighty tome was designed to explicate the various provisions of the new Constitution rather than to speculate on theoretical issues. However, it is possible to identify a relatively small number of instances where the authors' fundamental assumptions begin to emerge. For instance, Quick and Garran referred to the Constitution as 'founded on the will of the people who it is designed to unite and govern'.[60]

The most revealing passages in Quick and Garran appear in the section dealing with section 128, the constitutional amendment provisions. Here, they sounded much like Clement in Canada, emphasising the colonial and subordinate nature of the Australian Commonwealth in the spirit of Imperial theory:

> If . . . the Commonwealth were a sovereign and independent State, no amendment, duly passed in the prescribed form [following s. 128], would be beyond its powers; the amending power would have no limits. But the Commonwealth is only quasi-sovereign, and *the amending power*, though above the State Governments and above the Federal Government, *is below the Imperial Parliament. The Commonwealth is a dependency of the Empire; and the amending power—the highest legislature of the Commonwealth—is a colonial legislature.* It can therefore pass no law which is repugnant to any Act of the British Parliament extending to the Commonwealth, or repugnant to any order or regulation founded upon such Act; and on the other hand no law passed by the amending power will be void on the ground of repugnancy to the law of England unless it is repugnant to the provisions of some such Act, order, or regulation. (Colonial Laws Validity Act, 1865).[61]

One of the surprising, though logically comprehensible, consequences of this constitutional hierarchy was that the covering clauses of the Constitution, i.e. sections 1 to 9 of the Commonwealth of Australia Act 1900 (Imp.)—could be altered only by the Imperial Parliament.[62] As Quick and Garran put the matter, 'the amending power can amend the Constitution, but the Constitution Act is above its reach'.[63] Quick and Garran acknowledged that the Imperial Parliament was an alternative method of amending the Constitution, especially where the section 128 procedure was blocked for whatever reason. However, they warned that 'such a radical and drastic method of settling a deadlock, unsolvable by the Constitution itself, could only be justified by the gravest considerations of a most serious emergency'.[64]

Australian constitutional writing in the early period of the Constitution presented glimpses of independent-spirited writing but was orthodox in the main. We have seen that there were not-infrequent references to the people of Australia, but sustained analysis of the legal implications of this fact were rare.

---

[59] Quick and Garran (1901) (n. 3 above).
[60] Quick and Garran (1901) (n. 3 above) quoted in L. Zines, 'The Sovereignty of the People' in M. Coper and G. Williams (eds) *Power, Parliament and the People* (Annandale: Federation Press, 1997) 94.　　　　[61] Quick and Garran (1901) (n. 3 above) 994 (emphasis added).
[62] ibid., 989.　　　　[63] ibid., 989.　　　　[64] ibid., 991.

Writing in 1932, Robert Garran referred to the Conventions which drafted the Constitution Bill as 'a Parliament . . . summoned to frame one important Act',[65] but he refrained from developing this statement into an alternative view of the Australian Constitution's constitutional foundations.

One writer who developed a more sustained analysis of popular sovereignty in the early years of the Australian Constitution was Inglis Clark, author of *Studies in Australian Constitutional Law*.[66] In the opening sentences of chapter 2 of that work, on 'The Interpretation of a Written Constitution', Clark acknowledged that the Australian Constitution owed its binding force to the Imperial Parliament: 'The Constitution of the Commonwealth of Australia is contained in a written document which is an Act of the Imperial Parliament . . . and the ultimate authority for all the legislation enacted by the Parliament of the Commonwealth . . . must be found in it.' However he also recognised the people of Australia as 'possessors of sovereign power'. Clark's sense of each generation of the Australian people sustaining the Constitution has been referred to as 'his "living force" vision'.[67] The following sample from Clark's writing sets out both the 'living force' vision and the makings of a sophisticated theory based on popular sovereignty:

. . . the Constitution was not made to serve a temporary and restricted purpose, but was framed and adopted as a permanent and comprehensive code of law, by which the exercise of the governmental powers conferred by it should be regulated as long as the institutions which it created to exercise the powers should exist. But the social conditions and the political exigencies of the succeeding generations of every civilised and progressive community will inevitably produce new governmental problems to which the language of the Constitution must be applied, and hence it must be read and construed, not as containing a declaration of the will and intentions of men long since dead, and who cannot have anticipated the problems that would arise for solution by future generations, but as declaring the will and intentions *of the present inheritors and possessors of sovereign power*, who maintain the Constitution and have the power to alter it, and who are in the immediate presence of the problems to be solved. It is they who enforce the provisions of the Constitution and make *a living force* of that which would otherwise be a silent and lifeless document. *Every community of men is governed by present possessors of sovereignty* and not by the commands of men who have ceased to exist. But so long *as the present possessors of sovereignty* convey their commands in the language of their predecessors, that language must be interpreted by the judiciary consistently with a proper use of it as an intelligible vehicle of the conceptions and intentions of the human mind, and consistently with the historical associations from which particular words and phrases derive the whole of their meaning in juxtaposition with their context. *If the present*

---

[65] Garran (Sydney, 1932) (n. 1 above) 15.

[66] Andrew Inglis Clark, *Studies in Australian Constitutional Law* (1st edn, 1901) (reprinted Sydney: Legal Books, 1997). See J.A. Thomson, 'Andrew Inglis Clark and Australian Constitutional Law' in M. Haward and J. Warden (eds) *An Australian Democrat: The Life, Work and Consequences of Andrew Inglis Clark* (1995).

[67] F. Wheeler, 'Framing an Australian Constitutional Law: Andrew Inglis Clark and William Harrison Moore' (1997) 3 Aust J Leg Hist 237, 247.

possessors of sovereignty discover that the result so produced is contrary in particular cases to their will in regard to future cases of a like character, they will amend the language which they previously retained as the expression of their will. If they do not amend it they must be presumed to accept the interpretation put upon it by the judiciary as the correct announcement of their present commands.[68]

It would be a long time before such views would find their way back into the mainstream of Australian constitutional thinking.[69]

Balfour, Westminster and adoption debates

We have already seen in Chapter 2 that Australia did not adopt the Statute of Westminster until 1942 with effect from 1939. It had been agreed in London in 1930 that, except in the case of two Dominions—New Zealand and Newfoundland—the Statute would come into force on 11 December 1931. New Zealand, as we have seen in Chapter 8, was emotionally and politically set against the Statute, whereas Newfoundland was simply too small to cope with independence.[70] Australia was never enthusiastic, but the assumption seemed to be that if Canada, South Africa and the Irish Free State went ahead then Australia would not let itself be left behind. Nonetheless, some leading political and academic commentators were strongly against what they perceived as the weakening and blurring of the ties of Imperial unity.

As we have seen, the lead-up to the Statute of Westminster began with the Balfour Declaration of 1926. Even, or perhaps especially, the latter's supporters acknowledged that it was a 'masterpiece of ambiguity'. Harrison Moore, who was advising the Australian delegation, captured both the political ambiguity and the emerging legal confusion of the time: 'the relations of the several parts of the Empire to other countries, present us with a tangle in which the political has to be distinguished from the legal, and the legal may be on different planes'.[71] K.H. Bailey, Professor of Jurisprudence at Melbourne and Moore's former colleague, insisted that in legal terms Australia's constitutional position was basically unaltered since federation: 'Australia is not a sovereign state but a self-governing Dominion within the British Empire'.[72] Leading politicians, notably

[68] Clark (1901) (n. 66 above) 20–1 (emphasis added).

[69] See *Theophanous v The Herald Weekly Times Ltd* (1994) 182 CLR 104, 171–2 where Deane J quotes this same passage.

[70] W.J. Hudson and M.P. Sharp, *Australian Independence: Colony to Reluctant Kingdom* (Melbourne: Melbourne University Press, 1988) 118.

[71] W. Harrison Moore, 'Separate Action by the British Dominions in Foreign Affairs' in *Australian and New Zealand Society of International Law Proceedings*, Melbourne, 1935, 1, quoted in Hudson and Sharp (1988) (n. 70 above) 98.

[72] K.H. Bailey, 'Australia's Treaty Rights and Obligations' in P. Campbell, R.C. Mills and G.V. Portus, (eds), *Studies in Australian Affairs* (Melbourne, 1930) 156, quoted in Hudson and Sharp (1988) (n. 70 above) 98.

John Latham, the future Chief Justice, were equally intent on explaining away the Balfour Declaration. Latham's efforts were to prove decisive regarding the Statute of Westminster as well.

In the years immediately following the Balfour Declaration, Latham cultivated public opinion so as to de-emphasise the sense of strength and independent spirit that had emerged out of Australia's experience of World War I, Versailles and the League of Nations. In 1928, as Attorney-General, Latham made a point of insisting that 'the several parts of the Empire have not become independent states'.[73] He felt impelled to underline certain constitutional fundamentals: the Westminster Parliament remained supreme, and appeals from Australian courts could still proceed to the Judicial Committee of the Privy Council in London.[74] Neither Australia nor any other Dominion could be independent in such circumstances, and Latham assured Australians that this was a good thing. Latham's political agenda seemed to be one of convincing Australians that their country was still weak, for, once they recognised its weakness, they would see it could be truly strong only as a member of the British Commonwealth.

Once it became clear that a majority of self-governing Dominions had agreed to the Statute of Westminster, Latham, by then Leader of the Opposition, set about ensuring that it would not affect Australia. His first success was 'simply in having Australia also listed with Newfoundland and New Zealand as dominions to which the Statute would not apply'.[75] His second was 'in having Australia listed with Newfoundland and New Zealand as dominions whose parliaments could at any time repeal their own legislation adopting the Statute'.[76] As Hudson and Sharp note, echoing Geoffrey Palmer's reaction to New Zealand diffidence in the same period, 'the mind now boggles at the notion of an independent state unilaterally surrendering its independence and reverting to the status of a colony of the presumably now indifferent metropolitan power, but this is what was done'.[77] Latham's third success was 'in so rousing false fears in the states about the possible impact of the Statute on them as to ensure that speedy adoption by Australia of the Statute was unlikely, and celebration of it very unlikely'.[78]

By 1932 Latham was once again in government, this time as Deputy Prime Minister, Attorney-General and Minister for External Affairs.[79] When asked

[73] J.G. Latham, *Australia and the British Commonwealth* (London: Macmillan, 1929) 26, quoted in Hudson and Sharp (1988) (n. 70 above) 98–9.

[74] Hudson and Sharp (1988) (n. 70 above) 99.   [75] ibid., 118.

[76] ibid., 118. As noted in Ch. 1 above, Newfoundland's constitutional fate became joined to that of Canada as of 1949.   [77] Hudson and Sharp (1988) (n. 70 above) 118–9.

[78] ibid., 119.

[79] In 1931 Prime Minister Lyons had indicated that he favoured calling a Constitutional Convention to review the workings of the Australian Constitution. In April 1933, after consultation with his Attorney-General, John Latham, Lyons clarified his essentially orthodox views regarding constitutional possibilities before State representatives attending the Premiers Conference:

It is clear that a Convention cannot be used as an actual means of amending the Constitution although a Convention may make a recommendation for the consideration of the Federal

whether the government planned to adopt the Statute of Westminster, Latham replied that it did not, and he took the opportunity to explain his long-standing attitude:

I was a member of the Imperial Conference of 1926, and I consider real advances were made in the various relations of the British Empire. In 1930 another Conference was held and an effort was made in the Statute of Westminster to express this political under-standing in legal terminology. I have no enthusiasm for that expression . . . I do not view with any enthusiasm at all the attempt of 1930 to express in statutory form the political understanding of 1926. I was instrumental in the Australian parliament in introducing an amendment which makes it optional for Australia to adopt the Statute of Westminster. Up to the present we have not done so, and so long as I am Attorney-General with any influence, I do not know that we will.[80]

As it happened, Latham soon changed his mind.[81] He perceived that variable adoption of the Statute was creating undesirable disunity in the Commonwealth. And closer to home, with the Opposition now in favour of adoption, Latham saw that if he and his colleagues did not act, the Opposition might one day do so and make claim to having achieved independence for Australia. By then, how-ever, Latham was unable to persuade his colleagues of his new line of argument. He would in any event soon be leaving politics in order to become Chief Justice of the High Court of Australia.

Latham's successor, R.G. Menzies, also raised the issue of adoption in Cabinet, but he too was initially denied. Finally, in 1936, Menzies was allowed to proceed, but in that year, as in the next, the adoption Bills were allowed to lapse by a government which still gave them no real priority. A change of government in 1941, and the new circumstances of a second World War, eventually ensured that adoption occurred. Australia had not so much discovered nationalist fervour as recognised the need both to remove inconvenient obstacles and uncertainties[82] and to join the other leading Dominions which had already adopted the Statute.

Parliament and, if the Federal Parliament approved, for subsequent submission to the people. A great deal of misunderstanding exists because the Constitution was originally framed by a Convention. The principle Federation Conventions were elected under State laws, and their deliberations resulted only in proposals which were afterwards submitted to referendum in the several States. Even these referenda did not create the Constitution. The Constitution was created by the statute of the Imperial Parliament.
Quoted in U. Ellis, *A Federal Convention: To Revise the Constitution* (Canberra: Australian Office of Rural Research and Development, 1952) 28.

[80] Australia, *Commonwealth Parliament Debates*, Vol. 143, 5878 (8 December 1933), quoted in Hudson and Sharp (1988) (n. 70 above) 123.

[81] Hudson and Sharp (1988) (n. 70 above) 123–4.

[82] It was felt that adoption of the Statute would expedite the implementation of merchant shipping legislation and remove uncertainties about some of the government's security activities. Hudson and Sharp (1988) (n. 70 above) 125.

Adoption of the Statute of Westminster meant that sections 2, 3, 4, 5 and 6 of the Statute now applied to the Commonwealth of Australia.[83] However, as we have seen in Chapter 2, the *status quo ante* applied with regard to the Australian states. Section 9 of the Statute made clear that: 'Nothing in this Act shall be deemed to authorise the Parliament of the Commonwealth of Australia to make laws on any matter within the authority of the States of Australia, not being a matter within the authority of the Parliament or Government of the Commonwealth of Australia.' Given that the states controlled their Constitutions, adoption of the Statute of Westminster by the Commonwealth only affected the Commonwealth. The states continued to be governed by the Colonial Laws Validity Act, 1865 (Imp.) and the rules regarding repugnancy that went with it, by the extraterritoriality rules, and by other less significant though equally anomalous badges of continued subordination.

Writing in 1937, John Latham's son, Richard, noted that 'since the constitutions of the Commonwealth and the States are not contained in a single instrument, but in so many Acts of the Imperial Parliament', it would be difficult for Australia 'to sever her law from the Imperial root'.[84] Unlike his father, however, Richard Latham had no doubt that this was conceivable: 'It is not at all impossible that the law of a Dominion should come to regard the Imperial Parliament's legislative power within the borders of the Dominion as now derivative—delegated by tolerance, if not expressly—if only it can explain how its former supremacy was terminated.'[85] Explanations turned on interpretations of the Statute of Westminster that left Imperial theory orthodoxy behind. In Australia's case, replacement of the Imperial Parliament at the apex of the Australian legal system would also have to solve the state-Commonwealth problem just referred to: 'Accordingly, if the Imperial Parliament ceased to be looked to as the original source of law, there would have to be a novation of the federal compact, a new fundamental agreement between Commonwealth and States.'[86] Richard Latham took the view that such a situation was unlikely to occur, 'not from lack of nationalism, but because Australian nationalism has always been interested rather in the substance than the trappings and formal guarantees of independence'.[87]

We shall see in Part III that a number of constitutional commentators now designate 11 December 1931, the time when Australia acquired the power to

---

[83] It is worth noting that since 1931 there had been four United Kingdom Acts which purported to extend the powers of the Commonwealth Parliament: Whaling Act 1934, s. 15; Geneva Convention Act, 1937, s. 2; Emergency Powers (Defence) Act 1939, s. 5; and Army and Air Force (Annual) Act, 1940, s. 3. On the constitutional status of state constitutions after adoption of the Statute of Westminster, see A. Twomey, *The Constitution of New South Wales* (Annandale: Federation Press, 2004).

[84] R.T.E. Latham, 'The Law and The Commonwealth' in W.K. Hancock (ed.) *Survey of British Commonwealth Affairs*, Vol. 1 (London: Oxford University Press, 1937) 517, reprinted with a foreword by W.K. Hancock but with otherwise unaltered pagination as R.T.E. Latham, *The Law and the Commonwealth* (Oxford: Oxford University Press, 1949), 526–7.

[85] Latham (1937) (n. 84 above) 526.   [86] ibid., 527.   [87] ibid., 526.

adopt the Statute of Westminster, as the moment when Australia achieved its independence. For the time being, however, we will attempt to determine what Australian attitudes were in this period. A rare few were already convinced of Australia's constitutional independence,[88] but leading constitutional commentators took a traditional line. It will be convenient, and revealing, to consider in detail two writers who for very different reasons had an especially strong effect on the evolving Australian understandings of their constitutional fundamentals, notably those relating to sovereignty and the legal system. The first of these, Owen Dixon, was a judge, later Chief Justice, of the High Court, and was acknowledged to be one of the finest intellects that Australian law had ever produced. His speeches were widely reported and eventually collected in 1965 for even wider consultation.[89] The second was W. Anstey Wynes, author of *Legislative, Executive and Judicial Powers in Australia*. Wynes' text, which was widely used in Australian law schools, was first published in 1936[90] and went to five editions, the last appearing in 1976.[91]

[88] See, e.g., T.C. Brennan, *Interpreting the Constitution: A Politico-Legal Essay* (Melbourne: Melbourne University Press, 1935) 12–13. Brennan used the fact that his was 'a politico-legal essay' to consider 'material denied the High Court as judges'. He was accordingly not bound to the fiction that 'the Constitution is a document evolved by the Imperial Parliament and imposed by its sovereign on the people of Australia'. The people of Australia knew 'that the Constitution was drawn up by the representatives of the people, was adopted by the people themselves at a referendum, and was handed to the Imperial Parliament with the request that it should be given force of law'. For that reason, 'they know that . . . the Constitution as a whole . . . is the work of the people of Australia and not of the Parliament of Great Britain'. Despite the popular and independent spirit of this essay, Brennan's express self-dispensation from matters which would concern the High Court suggested that he might have expressed a different opinion if asked to advise as King's Counsel. 'Technically, then, the Constitution is an Act of the Imperial Parliament; really, it is the act of the people of Australia.'

[89] Rt Hon. Sir Owen Dixon, *Jesting Pilate: And Other Papers and Addresses* (Melbourne: Law Book Company, 1965).

[90] The 1st edn bore the shorter title *Legislative and Executive Powers in Australia* (Sydney: Law Book Company, 1936).

[91] See previous footnote for first edition. Subsequent editions bore the longer title: W. Anstey Wynes, *Legislative, Executive and Judicial Powers in Australia* (Sydney: Law Book Company) (2nd edn, 1956; 3rd edn, 1962; 4th edn, 1970; 5th edn, 1976).

10

Australia II: Westminster to Canberra

Australian constitutional understandings
after 1931: Owen Dixon[1]

Owen Dixon's work is in many ways a model for this book; however, his work is discussed here as exemplary of dominant Australian understandings of constitutional fundamentals in the middle part of the last century. Dixon had a clear sense of how seemingly obscure theoretical issues affected the working out of constitutional issues in a legal system whether or not these assumptions were acknowledged by their exponents:

The fundamental conceptions, which a legal system embodies or expresses, are seldom grasped or understood in their entirety at the time when their actual influence is greatest. They are abstract ideas usually arrived at by generalisation and developed by analysis. But it is a mistake to regard such ideas as no more than philosophic theories supplied ex post facto to explain a legal structure which has already been brought into existence by causes of some other and more practical nature. On the contrary, sometimes the conceptions, even though never analysed and completely understood, obsess the minds of the men who act upon them. Sometimes indeed they are but instinctive assumptions of which at the time few or none were aware. But afterwards they may be seen as definite principles contained within the ideas which provided the ground of action. Further, when such conceptions have once taken root they seldom disappear. They persist long after the conditions in which they originate have gone. They enter into combinations with other conceptions and contribute to the construction of new systems of law and government.[2]

[1] See P. Ayres, *Owen Dixon: A Biography* (Melbourne: Melbourne University Press, 2004), which unfortunately appeared too late to be included in this chapter's account of Dixon's influence on Australian constitutional thinking.

[2] O. Dixon, 'The Law and the Constitution' in O. Dixon, *Jesting Pilate: And Other Papers and Addresses* (Melbourne: Law Book Company, 1965) 38, originally delivered in Melbourne on 14 March 1935, as one of a series of lectures arranged by the University of Melbourne in commemoration of the centenary of the State of Victoria (hereinafter Dixon (1935). Dixon made a similar point in 'The Statute of Westminster 1931' (1936) 10 Australian LJ, Supplement, 96, a paper prepared for delivery during the second convention of the Law Council of Australia, 25 September 1936 and reprinted in Dixon (1965) 83 (hereinafter Dixon (1936) with citations to Australian LJ:

An inquiry into the source whence the law derives its authority in a community, if prosecuted too far, becomes merely metaphysical. But if the theoretical answer be adopted by a system of law as part of its principles, it will not remain a mere speculative explanation of juristic facts. It will possess the capacity of producing rules of law. Its incorporation into the body of the law may lead to consequences of much practical importance.

The 'doctrine that the supreme law of the United States derives its authority from the people'[3] was one example of such a fundamental conception, but not one shared by Australia and other British colonies, according to Dixon. Dicey's orthodox version of parliamentary sovereignty was another example. Dixon set out to make these fundamental conceptions clearer. In this respect, he too proved to be quite orthodox in his constitutional thinking, but usually subtle and profound as well.

Without using the loaded Diceyan vocabulary of 'subordinate legislatures' and the like,[4] Dixon was nonetheless clear that the fundamental conceptions differed depending on whether one was analysing the British or the Australian (and other colonial) Constitutions. Regarding the British Constitution, three rival conceptions had been in contention: the supremacy of the law; the supremacy of the Crown; and the supremacy of Parliament. After 1688 the supremacy of the Crown had necessarily to give way, receiving instead a new application as the somewhat mystical representation of the supreme authority of the State.[5] Supremacy of law in turn gave way to supremacy of Parliament in order for the latter to secure the former. However, Dixon was clear that it was the common law which recognised in Parliament that 'supreme *and* unlimited legislative power' that we associate with its sovereignty.[6] Furthermore, this sovereignty was clearly what we referred to in Chapters 1 and 3 as 'continuing'. 'It is, of course, a commonplace', Dixon stated, 'that if the British Parliament were to attempt to limit its own powers . . . it might the next day pass a valid law flatly inconsistent with the limitation.'[7] Its supremacy over the law meant that 'the last expression of its will must take effect notwithstanding anything to the contrary in the existing state of law'.[8] We saw in Chapter 3 that Dixon J appeared ready to contemplate manner and form limitations on even the United Kingdom Parliament; however, these comments, written four years after the *Trethowan* case,[9] revealed his essentially orthodox view of that Parliament's powers.

What of Australia and the other colonies? The common law 'conferred upon the Crown authority to constitute a legislature in any place . . . which the Crown acquired in right of its English sovereignty'.[10] But at common law, 'such a legislature was not supreme over the law'.[11] Its powers were limited by law, such limitations arising, as we have seen in Chapter 2, from the express terms of the instrument creating the legislature or from the doctrines of extraterritoriality and repugnancy. Furthermore, the courts of a colony were the King's courts

---

[3] Dixon (1936) (n. 2 above) 82.

[4] As we shall see, Dixon was more inclined to emphasise the unlimited power of colonial legislatures, once certain Imperial limitations had been taken into account.

[5] Dixon (1935) (n. 2 above) 40.   [6] ibid., 42 (emphasis in original).   [7] ibid., 48.

[8] ibid., 48.

[9] *Attorney-General for New South Wales v Trethowan* (1931) 44 CLR 395 (H Ct).

[10] Dixon (1935), (n. 2 above) 43.   [11] ibid., 43.

administering 'the common law which acknowledged only one sovereign legislature, the parliament at Westminster'.[12]

As noted earlier in the discussion of Dixon's notion of fundamental constitutional conceptions, when it came to the federal Commonwealth Constitution, Dixon was quite prepared to acknowledge the American influences on it. However, popular sovereignty was not part of the deal. In this respect, the Australian Constitution 'depart[ed] altogether from its prototype'.[13] It was 'not a supreme law purporting to obtain its force from the direct expression of a people's inherent authority to constitute a government'; rather it was 'a statute of the British Parliament enacted in the exercise of its legal sovereignty over the law everywhere in the King's Dominions'.[14]

Ruling out popular sovereignty and reasserting the overarching sovereignty of the Imperial Parliament did not necessarily shed light on what fundamental conceptions were at work in Australia, Commonwealth and states. Was it supremacy of the law or supremacy of the legislature(s)? Dixon noted that the Colonial Laws Validity Act, 1865 (Imp.) had empowered every colonial legislature to legislate with respect to its own Constitution, powers and procedure. He recognised recent attempts under this power to impose manner and form restrictions on certain types of legislation as 'a modern reconciliation of the conception of supremacy of law and the supremacy of Parliament'.[15] 'The law existing for the time being' was supreme when it prescribed conditions for making law.[16] However, provided that those conditions were fulfilled, Parliament was supreme over the law regarding what should be done with the law. The same sort of reconciliation could be seen as the foundation for federalism. The states and the Commonwealth were obliged by law to stay within the powers granted to them, but provided that they did so, they could legislate as they saw fit.[17] Dixon saw 'manner and form' limitations as 'perhaps...the most important legal development of the time'. Australian federation, with its accompanying assumptions regarding the supremacy of law, was 'the greatest event in our political and legal development'.[18] Whereas the conception of parliamentary supremacy over the law had dominated lawyers' thoughts in the past, more recently, the conception of supremacy of the law had triumphed.[19] Some of this gives the impression that Dixon was a signed up member of the 'new view'. However, it was crucial to remember that Dixon's discussion of the supremacy of the law in Australia was not intended by him to contradict the fundamental supremacy of the Westminster Parliament at the apex of the Imperial legal system.

What then did Dixon make of the Statute of Westminster, 1931? Here, once again, his orthodox but subtle approach appeared. He recognised that sections 2 and 4 of the Statute represented a clear 'legislative denial' or 'restriction' of the

---

[12] ibid., 43. [13] ibid., 44. [14] ibid., 44. [15] ibid., 50. [16] ibid., 50.
[17] ibid., 51. [18] ibid., 51. [19] ibid., 50–1, 56.

Imperial Parliament's supremacy. But he asserted that 'in a purely legal point of view supremacy of the law is a thing which from its very nature the law itself cannot restrict'.[20] This was pure Dicey, denying as it did even the possibility of Parliament limiting its own powers.[21] Regarding section 2 of the Statute, he concluded that it was 'no more than a restriction upon supremacy over the law here in force'.[22] This seemed to indicate that the Commonwealth could legislate inconsistently with then-existing Acts of the Westminster Parliament, but it could not necessarily do so with regard to future Westminster Acts. That seemed to make Australia's constitutional independence impossible or at the very least precarious. Section 4 was designed to take care of future Westminster legislation, and was also, therefore, 'a restriction upon British parliamentary supremacy' on its face.[23] Regarding section 4, Dixon stated somewhat ambiguously that it did 'no more than restate as a legal rule an existing constitutional convention'.[24] His earlier restatement of orthodox principles regarding Westminster's continuing sovereignty seemed to indicate that section 4 could not bind a future Westminster Parliament intent on passing legislation for Australia. In a subsequent essay, 'The Statute of Westminster 1931',[25] Dixon left no room for doubt on this point. Regarding section 4, he asserted that 'the proposed rule could not prevent the Imperial Parliament from afterwards enacting a statute containing some sufficient expression of intention that it should operate in a Dominion, notwithstanding any law of the Dominion to the contrary'.[26] Such a statute would 'necessarily prevail over the local statutes even if subsequently enacted'.[27]

However, Dixon was clearly aware of the political realities. He acknowledged that whereas before the Statute of Westminster 'the juristic sovereignty of the Empire theoretically resided in the Imperial Parliament', the main provisions of the Statute were clearly enacted 'for the purpose of altering this situation', whether that purpose could be achieved in law or not.[28] He emphasised that 'the

---

[20] Dixon (1935) (n. 2 above) 57.

[21] Dixon restated this Diceyan point about the impossibility of limiting sovereign power a year later in 'The Statute of Westminster 1931':

The purpose of the main provisions of the Statute is to abrogate the rules of law which were thought to be inconsistent with the existence of complete legal autonomy and complete legal equality. The accomplishment of this object by legislation was necessarily difficult. For . . . it brought the promoters of the Statute face to face with the only limitation there is upon the omnicompetence of the Imperial Parliament. The limitation necessarily arises from that Parliament's supremacy over the law. No law it makes can deprive it of supremacy over the law. The last expression of its legislative will repeals all prior inconsistent laws.

Dixon (1936) (n. 2 above) 98.

[22] Dixon (1935) (n. 2 above) 57.   [23] ibid., 57.   [24] ibid., 58.
[25] Dixon (1936), (n. 2 above) 96.   [26] ibid., 99.

[27] ibid., 99. Dixon was equally clear on this point later in the same article. In describing 'the manner in which the Statute deals with the indestructible sovereignty of the King in Parliament over the law throughout the King's Dominions', he asserted that however 'effectual' the Statute was likely to be 'in fact' in guaranteeing that the power of the Westminster Parliament would lie dormant, it '[did] not operate in law to diminish the power of that Parliament' (pp. 99–100).

[28] Dixon (1935), (n. 2 above) 59.

juristic sovereignty of the Imperial Parliament caused no uneasiness in Australia', but that the same was plainly not true elsewhere, notably in South Africa and in the Irish Free State.[29] Dixon's somewhat wry and wistful conclusion was politically astute and at the same time consistent with his ongoing orthodox views regarding the legal position of Australia and other well-behaved Dominions: 'It has been found that the unity of the British Commonwealth is not secured by the existence of an actual but latent power exercisable by one single authority over all its people.'[30] 'Not secured' for South African and Ireland, but still secure enough for Australia and its fellow well-behaved Dominions, Canada and New Zealand, so long as they were willing.

We see here Dixon's clear sense of the Empire as a legal system, unified in theory if not always in practice by the Imperial Parliament. Dixon developed this theme in a number of his extra-judicial writings. He emphasised that unlike America which maintained an 'abstract theory of the source whence the law derives its authority', the Imperial legal system tended not to engage in 'speculative or artificial explanation of its basis'.[31] 'Without inquiring why it should be so', British and (most) Commonwealth lawyers had 'accepted the traditional principle on which that system rests':[32] 'It was the accepted doctrine of our system that the King in Parliament had absolute authority over the law and that all places acquired by the Crown in right of the Crown's British sovereignty must be subject to that authority'.[33] And 'allegiance to the Crown carried with it subjection to the ultimate legislative authority of the King in Parliament'.[34] Dixon was here disarmingly frank about his Diceyan assumptions, but also characteristically subtle and profound in linking the idea of sovereignty to the concept of an Imperial legal system.[35] Ever-realistic, Dixon was well aware that most Australians, lawyers

---

[29] ibid., 59.   [30] ibid., 59.   [31] Dixon (1936), (n. 2 above) 96.   [32] ibid., 96.
[33] ibid., 96.   [34] ibid., 96.

[35] Dixon's speculations no doubt influenced R.T.E. Latham who, through his father, John Latham, was acquainted with Dixon personally and professionally. Latham met Dixon in London and no doubt they discussed many legal matters. Latham reported to his father in July 1939 that he had 'seen a good deal of Dixon J., and like[d] and admire[d] him very much'. *National Library of Australia Collection*, Sir John Latham Collection, Series 10/1 July 1939. Dixon was one of Latham's two referees when Latham applied for a Chair in Law at the University of Sydney in 1941. See P. Oliver, 'Law, Politics, the Commonwealth and the Constitution: Remembering R.T.E. Latham', 1909–43 (2000) 11 KCLJ 153, 172. Dixon seldom referred to other academic writers in his publications, but he made an exception for Richard Latham who was referred to more than once. See Dixon (1943) (n. 41 below) 200n and Dixon (1957) (n. 45 below) 210n. Latham could not help but notice the discomfort which constitutional developments in the Commonwealth had produced for Dixon's essentially orthodox legal mind: 'The reluctance with which an eminent Australian lawyer finds himself forced to realise that the Imperial *Grundnorm* is anywhere questioned as the root of Dominion law may be seen in Mr Justice Dixon's address in 10 Austr LJ, Supp. 96.' R.T.E. Latham, 'The Law and The Commonwealth' in W.K. Hancock (ed.) *Survey of British Commonwealth Affairs*, Vol. 1 (London: Oxford University Press, 1937) 517, reprinted with a Foreword by W.K. Hancock but with otherwise unaltered pagination as R.T.E. Latham, *The Law and the Commonwealth* (Oxford: Oxford University Press, 1949). Latham (1937) 526n. Latham noted the same discomfort in the Commonwealth Attorney-General, Mr Menzies, in the latter's reply to Dixon's address. Latham (1937) 526.

included, were largely unaware of the location of ultimate legal authority. The 'derivative character of colonial constitutional law' made it unnecessary for them to be so.[36] Furthermore, 'the British Parliament so sparingly exercised its residual authority' that it was difficult to see fundamental constitutional principles in practice.[37]

The Statute of Westminster, 1931 was therefore exceptional in pointing the spotlight on fundamental questions. And, in Dixon's view, 'anything that touches upon so profound a question arouses instinctive misgiving'.[38] Whether for that reason or 'because it was feared lest the Statute should prove a Greek gift or for deeper motives of policy',[39] Australia along with New Zealand and Newfoundland had sought to protect themselves from its application. Before long, however, Australia would want to adopt the Statute and one day it would also want to obtain or (if already obtained) explain its constitutional independence. How would it do that?

Dixon was particularly fascinated with Ireland and South Africa[40] which had seemingly transcended the powers given to them in the Statute of Westminster. In Dixon's memorable phrase, they had 'induced the [constitutional] stream to flow above its source'.[41] This phenomenon could only be explained on two grounds, in Dixon's view: 'It may mean that the complete supremacy over the law belongs to the Dominion legislature', meaning that the common law of those countries now recognised in the local legislature a supremacy equivalent to that formally held by the Westminster Parliament; presumably acquired by what H.W.R. Wade would later describe as a disguised revolution.[42] 'Or,' he continued, 'it may mean that the Imperial Parliament, retaining its supremacy over the law of the Empire, has exercised it by entrusting to the Legislature of the Dominion a new *and overriding* power of constitutional amendment'.[43] This second ground of explanation was full of possibility, and desperately in need of unpacking, but Dixon preferred not to do so himself, perhaps out of practised diffidence given his position as High Court justice. Was he not trying to have his constitutional cake and eat it too, suggesting that the Imperial Parliament would 'retain its supremacy' even as the Dominion acquired a 'new *and overriding*'

---

[36] Dixon (1936), (n. 2 above) 97.   [37] ibid., 97.   [38] ibid., 99.   [39] ibid., 99.

[40] In reply to Dixon's paper, Mr Menzies, the Attorney-General of the Commonwealth, noted wryly that South Africans had 'become unduly obsessed with notions of status and independence'. He speculated that 'its Ministers sleep with a copy of the Statute of Westminster under their pillows'. Dixon (1936) (n. 2 above) 108.

[41] Dixon (1936) (n. 2 above) 105. In a 1943 paper, 'Sources of Legal Authority' Dixon noted how the 'existence of a central legislative body' in the Empire 'with the requisite legal authority in reserve' made it 'possible without any break in the continuity of the constitutional legal system of a Dominion or self-governing colony to bring into being a new government'. In other words, 'the law of the British Commonwealth provide[d] a constituent authority'. O. Dixon, 'Sources of Legal Authority' in O. Dixon (ed.) *Jesting Pilate: And Other Papers and Addresses* (Melbourne: Law Book Company, 1965) 198, 200 (hereinafter Dixon (1943)).

[42] H.W.R. Wade, 'The Basis of Legal Sovereignty' [1955] CLJ 172, 191.

[43] Dixon (1936) (n. 2 above) 106 (emphasis added).

supremacy of its own? The stream was rising above its source if the Imperial Parliament's powers were definitively 'continuing' in nature. If, however, that Parliament possessed unexplored 'self-embracing' powers[44] (though perhaps only from the Dominion perspective) then the old Imperial stream was acting, in the normal way, as a source for a new Dominion stream, but one that would in future be fed by new waters. Such questions will be explored further in Part III. It is important here simply to point out that although Dixon appeared not to address in any detail the question of how constitutional independence could be obtained, his astute analysis pointed the way to fruitful avenues of inquiry.

Ultimately, Dixon's essentially orthodox constitutional understandings affected his sense of the limits of constitutional possibilities. He returned to a consideration of constitutional fundamentals in his 1957 article, 'The Common Law as an Ultimate Constitutional Foundation', still orthodox in his assumptions though aware of other openings.[45] First, however, he repeated and refined most of the points made earlier: the contrast between the United States' original constitutional and jurisprudential authority and Australia's derivative equivalent;[46] and the contrast between the United Kingdom's supremacy of Parliament and Australia's emphasis on supremacy of law. Regarding this last point, Dixon's earlier writing gave the impression that the contrast between the two types of supremacies was stark. His 1957 article was yet more subtle on this point. His 'thesis' there was that 'the common law is the source of the authority of Parliament at Westminster'.[47] It was a proposition of the common law that 'a court may not question the validity of a statute'.[48] That was just 'another way of expressing the doctrine of parliamentary supremacy over the law'. In his writing in the 1930s, Dixon had been inclined to accept Dicey's strictures about a sovereign Parliament being logically prohibited from limiting its own powers. By 1957 he had apparently abandoned that view. Too many lawyers, and here he perhaps included himself, had failed to understand that 'the principle of parliamentary supremacy was a doctrine of the common law as to the Parliament at Westminster and not otherwise a necessary part of the conception of a unitary system of government'.[49] 'To suppose otherwise' was 'to mistake what may be and often is for what must be'.[50] Again, these comments may have been

---

[44] On 'continuing' and 'self-embracing' sovereignty see discussion in Chs 1, 3 and 12. In reply to Dixon's 1936 paper, Mr Justice Evatt seemed quite willing to abandon what he referred to as 'the old dogma that the Parliament at Westminster is always able to nullify provisions of a Constitution purporting to bind that Parliament'; however, the Attorney-General, R.G. Menzies and Professor A.L. Campbell, also commenting on the paper, were more inclined to take the traditional view. See Dixon (1936) (n. 2 above) 106 et seq.

[45] O. Dixon, 'The Common Law as an Ultimate Constitutional Foundation' in O. Dixon, (ed.) *Jesting Pilate: And Other Papers and Addresses* (Melbourne: Law Book Company, 1965) 203 (hereinafter Dixon (1957)).   [46] ibid., 203.

[47] ibid., 206.   [48] ibid., 206.

[49] ibid., 206. *See Harris v Minister of the Interior* [1952] 2 SALR 428, 464.

[50] Dixon (1957) (n. 45 above) 206.

self-directed, and they opened up new possibilities, not all of which Dixon was prepared to explore.

It is easy to see why, if one accepts Dixon's thesis about the common law as the source of the Westminster Parliament's authority. Rather than being a logical requirement of sovereignty, what we have termed 'continuing' sovereignty was simply that which the common law had recognised for the Imperial Parliament. Dixon was now far clearer about there being historical (political and intellectual) rather than logical reasons for this fact: 'The development of the doctrine into its most absolute form may be traced and in that development may be seen the influence not only of the changes in political thought but also of more abstract questions of sovereignty.'[51] The recognition of the importance of history seemed to put Dixon in H.W.R. Wade's camp.[52] But Dixon was insistent that, however historically contingent, the absolute conception of parliamentary sovereignty was no less part of constitutional law, the common law of the constitution. Wade too referred to the doctrine of continuing parliamentary sovereignty as part of the common law, but he insisted that it was the only common law rule which could not change by legal means. Dixon acknowledged that Wade's 1955 article was 'powerful',[53] but Dixon was open and alive to the fact that even an ultimate common law rule can change: 'If there has been a shift in the understanding of the rule [regarding parliamentary sovereignty] and in the extent to which it is allowed an unqualified operation, that is characteristic of principles of the common law'. Dixon's reference to Wade's work was placed following the last comma in the preceding quotation; perhaps because the final phrase was inconsistent with Wade's admittedly 'powerful' argument. For Wade a change in the ultimate rule of a legal system was a 'disguised revolution'; for Dixon this was typical of the common law and fully legal.[54] And not only was it usual for the common law to evolve, sometimes it could be forced to do so by Parliament itself. Here Dixon squared up to the distinction between continuing and self-embracing sovereignty, though he did not use these terms. And again, the caution of the professional judge perhaps caused him to hold back on expressing a firm view. It is evident, however, that he saw the issue clearly: 'The proposition that it is a common law rule that the Parliament of the United Kingdom is supreme over the law is of course exposed to the objection that if it is a rule of the common law it may be altered by the supreme legislature.'[55] Wade, as we have

---

[51] Dixon (1957) (n. 45 above) 206–7.

[52] Wade (1955) (n. 42 above). See Ch. 4 above for discussion of Wade's views.

[53] Dixon (1957) (n. 42 above) 207n.

[54] ibid., 210: 'The first [step] is to treat parliamentary supremacy over the law as itself the creature of law ... The first step I would not be unwilling to concede. Indeed it is involved in the view that the principle of parliamentary supremacy formed part of the common law, true though it may be that it is an "ultimate" principle of the law.' This passage would seem to accept Wade's idea that parliamentary sovereignty is an ultimate principle, but reject Wade's further contention that the ultimate principle is immune to legal change. H.W.R. Wade (1955) (n. 42 above).

[55] Dixon (1957) (n. 45 above) 207.

seen, rejected this (Jennings-inspired) point, but Dixon was not inclined to foreclose the matter. He simply observed the paradox: 'It is the old theological and juristic riddle and the answer is that it is not so if you state the principle in full whether it be part of the metaphysics of the conception of sovereignty or part of the common law.'[56] This in turn implied that if the rule regarding the sovereignty of the Westminster Parliament had been already stated 'in full', and if that sovereignty was of the full 'continuing' variety, then Parliament would not be able to alter the rule. All Dixon's writing indicated that Parliament's powers were absolute and unlimited. But someone of Dixon's intellect probably saw that even absolute and unlimited power might disguise self-embracing possibilities, though he did not spell them out.[57] He simply referred to the possibility of 'placing upon the common law doctrine of the supremacy of Parliament the kind of qualification which of late has been discussed with so much learning'.[58] Here, in a footnote, he referred to articles by many of the exponents of the 'new' and 'revised' views, notably Hamish Gray and Richard Latham.[59]

It is worth pointing out that Dixon's new tendency to retain orthodox assumptions while exploring possible new qualifications on sovereignty was typical of another leading constitutional writer in the 1950s, Geoffrey Sawer, Professor of Law at the Australian National University. Sawer noted that 'the formal basis or *Grundnorm* of Australian constitutional law [was] still to be found in a series of British statutes',[60] and, in his assessment, 'few Australians find anything derogatory to Australia's status in continuing to attribute theoretical legal sovereignty to the Parliament at Westminster'.[61] It remained true that 'the formal source of Australian constitutional law [lay] in British statutes',[62] and there was an ongoing 'tendency to adopt the British principle of parliamentary supremacy, rather that the U.S. principle of popular sovereignty';[63] however, 'the realities of national autonomy'[64] would eventually prompt the question: 'assuming that the Mother of parliaments no longer claims sovereignty, where do

---

[56] ibid., 207.

[57] Dixon's reasons in the *Trethowan* case (1931) made clear that he saw clearly the 'new view'. 'Self-embracing' sovereignty, which included a substantive dimension, was part of what Geoffrey Marshall termed the 'revised' view. See Chs 1, 3, 4 above and 12 below for further discussion.

[58] Dixon (1957) (n. 45 above) 210.

[59] ibid., 210n. Subsequent comments indicated that Dixon was still willing to adopt the procedural qualification on parliamentary sovereignty emphasised in the 'new view':

It is therefore enough to say that the qualification upon the doctrine of the parliamentary supremacy of the law concerns the identification of the source of a purported enactment with the body established by law as the supreme legislature and the fulfilment of the conditions prescribed by the law for the time being in force for the authentic expression of the supreme will. If the qualification be law these are matters upon which the validity of a purported enactment may depend and they may accordingly be examinable in the courts.

It will be noticed that I have said 'if it be law'. Could the question of the nature, extent or existence of the qualification be regarded as anything but a matter of law?

[60] G. Sawer, 'Constitutional Law' in G.W. Paton (ed.) *The Commonwealth of Australia: The Development of its Laws and Constitution* (London: Stevens & Sons, 1952) 38, 78.

[61] ibid., (1952), 78.   [62] ibid., 78.   [63] ibid., 78.   [64] ibid., 78.

we find in Australia the person or combination of persons with authority to mark as law any proposed norm whatsoever?'[65] For Sawer there could only be one answer: 'The answer must be: the Federal Parliament and the electors, acting under s. 128 of the Constitution to amend the Constitution.'[66] Once this view was adopted, 'the theory of supremacy of parliaments may be qualified by a theory of sovereignty of the people'.[67]

Australian constitutional understandings after 1931: W. Anstey Wynes

Dixon (and Sawer) were eminent Australian lawyers. One had to read them quite carefully in order to pick out signs of the evolution in their thinking. Far more accessible for most students of Australian constitutional law were the various editions of W. Anstey Wynes.[68] However, regarding the fundamental constitutional questions which interest us, there was very little evolution in Wynes' thinking over almost forty years. It remained orthodox throughout in its espousal of what in Chapters 5 and 6 was termed the Imperial theory.

The first edition was published in 1936 prior to Australia's adoption of the Statute of Westminster, 1931, so traditional constitutional thinking was always more likely to appear here. Wynes' version was, however, strikingly full-blooded. In his chapter on 'The Commonwealth and States in Relation to the Empire', he was emphatic:

We begin with the principle of the supremacy of the Imperial Parliament over every portion of the British Empire. That Parliament may legislate for the whole or any portion of the Empire without restraint or limit of any kind. This matter needs no further elucidation since it is and always has been well recognised. This legal supremacy is not in any way lessened by the grant of a Constitution to a colony. Indeed the Dominions owe their Constitutions and their powers to the Legislature of Great Britain. In fact, however, the British Parliament has not for some considerable time exercised its rights of legislation for the Dominions without consulting their respective Governments ... [69]

This passage disappeared from subsequent editions, beginning with the second edition in 1956, and was replaced by a passage discussing the Balfour Declaration and the equality principle. Further mention was made of the fact that 'existing legal limitations' had been 'removed by the enactment by the Parliament of the United Kingdom, after consultation and agreement with the Dominions, of the

[65] Sawer (1952) (n. 60 above) 78.   [66] ibid., 78.   [67] ibid., 78.
[68] W. Anstey Wynes, *Legislative and Executive Powers in Australia* (Sydney: Law Book Company, 1936) and W. Anstey Wynes, *Legislative, Executive and Judicial Powers in Australia* (Sydney: Law Book Company) (2nd edn., 1956; 3rd edn., 1962; 4th edn., 1970; 5th edn., 1976).
[69] Wynes (1st edn 1936) (n. 68 above) 54–5.

Statute of Westminster'.[70] Wynes' first edition statement of the Westminster Parliament's unquestioned sovereignty was replaced by a similar, though more off-hand, statement on the relevant point:

It is unnecessary to dwell at length upon the legal supremacy of the Imperial Parliament in relation to Commonwealth and States alike, for the principle is and always has been well recognised. Indeed the Commonwealth Constitution itself was the creature of the Parliament at Westminster, as were the Constitutions of the several Colonies. *But, while the supremacy is not in any way lessened by the grant of a Constitution to a Colony,* its existence has not meant the subservence of the Colonies to the Imperial authorities; in point of fact . . . the United Kingdom had not generally exercised its powers of legislation in respect of the Dominions without prior consultation . . .[71]

Wynes had removed the first edition statement to the effect that 'the Dominions owe their Constitutions and their powers to the Legislature of Great Britain', probably because this was patently no longer true of Ireland, in more than one sense.[72] However, by merging the italicised sentence on supremacy and that regarding the constitutional convention regarding consultation, Wynes arguably made the legal position more emphatic, and all the more anachronistic by the time the fourth and fifth editions were published containing these passages in the 1970s.

What did Wynes make of the potentially liberating force of the Statute of Westminster, 1931? At the time of the first edition, the Statute could be taken as a confirmation of the *status quo* (because it did not yet apply to Australia), or as a harbinger of future independence (because the assumption was that it would eventually be adopted). Wynes took the unexpectedly traditional line, following Berriedale Keith,[73] of insisting that the Statute clarified and reaffirmed the Westminster Parliament's sovereign and continuing powers:

The Statute itself, while it contains a complete renunciation by the Imperial Parliament of any measure of control over, or interference with, Dominion affairs, is at the same time, as Professor Keith has expressed it, 'a singular assertion of the sovereign authority' of the British Parliament. For as is well known, it is legally impossible for the sovereign Parliament to limit itself in this way and there is nothing to prevent a future Parliament from repealing the Statute either expressly or by inconsistent legislation, however unthinkable such an exercise of Imperial power may be.[74]

The footnote to this passage stressed that 'this fact has been noted by every legal writer on the subject'. What then did subsequent editions make of legal writers

---

[70] Wynes (2nd edn, 1956) 73, (3rd edn, 1962) 72.

[71] Wynes (2nd edn, 1956) 76; (3rd edn, 1962) 73–4; (4th edn, 1970) 54. The 5th edn (1976) differs very little from the 4th edn; in fact, the 3rd edn was the last significant revision.

[72] Ireland had succeeded in creating a constitutional novation in the 1930s with no involvement by the Westminster Parliament, and by 1956, the date of the 2nd edn, the Republic of Ireland was neither a Dominion nor a member of the Commonwealth.

[73] See A. Berriedale Keith, *The Dominions as Sovereign States: Their Constitutions and Governments* (London, Macmillan, 1938) 62. [74] Wynes (1st edn, 1936) (n. 68 above) 74.

such as Jennings, R.T.E. Latham, Dixon, Marshall, Wheare or perhaps even Wade? The relevant passage disappeared from subsequent editions; however, a similar view appeared later in the reworked chapter, following a discussion of Dixon's explorations of new constitutional perspectives. Wynes dismissed out of hand the idea that a particular constitutional solution had to be preferred, because in the eyes of some nationalistic writers it was 'consonant with the status of a self-governing Dominion',[75] preferring Lord Sankey's distinction between formal if 'abstract law' and political if simply conventional realities.[76] At this point, he reverted to what he had said in the first edition, holding onto this view, once again, into the 1970s: 'It is, perhaps unnecessary, for the present writer to repeat the view taken in the first edition that the Statute was and remains [, in Keith's words,[77]] "a singular assertion of the sovereign authority" of the British Parliament.'[78]

It was not surprising, given these views, that Wynes took the view that the Statute of Westminster had altered Australia's constitutional fundamentals little. It is hard to imagine, for example, a more orthodox interpretation of section 4 of the Statute, unaltered in this case through all editions: 'In point of law, in so far as this section purports to limit the powers of the Imperial Parliament it is, as we have seen, of no effect.'[79] To this, he added the usual comment regarding the particular wording of section 4: 'even apart from this principle, so far as sec. 4 is concerned, the Parliament of the United Kingdom is only required to declare that the request and consent of the Dominion have been obtained; the Courts would not and could not go behind the declaration'.[80]

A further example of Wynes' orthodoxy was evident in his discussion of constitutional amendment. While other authors took the view that section 128 could be used to amend the covering clauses of the Constitution of the Commonwealth of Australia Constitution Act, 1900, Wynes was apparently blind to these arguments: 'it is admitted on all sides that section 128 does not permit of any amendment [to the covering clauses]'.[81] In point of fact, 'the Statute of

---

[75] Wynes (2nd edn, 1956) (n. 68 above) 73.   [76] ibid., 108–9.

[77] Removed as of Wynes (4th edn, 1970) (n. 68 above) 79.

[78] Wynes (2nd edn, 1956) 109, (3rd edn, 1962), 105, (4th edn, 1970) 79. Wynes found further support here for this claim in the view expressed by Latham CJ in *R v Sharkey* (1949) 79 CLR 136: 'This section [4 of the Statute of Westminster] expressly recognises the legislative authority with respect to the Commonwealth of the Crown and Parliament of the United Kingdom and provides for the manner in which that authority is to be exercised.' However, one should also note Dixon J in the same case:

[Before the Statute of Westminster] the ultimate legislative authority of the Parliament at Westminster was exercisable with reference to the Commonwealth and that may have provided a theoretical basis for a law safeguarding the institution against disaffection. The Statute of Westminster has, however, since provided against the exerciseability of the power unless with the consent and request of the Commonwealth as one of the Dominions: s. 4.

[79] Wynes (1st edn, 1936) 80, (2nd edn, 1956) 100, (3rd edn, 1962) 97, (4th edn, 1970) 74.

[80] Wynes (1st edn, 1936) 80, (2nd edn, 1956) 100, (3rd edn, 1962) 97, (4th edn, 1970) 74.

[81] Wynes (1st edn, 1936) 363, (2nd edn, 1956) 694, (3rd edn, 1962) 696, (4th edn, 1970) 505–6.

Westminster [did] not confer any new power of amendment'.[82] Only the 'Imperial Parliament itself' could alter these provisions.[83] Furthermore, all parts of the Constitution could be amended 'by Imperial enactment' 'at any time'.[84]

Contemplating constitutional independence: the view from the courts

As far as the Australian Commonwealth was concerned, one gets the impression from Dixon, Wynes and others that the existing constitutional arrangements were satisfactory, despite the ongoing theoretical possibility of Westminster legislation. That possibility was controlled at the very least by the rules of construction set out in section 4 of the Statute of Westminster and by the conventions of United Kingdom-Dominion relations. As Richard Latham had observed in 1937, Australians, while not lacking in nationalistic spirit, seemed more interested 'in the substance than in the trappings and formal guarantees of independence'.[85]

All this seemed to change in the late 1970s and early 1980s, mostly as a result of a series of awkward cases regarding the legal relationship between Imperial statutes with enduring force as part of Australian law, the states (who could not legislate repugnantly to such statutes) and the Commonwealth (which was intent on ending this anomalous situation to the extent that it was in its power to do so).[86] Three of these cases merit closer attention: *Bistricic v Rokov*,[87] *China Ocean Shipping Co v South Australia*[88] and *Kirmani v. Captain Cook Cruises Pty Ltd (No 1)*.[89]

In the *Bistricic* case, the plaintiff crew member had injured himself while working on a New South Wales registered ship. When he sued his employers for damages, they claimed that section 503(1) of the Merchant Shipping Act 1894 (Imp.), still applicable in New South Wales, limited Bistricic's damages to A\$1,489.75. As it happened, section 503(1) of the 1894 Act had been modified for United Kingdom purposes by section 2(4) of the Merchant Shipping (Liability of Shipowners and Others) Act 1958 (UK); and, if Bistricic had the benefit of this statute his damages would not be subject to the above-mentioned limit. The problem was that nothing in the 1958 Act stated that it should apply to

[82] Wynes (1st edn, 1936) 363, (2nd edn, 1956) 694, (3rd edn, 1962) 696, (4th edn, 1970) 506.
[83] Wynes (1st edn, 1936) 363, (2nd edn, 1956) 694, (3rd edn, 1962) 696, (4th edn, 1970) 506. The use of the term 'Imperial Parliament' was common in 1936, but by the 1950s, certainly the 1970s, it was arguably anachronistic and therefore inappropriate.
[84] Wynes (1st edn, 1936) 365, (2nd edn, 1956) 696, (3rd edn, 1962) 698, (4th edn, 1970) 507.
[85] Latham (1937), 526.
[86] The robust nationalism of the Whitlam government (1972–5) set a tone which other governments had to follow to a greater or lesser extent.
[87] *Bistricic v Rokov* (1976) 135 CLR 552.
[88] *China Ocean Shipping Co v South Australia* (1979) 145 CLR 172.
[89] *Kirmani v Captain Cook Cruises Pty Ltd (No 1)* (1985) 159 CLR 351.

Australia, though section 11(1)(c) indicated that the Queen might by Order in Council extend the Act to 'any colony, or any country or place outside Her Majesty's dominions in which for the time being Her Majesty has jurisdiction'. A unanimous High Court held that the 1958 modifications did not apply in Australia, and that that therefore the limitation on damages set out in 1894 continued to apply. In the course of his reasons, Mason J noted that section 11 of the Statute of Westminster, 1931 made clear that Australia was neither 'a colony' nor a 'country or place outside Her Majesty's Dominions', and he related this point to Australia's evolving nationhood:

The legislative policy which underlies section 11 of the Statute of Westminster is as important as the language of the section. This policy, which has evolved over the long history of constitutional development leading to responsible government, legislative autonomy and Australian nationhood, is that a statute of the United Kingdom Parliament, if it is intended to apply to an Australian State, will be expressed to apply to that State . . .

The appellant's case for saying that the 1958 Act has an unexpressed application to the Australian States, chiefly rests on the proposition that because the 1894 Act enunciated the law for New South Wales any amendment to that Act should be approached on the footing that it was intended to amend the law wherever the 1894 Act applied in 1958. If we were to turn our backs on the history of constitutional development which has taken place since 1894 and on the provisions of the 1958 Act which delimit with some particularity its spheres of operation, this would be an attractive argument. But in the light of all that has happened since 1894 and all that is provided by the 1958 Act the argument is quite unacceptable.[90]

Murphy J agreed with his colleagues but took a far more radical approach, one which he would adhere to and develop over a series of decisions and extra-judicial writings. This was an extreme version of the Independence theory which was identified in Chapters 5 and 6. In his view, not only did the United Kingdom Parliament have no power, whether in 1976 or in 1958, to make 'a law having force in any part of Australia',[91] it had not had any such power since 1901. Murphy J was well aware of the orthodox theory and what it meant: 'This doctrine reflects the constitutional theory and reality that the people of a nation (or their representatives) cannot irrevocably bind their successors or even themselves to any constitution or other law.'[92] However, the doctrine and the theory behind it were 'part of the United Kingdom's municipal law'. While that 'municipal law' included Imperial law applying to colonies, 'when a colony . . . ceases to be under the political control of the United Kingdom Government, the supremacy ceases, and with it all legislative authority over the former colony or subject territory'.[93] As a Crown colony, New South Wales had been subject to this authority, but no more:

This paramount force and the Imperial Parliament no longer exist for Australia. Australia is an independent and equal member of the community of nations. Its relationship with

[90] *Bistricic* (n. 87 above) 557.   [91] ibid., 565.   [92] ibid., 565.   [93] ibid., 565.

the United Kingdom has long ceased to be imperial-colonial and is now international. The change in relationship was not brought about by the Statute of Westminster 1931 . . . The Statute of Westminster dealt with the constitutional forms, not substance as was well recognised at the time.

The United Kingdom has no legislative or executive authority over Australia (or any part of it). Any authority over the people of a State would be incompatible with the integrity of the Australian nation which is an indissoluble union of the people of the Commonwealth . . . [94]

Murphy was willing to concede that the 1900 Constitution was based on an Act of the United Kingdom Parliament rather than on the sovereignty of the people, but that situation had quickly changed: 'The original authority for our Constitution was the United Kingdom Parliament, but the existing authority is its continuing acceptance by the Australian people'.[95] The new basis for authority ensured that the Australian Constitution was immune from repeal by the body that had enacted it. After citing Viscount Sankey's famous statement regarding the theoretical ability of the Westminster Parliament to pass any law for any Dominion, Murphy J delivered his rebuke, and reasserted Australia's independence as of 1901:

Any theory which has no relation to realities is suspect. The United Kingdom Parliament could of course repeal the Statute of Westminster. It could repeal the Commonwealth of Australia Constitution Act. But such repeals would have no effect in Australia. Their effect, if any, would be confined to the municipal law of the United Kingdom (including the residual Imperial-colonial system) . . . The United Kingdom can have no power to make laws for an independent nation which was a former colony unless its paramount force is restored.

   . . .

In my opinion (notwithstanding many statements to the contrary) Australia's independence and freedom from United Kingdom legislative authority should be taken as dating from 1901. The United Kingdom Parliament ceased to be an Imperial Parliament in relation to Australia at the inauguration of the Commonwealth.[96]

Needless to say, Murphy J's opinion caused quite a stir, even though none of his fellow judges in the *Bistricic* case had agreed with his argument. Constitutional writers took note, and so did litigants. Had not Murphy J left open, in the final paragraphs of his reasons in *Bistricic*, the question whether the Merchant Shipping Act 1894 (Imp.) had *any* continued application in Australia?

In the *China Ocean Shipping* case, this issue was raised. A ship owned by China Ocean Shipping Company had collided with a jetty owned by the government of South Australia. The state claimed damages, and the ship owners attempted to limit their liability by relying on the same section 503(1) that was raised in the *Bistricic* case. A four-judge majority of the High Court held that the 1894 Act was still applicable in Australia, though three judges took the view that

[94] ibid., 566.   [95] ibid., 566.   [96] ibid., 566–7.

the Act did not apply in the case, because, as a matter of construction, the limitation it imposed did not bind the Crown. Murphy J, dissenting, took the opportunity to amplify the views that he had stated in the *Bistricic* case (and in a subsequent case, *Robinson v Western Australia Museum*).[97] Chief Justice Barwick dismissed Murphy J's argument in somewhat barbed fashion,[98] but it was left to Stephen J to make the substantive rebuttal.

Stephen J also betrayed some impatience with Murphy J's argument. He noted that it was 'not only opposed to the expressed view of all other members of this Court who participated in those decisions, it also runs counter to all those earlier decisions of the Court over the past twenty-five years in which the application to Australia of Imperial legislation has either been expressly asserted or has provided an essential basis for decision'.[99] However, Stephen J then proposed to assess Murphy J's arguments on their own terms, i.e. according to 'the *realities* of the relationship this century between the United Kingdom and Australia'.[100] He observed that the Constitutional Conventions clearly indicated that 'those who were . . . concerned to bring about Federation' accepted that 'the establishment of the Commonwealth would not of itself involve either the ending of the application to Australia of existing imperial laws or the denial to the Parliament at Westminster of continued competence to legislate for Australia'.[101] Stephen J stated that the 'political realities' were that 'viewed in the perspective of the nineteenth and of the early part of the twentieth century . . . the preservation of the residual power of the Imperial Parliament was still acceptable to the peoples of many British possessions', including Australia.[102] Furthermore, Stephen J asserted that this 'long continued to be the basis of the relationship between Imperial and Australian governments, regardless of their respective, and fluctuating, political complexions'.[103] Echoing the view taken by Wynes and Berriedale Keith, Stephen J argued that the Statute of Westminster 'affords testimony, attested to by each of the Dominions, of the continuing operation of Imperial legislation in the Dominions'.[104] Citing section 4 of the Statute, he asserted that: 'Not only did the Statute not itself affect the application of existing Imperial law, it expressly preserved the power of the Parliament of Westminster to enact future Imperial law for a Dominion, so long as the enactment declared that it had been

[97] *Robinson v Western Australia Museum* (1978) 138 CLR 283.

[98] *China Ocean* (n. 88 above) 181:

I must say that when I heard this proposition [that the Parliament of the United Kingdom ceased to have any power to pass any law effective in Australia as on and from . . . 1 January 1901], it seemed to me to represent a very quaint aberration, not only unsupported by any authority but contradicted by decisions of this Court. Moreover, it seemed to me to betray a lack of appreciation of the constitutional history of this country.

[99] *China Ocean* (n. 88 above) 209 (emphasis added).   [100] ibid., 209.

[101] ibid., 209–10.

[102] ibid., 210, approving views expressed in A. Castles, 'Reception and Status of English Law in Australia' (1963) 2 Adelaide L Rev 1.   [103] *China Ocean* (n. 88 above) 210.

[104] ibid., 211.

requested and consented to by the Dominion.'[105] Stephen J was willing to go so far as to say that Westminster's power to legislate for Australia was still valid in 1979: 'The legislative power of the Parliament at Westminster albeit responsive only to prior Australian initiatives, remains, for Australia, a factor in present-day constitutional law, despite undoubted changes in relationships which have occurred and which are reflected in the current realities of national political power and in Australia's own nationhood.'[106] The mark of change in the relationship between Australia and the United Kingdom was therefore 'not the rejection of the legislative power of the Parliament at Westminster to make laws in future for Australia, still less the abrogation of existing Imperial laws' but rather 'the continued application of existing Imperial laws ... *subject now to the power of repeal or amendment by Commonwealth legislation*'.[107]

In 1979 the Commonwealth finally decided to grasp the nettle by expressly repealing section 503 of the Merchant Shipping Act 1894 (Imp.) in section 104(3) of the Navigation Amendment Act 1979 (Cth). This attempt to eliminate confusion once again turned on fundamental constitutional questions, such as where the Commonwealth obtained the power to do so, and, assuming that it had done so, whether it had the power to repeal all British Acts relating to Australia or just those within Commonwealth jurisdiction? In *Kirmani v Captain Cook Cruises Pty Ltd (No 1)* the High Court was given the opportunity to consider these fundamental questions.[108]

On 9 August 1981, just six months after the Commonwealth's legislation had come into force, Mrs Shawar Kirmani sustained an injury on a Sydney ferry, the *Captain Cook II*. She sued the ferry owners in negligence, claming substantial damages. The defendant company sought to limit its liability using section 503(1) of the 1894 Act. They claimed, first, that the Commonwealth Act of 1979 did not affect the 1894 Act as part of the law of New South Wales, and secondly, that the Commonwealth had no power to repeal section 503 in so far as it applied to New South Wales. On the first point, the High Court decided that as a matter of construction the Commonwealth had intended to repeal section 503 wherever it applied in Australia. Where, then, did the Commonwealth get its power to do so, four out of seven judges agreeing that it did? Brennan J argued that the Commonwealth's power lay in section 2 of the Statute of Westminster, 1931, and that it had 'no power apart from the Statute'.[109] This interpretation depended on the fact that section 2 of the Statute was more than a permission to eliminate repugnancy in areas where the Commonwealth had existing and independent powers. Brennan J was willing to adopt this interpretation on the basis that the

---

[105] ibid., 211–12.   [106] ibid., 212.

[107] As confirmed in s. 2 of the Statute of Westminster, 1931. *China Ocean* (n. 88 above) 212 (emphasis added).

[108] *Kirmani v Captain Cook Cruises Pty Ltd (No 1)* (1985) 159 CLR 351.

[109] *China Ocean* (n. 88 above) 405. Section 10 of the Statute implied a power in the Commonwealth to adopt the Statute, including s. 2.

Statute was 'an organic law . . . [conferring] the full measure of powers needed to make the Dominion Parliaments wholly independent'.[110]

Brennan J was alone in finding that section 2 of the Statute was sufficient to empower the Commonwealth. Three judges, however, Justices Mason, Murphy and Deane, concluded that repeal of section 503 was a valid exercise of the Commonwealth's external affairs power (section 51(xxix)). The logic behind viewing it as such was that 'it removed from Australian law not merely a part of our inherited law but a part expressly enacted for Australia by the United Kingdom Parliament, and to that end this intrusion concerned the relations between Australia and the United Kingdom (though the making of a new provision did not)'.[111]

Mason and Murphy JJ had shown their cards in the *Bistricic* case. In Kirmani it was Deane J's turn. Some of his comments were particularly apposite, even portentous:

It may . . . be necessary at some future time to consider whether traditional legal theory can properly be regarded as providing an adequate explanation of the process which culminated in the acquisition by Australia of full 'independence and Sovereignty'. Plainly there is something to be said for the view that any explanation of the legal nature of the process is incomplete if it fails to acknowledge and examine the relevance and importance, under both international and internal law, of that social compact, of those international agreements, of the 'established constitutional position' to which the Statute of Westminster expressly refers and of international recognition of Australia as an independent and sovereign state whose only de jure government is that which is locally based . . . *Those questions could become of some practical importance if the Parliament of the United Kingdom were, for example, to purport on its own initiative to repeal the provisions of the Constitution or the provisions of the Statute or otherwise to legislate for Australia.* Apart from such far-fetched examples, however, they lie largely in the realm of theory by reason of the scope of the power to amend the Constitution by the process which it itself contains (s. 128) and, at least since the Statute of Westminster, of the full ambit of the power under the Constitution to make laws, however extra-territorial be their operation and however repugnant they be to the law of another country, with respect to external affairs. The practical effects of that power to amend the Constitution and of that legislative power which the Constitution confers are that *whatever be the theoretical explanation, ultimate authority in this country lies with the Australian people* and that, subject to the Constitution and to the State Constitutions which it protects, the Commonwealth Parliament possesses legislative competence to preclude or exclude from Australia and from Australian law the direct operation of the laws, executive actions and judicial decisions of any other country including the United Kingdom.[112]

Deane J was to develop these ideas in decisions which will be discussed as part of the analysis of Australian explanations for constitutional independence post-1986 which appears in Chapter 11.

---

[110] *China Ocean* (n. 88 above) 409.

[111] M. Coper, *Encounters with the Australian Constitution* (North Ryde: CCH Australia, 1987) 14.

[112] *China Ocean* (n. 88 above) 442 (emphasis added).

One would have thought that a 4–3 victory for Kirmani in the High Court might have ended the case. However, the State of Queensland had intervened in the case at the High Court and now sought to argue the invalidity of the 1979 Act before the Privy Council. Queensland's action was 'doomed to failure'.[113] The Commonwealth, acting under powers conferred on it by section 74 of the Constitution, had succeeded in terminating appeals to the Privy Council from the High Court in 1975.[114] Queensland could in theory apply to the High Court for a certificate to appeal to the Privy Council, which it did, but in *Kirmani (No 2)*[115] a unanimous High Court confirmed that this power was obsolete.

The expansive interpretation of the external affairs power in *Kirmani (No 1)* now opened the door to the possibility of Commonwealth legislation abolishing the only anachronism relating to the Privy Council still remaining: direct appeals from State Supreme Courts to the Privy Council. This potential was never tested, however, as the termination of Privy Council appeals became wrapped up in the broader aims of the Australia Acts 1986 (Cth and UK). More important, perhaps, for most Australians was the fact that the High Court had so unambiguously confirmed that the United Kingdom still had the power to legislate for Australia. The Australia Acts 1986 also attempted to deal with this issue head on.

Before we consider the Australia Acts 1986, it may be helpful to examine how discussion of fundamentals in the High Court affected discussion of such issues in Australian constitutional commentary prior to 1986.

Anticipating constitutional independence in the lead-up to 1986

In 1977, the future Attorney-General, Gareth Evans, wrote an essay in which he discussed the various mechanisms that constitutional reform would involve.[116] Whereas he preferred the initiative for constitutional amendment to come from the Australian people, he recognised that implementation required more formal procedures. Evans was not one for Imperial nostalgia, but his survey of four legal means by which the Constitution could be amended included two options involving the Westminster Parliament. The two Australian-based options were, first and foremost, the section 128 procedure (which had proved difficult to achieve) and secondly, and more tentatively, the 'joint venture' between

---

[113] Coper (1987) (n. 111 above) 14.

[114] The Commonwealth had done so in two stages: first, the Privy Council (Limitation of Appeals) Act 1968, which abolished appeals from the High Court in federal matters, including matters involving the interpretation of the Constitution. Appeals from the High Court to the Privy Council in matters of state law were left untouched. In 1975, the Commonwealth passed the Privy Council (Appeals from the High Court) Act which abolished even these appeals.

[115] *Kirmani v Captain Cook Cruises Pty Ltd (No 2)* (1985) 159 CLR 461.

[116] G. Evans, 'Changing the System' in S. Encel, D. Horne and E. Thompson (eds) *Changing the Rules: Towards a Democratic Constitution* (Ringwood: Penguin, 1977) 141.

Commonwealth and states that was set out in section 51(xxxviii) of the Constitution. Evans acknowledged, regarding the latter, that 'nobody has ever been quite sure what this means, and the provision has never been utilized'.[117] Regarding recourse to the United Kingdom Parliament, Evans noted that 'the Westminster Parliament can, technically speaking, at any time amend' the Australian Constitution.[118] Evans seemed to take the view that Australian request and consent was now a legal requirement, but he was not as clear on this point as one might have hoped:

> In a spirit of self-denial encouraged by some of the imperial offspring (though not by Australia, which was to remain, for many years yet, British to its bootstraps), Britain passed in 1931 the Statute of Westminster, which, if its terms are to be believed (and not all constitutional lawyers think that they should be), has the effect that the British Parliament cannot in fact legislate so as to affect the constitution or anything else in this country, unless such legislation is requested by and consented to by the parliament and government of the commonwealth of Australia.[119]

Given that the request and consent had to be given by the Commonwealth alone, in Evans' view, this was no great problem. He recognised that 'the real hurdle' was that 'it would be universally regarded as quite ludicrously incompatible with Australia's integrity, maturity and independence as a nation for us to be going cap in hand to Britain asking the mother country to do our constitutional house-keeping for us'.[120]

This brought him on to the second Westminster-based idea. The nationalistic objection to requesting British legislation would have far less force, in his view, if what was requested was 'not ... a new constitutional text, but rather ... the wherewithal to make a new constitutional text ourselves'. Evans had in mind the Indian model from 1947 whereby the United Kingdom Parliament would authorise the creation of a local constituent assembly, which would be charged with the task of preparing a new Australian Constitution. The new Constitution could then be ratified by the people of Australia. It would then be 'a "We the people ..." rather than a "Made in Britain" constitution'.[121] Evans acknowledged that it was possible for the Commonwealth to enact legislation creating this constituent assembly, but this would amount to a legal revolution: 'The overriding claim to authority of the present constitution, and its formal creator the British Parliament, would simply be ignored: therein would lie the revolution.'[122] Despite the 'splendid romantic appeal' of the Commonwealth-enacted constituent assembly, Evans preferred the idea of requesting that Westminster do the job. He viewed this as 'an attractive model for Australia to contemplate, even at this late stage in our history'.[123] It would involve 'no abrupt severance of legal continuity', and it would free Australia from 'the mother country's apron strings'.[124]

---

[117] Evans (1977) (n. 116 above) 158.   [118] ibid., 158.   [119] ibid., 159.
[120] ibid., 159.   [121] ibid., 160.   [122] ibid., 161.   [123] ibid., 160.
[124] ibid., 160.

In his *Australia's Constitution* in 1978,[125] Colin Howard also considered the possibility of constitutional amendment via the United Kingdom. As Deane J would do in the *Kirmani case*, Howard raised the question 'whether it is open to the United Kingdom parliament to abolish the commonwealth of Australia by repealing the Commonwealth of Australia Constitution Act'.[126] The answer for him was that 'such an action might well abolish the commonwealth for the purposes of United Kingdom internal law but would be highly unlikely to persuade the high court of Australia that the same effect followed in Australian law'.[127] Some might conclude from this that 'no assistance can be looked for from the United Kingdom parliament in overcoming some of the difficulties of amending the constitution',[128] but Howard did not believe this to be the case. If the section 128 amendment procedure ever proved to be such an obstacle to constitutional change that Australians were willing to look for 'any manoeuvre to change or circumvent it', the United Kingdom might be 'asked to amend the constitution by amending its own act'.[129] This then raised the possibility that, as argued earlier by Howard, the High Court would not recognise such legislation; however, he did not believe this would be the case. The reason for this was that while section 4 of the Statute of Westminster made clear that the United Kingdom had 'renounced its former capacity to enact such laws as it saw fit for the dominions', that same section also indicated that 'the United Kingdom parliament remains available to assist the parliaments of the former dominions, by suitable legislative action, if this becomes necessary to dispose of legal obstacles', provided the necessary requests and consent were present.[130] Like Evans, Howard was prepared to suggest that 'the request and consent procedure would be available also as one means of replacing the present constitution altogether'.[131] The real problems with any of these Westminster-based schemes would be 'political rather than legal'.[132]

The difficult theoretical issues surrounding the issue of Australia's constitutional independence were considered in detail in a 1978 article by R.D. Lumb entitled 'Fundamental Law and the Processes of Constitutional Change in Australia'.[133] Unlike most of the sources which we have discussed, this was an in-depth study of constitutional fundamentals, which included discussions of, amongst others, Hart, Kelsen, Marshall and Wheare. We will want to return to Lumb as part of the discussion regarding how Australia now explains its constitutional independence. For now, we will examine it as indicative of prevailing attitudes leading up to the Australia Acts 1986.

---

[125] C. Howard, *Australia's Constitution* (Ringwood: Penguin, 1978) ch. 5, 'Amendment and Change'.   [126] ibid., 153–4.
[127] ibid., 154.   [128] ibid., 154.   [129] ibid., 154.   [130] ibid., 155.
[131] ibid., 155.   [132] ibid., 155.
[133] R.D. Lumb, 'Fundamental Law and the Processes of Constitutional Change in Australia' (1978) 9 Fed LR 148.

Lumb began his analysis in familiar, orthodox terms:

There is no doubt . . . that the Constitution Act and the Constitution which it established owed its legal validity to an Act of the Imperial Parliament and that the United Kingdom had legal supremacy over the Commonwealth of Australia which was considered to be a self-governing colony. This supremacy or sovereignty was a continuation (although admittedly in modified form) of the sovereignty which had been exercised over the colonies of the Australian continent since 1788.[134]

This meant that even after 1901 'the Imperial Parliament could have amended the Constitution Act including the provisions of the Constitution . . . even though an "indigenous" amending process was contained in section 128'.[135] Lumb acknowledged that Imperial conventions militated against Parliament doing so unrequested; however, 'at a theoretical level . . . in terms of the ranking of the norms of constitutional amendment . . . the rule that the Imperial Parliament had ultimate legal authority over the Australian federal system . . . had, for a certain period after 1900, superior status over the rule embodied in section 128'.[136] At some point in 'the first fifty years of federalism', however, 'this hierarchical relationship was reversed: the method of amendment based on the exercise of Imperial legislative power disappeared from the Australian rules of recognition of constitutional change'.[137] This 'disappearance or elimination' was 'the direct result of the development of dominion status reflected in various acts and events having constitutional significance, for example, the Balfour Declaration and the Statute of Westminster', and it was complete, at the latest, 'by the time the Statute was adopted'.[138] Lumb deployed a detailed analysis of the Statute of Westminster in order to conclude that by adopting the Statute, Australia had 'disabled the United Kingdom Parliament from legislating for an amendment of the Commonwealth Constitution in disregard of the procedure laid down in section 128'.[139] 'The growth of an exclusively Australian grund-norm or rule of recognition of constitutional amendment' then raised the question whether Australian courts would in 1978 'recognise the enactment by the United Kingdom Parliament of constitutional amendment legislation at the request of the Commonwealth Parliament'.[140] Lumb predicted that an Australian court would not recognise such an enactment, the reason being that 'presuppositions of legal supremacy embodied in the British system' were 'not embodied in the Australian federal system which ex hypothesi has matured into a legally separate system of norms of which section 128 is the apex'.[141] In Lumb's view, 'the Constitution has continuing legal validity separate from its enactment by the United Kingdom Parliament'.[142] Accordingly, he disagreed with Wynes

---

[134] Lumb (1978), 154. Regarding the rival 'popular sovereignty' explanation, Lumb noted that the 'democratic basis of the draft bill [was] indirectly recognised', but he pointed out that 'autochthony was not a concept which had attained the same status then as in more recent times' (p. 153).   [135] ibid., 154.

[136] ibid., 154.   [137] ibid., 154.   [138] ibid., 154.   [139] ibid., 157.

[140] ibid., 157.   [141] ibid., 157.   [142] ibid., 158.

and others regarding whether the covering clauses could be amended only by the Westminster Parliament, taking the view that 'they are so intertwined with the Constitution as a whole . . . that they may be regarded as part of its fabric'.[143] Lumb also took the view that section 128 could be used in order to sever all remaining ties between the states and the United Kingdom.[144]

We have already seen how the *Kirmani* decision opened up the possibility of Commonwealth legislation to end the Imperial link. In the early 1980s another constitutional grounding for such Commonwealth legislation emerged. We have also already seen how Harrison Moore had noted the mischievous potential of section 51(xxxviii) of the Constitution. That section provided as follows:

51. (xxxviii) The exercise within the Commonwealth, at the request or with the concurrence of the Parliaments of all the States directly concerned, of any power which can at the establishment of the Constitution be exercised only by the Parliament of the United Kingdom or by the Federal Council of Australasia.

Taken literally, this section would authorise a law concerning the exercise of power repugnant to Imperial legislation in matters within Commonwealth and state spheres. As Leslie Zines, writing in 1981, pointed out, there were two potential arguments against this literal interpretation: (1) section 51(xxxviii) should have the same meaning today as it had in 1900;[145] and (2) the phrase 'within the Commonwealth'.[146] Zines took the view that both of these arguments could be overcome. This seemed to present a further method by which the Imperial connection could be terminated without the need for legislation at the Westminster end.[147] Furthermore, regarding Westminster legislation, Zines took the view that that route was still open: 'So far as the legislative supremacy of the United Kingdom Parliament is concerned, it can only be said that it appears to be still accepted as an established rule, subject only to the Statute of Westminster.'[148]

Achieving constitutional independence: the Australia Acts 1986

By the early 1980s, Australian constitutional affairs were full of possibility even if they lacked clarity. Although Murphy J and some academic commentators

---

[143] ibid., 160.   [144] ibid., 163.

[145] Most constitutional writers admit, as does Zines, that in 1900 the meaning of section 51(xxxviii) had to be consistent with the fact that the Constitution of the Commonwealth of Australia Act was subject to the Colonial Laws Validity Act, 1865. 'Once the Imperial restraints had been lifted, the power can take effect to its full extent.' L. Zines, *The High Court and the Constitution* (Sydney: Butterworths, 1981) 246.   [146] ibid., 246.

[147] Not surprisingly, some were less certain. Sir Arnold Bennett rejected the notion that the Commonwealth Constitution could be amended by section 51(xxxviii), pointing out that all s. 51 powers were 'subject to this Constitution', one provision of which was s. 128, which in turn specified that 'This Constitution shall not be altered accept in the following manner.' Sir Arnold Bennett, 'Can the Constitution be Amended Without a Referendum?' (1982) 56 Austr LJ 358.

[148] Zines (1981) (n. 145 above) 252.

doubted it, the accepted view seemed to be that the Westminster Parliament could still legislate for Australia if need be, provided that the requirements of request and consent were fulfilled (whether as a legal or a conventional matter). Canada had recently offered an example of how Westminster legislation could achieve constitutional independence, thereby perhaps lessening the embarrassment of such an apparently subservient process for Australians.

There were also new possibilities for an all-Australian solution. A growing academic literature took the view that the Commonwealth, at the request of the states, could achieve constitutional independence for Australia by exercising powers given to it under section 51(xxxviii). Finally, we have seen that by 1985 there was support (even though not clear authorisation) in the High Court for the Commonwealth acting on its own under its external affairs power.

In June 1982, just months after Canada's patriated constitution had been proclaimed, the Premiers Conference decided that action to sever Australia's residual links with the United Kingdom was in order. Eventually this process resulted in the enactment of two substantially identical versions of the Commonwealth and Westminster Parliaments. As Blackshield and Williams have noted regarding this process, 'whatever doubt there may have been about the capacity of any one of the participating Parliaments . . . the doubt was eradicated by legislation at every possible level'.[149] Each state requested both the Australian and United Kingdom versions of the Australia Act.[150] The Commonwealth in turn communicated its request and consent to Westminster, as expressed in the Australia (Request and Consent) Act 1985 (Cth). And, finally, both the Commonwealth and Westminster Parliaments acceded to these various requests by enacting the Australia Act 1986 (Cth) and the Australia Act (UK). The long title of each Act was 'An Act to bring constitutional arrangements affecting the Commonwealth and the States into conformity with the status of the Commonwealth of Australia as a sovereign, independent and federal nation'. The Australian version stated in its Preamble that it was enacted pursuant to section 51(xxxviii).

Many of the Acts' provisions related to the states, giving to them that which had been given to the Commonwealth by the statute of Westminster, 1931. Therefore the states were expressly permitted to make laws having extraterritorial application (section 2). The states were removed from the application of the Colonial Laws Validity Act, 1865 (Imp.) and were therefore permitted to enact legislation repugnant to Imperial legislation (section 3). Problems regarding advice to the Queen by states were resolved by enacting that all the powers and

---

[149] T. Blackshield and G. Williams, *Australian Constitutional Law and Theory*, (3rd edn, Annandale: Federation Press, 2002) 167.

[150] See, e.g. Australia Acts Request Act 1985 (NSW) and Australia Acts (Request) Act 1985 (WA). For a detailed account of state participation in the process leading up to the Australia Acts 1986, see A. Twomey, *The Constitution of New South Wales* (Annandale: Federation Press, 2004).

functions of the Queen were to be exercised only by the governor,[151] except those regarding appointment of the governor (section 7). Provision for disallowance and reservation of state legislation was abolished (sections 8 and 9). Section 11 terminated all remaining appeals to the Judicial Committee of the Privy Council,[152] and repealed all the relevant Imperial legislation at the same time.

For our purposes, the main provision was section 1, which stated that 'No Act of the Parliament of the United Kingdom passed after the commencement of this Act shall extend, or be deemed to extend, to the Commonwealth, to a State or to a Territory as part of the law of the Commonwealth, of the State or of the Territory'.[153] Section 12 emphasised the new constitutional state of affairs by repealing section 4 (together with subsections 9(2) and (3) and 10(2)) of the Statute of Westminster, in so far as these were part of the law of the Commonwealth. Section 15 stated that the Australia Act 1986 and the remaining parts of the Statute of Westminster still in force in Australia 'may be repealed by an Act of the Parliament of the Commonwealth passed at the request or with the concurrence of the Parliaments of all the States, and subject to subsection (3) below, only in that manner'. Thus, in effect, the states and Commonwealth which had brought about the Australia Act 1986 could repeal or amend it. This seemed simple enough. However, the 'subject to section (3)' was to cause difficulties of interpretation. Section 15(3) was as follows:

15(3)   Nothing in subsection (1) above limits or prevents the exercise by the Parliament of the Commonwealth of any powers that might be conferred upon that Parliament by any alteration of the Constitution of the Commonwealth made in accordance with section 128 of the Constitution of the Commonwealth after the commencement of this Act.

It was clear after 1986 that neither the Westminster Parliament nor the Judicial Committee of the Privy Council were to have an active role in Australian constitutional affairs after 1986, but it was not clear whether it was the Westminster or the Commonwealth legislation which had achieved this. Furthermore, it was not clear whether the constitutional master key now lay in section 128 of the Constitution or whether certain areas, such as the Australia Act 1986 itself, were beyond access. And if that were the case, then it appeared that both the Westminster and the Commonwealth Parliaments had succeeded in binding themselves, though not everyone was willing to accept this conclusion. Furthermore, if section 15 affected amendment of the Constitution, then

---

[151] An exception to the rule that the Queen's powers can be exercised only by the governor is where alternative arrangements are made when she is within the state.

[152] Subject to the obsolete provisions of s. 74 of the Constitution.

[153] The Explanatory Memorandum noted regarding s. 1 that it 'achieves complete legislative independence of Australia from the United Kingdom'. Australia, Parliament, House of Representatives, Australia Bill 1986, Australia (Request and Consent) Bill 1985: Explanatory Memorandum (circulated by authority of the Hon. Lionel Bowen, Deputy Prime Minister and Attorney-General).

was it not possible that it had exceeded the powers in section 51(xxxviii)? These and other questions will be discussed in Chapters 11 and 13.

In presenting the Australia Bill and Australia (Request and Consent) Bill to Parliament, the Attorney-General, Lionel Bowen, stated that 'the Bills . . . seek the removal of the outmoded residual constitutional links that still exist between Australia and the United Kingdom Parliament, Government and judicial system'.[154] The proposed legislation would 'terminate any powers that *might* remain in the United Kingdom parliament to make laws having effect as part of Australian law'.[155] Passage of 'this long overdue legislation' would complete 'the process of constitutional development commenced at the beginning of this century'.[156] It would 'eliminate those laws and procedures which are anachronistic and substitute new arrangements which reflect Australia's status as an independent and sovereign nation'.[157]

In the debates which followed, some of the speakers noted the 'rather theoretical nature' of the Bills, and that 'the ordinary Australian would be surprised if he or she were told that theoretically [the power of the United Kingdom to legislate for Australia] existed'.[158] Some wrestled with why it was that a sovereign, independent nation such as Australia should have to go through this sort of procedure,[159] but most were happy to mark its occurrence with a wide range of rhetorical flourishes: 'we are about to divest ourselves of our convict shackles'; 'Britain laid the egg that was to yield the nation, but laid it in someone else's nest'; and 'this is . . . truly a coming of age'.[160] Much as in New Zealand, some members struggled to square what was happening with their Dicey-influenced legal education:

> While I support the thrust of this legislation . . . I believe that these Bills are fundamentally defective. We are once again being treated to the dubious spectacle of the Hawke Government seeking to pass legislation which is binding on a subsequent parliament. The Attorney-General is asking the Parliament to pass legislation which, following enactment by the Parliament at Westminster, will purport to bind succeeding parliaments at Westminster. This flies in the face of the accepted doctrine of parliamentary sovereignty which exists both in English and Australian constitutional law.

> I remind the House that under the doctrine of parliamentary sovereignty as outlined by constitutional authors such as Dicey, Wade and others and as accepted by courts both in the United Kingdom and in Australia, no parliament can bind a subsequent parliament so that the latter must follow the legislative fiat of the previous parliament. The contrary proposition is a nonsense.

> . . .

> There is no power on earth which can stop a future parliament either in Canberra or Westminster from repealing the Acts incorporating the Bills before the House. While some academic authors challenge the doctrine of parliamentary sovereignty, the fact

---

[154] Australia, Parliament, House of Representatives, Debates, 13 November 1985, 2693.

[155] Debates, 13 November 1985, 2693 (emphasis added).

[156] Debates, 13 November 1985, 2695.   [157] ibid.

[158] Debates, 25 November 1985, 3584 (Spender).

[159] See, e.g. Debates, 25 November 1985, 3587 (Ruddock).

[160] Debates, 25 November 1985, 3590 (Fitzgibbon); 3585 (Snow); 3592 (Tickner).

remains that it is clearly upheld by the courts. For as long as the system of jurisprudence which underlies our system of constitutional law remains in place, the doctrine of parliamentary sovereignty will remain a functioning part of our constitutional law.

. . .

Unfortunately the structure of the relationship between Westminster and Australia can still be changed by any future Federal government. An extremist government, whether of the far Left or Right, could tamper with the Constitution by making advances to an ideologically similar government in the United Kingdom, and persuading it to act legislatively. Our Constitution and our system of government are not safe from this possibility, far-fetched though it may be. It behoves this Parliament to ensure that the Australian Constitution and the system of constitutional monarchy that it enshrines emanates from *the Australian people, who are in reality the source of all power in this nation.* In this way, neither our Constitution nor our democracy will ever be threatened because they will be firmly guarded *by the ultimate source of power in this nation, namely, the Australian people.*[161]

In summing up the debate, the Attorney-General was happy to confirm that 'the people rule this country' and that 'Nothing can happen to the Constitution of Australia unless the people of Australia agree that it should happen'; however, he was less sympathetic regarding the member's more theoretical concerns. The Attorney-General emphasised that Britain too had moved on and was now part of Europe, so there was no reason 'to return to the days of the eighteenth century'.[162] One presumes that he was referring to the debates regarding the changing nature of parliamentary sovereignty that have occurred since the enactment of the European Communities Act 1972 (UK), and, which would later be confirmed, the House of Lords decision in the *Factortame* case.[163]

The debate on the Bills in the Senate saw two former Attorneys-General express their views. Senator Durack indicated that he was quite convinced that section 51(xxxviii) was sufficient to accomplish the task at hand, and that therefore it was 'not strictly necessary to have United Kingdom legislation'. Nevertheless, he agreed that it was 'very sensible' to have Westminster legislation 'because there is still a strongly held view in Australia . . . that there is still a residual power in the United Kingdom Parliament to pass laws with respect to the Australian States'.[164] He noted that this view was 'confined to legal circles but it [was] a view strongly held'.[165] Senator Durack was confident that the United Kingdom had divested itself of the power to pass laws for the Commonwealth as a result of the Statute of Westminster, but again he admitted that the matter was not free from doubt:

I suppose that there are even some theorists who will argue that, despite the Statute of Westminster, a subsequent United Kingdom parliament could repeal that and could in

---

[161] Debates, 25 November 1985, 3591–2 (Nehl) (emphasis added).
[162] Debates, 25 November 1985, 3603.
[163] *Factortame v Secretary of State for Transport (No 2)* [1991] AC 603.
[164] Debates, 2 December 1985, 2688.   [165] ibid.

fact even pass a new constitution for Australia or amend our present one. I think the time has long since gone when there is any reality to that argument, but it is one that is held and it is correct to have a symbolic act of severance of the powers of the United Kingdom Parliament which will declare that it no longer will exercise any powers over Australia. That is why I have said that this is truly historic legislation because it will put beyond all doubt, in the fullest possible way, the severance of those old constitutional links between the United Kingdom and Australia.[166]

The second former Attorney-General to speak to the Bill was Senator Gareth Evans. He clarified that successive Commonwealth governments had taken the view that United Kingdom legislation was not required; however, the states had 'lingering doubts' regarding Commonwealth competence in this area, and they preferred to put the matter 'beyond doubt' in the manner then being proposed.[167] In any event, in Evans' view, simultaneous promulgation of the Commonwealth Australia Bill and the United Kingdom Australia Bill would mean that 'the question as to what would have been the situation at law—whether the Australia Bill would have been effective on its own before the promulgation of the United Kingdom one—will remain a matter of entirely academic interest because it will not be capable of ever being tested'.[168]

It is now time to consider some of the academic debate, in this case post-1986, in order to discover the various ways in which constitutional independence is explained, now that the connection to the Westminster Parliament has been irreversibly terminated and constitutional independence thereby assured.

[166] ibid.   [167] Debates, 2 December 1985, 2692.   [168] ibid.

PART III

CONSTITUTIONAL INDEPENDENCE

11

Legal Continuity or Disguised Revolution?

Explaining constitutional independence

We have already seen how each of the countries under study anticipated and then acquired (at least in the mechanical sense) their constitutional independence. We have also seen to a limited extent how it was that government officials described what had occurred. In this Part we shall survey the various attempts to *explain* constitutional independence. In this chapter the focus will be on the academic and judicial explanations in each of Australia, Canada and New Zealand. We shall see that certain obstacles or preoccupations recur.[1] For example, a common set of concerns is that, where the United Kingdom Parliament has apparently terminated its power to legislate for the country in question:

(1) it may not have had the legal power to do so, in part due to the enduring effects of traditional Imperial theory (but assuming that it does have such a power);

(2) there is an explanatory void regarding the ongoing validity and supremacy of the Constitution; and

(3) there is a theoretical possibility, based in traditional constitutional theory, though not necessarily in the realm of real or likely possibilities, that even if the termination of power is initially valid, the United Kingdom Parliament could renege on that termination and reassert its old authority.

We shall see other concerns which relate to these main themes.

Chapter 12 will abstract itself from this Part in order to consider some of the theoretical aspects of these concerns in greater detail. Emerging from that chapter will be a possible explanation for how the United Kingdom Parliament could, at least as a matter of Australian, Canadian and New Zealand law, irreversibly terminate its constitutional role for those countries, without undermining either the validity or the supremacy of their Constitutions. It is, in other words, an explanation of how and why legal continuity need not imply

---

[1] For a recent example of such concerns, see J. Tate, 'Giving Substance to Murphy's Law: The Question of Australian Sovereignty' (2001) 27 Monash U L Rev 22.

continuing legal subordination, or of how respect for legality, even where that legality involves the United Kingdom Parliament, does not have to import an ongoing legal hold by that Parliament.

Chapter 13 will then attempt to apply some of the theoretical tools from the preceding chapter to the particular facts and circumstances of Australian, Canadian and New Zealand constitutional development. This final chapter of Part III may appear prescriptive, in that it sets out legal explanations for constitutional independence for countries which appear to favour 'revolutionary' explanations, but it is not intended to be so. There is much to be said about the pros and cons of 'revolutionary' explanations for constitutional independence, for example, though these will not be explored at any length. However, if 'revolutionary' (or other more complicated) explanations are preferred because of a sense that non-revolutionary or legal explanations of constitutional independence are excluded by the supposed logic of constitutional doctrines such as parliamentary sovereignty, then Chapter 13 is designed to show that at least one logical legal explanation is available, if not entirely self-sufficient.

In Part II, as in Chapter 2, the alphabetical approach to the countries under study was abandoned in favour of an ordering which was better suited to the analysis of those countries' constitutional development. The ordering of Part II—Canada, New Zealand and Australia—will be followed once again in this Part. It is appropriate to begin with Canada because, having acted first to achieve its constitutional independence, in 1982, it was also the first to attempt to explain its constitutional independence. Also, in many ways the Canadian process is the most straightforward, in that it involved only one enactment: the Canada Act 1982 (UK). New Zealand achieved its constitutional independence by means of a mix of British and New Zealand statutes enacted over a span of almost forty years. Australia also combined British and local enactments, i.e. the Australia Acts 1986 (UK and Cth), and there is still much debate over which of these Acts accomplished the task. It will be appropriate to analyse New Zealand's constitutional independence after Canada and before Australia. Whereas New Zealand's termination of the Imperial link shares lessons with Canada, the Australian experience is, for a number of reasons, quite unique. It will be appropriate simply to continue the ordering from the previous Part, in which New Zealand was considered second and Australia third.

We now turn to considering how constitutional commentators and courts in Canada, New Zealand and Australia attempted to explain both the events of 1982 and 1986 and the basis of their Constitutions' independent validity and supremacy.

Canada: the resurgence of the Independence theory

It is hardly surprising to discover that most constitutional writing after 1982 in Canada has not dealt with the theoretical questions canvassed in Chapter 1, the

Introduction to this book. The Charter of Rights and Freedoms, also enacted in 1982, has had the most profound effect on Canadian law and society and has accordingly attracted by far the greatest amount of attention. A few commentators have turned their minds to more obscure but equally fundamental questions regarding patriation and constitutional independence.

Bryan Schwartz and John Whyte were among the first to place the *Patriation Reference* (and by inference patriation and constitutional independence) in a new and transcendent light:

The importance of legal debate during 1980–81 can be underscored by noting that the definition of the rules for constitutional amendment for a nation is a debate over the proper definition of the nation's sovereignty. The rules which govern reformation of the constitution are the most basic expression of the legal nature of the country. That Canada's rules were so unclear was historically anomalous in light of the country's self-perception of independence and adherence to the rule of law. The legal debate revealed that independence may have been illusory and that the roots of our legal existence were virtually untraceable. These difficulties were resolved in part with the proclamation of the Constitution Act, 1982 on April 17, 1982.[2]

Schwartz and Whyte set out four different theories which were advanced by the provinces as part of the legal argument in the *Patriation Reference*. The theories were described as 'the theory of Canadian independence, the compact theory of the Canadian federation, the theory of provincial sovereignty, and the federalism theory'.[3] Each one of these came within the general category of the Independence theory, as discussed in Chapters 5 and 6, as they all would have required of the Supreme Court of Canada that it look upon constitutional amendment as a Canadian process, governed by Canadian rules of validity.[4] As Schwartz and Whyte noted, whatever the object of the legal aspect of the provincial challenge, 'the question whether Canadian sovereignty was discounted by British legal sovereignty was relevant'.[5] And such considerations might also have been relevant to the more limited claim against the right of the federal Parliament to pass a resolution and to send a proposed amendment to the United Kingdom. If, on the one hand, the United Kingdom Parliament was truly in full legal command, then there might have been some plausibility to the federal claim that the Canadian courts should no more have questioned or reviewed a joint resolution of the House of Commons and Senate seeking 'patriation' any more than they should have questioned or reviewed 'a motion extending birthday greetings to the Queen'.[6]

---

[2] B. Schwartz and J.D. Whyte, 'The Patriation Reference and the Idea of Canada' (1982–3) 8 Queen's LJ 158, 163.   [3] ibid., 163.

[4] Schwartz and Whyte note that the provinces which opposed the unilateral federal action to 'patriate' the Constitution probably feared the possibility of enactment by the United Kingdom Parliament prior to a decision by the Supreme Court of Canada. The authors point out that the question of the ultimate *legal* validity of the proposed amendments was therefore highly relevant. Any argument which challenged the validity of an enactment of the United Kingdom Parliament would have to rely to some extent on the premises of an Independence theory.

[5] Schwartz and Whyte (1982–3) (n. 2 above) 164.   [6] ibid., 164.

If, on the other hand, the validity of Canadian constitutional amendments passed by Westminster was in part dependent on an expression of consent from the proper Canadian authorities, then it would have been entirely justified for the Canadian courts to have questioned and reviewed the federal resolution.

The theory of Canadian independence, as described by Schwartz and Whyte, had provided the dissenting provinces with a means of overcoming the federal lawyers' arguments regarding the unlimited legal sovereignty of the Westminster Parliament. The provinces were able to acknowledge that no text, including the Statute of Westminster, 1931, had altered the legal authority of the United Kingdom Parliament with respect to amendment of the Canadian Constitution. The Provinces were also able to argue, however, that in reality Canada had been fully independent since well before 1981, and that at the highest level of constitutional analysis 'the reality is the law'.[7] The argument was made most persuasively by the Attorney-General of Manitoba who had relied on the arguments founded on H.W.R. Wade's 1955 article.[8] Schwartz and Whyte elaborated on the argument in a way which pointed to an important difference between the Imperial and Independence theories, Wade's insight belonging most particularly to the latter from their perspective:

Counsel for Manitoba cited an article by H.W.R. Wade which contended that there is no strictly legal way for a British colony to become fully independent. If one starts with the [Imperial theory] assumption that British Parliaments are supreme, with the one exception that they cannot bind their successors, it logically follows that no declaration by Great Britain declaring the independence of a former colony can ever legally prevent a subsequent Parliament from reasserting legislative control. Former colonies become legally independent in the eyes of their own courts because those courts [following an Independence theory] accept the fact that there has been a change in the fundamental legal order.[9]

According to the latter approach, it was possible to acknowledge the continuing resort to the Westminster Parliament for the purpose of amending the Canadian Constitution (consistent with section 7(1) of the Statute of Westminster, 1931), but, given the fact or reality of Canadian political independence, to look at the ongoing role of that Parliament up until 1982 as a strictly formal part of a *Canadian* process: 'just formal machinery to be used *by Canadians* to amend *their own Constitution*'.[10]

In the end, however, it had been up to the Supreme Court of Canada, as 'the ultimate arbiter of legal legitimacy',[11] to determine the nature of the United Kingdom Parliament's role in the Canadian amendment process. Schwartz and

---

[7] Schwartz and Whyte (1982–3) (n. 2 above) 165.

[8] H.W.R. Wade, 'The Basis of Legal Sovereignty' [1955] Camb LJ 172. This article was discussed in some detail in Ch. 4 above.   [9] Schwartz and Whyte (1982–3) (n. 2 above) 165.

[10] ibid., 166 (emphasis added). 'Just formal', of course, has more than one meaning, one of which—i.e. 'legal'—was adopted by the majority (law and convention). Here, 'formal' is intended to mean 'automatic'.   [11] ibid., 169.

Whyte noted that this had not been an easy task where no clear answer could have been said to present itself: 'But it must be conceded, neither history nor the texts dictate a single answer. Ultimately, a judicial opinion in the matter of whether Britain retained its plenary legal sovereignty had to turn on the political philosophy of the judges deciding the whole complex of issues at stake.'[12]

A majority of the Supreme Court of Canada in the *Patriation Reference* had been very reluctant to go beyond the legal texts, perhaps because the judges felt that even the highest Court in the land required a clear signal, by the appropriate legislative means, of a desire by Canadians to change the rules regarding constitutional amendment. It was easy to understand such a political or judicial philosophy; however, as Schwartz and Whyte indicated, it was harder to deal with its apparent implications:

> ... ultimately the court did not accept the validity of the legal claim of Canada's independence ... Although we hesitate to name it, the idea of Canada that this judgment comes perilously close to is Canada as colony. In light of this bleak characterization of our fundamental legal position we should be grateful that this same judgment induced the frenzy of political activity which led ultimately to the *Constitution Act, 1982* and to legal sovereignty.[13]

As perceptive as their analysis is, Schwartz and Whyte, like others, did not explain in what sense or how legal sovereignty was acquired in 1982.

The same critical and slightly exasperated attitude toward the Supreme Court of Canada judgment in the *Patriation Reference* was evident in a 1982 article by Eric Colvin, entitled 'Constitutional Jurisprudence in the Supreme Court of Canada'. Colvin criticised the Court for its 'failure ... to recognize the jurisprudential character of the issues at stake and to utilize the insights of contemporary legal theory in their resolution'.[14] For our purposes, the most significant missed 'insight' was 'that rules of constitutional law may have their source in constitutional practice',[15] by which he certainly meant a Canadian constitutional practice. Hence, this view also fell squarely within the Independence theory.

After chronicling Canada's acquisition of *de facto* or political independence, Colvin observed that the majority view in the Supreme Court of Canada was inconsistent with such independence. He then went on to criticise the dissonance which the Court's narrow, legalistic view created when put together with the most basic Canadian and British understandings of political reality:

> ... the approach taken by the majority necessitated the conclusion that Canadian law empowered the U.K. Parliament, of its own volition, to destroy Canadian federalism and even to destroy Canadian independence.

---

[12] ibid., 169.   [13] ibid., 187.
[14] E. Colvin, 'Constitutional Jurisprudence in the Supreme Court of Canada' (1982) 4 Sup Ct L Rev 3.   [15] ibid., 7.

We are entitled to be suspicious of a line of reasoning which produced conclusions at odds with the common understanding, on both sides of the Atlantic, of political realities. The proper characterization of the foundations of a legal system has long been a controversial issue in constitutional theory and jurisprudence. Nevertheless, it is now widely accepted that these foundations must be sought in patterns of social practice giving rise to rules of law which exist only in the sense that they are observed in fact. Demonstrations of this proposition typically proceed along a 'chain of validity', through which the existence of a legal rule is assessed by reference to the authority for its making which is conferred by a higher legal rule, which in turn also exists because there is authority for its making. To say that a legal rule is 'valid' means that the legal system authorizes its existence. Yet no chain of validity is infinite. Eventually a point is reached where there is no higher rule and analysis must turn from questions of validity to questions of observance.[16]

Colvin's analysis pointed to an aspect of the legal problem in the *Patriation Reference* which the Court did not explicitly address: that is, what was the ultimate rule of the Canadian legal system? Colvin noted that the Court seemed to be asserting that 'the problem could be resolved without reference to constitutional practice',[17] and this approach was in his view untenable. As we have seen in examining the Imperial theory, however, it appears that the majority (law) saw the amendment process, at least in its legal aspect, as Westminster-based and governed by the British rules of parliamentary supremacy. It would not have been appropriate, according to this view, for a Canadian court to inquire into the ultimate rule of the British legal system as determined, so the analysis went, by British constitutional practice. Colvin acknowledged this consideration, in part, in stating that 'At best the majority could only be interpreted as subscribing to the view that the colonial rule of recognition had not changed with the development of *de facto* Canadian independence.'[18] Colvin added that in its strongest version this view of things left the United Kingdom Parliament free to enact *any* legislation whatsoever for Canada, even by disregarding the request and consent recitals provided for in section 4 of the Statute of Westminster, 1931. And, of course, even the weaker version of this view, according to which only *constitutional amendments* enacted by Westminster without Canadian request and consent would be valid, left the pre-1982 Canadian legal system vulnerable to radical and unwanted change.[19]

Colvin then turned to the problem of how the seemingly immutable British rule of recognition could disappear and be replaced by a new Canadian rule. He observed that Canadians who believed in the 'patriation' process and in the reality of *constitutional* independence necessarily assumed that such a transition was possible, even by non-revolutionary means:

... the assumption that new criteria can be peacefully agreed to seems to have underlain the process of patriation which eventually culminated in the renunciation of British legislative power in section 2 of the Canada Act. Were this assumption not made, section 2

---

[16] ibid., 8–9.   [17] Colvin (1982) (n. 14 above) 9.   [18] ibid., 9–10.
[19] ibid., 10n.

could be repealed as part of Canadian law by the body which enacted it. The federal Parliament could by-pass the amending formula which is set out in the Constitution Act, 1982, and once again seek constitutional change through action by the U.K. Parliament. Moreover, the U.K. Parliament itself could still, of its own volition, intervene to destroy Canadian independence.[20]

Colvin was right, it seems, to observe that Canadians assumed that the link with the United Kingdom had been broken. Looked at in this way, the transition was no more complicated than a mere substitution of turtles (basic norms), to use Professor F.R. Scott's analogy.[21]

The process was in fact more complicated than the turtle-*Grundnorm* analogy indicated, and Colvin appeared to recognise this. He noted that such transitions placed the courts in a difficult position, and that this was especially so where the transition was said to have taken place over an extended period of time: 'More difficult issues are raised by the idea of evolutionary change in the rules of recognition, which was in essence what the dissenting provinces had asserted. Judges should be cautious in deciding that developments in political practice have outdated traditional legal formulations.'[22] Colvin went on to observe, however, that over the course of English constitutional history, such an evolution had taken place in response to various changes in the political context.[23]

In the end, Colvin concluded that the Supreme Court of Canada would have been fully justified in recognising an ultimate rule of the Canadian legal system based in Canadian social, political (and even theoretical) reality:

The Court would not have been departing from the traditions of the common law if it had insisted that the rules of recognition of the Canadian legal system, although hitherto unarticulated in some key respects, must be consistent with the existence of Canada as an independent federal state. It would have been no more dramatic an entry into the political arena than was countenanced by English constitutional history. And if the Court had proceeded in this way, it would have laid the foundation for understanding the significance of the subsequent Canada Act as a declaration of proper constitutional practice and it would also have provided guidance for the handling of such crises of government as may face future generations of judges.[24]

Colvin was quick to point out that this approach would not necessarily have produced a different result in the *Patriation Reference*. Clearly, however, it would have opened up a whole range of questions for legitimate consideration, including whether or not a constitutional amendment enacted by the United Kingdom Parliament without the request and consent of the proper Canadian authorities (however defined) could have been considered valid by a Canadian court applying the ultimate rule of an independent Canadian legal system.

---

[20] ibid., 10.
[21] See F.R. Scott, 'The Redistribution of Imperial Sovereignty' in *Transactions of the Royal Society of Canada*, June 1950, reprinted in F.R. Scott, *Essays on the Constitution* (Toronto: University of Toronto Press, 1977) 244 and discussion in Ch. 6 above.
[22] Colvin (1982) (n. 14 above) 10.   [23] ibid., 10–12.   [24] ibid., 12–13.

In an article entitled 'The Independence of Canada', Brian Slattery grappled with the difficult theoretical issues regarding patriation and constitutional independence in a particularly thorough and systematic way.[25] In answer to the question 'What . . . is the legal basis of the new Constitution?', Slattery stated that:

Superficially, it would appear that the Canadian Constitution derives it force in Canada from the power of the British Parliament. But if this is the case, how can it be said that Canada possesses a fully patriated Constitution, in the sense of one possessing a local root? Further, if the Constitution rests on the power of Westminster over Canada, can it be maintained convincingly that this power is at an end?[26]

These are the very concerns that have been identified at numerous points in this book.

Slattery's approach was far too thorough and subtle to be summarised adequately in just a few paragraphs. Essentially, his argument was that Canada's legal (and constitutional) independence was based neither on 1931 nor on 1982 nor on any other decisive legal event, but was 'at root a matter of fact'.[27] The acquisition of political independence sometime between 1919 and 1931 had the legal effect of ending the colonial rule of subordination and replacing it with one of equality. This meant in effect that a disguised legal revolution based on extra-legal factors took place, its true dimensions visible only over time. After the moment of independence, it was only necessary for the inevitable process of erosion to run its course and so eliminate the remaining fragments of Imperial authority. It was therefore political independence and not section 2 of the Statute of Westminster which ended the relationship of subordination between the Canadian and United Kingdom Parliaments,[28] and political independence rather than section 2 of the Canada Act 1982 which ended the latter Parliament's ability to legislate for Canada.[29] Furthermore, throughout the period leading up to 1982 the United Kingdom Parliament, on Slattery's view, could only legislate for Canada at the latter's request, and that as a matter of law, not merely convention.

Slattery's work was significant in that it identified the importance of Canadian attitudes regarding the fundamental rules of the legal system, but it was perhaps vulnerable to the criticism that it did not square with the legal account given by the Supreme Court of Canada. Far from recognising a relationship of equality between the United Kingdom Parliament and Canada, the Supreme Court of Canada in the *Patriation Reference* was at pains to emphasise one of subordination, as we have seen.[30] It may be, however, that some of Slattery's arguments could be redeployed to support an interpretation of the events of 1982 which

---

[25] Brian Slattery, 'The Independence of Canada' (1983) 5 Sup Ct L Rev 369.
[26] ibid., 403.   [27] ibid., 391.   [28] ibid., 394.   [29] ibid., 403.
[30] Slattery (1983) (n. 25 above) 397n acknowledges that the *Patriation Reference* contains disturbing evidence of the Court's hierarchical view of the legal relationship with the United Kingdom Parliament, but he prefers to extract a narrower ratio from the case.

was consistent with Canada's independence and fully sovereign status. Such an argument will be explored in Chapter 13.

Peter Hogg, author of the most influential constitutional law text in Canada, and a colleague of Slattery's at Osgoode Hall Law School, adopted a similar approach in an article entitled 'Patriation of the Canadian Constitution: Has It Been Achieved?'.[31] He discussed Wheare's concept of autochthony[32] and concluded that it was 'neither very clear nor very useful'.[33] In preference he borrowed and slightly modified Geoffrey Marshall's test for patriation: 'the question we should be asking is whether a legally effective termination of British legislative authority has occurred'.[34] Hogg took the view that although section 2 of the Canada Act 1982 appeared to be an obvious candidate for having accomplished this termination of authority, it could not have done so on its own. He agreed that the Supreme Court of Canada would not allow an Act of the United Kingdom Parliament passed after 1982 to extend to Canada as part of its law,[35] and that 'freedom, once conferred cannot be revoked',[36] but he asserted that it could plausibly be argued that 'it is not s. 2 but the fact of Canadian independence which has terminated the authority to enact laws for Canada'.[37] He essentially adopted Slattery's view that once Canada had acquired all the tools of its legal autonomy, then any future legislation by the United Kingdom Parliament would be treated as a nullity, in the same way that unwanted legislation from another country would be so treated.[38]

Both Slattery's and Hogg's analyses assumed that it was independence and not section 2 of the Canada Act 1982 which was the key to patriation and to constitutional independence. As Hogg stated, in accordance here again with Slattery: 'If this view is correct, then the United Kingdom Parliament had lost much of its authority over Canada before 1982: what it retained was only what was necessary to fill the gaps in Canadian domestic legislative power.'[39] In the footnote to this text, Hogg too acknowledged that it was difficult to reconcile this view with parts of the *Patriation Reference* which suggested, in Hogg's paraphrase, 'that there had been no diminution of the legal authority over Canada of the United Kingdom Parliament since colonial times'.[40]

Two Quebec constitutional writers, Jacques-Yvan Morin and José Woehrling, both of the University of Montreal, also agreed that the Supreme Court of Canada took a broad view of the Westminster Parliament powers. In fact, they

---

[31] P.W. Hogg, 'Patriation of the Canadian Constitution: Has It Been Achieved?' (1982–3) Queen's LJ 123. This article formed the basis of P.W. Hogg, *Constitutional Law of Canada* (4th edn (looseleaf) Toronto: Thomson Carswell, 1997) ch. 3, 'Independence'.

[32] K.C. Wheare, *The Constitutional Structure of the Commonwealth* (Oxford: Clarendon Press, 1960) 89. Hogg (1982–3) (n. 31 above) 125.   [33] Hogg (1982–3) (n. 31 above) 125n.

[34] ibid., 126.   [35] ibid., 127.

[36] ibid., 127 quoting *Ndlwana v Hofmeyr* [1937] AD 229, 237.   [37] ibid., 127–8.

[38] ibid., 128.   [39] ibid., 128.

[40] ibid., 128n. Hogg added: 'It is because of these dicta that this part of my text is expressed tentatively.'

observed that if we had only the *Patriation Reference* to go on, we would assume that the Supreme Court of Canada would respond in the same manner as a British court if presented with post-1982 Westminster legislation for Canada; i.e. it would accept its validity. In the end these authors concluded that the *Patriation Reference* was an essentially political decision and that in the equally political circumstances of the hypothesis noted above, the Court would find a way to reject the United Kingdom legislation, relying principally on the political fact of independence.[41]

The Supreme Court of Canada in the *Patriation Reference* was reluctant to acknowledge that the gradual attainment of political independence had at the same time changed the rules regarding amendment because such an admission could amount to an acknowledgement that conventions can 'crystallise' into law. If the Court had been forced to admit that the conventions of Dominion request and consent which protected independence had crystallised into a rule that the United Kingdom Parliament could only legislate for Canada according to the wishes of the Canadian government or Parliament, then it would have had greater difficulty in rejecting, as it was disposed to do, the argument that the conventions of *provincial* consent which protected the federal principle had also crystallised into law. If we assume, then, that the United Kingdom Parliament's powers *vis-à-vis* Canada were as unlimited and undiminished as the Supreme Court of Canada indicated in 1981, was there still not any way in which the Court could after 1982 explain, to adopt Hogg's test, that 'the legally effective termination of British authority ha[d] occurred'?[42] In Chapter 13, we shall explore the possibility that such an explanation existed, and that section 2 of the Canada Act 1982 and other sections of the 1982 legislation should be seen not as redundant but as fully effective.

It is worth noting that while many of the Canadian writers just surveyed were willing to rely on extra-legal factors in order to explain Canadian constitutional independence, they were disinclined to describe the process as revolutionary. As we shall see, constitutional commentators in New Zealand showed no such compunction.

New Zealand: a disguised revolution?

In a penetrating and informative essay written before the enactment of the Constitution Act 1986 (NZ), F.M. (Jock) Brookfield associated himself with those such as C.C. Aikman[43] who had expressed a preference for newer

---

[41] J.-Y. Morin and J. Woehrling, *Les Constitutions du Canada et du Quebec du Régime Français à nos Jours* (Montreal: Les Éditions Thémis, 1992) 464.

[42] Hogg (1982–3) (n. 31 above) 126.

[43] C.C. Aikman, 'Parliament' in J.L. Robson (ed.) *New Zealand: The Development of its Laws and its Constitution* (2nd edn, Stevens: London, 1967) 40.

approaches to sovereignty.[44] He wrote, for example, of 'the plenary constituent power' conferred on the New Zealand Parliament by the combined effect of section 1 of the New Zealand Constitution (Amendment) Act 1947 (UK)[45] and section 53 of the New Zealand Constitution Act 1852 (Imp.).[46] One would have thought, then, that Brookfield would have no difficulty with the logic which lay behind the Constitution Act 1986.

However, in 1992 he set out his criticisms of that Act in a section of an article entitled '1986: The year of the quiet revolution?'.[47] According to Brookfield, the possibility of a revolutionary break was attributable to two key provisions of the Constitution Act 1986: first, section 21(1) which declared, *inter alia*, that the (Amendment) Act 1947 (UK) 'shall cease to have effect as part of the law of New Zealand', despite the fact that, according to Brookfield, 'no power was conferred on the New Zealand legislature, either by the Act of 1947 or any other Act of the United Kingdom Parliament, to repeal the Act of 1947 itself';[48] and secondly, section 15(2) which administered the last rites to the United Kingdom Parliament's powers to legislate for New Zealand. He discounted the idea, noted in Chapter 8, that section 53 as amended by the New Zealand Constitution Amendment Act 1973 (NZ) embraced a plenary constituent power[49] of the type that Brookfield himself had identified in his 1984 article in describing the post-1947 powers of the New Zealand Parliament.[50] Brookfield therefore concluded that the two 1986 provisions taken together amount to 'an "ultimate proclamation of autochthony" . . . of the sort achieved by a revolutionary break'.[51] On this account, the validity of the New Zealand Constitution is not derived from an uninterrupted chain of legal processes but is instead 'self-existent', proclaimed in the declaratory terms of section 15(2).[52]

---

[44] F.M. Brookfield, 'Parliamentary Supremacy and Constitutional Entrenchment: A Jurisprudential Approach' (1984) 5 Otago LR 603.

[45] Hereinafter (Amendment) Act 1947 (UK).   [46] Brookfield (1984) (n. 44 above) 618.

[47] F.M. Brookfield, 'Kelsen, the Constitution and the Treaty' (1992) NZULR 163, 169: 'it is at least possible that the New Zealand Parliament made a revolutionary break [in New Zealand's constitutional links with the United Kingdom] in 1986'. He quoted with general approval Philip Joseph's statement that the 1986 Act 'though itself a product of New Zealand's legislative auto-nomy gifted by the Westminster Parliament, repudiates the source of that autonomy and denies the gift was ever made' (p. 169), quoting P.A. Joseph, 'Foundations of the Constitution' (1989) 4 Canta LR 58, 74.

[48] Brookfield (1992) (n. 47 above) 171. Section 2(2) of the Statute of Westminster, 1931 can be said to have provided this power. See K.C. Wheare, *The Statute of Westminster and Dominion Status* (5th edn, Oxford: Oxford University Press, 1953) 161 and Wheare (1960) (n. 32 above) 33.

[49] Brookfield (1992) (n. 48 above) 171n. See P.A. Joseph, *Constitutional and Administrative Law in New Zealand* (2nd edn, Wellington: Brookers, 2001) 134–7.

[50] Brookfield (1984) (n. 46 above).

[51] Brookfield (1992) (n. 47 above) 171 quoting Joseph (1989) (see n. 47 above) 74.

[52] On Brookfield's version this amounts to a change in what Hans Kelsen referred to as the *Grundnorm*, about which more will be said in Ch. 12 below.

Philip Joseph has touched on similar themes in a stimulating and thoughtful analysis of the foundations of the New Zealand Constitution.[53] His approach is a balanced one, as befits the writer of a general textbook. Essentially three approaches can be identified to the problem of New Zealand constitutional foundations, according to Joseph. First, it may be that the New Zealand Constitution is sustained by 'legal continuity: the Constitution "is" because it derives, with unbroken lineage, from an historically prior and superior authority',[54] i.e. the United Kingdom Parliament. This approach is unattractive in Joseph's view for various reasons. One of its 'unsettling implications'[55] is that 'insist[ing] New Zealand must remain legally *derived from (and historically subordinate to)* the United Kingdom manifestly contradicts public perception',[56] and Joseph, like Brookfield,[57] felt that: 'Lawyers must accommodate their concepts to the facts of political life.'[58] Furthermore, it was even possible that the appearance of legal continuity was deceptive, and this led Joseph to a second approach.

The second approach was simply to acknowledge that there had been a disguised revolution, a 'technical breach in continuity',[59] which may have occurred in either 1986[60] or 1973[61] but which passed unnoticed. On this view, the New Zealand Constitution could only be self-seeded, and the powers of the New Zealand Parliament self-proclaimed.[62]

The third approach built on the first but concluded in the same manner as the second. Legal continuity was acknowledged but the historical connection to a superior and sovereign United Kingdom Parliament was not allowed to obscure an evolution in the attitudes of New Zealand 'judges and officials (and ultimately the people)'[63] towards acceptance of the sovereignty of the Parliament in Wellington.[64] Once the new attitude took hold, the old *Grundnorm* could be said to have been replaced by the new;[65] the old ultimate rule of recognition

---

[53] Joseph's article 'Foundations of the Constitution' (1989) (n. 47 above) predates the second of the Brookfield articles just discussed. References in this essay are to the later, slightly altered version, which appeared in P.A. Joseph, *Constitutional and Administrative Law in New Zealand* (Sydney: Law Book Co., 1993), ch. 13. Chapter 13 is the same in its essentials as Joseph (2001) (n. 49 above).   [54] Joseph (1993) (n. 53 above) 307.

[55] ibid., 397.

[56] ibid., 397 (emphasis added). The Diceyan views expressed by Scott (see K.J. Scott and J.L. Robson, 'Parliament' in J.L. Robson (ed.) *New Zealand: The Development of its Law and Constitution* (London: Stevens, 1954) and, especially, K.J. Scott, *The New Zealand Constitution* (Oxford: Oxford University Press, 1962) (discussed in Ch. 8 above), are an example of this implication.   [57] See, e.g., Brookfield (1984) (n. 46 above) 626.

[58] Joseph (1993) (n. 53 above) 398.   [59] ibid., 121.

[60] See Brookfield (1992) (n. 47 above).

[61] On the basis that the former s. 53 was the sole source of legislative power for the New Zealand Parliament and that logically such a limited power could not be used to create 'full powers'. The contrary argument is discussed in Ch. 13 below and in Joseph (1993) (n. 53 above) 121, 408.

[62] By s. 53 of the Constitution Act 1852 as amended in 1973, if that is the moment when continuity was broken, or by s. 15(2) if the breach occurred in 1986.

[63] Joseph (1993) (n. 53 above) 398.   [64] ibid., 121, 398.

[65] ibid., 398, using Kelsenian terminology.

transformed into a version more attuned to New Zealand needs.[66] On Joseph's account, the process was evolutionary but the effect revolutionary.[67] Joseph's guarded conclusion was that the appropriate approach would not be known until the courts had reason to pronounce on the matter.[68]

This analysis proceeds from the assumption that New Zealanders, like Canadians and Australians, assume that their Constitution is derived from a history of constitutional continuity and that, nonetheless, constitutional independence has been achieved. It may also be fair to assume that a New Zealand court, conscious of its judicial role, would be reluctant to uncover breaches of continuity where other interpretations were available; and that such a court would be eager, at the same time, to attribute any change in the ultimate rules of the legal system to legal rather than extra-legal factors If that is so, then Brookfield's analysis and Joseph's second and third approaches would be less attractive to such a court. However, acceptance of the first approach would seem to justify a return to the United Kingdom Parliament, and that too would be unattractive. Was there not any way that New Zealand could have its constitutional cake and eat it too, i.e. account for both continuity and change in New Zealand's constitutional fundamentals?

Joseph seemed to ask a similar question in tantalising form in his conclusion regarding the effects of the 1986 Act. 'The Constitution Act 1986', he said, 'invites [an] analog[y]. [T]he axeman who, perched on the bough of a tree, severs the limb at the trunk. Does the axeman fall to the ground with the branch? Or can he defy gravity and remain suspended, though he has lost his means of support?'[69] These and other fundamental questions will be considered in Chapters 12 and 13.

A third important New Zealand constitutional writer and theorist is Paul McHugh, author of the highly influential *The Maori Magna Carta: New Zealand Law and the Treaty of Waitangi*.[70] McHugh's work was packed full of evidence regarding the over-bearing influence of those traditional conceptions of sovereignty associated with Dicey, and McHugh was very aware of the sorts of alternative conceptions presented by contemporary (as opposed to modern) constitutionalism.[71] McHugh admitted that his early work stood quite deliberately within the orthodox Diceyan compound.[72] However, for many years now

---

[66] ibid., 121 and 398, using Hartian terminology. [67] ibid., 122.

[68] ibid., 459. Joseph noted that in *Re Ashman and Best* [1985] 2 NZLR 224(n) Wilson J expressed the view that the 1973 amendment to s. 53 established New Zealand as 'an independent sovereign state', but that it was hard to draw any firm conclusion from these and other broad statements in that judgment.

[69] Joseph (1993) (n. 53 above) 114. Brookfield appeared not to be tempted by this analogy. Brookfield (1992) (n. 47 above) 171.

[70] P.G. McHugh, *The Maori Magna Carta: New Zealand Law and the Treaty of Waitangi* (Auckland: Oxford University Press, 1991).

[71] See P.G. McHugh, 'Constitutional Voices' (1996) 26 VUWLR 499, in which he discusses a leading proponent of contemporary constitutionalism, J. Tully, *Strange Multiplicities: Constitutionalism in an Age of Diversity* (Cambridge: Cambridge University Press, 1995).

[72] McHugh (1996) (n. 71 above) 503n.

McHugh's work took for granted, and in many cases moved beyond, the 'new' or 'revised' view of sovereignty discussed in Chapter 4. In *The Maori Magna Carta*, McHugh took for granted many of the points and arguments that have been made in this book, and which will be further developed in the remaining chapters in this Part. For instance, McHugh accepted that section 15 of the New Zealand Constitution Act 1986 successfully terminated the power of the United Kingdom Parliament to legislate for New Zealand. The 1986 Act 'highlighted the indigenous character of the New Zealand constitution and located full sovereign authority within this country'.[73] McHugh also accepted the 'supposition . . . that once New Zealand adopted the Statute of Westminster in 1947 its legislative organs obtained supreme sovereign power'.[74] However, despite accepting these constitutional developments within his own theoretical framework, McHugh was acutely aware that, along with a transfer of sovereignty from Westminster to Wellington in 1947, there had been a completion of the 'transplantations of [orthodox] English concepts of Parliamentary sovereignty'.[75] In particular these orthodox English concepts made it difficult for New Zealand lawyers and politicians to accept the idea that the Wellington Parliament's powers might be limited by the need to respect the Treaty of Waitangi.[76]

As has been done in this book, McHugh labelled the two opposing views of Parliamentary sovereignty 'the "continuing" view' and 'the self-embracing view'.[77] He noted that the New Zealand government had apparently endorsed the 'self-embracing' view[78] and that 'most lawyers in Australasia, Canada and other former British colonies' accepted it as well. Only 'English lawyers' and other 'determined diehards' in the Commonwealth 'stick doggedly to the "continuing" view'.[79] If McHugh was right, then it would be much easier to make the arguments regarding New Zealand's constitutional independence that are explored in Chapter 13. And McHugh must be right about the possibility of limited sovereignty and self-limitation by the Wellington Parliament if he is to make out his sophisticated arguments regarding New Zealand constitutional law and the status of the Treaty of Waitangi.[80]

---

[73] McHugh (1991) (n. 70 above) 63.   [74] ibid., 59.   [75] ibid., 59.

[76] ibid., 59.   [77] ibid., 55.

[78] See New Zealand, A Bill of Rights for New Zealand (White Paper presented to the House of Representatives by leave of the Hon. Geoffrey Palmer, Minister of Justice) (1985) 68.

[79] McHugh (1991) (n. 70 above) 55.

[80] In McHugh (1996) (n. 71 above) 503, McHugh characterised the division in approaches to sovereignty as one between 'modernist' and 'contemporary' constitutionalism, the latter as exemplified by the work of Tully (1995) (n. 71 above). McHugh described the 'modernist' view (which we have labelled 'orthodox', 'traditional' and 'absolutist') as follows:

The modernist . . . views fragmented constitutional form as historically retrogressive and fundamentally at odds with the unified and centralised character of sovereignty. Criticism of the 'rangatiratanga as a constitutional momentum' argument or *grundnorm motile* (as it has been disparagingly termed) reveals modernism's abhorrence of a haemorrhaging of political authority. Defenders of the modernist constitution cannot contemplate a form of sovereignty or means of organising ultimate political authority which is not concentrated and unitary in character. Modernists adopt the position that any change in the location of sovereignty can only be revolutionary and

It is ironic, considering that McHugh was such a critic of the orthodox tradition of parliamentary sovereignty and orthodox constitutional attitudes in general,[81] that within the field of aboriginal rights in New Zealand, McHugh was considered to be an exponent of the 'orthodox legal paradigm'.[82] This paradigm was characterised as 'orthodox' because, on its own account of itself, it rejected ' "politically correct" but "technically wrong" '[83] approaches to aboriginal rights. Whereas the proponents[84] of the orthodox legal paradigm attempted to make progress through the identification of technically valid legal arguments, critics of this paradigm from within the Marxist tradition, for example, were more inclined to question whether *any* legal paradigm can deliver justice.[85]

We have seen how, notably in New Zealand, acceptance of the Constitution by the people was an important concept, and one which was sometimes thought to have legal consequences. In Australia, popular acceptance is part of a full-blown theory of popular sovereignty. In the following section, we shall see how popular sovereignty competes with the sovereignty of the Westminster Parliament as a source of and explanation for constitutional validity and supremacy.

Australia: Imperial sovereignty and popular sovereignty—academic writing

As we saw in Chapter 10, Australia sought to acquire its constitutional independence by means of two virtually identical pieces of legislation: the Australia

---

(either) successive or secessive. It cannot be fissionary. In other words, modernists insist political authority once concentrated cannot be (re-)dispersed into the polity so much as replaced or partitioned by a deliberative act of those comprising or opposing the association.

[81] See, e.g., P.G. McHugh, 'The Historiography of New Zealand's Constitutional History' in P.A. Joseph (ed.) *Essays on the Constitution* (Wellington: Bookers, 1995) 344.

[82] See P. Havemann, 'The "Pakeha Constitutional Revolution?" Five Perspectives on Maori Rights and Pakeha Duties' (1993) 1 Waikato Law Review 53, 71 et seq. More generally, see P. Havemann (ed.) *Indigenous Peoples' Rights in Australia, Canada, and New Zealand* (Auckland: Oxford University Press, 1999) and A. Sharp, *Justice and the Maori: The Philosophy and Practice of Maori Claims in New Zealand since the 1970s* (2nd edn, Auckland: Oxford University Press, 1997).

[83] Havemann (1993) (n. 82 above) 71.

[84] Havemann (1993) 71 states that the Orthodox Legal Paradigm 'overlaps in methodology with the post-assimilationist paradigm and shares analysts and activists such as Professor Jock Brookfield, Gordon Orr, Judge E. Durie, Sir Geoffrey Palmer, Alex Frame, Sir Kenneth Keith, Sir Robin Cooke and Dr David Williams'. In Havemann's terms, those whom many lawyers would consider truly orthodox on constitutional issues, and far more conservative than McHugh on the question of indigenous rights, are labelled 'the Prendergast Paradigm' in memory of the judge in the *Wi Parata* case, which was discussed briefly in Ch. 2 above.

[85] See, e.g., the work of Jane Kelsey, including *A Question of Honour? Labour and the Treaty 1984–1989* (Wellington: Allen & Unwin, 1990), 'From Flagpoles to Pine Trees: Tino Rangatiratanga and Treaty Policy Today' in P. Spoonley, D. Pearson and C. McPherson (eds) *Nga Patai: Racism and Ethnic Relations in Aotearoa/New Zealand* (Palmerston North: Dunmore Press, 1996) and 'The Treaty of Waitangi and Maori Independence—Future Directions' (1990) 9th Commonwealth Conference Papers 249–256. Unlike Kelsey, Paul McHugh does not visualise

Act 1986 (UK) and the Australia Act 1986 (Cth). The validity of the Australia Act 1986 (UK) was based in the United Kingdom Parliament's long-standing power to legislate as it saw fit for Australia (and elsewhere). By convention, and according to the Statute of Westminster, United Kingdom legislation for Australia had to be preceded by Australian request and consent, and this had been provided, as we have already seen in Chapter 10. While there were few doubts as to the United Kingdom Parliament's power to legislate for Australia up to 1986,[86] explaining the acquisition of Australia's constitutional independence in that year presented a number of difficulties, some of which have been judged more serious than others. First, basing constitutional independence on an Act of the United Kingdom Parliament seemed to some to contradict the very idea of independence. Symbolically, this is hard to deny; however, as we shall see in Chapters 12 and 13, it is quite possible to interpret the United Kingdom Parliament as having validly enacted to the Australia Act 1986 (UK), and then entirely removed itself from the Australian legal system, consistently with real constitutional independence for Australia. To the extent that a United Kingdom version of the Australia Act 1986 was necessary, and that is increasingly in doubt, the colonial symbolism associated with such an Act was simply a by-product of the more familiar and, relatively speaking, neutral idea of respect for the rule of law. Secondly, basing constitutional independence on United Kingdom legislation presented Australian constitutional commentators with the enduring, and still powerful, arguments based in orthodox Imperial constitutional theory: whatever the United Kingdom Parliament could do it could also undo, thereby rendering supposed constitutional independence precarious.

The validity of the Australia Act 1986 (Cth) was based principally in section 51(xxxviii) of the Constitution, at least according to the Preamble to the 1986 Act,[87] though it is also claimed that its validity was based in the external affairs power (section 51(xxix)). There are two types of difficulties with the Australian version of the Australia Act 1986. First, if the Commonwealth

---

the abandonment of the technical constitutional doctrine of Parliament's sovereignty. See P.G. McHugh, 'Aboriginal Identity and Relations' in K.S. Coates and P. McHugh (eds) *Living Relationships: Kokiri Ngatahi: The Treaty of Waitangi in the New Millennium* (Wellington: Victoria University Press, 1998) 107, 178. For an account of the debate from what Havemann would call a 'post-assimilationist' perspective, see F.M. (Jock) Brookfield's *Waitangi and Indigenous Rights: Revolution, Law and Legitimation* (Auckland: Auckland University Press, 1999) ch. 7.

[86] We have already seen in Ch. 10 above that a small number of constitutional commentators in Australia, notably Murphy J and R.D. Lumb, took the view that, even before 1986, the United Kingdom Parliament could not alter the Australian Constitution, whether or not the Commonwealth Parliament provided its request and consent under s. 4 of the Statute of Westminster. (See also M. Byers, 'Conventions Associated With the Commonwealth Constitution' (1982) 56 Austr LJ 316, 318.)

[87] Australia Act 1986 (Cth), Preamble:

AND WHEREAS in pursuance of paragraph 51 (xxxviii) of the Constitution the Parliaments of all the States have requested the Parliament of the Commonwealth to enact an Act in the terms of this Act: . . .

(in conjunction with the states) was able to terminate United Kingdom powers over Australia in 1986, then presumably it was necessary to explain at what point it acquired that power. Was it in 1900, in 1931, in 1942 or simply at some unspecified moment before 1986? If United Kingdom Parliament action was decisive in granting that power to Australian institutions, then the same problems discussed in the previous paragraph regarding the orthodox Imperial theory of parliamentary sovereignty were relevant. Secondly, even assuming that, by whatever means, the Commonwealth had acquired the power to terminate the Westminster Parliament's ability to legislate for Australia, there have been considerable doubts over the years about the two Commonwealth constitutional powers in question (sections 51(xxix) and (xxxviii)) and what can and cannot be done under them. However, their meaning has been clarified considerably over the past twenty-five years or so, with expansive meanings favourable to the Commonwealth preferred. Notwithstanding the expansive interpretation of these powers, it may be that the Commonwealth exceeded them in enacting the Australia Act 1986, not only in its attempt to terminate the powers of the United Kingdom Parliament, but also in its attempt to provide for future amendment of the Australia Act 1986 and Statute of Westminster, 1931 in section 15 of the 1986 Act. To the extent that these attempts were beyond the powers of the Commonwealth, it would mean that only the United Kingdom Parliament could have had the power to enact the Australia Act 1986 as a whole. At present, as seen in the 1999 case *Sue v Hill*,[88] the High Court apparently assumes that the Australia Act 1986 (Cth) was sufficient to achieve constitutional independence.

Whether the United Kingdom or the Commonwealth version of the Australia Act 1986 was essential or sufficient, there must have been some moment, at or prior to 1986, when the power of the United Kingdom Parliament to legislate for Australia was subordinated to Australian constitutional mechanisms, notably section 128. Clearly, in 1986, if not before (according to the minority view),[89] the United Kingdom Parliament's powers to enact laws extending to Australia were terminated. Many commentators therefore ask what it is that is underpinning the Australian Constitution now that the United Kingdom Parliament, which originally enacted it, has been removed from the present-day Australian constitutional picture. We will see that by far the favourite candidate for successor to parliamentary sovereignty is the concept of popular sovereignty. However, understandings of popular sovereignty appear to be as various and diverse as understandings of parliamentary sovereignty. We shall canvass some of the former understanding in this chapter, and discuss the issue in greater detail in Chapter 13.

Popular sovereignty, at a minimum, means that the sovereignty of the Australian Constitution is now based in section 128 and the referendums which form part of the procedure for amendment of the Commonwealth Constitution.

---

[88] *Sue v Hill* (1999) 199 CLR 462.   [89] See n. 86 above for references.

At the other extreme of constitutional possibility, popular sovereignty may, as it does in the United States, refer to the sense in which the people of Australia are the true *pouvoir constituant*, or constituent assembly. As presently constituted, section 128 governs fundamental changes to the Australian constitutional system; however, if Australians chose to revisit those fundamentals, the ultimate constituent body would no longer be the United Kingdom Parliament but possibly the people of Australia meeting in Conventions much as they did in the 1890s. We know as a matter of historical fact that the Conventions and related referendums were not deemed sufficient in 1900 to confer legality on the Australian Constitution. However, we also know, better than ever it must be said, how genuine a popular process, relatively speaking, occurred in Australia just over a hundred years ago.[90] It may be possible to argue, even as a legal matter, that popular sovereignty, in the constituent sense, has always run alongside Westminster parliamentary sovereignty as an explanation for the validity and supremacy of the Australian constitution. In 1900 there was no desire to ride the popular sovereignty horse because it conveyed too much of a desire to be independent of the Empire; however, once Australians were convinced of their desire to be independent, it was possible to jump onto the popular sovereignty horse which was still running alongside, and even to leave the parliamentary sovereignty mount behind.

The Australian debate about constitutional foundations is by far the most complicated and developed of the three countries under study. With this introduction to the issue in mind, it may now be possible to wade into the Australian sovereignty debate. The main contributors to this debate are Geoffrey Lindell, George Winterton and Leslie Zines, although important insights have also been provided by James Thomson,[91] R.D. Lumb,[92] John Goldring,[93] Brian Galligan,[94] Paul Finn,[95] Michael Detmold,[96] Greg Craven,[97] Michael Coper[98]

---

[90] See H. Irving, *To Constitute a Nation: A Cultural History of Australia's Constitution* (Cambridge: Cambridge University Press, 1999).

[91] J.A. Thomson, 'The Australia Acts 1986: A State Constitutional Law Perspective' (1990) 20 WA L Rev 409.

[92] R.D. Lumb, 'The Bicentenary of Australian Constitutionalism: The Evolution of Rules of Constitutional Change' (1988) 15 UQLJ 3 and R.D. Lumb, 'Representative Democracy, Federalism and Constitutional Revision' in M.A. Stephenson and Clive Turner (eds) *Australia, Republic or Monarchy?: Legal and Constitutional Issues* (St Lucia: University of Queensland Press, 1994) 165.

[93] J. Goldring, 'The Australia Act 1986 and the Formal Independence of Australia' [1986] Public Law 192.

[94] B. Galligan, *A Federal Republic: Australia's Constitutional System of Government* (Cambridge: Cambridge University Press, 1995).

[95] P. Finn, 'A Sovereign People, A Public Trust' in P. Finn (ed.) *Essays on Law and Government*, Vol. 1 (Sydney: Law Book Company, 1995).

[96] M. Detmold, *The Australian Constitution* (Sydney: The Law Book Company, 1985).

[97] G. Craven, *Secession: The Ultimate State Right* (Melbourne: Melbourne University Press, 1986) and 'Australian Constitutional Battlegrounds of the Twenty-First Century' (1999) 20 UQLJ 250.

[98] M. Coper, *Encounters with the Australian Constitution* (North Ryde: CCH Australia, 1987) and M. Coper and G. Williams, (eds) *Power, Parliament and the People* (Annandale: Federation Press, 1997).

and others,[99] without forgetting the significant (if only for its importance if not always for its detailed elaboration) contribution of the High Court of Australia.

Geoffrey Lindell was one of the first Australian constitutional commentators to analyse the significance of the Australia Acts 1986, in an article entitled 'Why is Australia's Constitution Binding?—The Reasons in 1900 and Now, And the Effect of Independence'.[100] Lindell began with the assumption that even a legal answer to the question contained in his title should conform as much as possible with historical, political and social reality. He therefore further assumed that the answer would differ for 1900 as opposed to 1986. In 1900, 'the Constitution was legally binding because of the status accorded to British statutes as an original source of law in Australia and also because of the supremacy accorded to such statutes'.[101] He acknowledged that 'this explanation does not treat as legally relevant the agreement of the Australian people to federate however important such a factor may have been in explaining the political reason for the adoption of the Constitution'.[102]

In terms of post-1900 changes, Lindell identified, first, the development of Australian independence in the eyes of the international community, achieved some time after 1939 and certainly before 1986. Secondly, he identified the restrictions on the Westminster Parliament, including the Commonwealth's ability under section 2 of the Statute of Westminster to alter or repeal British statutes. However, he noted that the Statute did not terminate the power of the Westminster Parliament to legislate following Australian request and consent (real or stated). Thirdly, he identified the ability of both the Commonwealth and state Parliaments, perfected in 1986, to alter or repeal British statutes of any kind by normal legislative action (other than the Commonwealth Constitution, the Australia Act 1986 and the Statute of Westminster 1931 which required the special procedures set out in section 128 of the Constitution and section 15 of the Australia Acts 1986). The 1986 Act also, of course, put to an end the possibility of the United Kingdom Parliament legislating for Australia.[103]

In discussing the 'Answer in 1986' Lindell employed a term that has been used throughout this book: he confirmed that 1986 resulted in 'the attainment of

---

[99] See, e.g., Australia, *First Report of the Constitutional Commission*, Vol. 1 (Canberra: Australian Government Publishing Service, 1988) 72–84; J. Daley, 'The Bases for the Authority of the Australian Constitution' (Doctoral Thesis, Oxford, 1999); A. Dillon, 'A Turtle By Any Other Name: The Legal Basis of the Australian Constitution' (2001) 29 Fed LR 241; M. Moshinsky, 'Re-enacting the Constitution in an Australian Act' (1989) 18 Fed LR 134; John W. Tate, 'Giving Substance to Murphy's Law: The Question of Australian Sovereignty' (2001) 27 Monash U L Rev 21; A. Twomey, 'Sue v. Hill—The Evolution of Australian Independence' in A. Stone and G. Williams (eds) *The High Court at the Crossroads* (Annandale: Federation Press, 2000) 77; H.G.A. Wright, 'Sovereignty of the People—The New Constitutional Grundnorm?' (1998) 26 Fed LR 165.
[100] G. Lindell, 'Why is Australia's Constitution Binding?—the reasons in 1900 and Now and the Effect of Independence' (1986) 16 Fed LR 29.   [101] ibid., 32.
[102] ibid., 33   [103] ibid., 33–6.

complete *constitutional independence*.[104] He began his post-1986 analysis by emphasising that the attainment of constitutional independence need not have affected the nature of the explanation for the legally binding and fundamental character of the Australian Constitution. The Commonwealth and the states were still unable to legislate inconsistently with the Constitution 'whatever changes may have occurred in relation to the ability of those Parliaments to enact legislation which is inconsistent with other British Acts of Parliament'.[105] In Lindell's eyes, this explanation, emphasising as it did 'the essential continuity in the chain of legislative authority' was 'constitutionally and legally sound'.[106] However, he admitted that, due to its 'reliance on Australia's colonial past', there may have been some interest in searching for 'an additional, although not necessarily alternative way of explaining the legally binding and fundamental character of the Constitution'.[107] He found that additional way in the idea of the sovereignty of the Australian people:

In short the explanation can be found in the words of the preamble to the Constitution Act... namely, the agreement of the people to federate, supported by the role given to them in approving proposals for constitutional alteration under s 128 of the Constitution, as well as their acquiescence in the continued operation of the Constitution as fundamental law. According to this approach the Constitution now enjoys its character as a higher law because of the will and authority of the people. Such an explanation more closely conforms to the present social and political reality and has the advantage of ensuring that the legal explanation for the binding character of the Constitution coincides with popular understanding.[108]

What then might have been the problems with such an explanation? Lindell noted, first, that the fact that this interpretation was different from the one which would have been given in 1900 was not a terminal obstacle, because the High Court subscribed to a liberal and progressive interpretation of the Constitution. A more worrying potential obstacle to his mind was the question as to who was the ultimate beneficiary of the legal power previously exercised by the United Kingdom Parliament. The argument that the Australian people were the true successors by virtue of their powers in section 128 was vulnerable 'if it can be found that the power to alter the constitution also resides elsewhere, or that there are important matters... which lie beyond the scope of section 128'.[109] Lindell discussed possible limitations on section 128 and concluded that the High Court was unlikely to recognise such limitations if at all possible. He was more concerned by the possibility that section 15 of the Australia Act 1986 represented an alternative location for the power to amend the Constitution, and one not linked in to popular sovereignty; though again he assumed that the High Court would strain against such an interpretation.[110]

---

[104] Lindell (1986) (n. 100 above) 37 (emphasis added).   [105] ibid., 37.
[106] ibid., 37.   [107] ibid., 38.   [108] ibid., 38.   [109] ibid., 39.   [110] ibid., 39.

In a later article, responding to arguments made by S. Gageler and M. Leeming,[111] Lindell and Dennis Rose argued that section 15(3) did more than just qualify the power in section 15(1)—it made clear that the Statute of Westminster, 1931 and the Australia Act 1986 could be altered not only by section 15(1) but also by the procedure specified in section 15(3), i.e. section 128. They argued that section 15(3) was probably added as an after-thought to make clear that major national changes would not be held up by one state (under section 15(1)) but could still be done by section 128. This inter-pretation was 'more consistent with the high importance accorded to the role of the people under s. 128'.[112] The problem, specifically relating to section 15(1) and (3) of the Australia Act 1986, will be discussed later in considering the writing of Leslie Zines.

In 2003, Lindell returned to some of these issues in an article entitled 'Further Reflections on the Date of the Acquisition of Australia's Independence'.[113] Here Lindell followed George Winterton in choosing 1931 as the moment when Australia achieved its constitutional independence. He distinguished the *capacity* to end colonial links with the United Kingdom from the *exercise* of that capacity, dating acquisition of the former at 1931 and the latter at 1986. He deemed acquisition of *capacity* to be critical in so far as independence was concerned. And whereas Winterton argued, as we shall see, that capacity came from the Statute of Westminster, making Australia's adoption of that Statute or Commonwealth-state joint legislation under section 51(xxxviii) possible, Lindell saw section 2(2) of the Statute of Westminster and section 51(xxix) of the Constitution as critical. Significantly, he emphasised that freely *choosing* the legislature (executive and courts) of another country to exercise authority in Australia was not inconsistent with constitutional independence.[114] We have seen the same argument made with respect to Canada. The essential point was not the continued existence or operation of these extra-Australian forms of governmental authority, but rather the ability or capacity of Australian institu-tions to put an end to them.

George Winterton's early writing[115] on Australian constitutional independ-ence after 1986 established a theme that would persist in his writing on the subject through to the present. In two 1986 publications he emphatically rejected theories, such as those propounded by Murphy J, R.D. Lumb and

---

[111] S. Gageler and M. Leeming, 'An Australian Republic: Is a Referendum Enough' (1996) 7 Public Law Review 143.

[112] G. Lindell and D. Rose, 'A Response to Gageler and Leeming: "An Australian Republic: Is a Referendum Enough" ' (1996) 7 Public L Rev 155, 160.

[113] In G. Lindell, C. Saunders and R. French (eds) *Reflections on the Australian Constitution* (Annandale: Federation Press, 2003) 51–60.   [114] ibid., 54–5.

[115] Winterton's early writing on United Kingdom constitutional issues demonstrated that he was very familiar with the distinction between continuing and self-embracing sovereignty that has been emphasised throughout this book. See G. Winterton, 'The British Grundnorm: Parliamentary Supremacy Re-examined' (1976) 92 LQR 591.

Sir Maurice Byers QC, which tried to explain the termination of Westminster legislative powers *vis-à-vis* Australia prior to 1986 by employing extra-constitutional notions such as political independence.[116] Extra-constitutional notions were for Winterton 'a slippery slope' leading away (and down) from the rule of law.[117] Such notions needed to be approached, therefore, with 'extreme caution'.[118] The end of the Westminster Parliament's powers had to be based on a legal event for Winterton. The enactment of a new Constitution in 1900 including a new amending formula was one such possibility, though Winterton doubted whether section 128 constituted either an abdication of power or a strong manner and form redefinition of the legislature authorised to amend the Australian Constitution.[119] The Statute of Westminster and/or the Australia Acts 1986 represented far more likely legal pegs for constitutional independence. We shall return to Winterton's consideration of the appropriate date for constitutional independence once we have looked at his reaction to the debate regarding constitutional foundations and popular sovereignty.

Having rejected reliance on extra-constitutional notions for the termination of United Kingdom Parliament power *vis-à-vis* Australia, Winterton was also inclined to reject such extra-constitutional notions where new constitutional foundations were concerned. He was more than happy to acknowledge that 'Australia's constitutional system is clearly already founded *politically* upon popular sovereignty';[120] however, he was not inclined to convert this political foundation into a legal foundation. Writing in 1998, he chided constitutional commentators for too quickly claiming a 'glorious revolution' or 'fundamental paradigm shift' in Australia's movement from parliamentary to popular sovereignty.[121]

Winterton perceived that 'sovereignty'—a 'notoriously ambiguous concept' at the best of times[122]—was being used by commentators and courts in at least two different senses. The first referred to 'the source from which the Constitution derives its authority' and the second to 'the location of the power to amend the Constitution'.[123] In terms of the derivation of authority, Australia could claim two sources, one 'political' (the Australian people) and the other 'initially both legal and political, but in time only legal' (the Westminster Parliament).[124] Given that section 1 of the Australia Acts 1986 was prospective, it left the past legal authority of the Westminster Parliament untouched: 'This abdication of power for the future had no effect on the legal force of existing British legislation

---

[116] G. Winterton, 'Extra-Constitutional Notions in Australian Constitutional Law' (1986) 16 Fed LR 223 and G. Winterton, *Monarchy to Republic* (Melbourne: Oxford University Press, 1986) 127–8.   [117] Winterton, *Monarchy to Republic* (1986) 128.

[118] ibid., 128.   [119] ibid., 128.

[120] G. Winterton, 'The Constitutional Implications of a Republic' in M.A. Stephenson and Clive Turner (eds) *Australia, Republic or Monarchy?: Legal and Constitutional Issues* (St Lucia: University of Queensland Press, 1994) 15–16 (emphasis added).

[121] G. Winterton, 'Popular Sovereignty and Constitutional Continuity' (1998) 26 Fed LR 1.

[122] ibid., 4.   [123] ibid., 4   [124] ibid., 5.

applying to Australia by paramount force . . . Hence, at least as a matter of logic, it [was] difficult to see how the Australia Act could have affected the legal authority which the Constitution derived from enactment at Westminster.'[125] To those who were inclined to abandon distinctions between the legal and political sources of constitutional authority, Winterton argued, as he had for many years, that 'one ought to be wary of breaking the chain of legal authority or legitimacy, however obsolete it might seem to be'.[126] For Winterton, there was 'no national indignity in acknowledging legal continuity'.[127] Continuity did not necessarily imply subordination: 'The continuing legal authority of our Constitution derives its original authority from its original enactment at Westminster and subsequent retention (with amendments) by those empowered to amend it, which includes the Australian electors. But the latter derived their legal authority from the former.'[128]

Whatever authority grounded sovereignty in the first sense, it was clear that Australia possessed popular sovereignty in the second sense, i.e. the ability to amend the Constitution. Up until 1986, the Westminster Parliament represented 'an alternative route for amending the Commonwealth Constitution', though one that was 'largely theoretical, and was never used, at least not to effect a direct amendment'.[129] Winterton therefore found it difficult to understand how the termination of this theoretical power in 1986 had proved such a 'catalyst for recognition of Australia's popular sovereignty, which has surely existed since 1901', at least in the second sense.[130] 'In short, there has been no constitutional "revolution" or "paradigm shift" but rather remarkable continuity.'[131]

Writing in 2003, Winterton attempted to fix a date for Australian constitutional independence, and in doing so he developed his thinking further on some of these issues.[132] He identified 1931 and enactment of the Statute of Westminster as the relevant moment given that, from that point on, all the necessary levers for removal of all vestiges of colonialism lay within Australian hands, either through Commonwealth legislation, as in the Statute of Westminster Adoption Act 1942, or by joint legislation by Commonwealth and state legislatures, as in the Australia Act 1986 (Cth), enacted pursuant to section 51(xxxviii) of the Constitution.

Leslie Zines has considered issues of Australian independence at least since the appearance of the first edition of his highly influential and authoritative *The High Court and the Constitution*.[133] However, for our purposes, the most detailed elaboration of Zines' views on the subject emerged in two 1997 publications: an

---

[125] ibid., 6.   [126] ibid., 7.   [127] ibid., 7.   [128] ibid., 7.   [129] ibid., 8.
[130] ibid., 8.   [131] ibid., 12.
[132] G. Winterton, 'The Acquisition of Independence' in G.J. Lindell, C. Saunders and R.S. French (eds) *Reflections on the Australian Constitution* (Sydney: Federation Press, 2003) 31.
[133] L. Zines, *The High Court and the Constitution* (Sydney: Butterworths, 1981). See also L. Zines, 'The Growth of Australian Nationhood and its Effects on the Powers of the Commonwealth' in L. Zines (ed.) *Commentaries on the Australian Constitution* (Sydney: Butterworths, 1977) 1.

article entitled 'The Sovereignty of the People'[134] and the fourth edition of his *The High Court and the Constitution*.[135]

In 'The Sovereignty of the People', Zines readily acknowledged that the democratic origins of the Australian Constitution were very real, and that section 128 represented an important democratic element as well. However, he stressed that in 1900 enactment of the Constitution by the Imperial Parliament was considered legally essential. The 'traditional view', therefore, was that 'from a *political* point of view the Commonwealth came about as a result of the will of the people, however defined', but 'this political will could only be translated *into law* by the will of the legal sovereign of the British Empire, the Imperial Parliament'.[136] Zines observed that this bifurcated approach to sovereignty bore a resemblance to Dicey's distinction between political and legal sovereignty.[137]

Moving into the contemporary era, Zines observed that 'the concept of the British Parliament as the ultimate legal sovereign' sat uncomfortably alongside Australia's 'emergence . . . as a sovereign state of the world', and that not surprisingly new approaches which challenged the traditional view had emerged, notably from the High Court.[138] Whatever the uncertainties and differences regarding sovereignty prior to 1986, Zines was clear that the Australia Acts 1986 (Cth and UK) 'put an end to the principle that the Constitution was legally sustained by what Brennan J. has called "a stream of power flowing from a higher Imperial source"'.[139] And this in turn has prompted Australian constitutional commentators to propose new constitutional foundations, or new sources for the constitutional stream, the most popular of these being the Australian people.[140] Zines stressed, however, that 'from the point of view of legal theory there was no necessity to provide any norm higher than the Constitution and the other accompanying instruments, such as the Australia Act':[141]

It would be sufficient to conclude that the Constitution *was* law because it was enacted by the British Parliament. It is *now* law because it is accepted by the Australian people as their framework of government. In other words it is our fundamental law and needs no further legal justification. This explanation, however, does not satisfy those who feel the need for a 'sovereign'.

For the sake of argument, then, Zines proceeded to ask probing questions about 'the people' as a potential new sovereign. He summarised what he took to be the popular sovereignty argument as follows, always bearing in mind his recognition

---

[134] L. Zines, 'The Sovereignty of the People' in M. Coper and G. Williams (eds) *Power, Parliament and the People* (Annandale: Federation Press, 1997) 91.

[135] L. Zines, *The High Court and the Constitution* (4th edn, Sydney: Butterworths, 1997).

[136] Zines, 'The Sovereignty of the People' (1997), 92 (emphasis added).

[137] ibid., 92.   [138] ibid., 92.   [139] ibid., 93.

[140] Zines, ibid., 93, cites Lindell (1986) (see n. 100 above) and Finn (1995) (see n. 95 above) by way of example. A. Dillon, 'A Turtle by Any Other Name: The Legal Basis of the Australian Constitution' (2001) 29 Fed LR 241 has proposed the federal compact as the best substitute for the United Kingdom Parliament.

[141] Zines, 'The Sovereignty of the People' (1997) (n. 134 above) 93.

of the political relevance of the Australian people in the creation of the Constitution:

The argument seems to be that, by doing away with the authority of [the Westminster] Parliament, we are left with the people as the font and origin of our legal system. The grundnorm has shifted. The will of the people, having been a political precondition of the legal enactment of the Constitution, has become its fundamental legal basis, the ground of its validity (and not merely, as before, the source of its 'legitimacy' in the political sense).[142]

Zines, it is worth remembering, saw no need for a new 'ground of its validity'.

Pursuing the argument as made by others, however, Zines noted that 'the sovereignty attributed to the people' must have 'quite a different effect and probably a different meaning, from that previously possessed at Westminster'.[143] He identified four principal differences. First, 'the British Parliament is a clearly defined, legal institution which acts in accordance with reasonably clear rules', whereas 'the people is not such a body or institution'.[144] Secondly, a closely related point, 'unlike the Imperial Parliament, the people cannot as a matter of law or practical reality direct the institutions that it created and which act on its behalf to carry out its will'.[145] Thirdly, popular sovereignty now seemed to require that Commonwealth and state legislatures must 'listen to, and be accountable to, their political, and now constitutional masters'.[146] And yet, none of these legislatures owed such a duty to the Imperial Parliament. Fourthly and finally, if 'the constitutional sovereignty of the people co-existed with the legal sovereignty of the Imperial Parliament' from as early as 1901, as some (including the High Court) have suggested, then 'somehow or other, popular sovereignty as a legal concept was compatible with colonial status and a grundnorm of obedience to Imperial enactments'.[147] Zines' conclusion was that: 'Having regard only to literal meaning it is clear that there is a considerable fictional element in both concepts included in the new doctrine: "sovereign" and "people".'[148] It was important to determine whether sovereignty of the people was 'purely symbolic or a theoretical standard of sorts', because if it was the latter, then it may have a direct effect on interpretation of the Constitution.[149] In Zines' view, most of the results which the High Court of the 1990s was intent on achieving could have been accomplished by using the concept of representative government rather than a full-blown theory of popular sovereignty.[150] The risk of incorporating a broad political standard such as sovereignty of the people into constitutional law was that it represented 'a transfer of power, on a fairly large scale, to an arm of government that is not directly responsible to anyone'.[151]

Before leaving Zines' work, it may be important to consider his characteristically subtle arguments regarding whether the Commonwealth version of the Australia Act 1986 was sufficient to achieve constitutional independence; or,

---

[142] ibid., 95.   [143] ibid., 95.   [144] ibid., 95.   [145] ibid., 95.   [146] ibid., 96.
[147] ibid., 97.   [148] ibid., 98.   [149] ibid., 98.   [150] ibid., 99.   [151] ibid., 107.

put another way, whether the United Kingdom version was enacted out of abundance of caution, or whether it was legally essential. Zines dealt with this point in detail in the fourth edition of *The High Court and the Constitution*.

First, we need to know that Zines, like Lindell and Winterton, agreed that Australia obtained its independence prior to 1986, although Zines preferred not to designate any particular date. He took 1939 to be a key date, given that Australia's adoption of the Statute of Westminster took effect from that moment. Section 2 of the 1931 Statute gave the Commonwealth Parliament the power to override future Imperial legislation, and the external affairs power probably authorised the Commonwealth to prevent the application within Australia of laws of the United Kingdom Parliament, executive or courts. In terms of the analogy familiar to Australian constitutional lawyers, the stream had risen above its source as of 1939.[152] The United Kingdom Parliament could still legislate for Australia after 1939, as it would do in 1986, but it was no longer hierarchically superior. The *Grundnorm* or rule of recognition had seemingly shifted.[153]

Regarding 1986, Zines acknowledged that both sections 51(xxix) and 51(xxxviii) were strong candidates for having underpinned the Australia Act 1986 (Cth); however, he had concerns regarding section 15 of the 1986 Act.[154] Section 15(1) related to amendment of a constitutionally significant statute, and yet had been enacted by section 51 rather than section 128 of the Constitution, despite the former provision's being 'subject to this Constitution' and the latter provision's requiring that 'This Constitution shall not be altered except in the following manner.' And furthermore, if section 51(xxix) or 51(xxxviii) authorised the Australia Act 1986, then section 15(1) and (3) taken together appeared to mean that section 51 had been used to bind itself,[155] contrary to normal assumptions about the Commonwealth Parliament's inability in that regard. Zines concluded therefore that section 15 must have been underpinned by the United Kingdom version of the Australia Act 1986. Zines acknowledged that amendments to that Australia Act 1986 under section 15 would seldom be sought; however, the important point remained regarding the necessary nature of the United Kingdom legislation.[156]

This debate[157] is important if we are to attempt an explanation of Australia's constitutional independence so it may be useful to make two points at this stage. First, as noted earlier, Lindell and Rose read section 15(3) as confirming

---

[152] Zines (4th edn, 1997) (n. 135 above) 317.   [153] ibid., 307.

[154] ibid., 305 et seq.

[155] In that before 1986 the Commonwealth was free to legislate under s. 51(xxix) and 51(xxxviii), and after 1986 the Commonwealth was constrained by s. 15.

[156] Zines (4th edn, 1997) (n. 135 above) 306. The Australia Acts (Request) Act 1999 represented one such rare attempt. It was passed in identical form by all the states to repeal s. 7 of the Australia Act 1986 in so far as it applied to the states.

[157] Lumb (1988) (n. 92 above) 30–1, has observed regarding s. 15 of the Australia Act 1986:

It might be argued that no manner and form legislation can be imposed by Commonwealth legislation which diverges from that contained in the Commonwealth Constitution (i.e. as

that section 15(1) could not be exploited by one or a few states to block important constitutional change, and that section 15(1) could not be used to prevent section 128 being used to substitute that general amending formula for section 15(1). It may be, therefore, that section 15 is not incompatible with section 128. Secondly, it may be that Australian legislatures can bind themselves to a greater degree than has often been assumed. Michael Coper has argued that because section 5 of the Colonial Laws Validity Act, 1865 (Imp.) expressly permitted Commonwealth legislatures to bind themselves, the full potential of what we have called the 'new' and 'revised' views has been insufficiently explored in Australia.[158]

Finally, regarding the termination of Westminster Parliament powers *vis-à-vis* Australia, Zines stated that, from the Australian point of view, it was 'not in the field of practical politics to suggest that the Commonwealth or the States would attempt' to restore that power or any other British power.[159] And from the British point of view (and therefore according to the British version of the Australia

---

prescribed by s. 1, s. 57 or s. 128). If this view were accepted, the repeal of the Australia Act (Cth) would depend on the interpretation given to s. 51 (xxxviii) by the High Court. If it were held that the repeal of legislation passed under that section could be achieved by the ordinary legislative process the validity of the amending process prescribed by s. 15 of the Australia Act (Cth) would be in doubt. In that case, the validity of any amendment of the Australia Acts would be subject to determination under s. 15 of the Australia Act (U.K.).

Thomson (1990) (n. 91 above) 414–15, has stated:

Two sets of provisions in [the Australia Act 1986 (Cth)] are particularly vulnerable. First is section 15 . . . It is doubtful whether future Commonwealth Parliaments are bound by the requirements in section 15(1) that all State Parliaments must request or concur in Commonwealth legislation repealing or amending the Australia Acts. In so far as section 15(1) stipulates, through section 15(3), that only constitutional amendments which confer power on the Commonwealth Parliament can result in amendments to or repeal of the Australia Act or Statute of Westminster 1931, it unconstitutionally restricts the operation of section 128 of the Australian Constitution.

Tony Blackshield has summarised the debate as follows in the entry under 'Australia Acts' in T. Blackshield, M. Coper and G. Williams, *The Oxford Companion to the High Court of Australia* (Melbourne: Oxford University Press, 2001) 43–4:

. . . much academic commentary has assumed that the effectiveness of the Act depended on its UK version. The implication is that the Australian version alone could not have achieved its objective . . . The issue is symbolically important because, if the Australian version was sufficient, then even before 1986 Australia was arguably already independent: its sovereignty would not be negated by residual linkages with the UK, provided that the power to terminate them lay wholly within Australia. By contrast, if that objective could not be achieved without the assistance of UK legislation, then even in 1986 Australia was arguably not independent. It is therefore submitted that the joint judgment in *Sue v Hill* referred only to the Australian version—suggesting that the UK version was enacted 'out of a perceived need for abundant caution', and discounting any significance for Australia of the idea that, under the British conception of parliamentary sovereignty, the UK Parliament might retain the theoretical power to repeal its version of the Australia Act (and even the Statute of Westminster).

[158] See M. Coper, *Encounters with the Constitution* (North Ryde: CCH Australia Ltd, 1987) 88. However, the argument that the Commonwealth could bind itself using s. 51(xxxviii) has to address the issue of whether the Constitution had not already imposed binding manner and form by means of s. 128.   [159] Zines (4th edn, 1997) (n. 135 above) 306.

Act 1986), 'whatever effect the British Act has in Australia, it clearly amounts in British law to an abdication of all sovereign power and responsibility in relation to Australia'.[160] Accordingly, 'there is no way that the Commonwealth parliament, even acting with the concurrence of the States, could confer power, authority or responsibilities on the United Kingdom authorities'.[161] Zines was not inclined to find a new sovereign to replace the United Kingdom Parliament; however, if pushed he would find it in section 128 of the Australian Constitution:

> There is of course no logical or legal reason why we need to have a 'sovereign' at all, or to think or talk in those terms. For those who see a legal system as one which has at its base a 'Grundnorm' or 'rules of recognition', the rule of obedience to the British Parliament can be regarded as replaced by the rule of the Constitution and associated fundamental instruments, the Australia Act and what remains of the Statute of Westminster. If one were looking for a single fundamental rule it might lie in s. 128 used to make any alterations to the Australian legal system. If one insisted upon a 'sovereign', it could perhaps be seen as the persons and bodies referred to in s. 128, acting in accordance with the rules included in that provision, as qualified by s. 15 of the Australia Act.[162]

Before concluding this section on Australian explanations of constitutional independence, it may be helpful to look at what the High Court of Australia has had to say on these issues. The Court has led the way in particular on the principle of popular sovereignty, though it has not been as forthcoming as one might like on how that principle fits into the sort of legal, theoretical and historical account that has been the subject of this book. The principle of popular sovereignty was developed in a sustained way in a series of cases in the 1990s that are by now very familiar to Australian constitutional lawyers. Other readers may require a brief overview.

Australia: Imperial sovereignty and popular sovereignty—the High Court

Although there were earlier High Court references to the constitutional role of the Australian people, notably in the decisions of Murphy J discussed in Chapter 10, such references increased dramatically after 1986, notably in the early 1990s, initially in the reasons of Justices Deane and Toohey. In *Leeth v The Commonwealth of Australia*, they stated that it was 'the people of the federating Colonies' who were the 'parties to the compact which is the

---

[160] Zines (4th edn, 1997) (n. 135 above) 306.
[161] ibid., 306. In summarising his argument Zines stated, at 318:

Whatever force the United Kingdom version of the Australia Act 1986 is regarded as having in Australia, it clearly is an abdication by the United Kingdom of all governmental power in respect of Australia, similar to that in relation to other independent countries of the Commonwealth of Nations.

[162] Zines (4th edn, 1997) (n. 135 above) 415.

Constitution'.[163] A year later, in *Nationwide News Pty Ltd v Wills*, the same judicial pairing further developed their conception of the role of the Australian people:

The implication of the Constitution which is of central importance in the resolution of the present case flows from the third of those general doctrines of government which underlie the Constitution and form part of its structure. That doctrine can conveniently be described as the doctrine of representative government, that is to say, of government representatives directly or indirectly elected or appointed by, and ultimately responsible to, the people of the Commonwealth. The rational basis of that doctrine is that all powers of government ultimately belong to, *and are derived from*, the governed.[164]

Such views would have been uncontroversial, as Dawson J would later say,[165] if taken to describe the sort of abstract political doctrine which underlies most liberal-democratic constitutional systems. However, Deane and Toohey JJ were clear, as they themselves confirmed in the *ACTV* case, that the people's role had legal consequences: 'it is an implication of the doctrine of representative government embodied in the Commonwealth Constitution that there shall be freedom within the Commonwealth of communication about matters relating to the government of the Commonwealth'.[166] However, this sort of reasoning from constitutional principle, though with clear legal effects, did not necessarily engage the foundations of constitutional validity and supremacy. The reasons of Chief Justice Mason in the *ACTV* case came much closer to the mark in that respect:

The very concept of representative government and representative democracy signifies government by the people through their representatives. *Translated into constitutional*

---

[163] (1992) 174 CLR 455.

[164] (1992) 177 CLR 1 (emphasis added). Deane J repeated the italicised phrase in *Theophanous v The Herald and Weekly Times Ltd* (182) CLR 104, 180. Deane J elaborated further elsewhere in his reasons (p. 171), stating:

The present legitimacy of the Constitution as the compact and highest law of our nation lies exclusively in the original adoption (by referenda) and subsequent maintenance (by acquiescence) of its provisions by the people. While they remain unaltered, it is the duty of the courts to observe and apply those provisions . . . There is absolutely nothing in the provisions of the Constitution which suggests an intention on the part of the people either that the ordinary rules of construction should be ignored or that the failure to include a detailed list of their constitutional 'rights' should be treated as somehow precluding or impeding the implication of rights . . . from either the Constitution's express terms or the fundamental doctrines upon which it was structured and which it incorporated as part of its very fabric.

This passage was followed by discussion of and quotations from Andrew Inglis Clark, *Studies in Australian Constitutional Law* (1st edn, 1901)(reprinted Sydney: Legal Books, 1997).

[165] *Australian Capital Television Pty Ltd v The Commonwealth of Australia* (1992) 177 CLR 106 (hereinafter *ACTV* (1992)), 181:

No doubt it may be said as an abstract proposition of political theory that the Constitution ultimately depends for its continuing validity upon the acceptance of the people, but the same may be said of any form of government which is not arbitrary. The legal foundation of the Australian Constitution is an exercise of sovereign power by the Imperial Parliament.

[166] *ACTV* (1992) (n. 165 above) 168.

terms, it denotes that the sovereign power which resides in the people is exercised on their behalf by their representatives. In the case of the Australian Constitution, one obstacle to the acceptance of that view is that the Constitution owes its legal force to its character as a statute of the Imperial Parliament enacted in the exercise of its legal sovereignty; the Constitute was not supreme law proceeding from the people's inherent authority to constitute a government, notwithstanding that it was adopted, subject to minor amendments, by the representatives of the Australian colonies at a Convention and approved by a majority of the electors in each of the colonies at the several referenda. *Despite its initial character as a statute of the Imperial Parliament, the Constitution brought into existence a system of representative government for Australia in which the elected representatives exercise sovereign power on behalf of the Australian people.* Hence, the prescribed procedure for amendment of the Constitution hinges upon a referendum at which the proposed amendment is approved by a majority of electors and a majority of electors in a majority of the States *(s. 128).* And, *most recently, the Australia Act 1986 (U.K.) marked the end of the legal sovereignty of the Imperial Parliament and recognized that ultimate sovereignty resided in the Australian people.*[167]

This frequently-quoted passage clearly engaged the issues that are of interest to us, so it is worth unpacking it briefly. Mason CJ did not appear to wish to deny that the Australian Constitution came into existence as a statute of the Imperial Parliament; however, it seemed that the sovereignty of the Australian people could nonetheless supplement and succeed the sovereignty of Westminster. Mason CJ's references to the Convention and referendum process were ambiguous: it is not clear whether he was elaborating on the perceived obstacle or expressing his own view. He was clearly expressing his own view, however, when he stated that the statute of the Imperial Parliament which contained the Australian Constitution also contained provisions, notably section 128 on amendment, which expressed the sovereignty of the Australian people. There was nothing in the 1986 process which involved popular ratification. Therefore, his statement to the effect that the United Kingdom version of the Australia Act 1986 'recognised [the] ultimate sovereignty [of the] Australian people' must have referred to the fact that the Act left the section 128 amendment procedure, including its referendums, in an unopposed position at the summit of the Australian legal system. Given the dominance of the orthodox theory in the United Kingdom and in Australia, the assumed effectiveness of the Australia Act 1986 (UK) required more explanation, but assuming that it was effective even from a United Kingdom perspective, Mason CJ's views based on the pre-eminence of section 128 were comprehensible.

Dawson J in the *ACTV* case was more inclined not to muddy the constitutional waters by introducing the sovereignty of Parliament into an already crowded pool of legal ideas:

Whenever the question of implication is raised in relation to the Constitution it is well to bear in mind the nature of the instrument and the source from which it derives its

---

[167] ibid., 137–8 (emphasis added).

authority. The Constitution is contained in an Act of the Imperial Parliament: the Commonwealth of Australia Constitution Act (63 & 64 Vict. C. 12). Notwithstanding that this Act was preceded by the agreement of the people . . . 'to unite in one indissoluble Federal Commonwealth', *the legal foundation of the Constitution is the Act itself which was passed and came into force in accordance with antecedent law*. And the Constitution is itself a law declared by the Imperial Parliament to be 'binding on the courts, judges, and people of every State and every part of the Commonwealth'. It does not purport to obtain its force from any power residing in the people to constitute a government, nor does it involve any notion of the delegation of power by the people such as forms part of American constitutional doctrine.[168]

Dawson J thereby excluded popular sovereignty as a potential alternative or supplementary explanation for the validity and supremacy of the Constitution. Unlike Mason CJ, he did not wish even to emphasise the importance of section 128 in relation to popular sovereignty.

In *McGinty v The State of Western Australia*,[169] some members of the High Court began to pour cold water on the inevitable rush to imply all manner of constitutional rights based on representative democracy and popular sovereignty. They were determined to make clear that any implications from representative democracy were based in the text and structure of the Constitution not in any free-standing legal-political principle.[170] However, some were quite prepared to develop the line of thinking begun by Mason CJ in the *ACTV* case regarding the importance of the sovereignty of the people as a foundational, or at least fundamental, concept. McHugh J was particularly eloquent on this point:

The Constitution is contained in a statute of the United Kingdom Parliament. In the late twentieth century, it may not be palatable to many persons to think that the powers, authorities, immunities and obligations of the Federal and State parliaments of Australia derive their legal authority from a statute enacted by the Imperial Parliament, but the enactment of that statute containing the terms of the Constitution is the instrument by which the Australian people have consented to be governed. Since the passing of the Australia Act (UK) in 1986, notwithstanding some considerable theoretical difficulties, the political and legal sovereignty of Australia now resides in the people of Australia. But the only authority that the people have given to the parliaments of the nation is to enact laws in accordance with the terms of the Constitution.[171]

---

[168] *ACTV* (1992), 181 (emphasis added).
[169] *McGinty v The State of Western Australia* (1996) 186 CLR 140.
[170] ibid. *per* Brennan CJ at 168:

Implications are not devised by the judiciary; they exist in the text and structure of the Constitution and are revealed or uncovered by judicial exegesis. No implication can be drawn from the Constitution which is not based on the actual terms of the Constitution, or on its structure.

And *per* McHugh J at 235:

I regard the reasoning in *Nationwide News, Australian Capital Television, Theophanous* and *Stephens* in so far as it invokes an implied principle of representative democracy as fundamentally wrong and as an alteration of the Constitution without the authority of the people under s. 128 of the Constitution.

[171] *McGinty* (1996) (n. 169 above) 230.

Sovereignty of the people was contained within a post-1986 and intra-constitutional framework, the reference to 'the terms of the Constitution' including section 128. McHugh J made this point clearer later in his reasons, citing James Bryce,[172] but in this case with unorthodox effect:

Lord Bryce asserted that, in a country governed by a rigid Constitution which limits the power of the legislature to certain subjects or forbids it to transgress certain fundamental doctrines, the sovereignty resides in the body which made and can amend the Constitution. On that view, the sovereignty of Australia originally resided in the United Kingdom Parliament. Since the Australia Act (UK), however, the sovereignty of the Australian nation has ceased to reside in the Imperial Parliament and has become embedded in the Australian people. Only the people can now change the Constitution. They are the sovereign.[173]

Gummow J was even more guarded about the popular sovereignty argument, acceding only with conditions and qualifications attached. However, he too was prepared, however reluctantly, to situate popular sovereignty in section 128:

Broad statements as to the reposition of 'sovereignty' in 'the people' of Australia, if they are to be given legal rather than popular or political meaning, must be understood in the light of the federal considerations contained in s. 128.

   Those statements must also allow for the fact that none of the Australia Acts, Imperial, Commonwealth or State, followed approval at a referendum, in particular, any submission to the electors pursuant to s. 128 of the Constitution. Moreover, in s. 15 thereof, the Australia Acts provide their own mechanism for amendment or repeal by statute and without submission to the electors at State or Commonwealth level.[174]

In cases such as *Lange v Australian Broadcasting Corporation*,[175] *Levy v Victoria*[176] and *Kruger v Commonwealth of Australia*[177] the High Court continued the process of reigning in implication from constitutional principle, and references to sovereignty of the people seemed to be on the decline, at least in the judges' reasons if not always in plaintiffs' submissions. Some judges, such as Kirby J in the *Levy* case, approached the sovereignty issue with academic detachment;[178] whereas others, such as Brennan CJ in the *Kruger* case were

---

[172] See discussion of Bryce as a traditional or orthodox thinker on parliamentary sovereignty in Ch. 3 above.   [173] *McGinty* (1996) (n. 169 above) 237.
[174] ibid., 275.   [175] *Lange v Australian Broadcasting Corporation* (1997) 189 CLR 520.
[176] *Levy v Victoria* (1997) 189 CLR 579.
[177] *Kruger v Commonwealth of Australia* (1997) 190 CLR 1.
[178] *Levy* (1997) (n. 176 above) 634:

The notion that the ultimate foundation for constitutional norms is the common law is not a new one. However, it remains controversial. With the passage of time since federation in Australia and changing notions of Australian nationhood, the perception that the Australian Constitution is binding because of its imperial provenance has given way (at least since the Australia Acts 1986) to an often expressed opinion that the people of Australia are the ultimate repository of sovereignty. That view is not without conceptual and historical difficulties.

prepared, however tentatively, to reinforce and develop the earlier line of thinking: 'The Constitution, though in form and substance a statute of the Parliament of the United Kingdom, was a compact among the peoples of the federating Colonies, as the preamble to the Constitution declares.'[179]

The most significant recent development in the issue of constitutional dependence occurred in the 1999 case of *Sue v Hill*.[180] The case concerned a challenge to the election of a Senator on the basis that the person elected was a 'subject or citizen of a foreign power'—in this case a British citizen—within the meaning of section 44(i) of the Australian Constitution. In the words of Gleeson CJ, Gummow and Hayne JJ, it would not be possible to describe the United Kingdom as a 'foreign power' under section 44 (i) 'if Australian courts are, as a matter of the fundamental law of this country, immediately bound to recognise and give effect to the exercise of legislative, executive and judicial power by the institutions of government of the United Kingdom'.[181] The judges immediately stated that the *Commonwealth* version of the Australia Act 1986 prevented such a conclusion: 'whatever once may have been the situation with respect to the Commonwealth and to the States, since at least the commencement of the Australia Act 1986 (Cth) this had not been the case'.[182] With regard to recognition of United Kingdom legislative Acts, in particular, they argued that section 1 of the Australia Act 1986 (Cth) was sufficient to terminate Westminster's powers, and that section 1 was validly enacted under section 51(xxxviii) of the Commonwealth Constitution.[183] In contrast to Mason CJ, and others who had laid emphasis on the Australia Act 1986 (UK), they accepted that Dicey's 'dogma' regarding parliamentary sovereignty placed potential obstacles in the way of the ultimate effectiveness of the United Kingdom version of the 1986 Act in preventing any hypothetical post-1986 United Kingdom legislation for Australia. They noted that Dicey had never satisfactorily explained how the so-called abdication of Parliament's sovereignty was consistent with his assertion that no Parliament could bind a future Parliament.[184] The effectiveness of the United Kingdom Act was for the United Kingdom courts, according to Gleeson CJ, Gummow and Hayne JJ. However, 'whatever effect the courts of the United Kingdom may give to an amendment or repeal of the 1986 UK Act, Australian

---

[179] *Kruger* (1997) (n. 177 above) 41–2.

[180] (1999) 199 CLR 462 (hereinafter *Sue v Hill* (1999) cited to paragraph rather than page numbers).   [181] ibid., para. 59.

[182] ibid., para. 59.

[183] ibid., para. 62. Gaudron J agreed on this point (at para. 164). See also *Attorney-General (W.A.) v Marquet* (2003) 202 ALR 233, paras 67 and 70, *per* Gleeson CJ, Gummow, Hayne and Heydon JJ. See, however, Kirby J in *Marquet*, ibid., paras 202 et seq., in which he denied the constitutional validity of both the Australia Act 1986 (UK) and the Australia Act 1986 (Cth). In *Shaw v Minister for Immigration and Multicultural Affairs* (2004) 78 ALJR 203, para. 108, Kirby J acknowledged that his view was not adopted by the majority in the *Marquet* case. He therefore reluctantly accepted the validity of the Australia Acts.

[184] We have seen how even Dicey's apologist, H.W.R Wade had similar concerns. See H.W.R. Wade, 'The Basis of Legal Sovereignty' [1955] CLJ 172, 196.

courts would be obliged to give their obedience to s. 1 of the statute passed by the Parliament of the Commonwealth'.[185]

In Chapter 13, we will consider whether Australia can account for both constitutional continuity and constitutional independence, and whether the Australian people can be part of that account. We will also return to the issues raised in this Chapter regarding Canada and New Zealand. However, before doing so, it may be helpful to explore some theoretical writing on sovereignty and legal systems which may assist in the task.

[185] *Sue v Hill* (1999) (n. 181 above) para 64.

12

Theoretical Approaches to Sovereignty and Legal System

The comments of the range of constitutional commentators considered in Chapter 11 raise two key types of question regarding Australian, Canadian and New Zealand constitutional independence. First, how can it be said that those constitutions are independent of even the theoretical possibility of binding Westminster legislation if there has been no overt breach in legal continuity leading back to the Imperial Parliament? Was not that Parliament a 'continuing'[1] sovereign (Dicey's assertion that no Parliament may bind a future Parliament), and a perpetually superior law-maker at the same time? Secondly, if somehow it could be said that local mechanisms in Australia, Canada and New Zealand[2] were now sovereign in the ultimate sense that concerns us, then how was it possible to explain the validity and supremacy of those constitutional systems? Using Philip Joseph's analogy, and developing it slightly, was it possible for the Australian, Canadian and New Zealand constitutional branches to support themselves despite the exclusion of the axeman from those defiantly independent legal systems?[3]

These questions lead us initially to a brief re-examination of the traditional British theory of the sovereignty of Parliament in order to discover whether that theory has any way of making sense of legal continuity linking back to the

---

[1] P.A. Joseph, *Constitutional and Administrative Law in New Zealand* (Sydney: Law Book Company, 1993) 114.

[2] i.e. for Australia, s. 128 of the Australian Constitution (read together with s. 15 of the Australia Act 1986), for Canada, the Part V procedures on amendment in the Constitution Act 1982, and, for New Zealand, the Wellington Parliament.

[3] Of course, this question applies differently in the three countries in question. In Australia and Canada, the question relates to the exclusion from the present Australian and Canadian legal systems of the very body which enacted, or gave validity to, in the positivist sense, their Constitutions, there being no attempt to deny that the main constitutional texts are contained in enactments of the United Kingdom Parliament. In the New Zealand case, the question relates to the fact that the 1947 United Kingdom Parliament legislation for New Zealand that ostensibly empowered the New Zealand Parliament to enact the Constitution Act 1986 (NZ) has now been removed from the New Zealand statute book.

In Canada and New Zealand there was no significant popular participation in the enactment of their Constitutions, whereas in Australia the role of the public was crucial, politically, if not legally. What power is supporting and sustaining these three Constitutions, then?

United Kingdom Parliament and Australian, Canadian and New Zealand assertions of constitutional independence. If satisfactory answers are not forthcoming from within traditional British theory, we may want to consider the same issues in the larger context of new and revised theories of sovereignty, and of theories regarding the concept of a legal system more generally. From Australian, Canadian and New Zealand perspectives, the United Kingdom Parliament was both the constituent assembly, as Clement and others had noted,[4] and the ultimate or at least alternate amending mechanism of their legal systems. It is commonplace in the theory of legal systems to view both constituent processes and amendment of amending formulae as 'self-embracing', i.e. as capable of providing for their own replacement without any revolution or loss of continuity.[5] It may then be appropriate to examine the concept of self-embracing change and to consider how it provides for continuity and validity in law all the while accomplishing change at the pinnacle of the legal system. This Part concludes by applying the 'self-embracing' interpretation of constitutional change to the acquisition of Australian, Canadian and New Zealand constitutional independence.[6]

Sovereignty of Parliament revisited

Is there anything in the Australian, Canadian and New Zealand constitutional process described in Part II which could be said to terminate—i.e. truly and irreversibly terminate—the power of the United Kingdom Parliament to legislate for Australia, Canada and New Zealand? Asking the question in this way

[4] W.H.P. Clement, *The Law of the Canadian Constitution* (3rd edn, Toronto, Carswell, 1916) 3, 29.

[5] In a new state, when a constituent assembly produces a constitutional proposal and presents it for ratification by referendum, the referendum process may well confer validity on a Constitution containing its own procedures for constitutional amendment (e.g. two-thirds votes in two chambers followed by a referendum) which are from the moment of proclamation constitutionally binding (so as to exclude recourse to the simpler referendum-only procedure). The same is true of a process in an existing constitutional system whereby one amending procedure is used to amend itself (e.g. a two-thirds procedure used to institute a three-fifths procedure). Once the new procedure has been validly enacted there can be no recourse to the older, more flexible procedure. The latter, on this self-embracing interpretation, is no longer part of the active legal system from then on. Only the historian or the theorist of legal systems need consider it. The 'self-embracing' interpretation is no less logically coherent than its 'continuing' alternative, as argued in Ch. 1 above. This point will be developed further below. It is argued here and in Ch. 13 below that the self-embracing interpretation is more appropriate to the Australian, Canadian and New Zealand systems' present understanding of their constitutional fundamentals. Given the continued dominance of the traditional theory in the United Kingdom, acceptance of a self-embracing interpretation of their constitutional development may be dependent on the independence of Australian, Canadian and New Zealand constitutional theory.

[6] Though, as we shall see, its importance appears to be far greater in explaining Canadian and New Zealand constitutional independence. Australian constitutional independence may be explainable by other means.

provokes a standard response. As a matter of United Kingdom law the answer is probably 'no': the Westminster Parliament can legislate for Australia, Canada and New Zealand just as easily as it can legislate for Mexico and France,[7] and the British courts (or any courts which behave as such) will recognise that legislation to the extent possible.[8] As a matter of Australian, Canadian and New Zealand law, however, the answer is clearly 'yes', and the local courts would undoubtedly say so.[9] Where, however, the local courts have confirmed, as the Supreme Court of Canada did so clearly in the 1981 *Patriation Reference*, that the United Kingdom Parliament is a superior, unlimited, unimpaired, sovereign legislature which even a local court such as itself must heed, and to the extent that local constitutional theory continues to be dominated by traditional views of parliamentary sovereignty, the explanation for such an answer is far more difficult.

The dominant British theory of sovereignty of Parliament can be found in the writings of Dicey. The broad lines of this theory were discussed in Chapter 3. Following Dicey, certain writers began to develop 'new' or 'revised' views[10] which suggested that Parliament could shed a part of its sovereignty or at least bind itself as to the manner and form of its future legislation. These views were discussed in Chapter 4.

If Australian, Canadian and New Zealand courts were to continue in the future to be influenced by some of the more traditional aspects of British constitutional theory, then they might feel logically constrained by the classical version of

---

[7] See S.A. de Smith, *The New Commonwealth and its Constitutions* (London: Stevens & Sons, 1964) 4–5:

From the point of view of English courts, Parliament has the power to change the law of Mexico, because English judges, obliged to accept the sovereignty of Parliament, are obliged to recognise the formal efficacy of its legislation for any part of the world. But Mexican judges are under no such obligation . . .

See also I. Jennings, *The Law and the Constitution* (5th edn, London: University of London Press, 1959) who famously stated, at 170:

Parliamentary supremacy means . . . that Parliament can legislate for all persons and all places. If it enacts that smoking in the streets of Paris is an offence, then it *is* an offence. Naturally, it is an offence by English law and not by French law, and therefore it would be regarded as an offence only by those who paid attention to English law. The Paris police would not at once begin arresting all smokers, nor would French criminal courts begin inflicting punishments upon them.

It may be appropriate here to point out that British constitutional law often underestimates the significance of international law, although this trend may be in the process of being reversed. See, e.g., D. Feldman, 'The Internationalization of Public Law and its Impact on the United Kingdom' in J. Jowell and D. Oliver, *The Changing Constitution* (5th edn, Oxford: Oxford University Press, 2004) 117.

[8] See *Manuel v Attorney-General* [1983] Ch 77, 87 *per* Megarry V-C.

[9] Regarding the widely held view that local courts would simply ignore any attempt by Westminster to legislate as if its continuing sovereignty justified its doing so, see G. Marshall, *Constitutional Theory* (Oxford: Oxford University Press, 1971) 63; A.W. Bradley, 'The Sovereignty of Parliament—Form or Substance' in Jowell and Oliver (eds) (5th edn, 2004) (n. 7 above) 41.

[10] See, e.g., Jennings (5th edn, 1959) (n. 7 above), ch. 4; R.T.E. Latham, *The Law and the Commonwealth* (Oxford: Oxford University Press, 1949); G. Marshall, *Parliamentary Sovereignty and the Commonwealth* (Oxford: Clarendon Press, 1957) chs 2–4; and, generally, discussion in Ch. 4 above.

Westminster parliamentary sovereignty which dictates that even twenty-first century legislation for Australia, Canada or New Zealand would have to be recognised. According to the traditional view, a local court could not declare such legislation ultra vires any more than a British court could do so.[11] The conventions of Commonwealth relations certainly discourage such legislation without local request and consent; and, furthermore, it is easy to imagine that even with such request and consent, the United Kingdom Parliament might nonetheless refuse to act. These are, however, precarious pegs on which to hang the Australian, Canadian and New Zealand legal systems' constitutional independence— but perhaps there is no better solution. It seems highly unlikely, however, that the Australian, Canadian and New Zealand courts would accept this argument based in the absolute legal sovereignty of the Westminster Parliament limited only by convention, despite its classically neat logic, especially if a more attractive argument were presented.[12]

The apparent termination of the British link could also be explained within the confines of British theory by means of some of the views of the post-Dicey 'new' (and later 'revised') school. In 1984, Geoffrey Marshall summarised the possibilities.[13] Using the explanations put forward by adherents of the 'new' view, an Australian, New Zealand or Canadian court might reason, first, that the United Kingdom Parliament had in section 4 of the Statute of Westminster, section 2 of the Canada Act 1982, section 1 of the Australia Act 1986 (UK) or section 1 of the New Zealand Constitution (Amendment) Act 1947 (UK) bound itself to a strong manner and form requirement.[14] That is, it legally obliged itself

---

[11]   The Australian High Court has been taking a more independent line since the late 1970s, as we saw in Ch. 10 above. The Supreme Court of Canada showed its predilection for a traditional view in the *Patriation Reference* as discussed in Ch. 8 above. As long as New Zealand retained the Judicial Committee of the Privy Council as its final court of appeal, that court might have been tempted to accept the British, and therefore traditional, view of things, despite its imperial overtones, if for no other reason than that this would preserve the United Kingdom Parliament's ability to assist former colonies in an emergency if need be. The question regarding the Privy Council is now moot, given the recent enactment of the New Zealand Supreme Court Act which terminated appeals to the Privy Council. The attitude of the New Zealand Supreme Court is still to be revealed, however.

[12]   There are strong indications in the *Patriation Reference* that the Supreme Court of Canada saw the pre-1982 legal relationship between Canada and the United Kingdom Parliament in just these terms. (See Ch. 7 above for further discussion.) A similar attitude is expressed in New Zealand in the first pages of the Explanatory Notes accompanying the 1947 measures adopting the Statute of Westminster. (See Ch. 8 above for further discussion.) However, both the Canada Act 1982 (UK) and the Constitution Act 1986 (NZ) now provide strong reasons in both countries to take a different view.

[13]   G. Marshall, *Constitutional Conventions* (Oxford: Oxford University Press, 1984) 209.

[14]   In the *Manuel* (1983), Megarry V-C gave no precise opinion on this argument, but referred instead to an article on sovereignty by Professor H.W.R. Wade ('The Basis of Legal Sovereignty' [1955] CLJ 172) in which it was argued that 'there is one, and only one, limit to Parliament's legal power: it cannot detract from its own continuing sovereignty' (p. 174). Wade had strongly rejected Jennings' idea that there could be a 'manner and form exception' to the traditional doctrine of parliamentary sovereignty. Slade LJ in the Court of Appeal, (see *Manuel* (1983), 99–110), speaking on behalf of Cumming-Bruce and Eveleigh LJJ noted (at 110) that there was a clear division of opinion as to whether the United Kingdom Parliament could effectively tie the hands of its successors, but he did not find it necessary to deal with the issue. The House of Lords refused a petition for leave to appeal.

in future only to legislate for a former Dominion following the appropriate request and consent from the Dominion concerned, which presumably would have to be recited in the legislation (as even a weak manner and form argument would require). This approach might have been an improvement on an earlier state of affairs which, at least on one view, left a Dominion vulnerable at any time even to unsolicited legislation from Westminster, but the strong manner and form explanation still left the local legal system theoretically and legally tied to the United Kingdom Parliament, and this is not what most people in Australia, Canada and New Zealand understood to be the case. More importantly, if this interpretation found favour it would leave open the possibility that in the event of constitutional paralysis at some point in the future, the central government, as rightful representative of the former Dominion at the international level, could unilaterally seek an amendment to the Constitution via Westminster, a prospect which was particularly unacceptable for federal Australia and Canada. It seems unlikely that a local court would accept an explanation which left the door open to such a possibility.

A second and more popular line of reasoning, derived from Dicey according to some, and from the 'new view' of British parliamentary sovereignty according to others, involved the notion that, as of 1947, 1982 and 1986, the Westminster Parliament can be seen to have abdicated part of its sovereignty, more specifically, its power to legislate for New Zealand, Canada and Australia.[15] It seems odd that the United Kingdom Parliament should not be able to legislate for those countries when it might certainly legislate for Mexico or France, or anywhere else, according to the view still accepted by British courts. It has often been said that Mexican or French courts (and citizens) would certainly ignore such legislation, but that the British courts (*and* presumably those courts which still recognised that Parliament as part of their legal system) would have to recognise it.[16] In the *Patriation Reference*, the Supreme Court of Canada had taken the attitude of a British court in the face of legislation emanating from the superior and sovereign Parliament at Westminster. Did this mean, then, that Canadian courts, and other Commonwealth courts similarly positioned, were still bound to accept the continuing sovereignty of the United Kingdom Parliament? If that situation had changed as a result of independence legislation, then it seemed more appropriate to consider the matter not as a question of British constitutional theory regarding the sovereignty of the Westminster Parliament, but rather as a question of Australian, Canadian or New Zealand constitutional theory regarding the ultimate legal principles of each of those legal systems. The

---

[15] According to a careful reading of the traditional theory of Parliamentary sovereignty, Parliament can only abdicate its sovereignty entirely, i.e. by dissolving itself or by transferring all of its power to a new legislative body. See Marshall (1984) (n. 13 above) 209; A.V. Dicey, *An Introduction to the Study of the Law of the Constitution* 10th edn by E.C.S. Wade (London: Macmillan, 1959) 69 and Wade (1955) (n. 14 above) 196n.

[16] See sources cited in nn. 7 and 9 above.

New Zealand case is, of course, complicated by the fact that the United Kingdom Parliament never purported to *abdicate* its power to legislate for New Zealand. The most that can be argued is that the Westminster Parliament's powers were limited in terms of New Zealand laws of 1947, and that from that point on they were subject to termination at the discretion of the New Zealand Parliament, as occurred in 1986. If that was so, then it was again necessary to look beyond the confines of British constitutional theory in order to find an explanation that suited New Zealand (and perhaps also Australian and Canadian) needs.

The brief recapitulation of British constitutional theory above, and the fuller discussion in Chapters 2 and 3, indicated that while there are various theories dealing with the possibility of limiting the powers of the Westminster Parliament, there was no consensus on such matters. It may be useful at this point to isolate certain elements of Westminster parliamentary sovereignty that might be recognisable in more general theories of constitutional law.

Dicey's notion of parliamentary sovereignty can be divided into at least two aspects. First, there is the notion that Parliament cannot be limited as to the *ambit* of its legislation, the corollary being that the courts will recognise all manner of legislation passed by Parliament. There have always been rumblings which challenge this idea,[17] and clearly it should be conceded that there is nothing inevitable about the all-encompassing Diceyan version, but the notion is at least comprehensible. A further aspect of Dicey's sovereignty of Parliament is that Parliament cannot bind its successors, for if one Parliament at one moment in time can limit a second Parliament's ability to legislate at a later moment then the eternal 'Parliament' can no longer be said to be sovereign in the first sense.

It should be noted that the Supreme Court of Canada in the *Patriation Reference* referred only to the 'undiminished' or 'unimpaired' *ambit* of the United Kingdom Parliament's sovereignty prior to 1982. Such expressions implied acceptance of the first aspect of parliamentary sovereignty just noted. Did they necessarily mean that the Supreme Court accepted the second aspect? Is there any logical reason why the second should follow from the first?

In Australia and New Zealand, those with a traditional Diceyan perspective, such as Wynes and Scott, made no distinction between these two aspects of parliamentary sovereignty. They rejected the insights of the 'manner and form', 'new' or 'revised' view. Adherents of these views, such as Brookfield in New Zealand, made a similar distinction to the one set out above.[18] Brookfield distinguished between Parliament acting in its legislative capacity and Parliament acting in its constituent (constitution-making and -amending) capacity. Brookfield applied this distinction to the New Zealand Parliament, but perhaps

[17] For discussion and rebuttal of these ideas, see J. Goldsworthy, *The Sovereignty of Parliament* (Oxford: Oxford University Press, 1999).
[18] F.M. Brookfield, 'Parliamentary Supremacy and Constitutional Entrenchment: A Jurisprudential Approach' (1984) 5 Otago LR 603.

it was equally applicable to the Westminster Parliament, viewed from a local perspective if not from the British perspective.

In order to pursue this analysis, it will be necessary to go beyond the confines of the theory relating to the Westminster Parliament and to consider the notion of legal sovereignty generally. This discussion will take us into a consideration of the concept of a legal system. The approach favoured here is that the sovereign United Kingdom Parliament at the apex of the Imperial legal system earlier in this century should be treated in the same way as the rules governing validity and continuity in any legal system. Despite initial doubts in some theoretical writing, it seems clear now, in logic and in law, that just as one constitutional amending formula could be either permanent or amendable according to its own procedure so may a sovereign United Kingdom Parliament be viewed, at least from an Australian, Canadian or New Zealand point of view, as a permanent and continuing sovereign or as a self-embracing sovereign, one which could provide for its own replacement. It is argued here that the self-embracing interpretation is entirely coherent, and capable of explaining current constitutional assumptions in Australia, Canada and New Zealand.

Any discussion of the concept of a legal system requires that we consider briefly the highly influential writings of Hans Kelsen who identified the notion of a *Grundnorm* or basic norm, as well as the work of H.L.A. Hart who developed the idea of a rule of recognition.

General theories of law and legal system: Kelsen and Hart

In Kelsen's eyes the *Grundnorm*, or basic norm, was connected to the legal system by means of a chain of validity: 'All the norms whose validity may be traced back to one and the same basic norm form a system of norms, or an order.'[19] He suggested that all the laws in a legal system can be traced back to 'some constitution that is first historically'[20], and that the validity of this first constitution was the 'final postulate' upon which the validity of all the norms of the legal system depended: 'All these legal norms belong to one and the same legal order because their validity can be traced back—directly to the first constitution.'[21] The validity of the first constitution was dependent on the *Grundnorm*, or basic norm: 'That the first constitution is a binding legal norm is presupposed, and the formulation of the presupposition is the basic norm [*Grundnorm*] of this legal order.'[22]

Regarding the problem of Australian, Canadian and New Zealand constitutional independence, the *Grundnorm* had a potentially liberating effect. Once these countries could acquire their own basic norms, they would be free of the

---

[19] H. Kelsen, *General Theory of Law and State* (Cambridge, Massachusetts: Harvard University Press, 1949) 111.   [20] ibid., 115.
[21] ibid., 115.   [22] ibid., 115.

authority of the Imperial sovereign. F.R. Scott and Geoffrey Sawer had had this insight as early as the 1950s.[23] However, if all the norms which could be traced back to the basic norm formed part of the same legal system, then it was difficult to see how the Australian, Canadian and New Zealand penchant for following the rule of law as scrupulously as possible could ever separate these legal systems from the United Kingdom legal system.[24] According to Kelsen, 'the State and its legal order remain the same only so long as the constitution is intact or changed according to its own provisions'; or viewed in another way: 'A State remains the same as long as the continuity of the legal order is maintained . . .'[25]

Kelsen's theory of a legal system was found to be quite useful in justifying the fact that a revolution or *coup d'état* had successfully imposed a new legal order by virtue of having violated the provisions of the previous constitutional regime. It was difficult, however, to conceive of the Australian, Canadian and New Zealand experiences in such terms. Instead, the Australian, Canadian and New Zealand experiences indicated that historically the first constitution was the customary or common law British constitution, and that it had been respected. How then could it be said that the Australian, Canadian and New Zealand legal systems were separate and distinct from the British legal system? Kelsen's model appeared to make the fact of a historical legal link determinative. Rather than trying to untangle the analysis according to Kelsen and his (in)famous *Grundnorm*, it may be more useful to move on to those following Kelsen who adapted his ideas into what proved to be a more manageable model.

H.L.A. Hart rejected Kelsen's idea that the validity of a basic norm had to be assumed or postulated. For Hart, validity was a question of fact, specifically 'the actual practice of the courts and officials of the system when identifying the law which they are to apply'.[26] Hart underlined the importance of habitual and factual use by calling his substitute for the *Grundnorm* the 'rule of recognition'. The most basic of the rules of recognition he referred to as the 'ultimate rule of recognition'.[27]

In the absence of a revolution, Kelsen's *Grundnorm* would not change given its position at the pinnacle and, especially, at the source of the legal system. In contrast, Hart's rule of recognition could apparently change over time, in accordance with the courts' and officials' changing attitudes towards that which should

---

[23] See F.R. Scott, 'The Redistribution of Imperial Sovereignty' in *Transactions of the Royal Society of Canada*, 44, Series III, June 1950, 27–34, reprinted in F.R. Scott, *Essays on the Constitution* (Toronto: University of Toronto Press, 1977) 244, and G. Sawer, 'Constitutional Law' in G.W. Paton (ed.) *The Commonwealth of Australia: The Development of its Laws and Constitution* (London: Stevens & Sons, 1952) 38.

[24] John Finnis, 'Revolutions and Continuity of Law' in A.W.B. Simpson (ed.) *Oxford Essays in Jurisprudence*, 2nd Series (Oxford: Oxford University Press, 1973) 52, discusses how other Commonwealth countries deliberately broke the rules so as to sever the link to the Imperial *Grundnorm*.   [25] Kelsen (1949) (n. 19 above) 219.

[26] H.L.A. Hart, *The Concept of Law* (Oxford: Clarendon Press, 1961) (2nd edn, 1994) 245n (citations to 1st edn).   [27] ibid., ch. 6.

be recognised as valid law in the legal system.[28] Kelsen's theory placed considerable emphasis on the horizontal or temporal axis of the legal system, i.e. the tracing of validity through time in order to establish what Raz terms 'justified normativity'.[29] Hart's theory was far more concerned with what Kelsen's theory had referred to as the vertical 'hierarchy of norms' and the question of what was *considered* valid (from the internal perspective) at any given moment in the life of the legal system.

It is easy to see how the concept of a legal system spanning different periods of time was quite vital to Kelsen's approach though far less so for Hart. Kelsen's criteria for the existence of a legal system was, as we have seen, a juristic one: unblemished legal connection to the historically first constitution. Hart's analysis did not require a historically first constitution; validity could be determined by reference to the observable facts of the present. Hart gave little indication as to what, in his view, constituted a discrete legal system over time.

The closest Hart came to describing and distinguishing legal systems was in examining what he referred to as 'the pathology of the legal system'.[30] His discussion of Commonwealth developments provided useful material for our analysis of the Australian, Canadian and New Zealand situations. As difficult as it was according to Kelsen's criteria to explain how these countries got out from under the legal authority of the United Kingdom Parliament, on Hart's account the process was as simple as a change in the ultimate rule of recognition. The courts in any former colony simply ceased recognising enactments of the Westminster Parliament as a matter of observable fact.[31]

According to Hart's theory, then, the transition from the Imperial legal system to independent Australian, Canadian and New Zealand legal systems was clearly possible. That which was not clear was how the courts of the local legal systems could explain what had come about, how it was that the ultimate rule of recognition had simply evolved or shifted. If the process had been one of true revolution, as H.W.R. Wade had described similar processes,[32] one would not necessarily have expected such a legal explanation, but the Australian, Canadian

---

[28] ibid., 246n.   [29] J. Raz, *The Authority of Law* (Oxford: Oxford University Press, 1979).
[30] Hart (1961) (n. 26 above), 114.
[31] ibid., 117:

At the end of the period of development [from colony to independent nation] we find that the ultimate rule of recognition has shifted, for the legal competence of the Westminster Parliament to legislate for the colony is no longer recognised in its courts. It is still true that much of the constitutional structure of the former colony is to be found in the original statute of the Westminster Parliament: but this is now only an historical fact, for it no longer owes its contemporary legal status in the territory to the authority of the Westminster Parliament. The legal system in the former colony has now a 'local root' in that the rule of recognition specifying the ultimate criteria of legal validity no longer refers to enactments of a legislature of another territory. The new rule rests simply on the fact that it is accepted and used as such a rule in the judicial and other official operations of a local system whose rules are generally obeyed.

[32] Wade (1955) (n. 14 above), 191: 'the naked fact of revolution . . . beneath its elaborate legal dress'.

and New Zealand processes (as well as other Commonwealth decolonisation processes) had purported to be scrupulously legal and could presumably be explained in legal terms. We may readily accept that from the Australian, Canadian and New Zealand internal perspectives, the ultimate rule of recognition now excludes the United Kingdom Parliament, but Hart provided little insight into how that supposedly legal transformation might have taken place.

Taking Canada as an example, the ultimate rule of recognition for Canada pre-1982 undoubtedly included the United Kingdom Parliament, as the Supreme Court of Canada confirmed in the *Patriation Reference*. Could it be that even in 1981 the ultimate rule of the Canadian legal system was clear as to the *ambit* of the United Kingdom Parliament's powers, but uncertain as to the ability of that Parliament to bind itself? If so, then it was still possible for the Supreme Court of Canada to take a self-embracing interpretation of Westminster sovereignty, even while the British courts leaned in the direction of continuing sovereignty.[33] The consequence of this Canadian interpretation would be that the undiminished and unimpaired powers of the United Kingdom Parliament in relation to Canada in 1981 could, consistent with its self-embracing powers, simultaneously bestow validity on the Canada Act 1982 and provide for its own permanent replacement in the form of Part V of the Constitution Act, 1982 on amendment, at least as a matter of Canadian law.

And although the Australian and New Zealand courts had not been so clear and unambiguous as to the unlimited sovereignty of the Westminster Parliament so recently, a similar explanation of its self-embracing powers was available to them if necessary. The particular workings of this explanation for each country will be examined more closely in Chapter 13.

If this explanation is to be accepted, it will be necessary to consider three further questions. First, was a self-embracing conception of the ultimate rule of a legal system a coherent one? Some of the challenges to its coherence as a matter of legal authority have already been dealt with, but there were supposed logical objections to deal with as well. There were at one time considerable doubts on this score. Secondly, how could the United Kingdom Parliament simultaneously confer validity on local constitutions and the constitutional independence-granting legislation, and then, without undermining that validity, disappear from the legal map of the newly independent local legal system? Finally, on what basis could a local court in the newly independent country favour a self-embracing interpretation of the United Kingdom Parliament's powers, especially given that the local understandings earlier in the century had been almost unanimously in support of a 'continuing sovereignty' view. This question brings us back to a consideration of how it is that the ultimate rule of recognition evolves.

---

[33] Hart (1961) (n. 26 above) 118.

The possibility of self-embracing laws

In his book *On Law and Justice*, the Danish jurist, Alf Ross had looked more closely at Kelsen's basic norm and discovered a problem. The basic norm was, in Ross's first opinion on the matter, the norm which provided for the amendment of the constitution, there being no other higher legal norm which provided for the constitution's validity. Ross then argued that the basic norm could not provide for its own amendment without running into problems of self-reference. That is, if the rule on amendment were itself amended and replaced using the original rule then the new rule could not at the same time and without logical transgression both be based on the original rule and be the rule for which there is no higher justification. This complex logical argument produced the disturbing conclusion that self-embracing legal rules such as the constitutional amendment procedures of most countries (which were assumed to govern not only amendment of other constitutional provisions but also amendment of the amendment procedures themselves) were in fact logically impossible or self-contradictory; and in the Commonwealth case it cast doubt on whether the Queen-in-the-United Kingdom Parliament could provide for its replacement whether in 1931, 1947, 1982 or 1986. To the extent that it was commonly believed that the first rule on constitutional amendment *could* be used to amend itself, Ross stated that this was not in fact 'constitutional change' or change which could be related back to the basic norm, but rather a disguised legal revolution or 'magical act'.[34]

In order to understand Ross better we have to remember that he, together with Kelsen, was interested in examining the legal system in terms of its abstract logical or cognitive requirements. As a system based ultimately on the basic norm, a legal system by definition changed logically and in accordance with the basic norm. In that way the basic norm could explain the validity and norm-ativity of legal rules within the system and, at the same time, explain the coher-ence of that system over time.

In 1964, Professor Hart replied to Ross. With great care, he pointed out that self-embracing interpretations of the basic norm or ultimate rule of recognition were not only possible but logically coherent as well. Hart observed that Ross had ignored the temporal element which is relevant in legal as opposed to abstract logical problems. When, for example, a rule for constitutional amendment is used to provide for its own replacement, it is correct to view that as a legal change rather than as a magical act. The original rule on amendment is valid and effective until it is itself used to provide for a new rule on amendment which only at that moment becomes valid and effective and so replaces the old.[35] Accordingly, Hart argued as

---

[34] A. Ross, *On Law and Justice* (London: Stevens, 1958) 81.
[35] H.L.A. Hart, 'Self-Referring Laws' (1964) in H.L.A. Hart (ed.) *Essays in Jurisprudence and Philosophy* (Oxford: Oxford University Press, 1983) 170, 177 (hereinafter cited as Hart (1964).

he had before that continuing and self-embracing amendment procedures were 'both intelligible as constitutional arrangements'.[36]

If we remember Hart's comments regarding the indeterminate nature of the ultimate rule of recognition and the formalist error of assuming that every situation is covered in advance by a rule, his conclusions regarding the so-called problem of self-reference fall neatly into place.[37] Hart was more concerned with validity in legal systems as a question of fact or observance. He was more interested in momentary systems and validity than in dynamic systems and continuity.[38] Hart observed that the validity of legal rules in a system could be satisfactorily explained without necessarily determining in advance whether the ultimate rule of recognition (usually the procedure for constitutional amendment) was continuing or self-embracing in nature. That question would only arise if a legal answer became necessary. In the meantime, legal observers might make suggestions and predictions, but the validity of rules in the legal system could not be said to depend on clarity and certainty in advance of legal determination.

Ross replied to Hart and other critics in 1969. He acknowledged that Hart's 'temporal' refutation of the problem of self-reference was accurate in terms of legal considerations. Ross nonetheless insisted that, as a matter of logic, an original basic norm (relating to an amendment procedure) would naturally contradict a subsequent basic norm (relating to a new amendment procedure) which purported to replace it. While Hart was prepared to say that both continuing and self-embracing interpretations were potentially available for the ultimate rule, Ross's logical system required that 'the basic norm of the legal system must be unchangeable'.[39] Ross therefore recanted his earlier views identifying the amendment procedure as the basic norm and in its place he offered a norm requiring adherence to the original amendment procedure *or to any subsequent amendment procedure derived from and replacing that procedure.* This formulation of the basic norm allowed Ross to admit the possibility in law of self-embracing change, notably in the amendment procedure, while denying the possibility of a self-embracing basic norm.

In the end, then, both Hart and Ross acknowledged the possibility of self-embracing interpretations of the rule on constitutional amendment. For Hart it was just that—a *possible* interpretation of the penumbral content of the ultimate rule of recognition. Unless a question of validity arose involving the rule governing amendment, the core of the rule might be quite clear but the penumbra (i.e. continuing or self-embracing?) still uncertain. Ross's revised

---

[36] Hart (1964) (n. 35 above) 177.

[37] Hart dealt with the self-embracing/continuing sovereignty issue in his discussion of the uncertainty in the ultimate rule of recognition elsewhere in *The Concept of Law.* Hart (1961) (n. 26 above) 144 et seq.

[38] See Finnis (1973) (n. 24 above) 55, for an excellent discussion of these concepts.

[39] A. Ross, 'On Self-Reference and a Puzzle in Constitutional Law' (1969) 78 Mind 1, 21.

arguments admitted the possibility of a self-embracing amendment procedure, and we can presume that he could also have conceived of its 'continuing' alternative.[40]

If the Hart-Ross debate was helpful at all, despite its exasperating complexity, it did serve to highlight the fact that neither continuing nor self-embracing versions of sovereignty could be logically preferred but that one or the other version would have to be identified in any legal system if ever a question arose involving the true nature of that sovereignty.[41] Until that moment, at least on Hart's view of the matter, the question could remain safely unresolved.

If we return to the question that was being considered before discussing the Hart-Ross debate, it can now be stated with more sophistication. Depending on whether we take the Hart approach or the Kelsen-Ross approach, we will want to know how it is that courts (or legal commentators before them) can determine the following:

(1) What is the ultimate rule of recognition and how, if at all, can it change or evolve?

(2) What is the basic norm?

Before attempting to answer those questions, it may be useful to consider the work of John Finnis and Joseph Raz, in which the Kelsen-Ross approach was discredited and the Hart approach improved upon.

Continuity and legal systems

John Finnis's thoughts on this question were also useful in order to help to explain the type of constitutional transitions which took place in Australia, Canada and New Zealand. How was it that an Act of the Westminster Parliament could be said to sever the British legal link without disturbing the validity of existing local laws, constitutional or other, all of these having been brought into force—directly or indirectly—by the authority of that same Westminster Parliament? He agreed that Ross's problem of self-reference was not an insurmountable obstacle, but Finnis acknowledged that Ross had identified an important question regarding the validity of legal rules which derive from, but subsequently replace or eliminate, those validating rules.[42] Finnis proposed that

---

[40] According to the 'continuing' alternative, all amendments to the amendment procedure would be viewed only as subordinate 'statutes' and therefore amendable at all times using the *original* procedure. This corresponded with the system in the United Kingdom according to the prevailing view if one considered the Queen-in-Parliament as an amendment procedure. See also M.J. Detmold, *The Australian Commonwealth: A Fundamental Analysis of its Constitution* (Sydney: The Law Book Company, 1985) 201–210.

[41] R.T.E. Latham had made a similar point in 'The Law and the Commonwealth' in W.K. Hancock (ed.) *Survey of British Commonwealth Affairs*, Vol. 1 (London: Oxford University Press, 1937) 522, 524.   [42] Finnis (1973) (n. 24 above) 54.

the rule of recognition must include a general principle or rule of identification which could be expressed as follows: 'A law once validly brought into being, in accordance with criteria of validity *then in force*, remains valid until *either* it expires according to its own terms or terms implied at its creation, *or* it is repealed in accordance with conditions of repeal in force *at the time of repeal*.'[43] This principle truly seemed to 'make sense of the history and practice of legal systems and lawyers' and it provided 'a present guide to actions which take place and have effect in the future'.[44] Accordingly, it seems appropriate to adopt it.

In the Canadian context, for example, Finnis's analysis not only confirmed the validity of pre-1982 constitutional and ordinary laws passed at Westminster, but it also explained how the Canada Act 1982 could at one and the same time establish the validity of, *inter alia*, Part V of the Constitution Act, 1982 on amendment *and* terminate the power of Westminster to legislate for Canada, thereby leaving matters to be dealt with solely on Canadian terms. Effectively, this was Hart's point, examined earlier, in defence of self-embracing sovereignty; but Finnis's analysis also made clear that this was a point which applied beyond the self-reflexive provisions of a constitutional amendment procedure.

With Finnis, then, we can see how the process of achieving constitutional independence required different analysis at the level of history, logic and law. There was clearly no need to deny either the historical link to the Westminster Parliament or the conferral of legal validity which that link provided, and no need to fear that a rule of logic had been violated so as to have rendered the process incoherent and indefensible. In law there was a justification for a local court ignoring any new enactment by the Westminster Parliament, even one preceded by the repeal of the independence-granting legislation. There was nothing inevitable in this legal conclusion, of course, but it would have been surprising had there been no legal explanation for the prevailing local under-standings of the strictly legal processes by which constitutional independence has been achieved.

If a self-embracing interpretation of the highest rule in the legal system was logically possible and if that self-embracing process could indeed provide for a new rule and at the same time provide for the new rule's validity, then the only questions which remained were, first, how was it that the ultimate rule of recognition evolved, and secondly, how was it that the Australian, Canadian and New Zealand ultimate rules of recognition had evolved. The writings of Joseph Raz were relevant to the first question and were also useful in attempting to answer the second.

Raz first gathered together his ideas on this subject in *The Concept of a Legal System*. He rejected Kelsen's criterion of constitutional continuity as the proper

---

[43] Finnis (1973) (n. 24 above) 63 (Finnis's emphasis). Brian Slattery has proposed a similar principle in 'The Independence of Canada' (1983) 5 Sup Ct L Rev 384, 393.

[44] Finnis (1973) (n. 24 above) 63.

criterion for the identity of a legal system:

The continuity of legal systems is not necessarily disrupted by the creation of new original laws. Nor is the fact that the creation of law is *authorized* by a law belonging to a certain legal system a sufficient proof that the authorized law *belongs* to that system. A country may be granted independence by a law of another country authorizing its laws; nevertheless, its laws form a separate legal system.[45]

In a subsequent work, Raz also made clear that in his view Hart's rule of recognition did not provide an adequate analytical tool to solve the problem at hand:

Nor does the rule of recognition solve the problem of the continuity of legal systems. That one legal system comes to an end and another takes its place manifests itself in a change of rule of recognition, for each legal system has a different rule of recognition. The rule of recognition, however, is a customary rule; hence it is constantly in a process of change. What changes are consistent with the continued existence of the same rule, and what changes compel the admission that a new rule has replaced the old one? . . . Hart's theory provides no clue as to how to draw the conceptual distinction . . . If his theory fails to provide a complete solution to the problem of identity it is because he overlooked not only part of the answer but also a whole question: that of the relation of law and state.[46]

Like Hart, Raz acknowledged the importance of courts or 'primary law-applying institutions' and their view of legality from the internal perspective of that legal system,[47] but he went further. One needed to know something about the political system and 'to distinguish between the courts which are organs of that political system and those which are not'.[48] Therefore, in considering whether, and if so how, the ultimate rule of the Australian, Canadian and New Zealand legal systems have evolved, it is crucial (though not determinative) on Raz's terms to recognise that since 1926 or so they have been politically independent and that as of 2004 they are all now judicially independent. The Australian High Court, Supreme Court of Canada and New Zealand Supreme Court now consider themselves part of their respective local legal systems, not, as in the case of their predecessor, the Judicial Committee of the Privy Council, part of an Imperial or, subsequently, pan-Commonwealth legal system. Raz's observations seem to have a great deal of bearing on the type of prediction that we might wish to make regarding the evolution and present nature of the ultimate rule of the Australian, Canadian and New Zealand legal systems.

After asserting the fundamental interrelationship of a theory of state and a theory of law and legal system, Raz set out his own ideas on the problem of the

---

[45] J. Raz, *The Concept of a Legal System* (2nd edn, Oxford: Clarendon Press, 1980) 188 (emphasis added).   [46] J. Raz (n. 29 above) 98.

[47] '. . . a momentary legal system contains all, and only all, the laws recognised by a primary law-applying organ which it institutes.' Raz (1980) (n. 45 above) 192.

[48] Raz (1979) (n. 29 above) 80.

identity of a legal system:

It follows that since the continuity of a legal system is tied to the continuity of the political system, the former is affected by the fate of the non-legal norms that happen to form part of the political system concerned. However, emphasizing the importance of the fate of the non-legal norms to the continuity of the legal system does not mean that these are the only factors affecting continuity. The substance of my contention is that whatever form one's ultimate account of continuity takes, it must in view of the relation between law and state, be based on the interaction of legal and non-legal norms, and the extent and manner of their change; and secondly, that among the legal norms concerned some are more relevant than others. Since the continuity of the legal system is fundamentally a function of the continuity of the political system, political laws are more relevant than others.[49]

It seems fair to conclude from Raz that a principle similar to the ultimate rule of recognition is useful but must be supplemented by considerations of the under-lying and interrelated presence of social, political and historical factors before an explanation can be had for why the ultimate rule of recognition changes in such a way that it can be said that a new legal system exists independent of an older one.

It seems clear, following Raz, that social, political and historical factors must be brought to bear to some extent in order to determine the identity of a legal system. It is therefore important to know the politics and other allegiances of the judges who sit in the highest courts in Australia, Canada and New Zealand. At the most basic level, it is relevant that these judges are nationals of their coun-tries, with the politics and allegiances that usually flow from that fact. However, can it be right that change at the ultimate level is determined by judges?

Many would reply in the negative, including, for example, Jeffrey Goldsworthy.[50] Goldsworthy's recent book, *The Sovereignty of Parliament*, is dedicated to showing that judges historically have not had and philosophically should not have the power to impose limits on Parliament, or, in more theor-etical terms, to change the rule of recognition. Goldsworthy makes a strong and well-documented argument; however, he pays little attention to a different but closely related question which is of interest to us here. Even if courts should not impose limits on Parliament (and thereby change the rule of recognition) of their own volition, why should they not heed such limits if they are imposed by Parliament itself? What role does Parliament have in influencing a change in the rule of recognition? This is the question which interests us. Neil MacCormick's recent writing regarding the United Kingdom-European Community legal rela-tionship has addressed precisely this point.[51]

---

[49] Raz (1979) (n. 29 above) 100.

[50] J. Goldsworthy, *The Sovereignty of Parliament* (Oxford: Oxford University Press, 1999).

[51] For discussion of Goldsworthy's and MacCormick's recent work, see P. Oliver, 'Sovereignty in the Twenty-First Century' (2003) 14 KCLJ 137.

Change in the ultimate rule of recognition

It is worth considering MacCormick's work[52] in some detail for a number of reasons. First, he is one of those who has considered the concepts of sovereignty and legal system most carefully in recent years. Secondly, his familiarity with and affinity towards writers such as Kelsen, Hart, Finnis and Raz provide easy and obvious points of comparison with the arguments which have just been set out. Thirdly, though MacCormick focuses his analysis on the Member State-European Union relationship, it is easy to transpose that analysis to Commonwealth-United Kingdom relationships.

MacCormick's theoretical analysis applied to Europe worked at two different levels. First there was what we could call the 'micro' analysis in which he tried to explain the United Kingdom's relationship to the European Union in an extremely careful analysis of Wade, Hart (especially) and (to a much lesser extent) Dworkin. The emphasis here was on the United Kingdom's ultimate rule of recognition, and therefore the 'micro' focus was on the United Kingdom Parliament and its powers. MacCormick also provided a 'macro' analysis which set out to explain the creation and present structure of a new European legal order. We shall consider 'micro' analysis at some length, though the 'macro' analysis will be also noted briefly towards the end of this discussion.

At the 'micro' level, the debate was really about 'how it is possible to change a constitution in its fundamentals, while still acting in a constitutional and lawful manner and spirit'.[53] This was as much about respect for the rule of law (understood as respect for legality) as it was about sovereignty. According to MacCormick, it demanded 'some satisfactory account, necessarily a theoretical account, of what the foundations of a legal-constitutional order are, and how it was possible for these foundational elements in some way to regulate their own amendment or change'.[54] So far the Europe/Commonwealth analogy was completely intact. MacCormick was at pains to emphasise the role of the United Kingdom Parliament in accomplishing such change: 'The question is: can the *legislature* amended the rule of recognition by adding to it new criteria of recognition of valid law? Must the courts recognise and give effect to legislation that purports to bring this about? Is any special *legislative process* called for in this case?'[55] In the Commonwealth case, the legislature (the Westminster Parliament) amended the rule of recognition in order to remove an old criterion of recognition (itself); and the issue was not so much about whether a special procedure was required as about whether this was possible at all.

[52] See, in particular, N. MacCormick, *Questioning Sovereignty: Law, State, and Nation in the European Commonwealth* (Oxford: Oxford University Press, 1999) and 'Beyond the Sovereign State' (1993) 56 MLR 1.   [53] MacCormick (1999) (n. 52 above) 81.
[54] ibid., 81–2.   [55] ibid., 86 (emphasis added throughout).

MacCormick began his analysis of the United Kingdom/European Union relationship begun by the European Communities Act 1972 by asking a question which had strong Commonwealth resonances: 'Was there a revolution . . . ?'.[56] He noted that the main advocate of an affirmative response to this question was, in Europe as in the Commonwealth, H.W.R. Wade.[57] It may be helpful to recap Wade's views here with help from MacCormick, including Wade's more recent writing regarding Europe post-1972 and post-*Factortame*.[58]

MacCormick pointed out that in arguing that there was a revolution after 1972, Wade was not referring to 'bloodshed and violence and tumbrels rolling to the guillotine' but only to 'a "technical revolution" in the legal sense'.[59] In Wade's long-standing view of United Kingdom constitutional fundamentals,[60] parliamentary sovereignty in its traditional, absolute form was a pre-legal, historical, or political *fact*. As a pre-legal fact, it was immune from legal change either by Parliament or by the courts' moulding of the common law. Any purportedly 'legal' alterations to the traditional form of sovereignty (such as the *Factortame* rendition of the European Communities Act 1972) must therefore have been revolutions, in Wade's view, however respectful of law the relevant process may have appeared to be. It was precisely because of the 'atmosphere of harmony' that 'the naked fact of revolution was not so easy to discern beneath its elaborate legal dress', according to Wade.[61] Wade's rendering of the doctrine of parliamentary sovereignty pre-1972 and pre-*Factortame* was Dicey's traditional, continuing version: 'the rule was that an Act of Parliament in proper form had absolutely overriding effect, except that it could not fetter the corresponding power of future Parliaments'.[62] In Wade's view, when the House of Lords decided the *Factortame* case it recognised the 1972 Parliament's ability to fetter a later Parliament. As such, the legal basis of the United Kingdom Constitution had been altered by a procedure not contemplated in the previous rule. A legal revolution had therefore occurred. Wade adopted Hart's terminology to characterise this revolutionary change as a change in the United Kingdom's 'ultimate rule of recognition'.[63]

An alternative view, critical of Wade, acknowledged that a fundamental change had occurred but rejected the idea of a revolution, even in a technical sense. This line of argument has been pursued in a Dworkinian vein by T.R.S. Allan.[64] MacCormick's version, discussed below, used a Hartian framework. Whether inspired by Dworkin or by Hart, these approaches were of interest in the Commonwealth context because of their accent on constitutional

---

[56] MacCormick (1999) (n. 52 above) 79.

[57] ibid., 79. See H.W.R. Wade, 'Sovereignty—Revolution or Evolution?' (1996) 112 LQR 568.

[58] *Factortame v Secretary of State for Transport (No 2)* [1991] AC 603 (HL).

[59] MacCormick (1999) (n. 52 above) 79.   [60] Wade (1955) (n. 14 above).

[61] ibid., 191.   [62] Wade (1996) (n. 57 above) 574.   [63] Wade (1996), 574.

[64] See T.R.S. Allan, *Law, Liberty and Justice* (Oxford: Clarendon Press, 1993) and 'Parliamentary Sovereignty: Law, Politics and Revolution' (1997) 113 LQR 443.

continuity. We will have to see whether they can explain constitutional independence as well.

At the centre of MacCormick's 'micro' analysis, his argument is as follows. First, MacCormick described Hart as identifying 'whatever the Queen in Parliament enacts is law' as the ' "supreme criterion" of recognition within the "rule of recognition" '.[65] MacCormick's paraphrase of Wade's pre-1972 understanding of the doctrine of parliamentary sovereignty had a different emphasis: 'Parliament has an unrestricted and general power to enact valid law...'[66] MacCormick noted that whereas Wade focused on the *power* to enact laws, Hart's emphasis was the other way round: '[Hart's version] is explicitly about ascribing the status "law" to whatever (in the way of a rule) Parliament enacts, or has enacted.'[67] It was truly a 'rule of recognition', whereas Wade's power-based formula was a 'rule of change', again in Hartian language.[68] On MacCormick's analysis, the change (or power) aspect and the recognition aspect were two parts of the sovereignty (or supremacy) whole. MacCormick pointed out that 'a necessary condition for coherence in a workable constitution for a law-state' was that there had to be 'reciprocal matching between the criteria for recognising valid law, and the criteria for validly exercising the power to enact law'.[69] He concluded from this that: 'The doctrine of the sovereignty of Parliament is not itself a "rule", but indeed a "doctrine" with two aspects.... Parliament's power of change [and]... the judges' obligation... to implement any validly enacted Act of Parliament as a highest source of law.'[70] Wade's difficulties in explaining the process of the United Kingdom entry into the European Community arose, in MacCormick's eyes, as a result of his conflation of the rule of change and the rule of recognition. If MacCormick was right, then presumably Wade's difficulties in explaining the legal acquisition of constitutional independence in the Commonwealth lay in the same area.

MacCormick then faced up to the key questions of his 'micro' analysis. Once the supreme criterion in the rule of recognition had been identified, was it possible, as he conceived it, for the United Kingdom Parliament to use the power of change to amend the rule of recognition?[71] And if it was possible for

---

[65] MacCormick (1999) (n. 52 above) 83.   [66] ibid., 83.   [67] ibid., 84.

[68] Hart (1961) (n. 26 above) ch. 5.

[69] 'This necessary reciprocal reference belongs to what some consider the inevitable self-referential quality built into systems as such. MacCormick (1999) (n. 52 above) 85. See G. Teubner, *Law as an Autopoietic System*, A. Bankowska and R. Adler (trans), Z. Bankowski (ed.) (Oxford: Blackwell, 1993) 19–24.

[70] MacCormick (1999) (n. 52 above) 85–6. Both of these aspects—Parliament's power and the judges' obligation—are based in the common law according to MacCormick.

[71] MacCormick's vocabulary is unfortunate here. Parliament cannot literally amend or change the rule of recognition. The matter is more complicated than MacCormick indicates. Hart makes clear that the existence of the rule of recognition is a matter of fact not legal creation. It remains true, however, that by virtue of its position in the hierarchy of criteria in the rule of recognition, Parliament has a potentially unlimited ability to propose both new primary rules and new criteria for potential recognition as secondary rules. That is to say, Parliament has both a legislative and a constitution-making function. Where Parliament enacts, say, the Scotland Act 1998, we can be

Parliament to enact such an amendment would the courts then be obliged to recognise it?[72]

MacCormick must have been right in stating at the outset that there can be 'no all-purpose theoretical answer' to these questions.[73] He also came closer to our intuitive reactions in stating that 'nothing in the general theory of law should exclude the possibility of such change'.[74] It has always struck many as a point against Wade that a Parliament which has gone to great lengths to respect the rule of law at the highest constitutional level (in granting independence to colonies or in joining the European Community, for example) should be found to have done the opposite, i.e. to have engaged in an act of legal revolution or law-breaking, even of the merely technical sort.[75] MacCormick unambiguously accepted that 'Parliament's powers include power to enact changes to the rule of recognition . . . '[76] This was an outright endorsement of the 'revised' or 'self-embracing' view of parliamentary sovereignty. However, he then added what may seem an odd rider: 'but they do not include the power to change it in such a way as to disable Parliament from reversing in the future any such change

quite confident that the new proposal for recognition—Acts of the Scottish Parliament—will be recognised, because Parliament's power to enact laws of this type was already recognised, already part of the core of the rule of recognition. However, where Parliament enacted the European Communities Act 1972, its powers were uncertain, part of what Hart calls the penumbra of the rule of recognition. We had to wait for the *Factortame* case or its equivalent to confirm the fact of recognition. Where the United Kingdom Parliament enacted, e.g., the Canada Act 1982, in which Westminster terminated its powers *vis-à-vis* Canada, we had to wait until the *Quebec Veto Reference* (*Reference re Objection to a Resolution to Amend the Constitution* r [1982] 2 SCR 793) later that year to learn that it had been effective in doing so. Accordingly, it is wrong to imply, as MacCormick did, that having identified the power of change as a mirror-image to the rule of recognition all manner of constitutional change is possible. Significant constitutional change may indeed be possible where recognition can confidently be predicted, as with the devolution legislation and constitutional independence legislation; however, on more controversial matters, the proposed constitutional change is only confirmed when the courts eventually shed light on the rule of recognition's previously penumbral areas, as occurred in the *Factortame* case.

It was also wrong, however, to imply that when the courts do eventually recognise more controversial constitutional change of this type it is entirely a matter for the judges and the common law. (See, e.g., *Thoburn v Sunderland City Council* [2003] QB 151 (Div Ct)). The rule of recognition may well be a question of fact, but we know that in legal systems in the Westminster tradition it is constitutionally improper for courts to recognise law according to their own fiat. Put another way, the rule of recognition is duty-imposing not power-conferring in this respect. (See Raz (1980) (n. 45 above) 199.) If the rule of recognition in the United Kingdom eventually changed as a result of the United Kingdom's entry into the European Community, that was a result of both *Parliament's* proposal of a new criterion and a new hierarchy in the rule of recognition, as well as the *courts'* acceptance of that proposal. MacCormick overestimated the significance of the former, while others overestimated the importance of the latter. A true account lay somewhere in between, in the relationship between power and recognition. There is therefore both a legal and a political aspect to the roles of both Parliament and the courts which needs to be explored more carefully than is possible here. For a helpful analysis of the courts' political role in hard constitutional cases, see N. Barber, 'Sovereignty Re-examined: The Courts, Parliament, and Statutes' (2000) 20 OJLS 131.

In the analysis which follows, references to changing or amending the rule of recognition should be read in the light of the foregoing discussion.

[72] MacCormick (1999) (n. 52 above) 86.   [73] ibid., 86.   [74] ibid., 86.
[75] See, e.g., Finnis (1973) (n. 24 above) 52.   [76] MacCormick (1999) (n. 52 above) 86.

that it makes'. This rider did not present insurmountable obstacles in the European context, where other Member States have claimed something similar.[77] However, it did present difficulties in the Commonwealth context. Was the latter type of 'disabling' not exactly what the Westminster Parliament purported to do in granting independence to its colonies? Perhaps it only applied in the European context. We will have to look more closely at MacCormick's arguments in a moment in order to evaluate whether this conclusion regarding the limits of self-embracing legislation was correct, but first we need to complete our look at MacCormick's analysis of change in the rule of recognition.

MacCormick pulled these various strands of argument at the 'micro' level together and proposed a more credible alternative interpretation to the Wade 'revolution': 'What this interpretation says is that Parliament did in 1972 have the power it then exercised to amend the rule of recognition by adding a new criterion of validity at the highest sub-constitutional level.'[78] As argued earlier, the equivalent of this argument in the Commonwealth context is that the Westminster Parliament could also amend the rule of recognition by subtracting an old criterion of validity (itself) from the Australia, Canadian and New Zealand legal systems.

What should we make of MacCormick's analysis? It should be noted, first, that the identification of a rule of change as a matter of theoretical analysis does not necessarily lead to the conclusion that change to the supreme criterion of the rule of recognition is actually permitted in any given legal system. This is essentially the point made by Wade and other adherents to the traditional approach to sovereignty. Using MacCormick's revival of Hartian vocabulary, they might argue that the content of the power of change is a mirror image of the rule of recognition as *they* understand it, i.e. the power of change allows modifications to all criteria in the rule of recognition *other than* to the Queen-in-Parliament. So the Scotland Act 1998 could, for example, add Acts of the Scottish Parliament to the list of criteria in the United Kingdom rule of recognition, but it could not restrict or terminate the Westminster Parliament's ability to repeal that Act. On this view, Parliament's absolute, continuing sovereignty is reflected in both the rule of recognition and in the rule of change, making change to the supreme criterion impossible. Presumably MacCormick glossed over this point because, in his view, the *Factortame* case confirmed that the power of change was available even to modify the supreme criterion in the rule of recognition.

It was argued earlier, that contrary to long-standing assumptions about the nature of Parliament's sovereignty, much of that which has for so long been taken for granted is in truth what Hart would call a 'penumbral' issue, in the sense that the law has not yet taken a clear position on a range of important sovereignty-related issues, including whether those powers are ultimately

---

[77] See P. Craig, 'Britain in the European Union' in Jowell and Oliver (2004) (n. 7 above) 88, 103.
[78] MacCormick (1999) (n. 52 above) 89.

continuing or self-embracing.[79] We knew, because it was often stated by courts, academics and other constitutional commentators that Parliament could pass any law whatever. This was the first part of Dicey's rendition of Parliament's sovereignty. We did not know, however, whether this state of affairs could be changed. It was quite conceivable that it could not. Furthermore, it was reasonable for the courts to assume that they could not change this arrangement on their own initiative. This, then, explained the second part of Dicey's rendition of parliamentary sovereignty, i.e. the statement that no institution, notably the courts, could challenge Parliament's sovereignty. Confirmation of this proposition could also be found in the law books, of course. Thus far, the core of sovereignty seemed clear. What then of *Parliament's* powers of change?

Parliament's own claims to a power to change existing arrangements were much stronger than those of the courts or any other institution. We need to re-emphasise that the third part of Dicey's rendition of parliamentary sovereignty—the proposition that no Parliament can bind a future Parliament— was based on misleading logic[80] and exceptionally weak case law. The paucity of decent case law was based on an obvious factor, i.e. the extreme rarity of Parliament even attempting to bind future Parliaments. The fog here was thick. Or, to use Hart's terminology, the penumbra was dominant.

There has been a great deal of constitutional commentary on three cases which are said, by Wade amongst others, to confirm the proposition that no Parliament can bind a future Parliament: *Vauxhall Estates Ltd v Liverpool Corporation*,[81] *Ellen Street Estates Ltd v Minister of Health*[82] and *British Coal Corporation*.[83] These cases were discussed and their supposed authority doubted in Chapter 3.

---

[79] Hart (1961) (n. 26 above) 146:

Yet, as with every other rule, the fact that the rule of parliamentary sovereignty is determinate at this point does not mean that it is determinate at all points. Questions can be raised about it to which at present there is no answer which is clearly right or wrong. These can be settled only by choice, made by someone to whose choices in this matter authority is eventually accorded.

Hart (1961), 119–20:

. . . in relation to the high constitutional matter of a legal system's ultimate criteria of validity . . . All rules involve recognising or classifying particular cases as instances of general terms, and in the case of everything which we are prepared to call a rule it is possible to distinguish clear central cases, where it certainly applies and others where there are reasons for both asserting and denying that it applies. Nothing can eliminate this duality of a core of certainty and a penumbra of doubt . . . This imparts to all rules a fringe of vagueness or 'open texture', and this may affect the rule of recognition specifying the ultimate criteria used in the identification of the law . . .

[80] As we saw in Ch. 3 above, the 'logical' reason behind the rule that no Parliament could bind a future Parliament applied only if one assumed that Parliament had to remain sovereign in the continuing sense. Furthermore, the argument that each generation must be free to make its own constitutional arrangements overlooks the fact that, according to the idea of continuing sovereignty, each generation is *prohibited* from entrenching parts of its Constitution if that is what it deems sensible. For discussion of these and other points see Oliver (2003) (n. 51 above).

[81] *Vauxhall Estates Ltd v Liverpool Corporation* [1932] 1 KB 733 (KBD).
[82] *Ellen Street Estates Ltd v Minister of Health* [1934] 1 KB 590 (CA).
[83] *British Coal Corporation v The King* [1935] AC 500 (PC).

Nonetheless, we cannot ignore the fact that the *Vauxhall, Ellen Street* and *British Coal Corporation* cases had the potential to leave very different sorts of legal legacies. The first, and most popular (though least justified, it has been argued), was that they stood for categorical rejection of *any* attempt by Parliament to bind a future Parliament. Those who cite the broad proposition that no Parliament can bind a future Parliament usually cite these cases by way of support, thereby giving the impression that the matter is clear—part of the core of the rule of recognition—and thereby confirming the continuing nature of Parliament's sovereignty. However, they are anything but clear.

Therefore, a second sort of interpretation was possible. In all three cases, the judges' reasons on this interpretation extended only so far as the weak facts of each case. Focusing on the *Vauxhall* and *Ellen Street* cases in particular, they simply established that language such as that used in the Acquisition of Land (Assessment of Compensation) Act 1919 could not bind a future Parliament. Some of the judges, strongly influenced by the Diceyan dogmas of the early 1930s rather than by case law, doubted whether *any* language would suffice, but such views were clearly obiter dicta. Lord Sankey's famous words in the *British Coal Corporation* case were clearly obiter dicta as well, but it is often forgotten that they were said in the context of Canada's explicit decision in 1931 to retain the United Kingdom Parliament's unlimited legislative powers *vis-à-vis* Canada in order to guarantee amendment of its Constitution.[84] There is much to be said for this second interpretation, according to which the proposition that no Parliament can bind a future Parliament remains to the greatest extent penumbral for lack of clear attempts by Parliament to do so and clear case law in response.[85]

However, a third sort of interpretation is also possible, here seemingly favoured by MacCormick. This interpretation has a close affinity with the second, the main difference being the reading of the key cases. The third view is

[84] Statute of Westminster, 1931, s. 7.

[85] In one of the few cases (as opposed to the many commentaries) which considered the *Vauxhall* or *Ellen Street* cases after the 1930s, *Manuel v Attorney-General* (1983), the Court of Appeal was prepared to assume without deciding that 'Parliament can effectively tie the hands of its successors', although Slade LJ noted the potential conflict between this proposition and 'the general statement of the law made by Maughan L.J. in *Ellen Street*' and similar statements by Scrutton LJ. Slade LJ noted support available for the opposing argument (at 104–5). In *IRC v Collco Dealings Ltd* [1962] AC 1, 13 the House of Lords conveyed the meaning of the *Ellen Street* case in the most limited terms possible: 'see the observations of Scrutton and Maugham L.JJ. . . . on the effect to be given to subsequent legislation which is inconsistent with an earlier statutory provision'. If the latter interpretation reflected its true import, then there was considerable scope for Parliament to attempt other, clearer and more effective ways to bind future Parliaments.

Laws LJ in *Thoburn v Sunderland City Council* [2003] QB 151 (Div Ct) responded to counsel's suggestion that he 'forget the constitutional place in our law of the rule that Parliament cannot bind its successor, which is the engine of the doctrine of implied repeal' by stating that 'the law of England disallows any such assumption. Parliament cannot bind its successors by stipulating against repeal . . .'. (184) Laws LJ's singular boldness (compared to other judges at least) in stating the rule so categorically is perhaps explained by the fact that he was in the process of declaring that the common law had modified the 'traditional doctrine' (185).

that the *Vauxhall* and *Ellen Street* cases, and perhaps other more obscure authorities as well, did indeed establish the proposition that no Parliament can bind a future Parliament. That much was part of the core of the rule of recognition, on this interpretation. This *appeared* also to confirm that continuing sovereignty was the rule in the United Kingdom. However, the appearance was just that. For lurking in the penumbra was the possibility that Parliament had always retained a (self-embracing) power of constitutional change allowing it to alter the rule that no Parliament can bind a future Parliament if ever it wished (though perhaps not to the point of binding Parliament permanently and entirely). An important question, already identified in the second interpretation, was how Parliament had to indicate its wish to do so.

Famously, Parliament purported to bind future Parliaments in the European Communities Act 1972. The language was infinitely clearer than its precursor, the 1919 Act seen in the *Vauxhall* and *Ellen Street* cases, though the politics of the early 1970s (and perhaps even the enduring legacy of Dicey) encouraged a certain amount of convenient ambiguity in the drafting of the Act. In the *Factortame* case, the House of Lords confirmed the courts' willingness to recognise the wish of the 1972 Parliament. If the first interpretation of the *Vauxhall* and *Ellen Street* cases was correct then this was a revolutionary decision, at least in legal terms. However, under either the second or third interpretations it was as legal as could be, representing no more than the movement of certain previously penumbral questions into the core of United Kingdom legal understanding.

What are the implications of the subtle differences between the second interpretation, favoured in this book, and the third interpretation, favoured by MacCormick? First, MacCormick's version allowed the United Kingdom to bind itself though not permanently and completely. This sort of partial binding is sufficient for the time being for United Kingdom-European Union relations;[86] however, it is not enough for Australia, Canada and New Zealand which natur-ally want a permanent and complete binding of the Westminster Parliament with respect to their affairs, constitutional and other. Secondly, for the reason just mentioned, the second interpretation (for Commonwealth independence or European Union) and the third interpretation (for European Union) allow us to reject Wade's revolutionary explanation of Commonwealth independence legislation and European Union. If the second interpretation is correct then legal explanations of these events are all the easier: while it remained an uncertain matter until the *Factortame* case, it was always possible for Parliament to attempt to bind itself by any and all means so long as these means were clearer, ideally much clearer, than those employed in the 1919 Act.

---

[86] Admittedly it contradicts the views expressed by the European Court of Justice in cases such as *Costa* [1964] ECR 585, *Simmenthal* [1978] ECR 629 and *Factortame*; however, MacCormick and others point out that the European legal order can withstand conflicting claims to ultimate sovereignty so long as no claim is pushed to the limit.

If we accept the third interpretation, then it is still possible to conclude that something more fundamental, though not necessarily illegal, has occurred. As noted already, MacCormick, like Hart, conceded that the pre-1972 rule was that no Parliament could bind a future Parliament. For most commentators, this concession would have been enough to confirm and consolidate the continuing nature of Parliament's powers. However, MacCormick's identification of a rule of change opened up even more rarefied penumbral questions regarding whether Parliament ever had the power to change the most fundamental criteria of the rule of recognition, whether it had the power to amend the amending formula, so to speak. And it turned out that the answer was affirmative. This third interpretation then became available, in addition to the second interpretation, in order to explain the acquisition of Australian, Canadian and New Zealand constitutional independence. The logic of MacCormick's argument implied that such an explanation would be possible even from a United Kingdom point of view. However, while desirable perhaps, this was not essential, for it was sufficient, as we shall see, if the Australian, Canadian and New Zealand legal systems took this self-embracing view of the Westminster Parliament's powers of change, even if the United Kingdom persisted in taking a contrary view.

One way of understanding this embellished third interpretation was to say that, although the constitutional rules of the United Kingdom were once as Dicey described them, in addition to Parliament's legislative powers there was also what in other constitutional systems would be referred to as a power of constitutional amendment. In the United Kingdom this constitutional amendment power was disguised by the fact that it used the same machinery as the legislative power. However, although the machinery for constitutional amendment and legislation was the same, only the clearest words sufficed to accomplish the former, especially if the amendment was to have forward-reaching application.[87] Counsel in the *Vauxhall* and *Ellen Street* cases had tried to argue that the 1919 Act was sufficiently clear, whereas the judges in the cases remained wholly unconvinced, rightly it would seem. That which is required, then, was either a two-stage constitutional amendment (first, an enactment removing the pre-existing prohibition against binding future Parliaments and, secondly, the relevant attempt to do just that), or a single (constitutional amendment) enactment accomplishing both. The European Communities Act 1972 and Commonwealth constitutional independence legislation took the latter tack.

Some of the devices which have been discussed in MacCormick's 'micro' analysis of sovereignty were relevant at the 'macro' level, where he was more interested in the interaction of so-called sovereign legal systems at the national and supra-national level. The linkage between 'micro' and 'macro' considerations is made by MacCormick when he questioned whether 'it

---

[87] *Thoburn* (2003) (n. 85 above).

lies within the power of Parliament to enact legislation that will effect [a] fundamental alteration to [the] ranking of legal sources in the United Kingdom'.[88] That question could not be asked, let alone answered, without an investigation of what he called 'the institutional rules of the constitution'. These in turn were 'made intelligible through some general theory of legal systems and the constitutional framework of a state within the rule of law'.[89] This connection between the internal rules of the United Kingdom Constitution and general theories of legal systems was the link between 'micro' and 'macro' analysis.

Monist and pluralist perspectives on problems relating to legal systems

Essentially the problem for 'macro' analysis was that most legal theories—most notably Austin's influential writings—were monist and monocular. They sought to identify a single sovereign (therefore they are monist) and they looked at the question of sovereignty from the perspective of only one legal system (hence they were monocular). MacCormick argued that such methods of proceeding were ill-suited to present-day Europe if not the modern world, and what he had to say here was again relevant to Commonwealth constitutional independence.

In place of monism, a single sovereign and the inevitable zero-sum legal-political game which ensued from that analysis, MacCormick proposed a binocular (or multi-ocular) perspective, i.e. seeing the problem from the points of view of more than one legal system. This sounded like a recipe for confusion, yet MacCormick helpfully pointed out that the rush for certainty was not always warranted. It should immediately be noted that the problem of certainty was in one sense far more acute in the European as opposed to the Commonwealth context. In the former context, many legal systems were transferring sovereignty as they explored what it meant to be part of an 'ever closer union'. They shared sovereignty, without knowing who, if anyone, was the ultimate sovereign, and they also shared legal officials, judicial and other. The need for certainty was great, and yet MacCormick argued that uncertainty can be managed. In the latter context, many legal systems were acquiring sovereignty as part of an overall process of decolonisation. As of 2004, none of Australia, Canada, New Zealand or the United Kingdom share legal officials (other than the Queen), and therefore it is possible for them to go beyond managing uncertainty in the MacCormick fashion. They may go so far as to disagree outright as those disagreements take place in separate and distinct legal systems.

However, in another sense, the need for different legal system perspectives is more acute in the Commonwealth than in Europe. We have just seen in discussing MacCormick's 'micro' analysis that whereas Europe may only require

---

[88] MacCormick (1999) (n. 52 above) 92.   [89] ibid., 92.

the Westminster Parliament to bind itself partially and temporarily, Commonwealth countries need to be assured that Westminster powers are completely and permanently terminated. If British understanding of parliamentary sovereignty cannot stretch this far, then it may be necessary for Australia, Canada and New Zealand to adopt a different answer, notwithstanding British misgivings.

It was MacCormick's distinctive contribution to point out, first, that the sovereignty need not be a single, absolute concept, and, secondly, that different legal systems may take different views on where sovereignty lies or simply accept that the matter is uncertain. In the case of Member States and the European Union, the lack of a definitive answer encourages all parties to ensure to the greatest extent possible that circumstances do not arise which force the sovereignty question to be answered. In the Commonwealth context, notably in the years following the enactment and adoption of the Statute of Westminster, 1931, Dominions and colonies were prepared to live with considerable uncertainty regarding Westminster's sovereignty, in large measure due to constitutional conventions. Perhaps Europe can learn from this phase of Commonwealth history. However, normal reasons of national pride and a desire for clarity and certainty dictate that when Commonwealth countries acquire independence they eventually wanted that independence to be constitutionally beyond doubt. Therefore, even if the United Kingdom were to persist in assuming that its Parliament can, if ever it expressed a clear will to do so, legislate for Australia, Canada and New Zealand, those countries, through their courts, certainly assume the contrary. While the binocular perspective of the European Union and its Member States, as described by MacCormick, must ultimately produce a relatively clear focus, the binocular perspective of the United Kingdom and its former Dominions and colonies need do nothing of the kind. As stated earlier, the perspectives may flatly contradict each other, but no one in the Commonwealth will be any the worse off as a result. It may be that the United Kingdom perspective is finally shifting towards the sorts of self-embracing interpretations of Westminster Parliament sovereignty that may now be favoured in Australia, Canada and New Zealand. But there is no need for this to be so. Given their political, international and judicial independence, Australia, Canada and New Zealand are entitled to adopt distinct interpretations of the Westminster Parliament's powers in so far as that institution affects their own legal systems, just as they may adopt distinct interpretations of what was originally a common law of contract and tort.

Summary

The various theoretical perspectives explored in this chapter are in some cases difficult in themselves, and in other cases difficult to relate one to the other.

Accordingly, it may be appropriate to end this chapter with a summary of the most pertinent points:

(1) Despite initial doubts on the matter, it is accepted that both continuing and self-embracing interpretations of the ultimate rule of a legal system are possible.[90] This means that the United Kingdom Parliament can be seen either (on the continuing version) to remain perpetually at the apex of the Australian, Canadian and New Zealand legal systems, or (on the self-embracing version) to provide for its own replacement as the supreme amending procedure.

(2) Understood in self-embracing terms, the United Kingdom Parliament can simultaneously confer legal validity on the Australian, Canadian and New Zealand constitutional provisions, and, without undermining that validity, disappear (immediately or eventually) from the legal map of those constitutional systems. Finnis has described the 'principle of continuity' which underlies this process in the following terms: 'A law once validly brought into being, in accordance with criteria of validity *then in force*, remains valid until *either* it expires according to its own terms or terms implied at its creation, *or* it is repealed in accordance with conditions or repeal in force *at the time of repeal*.[91] If this principle is valid, applying either to the self-reflexive provisions of the constitutional amendment procedure or to legislation generally, then it seems to imply that there is no practical or theoretical need to keep the United Kingdom as an active component of the Australian, Canadian and New Zealand legal systems, or to keep the United Kingdom legislation on the those countries' books once it has performed its initial task of conferring validity on new, local constitutional texts.

(3) As Raz has pointed out, Hans Kelsen's use of constitutional continuity as the proper criterion for the identity of a legal system does not fit the facts: 'A country may be granted independence by a law of another country authorising its laws; nevertheless, its laws form a separate legal system.'[92] The *Grundnorm* is of interest in providing a genealogy of certain legal rules in the system, and for accounting for their initial validity and normativity; but if one accepts the possibility of self-embracing change, one should expect to uncover in Australian, Canadian and New Zealand constitutional history, institutions and laws which are no longer part of the present legal system, however vital their role may have been in the past. Constitutional continuity indicates respect for the constitutional

---

[90] A. Ross, *On Law and Justice* (London: Stevens, 1958) 81 and 'On Self-Reference and a Puzzle in Constitutional Law' (1969) 78 Mind 1, 21; H.L.A. Hart, 'Self-Referring Laws' in H.L.A. Hart (ed.) *Essays in Jurisprudence and Philosophy* (Oxford: Oxford University Press, 1983) 170, 177 and *The Concept of Law* (2nd edn, Oxford: Oxford University Press, 1994), 149–50 (in this summary, citations are to 2nd edn, 1994); J. Raz, 'Professor A. Ross and Some Legal Puzzles' (1972) 81 Mind 415, 420; G. Marshall, *Constitutional Theory* (Oxford: Clarendon Press, 1971).

[91] J. Finnis, 'Revolutions and Continuity of Law' in A.W.B. Simpson (ed.) *Oxford Essays in Jurisprudence*, 2nd Series, 63 (Finnis's emphasis).

[92] J. Raz, *The Concept of a Legal System* (2nd edn, Oxford: Clarendon Press, 1980) 188.

rule of law and, from a positivist perspective, a link to the historically first constitution and the *Grundnorm*. It does not indicate that all members of the family tree are alive and well and ready and able to assert their ancestral priority.[93]

(4) H.L.A. Hart's notions of the ultimate rule of recognition and of differing perspectives explain how the Westminster Parliament can be seen as having continuing sovereign powers from a United Kingdom perspective, and spent self-embracing sovereign powers from the Australia, Canadian and New Zealand perspectives.[94] However, Hart's account does not explain how or why the ultimate rule of recognition can be said to evolve, as clearly it must have done over the twentieth century.

(5) More recent writing regarding the concept of a legal system reveals that the allegiance of the primary law-applying agencies (courts) is an important factor in predicting how the ultimate rule of recognition will be perceived and where the boundaries of the legal system will be drawn.[95] Therefore, in considering whether, and if so how, the ultimate rules of the Australian, Canadian and New Zealand legal systems have evolved, it is crucial on Raz's terms to recognise that all three systems are now judicially independent. Raz emphasises that 'whatever form one's ultimate account of continuity takes, it must, in view of the relation between law and State, be based on ... the interaction of legal and non-legal norms, and the extent and manner of their change'.[96] Neil MacCormick's recent writing regarding Member State-European Union constitutional relations endorses the point about the interaction of legal and non-legal norms, but re-emphasises the role of primary law-making agencies (legislatures) in determining how the rule of recognition changes.[97]

(6) If the ultimate rule of recognition is a customary[98] or common law rule whose core content is judicially established (i.e. the Queen-in-Parliament is sovereign), but whose penumbra is uncertain (i.e. continuing or self-embracing sovereignty?),[99] one would expect it to evolve in advance of judicial determination in step with social and political developments in Australia, Canada and New Zealand. Furthermore, it seems reasonable to agree with Hart that it is a 'formalist error' to assume that every legal question is entirely covered in advance by a legal rule.

---

[93] See H. Kelsen, *General Theory of Law and State* (Cambridge, Massachusetts: Harvard University Press, 1949). 'All the norms whose validity may be traced back to one and the same basic norm form a system of norms, or an order.' (p. 111); 'All these legal norms belong to one and the same legal order because their validity can be traced back—directly to the first constitution.' (p. 115); 'the State and its legal order remain the same only so long as the constitution is intact or changed according to its own provisions' (p. 219); '[a] State remains the same as long as the continuity of the legal order is maintained ...' (p. 219).

[94] Hart (2nd edn, 1994) (n. 90 above) 121.   [95] Raz (1980) (n. 92 above) 192.

[96] Raz, *The Authority of Law* (Oxford: Oxford University Press, 1979) 80.

[97] N. MacCormick, *Questioning Sovereignty: Law, State, and Practical Reason* (Oxford: Oxford University Press, 1999).   [98] Raz (1979) (n. 96 above) 98.

[99] Hart (1994) (n. 90 above) ch. 7, section 4; ch. 6, section 3.

(7) The moment when the Westminster Parliament relinquishes its supreme constitution-making powers to Australia, Canada and New Zealand is 'a disguised revolution' if that Parliament's powers are irrevocably continuing in nature. However, it is also possible to argue that, while the Westminster Parliament's powers were apparently unlimited for some time, the question regarding whether these powers were continuing or self-embracing was either an open (penumbral) question, or a temporarily closed question capable of redefinition by Parliament itself using its power of change. These last self-embracing interpretations of Westminster's powers allowed Australia, Canada and New Zealand the possibility of claiming that while the principle of legality had been respected in transferring the supreme constitution-making powers for their respective legal systems, the process had also succeeded in terminating the Imperial link.

We now turn to considering whether and if so how such theoretical tools can assist in explaining constitutional continuity and constitutional independence in the three countries under study.

13

Constitutional Continuity and Constitutional Independence

New constitutional foundations

The first chapter in this Part surveyed the wide variety of different explanations for constitutional independence that exist in the three countries under study. Those explanations also had a bearing on these countries' understandings of constitutional foundations, i.e. ultimate questions of validity and supremacy. The different explanations can be summarised as follows. First, there was the idea of a constitutional revolution, based either in an abstract violation of constitutional rules at the highest level or in the more comprehensible substitution of popular sovereignty for parliamentary sovereignty. The great appeal of this explanation is that it confirms constitutional independence unequivocally; but it does so at the cost of excluding constitutional continuity and its positive (from most lawyers' perspective) associations with the rule of law. Secondly, by way of stark contrast, it was possible to include constitutional continuity by simply accepting the continuing sovereignty of the Westminster Parliament, and to base 'constitutional' (in the wider sense) independence on the conventions which restrain Westminster from enacting unwanted and unrequested legislation for former colonies. Not surprisingly, this explanation, despite its classical pedigree, has never been popular with local constitutional commentators. Thirdly, it was possible to view certain provisions of United Kingdom legislation as 'manner and form' limitations on the Westminster Parliament or as an 'abdication' of Imperial legal authority for the countries in question. The variations on this theme have been more popular, but the way in which they supposedly secure constitutional independence has always been in doubt,[1] making them considerably less attractive. Fourthly, following the 'revised' view of parliamentary sovereignty, it was possible to view such provisions of United Kingdom legislation as fully

---

[1] Even H.W.R. Wade, Dicey's apologist in so many respects, acknowledged that Dicey never adequately explained how abdication of sovereignty was compatible with the rest of his theory: 'How Dicey reconciled his assertions that Parliament could destroy or transfer its sovereignty with the proposition that it could not bind future parliaments is nowhere explained.' H.W.R. Wade, 'The Basis of Legal Sovereignty' [1955] CLJ 172, 196n. Manner and form limitations can be overcome simply by fulfilling the requisite manner and form for the legislation in question. They leave the Westminster Parliament substantively, if not procedurally, unrestricted.

self-embracing in effect, imposing legally valid and irreversible (at least by Westminster initiative) limitations on the United Kingdom Parliament. This approach, guaranteeing both constitutional continuity and respect for the rule of law, *and* constitutional independence seems attractive.

If a self-embracing approach is to be preferred, then a number of issues have to be dealt with. The first collection of issues is theoretical, and these have been discussed in the preceding chapter. That chapter concluded with a summary of these issues and the modes of analysis proposed, noting, for example, that if a self-embracing interpretation is to be preferred then it may be necessary for Australia, Canada and New Zealand to view United Kingdom legislation relating to them through their own separate legal perspectives rather than through the often dogmatic prism of Imperial theory. The present chapter represents an attempt to elaborate on what that unique perspective might look like in each of Canada, New Zealand and Australia. Canada and New Zealand are grouped together in the discussion which follows because of a similarity in those two countries' constitutional development. In both cases, general amendment procedures were transferred to them by the United Kingdom Parliament at discrete moments in their constitutional evolution *post-dating* the Statute of Westminster, 1931: 1982 in the case of Canada and 1947 in the case of New Zealand. The Australian general procedure for constitutional amendment[2] (section 128) was provided with the original Commonwealth of Australia Constitution Act 1900 (Imp.), and therefore analysis of Australian constitutional independence has less in common with that of Canada and New Zealand. Also, as we have already seen, Australia's debate regarding popular sovereignty distinguishes both the historical origins of its Constitution and its contemporary constitutional debates. We begin, as we did in Part II, with Canada, followed by New Zealand and Australia.

A final point may be necessary. The purpose of this chapter is not to insist on the explanations proposed. If Australia, Canada or New Zealand prefer to impose a legal revolution in their constitutional theory or retain a vestigial connection to the United Kingdom Parliament, then that is of course their prerogative. If, however, either of these options is preferred simply because there is thought to be no explanation which allows both constitutional continuity and constitutional independence, then an explanation something like that which appears below may be of interest.

Canada: amending the amending formula

Section 52 of the Constitution Act, 1982[3] indicates that amendments to the Constitution of Canada are now governed by Part V of that Act, and section 53

---

[2] Section 128 refers to 'alteration' rather than 'amendment' of the Constitution. Given that these are synonyms, the latter expression has been preferred in order to make the comparative aspect of this analysis clearer.   [3] Being Schedule B to the Canada Act 1982 (UK).

directs that sections 4 and 7(1) of the Statute of Westminster, 1931 are now repealed. On the face of the present Constitution, it appears that all that is amendable must be amended using the procedures set out in Part V. Section 41(e) indicates furthermore that any amendments to the Part V amending formula are to be accomplished only with the unanimous consent of all provincial legislatures together with the House of Commons and Senate.[4] Another way of asking the question which is the preoccupation of this chapter is as follows: do the procedures of Part V exhaust the possibilities for amendment of the Constitution of Canada, or is it still possible to have resort to an ultimate and continuing legal sovereign, i.e. the United Kingdom Parliament?

As we have seen, the Supreme Court of Canada in the *Patriation Reference*[5] referred frequently to the untrammelled and undiminished powers of the United Kingdom Parliament, but it did not say, and was not asked to say, whether those powers were based in continuing or self-embracing sovereignty.[6] Understood as a matter of British constitutional theory the answer could only be indefinite or qualified. British legal opinion leaned and arguably still leans toward continuing sovereignty. In the past, one might have wished to argue that for Commonwealth purposes as seen, say, from the point of view of the Judicial Committee of the Privy Council, it was best to stick to the assumption of continuing sovereignty in the event that any of the former colonies (or their courts) determined that it was politically desirable and legally possible once again to request legislation from the Mother Parliament. However, in Canadian terms, it seemed that, at least on the eve of patriation in 1982, the near-universal assumption was that the Westminster amendment procedure was being used to replace itself—for all time—with the Part V amendment procedure. If we were to put the assumption into the more obscure language of constitutional theory we would say that there was a 'self-embracing' assumption regarding the patriation process.

Regardless of popular assumptions, was there any legal explanation for this process of constitutional continuity characterised by the transfer and replacement of amendment powers? We have already seen in Chapter 12, that, despite Ross's initial doubts on the matter, both continuing and self-embracing understandings of sovereign power were logically coherent. Accordingly, was it possible to say that in Canadian constitutional theory Westminster's powers were self-embracing while in British or even Commonwealth terms they were continuing?

Some commentators have suggested that political independence or international recognition dictate such a conclusion (if not the same reasoning).[7] It is

---

[4] And proclaimed by the Governor-General under the Great Seal of Canada.

[5] *Reference re Resolution to Amend the Constitution* [1981] 1 SCR 753.

[6] G. Winterton, 'The British Grundnorm: Parliamentary Supremacy Re-examined' (1976) 92 LQR 591 argues persuasively that though there are in-between positions which can be identified, there is ultimately a fundamental choice between continuing and self-embracing sovereignty.

[7] See B. Slattery, 'The Independence of Canada' (1983) 5 Sup Ct L Rev 369. See also B. Colvin, 'Constitutional Jurisprudence in the Supreme Court of Canada' (1982) 4 Sup Ct L Rev 3.

argued here that independence by itself does not dictate any particular conclusion. There is no reason why a court in a newly independent country could not take the view that according to all relevant indicators it seemed clear that that country had decided to retain a system of constitutional amendment by the legal method of foreign enactment, however anomalous that might seem.[8]

In the Canadian case, as we have seen, there is no reason to assume that the mechanism of Westminster amendment was to be held in reserve even after a domestic procedure for amendment had been found. If one were to make such an assumption one might wish to return to 1931. As Peter Hogg has pointed out,[9] at that time it was not thought possible as a matter of law for the Imperial link ever to be truly severed. If that was the assumption in the past, then how can we say that it had changed by 1982?

Even though the fact of political independence did not lead to *necessary* legal results, it seems uncontroversial to say that independence should naturally lead to an independent legal theory. While the Judicial Committee of the Privy Council remained the highest court of appeal for Canada the development of such a theory might have been stifled, but certainly by mid-century when the Supreme Court of Canada had taken over the leading role in constitutional interpretation, it was natural that the Canadian court would occasionally take different views from the British or other Commonwealth courts on various legal and theoretical questions. And it would also be natural for it to do so on the basis of factors particular to Canadian political and social development, notably in constitutional 'hard cases'.[10]

---

[8] See G. Lindell, 'Further Reflections on the Date of the Acquisition of Australia's Independence' in G. Lindell, C. Saunders and R. French (eds) *Reflections on the Australian Constitution* (Annandale: Federation Press, 2003) 51, 54: 'The fact that a country chooses to allow the legislature, the executive and the courts of another country to exercise authority with respect to the affairs of the former country is not under this analysis seen as inconsistent with its independence.'

[9] P.W. Hogg, *Constitutional Law of Canada*, (4th edn. (looseleaf) Toronto: Thomson Carswell, 1997) 3–12.

[10] A Hartian rather than a Dworkinian approach to 'hard cases' is preferred here, though it is submitted that either approach would yield the same result in 2004. In 1934, however, it is quite possible to imagine, counterfactually, that as final court of appeal for Canada, the Judicial Committee of the Privy Council would have come to a different conclusion taking into account Dworkinian factors of 'fit' and 'justification' than the Supreme Court of Canada would have done in the same circumstances. The Privy Council would have quite naturally considered what was good for the Commonwealth as a whole, while the Supreme Court of Canada would have emphasised Canadian interests. Both courts would have been legally constrained in their decision-making to some extent, but a crucial part of their respective decisions would have been determined by an assessment of Canada's part in an evolving cultural, social and political story. Not surprisingly, the Privy Council and Supreme Court of Canada versions of this story would differ, despite the same cultural, social, political *and legal* raw material. Hart's analysis seems to provide a better account of constitutional law and constitutional 'hard cases'. See H.L.A. Hart, *The Concept of Law* (Oxford: Clarendon Press, 1961; 2nd edn, 1994) and R. Dworkin, *Law's Empire* (Cambridge, Massachusetts: Harvard University Press, 1985). This said, the Supreme Court of Canada has recently taken a more Dworkinian approach as evidenced by its fondness for discovering 'principles' in the Canadian Constitution. See, e.g., *Reference re Secession of Quebec* [1998] 2 SCR 217.

We have seen how the issue of continuing versus self-embracing sovereignty had not been resolved even in the United Kingdom by 1982.[11] It would have been surprising to see anything different. Such an arcane matter of constitutional theory would seldom be a matter for judicial determination. In the meantime, legal observers in the United Kingdom and Canada could have been expected to make predictions as to the likely view which a court might take.[12] But until a court pronounced on the issue, the true nature of that sovereignty, whether in British or in Canadian terms (and, as we have seen, the two need not have been the same), remained uncertain. In the meantime the matter was left to the constitutional theorists.

In Canada at some time after 1931 (significantly, it seems at about the time of the end of Privy Council appeals), Canadian constitutional commentators and political actors began to assume that there could be a final and irreversible transfer of constituent powers from Westminster to Canada at some time. This view had clearly crystallised by 1982. If the ultimate Canadian rule of recognition could ever have been said to contain a rule of continuing Westminster sovereignty (as counter-factual as that statement might be)[13] then it would seem that it had evolved, and by the 1950s (and certainly by 1982) it could be said to contain a rule of self-embracing Westminster sovereignty with the results that followed.

It may seem contrary to legal ways of thinking to say that the ultimate rule of recognition could have had one form at one time and then evolved into another form. Those who follow Kelsen and Ross's view might argue that the Canadian (and, as it happens, British) *Grundnorm* in 1982 would have to be the same as that which existed in 1867 and 1931. There had, after all, been no break in legal continuity. According to that view, the *Grundnorm* was probably one of continuing Westminster sovereignty from which there could be no legal escape.

The most telling criticism of Kelsen (and, implicitly, Ross) was suggested in the writings of Finnis and Raz, as we have seen in the preceding chapter. Finnis observed that the validity of present rules in a legal system was not

---

However, it may be possible, and preferable, to assimilate this approach into a Hartian analysis of the type proposed by Neil MacCormick in *Legal Reasoning and Legal Theory* (Oxford: Clarendon Press, 1978).

[11] The matter may be different in the United Kingdom today. See P. Oliver, 'Sovereignty in the Twenty-First Century' (2003) 14 KCLJ 137.

[12] P. Joseph and G. Walker, 'A Theory of Constitutional Change' (1987) OJLS 155, 172, have noted the importance of the institutional arrangement of the whole legal community—'the legal profession, the universities, a system of law courts, a judicial hierarchy, various law-making bodies and law reform agencies, parts of the state's political apparatus and the upper echelons of the state bureaucracy'—in the interpretation of the constitution and, in particular, rules of constitutional change.

[13] Raz points out that constitutional theory often asks questions regarding those laws which, according to the rule of recognition or other criterion, the courts of a particular system would recognise, even though it is only in the rarest sort of case that those courts ever come to consider these matters. See J. Raz, *The Concept of a Legal System*, (2nd edn, Oxford: Clarendon Press, 1980) 196 and *Authority of Law* (Oxford: Clarendon Press, 1979) 88.

dependent on uninterrupted connection to a *Grundnorm* lying deep in a country's constitutional past; rather validity was dependent on proper legal process at the time of enactment even if that process no longer continued to apply at some time in the future when the question was being asked. Raz pointed out that the continuity and identity of a legal system was not dependent on the *Grundnorm*; instead it was tied up with the continuity and identity of the social and political system. If the *Grundnorm* of the historically first constitution was not required to govern legal continuity and determine present legal validity, as Hart's and Raz's critiques indicated, then it seemed that it could indeed evolve over time. Of course, if one wished to have the ability to determine all the norms of a legal system at every moment in the life of that legal system then one would have to assign a specific content to the *Grundnorm* in advance of judicial determination. But if one agreed with Hart that it was a formalistic error to assume that all rules in a legal system have an entirely predetermined content, and if the most fundamental rules were linked to (changing) social and political factors, then it was possible to assume that thinking about the ultimate rule of recognition could evolve before a court was ever, if ever, asked to determine the matter conclusively. In the meantime, key questions regarding the ultimate Canadian rule of recognition were destined to remain penumbral, but court determination would eventually bring them into the core of that rule.

If a Canadian court were ever asked to determine whether, in 1982, the ultimate Canadian rule of recognition included a rule of continuing or self-embracing sovereignty,[14] it would naturally deal with the matter differently than the Judicial Committee or other British Court might have done. It might note that early Canadian thinking on the matter was conditioned by the perceived

---

[14] As we have seen in earlier chapters, the Supreme Court of Canada confirmed in the *Veto Reference* (*Reference re Objection to a Resolution to Amend the Constitution* [1982] 2 SCR 793, 806) that 'The Constitution Act, 1982 is now in force. Its legality is neither challenged nor assailable. It contains a new procedure for amending the Constitution of Canada which entirely replaces the old one in its legal as well as in its conventional aspects.' In the *Secession Reference* (*Reference re Secession of Quebec* [1998] 2 SCR 217, para 467) the Court confirmed that the 1982 process had removed the last vestige of British authority:

Canada's evolution from colony to fully independent state was gradual. The Imperial Parliament's passage of the Statute of Westminster, 1931 (U.K.) . . . confirmed in law what had earlier been confirmed in fact by the Balfour Declaration of 1926, namely, that Canada was an independent country. Thereafter, Canadian law alone governed in Canada, except where Canada expressly consented to the continued application of Imperial legislation. Canada's independence from Britain was achieved through legal and political evolution with an adherence to the rule of law and stability. The proclamation of the Constitution Act, 1982 removed the last vestige of British authority over the Canadian Constitution and re-affirmed Canada's commitment to the protection of its minority, aboriginal, equality, legal and language rights, and fundamental freedoms as set out in the Canadian Charter of Rights and Freedoms.

Legal continuity, which requires an orderly transfer of authority, necessitated that the 1982 amendments be made by the Westminster Parliament, but the legitimacy as distinguished from the formal legality of the amendments derived from political decisions taken in Canada within a legal framework which this Court, in the Patriation Reference, had ruled was in accordance with our Constitution.

limits of British constitutional theory, but that once it had become clear that both continuing and self-embracing sovereignty were logically possible, the Canadian assumption was in favour of the latter. And if the Court agreed with Raz that the continuity and content of a legal system is ultimately related to the continuity and content of the political system, then it might consider some of the following factors and add them to its reasons: that Canada had been an independent nation at least since 1926–31 and one which, despite its attachment to the monarchy and the Commonwealth, did not seek to rely unduly on the United Kingdom; that there was a presumption in favour of a close connection or correspondence between the Constitution and the political subjects of that Constitution; that the close connection between the Constitution and the government and governed is all the more important in a system of responsible government and democratic accountability; that ideally the Constitution should be perceived not only as legal but also as legitimate; that the larger historical context of a country's constitutional development should be relevant to the interpretation of the Constitution's most fundamental rules; and that certainly once the courts of a country are independent of any foreign control or supervision they should be free to develop legal rules and principles which are based on the above factors. Whether one conceives of these questions as cultural, social, political and historical considerations which courts are entitled to consider in resolving genuinely 'hard cases' in constitutional law, or whether one sees them as part of legal principle and legal reasoning, the conclusion is likely to be the same.

It is submitted that if ever a Canadian court were asked whether following the passage of the 1982 Act the United Kingdom Parliament could have a role, with or without request or consent, in the amendment of the Canadian Constitution, it would answer a resounding 'no'. It could, consistently with the *Patriation Reference*, conclude that although until 1982 the United Kingdom Parliament had absolute power to legislate for Canada, its powers were, at least as a matter of Canadian law, self-embracing, and that therefore Westminster could by means of the Canada Act 1982 both provide a new code on constitutional amendment in the form of Part V of the Constitution Act, 1982 and at the same time dictate that the Part V process entirely replace it as sovereign constituent legislature for Canada.[15]

If so, we may conclude that there is good reason to suppose that the 'patriation' process was successful and that the new amendment provisions set

---

[15] Accordingly, it may be more appropriate to say that s. 52 and especially s. 52(3) is the key provision in the 1982 legislation:

52(1)   The Constitution of Canada is the supreme law of Canada, and any law that is inconsistent with the provisions of the Constitution is, to the extent of the inconsistency, of no force and effect.

. . .

(3)   Amendment to the Constitution of Canada shall be made *only* in accordance with the authority contained in the Constitution of Canada.

The Constitution Act, 1982 is Schedule B to the Canada Act 1982 (UK).

out in the 1982 Act are now the only valid means of constitutional amendment. As we have seen, the Supreme Court of Canada seemed to assume as much as early as 1982, when it stated in the Quebec *Veto Reference* that Part V 'entirely replaced' the old system.[16]

This discussion of Canadian constitutional independence began with the question whether the United Kingdom Parliament is still a part of the Canadian legal system and an institution to which Canadians might have recourse in the event of future constitutional paralysis. An attempt has been made to justify the near-unanimous negative answer to that question in terms which conformed with logic, precedent and common sense. It has been argued that the *Patriation Reference* is only authority for the view that until patriation the *ambit* of the United Kingdom Parliament's sovereignty was unimpaired or undiminished. The Court was not asked to and did not comment on whether that sovereignty was continuing or self-embracing, although the statement in the *Veto Reference* that Part V 'entirely replace[d]' the former amending procedure pointed towards the latter interpretation. If the Court were ever asked to rule on the matter it might raise some of the considerations which have been discussed in this chapter: first, that both continuing and self-embracing conceptions of the ultimate rule of the legal system are coherent, there being no need to refer to 'magical acts' or 'revolutions in legal dress'; secondly, that within the self-embracing conception, the United Kingdom Parliament could simultaneously confer validity on the Canada Act 1982 and then, without undermining that validity, disappear from the post-patriation Canadian legal system; and thirdly, that the evolution from continuing to self-embracing conceptions as a matter of twentieth-century Canadian constitutional theory could be explained and justified in terms of Canadian social, political and historical development, both inside and outside the legal community. A legal understanding of the patriation process therefore included not only an evident respect for the existing constitutional rule of law, routed as it then was through the Parliament at Westminster, but also reference to factors particular and relevant to Canada and Canadians.

What then could Canadians do to extricate themselves from severe and apparently permanent constitutional paralysis? If the same occurred in another system following the replacement of one general amending procedure by another, too rigid procedure, for example, the solution would not be to return to the easier procedure, but rather perhaps to return to the type of extra-legal or legitimising process which created the Constitution in the first place—in many cases some combination of constituent assembly and popular consultation.[17]

---

[16] *Veto Reference* (1982), 806.

[17] This is not to suggest that *any* part of the Constitution could be amended by recourse to a 'legitimating' process. This would violate the constitutional rule of law. Furthermore, fundamental rights and freedoms would be particularly vulnerable to such super-majoritarian legitimising processes. What is contemplated here is a serious breakdown of the constitutional amendment process as a result of a persistent refusal by one or more provinces even or ever to participate in that process. In that context, a court might be willing to accept a highly 'legitimate' process as an

We shall see the pertinence of this point in the discussion of Australian constitutional independence.

In Canada, history does not point to any obvious source of legitimation. Strictly speaking, the only constituent assembly Canada ever had was the United Kingdom Parliament. Recourse to that body is now excluded as a matter of law, as argued in this chapter; and furthermore, it seems highly inappropriate to return to that foreign Parliament in search of extra-legal grounding or legitimation for the Canadian Constitution. It seems more acceptable to say that, beyond the new Constitution and Part V on amendment, the Canadian legal system has no easily identifiable roots. Rather, those roots and new roots have been and are being put down slowly—in popular sovereignty, in regional or provincial vetoes, in aboriginal consent, etc.—and a new Canadian constitutional theory will gradually uncover them.[18]

New Zealand's ultimate rule of recognition: cutting the Imperial link strand by strand

To what extent is the above analysis relevant to New Zealand constitutional independence? The critical years seem to be 1947 and 1986 and, to a lesser extent, 1973 and 2003.

It is possible to view the 1947 process as self-embracing in the same way as the 1982 process in Canada, with the crucial difference being the retention after 1947 of the potential for an ongoing United Kingdom role. According to the self-embracing interpretation of the events of 1947, the supreme Constitution-amending role was handed over to the New Zealand Parliament, with the United Kingdom Parliament thereafter representing a residual, alternative *but subordinate* constitutional amendment process. According to this interpretation, as supreme law-maker, the New Zealand Parliament was entitled to confirm and clarify its full powers in the text of the 1973 Act and, in 1986, to amend the rules of the New Zealand legal system so as to end the residual powers of the United Kingdom Parliament. Under the principle of continuity proposed by Finnis,[19] the New Zealand Parliament could use its powers given to it by the United Kingdom Parliament in 1852, 1931 and 1947 in order to achieve constitutional independence in 1986, and, having exhausted their usefulness,

---

unavoidable alternative in order to preserve the constitutional rule of law. Constitutions, we are told, are not intended to be a suicide pact. See, generally, *Reference re Manitoba Language Rights* [1985] 1 SCR 721.

[18] See, e.g., B. Slattery, 'First Nations and the Constitution: A Question of Constitutional Trust' (1992) 71 Can Bar Rev 261 and P. Russell, *Constitutional Odyssey: Can Canadians Be A Sovereign People?* (Toronto: University of Toronto Press, 1992).

[19] J. Finnis, 'Revolutions and Continuity of Law' in A.W.B. Simpson (ed.) *Oxford Essays in Jurisprudence*, 2nd Series, (Oxford: Clarendon Press, 1973) 44, 63. See Ch. 12 above for discussion.

revoke their continuing application under New Zealand law. None of this need be seen as creating a breach in continuity.

In this chapter, it is assumed that there was uncertainty in the penumbra of the ultimate rule (i.e. the sovereignty of the King-in-the-United-Kingdom Parliament) of the pre-1947 New Zealand legal system. Understandings at that time were heavily conditioned by Dicey's assumptions of continuing sovereignty, but as the question never required judicial clarification it remained penumbral. It seems legitimate, therefore, for New Zealanders in 1986 or 2004 to interpret the 1947 process in different terms than New Zealanders in 1947 might have done, in order to give more precise meaning to the many conflicting intentions of earlier legislators. In any event, in the 1947 debates in the New Zealand Parliament discussed in Chapter 8, one sees the expression of a desire to end the former relationship of superiority and subordination. It seems appropriate to interpret 1947 in the self-embracing terms which give effect to that desire.

Why might a New Zealand court prefer a self-embracing interpretation of the 1947 process? Most of the social, political and historical factors identified above regarding Canada apply equally to New Zealand. Even if political independence need not determine the answers to legal questions, it provides a strong indicator as to interpretations that should be preferred by local courts. And whereas continuing sovereignty as espoused by Dicey and later defended by Wade may be said to be preferable if it prevents the will of a bare majority of parliamentarians at one time from binding a future majority of that Parliament, viewed from a New Zealand perspective it is entirely appropriate that the will of the United Kingdom Parliament in 1947 should be the last to bind New Zealand. The self-embracing effect of the New Zealand Constitution (Amendment) Act 1947 (UK)[20] means that a future majority in the *New Zealand* Parliament can have the last word on constitutional matters in that country. Any diffidence the New Zealand courts might have had in coming to such a conclusion immediately after 1947 should be lessened by the removal of theoretical obstacles which has occurred since that time.

The approach summarised above may be reconstructed more precisely as follows with inspiration from (though not always the agreement of) the New Zealand commentators noted in Chapter 11. By section 1 of the (Amendment) Act 1947 (UK), Westminster gave to the New Zealand Parliament the power to 'alter, suspend, or repeal . . . all or any of the provisions of the New Zealand Constitution Act 1852'. At the same time, by adopting section 4 of the 1931 Statute, the New Zealand Parliament had recognised the United Kingdom Parliament's power to legislate at the request and with the consent of New Zealand. Section 2(2) of the 1931 Statute permitted the Parliament of a Dominion to repeal or amend any 'existing or future Act of the Parliament of the United Kingdom, or . . . any order, rule or regulation made

---

[20] Hereinafter (Amendment) Act 1947 (UK).

under any such Act . . . in so far as the same is part of the law of the Dominion'. The standard view is that this power amendment of repeal included the 1931 Statute.[21]

In order to determine whether the gift of power to the New Zealand Parliament by the (Amendment) Act 1947 (UK) included the supreme constituent or constitution-amending power, we would need to know whether the New Zealand Parliament or the Westminster Parliament was to be recognised as having the final word or trump card regarding law-making in the New Zealand legal system. Section 2(2) of the Statute of Westminster seemed to support the claim of the New Zealand Parliament.[22] But what if the United Kingdom Parliament could repeal the 1931 Statute? As noted in Chapter 11, there was a reply even to that far-fetched scenario. Section 4 of the 1931 Statute could be interpreted by a New Zealand court as instituting a substantive requirement of local request and consent before enactments of the Westminster Parliament could be treated 'as part of the law of the Dominion'. As long as New Zealand was capable of developing constitutional understandings which corresponded more closely with its own constitutional requirements, then it was not bound to interpret the Statute in the same manner as the British courts might have done.[23] Section 3 of the Statute of Westminster Adoption Act 1947 (NZ) gave this argument exceptional strength in the New Zealand context by stating that the request and consent provided for under section 4 of the 1931 Statute '*shall be made* and given by the Parliament of New Zealand, *and not otherwise*'.[24] On one view, this provided a legally enforceable gloss on section 4 of the 1931 Statute in its application to New Zealand and offered a further convincing basis[25] for saying that any post-1947 Westminster legislation for New Zealand which was not requested and consented to by the New Zealand Parliament was simply not 'part

---

[21] See Wheare, *The Constitutional Structure of the Commonwealth* (Oxford, Clarendon Press, 1960) 33.

[22] To the extent that the boundaries between the Westminster and Wellington Parliaments' powers regarding New Zealand were uncertain on a reading of the 1947 Acts, it was always possible for the local Parliament to clarify matters by legislating as permitted by s. 2(2) of the Statute so as to undo the purported effect of any United Kingdom legislation. Therefore if any Empire-wide legislation had been passed at the request of those colonies and Dominions still within the jurisdiction of the Westminster Parliament, Wellington could have put an end to the effect of that legislation as regards New Zealand. And so long as the Statute had a separate existence as a part of New Zealand law, s. 2 itself was immune from unrequested repeal by Westminster. These considerations also seem to support the self-embracing interpretation of 1947.

[23] This interpretation was not open to the Canadian courts in 1981 due to the fact that s. 7 of the Statute of Westminster, 1931 provided that s. 4 should not be deemed to apply to the 'repeal, amendment or alteration' of the main Canadian constitutional texts. It also seems unlikely that the new New Zealand Supreme Court would give effect to the theoretical musings of Lord Sankey in the *British Coal Corporation* case, which were in an event obiter dicta, and misunderstood obiter dicta at that. (For discussion see Ch. 3 above.)   [24] Emphasis added.

[25] It may be said that s. 3 does not add anything to the argument given that it was only intended to prevent any *New Zealand* entity other than the New Zealand Parliament from providing request and consent. However, even read in this light it does not detract from the argument based on s. 4 of the 1931 Statute. It seems more likely, however, that a New Zealand court would use s. 3 of the

of the law of that Dominion'. If this view held then it also meant that section 4 of the 1931 Statute in its application to New Zealand could not be repealed by the United Kingdom Parliament acting alone. In giving to the New Zealand Parliament the power to amend the central constitutional document of that country, Westminster was also effectively giving the master key of the Constitution to the local Parliament, just as it was to do for Canada in 1982.[26]

This analysis holds that, by section 1 of the (Amendment) Act 1947 (UK), the United Kingdom Parliament transferred to the Wellington Parliament its ultimate constituent power regarding New Zealand matters. Thus, even if the Wellington Parliament's powers were superficially limited by the text of the Constitution Act, 1852 there would be nothing to prevent it from altering the text so as to confirm and clarify its unrestricted powers. We can see the 1973 Act as doing just that: amending section 53 of the Constitution Act 1852 (Imp.) so as to confirm the New Zealand Parliament's 'full powers'. This expression was broad enough to take in not only the main purpose of the 1973 legislation (power over extraterritorial matters) but also the unrestricted constituent or constitution-amending powers which that Parliament had had since 1947. It was also broad enough to include the powers given under section 2(2) of the 1931 Statute to repeal or amend United Kingdom laws in so far they are part of the law of New Zealand.

We come then to 1986 in a context which included a fully competent New Zealand Parliament. If that Parliament had the supreme amending powers of the Constitution handed to it in a self-embracing process by the United Kingdom Parliament in 1947 (on the New Zealand view), and if those powers could be said to be included in the expression 'full powers' in the 1973 amendment, then it was not difficult to conclude that the New Zealand Parliament also had the power to amend the New Zealand constitutional amendment process in 1986 by eliminating from it any further role for the United Kingdom Parliament. And this is what it did in section 15 of the Constitution Act 1986 (NZ).

Adoption Act 1947 (NZ) to interpret the meaning that should have been given to s. 4 of the Statute of Westminster, which was being adopted by means of the same enactment. If the combination of s. 3 of the Adoption Act 1947 (NZ) and s. 4 of the Statute of Westminster, 1931 was deemed to be insufficient, then s. 1 of the (Amendment) Act 1947 (UK) was all the confirmation that was needed that the New Zealand Parliament was now the supreme constituent or constitution-amending body.

[26] It may be asked why New Zealand retained the possibility of recourse to the United Kingdom Parliament after 1947. A number of practical points come to mind. First, there was the immediate purpose of abolishing the New Zealand Legislative Council. Secondly, so long as the Empire or Commonwealth existed (and many New Zealanders still believed in its future as the 1947 debates indicate) it was convenient to retain the possibility of the Westminster Parliament legislating for the whole Empire or Commonwealth so as to provide directly effective measures for all from one source. That which was more important for our purposes is whether the supreme local legislator in New Zealand, the Wellington Parliament, was still subordinate ultimately to the Westminster Parliament. A continued role for Westminster after 1947 did not necessarily mean a legally superior role, if a self-embracing interpretation of the enactments of that year is preferred.

If the United Kingdom Parliament and key United Kingdom legislation were no longer part of the active legal system, then how could it be said that the New Zealand Parliament retained its own powers, which were after all derived from there? Was it entitled to eliminate the empowering United Kingdom legislation? If the constituent or constitution-amending power was already recognised in the new (1973) version of section 53 of the 1852 Act and was once again declared in the 1986 Act (also in section 15), then there was no difficulty in holding that the key United Kingdom Parliament legislation was no longer needed. If the principle of continuity could adequately underpin self-embracing change, then Westminster enactments (such as the (Amendment) Act 1947 (UK), section 2(2) of the 1931 Statute and section 53 of the 1852 Act) could, once they had provided the boost of legal validity that comes through following proper constitutional process, be dropped away like canisters of spent rocket fuel, at least in so far as the 'active' New Zealand legal system is concerned. On this view 1986 is clearly significant in that it removes the possibility of recourse to the United Kingdom Parliament, but it is not revolutionary. It is explained by a self-embracing interpretation of the 1947 process, an interpretation which was itself justified by many of the same factors that were listed above regarding Canada.

The approach adopted thus far provides a way of squaring the legal and the factual accounts. It allows Canada and New Zealand to assert convincingly that they are now constitutionally independent, while also asserting that this took place without any breach in legal continuity.

If one wishes to speak of the roots of the Canadian and New Zealand legal systems, then this approach acknowledges that in one sense these countries' roots lie in Westminster. But the analogy is deceptive for those roots did no more than provide Canadian and New Zealand legislation with bare legality. One needs to distinguish old but extinguished roots from roots which presently have the ability to affect the life of a living system. The force of the old Westminster roots is now spent, and they are now dead as far as the presently operating Canadian and New Zealand legal systems are concerned. Their past role in these legal systems is indicative of a general respect for the rule of law in Canada and New Zealand, but beyond that these dead roots are now only of interest to the legal historian or legal system theorist.

Unlike many modern constitutional systems, the Canadian and New Zealand systems have no constituent assembly that they can point to as a source of extra-legal legitimation. The United Kingdom Parliament was the only constituent assembly that they can be said to have had. The self-embracing interpretation of 1947 and 1982 and the inappropriateness of any continued role for the United Kingdom Parliament make it inconceivable that Canada and New Zealand would try to revive the old connection by returning to the Mother country in a constitutional crisis. If that is accepted, as undoubtedly it must be, and if it is recognised that it is the independence of Canadian and New Zealand constitutional theory that guarantees the independence of those legal systems, then it must be the proper role of constitutional writers in both countries to explore the new legal, political and social roots that have been and still are gradually being put down in local soil. In Canada, as noted earlier, that process is being affected, for example, by provincial claims to distinctiveness, assertion of aboriginal rights to self-government and, especially, by the Charter of Rights and Freedoms. In New Zealand the Bill of Rights, the ongoing debate regarding the Treaty of Waitangi, and even the recent changes in the electoral system may be part of the process.

The Imperial link was important in demonstrating a respect for the rule of law in high constitutional matters and in conferring bare validity or legality on the main institutions and texts of the Canadian and New Zealand Constitutions. But those Constitutions also derive their meaning and force from social, political and historical factors particular to those countries. Now that the Imperial link is cut, Canadian and New Zealand constitutional thinking is free to set off and explore in new directions. As we saw in Chapter 11, Australian constitutional thinking has already begun to do so, and it is to that country's constitutional independence and constitutional development that we now turn before concluding this story.

Australia: sovereignty of Parliament and sovereignty of the people

For a variety of reasons, Australia is a case apart, though a good one with which to conclude, because the Australian example forces us constantly to keep in mind the interlocking of political, social, historical and legal factors. Part of that which makes the Australian case unique is that, as far as the Australian Commonwealth was concerned, it was, to all intents and purposes, constitutionally self-sufficient as of 1901.[27] There is no point in ignoring the historical fact that the Commonwealth of Australia Constitution Act, 1900 was a statute of the Imperial Parliament and reliant on that fact for its validity and supremacy. However, unlike Canada and New Zealand, Australia had in section 128 a *general* constitutional amending procedure right from the beginning of its constitutional life. It also had in sections 51(xxix) and 51(xxxviii) provisions which, while not immediately fully effective because of the ongoing restrictions of the Imperial system (extra-territoriality and repugnancy in particular), nonetheless had clear potential to assume full effectiveness, as they would eventually illustrate in 1986. Furthermore,

---

[27] As the rest of this analysis makes clear, self-sufficiency here refers to the *constitutional tools* which were contained in the Australian Constitution even in 1901. The rules of the Imperial legal system prior to the Balfour Declaration and, especially, the Statute of Westminster, 1931, meant that there were important obstacles in the way of Australia actually using these tools. But once these obstacles were removed, Australia was constitutionally equipped in a way that was not true of Canada or New Zealand. Most significantly, Canada or New Zealand from the beginning lacked the full ability to amend their Constitutions.

Australia was the only country of the three under consideration which was founded as a result of a significant process of public involvement and public consultation, and in which the Constitution is amended using a procedure which involves referendums. The people of Australia were or are therefore involved both in the constitution-making process and in the Constitution-amending process.

It is impossible to deny the importance of Imperial Parliament enactment without rewriting the history of the Australian Constitution. Imperial sovereignty is unquestionably a critical part of Australia's story. However, unless one adopts a definition of sovereignty which requires clarity at every moment regarding one sole sovereign actor or institution,[28] it is possible also to infer that the Australian people have been an alternative source of sovereignty. This takes us into the realm of the counterfactual, or into what has already been referred to as the penumbra of the ultimate rule of recognition. The fact is that any sovereignty the Australian people might have had was never tested, and so any power they might have had in the early and middle part of the twentieth century is at best uncertain (though that situation has changed since 1986).

In order to understand the nature of the sovereignty of the Australian people, it is necessary to remind ourselves of the possible levels at which that sovereignty can work. First, popular sovereignty can operate as a powerful political principle, serving as a constant reminder, for the purposes of policy-making and constitutional interpretation alike, that the Constitution is designed not for the ease of the governors but for the benefit of the governed.[29] All commentators and judges agree that something like this principle is at work in Australia, though there may be important divergences as to, for example, whether the republican or the democratic variant of popular sovereignty is at work.[30] And while lawyers continue to emphasise an ongoing boundary between legal and political principle, there has never been any doubt that in 'hard cases' political principle often comes into play.[31]

---

[28] Contemporary constitutionalism no longer views sovereignty in this way. See, e.g., J. Tully, *Strange Multiplicity: Constitutionalism in an Age of Diversity* (Cambridge: Cambridge University Press, 1995); N. MacCormick, *Questioning Sovereignty* (Oxford: Oxford University Press, 1999); and P. Oliver, 'Sovereignty in the Twenty-First Century' (2003) 14 KCLJ 137.

[29] There is no shortage of high-quality information on this point in Australia due in particular to the influence of writers such as the political philosopher Philip Pettit (see P. Pettit, *Republicanism: A Theory of Freedom and Government* (Oxford: Oxford University Press, 1997), and 'The People in the Republican Tradition' in M. Coper and G. Williams (eds) *Power, Parliament and the People* (Annandale: Federation Press, 1997) 108); and the jurist Paul Finn, 'A Sovereign People, A Public Trust' in Paul Finn (ed.) *Essays on Law and Government* (Sydney: Law Book Company, 1995) 1. On the constitutional side of things, Jeremy Kirk, 'Constitutional Interpretation and a Theory of Evolutionary Originalism' (1999) 27 Fed LR is also insightful on these issues.

[30] See Pettit (1997) (n. 29 above) on the distinction between democratic and republican versions of popular sovereignty. Kirk (1999) discusses the difference between political sovereignty and popular sovereignty.

[31] Hart and Dworkin differ as to whether political principles are part of 'law' and 'legal reasoning' but both agree that judges often consider such principles in hard cases. For further discussion of this point see J. Raz, *Ethics in the Public Domain* (Oxford: Clarendon Press, 1984).

Secondly, popular sovereignty can operate at the constituent or constitution-*making* level. We know as a historical matter that the United Kingdom Parliament was seen as the constituent assembly for Australia, as it was for Canada, New Zealand and other colonies. However, we have also seen that Australia conducted a popular constituent process throughout the 1890s. We do not know whether, in a moment of constitutional crisis or paralysis in the period 1901–86, Australian judges would have recognised a new or radically revised Constitution drafted as a result of a renewed process of Convention and referendum,[32] and this not as a matter of emergency or necessity, but as a proper exercise of the *pouvoir constituant*.[33] The existence and wording of section 128 of the Constitution appears to militate against this possibility, but if a popular constituent process is truly hierarchically superior to the Constitution, in the same way as the Imperial Parliament was, then this apparent obstacle disappears. Furthermore, section 128 says 'This Constitution shall not be altered' which leaves room for a new or radically revised Constitution that is either no longer 'this Constitution' or no longer merely 'altered'. The purpose here is not to advance this possibility as the best interpretation, but rather to isolate a meaning for popular sovereignty which is legal in a relevant if rarefied sense, and different from section 128. Although the credibility of this interpretation is difficult to weigh up given the absence of a scenario in the period 1901–86 when it was played out and tested, it is at least a coherent concept. Understood in this way, popular sovereignty cannot be an *alternative* to the Imperial Parliament in the sense of 'either/or', because we know that the Imperial Parliament was clearly accepted as a constituent body and is therefore an essential constant in any picture of the Australian legal system. However, popular sovereignty in the sense here described can still be thought of as a possible *supplement* to the Imperial Parliament in the sense of 'both/and'.[34]

Thirdly, popular sovereignty can refer to the many places, most notably section 128, in which public participation appears in the Constitution. Section 128 is particularly important not just because it contains a referendum procedure, though that it undeniably significant, but also because the constitutional

[32] For discussion of this issue, see U. Ellis, *A Federal Convention: To Revise the Constitution* (Canberra: Australia Office of Rural Research and Development, 1952).

[33] In all legal systems which are the result of a constituent process leading to a Constitution, there is an issue as to whether the constituent process gives way to the Constitution in irreversible, and therefore self-embracing, fashion or whether the constituent process remains available, in reserve so to speak. This issue is therefore the same as the one we have been discussing in relation to the constituent power of the Imperial Parliament. A continuing interpretation of the constituent process is by no means excluded, therefore. See C. Klein, *Théorie et pratique du pouvoir constituant* (Paris: Presses Universitaires de France, 1996).

[34] Lindell makes a similar distinction where he refers to the 'search for an additional, although not necessarily alternative, way of explaining the reason for the legally binding and fundamental character of the Constitution'. G. Lindell, 'Why Is Australia's Constitution Binding?—The Reasons in 1900 and Now, and the Effect of Independence' (1986–7) 16 Fed LR 29, 37.

amendment process is usually the master key to the Constitution, as we have seen. Therefore, if everything that is amendable in the Constitution is amendable using a procedure involving the substantial participation of the Australian people, then the term 'popular sovereignty' is fairly apt (more so, it might be said, than in the United States). However, for the early period of Australian constitutional development, this sovereignty can only have been supplementary rather than truly alternative, in the sense just noted, unless we are intent on re-writing the historical record. In addition to the section 128 procedure, the Imperial Parliament was empowered to amend the Australian Constitution after 1901. When this power ended is a question that we will come to in a moment.

Finally, popular sovereignty can be a wide-ranging legal principle,[35] a synonym for representative democracy, and as such a principle by which all sorts of constitutional limitations can be divined by an activist High Court.[36] The High Court itself has now discouraged this sort of role for popular sovereignty, though it has not discouraged a more limited linking of popular sovereignty or representative democracy to the text and structure of the Constitution.[37]

What does this analysis of the concept of popular sovereignty add to our discussion of the acquisition of Australian constitutional independence? We have seen that in Canada and New Zealand there was some moment (1982 and 1947, respectively) when the United Kingdom Parliament granted to these countries the master key to amend their respective Constitutions. In Canada, the United Kingdom Parliament simultaneously handed over that master key and removed itself from Canadian constitutional amendment in 1982, whereas in New Zealand, the Wellington Parliament waited until 1986 to use the master key that it had been given in 1947 in order to remove the United Kingdom Parliament as a potential alternative (though subordinate) amending power for the New Zealand Constitution. It is hard to identify an equivalent moment in Australian constitutional development unless it is 1901, 1931 or 1986. 1901 would seem to be excluded because of the difficulty in re-writing a legal-historical record which acknowledged the supremacy of the Imperial Parliament until at least 1931. Many attempts have been made to pin constitutional independence on the Statute of Westminster, 1931 (adopted in 1942 with effect from 1939), but there was no equivalent in Australia to the New Zealand Constitution (Amendment) Act, 1947 (UK) to make this argument more credible. If we assume that the United Kingdom Parliament held the master key to the Australian Constitution until 1986, then the Australia Act 1986 (UK) would have been the essential part of the process of handing over the master key to Australia. We would have had to view section 1 of the Australia Act 1986 (UK) as a self-embracing

---

[35] It should be noted that the first interpretation of popular sovereignty concerned a political principle. This interpretation involves a legal principle, i.e. one with direct legal consequences.
[36] See the cases discussed in the final section of Ch. 11 above.
[37] See *McGinty v State of Western Australia* (1996) 186 CLR 140 and cases which followed it, as discussed in Ch. 11 above.

self-limitation by the Westminster Parliament, permanently and fully binding. However, there are a number of problems with this interpretation, some more serious than others. First, the High Court in *Sue v Hill*[38] has recently stated that it was the Australia Act 1986 (Cth) rather than the United Kingdom version which achieved Australia's constitutional independence. Secondly, both the High Court in *Sue v Hill* and the High Court of the early mid-1990s viewed the Australia Act 1986 (UK) not as the final act in an *Australian* constitutional process (as 1947 and 1982 were viewed from the New Zealand and Canadian perspectives just discussed) but as predominantly, if not solely, a United Kingdom Act directed at the United Kingdom and governed by United Kingdom constitutional theory. This is perhaps why it was so important for the High Court in *Sue v Hill* to make clear that even if British constitutional theory is still not up to concluding that the Westminster Parliament can bind itself, the Australia Act 1986 (Cth) is able to do the job.[39] Thirdly, if we assume that the United Kingdom Parliament held the master key until 1986, then we have to assume that, in theory, even after 1931 (or 1942),[40] it could have passed any legislation whatsoever for Australia. The Supreme Court of Canada left this possibility wide open in Canada's case in the *Patriation Reference*, but most Australian assumptions have been to the contrary at least since Australia acquired its political and international independence. Many Australian commentators would include a fourth problem associated with treating 1986 as the moment the Westminster Parliament handed over the master key to Australia: that is the implications for Australian perceptions of constitutional independence if such independence was achieved as a result of United Kingdom legislation. However, this is less of a *legal* problem than those commentators often assume. So long as the possibility of self-embracing legal change is accepted, there should be no problem with the fact that constitutional independence is granted by United Kingdom legislation where the United Kingdom Parliament is permanently and fully prohibited from interfering in Australian legal affairs, constitutional or other. Emotional or nationalistic objections are a different, though by no means irrelevant, concern.

If, however, we assume, as the High Court appears to at the moment, that the Australia Act 1986 (UK) is really for United Kingdom legal consumption—a United Kingdom restraint on the Westminster Parliament—and that the Australia Act 1986 (Cth) does the essential work in achieving Australian constitutional independence, then how do we explain what has occurred? As noted earlier, Australia is unique amongst the countries under study in having all the

[38] *Sue v Hill* (1999) 199 CLR 462. See also *Attorney-General (W.A) v Marquet* (2003) 202 ALR 233, paras 67 and 70 *per* Gleeson CJ, Gummow, Hayne and Heydon JJ.

[39] ibid., para. 64.

[40] It is worth noting that between 1931 and 1942 there were four United Kingdom Acts which purported to extend the powers of the Commonwealth Parliament: the Whaling Act 1934, s. 15; the Geneva Convention Act, 1937, s. 2; the Emergency Powers (Defence) Act 1939, s. 5; and the Army and Air Force (Annual) Act, 1940, s. 3.

essential tools of constitutional independence in its first and only Constitution. This did not mean that it was constitutionally independent in 1901, only that it was fully equipped. The Constitution set up all the essentials of a federal, democratic system of representative and responsible government under the rule of law.[41] More importantly, for our purposes, section 128 dealt with amendment[42] of the Constitution, section 51(xxix) provided jurisdiction over external affairs to the Commonwealth, and section 51(xxxviii) allowed the Commonwealth, at the request of all states directly concerned, to exercise 'any power which can at the establishment of this Constitution be exercised only by the Parliament of the United Kingdom'. So long as the doctrines of extra-territoriality and repugnancy were in place, the potential of these section 51 provisions could not be fully explored. However, when the Statute of Westminster, 1931 removed the obstacles of extraterritoriality and repugnancy, and when Australia adopted the Statute in 1942, these sections were ripe to assume their full potential.

In the case of the external affairs power, three judges in the *Kirmani* case had confirmed its potential *vis-à-vis* United Kingdom legislation just prior to the Australia Acts 1986. In the case of section 51(xxxviii), its potential, though often asserted in government and academic circles in the years leading up to 1986, was only confirmed in 1989,[43] and again in 1999 in *Sue v Hill*.[44] Effectively, the section 51 provisions, and especially section 51(xxxviii), were, much as Harrison Moore had feared regarding the latter,[45] sections which could grow into a meaning and potential that had constitutional independence as their object. In the case of section 51(xxxviii) that potential was no less than eventually to remove the United Kingdom Parliament from its position at the apex of the Australian legal system. In Imperial terms, understood through the prism of Imperial theory and Diceyan dogma, this was impossible. However, in

---

[41] It is assumed in this analysis either that the covering clauses were directly or indirectly amendable using s. 128, or that their existence was insignificant where constitutional independence was concerned. For discussion of differing views regarding amendment of the covering clauses, see Chs 9 and 10 above.

[42] As noted above, s. 128 speaks of 'alteration'; however 'amendment' is deemed to be a synonym in what follows and is used in order to maintain consistency of vocabulary, taking into account that 'amendment' is used in Canada and New Zealand.

[43] *Port MacDonnell Professional Fishermen's Assn Inc v South Australia* (1989) 168 CLR 340.

[44] *Sue v Hill* (n. 38 above) para. 61.

[45] W. Harrison Moore, 'The Commonwealth of Australia Bill' (1900) 16 LQR 35, 39–40:

There is one power conferred upon the Commonwealth Parliament . . . which seems to me more far-reaching and perhaps more dangerous than those which are merely concerned with external affairs. The 38th Article [the present section 51(xxxviii)] of legislation includes the power to 'exercise within the Commonwealth at the request or with the concurrence of the Parliaments of all the States concerned, any power which can at the establishment of this Constitution be exercised only by the Parliament of the United Kingdom . . .' This article may lead to serious trouble. Claims to legislative independence have been founded on lighter grounds than this; and . . . the theoretical power of the Imperial Parliament to recall constitutional powers is not one of great practical value. Under this article it would seem that the Commonwealth Parliament might, at the request of a

Australian terms, to the extent that its constitutional theory had become independent, this amounted to nothing more complicated than having a constitutional provision which said, in so many words: 'when the obstacles of extraterritoriality and repugnancy have been removed this provision may be used by the Commonwealth, at the behest of the States, to amend the Constitution so as to replace the United Kingdom Parliament in whatever constitutional role or roles it continues to play at that time'. Normally such a provision would be found in the amending formula itself, i.e. in section 128; however, it was appropriate given the significance and potential of section 51(xxxviii) that it was governed not by the qualified majorities of section 128 but by unanimous state consent (as all states would be concerned). Section 128 and section 51(xxxviii) need to be interpreted in a manner which takes into account their respective constitution-making potential.

Section 128 refers to the fact that '*this Constitution* shall not be altered except in the following manner'. Strictly speaking, the Commonwealth in enacting the Australia Act 1986 under section 51(xxxviii) did not alter the Constitution, i.e. the text bearing that name.[46] And similarly section 51(xxxviii) which must be exercised 'subject to this Constitution' did not in that light conflict with section 128. Section 15(1) of the Australia Act 1986 dealt with alteration not of the Constitution but of the Australia Act itself and of the Statute of Westminster.[47] The closest it came to amending the Constitution was in clarifying in section 15(3)

State Parliament, repeal any Act of the Imperial Parliament applicable in the colony; in other words, the Commonwealth and State parliaments, acting together, might nullify Imperial legislation. Here, if anywhere, the Imperial Parliament may in future be said to have intended to divest itself of authority. It is not enough that we may be able to show by abstract reasoning that this is not or could not be the case.

[46] The Australia Act 1986 amends, restricts or repeals (in their application to Australia) all or part of the Statute of Westminster, 1931 (UK), the Merchant Shipping Act 1894 (UK), the Colonial Courts of Admiralty Act 1890 (UK), the Colonial Laws Validity Act, 1865 (UK), the Australian Constitutions Act 1850 (UK), the Judicial Committee Act 1844 (UK), the Judicial Committee Act 1833 (UK), the Australian Courts Act 1828 (UK) and the Australian State Constitutions. There is no mention of any amendment or alteration to the Commonwealth Constitution.

[47] Section 15(1):

15(1) This Act or the Statute of Westminster 1931, as amended and in force from time to time, in so far as it is part of the law of the Commonwealth, of a State or of a Territory, may be repealed or amended by an Act of Parliament of the Commonwealth passed at the request or with the concurrence of the Parliaments of all the States and, subject to subsection (3) below, only in that manner.

It should be noted that s. 15(1) requires the concurrence of 'all the States', whereas s. 51(xxxviii) requires the concurrence of 'all the States directly concerned'. If s. 51(xxxviii) is understood to have discrete constitution-making power, then s. 15 represents a slight amendment to the former power, apparently in contradiction with s. 128: 'this Constitution shall not be altered except...'. However, if s. 51(xxxviii) does indeed contain constituent powers, then those powers should be capable of amendment. That is, just as s. 128 can be used to amend itself, the discrete constitution-making powers of s. 51(xxxviii) should be available to amend that same section. Section 15(3)

that nothing in section 15(1) prevented the Commonwealth Parliament from exercising powers conferred on it by section 128.[48] As a clarification of section 15(1) it did not, again, amend the Constitution. However, it did helpfully confirm that section 128 can be used to amend and, if desired, replace section 15.[49] This would seem to make clear that section 128 is the master key to the Australian Constitution.[50]

If section 15(1) is deemed to be an amendment to the Constitution, or if the Commonwealth acting under section 51(xxxviii) really cannot bind itself, as Leslie Zines and others have stated,[51] then it may be that the Australia Act 1986 (UK) does more than the High Court indicated in *Sue v Hill*. The Court was there concerned with section 1 rather than with section 15 of the Australia Act 1986, so this would have been understandable. In that case, following the examples of Canada and New Zealand, it would seem appropriate to look at the Australia Act 1986 (UK) as a self-embracing Act, at least from an Australian perspective, according to which sections 1 and 15 together make clear that the

makes clear that such Commonwealth powers (in conjunction with all states) are ultimately controlled by s. 128, which is therefore the master key to the Australian constitution.

[48] Section 15(3):

15(3) Nothing in subsection (1) above limits or prevents the exercise by the Parliament of the Commonwealth of any powers that may be conferred upon that Parliament by any alteration to the Constitution of the Commonwealth made in accordance with section 128 of the Constitution of the Commonwealth after the commencement of this Act.

[49] In this respect, see the debate between Gageler and Leeming and Lindell and Rose which was summarised in Ch. 11 above. Tony Blackshield has made a recent helpful attempt to cut through this debate, in a way which differs from the analysis proposed here, in the 'Australia Act' entry to T. Blackshield, M. Coper and G. Williams (eds) *The Oxford Companion to the High Court of Australia* (Melbourne: Oxford University Press, 2001) 45:

[There have been] suggestions that the Australia Act, or the circumstances of its enactment, may have opened up an alternative method of amending the Constitution, bypassing the referendum process required by section 128.

. . .

Clearly, no ordinary exercise of Commonwealth-state co-operation under section 5(xxxviii) of the Constitution could circumvent section 128, which emphatically declares: 'This Constitution shall not be altered except in the following manner.' To make sense of the argument about the Australia Act, we must assume that the formula used in section 15(1) (request or concurrence 'of all States') is *different* from the formula in section 51 (xxxviii) of the Constitution (request or concurrence 'of all the States directly concerned'. But this seems unduly strained. If, as seems likely, the Australia Act does not create a new independent alternative to section 51 (xxxviii), but simply allows section 51 (xxxviii) to be used for the specified purposes, any use of section 15(1) would still be 'subject to this Constitution'.

. . .

It is hardly likely that section 15(1), construed upon [a foundation of popular sovereignty recognised by the High Court], would be found to have subverted that foundation.

[50] It would also seem to permit an alteration to the Constitution to allow for amendment to the covering clauses to the Constitution.

[51] See discussion in Ch. 11 above. See also A. Twomey, *The Constitution of New South Wales* (Annandale: Federation Press, 2004) 110, 123–5.

United Kingdom Parliament is no longer an active component of the Australian legal system. If the interpretation of section 15(3) favoured above is correct, then section 15(1) is ultimately subject to alteration and even replacement by section 128. In that sense, if not in the more fundamental senses discussed above, the people of Australia are now sovereign.

14

Conclusion

Much of this book has been about how the well-behaved Dominions of the former British Empire—Australia, Canada and New Zealand—acquired their constitutional independence: how they contemplated it, how they achieved it practically speaking, and how they subsequently explained what they had done. Each stage was greatly affected by often unacknowledged and contestable assumptions about central concepts such as sovereignty and legal system. One of the main purposes of this book has been to shed light on those assumptions, to illustrate how such ingrained or dogmatic doctrines affected assessments regarding possible options, and to point out alternative conceptions and the options that emerge as a consequence.

It is often assumed, in law as in other disciplines, that we can learn a great deal by looking at 'pathological' situations, or circumstances of abnormal legal-constitutional behaviour—revolutions, *coups d'état*, unilateral declarations of independence (UDI), civil war or secession—and an abundant literature illustrates that assumption wonderfully well.[1] However, it is often forgotten that normal behaviour, like good health, is also full of lessons when studied closely, though the temptation, quite naturally, is to simply take it for granted. Bearing this in mind, it may have been helpful in our consideration of concepts such as sovereignty and legal system, that Australia, Canada and New Zealand present themselves, in the main, as well-behaved, rule-of-law-following countries. What then have we learned from them regarding sovereignty and legal systems, and how have these lessons played out in Australia, Canada and New Zealand? Many of the detailed lessons have been explored in corresponding detail in the chapters which precede. It may now be helpful to isolate some more general lessons from this study. Accordingly, we shall examine some of the lessons regarding sovereignty and legal system, before summarising the arguments put forward in the book as a whole. We then conclude with a discussion of the importance of assumptions in constitutional law.

---

[1] See, e.g., Hart, *The Concept of Law* (Oxford: Clarendon Press, 1961; 2nd edn, 1994) ch. 6; J. Finnis, 'Revolutions and Continuity if Law' in A.W.B. Simpson (ed.) *Oxford Essays in Jurisprudence*, 2nd Series (Oxford: Clarendon Press, 1973) 44.

'Normal' constitutional development and 'micro' analysis: sovereignty

Pathological constitutional situations often ignore traditional claims to sovereignty and instead cry out for legitimacy and efficacy, factors which are usually marginalised or even banished from mainstream legal analysis. Normal constitutional situations take legitimacy and efficacy for granted and heed traditional claims to sovereignty—until, that is, traditional claims to sovereignty put obstacles in the way of explaining that which is perceived to be normal constitutional development. This was the case in Australia, Canada and New Zealand, as we have seen, when it came to anticipating, achieving and, especially, explaining the normal rite of passage from colony to independent nation. When the dominant orthodox or Imperial theory of sovereignty offered up weak or inadequate explanations for constitutional independence, constitutional commentators were naturally inclined to emphasise the legitimacy and efficacy side of things. For example, the Australian Constitution is rooted in the sovereignty of the people, the Canadian Constitution dependent on acceptance by the international community of Canada's independent status, and the New Zealand Constitution is based more generally in popular acceptance in both the *Māori* and *Pākehā* communities. It would be foolish to ignore the importance of these factors, given their undoubted contribution to those countries' current convictions regarding the strength and security of their constitutional independence.

However, Australia, Canada and New Zealand had not just set out to achieve constitutional independence in the 1980s. They had purported, and emphatically so in the case of Canada, to be doing so with appropriate respect for existing constitutional rules. In Chapter 1, the Introduction, we questioned whether it was possible to explain constitutional independence with due account for constitutional continuity and the rule of law associations that accompany it. We saw how the orthodox Diceyan conception of continuing sovereignty made this explanation difficult, or at best precarious; whereas a 'revised' or self-embracing interpretation of sovereignty did so satisfactorily. And even if the United Kingdom was still unclear on whether its Parliament ultimately had continuing or self-embracing powers, it was open to independent Australian, Canadian and New Zealand legal systems, topped by independent supreme courts, to secure constitutional continuity and constitutional independence by adopting discrete interpretations of the Westminster Parliament's powers. After all, viewed from Australian, Canadian and New Zealand perspectives, the Westminster Parliament had acted not as a foreign Parliament, but as an essential component part in the machinery of those countries' Constitutions, admittedly a component which by the choice of those countries had remained located in the

United Kingdom. Interpretation of that component's powers as part of the local legal system was a matter for local constitutional actors, courts and constitutional amendment procedures. It was argued that there is every reason to expect that local constitutional actors will choose the self-embracing interpretation of the Westminster Parliament's powers that satisfactorily explains these countries' constitutional independence.

If this, or some similar independent-spirited variation on it, is a satisfactory legal explanation of Australia, Canada and New Zealand's constitutional continuity and constitutional independence, then the government advisers who devised the legal side of 1982 and 1986 should feel vindicated. They accomplished the task that they were assigned, and it should be clear from this account that it was by no means an easy task to perform. However, others, constitutional experts amongst them, may be struck by how 'thin' or unsatisfying this explanation is, whatever its legal merits. How can it be, they might ask, that the validity and supremacy of their countries' Constitutions turns on a 'micro' interpretation of the Westminster Parliament's powers rather than on something more inspiring? And even if one ignored the 'micro' explanation and focused on the legal machinery alone, how can it be that merely jumping through a legislative procedural hoop in the United Kingdom justifies the exalted status of each country's constitutional arrangements? It is not surprising, then, that constitutional experts, who are citizens before they are experts, look for more inspiring and convincing explanations in popular sovereignty, international recognition and inter-societal acceptance, for example.

Because the foregoing analysis has been intent on illustrating the effects of hidden, often unacknowledged assumptions on our sense of constitutional possibility, it may also have given the impression that a 'micro' legal analysis based on a self-embracing interpretation of the United Kingdom Parliament's powers was a sufficient explanation for the supremacy and validity of Australia, Canada and New Zealand's Constitutions. That would be an entirely understandable impression given the time devoted to such 'micro' arguments in this book; however, it would be mistaken. It may be helpful, therefore, to explain why.

Choosing between continuing and self-embracing sovereignty: the inadequacy of legal reasons

Because of the dominance of the orthodox Diceyan doctrine of continuing sovereignty, it was necessary to spend some time clarifying and defending the self-embracing alternative. That done, it was also noted that there is no abstract logical reason to prefer either the continuing or the self-embracing interpretation of sovereignty. They are equally coherent. Political reasons are often presented for preferring one or the other, but not surprisingly the arguments divide on either side of the debate. The choice between continuing and self-embracing sovereignty relates to the fact that sovereignty itself is a paradoxical concept. This in turn relates to the fact that both law and legal system are self-referential or circular concepts by nature. Whether the circle is vicious or virtuous is for each of us to decide; however this circularity is the way that law and legal system do their work. We shall discuss the concept of legal system in a moment.

Remaining with law for the moment, we know that officials, principally judges, recognise some but not other sources as law. This is the way that the legal circle begins to close. We have seen how significant it was that Imperial officials and judges on the whole recognised British law rather than aboriginal law in the early period of discovery, settlement, conquest or cession. We also know, though we do not consider its implications sufficiently, that the same judges who recognise the law recognise *themselves* as valid sources of law. They also recognise the ability of the legislature to determine the law, and it is one of the most important variables in any constitutional system to know whether the judges defer to or control the legislature.

In the United Kingdom the judges generally defer to the legislature where the legislature speaks clearly. It was one of the insights of the 'new' and 'revised' view of sovereignty to note that before judges can recognise a legislature they need to know what the legislature is, how it communicates and what it may say. Not surprisingly, the legislature often attempts to influence the courts by suggesting or 'trying on' different modes and kinds of communication in the hope and expectation that the judges will defer to the legislature's democratic will. What we have noted with regard to continuing and self-embracing sovereignty is that, prior to the middle part of the twentieth century, the United Kingdom Parliament seldom if ever tried to bind itself (certainly not in clear, effective terms), and therefore, contrary to the orthodox view, we never had any clear, binding ruling from the courts on whether it was possible to do so. Saying that Parliament may legislate on any matter whatever simply begged the question: what if Parliament clearly stated that it wished to limit itself? The clearest attempts of this type came with the multiple Westminster-enacted independence Acts and, more recently, with the European Communities Act 1972.

As stated earlier, again contrary to the orthodox view, there was no abstract logical reason to choose between the continuing and self-embracing versions of Parliament's power. The fact that a democratic Parliament purported to bind itself in independence-granting Acts and in the European Communities Act 1972 might seem to dictate an answer to unelected judges, but if continuing sovereignty was the rule then the judges would simply have to refuse the attempt by one Parliament to bind itself in order to preserve the full democratic discretion of future Parliaments. The fact that such Parliaments would not be able democratically to choose certain forms of entrenchment was a pertinent and troubling point, but one which simply indicated that in the end the democratic arguments seemed to cancel each other out. Remaining with the independence example, if we assume that the obscure question regarding the true nature of

Parliament's powers was still penumbral, at least from the perspective of local legal systems, this would mean that the courts would have to choose between equally viable alternative conceptions of Parliament's powers. The courts of Australia, Canada and New Zealand, most notably the Supreme Court of Canada in the *Patriation Reference*, had shown a disturbing tendency to view themselves as deferential colonial courts in this matter, but presumably in the twenty-first century they would be able to take an independent view.

It was suggested in Chapter 12 that if the choice between continuing and self-embracing sovereignty was penumbral and therefore still open, and if there was no abstract logical reason to favour one or the other type of sovereignty, the courts would eventually have to choose. That is not to say that the choice was unregulated by law. It was at least clear, for example, that neither a compact of states or provinces nor a majority of Commonwealth countries could dictate a constitutional arrangement for Australia, Canada and New Zealand. However, there was an important level of uncertainty or open texture regarding the nature of the sovereignty of the Westminster Parliament. In Chapter 12 it was suggested that an Australian, Canadian or New Zealand court would resolve the uncertainty by choosing the solution which was most fitting according to an amalgam of cultural, social, political and historical factors, including the issues of popular sovereignty, international acceptance and inter-societal acceptance and legitimation that were emphasised by local constitutional commentators and noted earlier. It was important in this respect that the interpreter was a local court given that the High Court of Australia, Supreme Court of Canada and New Zealand Supreme Court are likely to read the story of their countries' past and future constitutional development differently than the Judicial Committee of the Privy Council might have done, despite the presence of the same, apparently neutral facts. It seems clear that the local courts would choose the self-embracing interpretation of the Westminster Parliament's powers if that preserved constitutional continuity and guaranteed constitutional independence, and if the choice was also dependent on such cultural, social, political and historical factors.

We see here that it is impossible to choose between continuing and self-embracing sovereignty in a vacuum. Dicey attempted to close the choice down by presenting abstract logical reasons why the former had to be preferred ahead of the latter. We have seen that those reasons do not necessarily avail. The law presents a choice, then, but one where neither clear, binding precedent nor abstract logic dictate an answer. Here, the lawyer, judge and citizen are forced to return to the factors which they know best in order to choose the answer which most suits their constitutional arrangements. It is as if constitutional law and theory finally come up for air. Having done so, it is clearly important to bear in mind the relationship between law and legitimacy in matters as important as the foundations of the Constitution, rather than return to the oxygen-deprived waters of legal analysis based on excessively rigid approaches to logic and precedent alone.

As a final general point, it is an abiding characteristic of constitutional rules that so many of them are never tested. The core of their legal meaning relies on their comprehensibility. However, given that so many of these rules are unlikely ever to be commented on or clarified by a court, it seems unreal to speak in terms of a rule of recognition. In order to understand these rules and how, if at all, they work, we need to go beyond official recognition and consider what it is that gives these rules authority. Constitutional authority appears to go beyond Hart's 'internal aspect of rules',[2] and beyond Raz's exclusionary reasons,[3] to whatever quality it is that makes such rules seem legitimate and authoritative in the largest sense of those words. Such considerations are for another day, or perhaps for another book. They do, however, point to a sense in which factors such as popular sovereignty, international recognition or inter-societal accept-ance are highly relevant, if not entirely determinative.

'Normal' constitutional development and 'macro' analysis: legal system

The foregoing discussion has an analogue in thinking about legal systems, the 'macro' level of analysis, as it was referred to in Chapter 12. According to a familiar analysis, developed by Kelsen but also ingrained in much of our legal education, the normative or obligatory force of a by-law in Sydney, Vancouver or Auckland is explained by following a chain of legal validity which leads upwards (in constitutional terms) and backwards (in temporal terms) to (a) the state, province, regional or national authority; (b) the Constitution; (c) any previous Constitution; (d) the body which enacted the first Constitution; and (e) (in the case of a customary or common law constitution) and so on into the mists of time. In most legal systems the recursive analysis comes to a halt at (d). Whether stopping at (d) or (e), we eventually run out of links in the chain of validity, so (f) we take the final vital step of presuming the validity of the first historical Constitution. Here we have reached the basic norm, or *Grundnorm*.[4]

The virtue of this analysis is that it tells a story not only about legal validity and normativity, but also about the unity or identity of a legal system. So far so good. This is part of the attraction of theories of legal system in preference to theories of sovereignty standing alone. The problem is, however, that the story is not a very convincing one. First, regarding both legal validity and normativity, the Kelsenian chain is thin and unsatisfying. The citizen of Sydney, Vancouver or Auckland, apprised of this theory when asked to pay his or her parking fine, for example, probably expects something grand and impressive at the end of the

---

[2] Hart (n. 1 above) ch. 5.
[3] J. Raz, *The Authority of Law* (Oxford: Oxford University Press, 1979) ch. 1.
[4] See H. Kelsen, *General Theory of Law and State* (Cambridge, Massachusetts: Harvard University Press, 1949) ch. 10.

chain. The *Grundnorm* borrows some force from German capitalisation rules, but as a reason for validity and normativity it is a disappointment. Once we add considerations such as legitimacy and respect for the rule of law it begins to come to life. The original constitution-making process may have been so impressive and widespread a democratic consultation that this initial legitimacy continues to animate the Constitution in its day-to-day work many links and years along the chain. Or perhaps the original process was more prosaic in nature, but the many years of rule-following may have set up an impressive and widespread respect for the rule of law in the system in question. While Kelsen's simple model may be enough to identify valid law and explain its normativity in basic terms, other factors must be brought to bear in order to bring the law, especially the law of the constitution, to life, i.e. to understand how validity and normativity actually come about. Hart's internal aspect successfully took us beyond orders backed by threats, but Hart was reluctant to pour the sort of content into the 'internal aspect' that would make it understandable in the deeper sense just discussed.[5]

A second problem with Kelsen's theory, more directly relevant to this book, is that its explanation for the unity or identity of the legal system is overbearing. As we saw in Chapter 12, Kelsen states that a legal system includes all rules which are connected to the *Grundnorm* by an unbroken chain of legal rule-following. Given that Australia, Canada and New Zealand purported to follow the then-existing legal rules in order to achieve their constitutional independence, that independence would seem to be illusory. If, on the one hand, Ross was right about self-embracing attempts to, effectively, amend the amending formula being logically impermissible and therefore 'magical' or, as Wade would say, 'revolutionary', then constitutional independence was secure but only at the cost of a breach in legality and a new *Grundnorm*. This was not the sort of constitutional story that Australia, Canada and New Zealand were trying to tell. If, contrary to Ross, Hart was right about the logical coherence of self-embracing change, then the self-embracing manner in which Australia, Canada and New Zealand may have acquired their constitutional independence left them connected to the first historical Constitution in an unbroken chain of rule-following and therefore seemingly part of the British (or Imperial) legal system.

It is here that we need to look at the situation with more subtlety. There seem to be two different senses of legal system at work here. If Australia, Canada and New Zealand believe in rule-following and constitutional continuity, then there should be no embarrassment about being part of one sort of 'legal system' the one which leads back at least to 1688–9 if not to the distant and partly mythical origins of the English Constitution. In fact, such an account may serve an important symbolic purpose and even be inspiring to some. There are many countries in the world which would like to look back at their constitutional past and see such a story of respect for the rule of law. This sense of legal system is

---

[5] Hart (n. 1 above) ch. 5.

much like a family tree. It is the historical record. If it is more than a historical record then we will need to know more about the legal system in question, just as we would need to more about the family in question, before we concluded that the ancestors' influence on the living is still strong.

A second sense of legal system is the set of rules which are presently active, in the sense of their acting on legal subjects and being capable of recognition by judges and officials. This sense of an active 'legal system' may be overly narrow, but it is has sufficient distinctiveness for present purposes. If self-embracing constitutional change is possible, and there is no reason to assume the contrary, then we should expect to find in Australia, Canada and New Zealand, legal rules, such as those relating to the power of the Westminster Parliament, which are important components of the legal system in the first sense, but irrelevant in the second sense.

This brings us to the point where the 'micro' and the 'macro'—sovereignty and legal system—meet again. Where continuing sovereignty is the rule, we should expect to find that the two senses of legal system substantially overlap. However, where self-embracing change has occurred, notably at the highest constitutional level, the legal system in the second sense may be separate and distinct from much of the earlier part of the legal system understood in the first sense. This explains why Australia, Canada and New Zealand can be proud of both their respect for constitutional continuity and their achievement of con-stitutional independence.

However, as was stated earlier, there is no inevitability about either the continuing or the self-embracing interpretation, and therefore about the way in which the legal system evolves. Therefore, in order to understand and interpret the evolution of a legal system, it is necessary to know a great deal about the culture, politics, history and law of the society in question, just as was true in the case of understanding and interpreting sovereignty. It will also be important to know which legislatures can influence the telling of that story and which courts can influence its interpretation.

The development of constitutional theory in Australia, Canada and New Zealand

It should now be clear why it has been necessary to bring so many different elements together in the discussion of the development of constitutional theory in Australia, Canada and New Zealand, and the constitution of their independence.

In Part I, it was necessary to explain how British (or English) law supplanted aboriginal or other European legal systems in the territories that now make up Australia, Canada and New Zealand. Experts in aboriginal rights and legal historians have uncovered a remarkable and surprising pluralism in the way that law was actually practised. However, for our purposes, it was important to know that if and when push came to shove, the courts and law-enforcement agencies would heed the wishes of the British Crown, and ultimately, the British Crown-in-Parliament. The Imperial legal system which developed, contained as part of its constitutional set up important rules regarding, for example, repugnancy and extraterritoriality, which controlled the ambitions of the new colonies that emerged in the nineteenth century. These obstacles were removed by the Statute of Westminster, 1931, but certain theoretical assumptions lingered on. It was also necessary, therefore, to demonstrate the extent to which the Imperial legal system was dominated by dogmatic assertions of the Westminster Parliament's absolute and continuing sovereignty. This dogma made it easy to comprehend why colonies, even Dominions, had subordinate legislatures, and difficult to explain how the Westminster Parliament could ever terminate its legal authority over them. 'New' and 'revised' theories of parliamentary sovereignty emerged but these never took firm hold. It came to be accepted that the Westminster Parliament could terminate its powers relating to a colony and thereby grant independence; however, the dominant view in British constitutional theory was that such action was 'revolutionary'. At best, it could be said that the local courts would no longer recognise Westminster enactments, but there was no consensus on what the explanation might be. This was particularly problematic in countries like Canada where, as late as 1981, on the eve of independence, the Supreme Court of Canada had confirmed that the Westminster Parliament's powers *vis-à-vis* Canada were undiminished, and that a court such as itself could not judicially review its enactments.

If Imperial constitutional theory had had no impact on Australia, Canada and New Zealand that was one thing, but to the extent that Imperial ideas had taken hold in the Empire (later the Commonwealth), they too would need to be considered. Part II therefore examined the way in which these Imperial ideas influenced Australia, Canada and New Zealand, notably in the contemplation of constitutional independence and in the mechanics of setting out to achieve it. The Canadian context was distinguished by the fact that Canada lacked a general formula for constitutional amendment from the earliest days of Confederation. By default, the body which enacted the Constitution Act, 1867, the Westminster Parliament, would amend it. The Statute of Westminster, 1931 left this situation untouched. Some Canadian constitutional commentators therefore tended to look at the amendment procedure as a British matter, governed by British constitutional understandings. To the extent that there was any difference between Canadian and British constitutional understandings, and until 1950 or so these were rare, the British understanding prevailed. This approach was termed the 'Imperial theory'. Other Canadians saw the Westminster Parliament as part of a *Canadian* procedure for constitutional amendment, and one that was therefore subject to distinctive Canadian interpretations. This approach was termed the 'Independence theory'. As just noted, when the Supreme Court of Canada came to consider the matter in 1981 it showed all the tendencies of an institution which was influenced by the Imperial theory. By means of the Canada Act 1982, the Westminster Parliament renounced its authority to legislate for Canada and substituted a new domestic code on constitutional amendment. The Supreme Court of Canada gave the impression of having taken on board some element of the Independence theory when it confirmed in the *Veto Reference* that the new code on amendment had entirely replaced the Westminster Parliament.

New Zealand constitutional theory was also heavily dominated by Imperial theory. Most significantly, this accounted in part for the mid- and late-nineteenth-century downgrading of the Treaty of Waitangi from foundational to historical status. Some independence was manifested in New Zealand interpretations of section 5 of the Colonial Laws Validity Act, 1865 (Imp.), but on the whole New Zealand politicians and constitutional commentators were comfortable with the overarching sovereignty of the Westminster Parliament, as reflected in the fact that New Zealand did not adopt the Statute of Westminster, 1931 until 1947. When it did so, however, it also acquired the ability to amend its Constitution. Although at a later point 1947 could be viewed from a New Zealand perspective as a self-embracing handing over of the constitutional master key to the Wellington Parliament, the fact that the United Kingdom Parliament maintained a legislative role for New Zealand under section 4 of the Statute of Westminster, 1931 (subject to its New Zealand gloss) meant that the matter remained uncertain. Some New Zealand constitutional commentators began to move in the direction of 'new' and 'revised' understandings of parliamentary sovereignty in the 1960s, and in 1973 the New Zealand Parliament used its constituent or amending powers to confirm and clarify that its powers under the Constitution Act, 1852 (Imp.) were unlimited. The Constitution Act 1986 then terminated the residual powers of the Westminster Parliament where New Zealand was concerned.

Australian constitutional theory too was dominated by Imperial theory. However, even at the earliest stages of its national development, Australian constitutional commentators also noted that the Australian constitution-making process had been distinguished by the participation of elected representatives in Conventions and the ratification of the proposed Constitution in referendums. While it was clear that virtually all Australians observers at the time explained the validity of the Commonwealth of Australia Constitution Act, 1900 (Imp.) in terms of its enactment by the Westminster Parliament, the importance of popular participation in Australia's constitutional founding was to re-emerge as an important justificatory factor at a later stage. However, even after enactment of the Statute of Westminster, 1931 and Australia's adoption of it in 1942, mainstream Australian writing adopted the traditional Imperial theory. Owen Dixon, one of Australia's finest thinkers, was subtle and sophisticated in his approach to the issue, but, either because of his judicial responsibilities or because of his own fundamental legal and constitutional assumptions, his assessment of independent Australian understandings of Westminster sovereignty was limited to the 'new' view and did not proceed to its 'revised' extension. Wynes, the leading textbook writer from the 1930s until the 1970s, was as orthodox as could be imagined in his approach. Only in the 1970s and 1980s did a series of High Court decisions and constitutional comment seize upon a wide range of potential for independent Australian understandings of sovereignty-related issues. Doubts based on orthodox Imperial understandings were sufficiently great that when Australia sought its constitutional independence in 1986 it did so by means of two enactments: the Australia Act 1986 (Cth) under powers based in section 51(xxxviii) and possibly section 51(xxix); and the Australia Act 1986 (UK) under the traditional power of the United Kingdom Parliament.

A great deal changed as of the 1980s and Part III set out to survey and evaluate the changes and their implications. In all three countries, legislation, whether United Kingdom or local, had purported to terminate any ongoing role of the Westminster Parliament in these countries. Although the achievement of constitutional independence in this manner was overshadowed by other events in some cases or virtually unnoticed in others, those who studied constitutional law closely were presented with questions which went to fundamentals. In particular, if the United Kingdom no longer had any ongoing role in these countries, what was it that now explained the validity of their Constitutions? The period since 1982 in Canada and since 1986 in Australia and New Zealand has seen a fascinating range of new thinking on constitutional fundamentals in these countries.

In Canada, those who have examined these issues most closely have argued that constitutional independence was tied to recognition of Canada as a sovereign and independent nation and that therefore it was achieved before 1982. On this view, the key provisions of the Canada Act 1982 were probably redundant. Others, however, preferred not to raise questions about the influence of extra-legal considerations on the acquisition of Canadian constitutional independence. The unstated fear was that if Canada could be said to have acquired its independence by extra-legal means then separatist elements in Quebec might claim the same if ever that province were to leave Confederation. The Supreme Court of Canada's decision in the *Secession Reference* was designed to pre-empt that implication, but that was perhaps not the end of the matter.

In New Zealand, those who have analysed the Constitution Act 1986 (NZ) most closely have concluded that a constitutional revolution must have taken place, in part because of the supposed continuing nature of Westminster sovereignty, but also because of the removal of key United Kingdom statutes from the New Zealand statute book. The latter action was said to remove the constitutional underpinning for the New Zealand Constitution. Because the 1986 process was revolutionary, according to this view, the New Zealand Constitution must be based on acceptance by the New Zealand people, that is on considerations of legitimacy. Other writers confirmed the effectiveness of the

Constitution Act 1986 but call for more pluralistic conceptions of sovereignty in order to accommodate aboriginal claims and the Treaty of Waitangi.

The Australian debate on new constitutional foundations is the most active and in many ways the most complicated. Arguments range from the occasional espousal of orthodox Imperial assumptions through to 'revolutionary' explanations based on the sovereignty of the Australian people. In between, one finds explanations which attempt in varying ways to harness popular and Westminster parliamentary sovereignty together as justifications for the validity and supremacy of the Australian Constitution. Some of those 'harnessed' explanations use 1900 as the starting point for Australian-based sovereignty, popular or other, while others use 1931, 1939 or 1942. Still others use 1986, in which case the horses of popular and parliamentary sovereignty were not so much harnessed as staged. Perhaps the most difficult analysis regarding 1986 concerns the proper interpretation of section 15 of the Australia Acts 1986. If this section attempts to amend the Australian Constitution and bind the Commonwealth, then some commentators take the view that only the Australia Act 1986 (UK) could have justified it. Finally, it was necessary to consider some of the High Court of Australia's jurisprudence, first, on the central concept of popular sovereignty, and secondly the seminal decision in *Sue v Hill* in which the Court confirmed that Australia's constitutional independence is based on the Australia Act 1986 (Cth).

It is quite clear from this summary that a large number of the explanations for constitutional independence in Australia, Canada and New Zealand are based on some sort of 'revolutionary' or extra-legal grounding. These were surprising conclusions given that all three countries purported to achieve constitutional independence through constitutional continuity and respect for the rule of law. Was there not some explanation that could account for both constitutional independence and constitutional continuity and respect for the rule of law? It was necessary then to survey, on the one hand, whether there were explanations within the orthodox theory of sovereignty, and not surprisingly such explanations had been proposed. However, on closer examination, each explanation seemed either to rely on United Kingdom self-restraint or to otherwise hang itself on a precarious peg. This was also true of 'manner and form' explanations based in the 'new' view. None of these explanations, orthodox or new, was satisfactory in terms of the need to establish convincingly the main objective of constitutional independence. In contrast, it seemed that the 'revised' or self-embracing approach to parliamentary sovereignty offered a convincing account of both constitutional independence and constitutional continuity. It was essential therefore to consider whether there were any reasons based in legal authority or the logic of constitutional change which would prevent such an account being applied to Australia, Canada and New Zealand, and no such reasons emerged.

Consequently, a self-embracing approach was applied to the constitutional development of each of these countries. In Canada, the Westminster Parliament through the Canada Act 1982 simultaneously validated a new Canadian code on constitutional amendment and terminated Westminster's ability to legislate as part of Canadian law. In New Zealand, the Westminster Parliament through the New Zealand Constitution (Amendment) Act 1947 handed over the master key to the New Zealand Parliament without, however, terminating Westminster's ability to legislate as part of New Zealand law. The New Zealand Parliament used the master key in order to confirm and clarify its power in 1973 such that thirteen years later when it enacted the Constitution Act 1986 it had the power by then to terminate Westminster's residual ability to legislate as part of New Zealand law. Across the Tasman Sea, if worries regarding section 15 of the Australia Acts 1986 turned out to be justified, Australia would then have to rely on a self-embracing interpretation of the Westminster Parliament's enactment of the Australia Act 1986. In that Act, the Westminster Parliament simultaneously validated section 15 of the 1986 Act which provided for amendment of the Australia Act 1986 and of such parts of the Statute of Westminster, 1931 as remained in force as part of the law of Australia, and in section 1 terminated its ability to legislate as part of Australian law. However, if section 15 worries turned out to be unwarranted, then it was quite conceivable, as the High Court of Australia suggested in *Sue v Hill*, that the Australia Act 1986 (Cth) accomplished the task of achieving constitutional independence on its own. Unlike Canada and New Zealand, Australia had had all the tools it needed to be constitutionally independent as of 1 January 1901, the day the Commonwealth of Australia came into existence: section 128, sections 51(xxxviii) and 51(xxix) and its own High Court of Australia. There were a number of important obstacles in the way of using these tools, notably rules regarding repugnancy and extraterritorial legislation; however, with the enactment of the Statute of Westminster, 1931 and its adoption by Australia in 1942, these obstacles were no more. Although the matter was unclear at the time, it later became apparent that, like Dorothy in the Land of Oz, Australia had had the power to achieve its constitutional independence all along.

None of these explanations is presented as the one and only viable explanation for Australia, Canada and New Zealand to account for their constitutional independence. Rather, they are proposed as one way in which constitutional independence can be explained together with constitutional continuity and respect for the rule of law. Any such explanation is made more likely and viable in each case by the end of appeals to the Judicial Committee of the Privy Council, accomplished only recently in New Zealand with the creation of its new Supreme Court.

The importance of constitutional theory

Even if one disagrees with the proposed explanations for Australian, Canadian and New Zealand constitutional independence, this account should have succeeded in revealing the importance of the theoretical assumptions that are embedded in supposedly untheorised, pragmatic or events-driven constitutional practice. It is true that lawyers and politicians will usually find a way to do what they want regardless of theoretical obstacles. However, the account set out in this book should demonstrate the extent to which theoretical assumptions can influence the course of events and the sense of constitutional possibility for surprisingly long periods of time, especially when put forward by determined and persuasive communicators such as Dicey. As any teacher of first year constitutional law will know, once Dicey's doctrine is in place in the minds of law students it is very difficult to dislodge it. The same proved true in the Commonwealth where students of Dicey were many.

Despite the claims just made to the effect that the self-embracing explanation of parliamentary sovereignty is just one explanation amongst many, it would be disingenuous not to confess that self-embracing explanations are here presented as compelling and attractive. To that extent, if not in many other ways, this book too is influenced by its own theoretical assumptions. If we are not careful, theoretical explorations can cause yet further confusion. However, even if they do not provide clear pre-packaged answers, if done properly—and the hope is that that has been the case here—they can at least shed some light on a range of viable options. It seems vastly preferable to make constitutional choices in the awareness that there are other viable options, rather than in the blind assurance that one option is the only possible way. Choosing from viable options requires a certain amount of courage and conviction. Recognising that there are other viable options imposes a certain impulse towards humility as well. This mix of courage and humility is perhaps the best spirit in which Australia, Canada and New Zealand can explore their constitutional futures.

Bibliography

BOOKS AND ARTICLES

Aikman, C.C., 'Parliament' in Robson, J.L. (ed.) *New Zealand: The Development of its Laws and its Constitution* (2nd edn, London: Stevens, 1967) 40.

Allan, T.R.S., 'The Limits of Parliamentary Sovereignty' [1985] Public Law 614.

——, *Law, Liberty and Justice: The Legal Foundations of British Constitutionalism* (Oxford: Clarendon Press, 1993).

Ayres, P., *Owen Dixon: A Biography* (Melbourne: Melbourne University Press, 2004).

Bailey, K.H., 'Australia's Treaty Rights and Obligations' in Campbell, P., Mills, R.C. and Portus, G.V. (eds) *Studies in Australian Affairs* (Melbourne, 1930) 156.

Banting, K. and Simeon, R., *And No One Cheered: Federalism, Democracy and the Constitution Act* (Toronto: University of Toronto Press, 1985).

Beaglehole, J.C. (ed.) *New Zealand and the Statute of Westminster* (Wellington: Victoria University College, 1944).

Beaudoin, G.-A., *et al.* (eds) *Mécanismes pour une nouvelle constitution* (Ottawa: Éditions de l'université d'Ottawa, 1981).

Bennett, A., 'Can the Constitution be Amended Without a Referendum?' (1982) 56 Austr LJ 358.

Berriedale Keith, A., *Responsible Government in the Dominions*, Vols 1–3 (Oxford: Clarendon Press, 1912).

——, *The Sovereignty of the British Dominions* (London: Macmillan, 1929).

——, *The Constitutional Law of the British Dominions* (London: Macmillan, 1933).

——, *The Governments of the British Empire* (London: Macmillan, 1935).

——, *The Dominions as Sovereign States: Their Constitutions and Governments* (London: Macmillan, 1938).

Black, E.R., *Divided Loyalties* (Montreal: McGill-Queen's Press, 1975).

Blackshield, T., 'Australia Acts' in Blackshield, T., Coper, M. and Williams, G. (eds) *The Oxford Companion to the High Court of Australia* (Melbourne: Oxford University Press, 2001) 43.

Blackshield, T. and Williams, G., *Australian Constitutional Law and Theory* (3rd edn, Annandale: Federation Press, 2002).

Bogdanor, V. (ed.) *The British Constitution in the Twentieth Century* (Oxford: Oxford University Press, 2003).

Borrows, J., ' "Because It Does Not Make Sense": Sovereignty's Power in the Case of *Delgamuuk v The Queen 1997*' in Kirkby, D. and Coleborne, C. (eds) *Law, History, Colonialism: The Reach of Empire* (Manchester: Manchester University Press, 2001) 190.

——, *Recovering Canada: The Resurgence of Indigenous Law* (Toronto: University of Toronto Press, 2003).

Bradley, A.W., 'The Sovereignty of Parliament—Form or Substance' in Jowell, J. and Oliver, D. (eds) *The Changing Constitution* (5th edn, 2004) 26.

——, 'Sir William Ivor Jennings: A Centennial Paper' (2004) 67 MLR 716.

Bradley, A.W. and Ewing, K.D., *Constitutional and Administrative Law* (13th edn, Harlow: Pearson, 2003).

Brennan, T.C., *Interpreting the Constitution: A Politico-Legal Essay* (Melbourne: Melbourne University Press, 1935).

Brookfield, F.M., 'Parliamentary Supremacy and Constitutional Entrenchment: A Jurisprudential Approach' (1984) 5 Otago LR 603.

——, 'The New Zealand Constitution: The Search for Legitimacy' in Kawharu, I.H. (ed.) *Waitangi: Māori and Pākehā Perspectives of the Treaty of Waitangi* (Auckland: Oxford University Press, 1989) 1.

——, 'Kelsen, the Constitution and the Treaty' (1992) NZULR 163.

——, *Waitangi and Indigenous Rights: Revolution, Law and Legitimation* (Auckland: Auckland University Press, 1999).

Brown, J., 'The Australian Commonwealth Bill' (1900) 61 LQR 24.

Bryce, J., *Studies in History and Jurisprudence*, Vols I and II (Oxford: Oxford University Press, 1901).

Byers, M., 'Convention Associated With the Commonwealth Constitution' (1982) 56 Austr LJ 316.

Campbell, P., Mills, R.C. and Portus, G.V. (eds) *Studies in Australian Affairs* (Melbourne, 1930).

Campbell, T., Ewing, K.D. and Tomkins, A. (eds) *Sceptical Essays on Human Rights* (Oxford: Oxford University Press, 2001).

Castles, A., 'The Reception and Status of English Law in Australia' (1963) 2 Adelaide L Rev 1.

——, *An Australian Legal History* (Sydney: Law Book Company, 1982).

Clark, Andrew Inglis, *Studies in Australian Constitutional Law* (1st edn, 1901) (reprinted Sydney: Legal Books, 1997).

Clement, W.H.P., *The Law of the Canadian Constitution* (Toronto, Carswell, 1892) (2nd edn, 1904; 3rd edn, 1916).

Cohen, L., Smith, P. and Warwick, P. (eds) *The Vision and the Game: Making the Canadian Constitution* (Calgary: Detselig Enterprises Ltd, 1987).

Colvin, E., 'Constitutional Jurisprudence in the Supreme Court of Canada' (1982) 4 Sup Ct L Rev 3.

Conklin, W., *Images of a Constitution* (Toronto: University of Toronto Press, 1989).

Cooke, R., 'Fundamentals' (1988) NZLJ 158.

Coper, M., *Encounters with the Australian Constitution* (North Ryde: CCH Australia, 1987).

Coper, M. and Williams, G. (eds) *Power, Parliament and the People* (Annandale: Federation Press, 1997).

Craig, P., 'Britain in the European Union' in Jowell, J. and Oliver, D., *The Changing Constitution* (5th edn, Oxford: Oxford University Press, 2004) 88.

Craven, G., *Secession: The Ultimate State Right* (Melbourne: Melbourne University Press, 1986).

——, 'Australian Constitutional Battlegrounds of the Twenty-First Century' (1999) 20 UQLJ 250.

Curie, A.E., *New Zealand and the Statute of Westminster 1931* (Wellington: Butterworth, 1944).

Daley, J., 'The Bases for the Authority of the Australian Constitution' (Doctoral Thesis, Oxford, 1999).

Dawson, R. MacGregor (ed.) *Constitutional Issues in Canada* (London: Oxford University Press, 1933).

Derrida, J., 'Force of Law: The "Mystical Foundation of Authority"' in Cornell, D., Rosenfeld, M. and Carlson, D. (eds) *Deconstruction and the Possibility of Justice* (New York: Routledge, 1992) 1.

de Smith, S.A., *The New Commonwealth and its Constitutions* (London: Stevens & Sons, 1964).

Detmold, M.J., *The Unity of Law and Morality: A Refutation of Legal Positivism* (London: Routledge & Kegan Paul, 1984).

——, *The Australian Commonwealth: A Fundamental Analysis of Its Constitution* (Sydney: Law Book Company, 1985).

Dicey, A.V., *A Leap in the Dark: A Criticism of the Principles of Home Rule as Illustrated by the Bill of Rights 1893* (1st edn, 1893; 2nd edn, London: John Murray, 1911).

——, 'Book Review' (1898) 14 LQR 199.

Dicey, A.V., *An Introduction to the Study of the Law of the Constitution*, 10th edn by Wade, E.C.S. (London: Macmillan, 1959).

Dillon, A., 'A Turtle By Any Other Name: The Legal Basis of the Australian Constitution' (2001) 29 Fed LR 241.

Dixon, O., 'The Statute of Westminster 1931' (1936) 10 Australian LJ, Supplement, 96.

——, 'The Law and the Constitution' in Dixon, O. (ed.) *Jesting Pilate: And Other Papers and Addresses* (Melbourne: Law Book Company, 1965) 38.

——, *Jesting Pilate: And Other Papers and Addresses* (Melbourne: Law Book Company, 1965).

——, 'Sources of Legal Authority' in Dixon, O. (ed.) *Jesting Pilate: And Other Papers and Addresses* (Melbourne: Law Book Company, 1965) 198.

——, 'The Common Law as an Ultimate Constitutional Foundation' in Dixon, O. (ed.) *Jesting Pilate: And Other Papers and Addresses* (Melbourne: Law Book Company, 1965) 203.

Dworkin, R., *Law's Empire* (Cambridge, Massachusetts: Harvard University Press, 1985).

Ellis, U., *A Federal Convention: To Revise the Constitution* (Canberra: Australian Office of Rural Research and Development, 1952).

Encel, S., Horne, D. and Thompson, E. (eds) *Changing the Rules: Towards a Democratic Constitution* (Ringwood: Penguin, 1977).

Evans, G., 'Changing the System' in Encel, S., Horne, D. and Thompson, E. (eds) *Changing the Rules: Towards a Democratic Constitution* (Ringwood: Penguin, 1977) 141.

Ewart, J.S., *The Kingdom of Canada, Imperial Federation, The Colonial Conferences, the Alaska Boundary and other Essays* (Toronto: Morang & Co, 1908).

Ewing, K.D., 'The Law and the Constitution: Manifesto of the Progressive Party' (2004) 67 MLR 734.

Evatt, H.V., 'The Legal Foundations of New South Wales' (1938) 11 Austr LJ 409.

Favreau, Hon. Guy, *The Amendment of the Constitution of Canada* (Ottawa: Queen's Printer, 1965).

——, 'Constitutional Amendment in a Canadian Canada' (1966–7) 12 McGill LJ 384.

Feldman, D., 'The Internationalization of Public Law and its Impact on the United Kingdom' in Jowell, J. and Oliver, D., (eds) *The Changing Constitution* (5th edn, Oxford: Oxford University Press, 2004) 117.

Finn, Paul (ed.) *Essays on Law and Government* (Sydney: Law Book Company, 1995).

——, 'A Sovereign People, A Public Trust' in Finn, Paul (ed.) *Essays on Law and Government* (Sydney: Law Book Company, 1995) 1.

Finnis, J., 'Revolutions and Continuity of Law' in Simpson, A.W.B. (ed.) *Oxford Essays in Jurisprudence*, 2nd series (Oxford: Clarendon Press, 1973) 44.

——, 'Scepticism, Self-Refutation and the Good of Truth' in Hacker, P.M.S. and Raz, J. (eds) *Law, Morality and Society: Essays in Honour of H.L.A. Hart* (Oxford: Clarendon Press, 1977) 247.

Forsey, E., *Freedom and Order* (Toronto: McClelland & Stewart, 1974).

French, R., 'The Constitution and the People' in Lindell, G.J., Saunders, C. and French, R.S. (eds) *Reflections on the Australian Constitution* (Sydney: Federation Press, 2003).

Fuller, L., 'Positivism and Fidelity to Law—A Reply to Professor Hart' (1958) 71 Harvard L Rev 630.

Gageler, S. and Leeming, M., 'An Australian Republic: Is a Referendum Enough?' (1996) 7 Pub L Rev 143.

Galligan, B., *A Federal Republic: Australia's Constitutional System of Government* (Cambridge: Cambridge University Press, 1995).

Garran, R., *The Making and Working of the Constitution* (Sydney: New Century Press, 1932).

Gélinas, F., 'Les conventions, le droit et la Constitution dans le renvoi sur la "sécession" du Québec: le fantôme du rapatriement' (1997) 57 Rev du Barreau 291.

Gérin-Lajoie, P., *Constitutional Amendment in Canada* (Toronto: University of Toronto Press, 1950).

——, 'Du pouvoir d'amendement constitutionnel au Canada' (1951) 29 Can Bar Rev 1136.

Goldring, J., 'The Australia Act 1986 and the Formal Independence of Australia' [1986] Public Law 192.

Goldsworthy, J., *The Sovereignty of Parliament* (Oxford: Oxford University Press, 1999).

Gooch, J., *Manual or Explanatory Development of the Act for the Union of Canada, Nova Scotia and New Brunswick in one Dominion under the Name of Canada, Synthetical and Analytical: With the Text of the Act Etc, and Index to the Act and the Treatises* (Ottawa: G.E. Desbarats, 1867).

Goodrich, P., 'Terminal legality: Imperialism and the (de)composition of law' in Kirkby, D. and Coleborne, C. (eds) *Law, History, Colonialism: The Reach of Empire* (Manchester: Manchester University Press, 2001) 1.

Gustafson, B.S., *Constitutional Changes Since 1870* (Auckland: Heinemann, 1969).

Hacker, P.M.S., and Raz, J. (eds) *Law, Morality and Society: Essays in Honour of H.L.A. Hart* (Oxford: Clarendon Press, 1977).

Hart, H.L.A., *The Concept of Law* (Oxford: Clarendon Press, 1961; 2nd edn, 1994).

——, 'Self-Referring Laws' in Hart, H.L.A. (ed.) *Essays in Jurisprudence and Philosophy* (Oxford: Oxford University Press, 1983) 170.

Havemann, P., 'The "Pakeha Constitutional Revolution?" Five Perspectives on Maori Rights and Pakeha Duties' (1993) 1 Waikato L Rev 53.

—— (ed.) *Indigenous Peoples' Rights in Australia, Canada, and New Zealand* (Auckland: Oxford University Press, 1999).

Haward, M. and Warden, J., *An Australian Democrat: The Life, Work and Consequences of Andrew Inglis Clark* (1995).

Heuston, R.F.V., *Essays on Constitutional Law* (2nd edn, London: Stevens, 1964).

Hight, J. and Bamford, H.D., *Constitutional History and Law of New Zealand* (Christchurch: Whitcombe and Tombs, 1914).

Hogg, P.W., *Constitutional Law of Canada* (Toronto: Carswell, 1977).

——, 'Patriation of the Canadian Constitution: Has It Been Achieved?' (1982–3) Queen's LJ 123.

——, *Constitutional Law of Canada* (4th edn (looseleaf) Toronto: Thomson Carswell, 1997).

Hood Phillips, O., 'Book Review' (1964) 80 LQR 290.

Howard, C., *Australia's Constitution* (Ringwood: Penguin, 1978).

Hudson, W.J. and Sharp, M.P., *Australian Independence: Colony to Reluctant Kingdom* (Melbourne: Melbourne University Press, 1988).

Hurley, J. R., *Amending Canada's Constitution: History, Processes, Problems and Prospects* (Ottawa: Canada Communication Group, 1996).

Irving, H., *To Constitute a Nation: A Cultural History of Australia's Constitution* (Cambridge: Cambridge University Press, 1999).

Jennings, W. Ivor, *The Law and the Constitution* (3rd edn, London: University of London Press, 1943).

——, *The Law and the Constitution* (5th edn, London: University of London Press, 1959).

Joseph, P. and Walker, G., 'A Theory of Constitutional Change' (1987) OJLS 155.

——, 'Foundations of the Constitution' (1989) 4 Canta LR 58.

——, Constitutional and Administrative Law in New Zealand (Sydney: Law Book Company, 1993).

—— (ed.) *Essays on the Constitution* (Wellington: Bookers, 1995).

——, *Constitutional and Administrative Law in New Zealand* (2nd edn, Wellington: Brookers, 2001).

Kawharu, I.H., *Waitangi: Māori and Pākehā Perspectives of the Treaty of Waitangi* (Auckland: Oxford University Press, 1989).

Kelsen, H., *General Theory of Law and State*, Wedberg, A. (trans.) (Cambridge, Massachusetts: Harvard University Press, 1949).

Kelsey, J., *A Question of Honour? Labour and the Treaty 1984–1989* (Wellington: Allen & Unwin, 1990).

——, 'The Treaty of Waitangi and Maori Independence—Future Directions' (1990) 9th Commonwealth Conference papers, 249.

——, 'From Flagpoles to Pine Trees: Tino Rangatiratanga and Treaty Policy Today' in Spoonley, P., Pearson, D., and McPherson, C. (eds) *Nga Patai: Racism and Ethnic Relations in Aotearoa/New Zealand* (Palmerston North: Dunmore Press, 1996).

Kennedy, W.P.M., *The Constitution of Canada: An Introduction to its Development and Law* (London: Oxford University Press, 1922).

——, *The Constitution of Canada: An Introduction to Its Development and Law* (2nd edn, London: Humphrey Milford, Oxford University Press, 1931).

Kennedy, W.P.M., *Some Aspects of the Theories and Workings of Constitutional Law* (New York: Macmillan, 1932).

——, 'The Imperial Conferences, 1926–1930' (1932) 190 LQR 191.

——, 'Interpreting the Statute of Westminster' in Kennedy, W.P.M. (ed.) *Essays in Constitutional Law* (London: Oxford University Press, 1934).

——, *The Constitution of Canada 1534–1937: An Introduction to its Development, Law and Custom* (2nd edn, London: Oxford University Press, 1938).

Kirk, Jeremy, 'Constitutional Interpretation and a Theory of Evolutionary Originalism' (1999) 27 Fed LR.

Lang, J.D., *Freedom and Independence for the Golden Lands of Australia* (London: Longman, Brown, Green & Longmans, 1852).

Latham, J.G., *Australia and the British Commonwealth* (London: Macmillan, 1929).

Latham, R.T.E., 'The Law and The Commonwealth' in Hancock, W.K. (ed.) *Survey of British Commonwealth Affairs*, Vol. 1 (London: Oxford University Press, 1937) 517, reprinted with a foreword by W.K. Hancock but with otherwise unaltered pagination as Latham, R.T.E., *The Law and the Commonwealth* (Oxford: Oxford University Press, 1949).

Laws, J., 'Law and Democracy' [1995] Public Law 72.

——, 'The Constitution, Morals and Rights' [1996] Public Law 622.

Lederman, W.R., 'The Process of Constitutional Amendment for Canada' (1966–7) 12 McGill LJ 37, reprinted in Lederman, W.R. (ed.) *Continuing Constitutional Dilemmas* (Toronto: Butterworths, 1981) 81.

——, 'Constitutional Amendment and Canadian Unity' in Special Lectures of the Law Society of Upper Canada (Toronto, 1978), reprinted in Lederman, W.R. (ed.) *Continuing Constitutional Dilemmas* (Toronto: Butterworths, 1981) 91.

——, 'Canadian Constitutional Amending Procedures: 1867–1982' (1984) 32 Amer Jo Comp L 339.

——, 'The Supreme Court of Canada and Basic Constitutional Amendment' in Banting, K. and Simeon, R. (eds) *And No One Cheered: Federalism, Democracy and the Constitution Act* (Toronto: University of Toronto Press, 1985) 176.

Lefroy, A.H.F., *The Law of Legislative Power in Canada* (Toronto: Toronto Law Book and Publishing, 1897–8).

——, 'The Commonwealth of Australia Bill' (1st Article) (1899) 58 LQR 155; (2nd Article) (1899) 59 LQR 281.

——, *Canada's Federal System* (Toronto: Carswell, 1913).

——, *Leading Cases in Canadian Constitutional Law* (Toronto: Carswell, 1914; 2nd edn, 1920).

——, *A Short Treatise on Canadian Constitutional Law* (Toronto: Carswell 1918).

Lindell, G., 'Why is Australia's Constitution Binding?—The Reasons in 1900 and Now, and the Effect of Independence' (1986) 16 Fed LR 29.

——, 'Further Reflections on the Date of the Acquisition of Australia's Independence' in Lindell, G., Saunders, C. and French, R. (eds) *Reflections on the Australian Constitution* (Annandale: Federation Press, 2003) 51.

Lindell, G. and Rose, D., 'A Response to Gageler and Leeming: "An Australian Republic: Is a Referendum Enough"' (1996) 7 Public L Rev 155.

Lindell, G., Saunders, C. and French, R.S. (eds) *Reflections on the Australian Constitution* (Sydney: Federation Press, 2003).

Livingston, W.S., *Federalism and Constitutional Change* (Oxford: Oxford University Press, 1956).

Loughlin, M. *Public Law and Political Theory* (Oxford: Clarendon Press, 1992).

——, *The Idea of Public Law* (Oxford: Oxford University Press, 2003).

Lumb, R.D., 'Fundamental Law and the Processes of Constitutional Change in Australia' (1978) 9 Fed LR 148.

——, 'The Bicentenary of Australian Constitutionalism: The Evolution of Rules of Constitutional Change' (1988) 15 UQLJ 3.

——, 'Representative Democracy, Federalism and Constitutional Revision' in Stephenson, M.A. and Turner, C. (eds) *Australia, Republic or Monarchy?: Legal and Constitutional Issues* (St Lucia: University of Queensland Press, 1994) 165.

MacCormick, N., *Legal Reasoning and Legal Theory* (Oxford: Clarendon Press, 1978).

——, 'Beyond the Sovereign State' (1993) 56 MLR 1.

——, *Questioning Sovereignty: Law, State, and Practical Reason* (Oxford: Oxford University Press, 1999).

Marshall, G., *Parliamentary Sovereignty and the Commonwealth* (Oxford: Clarendon Press, 1957).

——, *Constitutional Theory* (Oxford: Clarendon Press, 1971).

——, *Constitutional Conventions* (Oxford: Oxford University Press, 1984).

——, 'The Constitution: Its Theory and Interpretation' in Bogdanor, V. (ed.) *The British Constitution in the Twentieth Century* (Oxford, Oxford University Press, 2003) 29.

McGechan, R.O., 'Status and Legislative Inability' in Beaglehole, J.C. (ed.) *New Zealand and the Statute of Westminster* (Wellington: Victoria University College, 1944) 65.

McGee, Thomas D'Arcy, *Speeches and Addresses: Chiefly on the Subject of British American Union* (London: Chapman and Hall, 1865).

McHugh, P.G., 'The Aboriginal Rights of the New Zealand Maori at Common Law' (Doctoral Dissertation, Cambridge University, 1987).

——, *The Maori Magna Carta: New Zealand Law and the Treaty of Waitangi* (Auckland: Oxford University Press, 1991).

——, 'The Historiography of New Zealand's Constitutional History' in Joseph, P.A. (ed.) *Essays on the Constitution* (Wellington: Bookers, 1995) 344.

——, 'Constitutional Voices' (1996) 26 VUWLR 499.

——, 'Aboriginal Identity and Relations' in Coates, K.S. and McHugh, P.G. (eds) *Living Relationships: Kokiri Ngatahi: The Treaty of Waitangi in the New Millennium* (Wellington: Victoria University Press, 1998) 107.

McNeil, K., *Common Law Aboriginal Title* (Oxford: Clarendon Press, 1989).

McWhinney, E., 'The How, When and Why of Constitution-Making: The Machinery for Developing a New Constitution' in Beaudoin, G.-A. *et al.* (eds) *Mécanismes pour une nouvelle constitution* (Ottawa: Éditions de l'université d'Ottawa, 1981).

——, *Canada and the Constitution, 1979–82* (Toronto: University of Toronto Press, 1982).

Moore, W. Harrison, 'The Commonwealth of Australia Bill' (1900) 16 LQR 35.

——, *Constitution of the Commonwealth of Australia* (London: John Murray, 1902).

——, *Constitution of the Commonwealth of Australia* (2nd edn, Melbourne: Charles F. Maxwell, 1910) (reprinted by Legal Books, 1997).

——, 'Separate Action by the British Dominions in Foreign Affairs' in *Australian and New Zealand Society of International Law Proceedings*, Melbourne, 1935.

Morin, J.-Y. and Woehrling, J., *Les Constitutions du Canada et du Quebec du Régime Français à nos Jours* (Montreal: Thémis, 1994).

Moshinsky, M., 'Re-enacting the Constitution in an Australian Act' (1989) 18 Fed LR 134.

Northey, J.F. (ed.) *The A.G. Davis Essays in the Law* (London: Butterworths, 1965).

——, 'The New Zealand Constitution' in Northey, J.F. (ed.) *The A.G. Davis Essays in the Law* (London: Butterworths, 1965) 149.

O'Hearn, Hon. P.J.T., 'Nova Scotia and Constitutional Amendment' (1966–7) 12 McGill LJ 433.

Oliver, P., 'Law, Politics, the Commonwealth and the Constitution: Remembering R.T.E. Latham' 1909–43' (2000) 11 KCLJ 153.

——, 'Canada, Quebec and Constitutional Amendment' (2000) 49 UTLJ 519.

——, 'Sovereignty in the Twenty-First Century' (2003) 14 KCLJ 137.

Ollivier, M., *L'avenir constitutionnel du Canada* (Montreal: Albert Lévesque, 1935).

O'Regan, Tipene, 'The Ngāi Tahu Claim' in Kawharu, I.H. (ed.) *Waitangi: Māori and Pākehā Perspectives of the Treaty of Waitangi* (Auckland: Oxford University Press, 1989) 234.

O'Sullivan, D.A., *A Manual of Government in Canada; or, The Principles and Institutions of our Federal and Provincial Constitutions* (Toronto: J.C. Stuart, 1879).

——, *Government in Canada: The Principles and Institutions of our Federal and Provincial Constitutions: The BNA Act 1867 Compared with the United States Constitution, With a Sketch of the Constitutional History of Canada* (2nd edn, Toronto: Carswell, 1887).

Palmer, G., *New Zealand's Constitution in Crisis: Reforming Our Political System* (Dunedin: John McIndoe, 1992).

Paton, G.W. (ed.) *The Commonwealth of Australia: The Development of its Laws and Constitution* (London: Stevens & Sons, 1952).

Pelletier, B., *La Modification Constitutionnelle au Canada* (Scarborough: Carswell, 1996).

Pettit, P., *Republicanism: A Theory of Freedom and Government* (Oxford: Oxford University Press, 1997).

——, 'The People in the Republican Tradition' in Coper, M. and Williams, G. (eds) *Power, Parliament and the People* (Annandale: Federation Press, 1997) 108.

Pigeon, L.-P., 'Le sens de la formule Fulton-Favreau' (1966–6) 12 McGill LJ 403.

Pope, J., *Confederation: Being a Series of Hitherto Unpublished Documents Bearing on the British North America Act* (Toronto: Carswell, 1895).

Raz, J., 'Professor A. Ross and Some Legal Puzzles' (1972) 81 Mind 415.

——, *Practical Reason and Norms* (Oxford: Oxford University Press, 1975) (reprinted with new postscript, 1990).

——, *The Authority of Law* (Oxford: Oxford University Press, 1979).

——, *The Concept of a Legal System* (2nd edn, Oxford: Clarendon Press, 1980).

——, *Ethics in the Public Domain* (Oxford: Clarendon Press, 1984).

Rémillard, G. *Le Devoir [de Montréal]*, 26 June 1980, 13.

——, 'L'historique du rapatriement' (1984) 23 C du D 1.

Risk, R.C.B., 'A.H.F. Lefroy: Common Law Thought in Late Nineteenth-Century Canada: On Burying One's Grandfather' (1991) 41 UTLJ 307.

——, 'Constitutional Scholarship in the Late Nineteenth Century: Making Federalism Work' (1996) 46 UTLJ 427.

——, 'The Scholars and the Constitution: P.O.G.G. and the Privy Council' (1996) 2 Manitoba LR 496.

——, 'The Many Minds of W.P.M. Kennedy' (1998) 48 UTLJ 353.

Robinson, K.E., 'Autochthony and the Transfer of Power' in Robinson, K.E. and Madden, A.F. (eds) *Essays in Imperial Government* (Oxford: Blackwells, 1963).

Robinson, K.E. and Madden, A.F. (eds) *Essays in Imperial Government* (Oxford: Blackwells, 1963).

Robson, J.L. (ed.) *New Zealand: The Development of its Law and Constitution* (London: Stevens, 1954).

——, (ed.) *New Zealand: The Development of its Laws and Constitution* (2nd edn, London: Stevens, 1967).

Rogers, N. McL., 'The Constitutional Impasse' (1934) 41 Queen's Q 482.

Ross, A., *On Law and Justice* (London: Stevens, 1958).

——, 'On Self-Reference and a Puzzle in Constitutional Law' (1969) 78 Mind 1.

Russell, P., *Constitutional Odyssey: Can Canadians Be A Sovereign People?* (Toronto: University of Toronto Press, 1992).

——, 'High Courts and the Rights of Aboriginal Peoples: The Limits of Judicial Independence' (1998) 61 Saskatchewan L Rev 247.

Sawer, G., 'Constitutional Law' in Paton, G.W. (ed.) *The Commonwealth of Australia: The Development of its Laws and Constitution* (London: Stevens & Sons, 1952) 38.

Schwartz, B. and Whyte, J.D., 'The Patriation Reference and the Idea of Canada' (1982–33) 8 Queen's LJ 158.

Scott, F.R., *Essays on the Constitution* (Toronto: University of Toronto Press, 1977).

——, 'The Redistribution of Imperial Sovereignty' in *Transactions of the Royal Society of Canada* (June 1950), reprinted in Scott, F.R., *Essays on the Constitution* (Toronto: University of Toronto Press, 1977) 244.

Scott, K.J., *The New Zealand Constitution* (Oxford: Oxford University Press, 1962).

Scott, K.J. and Robson, J.L., 'Parliament' in Robson, J.L. (ed.) *New Zealand: The Development of its Law and Constitution* (London: Stevens, 1954).

Scott, S.A., 'Constituent Authority and the Canadian Provinces' (1966–7) 12 McGill LJ 528.

Sifton, C., 'Some Canadian Constitutional Problems' (1922) 3 Can Hist Rev 3.

Sharp, A., *Justice and the Maori: The Philosophy and Practice of Maori Claims in New Zealand since the 1970s* (2nd edn, Auckland: Oxford University Press, 1997).

Slattery, B., 'Land Rights of Aboriginal Canadian People, as Affected by the Crown's Acquisition of Their Territories' (Doctoral Dissertation, Oxford University, 1979).

——, 'The Independence of Canada' (1983) 5 Sup Ct L Rev 369.

——, 'Ancestral Lands, Alien Laws: Judicial Perspectives on Aboriginal Title' (Saskatoon: University of Saskatchewan Native Law Centre, 1983).

——, 'Understanding Aboriginal Rights' (1987) 66 Can Bar Rev 727.

——, 'Aboriginal Sovereignty and Imperial Claims' (1991) 29 Osgoode Hall LJ 1.

——, 'First Nations and the Constitution: A Question of Constitutional Trust' (1992) 71 Can Bar Rev 261.

Stone, A. and Williams, G. (eds) *The High Court at the Crossroads* (2000).

Strayer, B., *Patriation and Constitutional Legitimacy* (Saskatoon: College of Law, University of Saskatchewan, 1982).

Swinfen, D.B. *Imperial Appeal* (Manchester: Manchester University Press, 1987).

Tate, J., 'Giving Substance to Murphy's Law: The Question of Australian Sovereignty' (2001) 27 Monash U L Rev 22.

Teubner, G., *Law as an Autopoietic System* in Bankowska, A. and Adler, R. (trans), Bankowski, Z. (ed.) (Oxford: Blackwell, 1993).

Thomson, J.A., 'The Australia Acts 1986: A State Constitutional Law Perspective' (1990) 20 WA L Rev 409.

——, 'Andrew Inglis Clark and Australian Constitutional Law' in Haward, M. and Warden, J. (eds) *An Australian Democrat: The Life, Work and Consequences of Andrew Inglis Clark* (1995).

Tomkins, A., *Public Law* (Oxford: Clarendon Press, 2002).

Twomey, A., 'Sue v. Hill—The Evolution of Australian Independence' in Stone, A. and Williams, G. (eds) *The High Court at the Crossroads* (Annandale: Federation Press, 2000) 77.

——, *The Constitution of New South Wales* (Annandale: Federation Press, 2004).

Wade, H.R.W., 'The Basis of Legal Sovereignty' [1995] CLJ 172.

Walker, R.J., 'The Treaty of Waitangi as the Focus of Māori Protest' in Kawharu, I.H. (ed.) *Waitangi: Māori and Pākehā Perspectives of the Treaty of Waitangi* (Auckland: Oxford University Press, 1989) 263.

Walters, M.D., 'British Imperial Constitutional Law and Aboriginal Rights: A Comment on *Delgamuukw v. British Columbia*' (1992) 17 Queen's LJ 350.

Wheare, K.C., *The Statute of Westminster and Dominion Status* (5th edn, Oxford: Oxford University Press, 1953).

——, *The Constitutional Structure of the Commonwealth* (Oxford: Clarendon Press, 1960).

Wheeler, F., 'Framing an Australian Constitutional Law: Andrew Inglis Clark and William Harrison Moore' (1997) 3 Aust J Leg Hist 237.

Windeyer, V., ' "A Birthright and Inheritance"—The Establishment of the Rule of Law in Australia' (1962) Tasmanian Univ L Rev 635.

Winterton, G., 'The British Grundnorm: Parliamentary Supremacy Re-examined' (1976) 92 LQR 591.

——, *Monarchy to Republic* (Melbourne: Oxford University Press, 1986).

——, 'Extra-Constitutional Notions in Australian Constitutional Law' (1986) 16 Fed LR 223.

——, 'The Constitutional Implications of a Republic' in Stephenson, M.A. and Turner, Clive (eds) *Australia, Republic or Monarchy? : Legal and Constitutional Issues* (St Lucia: University of Queensland Press, 1994).

——, 'Popular Sovereignty and Constitutional Continuity' (1998) 26 Fed LR 1.

——, 'The Acquisition of Independence' in Lindell, G.J., Saunders, C. and French, R.S. (eds) *Reflections on the Australian Constitution* (Sydney: Federation Press, 2003) 31.

Woolf, H., 'Droit Public—English Style' [1995] Public Law 57.

Wright, H.G.A., 'Sovereignty of the People—The New Constitutional Grundnorm?' (1998) 26 Fed LR 165.

Wynes, W. Anstey, *Legislative and Executive Powers in Australia* (Sydney: Law Book Company, 1936).

——, *Legislative, Executive and Judicial Powers in Australia* (Sydney: Law Book Company, 2nd edn, 1956; 3rd edn, 1962; 4th edn, 1970; 5th edn, 1976).

Zines, L., 'The Growth of Australian Nationhood and its Effects on the Powers of the Commonwealth' in Zines, L. (ed.) *Commentaries on the Australian Constitution* (Sydney: Butterworths, 1977) 1.

——, *The High Court and the Constitution* (Sydney: Butterworths, 1981).

——, *Constitutional Change in the Commonwealth* (Cambridge: Cambridge University Press, 1991).

——, *The High Court and the Constitution* (4th edn, Sydney: Butterworths, 1997).

——, 'The Sovereignty of the People' in Coper, M. and Williams, G. (eds) *Power, Parliament and the People* (Annandale: Federation Press, 1997) 94.

OFFICIAL PUBLICATIONS

Australia

Australia, Parliament, House of Representatives, Australia Bill 1986, *Australia (Request and Consent) Bill 1985: Explanatory Memorandum* (circulated by authority of the Hon. Lionel Bowen, Deputy Prime Minister and Attorney-General).

Australia, *First Report of the Constitutional Commission*, Vol. 1 (Canberra: Australian Government Publishing Service, 1988).

Canada

Canada, Senate, *Report*, by W.F. O'Connor (Ottawa, 1939; reprinted 1961). Canada, Communiqué of the Federal-Provincial Conference (14 October 1964), reprinted with attachment: An Act to Provide for the Amendment in Canada of the Constitution of Canada.

Canada, Constitutional Conference, Statement of Conclusions (8–9 February 1971). Canada, Parliament, Special Joint Committee of the Senate and the House of Commons on the Constitution of Canada, *Final Report*, 16 March 1972 (Chairmen: Senator G.L. Molgat, Mr Mark MacGuigan, MP).

Canada, Federal-Provincial Relations Office, *The Canadian Constitution and Constitutional Amendment* (1978).

Canada, Parliament, *Minutes and Proceedings of the Special Joint Committee of the Senate and House of Commons on the Constitution of Canada* (Chairs: Senator Harry Hays and Serge Joyal, MP) (1980–81).

Canada, *Report of the Royal Commission on Aboriginal Peoples* (1996).

New Zealand

New Zealand, House of Representatives, *The Statute of Westminster: Notes on the Purpose and Effect of the Adoption by New Zealand Parliament of Sections 2, 3, 4, 5 and 6 of the Statute of Westminster and the New Zealand Constitution Amendment (Consent and Request) Bill* in New Zealand, House of Representatives, *Journals*, 1st Session, 28th Parliament, 1948, Appendix, Vol. 1.

New Zealand, Parliament, *Explanatory Note to the New Zealand Constitution Amendment Bill, No 57–1*, 1973.

New Zealand, *A Bill of Rights for New Zealand* (White Paper presented to the House of Representatives by leave of the Hon. Geoffrey Palmer, Minister of Justice) (1985).

United Kingdom

United Kingdom, House of Commons, *First, Second and Third Reports of the Foreign Affairs Committee* (21 January, 15 April, 22 December, 1981) (London: HMSO, 1981).

United Kingdom, Scottish Office, *Scotland's Parliament* (White Paper) (1997) (Cm 3658).

United Kingdom, Home Secretary, *Rights Brought Home: The Human Rights Bill* (White Paper) (October 1997) (Cm 3782).

Index